Tell Balâṭah from the air near the summit of Mt. Gerizim, looking north.

SHECHEM III
THE STRATIGRAPHY AND ARCHITECTURE OF SHECHEM/TELL BALÂṬAH

VOLUME 1: TEXT

American Schools of Oriental Research
Archaeological Reports

Gloria London, editor

Number 06

Shechem III: The Stratigraphy and
Architecture of Shechem/Tell Balâṭah

Shechem III

The Stratigraphy and Architecture of Shechem/Tell Balâṭah

Volume 1: Text

Edward F. Campbell

Illustrated by Lee C. Ellenberger, photographer
and G. R. H. Wright, architect

shechem

Archaeological Excavations

AMERICAN SCHOOLS OF ORIENTAL RESEARCH • BOSTON, MA

Shechem III
The Stratigraphy and Architecture of Shechem/Tell Balâṭah
Volume 1: Text

Edward F. Campbell

© 2002
American Schools of Oriental Research

Billie Jean Collins
ASOR Director of Publications

ISBN: 0-89757-062-6 [set]
ISBN: 0-89757-058-8 [volume 1]
ISBN: 0-89757-061-8 [volume 2]

Library of Congress Cataloging in Publication Data is available.

*Dedicated to the memory of
Professor G. Ernest Wright,
mentor and friend to all who worked at Shechem*

CONTENTS

List of Figures xi

Acknowledgements xxi

Introduction 1

Chapter 1: The Earliest Strata: Chalcolithic/Early Bronze I and Middle Bronze IIA 11

Chapter 2: The Middle Bronze IIB Period 27

Chapter 3: The Middle Bronze IIC Period 105

Chapter 4: The Late Bronze Age to Early Iron I 169

Chapter 5: The Iron Age 235

Chapter 6: The Hellenistic Period 311

References 343

LIST OF FIGURES

Frontispiece: Tell Balâṭah from the air near the summit of Mt. Gerizim, looking north.

Fig. 1 Shechem: Uncrowned Queen of Palestine, Navel of the Land.
Fig. 2 Plan of Balâṭah village and environs, with inset showing location of tombs.
Fig. 3 Field IX, Stratum XXIV remains, looking west in Area 4.
Fig. 4 Section in 3 EF as drawn in 1960, now reversed and serving as part of VI BB. Note the sequence of street numbers placed on the profile of Wall 900, and the layering beneath the foot of Wall 900.
Fig. 5 Section 3 EF, cut back in 1964.
Fig. 6 Key plan of Field VIII, showing lines of sections on Areas 1 and 3. "Area 2" was not assigned.
Fig. 7 Section AA on north face of Area 1 in Field VIII, to bedrock.
Fig. 8 Field IX, Area 4, looking north. Note Stratum XXI drainage channel 9630 met by Wall 9628 at its north end, plaster-lined installation against Wall 9631 and Firepit 9632.
Fig. 9 Looking down at the west face of Wall 968 in Field VI, Area 25. The meter stick rests on the fill of the platform retained by Wall 968. Note the smashed MB IIA storage jars fallen from the top of the platform.
Fig. 10 Silo 130 sunk into MB IIA Surface 122, as filled at left and with its packing removed and bones displayed at right.
Fig. 11 Section VI PP on the north face of Field VI.2.
Fig. 12 Section VI RR on the west face of Field VI.2.
Fig. 13 Structures at the north end of Field VI, showing location of Field VI.2
Fig. 14 Section VI LL, showing Wall 935 beneath Wall D.
Fig. 15 Wall 935 as it runs beneath Wall D; diagrammatic view, north end of VI BB section.
Fig. 16 Drain 402 looking north in Field VI, Area 24.
Fig. 17 Field V section through Wall D and layers leading to it, looking north.
Fig. 18 The north face of the VI.2 trial trench, revealing Wall D at lower right.
Fig. 19 Wall 900 viewed looking east at the seam to the right of the strip of balk. The numbers painted on rocks in the wall show the elevations of some of the streets.
Fig. 20 Auxiliary section on Field VI AA I/1, streets and drainage between Walls 900 and 901/902.
Fig. 21 Segments of Street 9 along Wall 900, with unpaved drainage path to its left (west).
Fig. 22 Cylinder seal impression on an MB IIB storage jar handle, according to Edith Porada showing the Ishtar of War and other motifs, probably Syrian.
Fig. 23 MB IIB smashed storage jars Locus 436 on Floor 433 in Room 23 of Field VI.
Fig. 24 Human skeleton lying on Floor 611A in Room 28 of Field VI.
Fig. 25 Oven 606A in Room 28 on Floor 16:9 of Stratum XXA.
Fig. 26 Elevation drawing of pillar bases against Wall 958a in the Entrance Hall.
Fig. 27 Seven pillar bases as preserved in the Entrance Hall, viewed from the south.
Fig. 28 Flagstone Floor 605 in the Entrance Hall.
Fig. 29 Base of storage jar sunk in Floor 556 of Courtyard 35.
Fig. 30 Oven 559 in Floor 556 of Courtyard 35.
Fig. 31 Detail of the construction of Oven 559, with layering of sherds on its exterior.
Fig. 32 Stratum XX pottery forms, as prepared by Dan P. Cole (Cole:pl. 46).
Fig. 33 Sections beneath North Gate, loci 4003 (left) and 4002 (right), looking east.
Fig. 34 Key plan of the Northwest Gate, after Welter.
Fig. 35 Lawrence Toombs' field sketch of subsidiary section in Field XIII, Area 3, showing at its base the tiplines of the C Rampart, locus 3564.
Fig. 36 Overview of the acropolis, bounded by Wall 900 at the left margin. The streets ran between Wall 900 and the succession of walls to its right. The tongue of the Temple forecourt is in the center. The Hellenistic structure in Field II is at the upper left.
Fig. 37 The balk between Areas 3D and 3E with Wall 900 at left. Street 6 is marked by numbers on the wall at left margin.
Fig. 38 Looking south at Stratum XIX Wall 924A,

resting on the mudbrick topping of Stratum XX Wall 976, in Field VI, Area 24. Wall 924A was preserved for only two to three courses of stone; riding immediately upon it is Wall 924 of Stratum XVIII. Note the door socket stone reused in 924A. In the foreground is a segment of Stratum XX Floor 451 with the stones of Wall 965 nearest the camera. Floor 406 of Stratum XVIIIB is the white surface approaching Wall 924 at the sixth decimeter from the bottom of the meter stick propped against Wall 924A-924. Surfaces of Stratum XIX were not preserved, due to the intrusions of Pit 431 and Trough 410.

Fig. 39   Flagstone Paving 602 of Stratum XIX, in the Entrance Hall.
Fig. 40   Jar Burial 608 in Stratum XIX Entrance Hall, looking southeast
Fig. 41   Jar 614, in which was Burial 608, with four MB IIB found within.
Fig. 42   Remains of the skeleton in Burial 608, oriented as in fig. 40, head to southeast.
Fig. 43   Crystal and agate beads with scaraboid, strung as they lay in Burial 608.
Fig. 44   Four MB IIB vessels in Burial 608.
Fig. 45   Burial 612, at junction of Walls 951A and 924A in the Entrance Hall.
Fig. 46   South face of Wall 903A topped by Wall 903; note the two phases of building.
Fig. 47   Wall 915 of Stratum XIX, showing mudbrick topping. Above it, a column base of Stratum XVIII.
Fig. 48   Brick topping of Wall 916 at right, south boundary of Room 10, Stratum XIX.
Fig. 49   Brick topping on Wall 921 at its junction with Wall 919 at left margin, Room 13. Note the plaster covering the overlapping bricks.
Fig. 50   Top plan of Rooms 8 and 9 of Stratum XIX.
Fig. 51   Section BB II/1 between Walls 904 and 901-902-939. Floor 16.8 of Room 9 at top of undisturbed soil.
Fig. 52   A kneading rock lying of Surface 16.8 in Room 9.
Fig. 53   Ovens on Surface 16.8 in Room 9, with kneading block in foreground.
Fig. 54   Storage jar Burial 16.21 covered over by Floor 16.8 in Room 9.
Fig. 55   Burial 16:21, with fragments of bones in its base.
Fig. 56   Sheep or goat burial, locus 6:18, beneath Floor 509B in Room 8.
Fig. 57   Deep carinated MB IIB bowl #1528 from Stratum XIXA, Floor 6:8 in Room 8.
Fig. 58   Stone-lined pit with stone mortar as its base in Floor 6:8, Room 8.
Fig. 59   Looking south at the junction of Walls 919 (foreground) and 908A in the southeast corner of Room 13. Wall 915 runs away from the pillar at upper left.
Fig. 60   Looking slightly west of north from within the southwest corner of Room 11, into Room 13. The pillar of 908A is at left center, constituting the south jamb of the door from Room 11 to 13. Wall 919 runs away from the pillar at the upper left.
Fig. 61   The northeast face of Wall 919 in Room 13, joining southeast face of Wall 921 at right. The surface on which the meter stick rests is Stratum XIXB Floor 332, its plaster evident in the probe trench through the floor to left of center.
Fig. 62   Looking southeast from the Fortress Temple elevation toward Wall 900, with Field II Hellenistic House in upper right corner. The bow in Wall 919 is visible in the center foreground.
Fig. 63   Looking east at the junction of Wall 903/903A and Wall 904/904A in the northeast corner of Room 11. The meter stick stands on a flagstone of Stratum XIXA surface.
Fig. 64   Looking north into the northeast corner of Room 11, at junction of Walls 922/922A and 903/903A, with flagstones of Stratum XIXA surface under the meter stick.
Fig. 65   Section VI FF, through the forecourt (Area 13) of Field V.
Fig. 66   Flagstones of Floor 8:8 of Stratum XIXA in Room 12, looking west from the top of Wall 908 visible in the lower left corner.
Fig. 67   Range of Stratum XIX pottery forms, from Floors 8:6 in Room 13 and 8:8 in Room 12, reproduced from Cole:pl. 47.
Fig. 68   Looking south along Wall 914, with Wall 925 in the center. Note the phasing in Wall 914: 914A of Stratum XVIII is the battered segment at the top of which are large semi-hewn *mizzi* blocks.
Fig. 69   Looking northeast into the junction of Wall 902 (right) and Wall 906 (left). Floor 17:7 runs beneath Wall 906. Wall 906 is the south wall of Room 1, Stratum XVIII.
Fig. 70   Bench 6:5 along Wall 901 in Room 1.
Fig. 71   Six column bases in the north part of Court 2

	viewed looking north.	Fig. 87	Streets 2, 3, 4 and 5 against Wall 900 in Area 3E. The meter stick lies on Street 3
Fig. 72	Stratum XVIII column base on stylobate. Walls 970 and 934 of Stratum XX are visible at bottom of photograph.	Fig. 88	Range of pottery forms from makeup for Stratum XVII, drawn from Pit 4:4 dug at the start of Stratum XVII.
Fig. 73	Burial 11:5b in a storage jar in the northwest corner of Court 2 where Walls 903 (right) and 922 meet (left).	Fig. 89	Drain in Field IX, its edges made of Walls 9621 and 9622, with cover stones at its south end. Wide Wall 9623 is to its east (left).
Fig. 74	Looking down at the succession of walls on the east of the Central Court. Wall 938 of Stratum XVIII on Wall 938A of Stratum XIX on Wall 983 of Stratum XX (on which the meter stick lies).	Fig. 90	White and red bricks on top of stones of Wall 9611.
		Fig. 91	Brick platform 9616, in parquet style.
		Fig. 92	Post hole scars shown in section, adjacent to 9616.
Fig. 75	Looking east from the top of Wall 914, with Wall 925 in foreground. The cubicle in the southwest corner of the Central Court ran from Wall 925 to the stretch of Wall 985 and the doorway against the north face of Wall 984 at right.	Fig. 93	Installation on Floor 9614, constructed of upright bricks with their faces plastered.
		Fig. 94	Vertical face at south edge of Room B, showing bricks of a second possible brick platform.
Fig. 76	Isolated column base 8-9:18, immediately south of and below Wall 927. The context is quite disturbed.	Fig. 95	Looking east in Field IX, Area 4, at Wall 9878 (meter stick is lying on it). Note the plaster line in the balk at right margin; Wall 9878 was covered with mud brick and then plastered on its face.
Fig. 77	Comparative block drawings of the two interpretations of the Stratum XVIII Central Court. Ernest Wright's interpretation is A; the more plausible Ross interpretation is B.	Fig. 96	Looking north in Area 4 of Field IX. Note the mark of robbed Wall 9889, separating plaster floorings of Rooms A and E (9882=9877A and 9888, respectively). The scraps of Wall 9880 separate these from Room C in which the base of a storage jar is set.
Fig. 78	G. R. H. Wright's drawings of the layout of Stratum XVIII in Field VI, based on Ernest Wright's interpretation.		
Fig. 79	Flagstone Floor 8R/9R against upper courses of Walls 938 and 984.		
Fig. 80	Balk face at the north edge of forecourt tongue left by Sellin. Junction of Stratum XVIII Walls 932 and 925. Stones of 932 are at the base of the balk, while stones of 925 are in the niche at right.	Fig. 97	Handle from a complete storage jar crushed near parquet platform of hearth 9616, with stamp impression and possible marks of quantity.
		Fig. 98	Praschniker's measurements of the course of Wall A, by taped distances, from his notebook, dated Sept. 17, 1913.
Fig. 81	Within the cut in the forecourt tongue, Walls 925 (foreground), 985 (center) and 984 (with meter stick resting on it) all show rebuilds belonging to Stratum XVIIIA.	Fig. 99	Section based on the work of C. Praschniker in 1913 against the exterior face of Wall A, showing the batter of the wall and the tiplines of fill against it.
Fig. 82	Oven 5082 adjacent to the top of Wall 985 in Central Courtyard cubicle.	Fig. 100	Schematic reconstructions of the Northwest Gate: longitudinally- and cross-sectioned.
Fig. 83	Sunken storage jar base 5081 in junction of Walls 984 and 925, probably of Stratum XVIIIA+.	Fig. 101	The bank of earth against the exterior of Wall A as it looked in 1960. There is no indication of sectioning through it by Sellin or Welter.
Fig. 84	Selection of pottery from Locus 35, makeup for Street 4, reprinted from Cole:pl. 48.	Fig. 102	Tannur with two layers of lining from surfacing within Court I in Field I.
Fig. 85	Surface of Street 3 between Wall 900 (right) and Wall 901 (left).	Fig. 103	Tannur 534 built into the junction of Walls 640 and 641, Field III, probably in use with MB IIC Floors 548 and 531.
Fig. 86	Balk through the streets in Area 3A, looking south. Wall 900 to left, 901 to right. The trench at left cleared fill from the Sellin dig along Wall 900. Street 3 is marked.	Fig. 104	Looking south in Field III toward the DD

Fig. 105 balk. The rocks in center are fallen from the top of Wall 640 at left onto Floor 533. The crush of pottery lay to the right of the fallen rocks, close to Wall 657, hidden in the temporary balk at the right margin.

Fig. 105 Looking west in Field IV, 7200 complex. Wall B/1 in center, with the doorway to the "postern gate" to its left. Dever's inked designations identify the elements.

Fig. 106 The opening in Wall A permitting visual coverage of approaches from the north to the Northwest Gate. Note the flat flooring slabs, covered with a layer of plaster.

Fig. 107 MB IIC pottery forms from Field IV phasing. Note jar rim forms in Phase 3 panel, ##11–13.

Fig. 108 More MB IIC forms, and 2 cooking pot rims from Iron I found in Field IV. The find spot of the two platter bowls (##13 and 15) is marked in fig. 105.

Fig. 109 Looking west in Field III, with Wall 654 at bottom margin, Wall 646 on top of 646A in center.

Fig. 110 Looking northwest in Field III, with Wall B at the right and part of Wall 649 in lower right corner. Bench 729 is the group of flat stones against the lowest course of Wall B, left of the meter stick. Note the striated soil layer beneath Wall B.

Fig. 111 Looking west at the center part of balk on which the III BB section was drawn. Wall 649 at left, Floor 738 at 0.70 m from the top of the meter stick.

Fig. 112 Looking west inside Wall B in the domestic complex of Field III. Wall 634 in the back, 650 in the foreground. The meter stick stands on Floor 734.

Fig. 113 Looking northwest in the room just inside Wall B. The balk with section III BB left of center. The succession of cobblestone surfaces, 708, 710, 711 show in the balk, while the meter stick lies on Floor 714.

Fig. 114 The central portion of the south balk of Field III, on which III DD is drawn. Wall 657 at far right, and the layering between Walls 642 and 640 to left of center. Note the thick layer of ḥuwwar, locus 515 running from the base of Wall 613 eastward.

Fig. 115 Looking west in Field III. The meter stick leans against Wall 634. Behind and above Wall 634 is Wall 631. A fragment of Wall 635 is at the right center, and across the deep trench from it is Pit 720, set down into the point where Wall 635 would meet the uppermost course of 634.

Fig. 116 Block plan of the uppermost Stratum XV phase in Field III.

Fig. 117 Looking north in Field III. Steps to platform 705, with Wall 639 in center. Parallel to 639 is Wall 638, to its left. In the lower left is the upper part of the balk on which III BB is drawn. The meter stick lies on Floor 702.

Fig. 118 Brick fall over Floor 702 in Field III, from Wall 647 southward, dating to the destruction of Stratum XV.

Fig. 119 Brick debris in south balk of Field III. Wall 635 is at right. Marks of burned beams show throughout the debris, which lies on Floor 702, Stratum XV.

Fig. 120 Smashed MB IIC cooking pot on Floor 702.

Fig. 121 Basalt tripod brazier from destruction on Floor 702, Stratum XV.

Fig. 122 Schematic reconstructions of the East Gate: roof plan, longitudinal section, ground plan, and cross section, as proposed by G. R. H. Wright.

Fig. 123 Axonometric view of reconstruction of the East Gate as though it had four turrets.

Fig. 124 Axonometric view of reconstruction of the East Gate as though with two lateral massifs.

Fig. 125 Looking north between East Gate tower on left and Wall 112 (originally designated "A-2"), showing stone working surfaces 1–5, with seven more below in the section at foot of photograph.

Fig. 126 The threshold wall for the outer orthostats in the East Gate, resting on a row of stones of gate surface of Foundation phase.

Fig. 127 Section through the East Gate showing phases of usage throughout its existence.

Fig. 128 Section through approach to the East Gate, set back 0.50 m from the line of I BB, as revealed by Lapp and drawn by Voelter in 1962.

Fig. 129 The orthostats in the East Gate as measured and drawn by Talbert.

Fig. 130 The East Gate looking from the northwest, showing the orthostat phase and steps leading down into the city.

Fig. 131 Elevation of southwest orthostat complex.

Fig. 132 Elevation of northwest orthostat complex.

Fig. 133 Pottery forms from Foundation phase of the East Gate (Seger 1974: fig. 3).

Fig. 134 Pottery forms from debris covering the steps

Fig. 135   Pottery and bones from the cobbled surface at the foot of steps at East Gate.
Fig. 136   Pottery forms from Stratum XV destruction in East Gate (from Seger 1974: fig. 5).
Fig. 137   Pottery forms from Stratum XV destruction in East Gate and from beneath brick collapse in Field III (from Seger 1974: fig. 6).
Fig. 138   Section F/2-F/2 through the Temple forecourt (Area 13), showing fills and the "via sacra."
Fig. 139   Schematic reconstructions of the Fortress Temple by G. R. H. Wright: front elevation, cross section, ground plan, roof plan and perspective view. Note that these renderings presume the central pillar in the doorway.
Fig. 140   Looking west along the south wall of the Temple structure. Wall 5603 is the well-hewn wide wall, its south face farthest to the left. Wall 5703 is above it, with the meter stick. There is an approximately five degree shift clockwise of the line of 5703 off that of 5603. Wall 5603 is of *mizzi* rock. Boulders on the right, north edge of 5703 represent the Iron Age Granary. Both 5703 and 5903 rocks are of *nari* limestone.
Fig. 141   Cistern/silo 5099A, with the mouth of 5099B at its base.
Fig. 142   Section through the granary and temple phases in Field V (portion of V BB).
Fig. 143   Curbing of whole white and grey-white bricks for the altar in the forecourt of the later phase of the Fortress Temple.
Fig. 144   Dever's block plan of Field IV, Northwest Gate and structures to either side.
Fig. 145   Column base spotted by Sellin in 7300 room, after cleaning by Dever in 1973. Wall A is to the right, Wall E outer face to left. Looking south. Photo: W. G. Dever.
Fig. 146   Second rhomboid-shaped column base in line with the one in foreground, just above meter stick, built into Wall E. Note the two building phases of Wall E. Photo: W. G. Dever.
Fig. 147   Looking north along the axis of the 7300 temple, its colonnaded wall in foreground, antechamber beyond it, and main room with pillar base. Note the altar podium against the back wall of the main chamber.
Fig. 148   Aerial view of the new homes covering over part of the Tananir structure, partially visible following Boling's excavation in 1968.
Fig. 149   Plan of the Tananir complex (Based on Welter's drawing [1932:313, fig. 14], from into the city at East Gate (Seger 1974:fig. 4).
Boling 1975b.)
Fig. 150   Top-plan of Tananir remains found by the Boling expedition in 1968, drawn by Oliver M. Unwin.
Fig. 151   North–south section through Tananir ruins, drawn by Oliver M. Unwin.
Fig. 152   Drain 3542 emerging from the corner of Building A in Field XIII (upper right).
Fig. 153   Destruction debris of Stratum XV in Room A of Field XIII, including a tripod brazier. This crush probably represents objects from the second floor or roof.
Fig. 154   Fragments of decorated bone inlay from the floor of Room A, Field XIII.
Fig. 155   Range of designs on bone inlay from Room A, Field XIII, Stratum XV destruction.
Fig. 156   Installation 16.129 against north balk of Field VII, Area 9.
Fig. 157   Block plan showing outline of the LB/Iron I gate tower along with later features.
Fig. 158   Junction of Wall 127 at right with Wall 126 within the LB/Iron I gate tower. Note that 126 abuts 127, and is founded higher.
Fig. 159   Plan of features inside town from the LB/Iron I gate tower. Note the proposed collapse of a secondary skin on Wall 127, and the positions of Walls 179 and 178.
Fig. 160   The tightly fitted Cobbled Surface 509, flush against Wall 127 at right margin.
Fig. 161   Plan of Field I Areas 16 and 17, showing Cobbling 509 and jumble of fallen rock over it to the north.
Fig. 162   Sketch drawing of section on north face of Field I, Area 17. Layer 508 represents destruction debris of Stratum XIII. Floor 503A runs east from Wall 179, its connection to Wall 127 severed by a pit.
Fig. 163   Layering of plaster floors within the Late Bronze gate tower.
Fig. 164   Equine skeleton on the uppermost LB floor in the gate tower guard room.
Fig. 165   Sketch plan of LB temple built over ruins of the Fortress Temple, after drawings by Bull.
Fig. 166   Wall 5703 with meter stick on it and several boulders of the 5903 granary wall still in place.
Fig. 167   Wall 5704 of the LB Temple phase.
Fig. 168   Bowl of LB IIB from beneath plastered Stratum XII LB surface in the LB Temple.
Fig. 169   Stone steps probably of Stratum XIV LB Temple, from disturbed flooring within the bounds of the MB IIC Fortress Temple; note

MB IIC foundation at right.

Fig. 170 Socket with *maṣṣebah* restored, south of entrance to Fortress Temple 1b.

Fig. 171 Socket for second flanking *maṣṣebah*, north of entrance to Fortress Temple 1b.

Fig. 172 Kurt Galling's 1926 photograph, with the flat altar platform in place in the temple forecourt, and *Maṣṣebah* 1 leaning in what is probably the position as found. The squared and well-preserved corner of the Fortress Temple walls is at right center.

Fig. 173 Re-erecting *Maṣṣebah* 1 on the tongue of temple forecourt. A large piece of the socket stone lies in the ruins of Field VI where it was pushed in the altercations between Sellin and Welter.

Fig. 174 *Maṣṣebah* 1 as the Joint Expedition remounted it.

Fig. 175 Looking west at the reconstructed ruin of the Fortress Temple. The consolidating wall around the tongue of forecourt on which *Maṣṣebah* 1 stands was built by the Joint Expedition. The two flanking *maṣṣeboth* are visible against the front wall of the Temple.

Fig. 176 Storage pit 5094 filled with rubbish that includes Iron I pottery. Note the plaster floor of the 5900 Granary sealing its top.

Fig. 177 Plan and section of Kiln 3396 in Field XIII, Area 2.

Fig. 178 Looking west at upper layer contents of Kiln 3396. Calcined limestone rock below meter stick; another to its left, nearer camera.

Fig. 179 Looking west at lower phase of Kiln 3396, with crushed MB II storage jar *in situ*.

Fig. 180 Looking north, with stone-lined pit set into the west end of the lower phase hearth, Kiln 3396. The meter stick lies on the hard-baked brick cap of the kiln. To the right of the meter stick is a portion of the lining of the kiln wall.

Fig. 181 Looking east at Kiln 3396, with meter stick on its collapsed cap, pit 03202 beyond.

Fig. 182 Slab of cap of Kiln 3396, removed from its position.

Fig. 183 Bullae B68 ##906-909, 912, from debris in Kiln 3396. It is not clear whether these belong to the kiln's use phase or are MB IIC residuals.

Fig. 184 Firepits 13.170 on top of 13.169 in Field VII, Area 6, of Strata XIV and XIII.

Fig. 185 Looking west in Room D of the eastern complex in Field XIII. Wall 3663 is at the top margin, and Wall 3667 along left margin.

The meter stick lies on Floor 3763. The hole in the foreground is of unknown purpose. The earth stack at lower right is the filling of Silo 3734, left in place as the excavation proceeded to its base.

Fig. 186 Crater smashed by brick lying on it, part of debris 3759 on Floor 3763. Wall 3667 (left) abuts Wall 3663 (right).

Fig. 187 Fragment (Object B68 #546) of fluted column from locus 3536 rubble on Surface 3537 in Room B of the Field XIII, Stratum XIV complex. The column matches those found in the temple ruins of Field V to the south.

Fig. 188 Surface 3528 in Sector C of Field XIII Stratum XIV complex. The marl ring was placed flush with the surface. The second view shows an LB *zir* base that would have fit it with chinking of sherds.

Fig. 189 Walls 16.110 and 16.110A of Stratum XIV in Field VII, Area 9. The structure was set into a saucer excavation, with Flagstone 16.118 to the right.

Fig. 190 North balk of Field VII Area 9. The meter stick rests on Block 16.118A. Note the vertical mark of the saucer into which the 16.110 complex was set, approximately 0.35 m to the right of the meter stick. The stones at the second decimeter from the bottom of the stick lie in the crushed remains of tannur 16.114 of Stratum XIV, reused in Stratum XIII.

Fig. 191 Segment of Floor 16.107A under meter stick against upper stones of Wall 16.110. Tannur 16.114, first laid with 16.107 of Stratum XIV and reused in Stratum XIII, is half hidden in the balk at center right.

Fig. 192 The west face of Wall 9588 in Field IX, showing both headers and stretchers.

Fig. 193 Looking north in Field IX Area 3, Wall 9588 to right and Wall 9585 to left. Alley surfaced by 9600 runs between them. Notice the building technique of Wall 9588 as viewed from above.

Fig. 194 Profile of stratigraphy in east balk of Field IX Area 3. Compare IX CC section. The brick topping of Wall 9611 shows Jar 9606B buried in it with the line of Stratum XIV plaster floor running just over it.

Fig. 195 Pottery profiles from loci in Fields VII and IX belonging to Stratum XIV.

Fig. 196 Looking south at south balk of Field VII Area

9. Stratum XIII Wall 16.109 in center, emerging from balk. White plaster on the surface beneath it marks Floor 16.107. Resurfacings 16.107A of Stratum XIII barely visible in the balk to west (right) of 16.109.

Fig. 197 Views of bronze figurine from Stratum XIII debris in Field VII.

Fig. 198 Looking east at the walls, bonded to one another, of the Sub-Floor Chamber in Field XIII, now completely cleared of its contents.

Fig. 199 Electrum pendant (B68 #821) from the silt layer at the base of the Sub-Floor Chamber.

Fig. 200 Sample of the complete vessels recovered from the filling of the Sub-Floor Chamber.

Fig. 201 Looking east at the pottery beneath surface 3745, within the top layering of the Sub-Floor Chamber. The hump above the meter stick contains the skeleton, its backbone discernible.

Fig. 202 Pottery crush on Floor 3745, the surface over the Sub-Floor Chamber. Among the vessels was the pitcher with gazelles painted on it shown in fig. 203.

Fig. 203 Reconstructed monochrome-painted pitcher with theme of animals, including gazelle (B68 Obj. #581).

Fig. 204 Painted biconical vase as crushed on Floor 3355.

Fig. 205 The biconical vase as reconstructed by Ruth Amiran and Miriam Tadmor, seated in its ceramic collar stand.

Fig. 206 Typical LB IIA (Stratum XIII) bowl from crush on Floor 3355.

Fig. 207 Looking east at the east balk of Field XIII, Area 2, showing the striated surfacings in Room M of the Stratum XIII complex.

Fig. 208 East balk of Field IX, Area 3. The Stratum XII surface runs from the foot of the scar just right of center where the *maṣṣebah* lay, north to the brick platform with plaster facing on the bricks, and beneath the bricks. Note that the upper courses of Wall 9588 had been removed prior to this photograph.

Fig. 209 The standing-stone or *maṣṣebah* on plastered floor of Stratum XII sanctuary.

Fig. 210 Obverse face, dressed, of the Stratum XII *maṣṣebah*, removed from context.

Fig. 211 Reverse face of Stratum XII *maṣṣebah*.

Fig. 212 Looking north in Field VII Area 9, at the contact of Wall 1679 (east–west) and Wall 1695 (north–south). The meter stick lies on Floor 1694. Pit 1690 is in foreground. Stump of Wall 16.101 extends west from Wall 1695 for 0.70 m; Wall 16.102 continues its line westward.

Fig. 213 Packing of post-holes 17.159, which appeared as rings in Floor 17.158 at the elevation of their tops. Packing is of clay and sherds.

Fig. 214 Configuration of the walls in Stratum XII later phase, in Field VII Area 9.

Fig. 215 Close-up of north balk, Field VII Area 9. Debris of locus 1688 fell to Floor 1699, which runs to the top of and over Wall 1695.

Fig. 216 Uppermost phase of Stratum XII. Wall 1679 is now rebuilt by the addition of boulders. The meter stick lies on Floor 1691. Wall 1672 runs north from its junction with Wall 1679. Wall 1675 at back and Wall 1670 at front of small room at east.

Fig. 217 Looking east in Field VII Area 2 in the Stratum XII (?) 11.156 complex. Note the post at the north end of Wall 11.139 in upper center. The meter stick lies on Floor 11.156, with pile of bones in lower right.

Fig. 218 Stratum XI white-lined Saucer 10.106 in Field VII Area 2.

Fig. 219 Looking northwest in Field VII Area 2 at destruction debris, Stratum XI.

Fig. 220 Looking west in Field VII Area 2, showing 11.108 burn on 11.111 stone platform. Surface 1196 is preserved in upper right.

Fig. 221 Looking west in Field VII Area 2 after cleaning of Platform 11.111. Note calcined rock and burn in balk over Wall 11.126.

Fig. 222 Looking north in Field VII Area 5 at Brickfall 14.129 on Surface 14.134, with shattered jar in foreground, all evidence of Stratum XIA destruction.

Fig. 223 Crush of Stratum XIA pottery on Floor 3261, Field XIII Room C.

Fig. 224 Vat 1770, with its rim heightened by rows of stones for use in Stratum XB. Looking west in Field VII Area 8, Wall 17.100 at right, Floor 1794 with meter stick. A small shelf of Floor 1791 is preserved at upper center against the balk.

Fig. 225 Looking north over Field VII Areas 3 and 6. A fragment of Floor 1077 is preserved where Wall 1071 nearest the camera and Wall 1069 at right margin, with a jar base and a flat stone (kneading block?) set into it.

Fig. 226 Platter Bin 1769 next to Vat 1770. Floor 1758 is in the foreground, a portion of Floor 1753 behind the bin.

Fig. 227 Tower view of Field II, showing remains of Stratum X structure beneath the Hellenistic House. Wall 7051 runs at an oblique angle to the Hellenistic walls near the top of the view.

Fig. 228 Sections on south and west faces of Field VIII. Wall 8006 appears on the south face near the top, flanked by later Iron II pits. Flagstones 8013 slope down beneath the fill of "hard grey" on the west face.

Fig. 229 Plan of upper segment of Field VIII, with Wall 8006 and Flagstones 8013 tentatively assigned to Stratum X.

Fig. 230 Plan of Field I Areas 16 and 17 showing Iron Age features. The Stratum X surface ran from Wall 175 to a point where it was interrupted near Wall 181, *under* Wall 176.

Fig. 231 Section on east face of Field I Areas 16 and 17. Surfaces in the left portion, cut by robbing from reaching Wall 181, represent Stratum X.

Fig. 232 View of Field IV, looking south southeast. Wall A in foreground. Nasr Dhiab Mansoor and Jeber Muhammad Hasan Salman stand at the exterior face of Wall E, their hands on the separation between the MB IIC and Iron Age phases of the wall. Photo by W. G. Dever.

Fig. 233 Balk in Field V beneath stones of granary wall 5905, showing thick plaster layer 5001 into which the granary stones were pressed.

Fig. 234 Block plan of phasing in Field IX, Stratum IX. Wall lines with double hatching continued throughout the period. Walls with single hatching were original, then went out of use in Stratum IXA. Stippled walls are Stratum IXA additions.

Fig. 235 Looking west in Field IX Area 1, the yard. Pit 9079c cuts into Surface 9077 running to Wall 9073 in the background.

Fig. 236 Detail of Field IX AA section.

Fig. 237 Block plan of Field VII in Stratum IX. Solid walls were in use throughout Stratum IX. Single-hatched walls are later additions, and crosshatched walls are the latest additions. Drawing by K. Djerf.

Fig. 238 Overview of Field VII Areas 3 and 6, with Terrace Wall 1640 at left. Houses A and B are depicted.

Fig. 239 Schematic stone-for-stone drawing of Field VII showing Stratum IX rooms. Drawing by K. Djerf.

Fig. 240 Looking north in Field VII Area 8 at Platter Bin 1769 and Vat 1770 (augmented) as reused in Stratum IX. The bands of red clay spilling into Vat 1770 appear in the small vertical cut at the extreme right edge.

Fig. 241 Looking south in Field VII Area 8. The two decayed limestone pillars 1743 are at left center, on Stratum IX Floor 1744. The meter stick lies on Stratum VIII Floor 1739.

Fig. 242 Looking south at Field VII Area 5. Stone Platform 1471 left of center, with Floor 1463 of Stratum IXB in Room 9 to the right (west) of the platform. Wall 1461 separates the platform from Room 9 running toward the camera in the center.

Fig. 243 Looking west into Room 14 paved with Flagstones 1153. Wall 1152 at right. The other walls pictured belong to higher strata.

Fig. 244 Looking north at Stratum IX remains in Field VII Areas 2 and 5. The meter stick lies on Flagstones 1153 in Room 14, Surface 1142 in Yard 18 in foreground. Later Stratum IX features added (cf. Ills. 102 and 103) include Wall 1159 between Room 14 and Yard 18, Pillar 1150 to which the left end of the meter stick points, at its west end, the upright slabs of 1157 creating bins against the south face of 1159. Complex 1155 in lower right corner on Floor 1142, against Wall 1154.

Fig. 245 Floor 1142 with broken Stratum IX cooking pot on it, as it comes to the west balk of Field VII Area 2. In the balk is Fill 1139.

Fig. 246 Looking east at Field IX Areas 3 and 6, Houses A and B, Rooms 3–7.

Fig. 247 Plan and section of Complex 1395-1396.

Fig. 248 Vat 1395 and Platter 1396. The channels in 1396 lead to groove emptying into the buried jar above the right end of the meter stick.

Fig. 249 Detail of section BB in Field VII, displaying Strata IX through VII layering around Complex 1395-1396.

Fig. 250 Walls and surfaces of House 1727 in Field VII.

Fig. 251 Block plan and section of Stratum VII House 1727.

Fig. 252 Packing of sherds and pebbles in Sump 1431.

Fig. 253 Early view of the emerging House 1727 in Field VII. Wall 1619 has the meter stick leaning against it in the upper center. Note dressed block in the third course.

Fig. 254 Looking south at surfaces in the balk between Areas 8 and 5 in Field VII. The balk is at the level of House 1727's central room. A small portion of Surface 1738 (Stratum VIIB) is preserved adjacent to it partially in the shadow of the boulder in the upper left. The next shelf down is Surface 1739 of Stratum VIII, and the meter stick is on Stratum IXA Floor 1744. Note the decayed pillars 1743 left of center.

Fig. 255 Looking north at Stratum VII Hearth 1443.

Fig. 256 Looking west at Room 2 of House 1727 with stone-paved floor. Note entrance pillars at left center.

Fig. 257 Collapse of brick Wall 1319 from the top of stone Wall 1323 in Room 5, viewed from the north. Note crushed cooking pot and jug on Floor 1320.

Fig. 258 Saddle quern and muller in the work area off the southeast corner of House 1727. Note the opening for Silo 1039 near left margin, beyond post with flagstones.

Fig. 259 Looking east at the west balk of Field VII Area 5. Pottery and brick fall from the upper story of House 1727 as first encountered above the floors of Rooms 6 and 1.

Fig. 260 Slab of roofing material fallen into Room 5 of House 1727.

Fig. 261 Debris in Room 1 of House 1727. The flat "terrazzo" slabs lie on brick detritus, at the foot of which are the burned half-round beams that supported the ceiling.

Fig. 262 Looking north at Scree 1539, the collapse of the east wall of House 1727.

Fig. 263 Obverse, impression, and side view of Assyrian adorant seal found in Scree 1539.

Fig. 264 Field VII south balk of Areas 2 and 3. The saucer containing House 1048 is marked with white.

Fig. 265 Looking north in Field II, out the door in Wall 7007. Cobble floor 7024 at right and left, and in the balk beneath the threshold of the door.

Fig. 266 Looking north in Field II with the meter stick on Wall 7026. Crush of pottery at right lies on Floor 7035, decayed brick to left of the wall.

Fig. 267 1956 plan by Robert J. Bull, showing "Wall c'" of the Iron Age, over the East Gate tower.

Fig. 268 Chalcedony *lmbn* seal from Hellenistic fill 1202, dated paleographically to the time of Stratum VI.

Fig. 269 Looking north at Field IX Area 1 balk, with the meter stick on plaster Floor 9037.

Fig. 270 Looking south in Field VII Area 7. Tannur 1828 is in the lower right corner, with Hellenistic Wall 1817 resting on its rim.

Fig. 271 Looking east in Field VII Area 4, with oval installation 1544-1545 at right. The thick plaster layer in the balk is Hellenistic Floor 1521, interrupted just above the meter stick by Pit 1522, cut down almost to the top of 1544-1545.

Fig. 272 Looking north in Field VII Area 2 at Installation 1127.

Fig. 273 Jar forms of Stratum V, Fields VII and IX, from N. Lapp (1985:fig. 4).

Fig. 274 Jug, bowl and crater forms of Stratum V, from Fields VII and IX, from N. Lapp (1985:fig 5).

Fig. 275 Stratum V crater forms of Stratum V, Fields VII and IX, from N. Lapp (1985:fig. 6).

Fig. 276 Cooking pot and lamp forms of Stratum V, Fields VII and IX, from N. Lapp (1985:fig. 7).

Fig. 277 Examples of Attic wares from Stratum V, from N. Lapp (1985:fig. 10).

Fig. 278 Electrum coin minted on Thasos, dated to Stratum V period.

Fig. 279 Impression of a Persian period seal on a bulla. The reverse shows the imprint of papyrus fiber.

Fig. 280 Impression of a lion figure on a Stratum V jar handle, B62, Object #349.

Fig. 281 Seven of the stamp impressions probably from Stratum V, showing an oval with a crossbar (resembling a "theta") with lines running away from the top of the oval. The vertical strokes have been interpreted as signifying "26".

Fig. 282 Fragment of Hellenistic wall on the MB IIC tower wall of the East Gate, Field I.

Fig. 283 Stone-lined flagstone bin outside the fortifications east of the East Gate, assigned to a domestic complex belonging to Stratum IV. Robert J. Bull serves as scale.

Fig. 284 Latest Hellenistic walls overlying the East Gate south tower (after 1956 drawing by Bull).

Fig. 285 Looking north in Field VII Area 4 at Stratum IV plastered Floor 1521. Metalled surface 1530 is in the upper left corner. The wall is 1531.

Fig. 286 Press installation 1525 and Jar 1526, with segments of Floors 1521, 1527 and 1523 (lowest to highest), all of Stratum IV. Looking east in Field VII Area 4.

Fig. 287 Looking north in Field VII Area 3. Stratum IVA Wall 1025 runs through the center from north to south; Wall 1026 abuts it on the right and Wall 1027 abuts it at upper left. Crushed oven or kiln 1024A with segments of Floor 1021 lie to the west of Wall 1025 (left).

Fig. 288 Column Base 23.004 in Field VII Area 23, looking north. Flagstones 23.009 at center.

Fig. 289 Field VII Areas 4 and 7, looking west. Room A of Stratum IIIB is in the center, Room B in the foreground.

Fig. 290 Plastered Bin 1520 at the south edge of Room B, Stratum IIIB. The plaster runs up the face of Wall 1506, upon which the meter stick lies.

Fig. 291 Looking east in Field VII Area 4 at Tannur 1509 and Bench 1518, in Room C.

Fig. 292 Looking south in Field VII Area 4 at the two phases of Stratum III. The junction of Walls 1505 and 1510 dominate the center, the northeast limit of Room E of Stratum IIIA. Stratum IIIB Wall 1516 runs parallel to 1505 at the top center. The rim of Tannur 1509 appears under the east (left) face of 1505 at left center.

Fig. 293 Looking south at the top of the balk in Field VII between Areas 8 and 9. Wall 1701 is in foreground, 1734A behind the meter stick, which lies on Floor 1603, all of Stratum IIIA.

Fig. 294 Field VII Area 6 within the disturbed area of Stratum IIIA. Cobbling 1306 and 1307 appear at the center near the cross balk.

Fig. 295 Cache of silver Ptolemaic tetradrachmas from the edge of the street in Field VII Area 5.

Fig. 296 Looking south over Field IX Areas 1 and 3, at the 9514 complex of Stratum IVA.

Fig. 297 Looking west in Field IX Area 1 at Wall 9514, interrupted by Islamic burial. Random rocks in foreground came to rest on probable IVA surface.

Fig. 298 Looking east at Field IX Area 4 showing cobbling 9760 of Stratum IVA.

Fig. 299 Looking south in Field I Area 7. The meter stick lies on Floor 205 inside the elbow of Wall 160 at left and 160A across the center. Floor 206 lies in the space beyond 160A.

Fig. 300 Field II, Room 1 of the Hellenistic House, looking to the northeast. The black line in the balk at right marks the bottom of the modern overburden.

Fig. 301 Structure 7015, dividing Rooms 2 and 3 in the Hellenistic House, Field II.

Fig. 302 Crushed jars on Floor 7099, Field II, Room 3, probably of Stratum II.

Fig. 303 Field II looking west. Wall 7104 well above chalk surface marking uppermost use of the yard with the Hellenistic House. Wall 7104 is assigned to Stratum IA.

Fig. 304 Field IX Area 1 looking south. Islamic burial oriented with head to west, face turned to the south.

ACKNOWLEDGEMENTS

THEIR NUMBERS ARE LEGION—THOSE WHO have contributed to the appearance of these volumes on Tell Balâṭah/Shechem; indeed it is almost certain that some names deserving appreciation will have been omitted inadvertently. Almost the entire archaeological community has been involved in some way or other, and about half the rest of the world also, it would seem.

The Introduction lists the names of the scholars and students who actually moved and studied the soil of the ancient *tell*. Special thanks must go to a group involved in assessing, checking, editing and producing this report: Phyllis K. Campbell, Billie Jean Collins, Michael D. Coogan, Nancy L. Lapp, Gloria London, Chris Madell, James F. Ross, Karen I. Summers, Joe D. Seger, Lawrence E. Toombs, Prescott H. Williams, Jr., and an anonymous reader who was among those in the early assessment. I have no wish to rank these colleagues for the extent of their contributions, but each of them will know what they did, will appropriately felicitate themselves for the good things, and will blame me for the errors not caught! Out of this group, my warmest gratitude to Billie Jean and Chris for composition, Prescott for giving one last thorough proofreading, and Phyllis for seeing it to the end.

Without the support of McCormick Theological Seminary over a couple of decades, the goal of publication would not have been reached. It required the attention of three presidents: David Ramage, G. Daniel Little and Cynthia M. Campbell; four deans: Robert Worley, Heidi M. Hadsell, Homer U. Ashby and David Esterline; and three business managers: Anthony Ruger, Kris Ronnow and Kurt Gabbard with their helpful staff. McCormick's role as a center for archaeological research has been noteworthy and long-standing; for an urban seminary with profound commitments to the education of men and women for ministry to have kept the importance of discovery and research an integral part of its work deserves high accolades.

Other institutions have been immensely helpful: ASOR, the American Schools of Oriental Research, has housed and nourished archaeological inquiry for over a century now, seeing to the start and guidance and publication of a host of undertakings. Its affiliates: AIAR, the W. F. Albright Institute of Archaeological Research in Jerusalem; ACOR, the American Center for Oriental Research in Amman; and CAARI, the Cyprus American Institute of Archaeological Research in Nicosia, have provided shelter and stimulus to Shechemites involved in producing this report on innumerable occasions. Personal thanks are due to St. George's College and Dean John L. Peterson for a research appointment in 1994 that permitted regular access to Tell Balâṭah and a pleasant place to write.

And then there is money. This work is costly. All of the following have contributed. I name them with profound appreciation, but will not embarrass them with greater detail:

The ASOR Harris Grants, through its Committee on Archaeological Policy
The Luther I. Replogle Foundation
The S. H. and Helen R. Scheuer Family Foundation
The Association of Theological Schools (TS & R Grant)
McCormick Theological Seminary
Betsey Bobrinskoy
Kew Sun Chai
Mary Louise Ellenberger
H. Burr Grumman
James L. and Patricia Macdonald
James B. and Mary Moffatt
Christopher and Marcia Pottle
James and Miriam Ross
Richard J. Scheuer

Then there is one person who has contributed on every front, by sacrifice of time and money, by encouragement, by appropriate critique, by shared frustration and the finest of loyalty. I cannot thank enough my wife Phyllis Kletzien Campbell. She has lived, endured and supported Shechem as fully as anyone who dug it, wrote its field reports, paid for it, and cheered it on—from the start and through to this fruition. I dare to hope for yet more miles to travel with her and with the family we have raised together.

Edward F. Campbell, Jr.
Winter, 2002

INTRODUCTION

THERE ARE SEVERAL ISSUES TO ADDRESS at the beginning of this two-volume set. They have to do with their intent, why they take the form they do, what methods the dig followed and what that means for this presentation, and who really has written it. Clarity on these matters should help the reader in using it.

THE BOOK'S INTENT

What I have set out to do is to present the stratigraphy and architectural remains of the tell of ancient Shechem, Tell Balâṭah, on the eastern outskirts of the modern municipality of Nablus, in what was at the time of excavation the independent village of Balâṭah (Frontispiece, Ill. 1, figs. 1 and 2). Attention focuses on the 24 strata found at the tell itself, leaving to other volumes reports on the surrounding region, indications of Roman/Byzantine settlement off the tell under modern Balâṭah, the related site of Tell er-Râs, and the search for adjacent cemeteries (cf. Campbell 1991 and the forthcoming volumes on Tell er-Râs by Robert Bull with W. Jack Bennett). Except for plates that sample pottery assemblages from certain key loci, I have left the reports on ceramics and the small finds for other volumes as well (such as Cole 1984).

The site of Tell Balâṭah, first identified as an ancient ruin and proposed as ancient Shechem in 1903, was excavated by an Austro-German team in the period between 1913 and 1934, and by the Drew-McCormick Archaeological Expedition, later named the Joint Expedition, between 1956 and 1973 (Ills. 3 and 4).

Through a series of circumstances, there has not been published a full portrayal of the site's stratigraphy. In hindsight, it is probably the first thing that an archaeological expedition should do, and do it immediately upon cessation of the field work as a pure description with such drawings as are ready and many photographs. Now, 89 years after Ernest Sellin began the dig, and 29 years after the expedition mounted by G. Ernest Wright left the field, this volume sets out to give that sort of portrayal to this mound of ancient cities that began its history at least 4000 years BCE and ended its pre-modern history in 107 BCE. Explanations for delays could be given at great length, but to no valuable purpose.

THE FORMAT

The publication plans of both the Sellin team and Wright's Joint Expedition encountered complex difficulties. Sellin's efforts and most of his records, including a manuscript describing his findings, were destroyed in a bombing attack on Berlin in 1943, and within two years Sellin was dead. The deaths of G. Ernest Wright and of a number of his staff, and the diversion of other staff members to major responsibility with other expeditions, have disrupted the fulfillment of the publication schedule of the Joint Expedition.

That schedule called for publication of pottery corpora from each era of the site's history. Pottery studies were to be distributed among volumes on Chalcolithic/Early Bronze (Strata 24–23), MB IIA (Strata 22–21), MB IIB (Strata 20–17), MB IIC (Strata 16–15), LB/Iron I (Strata 14–11), Iron II (Strata 10–6), and Persian/Hellenistic (Strata 5–1). Substantial progress has been made on these seven pottery volumes, one of which (Cole 1984) on MB IIB has been published. The doctoral dissertations of Seger (1965) on MB IIC, Holladay (1966) on Iron II, and P. Lapp on Hellenistic (published as Lapp 1961) serve as good introductions to Shechem ceramics for these periods, and both Paul and Nancy Lapp have presented important groups of Persian period pottery from Shechem (P. Lapp 1970; N. Lapp 1985).

Volumes were also planned on the Fortifications, the Public Buildings, and the Domestic Quarters. A volume presenting the non-ceramic "small

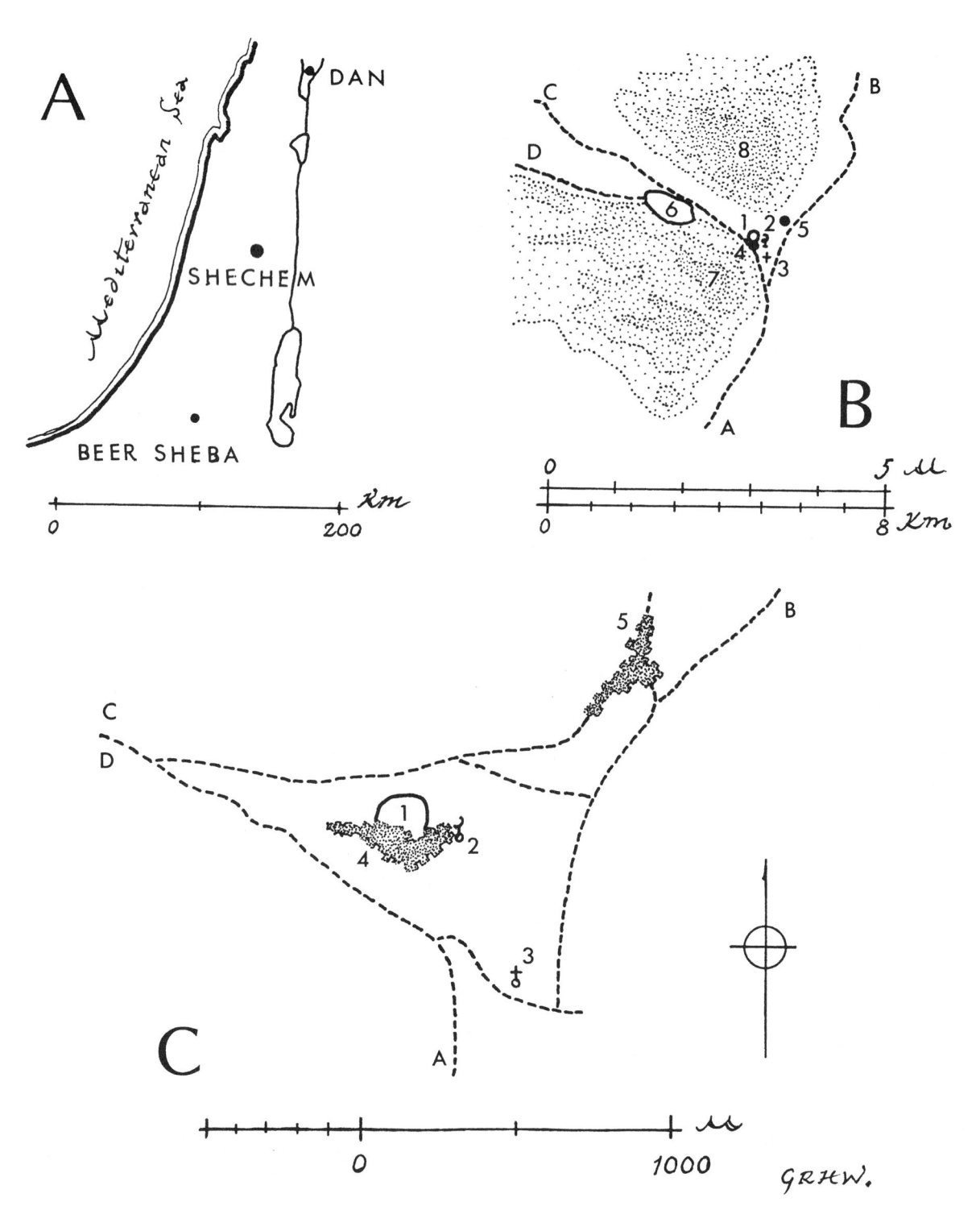

Fig. 1. Shechem: Uncrowned Queen of Palestine, Navel of the Land. Map A: Shechem between Dan and Beersheba. Map B: Tell Balâṭah (1) adjacent to the Qubr Yusuf (Joseph's Tomb, the weli at 2); the Church at Jacob's Well (+ at 3); Tell er-Râs on a forward spur of Mt. Gerizim (4); Askar village (• at 5); Nablus center (6); summits of Gerizim (7) and Ebal (8). Map C: Tell Balâṭah (1) partly covered by Balâṭah village (4), with Joseph's Tomb (2) and Jacob's Well (3). Askar village at 5.

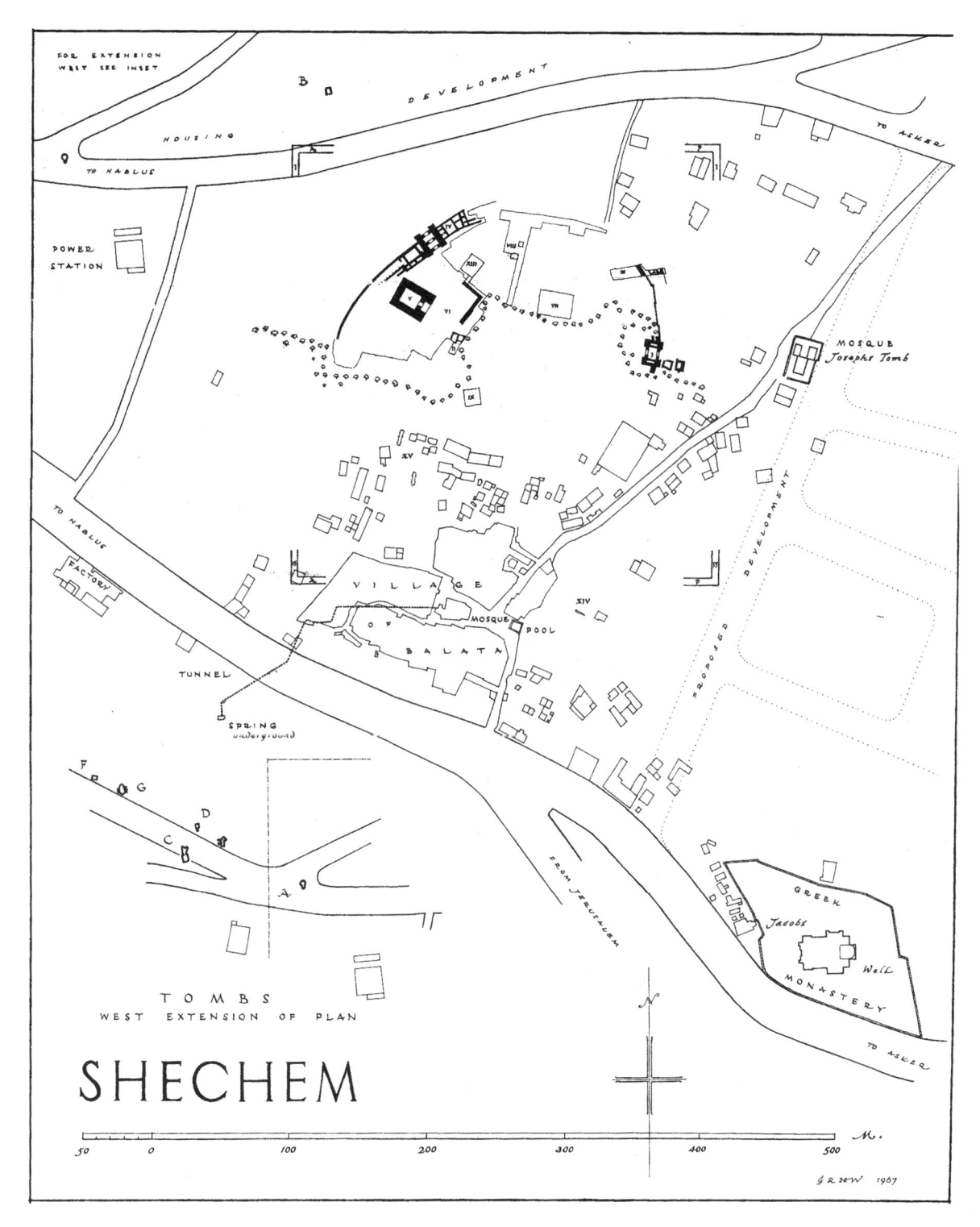

Fig. 2. Plan of Balâṭah village and environs, with inset showing location of tombs.

finds" was to be followed then by an interpretive volume on the site's contributions to reconstructing the history of the city—bringing the total to twelve. When the study of Tell er-Râs, located above Tell Balâṭah on a spur of Mt. Gerizim, was added to the research plan, a thirteenth volume was included. And with the addition of a regional survey to the program came plans for a fourteenth, since published as Campbell (1991).

As time has passed, it has become clear that what scholars now need involves combining the projected volumes on the fortifications, public buildings and domestic quarters into a guide to the tell's stratigraphy. Shechem's remains provide important data to the comparative study of the archaeology of the Levant and even incompletely published have already played a significant role in scholarship. This two-volume work brings together the data. It will also serve as the backbone for the ceramic typologies yet to be completed. New researchers are now joining the team, who must depend upon records rather than field participation. This work will provide a source for their work. Researches representing both these scenarios are in process.

The format of the work is designed to make it easy for readers to study the narrative while having the pictures and plans open before their eyes. The second volume, by G. R. H. Wright, contains 175 plans, sections and drawings, along with his illuminating description of the process and perils of recording the finds. Here in the first volume, the text is interwoven with photographs and more of G. R. H. Wright's work depicting more specific features.

As publication coordinator after Ernest Wright's death in 1974, I have sought in the narrative to bring the fruits of many people's labors and a multitude of field reports and notebooks into one account. There are many resources:

1. Sellin and Welter wrote preliminary reports on their seasons in the field. These reports served to inform the research design of the Joint Expedition. A small corpus of plans and sections were drawn of parts of the Austro-German work and were recovered for the use of the Joint Expedition. Every effort has been made to incorporate their findings. Early in the work of the Joint Expedition, Siegfried Horn prepared a translation of all their writing and of other German commentary, as well as of the Dutch reports of Böhl, for the use of the Joint Expedition.

2. Between the Joint Expedition's field seasons of 1962 and 1964, G. Ernest Wright authored a volume entitled *Shechem: The Biography of a Biblical City* (hereafter *SBBC*) which in semi-popular style told the story of the site's excavation history, including a thorough summation of Sellin and Welter's work and the first four American field seasons. The galleys of this work went into the field with the staff for the 1964 season and were corrected slightly during that campaign.

3. For each season, in each sector of work (designated "Fields," of which I–IX, XIII and XV were on Tell Balâṭah itself), field supervisors wrote a detailed report with a locus list arranging pottery and object and stating the field analyses of the pottery. From these, first Ernest Wright and later teams of staff prepared preliminary reports which appeared in the *Bulletin of the American Schools of Oriental Research* in numbers 144, 148, 161, 169, 180, 190, 204, 205 and 216. Using these preliminary reports, scholars could follow the dig's discoveries and, with careful attention, note corrections and augmentations. Not every feature of these reports was well published; a few plans and photographs were incorrectly captioned and last minute, but important, changes were located out of place or placed in little noticed addenda. One responsibility of the current volume is to resolve discrepancies, explain and correct erroneous descriptions and interpretations, and provide coherence. Sometimes this has extended to correcting the publications of others, who depended on an incomplete or confusing presentation of data.

4. Daily notebooks of all sectors dug, kept by area supervisors for the information of the field supervisor, are archived and have been used in this volume to check data and interpretations.

5. A number of encyclopedia and dictionary articles on Shechem have appeared, authored by members of the Shechem staff (Campbell 1993; Toombs 1985a, 1992, 1996; G. E. Wright 1978b). As with *SBBC*, these combine description, archaeological interpretation and biblical interpretation. It was a hallmark of the Joint Expedition's director, Ernest Wright, to think and to write in this fashion, and his style tended to influence all those who worked with him and wrote about Shechem—and it was his habit to encourage the staff to participate in all the writing about the dig. While I have aimed in this narrative volume to be

primarily descriptive, I have not avoided attention especially to problems of interpreting the archaeological remains, building on Ernest Wright's interpretation and staff deliberations.

In short, then, as a representative of a large team I have taken all the resources available and tried to present them in sequence. The sequence begins at the bottom of the tell and works its way to the top; chronology governs the flow. In each period, description is given of the data from the various fields of excavation, usually working with fortifications, then public buildings, and finally regions of domestic housing, highlighting digging loci that give the clearest picture and describing all the recorded architecture. Summaries are frequently given of the most firmly established loci that define strata.

An unusual feature of the presentation, which may at first seem odd or even distracting, is that indication is often given of the amount of available registered pottery first analyzed and dated in the field and now available for review and more precise study. The purpose is to encourage future researchers to join the effort and afford them guidance about good places to begin while the memories of the excavators are still in play.

METHODS

The Joint Expedition followed a field technique to which its staff members have kept their allegiance and upon which they have built. More sophisticated field techniques have been developed, and as some of them came into play the Joint Expedition adopted them, although the Expedition was in the field just at the cusp of movements into what is termed the "New Archaeology." Furthermore, much greater rigor has been introduced into methods of interpreting archaeological results. Some of that rigor has hopefully found its way into this volume and some new ventures at interpretation appear from time to time.

The Joint Expedition's field technique wedded the Wheeler-Kenyon method of tracing soil deposition to the ongoing typological study of pottery forms as they emerged from the stratified deposits. Conversation took place between the digging of the soil and the reading of the pottery.

Stratified deposits provided groups of contemporary pottery forms, but pottery in such groups could not always be counted upon to be homogeneous because of the tricks a mound can play in churning up early material and the intrusions that later people can introduce into what seem "sealed" stratified layers. Notable at Shechem were immense efforts at leveling the site and using fill to cover older remains. As a result, the Expedition sometimes found recognizably anachronistic sherds in pottery analysis and were able to go back to discover intrusions in the soil not perceived at the time of digging. The candor with which attention is drawn to unnoticed intrusions during excavation may seem overstated, but we may just as well admit to the vicissitudes of even the most careful excavation work.

A second Shechem procedure intentionally worked with sherds. The vast majority of pottery in a stratified mound consists of broken fragments, not complete or restorable vessels. Most of the judgments about the date of pottery were made from deposits of broken sherds, rather than from whole vessels *in situ*. The site presented a relatively small number of complete forms in crushes upon floors or the like, although these of course became strong anchors for the pottery sequences developed.

In a site with so many fills and intrusions, mixed deposits of pottery were the rule rather than the exception. Pottery in fills and in thin makeup layers for new surfaces had to be analyzed by judging what were the latest sherds sealed beneath a defined surface or structure and what were the earliest sherds *later than the latest below*, found above the sealing feature. A lucid rationale for the various elements in this procedure of working with fragments is given in Cole 1984:1–7.

Always a problem in modern excavation of large sites is the coordination of the stratigraphy in widely separated excavation plots across the sites. The conversation between stratigraphy and pottery analysis has special pertinence to this task. Where layering was very thin and strata separated by only a few centimeters, coordination with layers in another location is acutely difficult and pottery groupings may not tell their tale properly. Indeed, it is not inconceivable that two floorings reaching the opposite sides of the same wall are not quite contemporary, to take an extreme example. Much more of a problem is to coordinate a surface or structure in a field at the center of the tell with a surface or structure built on top of the fortifications, or with the floors of a public building on the acropolis.

The Joint Expedition embraced this problem and took the risks it entails seriously. Here the pottery analysis that was going on throughout each season, in between seasons, and from one field season to another provided the basis for coordination of the stratigraphy. Staff members became expert at recognizing forms and wares, admittedly using only macro-analysis. But their work enabled Lawrence Toombs to bring the site into a coordinated matrix with articles published in 1972 and 1976 and displayed with minor corrections in the accompanying chart.

Toombs's coordination governs the presentation made in this volume. There may yet remain some problematic coordinations. And it will be seen that sometimes one field does not display the same number of separations within a given period as does another field. Further research with the pottery may yield refinements, but again this volume gives the basis for such research.

AUTHORSHIP

The title pages of the two parts contain my name and the name of G. R. H. Wright as author. This is manifestly misleading, but someone must take responsibility for the presentation as here given. Each field supervisor is a primary author as well. In alphabetic order, they are:

Bernhard W. Anderson and William R. Farmer (Field I, 1957)

†Robert G. Boling (Tananir, 1968)

Robert J. Bull (Field I, 1956; Field V, 1957, 1960, 1962)

†Joseph A. Callaway (Field IX, 1962, 1964)

Edward F. Campbell, Jr. (Field VII, 1960, 1962, 1964)

William G. Dever (Field IV, 1972, 1973)

Robert W. Funk (Field III, 1957)

†Siegfried H. Horn (Field VII West, 1962)

Horace D. Hummel (Field VIII, 1957; Field IV, 1966)

H. Darrell Lance (Field I, 1964)

†Paul W. Lapp (Field I, 1962)

†H. Neil Richardson (Field II, 1957)

James F. Ross (Field II, 1968; Field III, 1964; Field VI, 1960, 1962, 1964)

Joe D. Seger (Field XIII, 1969)

Lawrence E. Toombs (Field I, 1957, 1966; Field XIII, 1968),

†G. Ernest Wright (throughout).

To realize that of these seventeen, six are deceased is no small source of sorrow, for the Shechem team was and remains a team, and the report of their work a labor of love. As this volume came into being, I lost certain opportunities to consult these colleagues personally about their records.

Among the roster of authors, some have been especially crucial to the completion of the narrative volume: James Ross, Lawrence Toombs, Robert Bull, John S. Holladay and Joe Seger, as well as Nancy L. Lapp who took up her husband's work at his death and has carried forward on Hellenistic materials. These six have read and corrected text, reviewed newly drawn plans, and made sure I understood what they learned from the site and wrote in their reports. Two other persons who are truly authors are G. R. H. Wright the dig's architectural draftsman and authority on architecture, and Lee C. Ellenberger, the dig photographer (deceased).

Each of these authors, however, would in turn mention the staff members of the expedition who worked with them. This seems an appropriate place, then, to list all who worked on the Shechem research staff, listed by the campaigns when they played their valuable parts.

1956: Bernhard W. Anderson, Hasan 'Awad (Jordan Department of Antiquities, foreman), Robert J. Bull, Douglas Trout, G. Ernest Wright

1957: Bernhard W. Anderson, Jean G. Boling, Robert G. Boling, George W. Buchanan, Robert J. Bull, Edward F. Campbell, Jr., Lee C. Ellenberger, William R. Farmer, Robert W. Funk, David M. Graybeal, Paul Hollenbach, Spiridion Jahshan (foreman), Howard C. Kee, Nancy L. Lapp, Paul W. Lapp, Far'ah Ma'ayeh (Jordan

Department of Antiquities), H. Neil Richardson, Ovid R. Sellers, Lawrence W. Sinclair, Hans H. Steckeweh, James T. Stewart, Arthur E. Talbert, Lawrence E. Toombs, G. Ernest Wright, G. R. H. Wright

1960: Robert J. Bull, Vivian J. Bull, Joseph A. Callaway, Edward F. Campbell, Jr., J. Stanley Chesnut, Dan P. Cole, Lee C. Ellenberger, John S. Holladay, Jr., Siegfried H. Horn, Herbert B. Huffmon, Mary Lou Huffmon, Horace D. Hummel, Jack R. Irwin, Spiridion Jahshan (foreman), Nancy L. Lapp, Paul W. Lapp, J. Patterson Lockwood, J. Tracy Luke, Maurice Luker, Jr., James L. Mays, Clinton D. Morrison, Sami Rashid (Jordan Department of Antiquities), H. Neil Richardson, James F. Ross, Ovid R. Sellers, Henry O. Thompson, Lawrence E. Toombs, E. Jerry Vardaman, G. Ernest Wright, G. R. H. Wright

1962: Roger S. Boraas, Robert J. Bull, Vivian J. Bull, Joseph A. Callaway, Sara Callaway, Edward F. Campbell, Jr., J. Stanley Chesnut, Dan P. Cole, Rafiq Dajani (Jordan Department of Antiquities), William G. Dever, Lee C. Ellenberger, Albert E. Glock, Carl Graesser, Jr., Mustafa Tawfiq Hazim (foreman), Delbert R. Hillers, John S. Holladay, Jr., Siegfried H. Horn, Hanna E. Kassis, H. Darrell Lance, Carol Landes, George M. Landes, Paul W. Lapp, Murray B. Nicol, James F. Ross, Robert F. Schnell, Joe D. Seger, Ovid R. Sellers, Byron E. Shafer, Aia Soggin, J. Alberto Soggin, Henry O. Thompson, Lawrence E. Toombs, David L. Voelter, Prescott H. Williams, Jr., G. Ernest Wright, G. R. H. Wright, Bishara G. Zogbi

1964: Nicola B. Antar (Jordan Department of Antiquities), Dewey M. Beegle, Marian Beegle, Roger S. Boraas, Robert J. Bull, Vivian J. Bull, Joseph A. Callaway, Sara Callaway, Edward F. Campbell, Jr., William G. Dever, Lee C. Ellenberger, Mary Louise Ellenberger, James M. Fennelly, Mustafa Tawfiq Hazim (foreman), John S. Holladay, Jr., William L. Holladay, Siegfried H. Horn, Dan T. Hughs, James Kirby, H. Darrell Lance, Paul A. Riemann, James F. Ross, Joe D. Seger, Ovid R. Sellers, Henry O. Thompson, Oliver M. Unwin, Prescott H. Williams, Jr., G. Ernest Wright, G. R. H. Wright, Kyle M. Yates, Jr.

1966: Nicola B. Antar (Jordan Department of Antiquities), W. Jack Bennett, Edward P. Blair, Robert G. Boling, Roger S. Boraas, William H. Brownlee, Robert J. Bull, Vivian J. Bull, Dan P. Cole, Stuart D. Currie, Bruce T. Dahlberg, Lee C. Ellenberger, Robert W. Fisher, Holt H. Graham, Mustafa Tawfiq Hazim (foreman), D. Larrimore Holland, Dan T. Hughs, Horace D. Hummel, Howard C. Kee, Charles F. Kraft, David A. Lutz, ʻAbdel-rauf Majid (Jordan Department of Antiquities), ʻAli Nazmi Saʻidi (Jordan Department of Antiquities), Ovid R. Sellers, Albert Sundberg, Jr., Henry O. Thompson, Lawrence E. Toombs, Oliver M. Unwin, Barbara Vesper, Walter Vesper, David L. Voelter, Prescott H. Williams, Jr., John Worrell, G. Ernest Wright

1968: W. Jack Bennett, Edward P. Blair, Robert G. Boling, Roger S. Boraas, William H. Brownlee, Robert J. Bull, Vivian J. Bull, Reuben C. Bullard, Edward F. Campbell, Jr., Sara Currie, Stuart D. Currie, Lee C. Ellenberger, Ibrahim el-Fanni (Department of Antiquities), Holt H. Graham, Rebecca Graham, Ralph O. Hjelm, Dan T. Hughs, Aziz Jedullah (foreman, Tell er-Râs), Charles F. Kraft, Leroy A. Miltner, Robert Northup, Wolfgang M. W. Roth, Tawfiq Salman, Joe D. Seger, Edward Tango (foreman, Tell Balâṭah), Henry O. Thompson, Carol Toombs, Lawrence E. Toombs, Oliver M. Unwin, George C. Whipple, G. Ernest Wright, G. R. H. Wright

1968 Tananir: Frank Benz, Robert G. Boling, James Charlesworth, Eduardo D'Olivera, Lee C. Ellenberger, Margaret McKenna, Karin E. Rabkin, John Ribar, Edward Tango (foreman)

1969 Tell Balâṭah: Frank Benz, Ibrahim el-Fanni (Department of Antiquities), Andrew Klein, John Landgraf, Janet MacLennan, Dean Moe, Karen E. Rabkin, Joe D. Seger

1972–73: William G. Dever, Nasr Dhiab Mansoor (foreman)

It will not have escaped the attention of the readers of this list of 115 different names that they represent a remarkable cross section of biblical and archaeological scholarship in the second half of the twentieth century. My great hope is that this volume honors them all, embarrasses them little, and reminds them of adventurous times getting Balâṭah soil beneath our fingernails and Balâṭah dust into our lungs.

8 SHECHEM III. INTRODUCTION

Stratum	Date	Field I Gate	Field I Interior	Field II	Field III	Field IV 7200	Northwest Gate	Field IV 7300
Zero	ca. 650-1000 C.E.	Plow Zone	Plow Zone		Plow Zone			
I A	Post-100 B.C.E.			7111		SELLIN EXCAVATION		
I	ca. 150-107		154-155 Complex	7104-7105?				
II	ca. 190-150			House, 1-3	Upper phase			
III A	ca. 225-190	Hellenistic Tower	160 and 170 Complexes	House, Room 1	Lower phase 609-612			
III B	ca. 250-225							
IV A	ca. 300-250	Reuse East Gate						
IV B	ca. 325-300							
A B A N D O N M E N T ca. 475-331 B.C.E.							
V	ca. 600?-425							
VI A	ca. 724-600	Rebuild? Wall c′				SELLIN EXCAVATION		
VI B								
VII	ca. 750-724	Sherds in spill down slope	Fl. 420-421	House	Sherds in spill down slope			
VIII	ca. 810-750		Floor 419					
IX A	ca. 860-810		176 Complex					
IX B	ca. 920-860							
X A	ca. 950-920		175 Complex	Scraps of 7051 house				
X B	ca. 975-950							
A B A N D O N M E N T ca. 1150/25-975 B.C.E.							
XI	ca. 1200-1150/25	LB/Iron I Gate Tower 127	178 Complex	Unexcavated			Gate perhaps in reuse	
XII	c. 1325-1200		Comp. 179					
XIII	c. 1400-1325		Plaza 509					
XIV	c. 1450-1400		Flags. 127B		Reuse Wall B			
A B A N D O N M E N T ca. 1550-1450 B.C.E.							
XV	c. 1600-1550	Wall B			Wall B	7200	Gate built and in use	7300 temple
XVI	c. 1650-1600	Wall A			Wall A	Tower 7287		Plaza 7318
XVII	c. 1675-1650	C Rampart			C Rampart	C Rampart		C Rampart
XVIII	c. 1700-1675							
XIX	c. 1725-1700							
XX	c. 1750-1725							
XXI	c. 1800-1750		Unexcavated					
XXII	c. 1900-1800							
UNOCCUPIED ca. 3200-1900 B.C.E.							
XXIII	EB IA							
XXIV	EB IB		Unexcavated					
Bedrock								

Stratum	Field V	Field VI	Field VI.2	Field VII	Field VIII	Field IX	Field XIII	Field XV
Zero	SELLIN EXCAVATION			Plow Zone	SELLIN TRENCH H 1913-14	Islamic Cemetery	STECKEWEH AND SELLIN 1934	Trench 1 7505
I A						Phase 2		Trench 2 7529
I				I				Unexcavated
II				II				
III A				III A				
III B				III B				
IV A				IV A				
IV B				IV B				
A B A N D O N M E N T ca. 475-331 B.C.E.							
V	SELLIN EXCAVATION	SELLIN EXCAVATION		V	SELLIN TRENCH H 1913-14	Phase 5	STECKEWEH AND SELLIN 1934	Unexcavated
VI A				VI A		Phases 6 a-b		
VI B				VI B				
VII				VII A-B		Phase 7		
VIII				VIII		Phs. 8a-b		
IX A	5900 Granary			IX A	Phase 1	Phase 9a		
IX B				IX B		Phase 9b		
X A	Storage Pits			Layer 1	Phase 2	Phase 10		
X B				Layer 2			Scraps	
A B A N D O N M E N T ca. 1150/25-975 B.C.E.							
XI	5700 Temple 2a		Phase 1	Layers 3-4	Phase 3	Phase 11	Phase 1	Unexcavated
XII								
XIII	5700 Temple 2b		Phase 3	Layer 6a	Phase 4		Amarna	
XIV			Phase 4	Layer 6b		Phs. 13-14?	Pre-Amarna	
A B A N D O N M E N T ca. 1550-1450 B.C.E.							
XV	Migdal Temenoi 7-6	930 Complex?	MB IIC Phase 1-3	Layer 7	Phases 5-6	Phs. 13-14?	Terraced Housing	Unexcavated
XVI						Phase 15		
XVII		Temenos 5			Area 1 C Rampart	Phase 16	Areas 5-6	
XVIII		Temenos 4		Unexcavated				
XIX		Temenos 3	C Rampart				C Rampart	
XX	Wall D	Temenos 2	Wall D			Phase 17	Unexcavated	
XXI		Temenos 1b			Fill	Phase 18		
XXII		Temenos 1a				Phs. 19-20		
UNOCCUPIED ca. 3200-1900 B.C.E.							
XXIII	Pit 5062				Fill			
XXIV		Unexcavated	Unexcavated			Phs. 21-22	Unexcavated	Unexcavated
Bedrock	Reached	Reached			Reached	Reached		

Stratification by field at Shechem. The terms used in each box are from preliminary reports in BASOR and from field reports in the Shechem archive, as well as from the text in this volume. This should allow correlation to other Shechem resources.

CHAPTER 1

THE EARLIEST STRATA: CHALCOLITHIC/EARLY BRONZE I AND MIDDLE BRONZE IIA

THE FOURTH MILLENNIUM

FOURTH MILLENNIUM STRATIGRAPHY was reached at two locations on Tell Balâṭah, just above sterile soil on bedrock. The sites are in Field IX, Area 4, where a Chalcolithic complex seals a makeup which also contains artifacts, and Field V, beneath the cella of the Fortress Temple, where soundings encountered cobbled and chalk segments of flooring and a clay-lined pit adjacent to a bedrock outcrop. In Field VI, Area 3EF, deep beneath Temenos Wall 900, bedrock was reached with a deep fill above it heavy with Chalcolithic/EB I pottery, always with a small admixture of MB IIA. For the positions of the fields, see Ill. 2.

Field IX (Ills. 141, 142, 145)

In 1964, work in Field IX reached bedrock in the northwest square of the field, in a 2.00 m probe in its southwest corner (Ill. 141, the IX AA section). Water sprang from a fissure in the rock, and the 0.50 to 0.65 m thick layer (IX AA:#126) of brown earth on the rock was wet. Heavy with pebbles, it was sterile of artifacts. Above it was an accumulation more than 1.00 m thick (IX AA:#125) of brown and grey soil of clay-like consistency; devoid of pottery, it produced a flint sickle blade. These two layers account for from 1.55 to 2.10 m of soil above bedrock, which here lies at elevation 1.40, more than 12 m lower than the bedrock of the knoll in Field V, 75 m to the northwest (correcting Bull, *et al.* 1965:17, which places the two bedrock elevations as approximately the same).

Rubbly soil in two distinguishable layers, 9925 and 9924 (IX AA:##124 & 123 and Ill. 145 = IX EE:##91 & 92) overlay the accumulation on bedrock. Loci 9925 and 9924 contained Chalcolithic and Early Bronze I sherds in substantial quantity: 16 from 9925 and 26 from 9924 were registered and saved. The evidence suggests fourth millennium Chalcolithic settlement uphill and nearby, from which material washed to its present location. Upon this eroded material lay locus 9921 (AA:#122, EE:#89), dark brown earth flecked with lumps of charcoal, rich in Chalcolithic sherds (140 registered) along with a bone gaming piece (B64 Obj. #707), a bone pendant (#706) and a fragment of a granite bowl rim (#682). Locus 9921 was makeup for the structures collectively designated locus 9917. These erosion layers and makeup evidenced an earlier phase of Chalcolithic use of the site, while the structures represented a later phase.

The configuration of locus 9917 is shown in Ill. 122 and fig. 3. The complex extended beyond the excavated area in every direction. In the northwest corner was a segment of wall, suggesting a standing structure barely encroaching into the square. The uppermost stones in the wall were 0.50 to 0.60 m above the adjacent cobbling. The cobbling did not continue under the wall; the two ingredients were apparently a unit. The cobbling stones were water-worn, unlike most stones in fills at Shechem, and were presumably intentionally selected for a surface upon which to live and walk.

Fig. 3. Field IX, Stratum XXIV remains, looking west in Area 4.

Four curvatures of slightly larger stones rose 0.10 to 0.30 m above the cobbling but were integrated with it. Three, A, B and C on Ill. 122, appeared to be bases of dwelling pits, perhaps originally covered by skin-on-frame superstructure. Curvature D was thought in the field to be the result of water erosion coursing around the adjacent wall, but it may also represent a dwelling pit. Curvature B if extrapolated would have had a diameter of ca. 2.60 m, more than sufficient for a recumbent human; A and C would both have been less than 1.60 m in diameter, rather cramped for human occupation. This complex constitutes Stratum XXIV, the earliest coherent architectural feature on the tell.

Locus 9916 (AA:#120) was the blanket of soil, at least 0.50 m to as much as 0.80 m thick, covering the entire 9917 complex. No distinction was discerned between the ceramic forms lying directly on 9917 cobbling and those throughout the sticky brown soil of 9916. Sherds were small; none could be reconstructed toward whole vessels. The expedition registered 44 indicator sherds sealed in the layer. An ivory gaming piece (B64 Obj. #675) came from 9916.

While locus 9916 cannot be appropriately designated occupation debris, it is more likely to have been *in situ* accumulation than erosion debris. It was topped by two distinguishable layers of rubbly soil, loci 9915 and 9914 (AA:##119 & 118, EE:##:85 & 86). The lower, 9915, was characterized by fine grains of soil along with rubble, suggesting erosion by wind and water. Fifty-two registered sherds from this layer received the field call "Chalcolithic/EB," and now demand restudy. From locus 9914, which contained in its rubble

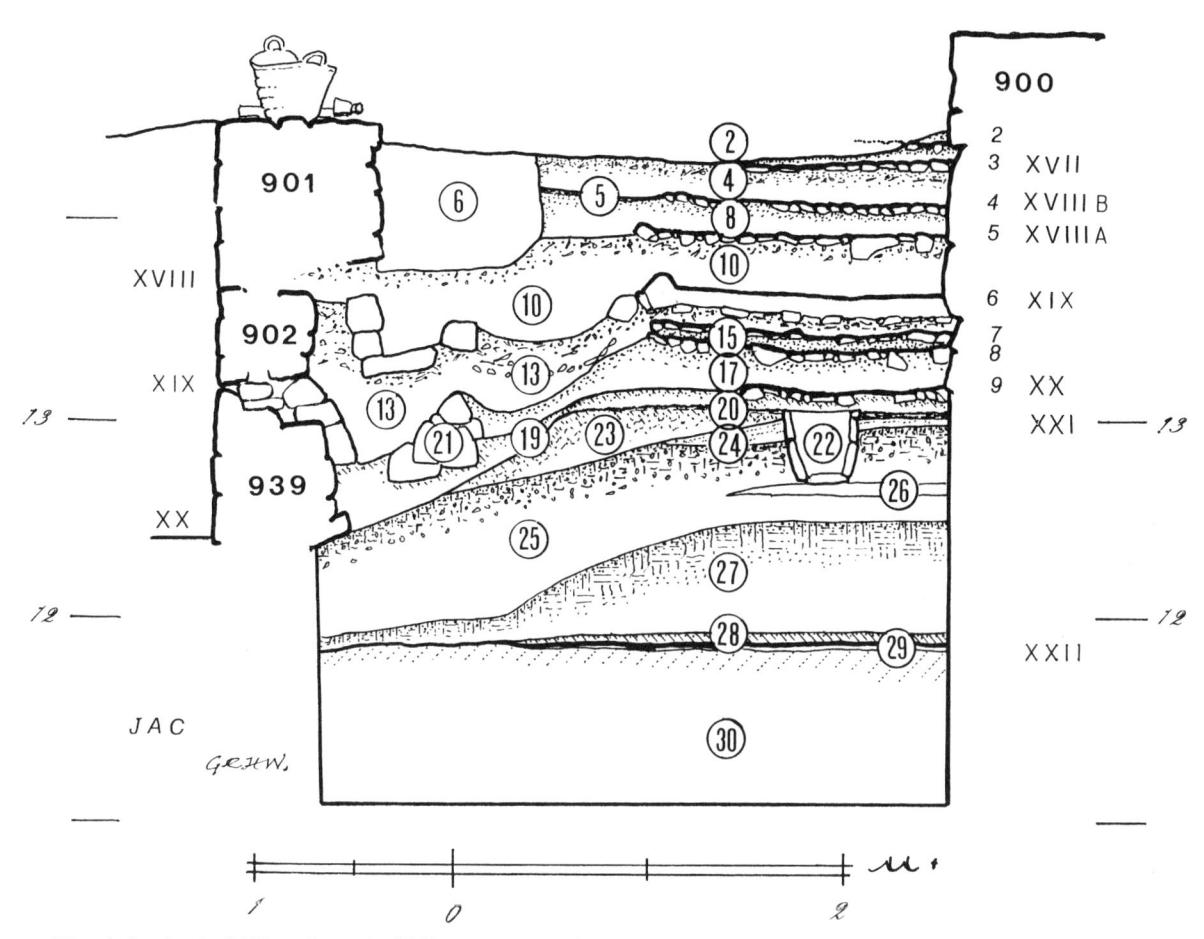

Fig. 4. Section in 3 EF as drawn in 1960, now reversed and serving as part of VI BB (see Ill. 83 with revised key). Note the sequence of street numbers placed on the profile of Wall 900, and the layering beneath the foot of Wall 900.

many lumps of charcoal, 89 indicator sherds were also analyzed as "Chalcolithic/EB." The charcoal ingredient in 9914 suggests nearby camping activity, but there were no architectural remains.

The present assessment of the pottery in layers 9916, 9921, 9924 and 9925, that is, with the two phases which have the cobbled structure 9917 and its makeup as interface, is Chalcolithic with associations to the Beersheban tradition. The prevailing impression is that the material culture is earlier than what was at first called Chalcolithic during the 1960 campaign in Fields VI and V (Bull, et al. 1965:16–17).

Field V (Ills. 8, 67)

Deep beneath the Fortress Temple, two trenches (5052 and 5051) in soil undisturbed by Austro-German digging reached a rock outcrop deemed to be bedrock at site elevation ranging from 14.11 through 13.93 to 13.76—an indication that there is a knoll with angular rock facets at this point in the hill's topography (Ill. 8). Adjacent, but not touching bedrock, was a clay-lined pit (locus 5062) with nearly vertical sides that showed a slight concavity. Only about two-thirds of the pit was encountered in the sounding, enough to show that its diameter varied from 1.02 m to 1.25 m. It was 0.35 m deep at the sides, 0.45 m in the center. The clay lining was 0.04 to 0.05 m thick and covered the sides and the bottom. Spilling into the pit, and carrying over to cover the nearby rock outcrop, was a layer of chocolate brown wet clay/soil of as much as 1.00 m thickness, the lowest layer above bedrock on the sections. It contained Chalcolithic pottery throughout; included are two cornets of Ghassulian style and other ware resem-

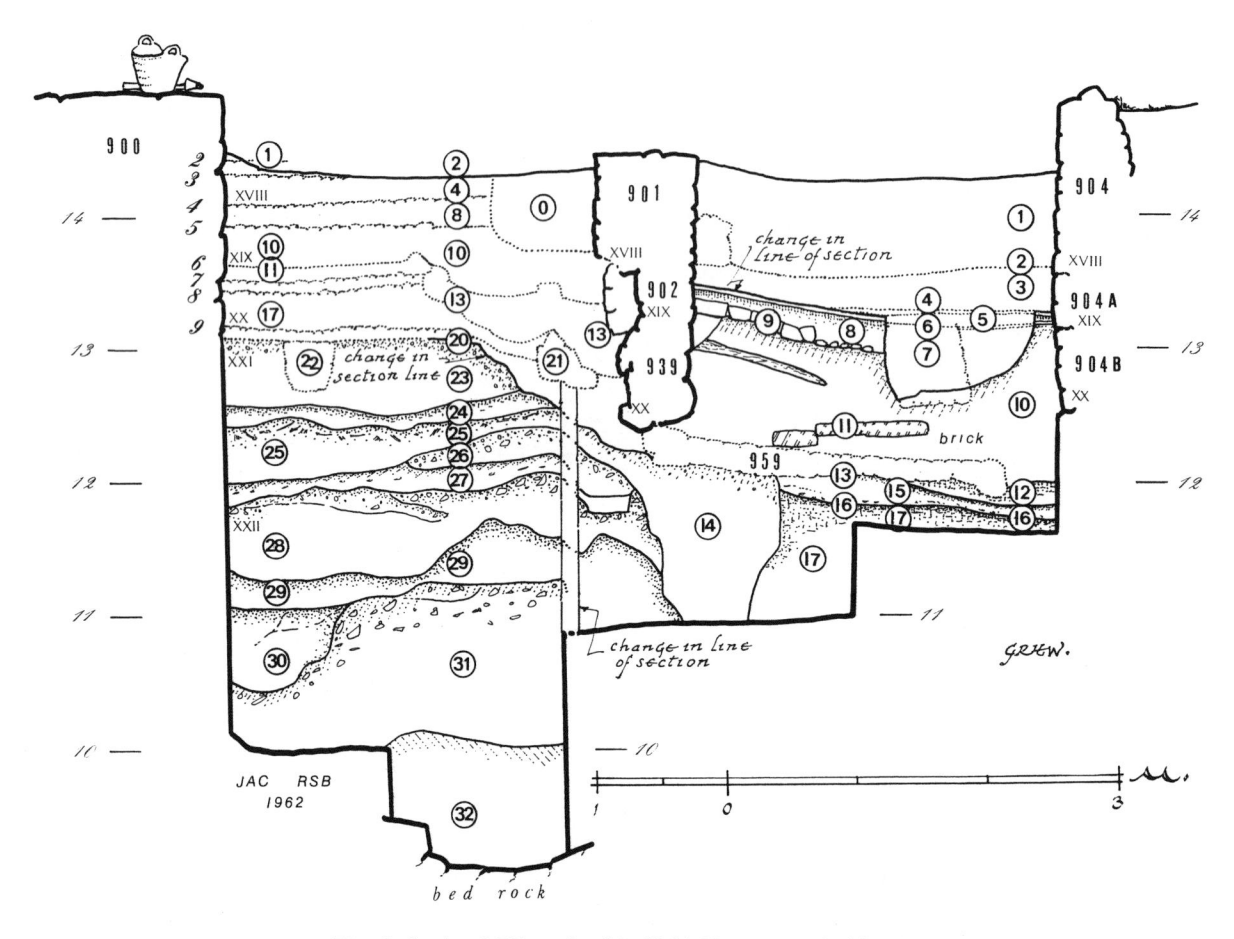

Fig. 5. Section 3 EF, cut back in 1964. Note reversal of fig. 4.

bling Ghassulian. Pit 5062 did not reach the balk on which Ill. 8 = V AA is drawn.

The top of the wet clay layer was marked by white chalk and a small segment of cobbling. All layering in the "fine damp brown earth" and "*ḥuwwar* fill" above the chalk layer and the cobbling contained MB II sherds, though fewer in number than the Chalcolithic/EB sherds found dispersed throughout layers all the way up to the MB IIC floorings of the Fortress Temple. These layers were probably part of the MB IIB Rampart of the C system, covered by fill laid in to prepare for building the temple (cf. Toombs and Wright 1961:36–37, fig. 14, where horizontal layers in the fine damp earth zone designated 5052A through E were posited as living surfaces; in fact, there was MB II pottery throughout this layering down to 5052E, below which was only Chalcolithic).

Field VI *(Ills. 71, 72, 82–84, 87)*

In 1960, a deep sounding beneath the streets of the Courtyard Complex in Field VI reached what were at first thought to be Chalcolithic layers below where Temenos Wall 900 was later to be built. The sounding was at the foot of Area 3EF, and a section drawn by Joseph Callaway was published in the preliminary report of that season, along with interpretation (Toombs and Wright 1961:18–22). Its left portion appears here, reversed, as fig. 4. Layer #29 was a beaten earth surface atop a thick layer, #30, of fine brown earth mixed with loose stones. Layer #28 was analyzed as occupation debris although no structures were encountered. The three layers contained Chalcolithic/EB I pottery, and #29 was taken at the time to be a Chalcolithic living surface. In 1964, further work here, and in another sounding five meters south, shown in the

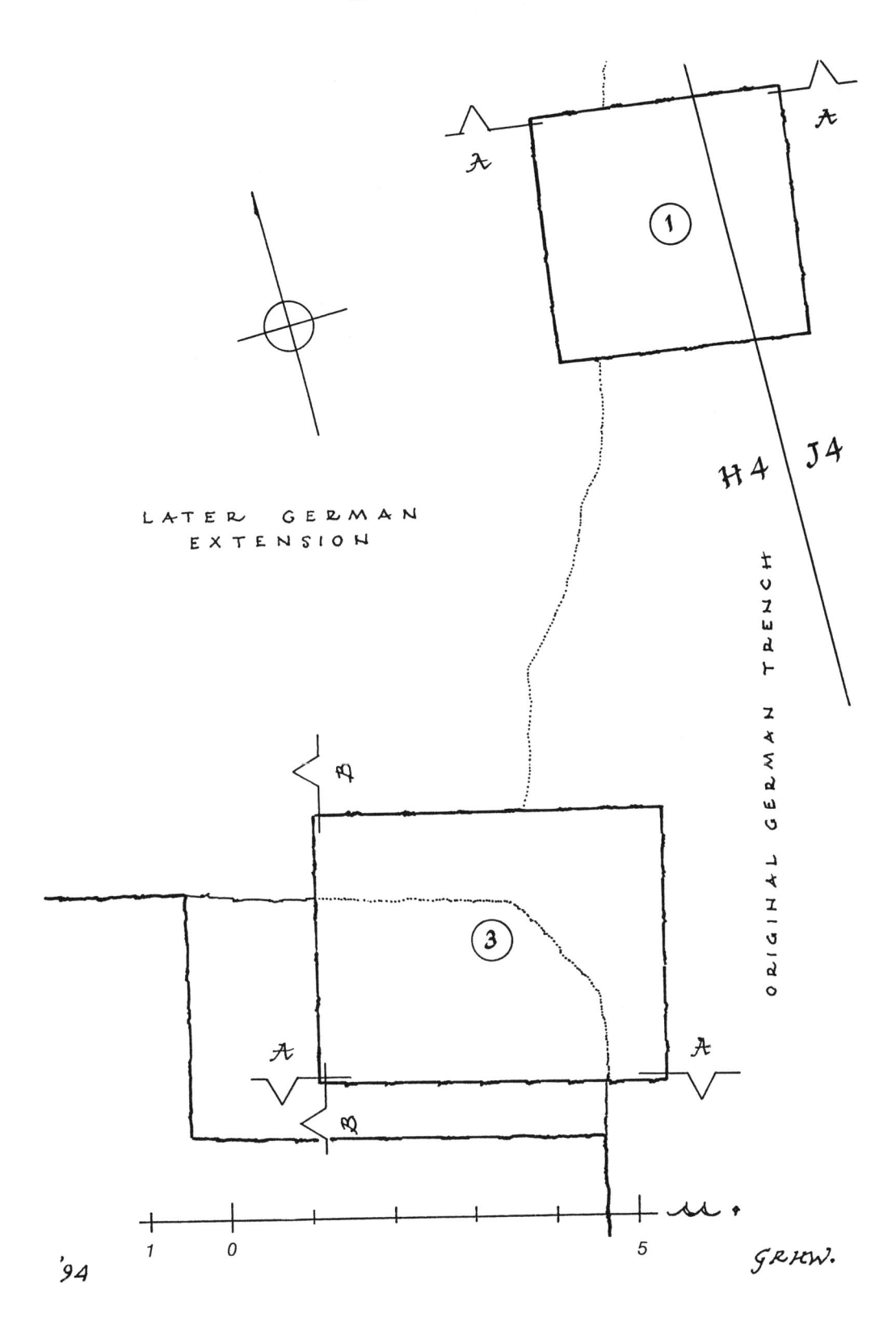

Fig. 6. Key plan of Field VIII, showing lines of sections on Areas 1 and 3. "Area 2" was not assigned.

extended section in fig. 5, checked this interpretation, and it was recognized that MB IIA sherds were also present in these deep layers; what had appeared to be a floor was apparently only a stopping surface in the laying in of the fill. The interpretation in Toombs and Wright (1961:21): "Phase 6. Chalcolithic occupation, possibly as a camp site, ca. 4000 B.C.," no longer stands, but the frequency of Chalcolithic sherds remains a clear datum.

Bedrock under the northern end of the region later occupied by the streets was reached at site elevation 9.02 (fig. 5), while a probe five meters to the south of the line of Wall 995 at the south end of the Courtyard Complex reached it at 8.87 m (Ill. 72). Field V bedrock beneath the Fortress Temple was as high as 14.11. The knoll under Field V must have had a shallow valley to its north and a slope to the south. The south slope presumably continues to the region of Field IX. The valley on the north was confirmed by findings in Field VIII, 60 m to the northeast of the north end of Field VI.

Field VIII

Field VIII was opened in 1960 at the bottom of the partially back-filled Trench H (cf. *SBBC*:65, which erroneously speaks of Trench L), dug by the Austro-German expedition in 1913 and 1914, then widened in 1926. Field VIII, Area 1, deep in the earlier trench (fig. 6), encountered undisturbed layers heavy with Chalcolithic and EB I pottery, always with some MB IIA and occasional MB IIB sherds, all the way to sterile soil at 10.35 of site elevation (fig. 7). There then appeared boulders presumed to be tumble from Mt. Ebal and taken as bedrock, at 10.15. In short, Chalcolithic and/or EB I *settlement* did not occur in Field VIII or in the north of Field VI, but the fill for the MB IIA settlement and for the C Rampart of MB IIB (see below) always contained sherds of these periods.

Dating Shechem's Fourth Millennium Evidence

Interpretation of Chalcolithic and EB I occupation requires a new assessment of the data. There are only two structural complexes to be dealt with, the pit and filling in Field V and the stratigraphy in Field IX. In the decades since Shechem was dug, a significant change has been introduced in both the nomenclature and the ceramic definition of fourth millennium cultures in Palestine (Stager 1992). These factors pertain:

1) Field calls on pottery from all the deep layers at Shechem vacillated between "Chalcolithic" and "Chalcolithic/EB." With the proposal and demonstration of Stager (1992:28–32; fig. 16) that "early EB I" now designate the post-Ghassulian, post-Beersheban cultures of Palestine, covering the period ca. 3500–3300 BCE, and that the term "late Chalcolithic" be dropped in view of the continuity of EB I early pottery with the rest of the EB ceramic tradition, it is clear that there was EB I at Shechem, and it is necessary to reassess the assignment of the Field V and Field IX features.

2) In 1964, when the Field IX Chalcolithic layering emerged, G. E. Wright in consultation with Israeli colleagues revised his reading of Shechem's early remains in two respects: the Field IX Chalcolithic was deemed older than that found in 1960 in Field V, and the Field V forms were seen as contemporary with the Beersheban culture Wright was able to observe for the first time in Israel—which he dated to 3500–3200 BCE in Bull, *et al.* 1965:16–17.

3) One of the clear Chalcolithic indicators is the Ghassulian "cornet" base. There are cornets of Ghassulian style in the Field V materials. On preliminary reinvestigation of Shechem Chalcolithic/EB I collections in 1993, it was clear that at least some of these cornets are slipped with red and burnished, possibly suggesting transition to EB I. Among pieces from the makeup and fill beneath Cobbling 9917 in Field IX are sherds clearly belonging to Stager's early EB I. There is, then, the prospect that one or the other of the Shechem stratified deposits belonged to early EB I; there is even the prospect that both do. Or both may prove to be Chalcolithic, while EB settlement has not yet been touched on the tell, but is present somewhere. And as has been noted above, Field IX in fact attested two phases, below and with the cobbled structure 9917.

4) Cave Tomb T-3, excavated on the flanks of Mt. Ebal in 1975 (Clamer 1977; 1981) was first used in the fourth millennium. Its materials require

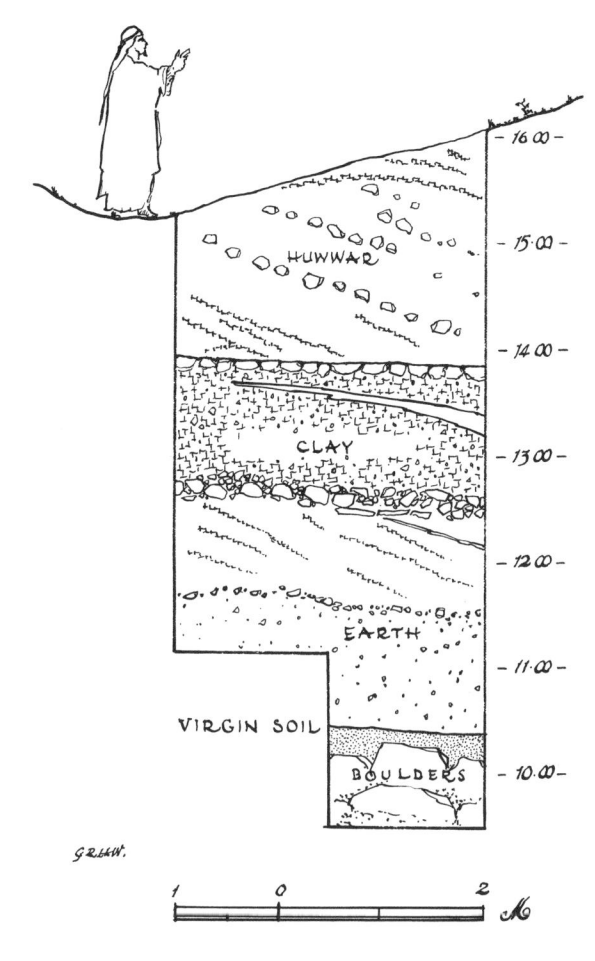

Fig. 7. Section AA on north face of Area 1 in Field VIII, to bedrock.

new analysis in connection with reassessment of the mound materials.

5) Shechem data, lacking sequential stratification as they do, will not go far to clarify the chronology of Chalcolithic and early EB I, but some 400 indicator sherds from sealed loci are pertinent to the ceramic typology of the period. In no case does the Shechem repertoire provide whole or reconstructible vessels.

The sherds are stored at the Harvard Semitic Museum. A sampling from Fields V and VI, usually of smaller pieces, is in the Chalcolithic study collection at the Museum.

MIDDLE BRONZE IIA = STRATA XXII–XXI

Middle Bronze IIA remains at Shechem fall into two distinct strata separated by erosion debris. The picture is clearest in Field IX, Area 4, where there was architecture and occupation accumulation in two sub-phases representing Stratum XXII, a blanket of fill 0.40 to 0.50 m thick, and then a completely different architectural layout with pottery suggesting close chronological proximity to the urban developments of MB IIB. Field IX evidence guides the interpretation of the evidence in Field VI. These two locations are the only ones where MB IIA settlement was encountered. MB IIA sherds, however, are ubiquitous in fills throughout the site.

Field IX (Ills. 123–124, 141–143, 145)

Two erosion layers, 9915 and 9914 (Ill. 141 = IX AA:##119 & 118; Ill. 142 = IX BB:##94 & 95), covered the Chalcolithic/EB I remains in Field IX. No MB IIA sherds appeared in these layers. What then developed can be seen on IX AA and IX BB of Area 4. On top of 9914, occupation debris accumulated as locus 9913 (AA:#117) on the west and 9923 (AA:#116; BB:#93) on the east of Wall 9919B which runs north–south through the area (Ill. 123 and IX BB). The wall was built shortly *after* this debris began to accumulate; the wall showed no foundation trench and loci 9913 and 9923 built up against its faces. At right angles to 9919B was Wall 9922. Both walls were built with outer faces and a rubble core, and were 1.00 m wide. Locus 9913 west of the combination of walls was of dense earth with charcoal flecks, but no clear floorings were discerned in its 0.30 to 0.60 m thickness. It persisted around the west end of Wall 9922 to the north edge of the area, where it encountered Wall 9918; this wall probably also had an earlier "B" phase to go with 9922 and 9919B. Locus 9913, then, was in the interior of a building; locus 9923, of silty and stony character, was outside accumulation. The pottery from 9923 is Chalcolithic and EB I (19 indicator sherds). It is the pottery in 9913 that dates the structure: MB IIA regularly appeared along with Chalcolithic and EB I. A granite bowl rim (B64 Reg. Obj. #601) came from this layer. When Wall 9918B was dismantled, MB IIA sherds were present in its rubble core.

Illustration 123 also portrays the second phase of Stratum XXII. Wall 9919A had been widened,

Fig. 8. Field IX, Area 4, looking north. Note Stratum XXI drainage channel 9630 met by Wall 9628 at its north end, plaster-lined installation against Wall 9631 and Firepit 9632.

Wall 9922 put out of use, and Wall 9918 at the north edge now was clearly established. Locus 9912 (AA:#115) was the occupation debris layer inside, to the west of the walls; locus 9920 (AA:#114; BB:#92) to the east lay outside. Again the soil character dictates this conclusion; again specific floorings were not discerned. Locus 9912 yielded 64 indicator sherds, the majority of which are MB IIA, with the usual Chalcolithic/EB I admixture. Locus 9920 yielded 17 sherds in the same proportions. A granite pestle (B64 Obj. #566) was in 9912.

Two distinguishable layers of erosion debris covered this complex. Locus 9911B (AA:#112) was a layer rarely more than 0.20 m thick and uniform throughout the area; it was silty with rubble and contains the rubbish of occupation, including a number of canine jaw-bones. Sixty sherds registered from it were predominantly MB IIA. This suggests there was ongoing MB IIA settlement nearby, wash from which covered Field IX. Locus 9911A (AA:#111) of roughly the same thickness blanketed 9911B; it was pebbly with chunks of chalk and an absence of rubbish, but was heavy with pottery, of which 203 sherds, mostly MB IIA, were registered. This locus suggests abandonment and erosion.

Covering locus 9911A was a thin layer of makeup for a new stratum, topped in a few places by a definable surface. Makeup and surface are designated 9910/9909 (AA:##110 & 109). These two merge with one another on the section and appear to have belonged to one process. Along the north and west balks of the area, a red bricky lens was also an ingredient (visible as part of IX BB:between #90 and #89). Loci 9910/9909 yielded 156 indicator sherds, preponderantly MB

Fig. 9. Looking down at the west face of Wall 968 in Field VI, Area 25. The meter stick rests on the fill of the platform retained by Wall 968. Note the smashed MB IIA storage jars fallen from the top of the platform.

IIA with a few Chalcolithic/EB I. Set into 9910/9909 at the east edge of Area 4 was a small arc of the circumference of Firepit 9632, the larger proportion of which is in Area 3 at the point of its deepest excavation. Illustration 124 depicts Stratum XXI in Field IX.

Area 3 features and layering of Stratum XXI are not undergirded stratigraphically; as always, that makes description of the stratigraphy difficult and tentative. The earliest installation was probably Firepit 9632, set into 9910/9909. Of cobbled construction, it was covered with ash. It probably related to the construction phase of Stratum XXI, especially since a subsequent wall of the stratum, Wall 9628, was laid directly on it. Stone-lined drain 9630 lay nearby to the east. The lining stones of the drain were set on edge. There was a drop of 0.26 m from its northernmost preserved point to its point of entry into the south balk.

To the east lay Wall 9631, the stone foundation for a probable brick superstructure. Wall 9631 established a line upon which a succession of stone walls were built throughout the remainder of the Bronze Age—presumably the western limit of a major building. It is basal and shown in elevation on Ill. 143 = IX CC. Against its west (exterior) face was the curious brick structure lined with white plaster seen in fig. 8. Wall 9628, at first thought to be a subsidiary channel of Drain 9630, but concluded to be a solid wall, did not connect with Wall 9631, and the stratigraphic circumstances in the north of Area 3 eluded field observation and interpretation. Illustration 124 suggests traces of an intrusion aimed at robbing Wall 9628 as it emerged into Area 4, but none was observed in section on IX BB.

Fig. 10. Silo 130 sunk into MB IIA Surface 122, as filled at left and with its packing removed and bones displayed at right.

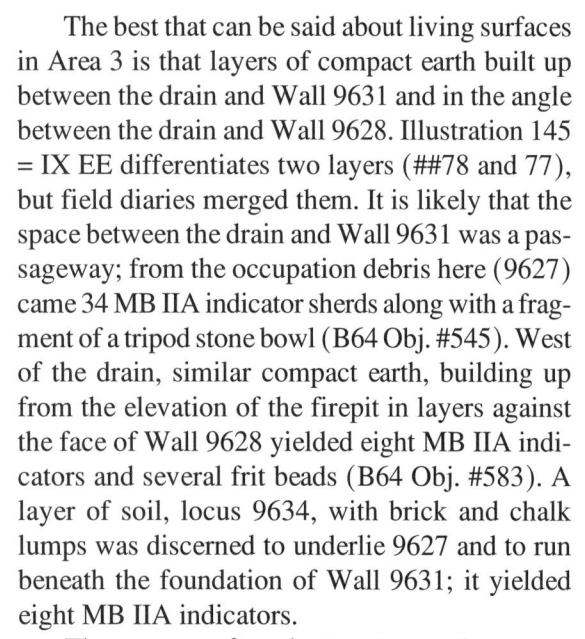

The best that can be said about living surfaces in Area 3 is that layers of compact earth built up between the drain and Wall 9631 and in the angle between the drain and Wall 9628. Illustration 145 = IX EE differentiates two layers (##78 and 77), but field diaries merged them. It is likely that the space between the drain and Wall 9631 was a passageway; from the occupation debris here (9627) came 34 MB IIA indicator sherds along with a fragment of a tripod stone bowl (B64 Obj. #545). West of the drain, similar compact earth, building up from the elevation of the firepit in layers against the face of Wall 9628 yielded eight MB IIA indicators and several frit beads (B64 Obj. #583). A layer of soil, locus 9634, with brick and chalk lumps was discerned to underlie 9627 and to run beneath the foundation of Wall 9631; it yielded eight MB IIA indicators.

The sequence from bottom to top, then:
    Firepit 9632 with layer 9634
    Drain 9630 and the earliest part of 9627/9626
    construction of Wall 9631
    continued buildup of 9627/9626.

In Area 4, as Ill. 124 indicates, only traces of mudbrick walls were found. For the most part the brick had degenerated, but a few were detectable *in situ* in Wall 9908. Indications of a surface to go with this wall appeared north and south of it and constituted the top of layer 9909, at elevation 6.02; above this possible flooring accumulated soil layer 9906, as much as 0.40 m thick, from which 57 indicator sherds, predominantly MB IIA with some Chalcolithic/EB I admixture, were registered. One sherd is incised (B64 Obj. #541). Stratum XXI remains in Area 4 were ephemeral and nondescript; perhaps the mudbrick walls defined a hut or house but field notes observe that the pattern displayed on Ill. 124 is largely conjectural.

Stratum XXI in Field IX finds its only real coherence in relation to Wall 9631 and the preparations for its building in Area 3. Since this wall began a building tradition that would last for as much as 800 years, close proximity in time between Strata XXI and XX is indicated, to be noted again in Field VI.

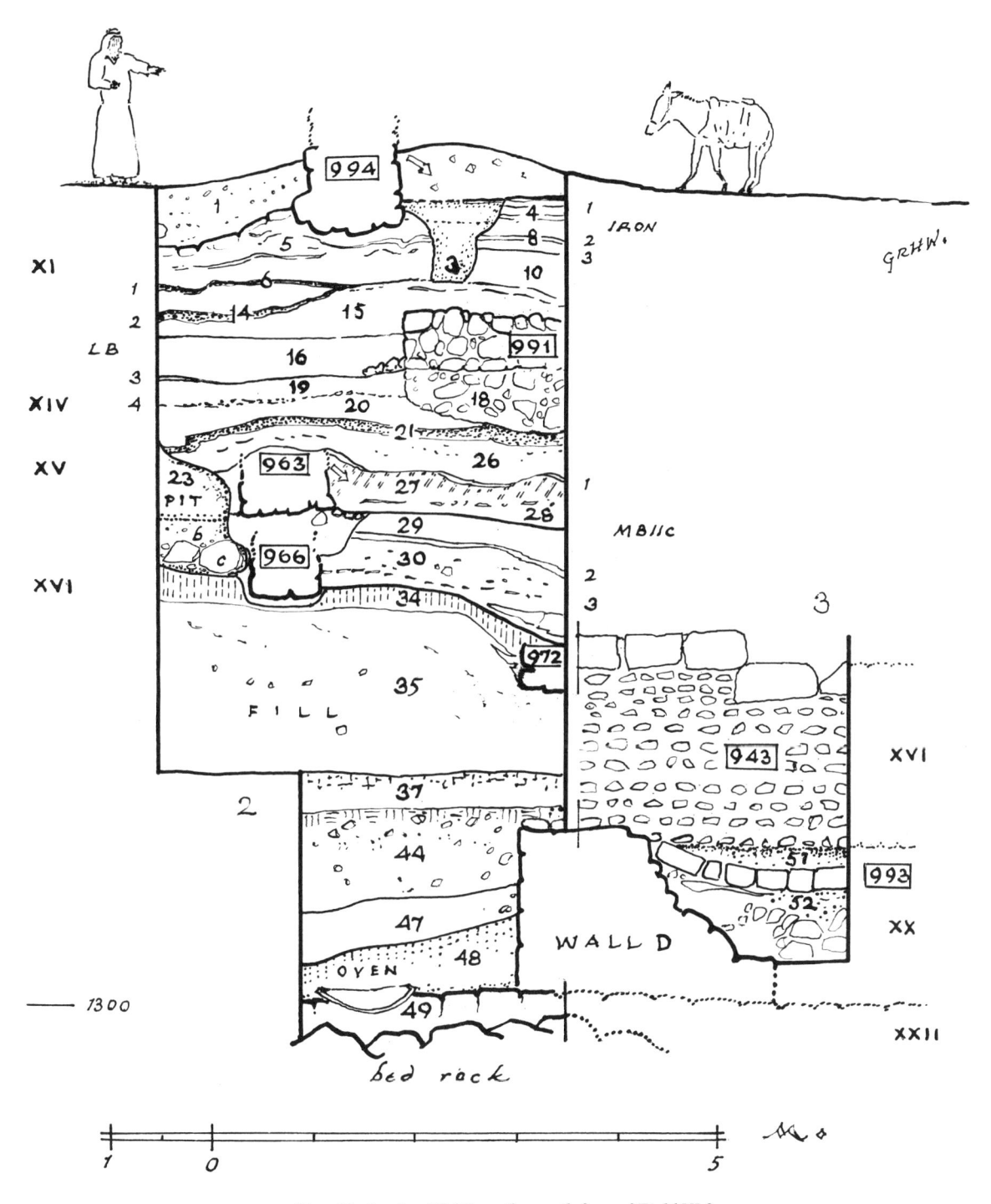

Fig. 11. Section VI PP on the north face of Field VI.2.

Field VI (Ills. 71, 82–84, 87)

In Field VI, MB IIA settlement was prepared for by the placement of a thick, striated leveling fill, covering bedrock, virgin soil, and the isolated Chalcolithic features on the knoll beneath the Fortress Temple. This fill was encountered deep beneath where Wall 900 would later be sited (fig.

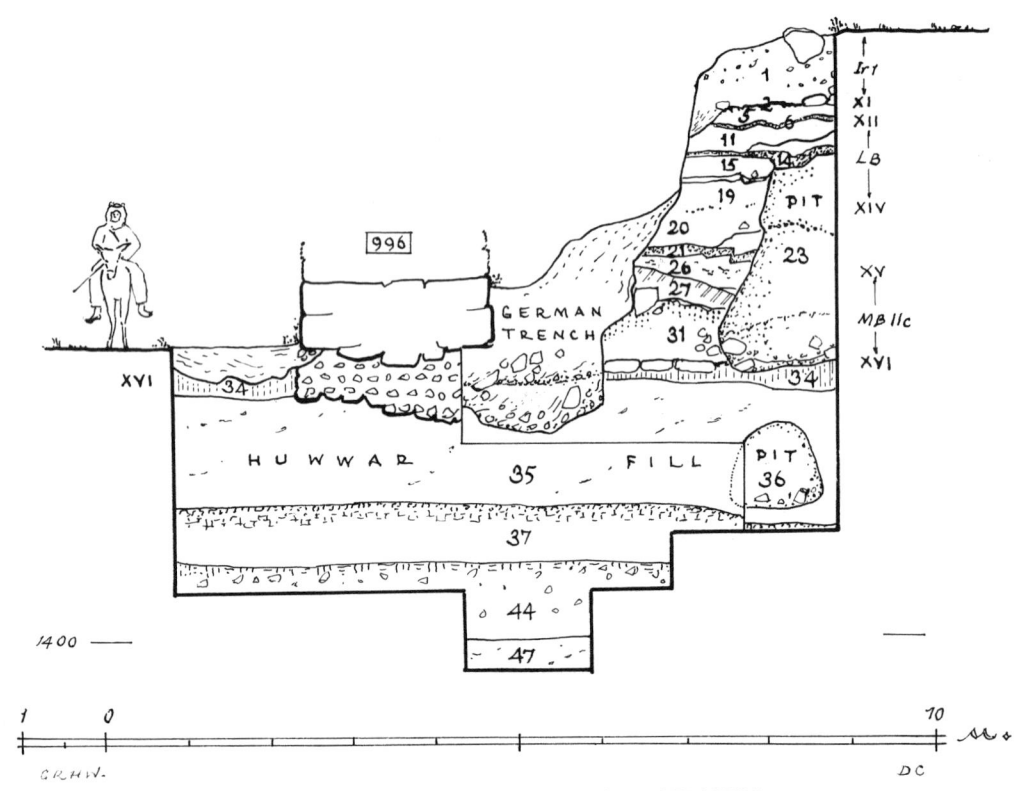

Fig. 12. Section VI RR on the west face of Field VI.2.

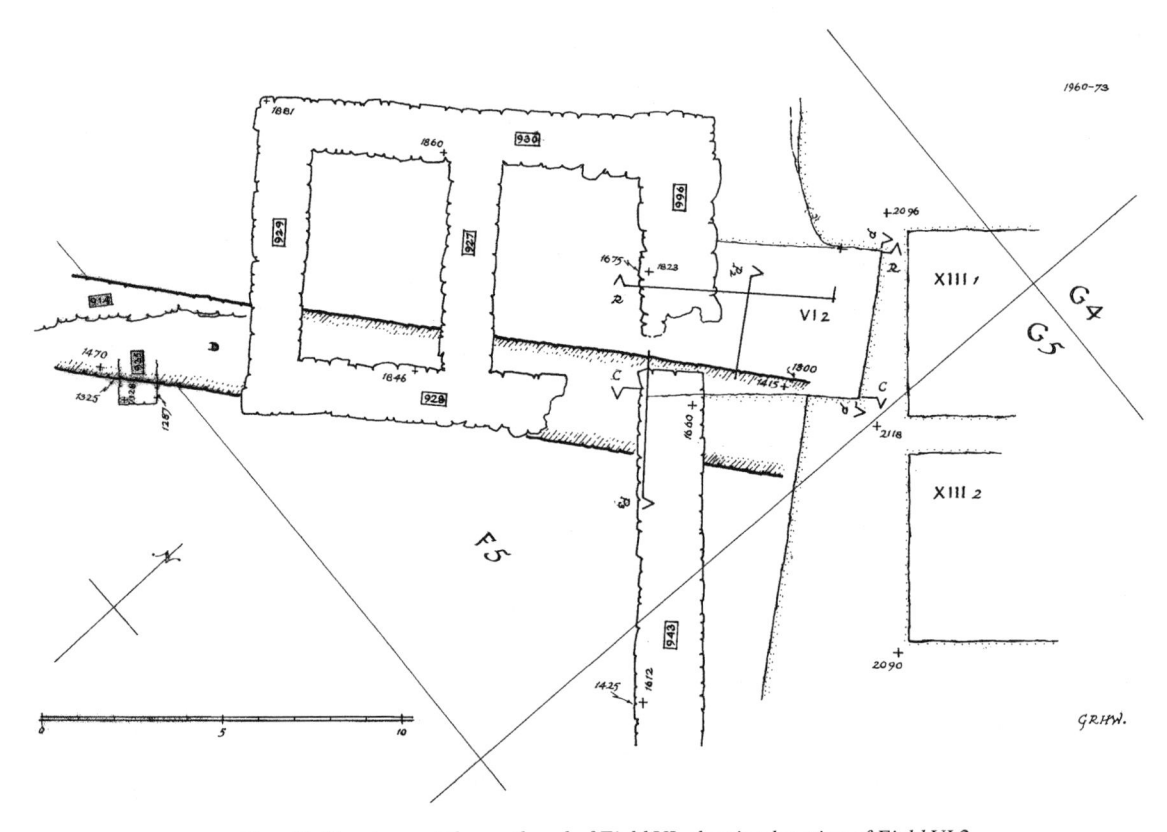

Fig. 13. Structures at the north end of Field VI, showing location of Field VI.2.

4:##28–30 with the VI BB section = Ill. 83, and the VI AA section = Ill. 82:#29), and was as much as 3.00 m thick. Apparently it was designed to level the shallow valley in the base topography. Pottery was predominately Chalcolithic/EB I, but always with MB IIA sherds present. A makeup of damp brown earth (fig. 4:#27, AA I:#28, AA II:#18, and regularly elsewhere where MB IIA installations were reached) covered the deep fill. In this layer, MB IIA sherds became proportionally more frequent. Upon it, Stratum XXII installations 968 and 977 were founded.

Installation 968 is designated after the wall which retained it on the west (Ill. 71) and made a right angle return at its north end to run beneath Wall 900. The installation seems to have been an elevated platform measuring at least 10.0 m north–south and 9.00 m east–west, rising 1.0 m above its footing on the west. No southern limit of the 968 installation was preserved; it had apparently eroded away. It was recognized on both sides of Wall 900 by a characteristic orange to yellow rocky filling (locus 222), visible in section on Ill. 87 = VI FF II and III:#13, FF I:#17. Wall 968 was very slightly battered on the west and north, indicating that the fill was piled first and then retained by the wall. A spill of debris against the west face of the wall is represented by VI AA II:##15 and 16. Fig. 9 shows the batter on the north face and two smashed MB IIA storage jars fallen mouth down and base up (B62 pottery ##971-974), probably from the top of the platform.

A segment of wall, 977, commencing at a point 8.50 m north of the northwest corner of 968 retained what is probably a similar elevated platform. Its fill (locus 624) was yellowish-white and chalky, mixed with reddish-brown clay, and the installation rode on the same damp brown earth bedding observed beneath 968. What these structures were is undetermined. Suggested comparison to the Megiddo MB IIA stone-lined earthen altar (Loud 1948:78ff.; *SBBC*:111) now seems excluded. There were two such structures at Shechem; artifacts do not suggest sacrificial, but rather domestic use; there were no steps on them; and domestic housing was constructed on top of both 968 and 977 within the period. Furthermore, they were not within a defined city fortification.

Upon an accumulation of soil (VI FF I:#16) which was stratigraphically subsequent to the 222 filling of 968, the next phase of settlement in MB IIA involved Wall 998, which had a mudbrick superstructure upon an earth cushion upon a stone foundation. Wall 998 ran perpendicular to Wall 999A, which originally extended under Wall 900 on top of Platform 968; the foundation trench for Wall 900 (FF I:#11) cut its extension. In the segment of Room 38, west of Wall 998 and south of Wall 999A, was flagstone paving at elevation 12.80 (FF I:#14) of fine quality (see Ill.71). Room 39 lay adjacent east of Wall 998 and had a beaten earth floor on a stony makeup (Floor 521 = FF I:#15 on #16a). The floor covered an infant burial in one half of an MB IIA storage jar, with a piriform juglet at the skeleton's feet (B64 pottery ##9925-9930). Rooms 38 and 39 were the north ends of two rooms of a home.

On 977, two poorly preserved stone wall segments, 959 and 960, formed the southwest corner of badly disrupted Room 40. A segment of flooring (locus 511) at elevation 12.16, with a complete MB IIA storage jar rim embedded, connected to Wall 960. (The elevation on Wall 960 at 12.17 may be in error, a mere centimeter above the floor.) On Floor 511 lay two preserved mudbricks, one measuring 0.37 by 0.43 by 0.12 m.

Into a nearby segment of flooring just to the east, locus 122, possibly a continuation of 511 but at an elevation recorded at 13.05, was sunk Silo 130, lined with hexagonal-shaped flat stones pressed into a plaster matrix (fig. 4:#22 sunk from #20). The silo had an outside diameter of 0.40 m and a depth of 0.30 m; it is pictured in fig. 10, with the animal bones from within it arranged on the adjacent floor. The makeup beneath floors 511 and 122 was identical in spite of the 0.88 m difference in elevations, suggesting that the silo was in an elevated platform—but note the caution above about the elevation readings.

Platform 968 and Room 40 on the similar height retained by Wall 977 are the two places where Field VI presents a succession of MB IIA phases, and the logical inference is that they correspond with Strata XXII and XXI as defined in Field IX—though the equation cannot be established. Preliminary analysis observes that the

24 SHECHEM III. THE EARLIEST STRATA

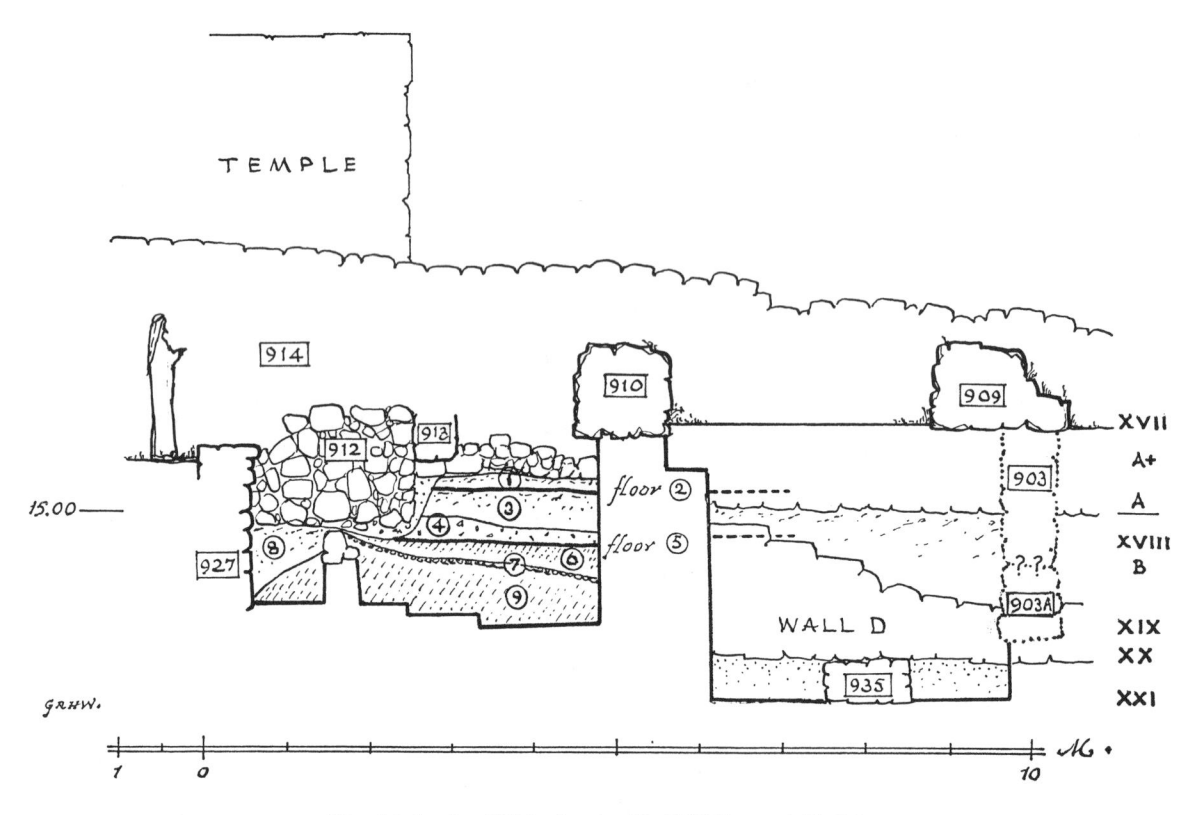

Fig. 14. Section VI LL, showing Wall 935 beneath Wall D.

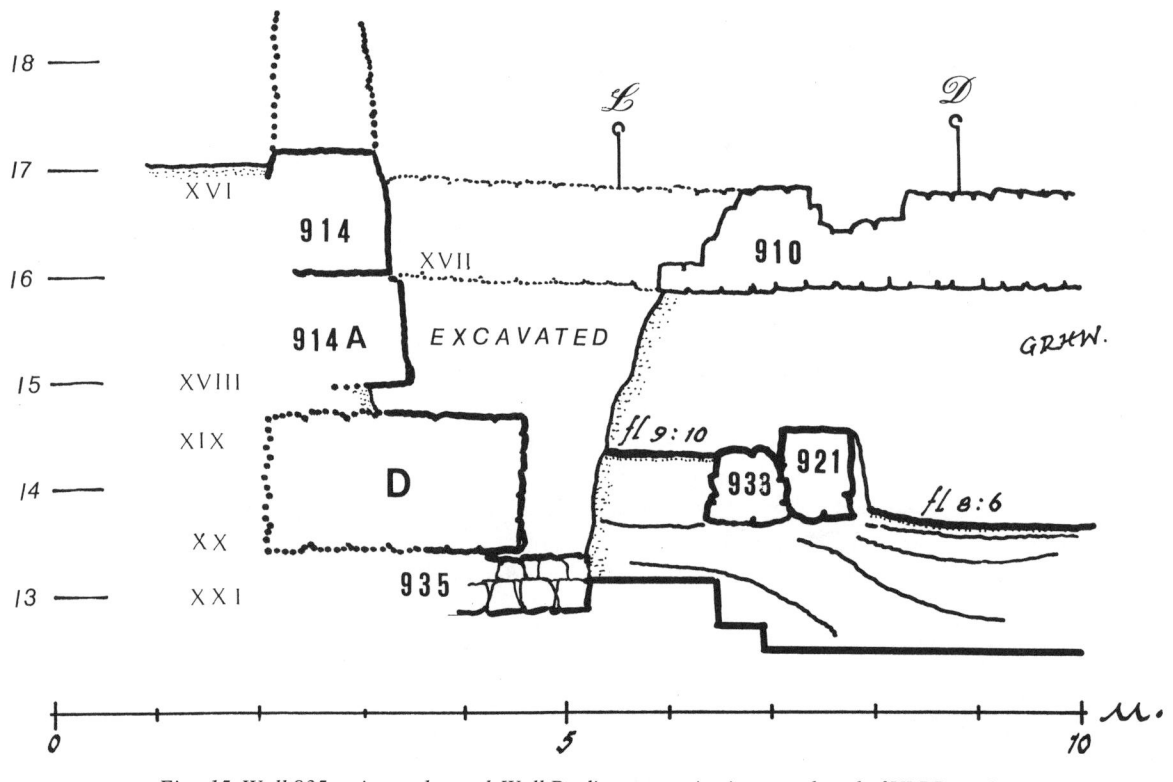

Fig. 15. Wall 935 as it runs beneath Wall D; diagrammatic view, north end of VI BB section.

sherds from the upper stratum in both sequences belong close to the transition to MB IIB.

Four isolated finds at the base of soundings and trenches throughout Field VI augment the finds already described. None shows more than one phase, so assignment to Stratum XXII or Stratum XXI cannot be certain. But since each lay close beneath Stratum XX remains, they probably are to be assigned to Stratum XXI. All are displayed on Ill. 71.

In the northwest corner of Field VI, a vertical cut in the eroded side of the Austro-German excavation was made in 1962 to gain control of the stratigraphy the earlier excavators had removed; it came to serve as the guide for digging Field XIII in 1966, 1968 and 1969. This cut is Field VI.2; the stratigraphy is displayed on Ill. 84 = VI CC and figs. 11 = VI PP and 12 = VI RR and the location in fig. 13. Wall D on these sections was the site's earliest known fortification. A flagstone and cobbled surface with the base of an oven set into it (VI PP:#49) ran under Wall D. It not only predated the earliest fortification, then, but also lay outside its line, showing that occupation extended beyond the perimeter later chosen for the fortification line. Under the stone surface was a layer of soil containing MB IIA pottery with forms close to those characteristic of the MB IIB stratification to come. This layer was 0.10 to 0.30 m thick lying upon huge nari limestone boulders characteristic of the geological strata adjacent on Mt. Ebal and taken as bedrock.

Wall 935 was a segment of a 1.10 m wide wall, preserved for one course only, running just under the east founding of Wall D (fig. 14 = VI LL; figs. 13 and 15). Trenching along Wall D by the Austro-German excavators removed any associated surfaces and cut off the prospect of interpreting this substantial wall in relationship to Wall D. Logically, it is a remnant of the same stratum as the Field VI.2 flagstone surface.

An east–west wall segment, 988, was an orphan, extending westward from a point 3.75 m west of the west edge of Platform 968. Excavation did not reach any preserved flooring with it. It can be seen at the base of VI CC III, covered by #33 = locus 351, a layer of rubbly earth which may have been makeup for surfaces against the wall;

Fig. 16. Drain 402 looking north in Field VI, Area 24.

the system is not held up from below stratigraphically. The one basket of pottery from locus 351 became mixed on the drying mats with other sherds and had to be dismissed as evidence. Makeup for Stratum XXB Floor 556 above it (CC III:#27) clearly covered the Wall 988 system.

In the north central part of Field VI near the future line of Wall 943, an open stone drain running due north and south was traced for 2.40 m. A perpendicular branch ran east–west away from it for 1.00 m—together the system is Drain 402. Both drains were lined with large MB IIA storage jar sherds (fig. 16). The pitch of the system was to the north and to the west—not what would be expected from the general slope of the mound, but indicative of the lie of the leveling operation preparatory to MB IIA occupation and probably of the topographic knoll to the south. Drain 402 lay below Stratum XX makeup. Associated surfacing was not discerned. Sealed beneath the drain was a fill of brown-yellow earth yielding 24 indicator sherds, half of them MB IIA and the rest Chalcolithic/EB I.

Since two of these four features clearly predate Wall D, and since any indication of fortification prior to Wall D is lacking, the MB IIA settlement seems to have been unprotected.

Stratum XXII pottery is firmly MB IIA; the proposed date is from ca. 1900 BCE on. Stratum XXI pottery shows an increasing degree of continuity with MB IIB forms as studied by Cole (1984; compare Dever 1989:87), and probably belongs to the first half of the nineteenth century. Closest definition of Stratum XXII will come from leveling layer 224; from locus 222, the filling for Platform 968, and locus 624, the filling behind Wall 977; and from the crush down the face of Wall 968. For Stratum XXI, closest definition should emerge from the makeup and occupation of the floorings in Rooms 38, 39 and 40; from Drain 402 and its makeup; and from the flagstone locus 49 running beneath Wall D, with its makeup layer 50, in Field VI.2. A new analysis of the MB IIA pottery is a desideratum for future researchers.

CHAPTER 2

THE MIDDLE BRONZE IIB PERIOD

DEFINITION OF THE STRATA BELONGING to Middle Bronze IIB, a designation the Joint Expedition still finds useful and dates between 1750 and 1650 BCE, derives from the west side of the tell in the fortifications and the acropolis. Since major effort was expended on these public features, and since there are four clear stages, they define Strata XX–XVII. Inside the town, evidence of domestic occupation can be traced only in Field IX and at the uppermost layering in Field XIII. For this reason, this chapter attends to the entire sequence in the public precincts before turning to the housing and use phases downtown.

STRATUM XX

The Wall D Fortification (Ills. 7, 9, 10)

The earliest fortification wall at Shechem so far attested by excavation is the free-standing Wall D (for orientation, see Ill. 9). Gabriel Welter, newly placed as director of the Austro-German expedition in the summer of 1928, discovered it (Welter 1932:293–94). His description fails to make clear how much of the wall he exposed, but one of his plans (redrawn), suggests that he traced it throughout the entire acropolis region, except directly beneath the entrance and the southern front tower of the Fortress Temple. A long section he prepared, redrawn and augmented now as Ill. 10, shows it beneath the front wall of the temple, its stone base topped by a brick superstructure.

At two locations where the Joint Expedition reached Wall D, the outline of the earlier clearance was evident, removing connections to adjacent soil layering. But at the north edge of the Austro-German exposure, in Field VI.2, work in 1962 was able to study a short segment north of where Welter had worked (Ill. 7). Welter's plan shows it following a straight line from just north of the line of Wall 943 to the front wall of the Fortress temple and under the temple to its south wall, where it makes a slight bend to the southeast. Measurements of the Joint Expedition suggest a bend eastward near the north preserved end.

The recognition of Wall D as the start of fortification depends on the relation it bore to a massive earthen rampart attested at a number of points around the tell's perimeter. This is the C Rampart system, which served (with augmentation) as fortification for the MB IIB Strata XIX–XVII. While the truncated top of the rampart has been identified at the west, north and east of the site, Wall D is known only from the northwest, in the acropolis region. It is presumed to have served as the interior retainer of the C Rampart around the whole tell.

The Joint Expedition reached the free-standing Wall D in Field V, Area 9, a 1.50 m wide probe trench placed nearly parallel to the south wall of the Temple, 7.50 m to its south; at a point 33 m to the northeast, 7 m east of the northeast corner of the Fortress Temple; and in Field VI.2 at the north edge of the acropolis exposure, another 16 m to the northeast.

Fig. 17 presents the conditions encountered in the probe south of the temple, dug in 1960, viewed looking north, so that the soil bank to the left is outside the fortification, the human figure at the right inside. Welter had apparently trenched all along the wall on both sides, cutting off the soil layers to it except for the lower ones on the outside (left); these layers were of virtually sterile soil with no indicator sherds to permit dating.

At this place, Wall D, 2.85 m wide at its base tapering to 2.65 m at its preserved height, was founded on a layer of damp clay. Its two exterior

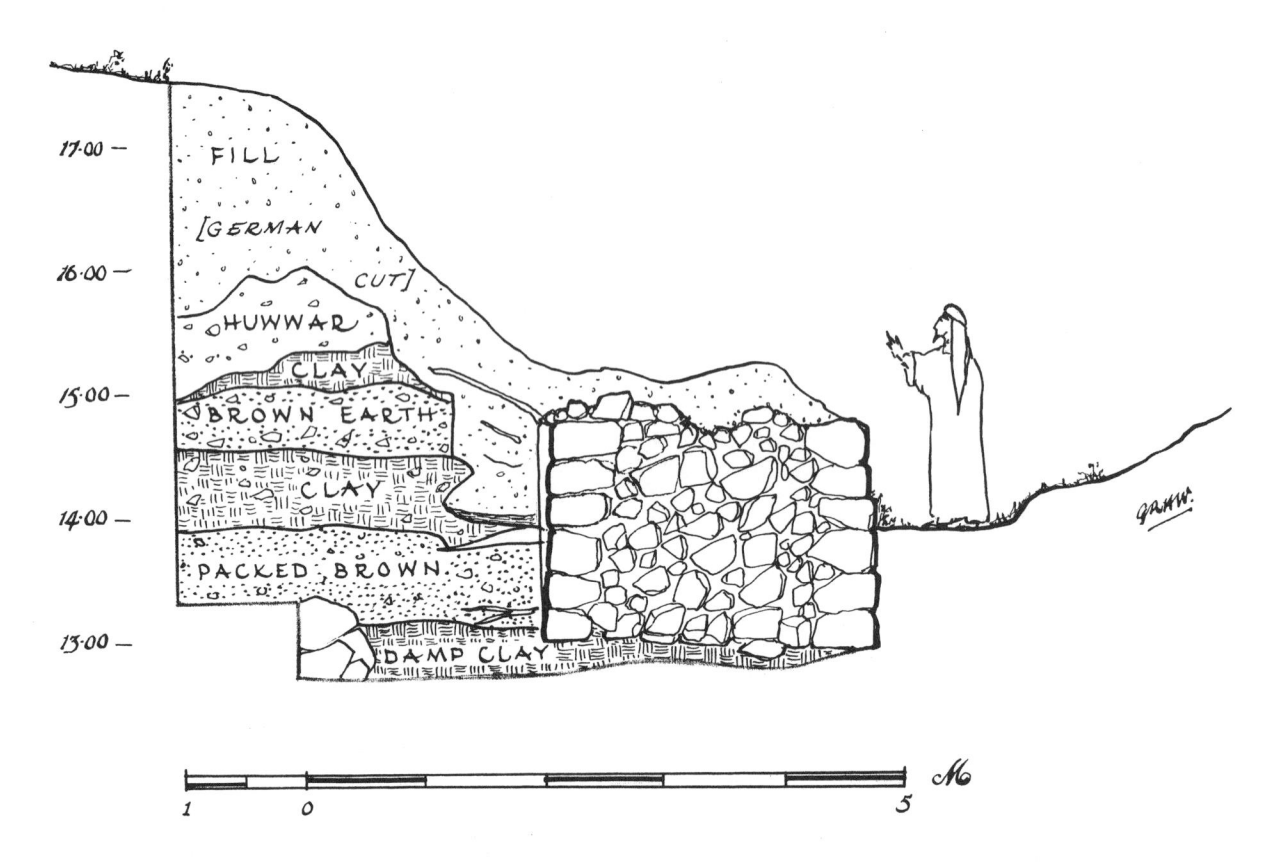

Fig. 17. Field V DD section through Wall D and layers leading to it, looking north (cf. Ill. 66).

faces were of selected and coursed stones, laid so that natural or possibly shaped facets produced a vertical surface. The core was of smaller stones and loose earth. The wall was dismantled to discern its construction and to secure any sherds included in the core. Six rims, one handle, and 5 ware sherds were registered; one rim is Chalcolithic/EB I, 3 rims and one ware sherd belong to the MB IIA/MB IIB transition, including a sharply carinated bowl profile, while the rest are analyzed as belonging with Strata XXII–XXI, MB IIA. The preserved stone base stands 1.70 m high, its top at elevation 14.78, probably as Welter found it. His description speaks of finding flat stones on top of the stone base, topped with preserved mudbricks; in Area 9, indications of the flat top were not certain, and no brick was preserved. The compass direction here was 45 degrees, due northeast.

Field VI.2 at the north edge of the Austro-German exposure encountered Wall D at the east edge of the excavation (figs. 11 and 18). Here the top was distinctly flat, and was first thought to be a pavement—fitting the description of Welter. The width of the wall here was 1.40 m, its west face resembling in construction that of the segment in Field V, Area 9. However the east face was discerned as only 0.40 m in height, above a layer of rubble spreading 3.00 m eastward. Conceivably this rubble is a collapse of the east face of Wall D, originally as wide here as in the south, although the excavation did not penetrate deeply enough to hold the stratigraphy up from below. A section against the east face of Wall D appears as the right segment of fig. 11 (offset 6.60 m to the south); it suggests the probable conditions just proposed.

In the description of Stratum XXI, it was noted that a flagstone surface of MB IIA with an oven embedded lay just beneath Wall D here. Loci 48 and 47 of fig. 11 (note that this section uses locus numbers, not a consecutive key, as does fig. 12, adjacent on the west [left]) accumulated against the west face of Wall D, both of which appear to be fill layers and neither of which was topped by

Fig. 18. The north face of the VI.2 trial trench, revealing Wall D at lower right.

what could be called a floor. There was a paucity of pottery in them, mostly Chalcolithic with a few MB IIA/B. These two layers are tentatively seen as part of the filling which in Stratum XIX will produce the C Rampart. When the probe to the east of Wall D was dug, a second cut was made through the wall which yielded the ever-present Chalcolithic/EB I pottery, with a preponderance of MB IIA and other indistinguishable early MB II forms.

A probe in Field VI along the line of Wall D, which exposed Wall 935 of Stratum XXI (see Chapter 1 and fig. 14), encountered the interior face of Wall D and discerned again that Welter's work along it had removed stratigraphic connections of any soil layers.

The information these probes contribute to the course of Wall D amounts to this: In Field VI.2, the course of the wall was at 51 degrees 43 minutes, 6 degrees more east of north than the segment in Field V, Area 9, south of the temple. In 1969, a deep probe by Joe D. Seger at the far north edge of Field XIII, placed on the extrapolated line where Wall D should have been, did not encounter it, suggesting that it had made another turn to the east. Welter's sense that it was straight throughout the stretch he traced, except at the south limit, must then be augmented by these indications that the fortification was tracing a roughly curved path much like those of the walls which followed. Sherds from within the wall showed that the beginning of MB IIB is the earliest possible date for its construction. This information goes with what is to be learned from Field VI to establish Wall D as the Stratum XX fortification—Shechem's earliest.

A free-standing fortification wall, with brick upon a stone base, conforms to the fortification tradition of the Early Bronze Age elsewhere in the land; walls of MB IIA most comparable to Shechem's Wall D are to be found at Megiddo, Aphek, Gezer, and Tell Beit Mirsim (Kempinski 1992:127–28; cf. *SBBC*:62–63). These walls have towers spaced along them or consist of offsets and insets. Along the roughly 52 m of Wall D traced at Shechem, Welter's evidence and that of the Joint Expedition found neither towers nor offsets—though the failure to find Wall D at the north edge of Field XIII might mean an inset was present there. Further, the free-standing fortification walls at other sites do not become incorporated as the interior line of a rampart system. Shechem's Wall D is thus far unparalleled in character for its period.

The Acropolis in Stratum XX (Ills. 72, 78, 82–83, 86–87, 90)

Middle Bronze IIB appeared at Shechem in four strata, defined by the tight stratigraphy in Field VI, adjacent to Wall D at the west edge of the site. Field VI uncovered what amounts to being the acropolis of the developing urban center, with successive complexes of rooms and courts between Wall D and Wall 900 (Ill. 78), the "temenos" or precinct wall separating the acropolis from the rest of the city. Wall 900 ran at an angle to Wall D, distant from it in the area excavated by 16.30 m at the north to 21.30 m at the south preserved end of Wall 900, and 24.70 m if Wall 900 is extrapolated to a point opposite the southernmost exposure of Wall D. The north–south extent unearthed is ca.

Fig. 19. Wall 900 viewed looking east at the seam to the right of the strip of balk. The numbers painted on rocks in the wall show the elevations of some of the streets.

43.60 m. The result is the trapezoid portrayed in the succession of Field VI period plans. Floors in the MB IIB structures on the acropolis were 6 to 7 m higher in elevation than house floors of the period in Field IX only 30 m away to the southeast.

Wall 900 had a long and complicated history. Its foundation trench near the south preserved end intruded upon Stratum XXI floor 510 and Wall 999A (Ill. 87 = VI FF I:#11; for the position of section lines, see Ill. 78); the base of the wall is at elevation 12.45. On the west face of Wall 900, in the FF II zone, the foundation is at elevation 12.55 and rested on the makeup for Street 9 (see below) which in turn lay on the fill of Stratum XXII Platform 968 (VI FF II:##11 and 13–14). North another 10 m at the line of the BB section, the Street 9 makeup ran under Wall 900 here founded at 12.25, and filled the foundation trench for Wall 939, the east defining wall of the structures inside the acropolis (Ill. 83 = VI BB I:#20), while covering the Stratum XXI Floor 122 and Silo 130 just below.

The sequence: foundation trench for 939, then laying of street makeup locus 125, then construction of Walls 900 and 939 at close to the same time, all soon after the close of Stratum XXI.

North another 5 m at the VI JJ line (Ill. 90), the founding of Wall 900 was much higher, at 13.90; no contemporary earth layers could be traced here because of Austro-German trenching along the wall face. At VI EE (Ill. 86) 4 m farther north, Wall 900 was founded at 14.00 on a layer of small stones which ran over Wall 981, part of the Stratum XX complex. The stone layer, locus 601 (VI EE:shown as stones between the line of Wall 981 and Wall 900, beneath #2) seems to have been a consolidation for a rebuilding of Wall 900. Three other observations support the hypothesis of a rebuild:

1) Streets 9–7, all of Stratum XX, could be traced along Wall 900 for 10 m as Ill. 72 shows, but were interrupted at a point just north of the VI BB section line, with only the makeup for Street 9 preserved north of that. Street 6 of Stratum XIX was preserved here, however, riding on a fill layer (locus 118) over the Street 9 makeup 125.

2) At almost exactly this point there was a seam in the west face of Wall 900 (fig. 19); from the south (right) the regular courses of semi-hewn stones proceeded to the seam, but to the north the courses were less regular, suggesting a rebuild using the original stones but with less careful construction.

3) Although the southern (original) portion was 2.20 m wide, the northern rebuild narrowed to 1.90 m from a point about 3 m north of the seam. The Joint Expedition did not re-excavate to determine this, but concluded it from the German plans

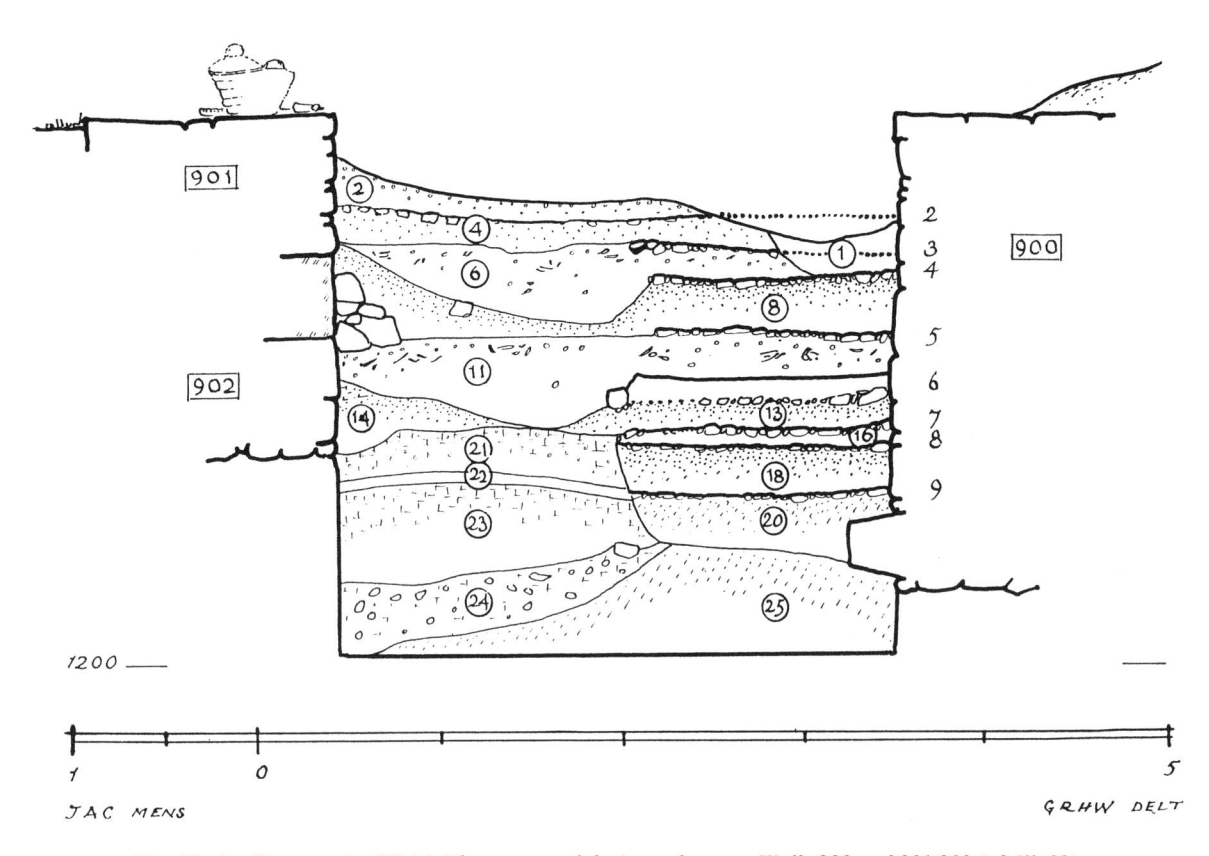

Fig. 20. Auxiliary section VI AA I/1, streets and drainage between Walls 900 and 901/902 (cf. Ill. 82).

published with the preliminary reports of 1926 and 1927. The narrowing is shown on the Stratum XIX plan (Ill. 73), while the current appearance of the wall is shown on Ill. 72.

The north segment of Wall 900 was probably, then, a rebuild, done in Stratum XIX because the street of that Stratum, Street 6 (Pavement 602), continued beyond the seam, and because the paving of the Stratum XIX phase of the Entrance Hall ran to the base of Wall 900. It was not possible to investigate the narrow stretch between Wall 981, the east wall of the Entrance Hall of Stratum XX, and Wall 900, because the consolidating stone layer 601 could not be safely removed. The relationship between wall 981 and Wall 900 was probably thoroughly disrupted by the rebuild, and the earlier history of Wall 900 in the north will probably never be known. It cannot be ruled out, on the basis of present data, that Wall 900 stopped to the south, and Wall 981 of the Entrance Hall was the limit of the acropolis in Stratum XX.

Wall 900 went through at least one more rebuilding within MB II. The two courses of its northern end, as now preserved, were bonded into Wall 943, known to belong to MB IIC. Most probably, the top of Wall 900 was reconstructed when the great fill for the Fortress Temple of Stratum XVI was laid in (see below).

The Streets. Between Wall 900 and the walls that successively formed the eastern border of the acropolis complex at least from the Entrance Hall south, there was a series of street surfacings and drains. To Stratum XX belong the lowest of these, Street 9, and the next two resurfacings, Streets 8 and 7. A layer of brownish-grey earth with a large admixture of ash and bone, locus 125, was the makeup for Street 9 and underlay Wall 900 while filling the foundation trench (locus 547) of Wall 939 (Ill. 82 = VI AA I:#24, fig. 20 = AA I/1:#20; Ill. 83 = VI BB I:#20; Ill. 87 = FF II:#11). This established the contemporaneity of these two walls. At the line of (later) Wall 906, to the south, Wall

Fig. 21. Segments of Street 9 along Wall 900, with unpaved drainage path to its left (west).

Fig. 22. Cylinder seal impression on an MB IIB storage jar handle, according to Edith Porada showing the Ishtar of War and other motifs, probably Syrian.

939 was razed and rebuilt as Wall 902 of Stratum XIX; no earth layer connections were preserved there to link Wall 900 and the Stratum XX remains.

Street 9 occupied only the east half of the corridor between Wall 900 and Wall 939; the paving of cobblestones 0.10 to 0.15 m in diameter stopped at a sharp line 1.50 m from wall 900. From there west to Wall 939 was an open, unpaved drain (fig. 21). About 0.50 m from Wall 939 was a curb, locus 532 (VI BB I:#19; VI FF II:#10) probably designed to keep water from undermining the wall. Street 9 dropped 0.35 m in the 14.50 m of its excavated length from north to south. The general topography here at the west had clearly been altered since Stratum XXI (see Drain 402, which ran northwards), of which more below. The northern end of Street 9 most probably led into the Entrance Hall; the Entrance Hall's paved interior is at elevation 13.00, while Street 9 is at 13.20 at its door.

Over Street 9 lay a 0.25 m thick makeup of compact grey earth with little ash and bone (VI AA I:#21; fig. 20:#18; VI BB I:#17; VI FF II:#8), topped by Street 8 (AA I:#20) of cobblestones 0.20 to 0.30 m in diameter. The makeup ran to the top of the curb for the drain of the Street 9 system, so Street 8's drain probably extended to the face of Wall 939. Over Street 8 was a thin layer of grey ashy soil (AA I:#19), upon which lay Street 7, simply a repair of Street 8. Layer AA I:#22 was a thick deposit of reddish brown clay and pebbles that accumulated in the open drain. Gullies in the drain cut down almost to the level of Street 9.

There is no question that Street 9 belonged to the 939 system and thus to Stratum XX; with Streets 7 and 8 there were no layers connecting them with Wall 939 because the foundation trench for Stratum XIX Wall 902 severed them. They were thus earlier than Wall 902, definitive of Stratum XIX, and must have belonged to Stratum XX. Street 7 may have gone with Phase A of Stratum XX, when new floors were laid and a new partition wall built within the interior complex—the phase distinction will be discussed below.

The three street surfaces assigned to Stratum XX provided effective sealed loci for the preservation of pottery of the stratum, although it cannot be known from whence the makeup material was gathered (cf. Dever 1989:87). When Cole developed the typology of earliest MB IIB pottery for his corpus, he selected 43 of his 64 illustrated forms from the street stratigraphy (Cole 1984:31, master loci 41, 43, 44, 70, 125, 127 [sherds from area baskets B60.VI.204, 211]; 3A:23 and 25 [sherds from baskets B60 VI.30, 34]; 3EF:121 [a sherd from B60.VI.196]; and 2:49 of Area VI.2 dug in 1962, from basket B62.VI.247—the last of these is from beneath a Stratum XXI floor and is stratigraphically dubious for a Stratum XX corpus.)

Structures on the Acropolis. Inside the complex bordered by Wall 900 and the adjacent streets, the stratigraphy and architecture was as depicted in Ill. 72 and in nine primary and secondary sections whose positions in the field are indicated on the plan—designated by letters and by roman numeral references to zones within the longer sections (e.g. VI CC III:#14).

Stratum XXI had existed for a relatively short period, judging especially from the accumulation under rooms 36 and 37 of Stratum XX where Stratum XXI wall-lines 998 and 999 were reused in XX, and from the minor shift in the pottery typologies from XXI to XX. No destruction debris separated the strata, nor were there indications of layers of wind-blown earth or silt. The topography was altered, however, by the laying of a leveling fill, thickest in the northern half of the complex, under Rooms 21–24. The lowest layer of this fill in this sector, Ill. 84 = VI CC II:#26, consisted of dark brown rubbly earth containing much Chalcolithic pottery; successive ingredients of the fill were a lens of pebbly chalk (#25) continuous with an intermittent layer of greyish red bricky soil and streaks of ashy debris. The uppermost ingredient was hard brown earth, #23, from which came a cylinder seal impression on a storage jar handle tentatively identified as from the Twelfth Dynasty (fig. 22). It appears to show the Ishtar of War known from Old Babylonian seals along with other motifs that are probably Syrian. Dr. Edith Porada provided this insight when the seal was first published by Campbell and Ross (1963:4) and mistakenly described as showing Egyptian motifs (personal communication, May 25, 1963). The total depth of the fill from which it came was at least 0.90 m.

As it spread south and east the fill was progressively thinner and humped over earlier fea-

Fig. 23. MB IIB smashed storage jars Locus 436 on Floor 433 in Room 23 of Field VI.

tures to attain a roughly level top. Under Room 25, it was hard-packed brown clay (VI CC III:#31) topped by coarse rocky brown (#30). Beneath Corridor 29 and Room 32 it is the damp brown of #32, covering the stump of Wall 988 of Stratum XXI. Under the Entrance Hall it consisted of light reddish brown earth with intermittent layers of rubble (Ill. 86 = VI EE:#10), petering out just west of Stratum XX Wall 981 and overlying Stratum XXII features, Wall 977 and its collapse (#15) and subsequent accumulations (#16). The depth here tapered from 0.85 m to just a few centimeters. At the southeast corner of the field, either side of Wall 900, the Stratum XX fill was loose rocky brown earth of Ill. 87 = VI FF III:##11–12 and FF II:#12, averaging 0.60 m thick over Platform 968 of Stratum XXII. Under Rooms 36 and 37, the rebuild of Stratum XXI rooms, it is FF I:#13, locus 509, about 0.55 m thick; this was the makeup for Floor 503.

The character and extent of the leveling fill under Stratum XX points both to continuity and discontinuity between Strata XXI and XX. At some points the fill obliterated any traces of the earlier period, while at others it permitted the reuse of tops of Stratum XXI walls for anchorage.

Over this fill, bounded by Wall D and Temenos Wall 900, two structural complexes were built. Wall 934 separated them. The Northern Complex consisted of small rooms, 21–28, and the Entrance Hall. Most appear to have been for storage, though Room 28 contained Oven 606A and may have been a kitchen. The southern block, Rooms 25–28, had two floor levels in each room. Wall 997 at the west edge of rooms 25 and 26, was built at the time of the later floorings, while the first floorings ran deep beneath it (Ill. 90 = VI JJ). In Room 25, the lower floor was 611A, the upper was 480 (VI JJ:##14 and 7; CC III:##20 and 18); in Room 26, the lower was 408A, the upper 11:16 (CC III:##21 and 19; Cole assigned this large jar rim 34:b to 11:16, but should have placed it in locus 301, the fill above the floor belonging to his "XIXs;" see his page 31). On this basis, Stratum XX had two phases, A and B; Streets 8 and 9 go by hypothesis with the lower Phase B, Street 7 with Phase A.

The Southern Complex ran south from Wall 934. Its southern limit is not determined. Its most prominent feature was the open courtyard 35; along its northern edge were three small rooms, 31–33, with Corridor 29 between them and Wall 934 and Corridor 30 along their west edge. At the western edge of Courtyard 35 was evidence of a smaller court, 34, but at this point Stratum XVIII structures intruded and robbed much of the evidence.

The Northern Complex. Description begins with Rooms 21–24. Only the eastern portions of these rooms were excavated, with one probe on the VI HH (Ill. 89) line in the western limit of these rooms, and no excavation in the northeast quadrant to the east of their east boundary in Wall 989.

Wall 989 was 1.10 m wide, preserved as high as 1.50 m. Its foundation was three courses of heavy unhewn stones facing a rubble interior, leveled off with small flat stones on which was a superstructure of mudbricks. The bricks are preserved to a height of 0.80 m and were laid in alternating courses of light and dark colors.

Partition walls 967, 974 and 965 were similar to one another in construction and were fairly evenly spaced. The stone foundations of 967 and 965 were 0.50 m wide; that of 974 was 0.40 m wide. All three stone foundations were two to three courses high, and 965 and 974 showed remains of brick superstructure; 967 can be assumed to have been brick-topped also.

Wall 976 at the south of this sub-complex had a foundation 0.90 m wide and three courses high, with a superstructure of brick preserved for 0.90 m and plastered on its north face, which was set back slightly from the foundation line.

The western wall of the sub-complex has not been excavated. It must have lain near Wall D, since the probe reaching to within 2.20 m of Wall D that revealed Wall 975 and the Floor 433 of Room 23 (Ill. 72; Ill. 89 = HH:#15) showed no sign of it; indeed Wall D itself may have been the western limit. As for the wall fragment 975, its construction was similar to that of the partition walls to its east but it was oddly located, apparently as a divider within Room 23. The Stratum XX floor here, Floor 433 on VI HH, touched both sides of it.

The portions of Rooms 21–24 excavated had clearly discerned floorings. Floor 406B of Room 21 was hard-packed earth overlaid with a thin deposit of ashy debris (CC II:#21) laid upon a makeup of fist-sized stones (405) topping the leveling fill 476 (#23) already described. Floor 446 of Room 22 was of packed limestone (#18) 0.04 m thick; occasionally, dark brown occupation debris (439) could be discerned upon it. Makeup was again a layer of small stones (473). Floor 433 of Room 23 (CC II:#19 and HH:#15) was hard-packed earth upon which lay smashed large storage jars shown in fig. 23 (locus 436; see Cole 1984: pl.37g). Makeup for Floor 433 varied from hard dark brown earth at the east to loose grey stony soil near Wall 975 (CC II:#22, HH:#16). Floor 451 of Room 24 was packed limestone as much as 0.13 m thick (CC II:#20) on makeup 405B (#22).

Silo 411B in Room 24 (CC II:#24) was constructed with its lip at Floor 451 which ran right to it; the silo was laid in before the floor was established. It was roughly circular, the inside diameter tapering from 0.92 to 0.72 m top to bottom. The depth, to a layer of flat stones at the bottom, was 1.46 m, cutting through the makeup and fill layers already described and continuing lower into unexcavated soil. On the bottom stones was hard-packed brown earth, locus 415B, topped by a loose crumbly grey earth mixed with decomposed chalk (411B proper) that contained whole pottery vessels (locus 436) designated Registry Objects 557, 558, and 553 (Cole 1984: Pls. 27f, 15c).

The presence of Silo 411B and the storage jars, along with the indications that Rooms 21–24 were long narrow enclosures of similar dimensions within a more strongly built perimeter, suggest that this sub-complex was a storage area.

Rooms 25–28. A second complex was made up of Rooms 25–28, showing two phases with two flooring systems. The western limit of the earlier phase, Stratum XXB, is not known, since Wall 997 is a later construction, belonging to XXA. Wall 970 was bonded into Wall 976, tying this group to the Northern Complex. Wall 980 abutted Wall 924B, indicating that the south wall of the Entrance Hall was in place when 980 was built. These connections suggest that Rooms 25–28 came to link the Northern Complex, the Entrance Hall and the Southern Complex into one large unit.

The sequence of construction of the XXB features in this sub-complex is unusual. Phase B Floor 611A extended from the foot of Wall 939 westward beyond the line which Wall 997 would later take (Ill. 90 = VI JJ:#14; Ill. 84 = VI CC III:#20). This lower floor was at elevations between 12.60 and 12.75 throughout Rooms 28, 27 and 25. Walls 939 and 976 were in place when it was laid, but it cannot be proven that the floor reached Wall 924B of the Entrance Hall, founded at elevation 12.75 at one point.

Walls 970 and 980 were built directly on Floor 611A, apparently without foundation trench (note the subsidence under Wall 980 on VI JJ), while 941 was probably set down into it with a foundation trench. Intrusion of Austro-German trenching along Wall 941 means that the 941 foundation trench is conjectural and that the connections of the flooring in Rooms 25 and 26 are broken.

Preserved segments of Floor 408A in Room 26 (VI CC III:#21) were at the same elevation as that of Floor 611A and it is most likely that they were the same floor—see the dashed line on CC III. Since Floor 408A ran to Wall 934, that would mean Wall 934 was also in place when the flooring here was first laid.

An early Joint Expedition suspicion that Floor 611A belonged to Stratum XXI was dispelled by its connection to Wall 939 and by its lying upon the Stratum XX fill locus 616A (VI JJ:#15). While the sequence of construction is unusual, it is clear that seven walls and Flooring 611A = Floor 408A all existed in one phase, XXB. The seven walls are 939, 976, 934 and probably 924B in place as the surface was established, 970, 980, and 941 then built on or into the surface.

Makeup for Floor 611A (locus 609A; VI JJ:#16 = CC III:#28) was a thin layer of coarse grey earth with an admixture of gravel and small stones, at least in the region west of Wall 970. This makeup contained an animal figurine fragment and a bone pendant. Floor 611A (JJ:#14) was of packed limestone from Wall 939 to Wall 980 (Room 28), with brownish-grey occupation debris and some ashy deposits on it (#11). In Rooms 25 and 27, Floor 611A was made of a thin layer of reddish crumbly soil and topped by occupation debris similar to that in Room 28 (#12).

Wall 980 butted both Walls 924B and 934. Its stone foundation was 0.60 m thick and is preserved as high as 1.00 m. Wall 970, which butted Wall 934 but bonded with Wall 976, was of quite different construction: a single course of massive unhewn foundation stones on which rode seven or eight courses of somewhat smaller stones. A mudbrick superstructure averaged 0.60 m in width and brought the preserved wall to as high as 1.25 m. Wall 941 was 0.50 m wide and was preserved through five courses to as high as 1.50 m; it was bonded to Wall 970. Wall 924B, only 2.60 m long from its butt join against Wall 989 to its eastern end, was 1.00 m wide and preserved for four courses to a height of 1.10 m. Its top was leveled off with flat stones, probably to carry a mud brick superstructure which was later removed, presumably to permit anchoring Stratum XIX Wall 924A on a rock foundation.

Fig. 24. Human skeleton lying on Floor 611A in Room 28 of Field VI.

In Room 28, a human skeleton lay on Floor 611A (locus 612A, fig. 24). The head lay to the east, and the knees were contracted; the hands were drawn up beneath the chin. No artifacts were found with the body and there was no sign of an interment trench. Apparently Phase A builders simply covered the body with makeup and new Floor 16:9.

The later phase, Stratum XXA, floors in Rooms 25–28 varied in their composition. In Room 25, makeup 481 (VI JJ:#13) of crumbly grey soil underlay Floor 480 (#7); on the floor was occupation debris (#5). In Room 26, in the very limited undisturbed soil, a makeup of rocky brown earth separated Floor 408A from a thin bricky layer, locus 11:16 (VI CC III:#19), which probably represented the floor and occupation here. In Room 27, on a makeup of crumbly, stony soil 604A (JJ:#9) was hard-packed earth Floor 602A

Fig. 25. Oven 606A in Room 28 on Floor 16:9 of Stratum XXA.

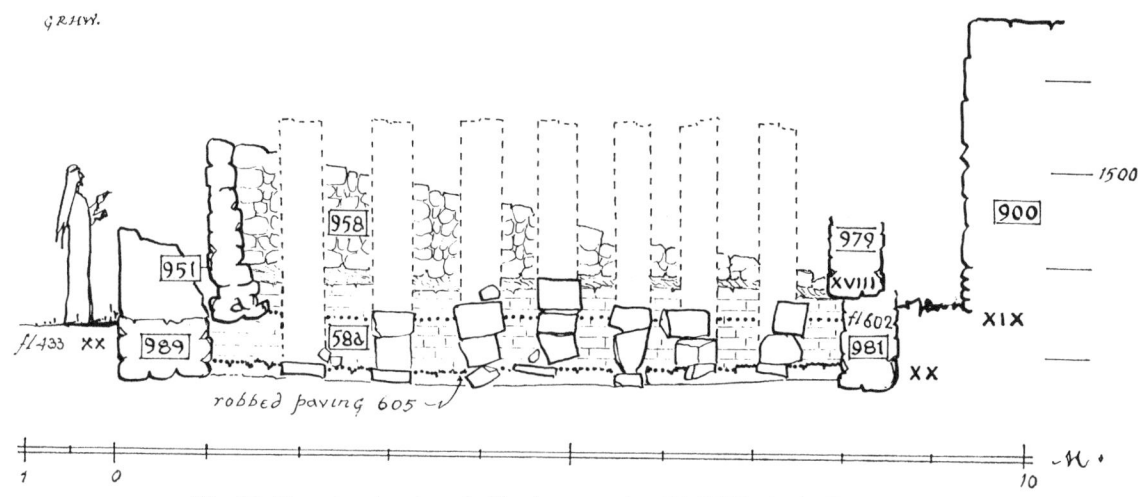

Fig. 26. Elevation drawing of pillar bases against Wall 958a in the Entrance Hall.

(JJ:#6). Found in the makeup was a fragment of a limestone weapon mold, comparable to a whole example found by Sellin. In Room 28, the makeup for the Phase A floor was locus 607A (JJ:#8; Ill. 91 = KK:#13), topped by Floor 16:9 of hard-packed earth with intermittent patches of packed limestone (KK:#12); this stratigraphy could be traced only in the southern half of the room near Wall 934. An ashy layer on the floor (KK:#11) no doubt resulted from the use of Oven 606A in the corner of Walls 980 and 934, of which only the base with an outside diameter of 0.50 m was preserved (fig. 25). This oven is the one hint that Rooms 25–28 constituted a living area, even while serving as the means of access from the Entrance Hall to the Southern Complex. Phase A floor levels, indicated on Ill. 72 with denser shading than that used for Phase B floors, ran at elevations between 13.00 and 13.20, some 0.30 to 0.40 m higher than Phase B floors.

The storage sub-complex and the possible living area made up of Rooms 25–28 flanked the

Fig. 27. Seven pillar bases as preserved in the Entrance Hall, viewed from the south.

Fig. 28. Flagstone Floor 605 in the Entrance Hall.

Entrance Hall. As preserved, Walls 924B and 939 suggest that a wide doorway ran from the Entrance Hall into Room 28, while a somewhat narrower one permitted access from the end of the streets into the Entrance Hall.

The Entrance Hall. The Hall was bounded by Walls 989 on the west and 924B on the south—both walls of high quality construction. It was paved with well-laid flagstones (Floor 605; Ill. 86 = VI EE:#7) running to a row of seven pillars standing close to Wall 958A (figs. 26 and 27). As preserved, the pillars are three rough-hewn drums high, although three of the seven have partially collapsed. The maximum preserved height is 1.15 m. The average diameter of the drums was 0.45 m, but six of the seven were roughly square in section, the seventh, second from the west, being rounded. Each rested on a flat foundation stone. They were evenly spaced, although there was a slightly wider gap between Wall 989 and the westernmost pillar than there was between Wall 981 and the easternmost. No stone of Floor 605 actually touched a pillar, but there can be no doubt they were contemporary; elevation on 605 at 12.95 is exactly that on the flat foundation stone.

There was a gap of only 0.02–0.03 m between the pillars and the face of Wall 958A. Wall 958A lay beneath Stratum XVIII Wall 958 which has not been removed, so Wall 958A is technically unexcavated. It is surmised to have run from Wall 989 to Wall 981 and to have been of the same width as its successor, 0.70 m. Its mud brick superstructure was visible and like Wall 989 shows alternating light and dark colored bricks. Presumably the pillars served to bear roof beams spanning the Hall (cf. comparable pillars in Room 2 of Stratum XVIII, below).

Before laying the flagstones of 605, Stratum XX builders laid a bedding layer 621 (Ill. 86 = VI EE:#8) on top of the leveling fill (#10). Floor 605 was not completely intact; Stratum XIX Burial 608 intruded upon it, and some of the flags quite possibly were reused in Stratum XIX Floor 602. The flagging was preserved to make contact with Walls 981 and 924B; some of the stones approached 0.70 m square (fig. 28).

Calling this room an Entrance Hall implies both its role as access and its ceremonial role as the point of first encounter with the interior of the acropolis. Street 9, at its nearest point of preservation was at elevation 13.16, 0.21 m higher than the floor of the Hall. One stepped down from the street into the Hall. Phase B Floor 611A in Room 28 was at 12.60 m, so one stepped down into it from the Hall. In Phase A, Floor 16:9 in Room 28 was at site elevation 13.00 (Ill. 91 = VI KK:#12), virtually on a level with the Hall. As to how one gained access to other rooms in the south, the data are lost. Wall 980 was preserved only to two courses in places, so there may have been a door in it allowing access from Room 28. Wall 934 was heavily robbed out by Stratum XIX builders, and it too may have had a door no longer discernible from Room 28 into the Southern Complex (see below).

As to the "ceremonial" nature of the Entrance Hall, the fine flagstones, the sturdy walls and the row of pillars speak for themselves.

The Southern Complex. Walls 939, 934 and 933 bounded the Southern Complex; no southern boundary has been identified, and erosion since the Austro-German excavations has removed any prospect of success in searching further. Many of the walls in this complex are known only from Welter's plan of the Sellin work and his own probing. For example, Stratum XIX Wall 995A, is from their plans, and the Joint Expedition posits a Wall 995 for Stratum XX that served as southern limit. It is to be noted that the preserved tongue of forecourt for the Fortress Temple remains largely uninvestigated; the small portions of wall on the plan for Stratum XX were found in probes deep into that tongue.

Wall 939 formed the west boundary of the streets; it has been noted above that the makeup for Street 9, locus 125, filled the foundation trench for 939 at a point just south of the line of Wall 934 (Ill. 83 = VI BB I:#20; Ill. 82 = AA I:#24; fig. 20:#20; Ill. 87 = FF II:#11). At this point, Wall 939 was founded 0.85 m lower than Wall 900. The north end of 939 as preserved was at the south edge of the interior of the Entrance Hall. South of the point of preservation shown on Ill. 72, it had been rebuilt as Stratum XIX Wall 902; the rebuild probably commenced at the line of XIX Wall 926, where Wall 902 made a slight jog and became wider (note Ill. 73). North of the line of Wall 926, Wall 939 was immediately overlaid by Wall 902. For most of its preserved length, Wall 939 was 0.60 m wide, built of two rows of stones; its maximum preservation is five courses to a height of 0.95 m above foundation.

Wall 934 was bonded into Wall 939, and ran west until cornering with Wall 933. Wall 904B was bonded into Wall 934, in contrast to Walls 970 and 980 of Rooms 25–28 which butted it. Between Wall 939 and Wall 904B, a segment of 934 was robbed out to its lowest course, leaving robber trench 605A (Ill. 91 = VI KK:#10). In VI KK, note that Floor 611A reached a flat stone in Wall 934 which may have been the threshold of the proposed doorway into Room 33. Wall 934 averaged 0.70 m in width, and was preserved through six courses to a height of 1.35 m at its junction with 939.

Wall 933 formed a corner with Wall 934 and ran south, with a distinct jog, under the forecourt of the Fortress Temple. It probably formed the western boundary of the complex in Strata XX and XIX, but probes in the forecourt did not establish this. The wall was seldom preserved above two courses, to a height of 0.60 m. The width varied from 0.45 to 0.70 m. There are a few traces of brick superstructure, which may, however, have come from the Stratum XIX reuse.

Partition walls in the Southern Complex were generally of slighter construction than those in the Northern. Walls 962 and 969 bounding Corridors 29 and 30 were only one stone wide, at about 0.40 m. Wall 962 survived as high as five courses, whereas Wall 969 was for the most part only one course and untraceable south of where Stratum XIX Wall 919 intruded on it. Wall 904B was 0.70 m wide and preserved for three courses, 0.50 m. It extended from a bonded junction with Wall 934 to a corner with Wall 961, preserved in only one course, at a width of 0.40 m. What was preserved is probably the full foundation; fragments of brick superstructure rode on this course. The founding level of Wall 961 rose slightly to the west to the location of its corner with Wall 922B, also preserved in only one course, 0.50 m wide. Walls 904B and 922B both were succeeded by Stratum XIX walls anchored on them.

The five walls just described formed a series of rooms and corridors at the north edge of a large courtyard, 35. Corridor 29 (see plan) was originally paved with cobblestones, preserved in two layers (Floor 566 = VI BB III:#10). Continuous with the lower layer of cobblestones was hard-packed earth Floor 568 (BB III:#9, CC III:#22; Ill. 85 = VI DD:basal) laid on a makeup of dark brown ashy earth locus 314 (BB III:#11 = CC III:#23), which in turn lay on the leveling fill for

Fig. 29. Base of storage jar sunk in Floor 556 of Courtyard 35.

Stratum XX. Stratum XIX intrusions destroyed all traces of Stratum XX surfaces in Corridor 30.

Room 31 had a preserved segment of hard-packed earth flooring, locus 328, laid on makeup 341, brown rocky soil. Ashy debris lay on the surface. In Room 32, Floor 312 (VI CC III:#24), also of packed earth with ash on it, lay on makeup 313 of loose rocky earth (not visible on VI CC III). The floor was preserved only in the northwest and southeast of the room; it was cut near Wall 961 by a (probably Stratum XIX) pit (CC III:#15). In Room 33, hard-packed earth floor 507 rode on makeup 508, of grey-brown bricky earth with patches of ash (VI BB II:#11 on ##12–13; KK #17 on #18). (Burial 16:21 cut through it on VI BB as #6 and KK as ##3 and 4.) Floor 507 was the surface onto which one would have stepped if coming south out of the Entrance Hall, through Room 28.

Courtyard 35 was the largest feature of the Southern Complex. It apparently occupied the full width from Wall 939 to Wall 969 extended. Court 34, marked off by the fragments of wall in the southwest, may have been open northward to Courtyard 35, just as Rooms 31 and 33 were open to it southward.

Floor levels in Courtyard 35 were reached in only a few probe trenches; since they were not connected, different locus numbers were assigned to each. South of Wall 961, Floor 556 could be traced southward to the limit of excavation (CC III:#26). Of hard-packed ashy earth, it rode on a makeup of brown earth containing decomposed chalk and small stones (locus 305 = CC III:#27). The base of storage jar Locus 553 was embedded in the floor, cut off exactly flush with its elevation (fig. 29; Cole 1984: pl. 37a). Possibly it held the flour used for bread baked in Oven 559. The oven was of the usual bee-hive shape, preserved to its original height 0.40 m above the floor (fig. 30). Its base was sunk 0.10 m into the floor and was oval, 0.60 m east–west and 0.50 m north–south in diameter. Its mouth—about half the rim was preserved—had an inside diameter of 0.20 m. A vertical opening 0.20 m wide cut out of the side wall may have been the loading door, or simply a fracture from the destruction of the complex. Three distinct layers of body sherds wrapped the outside, probably for insulation (fig. 31), where can be seen the rim of a large jug (Cole 1984: pl. 34e) leaning against the east side. A rim fragment of a flat-bottomed cookpot came from the oven (Cole 1984: pl. 23a). A section through the oven showed it was set on a base of small, flat stones. On top of 0.02 m of earth inside was a layer of grey fluffy ashes 0.04 m thick, above which was the hard brown

Fig. 30. Oven 559 in Floor 556 of Courtyard 35.

earth characteristic of the fill for Stratum XIX mixed with oven wall fragments. The walls were 0.06–0.07 m thick at the base (which showed a slightly inverted rim) but 0.02–0.03 m thick above the level of the floor.

Floor 556 continued past the corner of Room 32 and was most probably continuous with Floor 511A against Wall 939 to the east, again of hard-packed earth on a makeup of looser grey soil, locus 513A (not displayed on section); Stratum XIX walls rode above this small segment of floor and preserved it.

Further south, Floor 17:12 was found near the line of Wall 939 extrapolated; it was at a higher elevation (13.10 to 13.22) than 556 (12.70–12.75), probably because it rode on a hump over Stratum XXII Platform 968 (Ill. 82 = AA II:#8). Stratum XIX Walls 940, 937 and 926 all lay above Floor 17:12; the foundation trench for Wall 902 (AA II:#7) cut through it. Makeup for 17:12 was brownish clayey earth with small pebbles, locus 17:15 (AA II:#9). Three meters further south was a segment of flooring designated 214 (Ill. 88 = VI GG:#12; Ill. 87 = FF III:#9), which also ran beneath Stratum XIX Wall 940 and was at close to the same elevation as that of 17:12 (13.20–13.30 as compared to 13.10–13.22); there seems little doubt they were connected. Floor 214 was of packed earth with occasional patches of packed limestone (seen elsewhere, although rarely, in Stratum XX), riding on damp greyish-brown earth with interlaced layers of looser brown rocky soil (VI FF III:#9 on #10; GG:#13).

Court 34 was at the west edge of the excavation field, and was separated from Courtyard 35 to the east by Wall 983; Wall 986 was its south boundary. Wall 933 extended was probably its western boundary; if that wall made a jog back eastward, it may have continued as Wall 982, of which only 2 m were preserved. Alternatively, Wall D may have been the western boundary of Court 34. The court was probably open to the north.

Wall 983 is a short fragment; no trace of it was encountered to the north of the preserved segment. However, the combination of Walls 983 and 986 began a building tradition that continued through Strata XIX and XVIII, suggesting that the location of Court 34 was important for the history of the MB IIB acropolis; only three other interior walls in the complex, 958, 922 and 904 showed the same continuity.

West from the top preserved course of Wall 983 ran a fine, packed limestone segment of flooring (VI FF IV:#22), resting on a makeup of dark brown earth. Its elevation at 13.10 was higher than the 12.75 reading on Floor 556 but compared well

Fig. 31. Detail of the construction of Oven 559, with layering of sherds on its exterior.

with that of 17:12 (13.10 to 13.22) and of 214 (13.20 to 13.30) and with the elevations of Streets 9–7.

East of Wall 900. Stratum XX reuse of Stratum XXI remains was found only in Rooms 36 and 37. Stratum XXI Wall 998 was reused as the dividing wall of the two rooms, while Wall 999 was the rebuild of Stratum XXI Wall 999A slightly offset to the north. Between Wall 999A and Wall 999 was a 0.15 m layer of dark brown earth. The foundation trench for Wall 900, locus 512 = VI FF I:#11 cut through Stratum XXI Floor 510 and Wall 999a; Wall 900 thus became the west boundary of narrow Room 36.

In Room 36, hard-packed earth Floor 505 (VI FF I:#9) at elevation 13.10 overlay occupation debris on the Stratum XXI Floor 510 and the fill of the Wall 900 foundation trench. On 505 was occupation debris shown as FF I:#8. On the other side of Wall 988, in Room 37, Floor 503 was of well-laid cobblestones at elevation 13.25, resting on a 0.60 m thick makeup of fine damp brown and grey bricky earth, locus 509 (FF I:#10 on #13). Floor 503 was covered with ashy debris (FF I:#7) perhaps deriving from an oven outside the excavated area. The room was resurfaced with cobblestone floor 500 (FF I:#6); the accumulated occupation debris is FF I:#5. The superstructure of Wall 999 was robbed out after both floors were laid; they ran only to the robber trench.

It is significant that east of Wall 900 Stratum XX builders reused remains of their MB IIA predecessors, while west of the Wall 900 there was a completely new orientation of structures. Rooms 36 and 37 probably are to be related to the MB IIB remains in Field IX 30 m to the southeast and at an elevation nearly 7 m lower. With Wall 900 and Wall D, however, there was now a defined acropolis, separated from the rest of the city.

As noted, Field VI Stratum XX anchors the MB IIB typologies in Dan P. Cole's presentation of the MB IIB ceramic study (1984). Stratum XX fill and makeup had a number of loci (216, 313, 314, 405B, 484, 621) which contained what was analyzed in the field as pure MB IIA pottery. Other loci from Stratum XX preparation had an admixture of MB IIB forms (44, 17:15, 305, 444, 508, 509, 609A). Locus 125, the makeup for Street 9 and the fill in the 939 foundation trench, contained an even mixture. The impression is that Stratum XX began with the change from MB IIA to MB IIB, and that there was clear continuity in ceramic tradition. With the surfaces and occupation debris of Stratum XX, Phase B, the pottery becomes de-

EDWARD F. CAMPBELL

STRATUM XX: LOCI 41, 43, 44

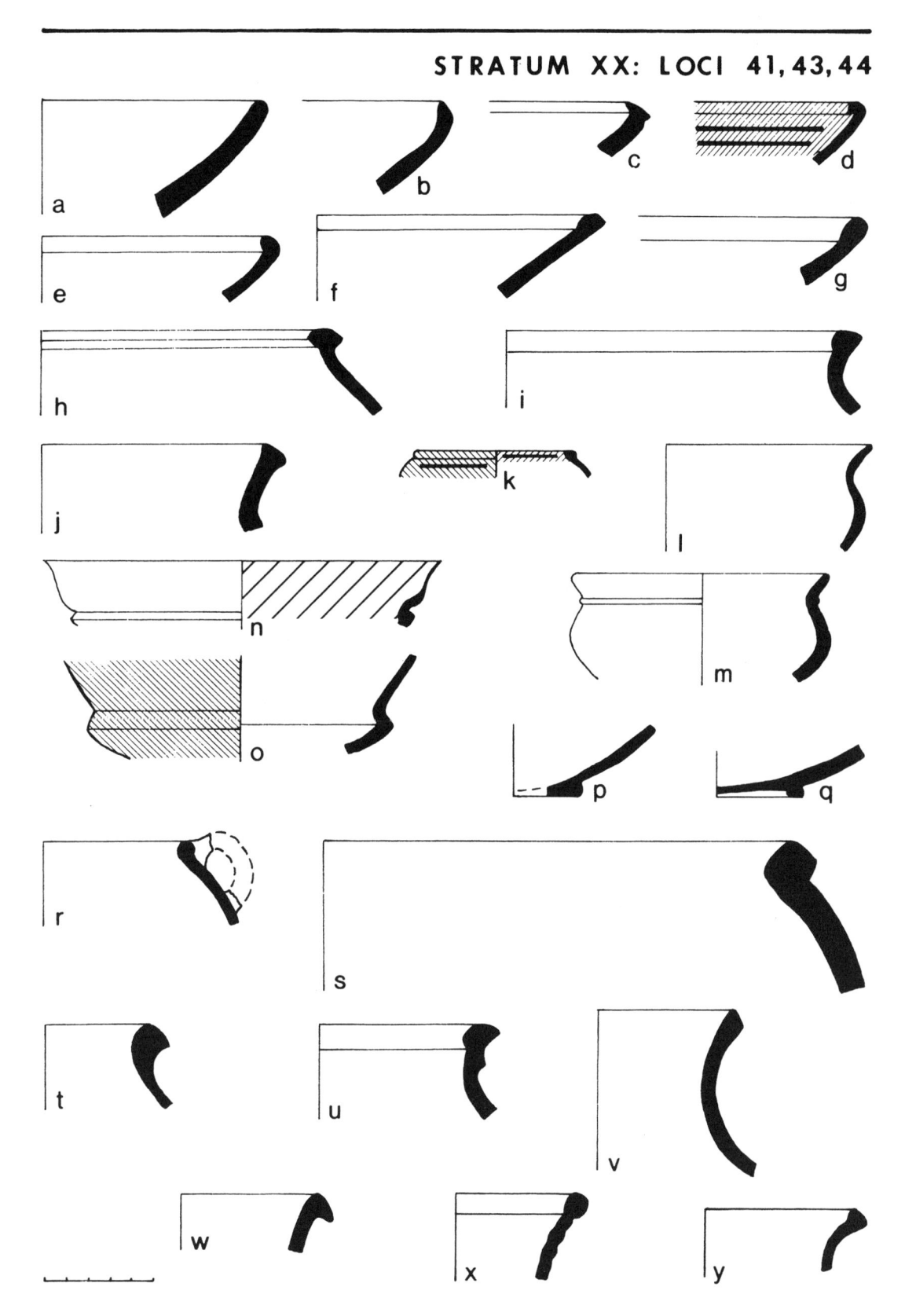

Fig. 32. Stratum XX pottery forms, as prepared by Dan P. Cole (Cole:pl. 46).

finitive for what the Expedition offers as early MB IIB, dating around 1750 BCE. The Cole volume presents the details; see especially Cole 1984:31 and pl. 46 reproduced here as fig. 32. As for Stratum XX Phase A, the best locus for discerning a terminus ad quem is the fill of Silo 411B of Room 24. The Expedition proposes 1750–1725 BCE for the date range of Stratum XX.

STRATA XIX–XVII

The Sequence of Fortification

At no point did the Joint Expedition make a cut completely through the successive systems of fortification so as to reach their base and display them in sequence. Nor had the Austro-German Expedition. The nearest approach to doing this was that of Welter, working in 1928 and 1931. His 1928 work, in some seven probe trenches through the acropolis, had traced Wall D and established its primacy, and had encountered Wall C, a wall whose exterior face was sloped inward, battered against fill behind it; the interior face was rough, the boulders pressed into the backing of what Welter termed "calcareous marl" (1928)—probably *ḥuwwar* soil pulled in from the slopes of Mt. Ebal (Ill. 10).

Stratum XIX: The Wall C Rampart

Field V (Ills. 10, 68). Welter published a section tying Walls A and C to the back wall of the Fortress Temple (1932:297–98, Abb. 5) and prepared another section carrying over to Wall D, which serves as the basis for Ill. 10. His text presents the correct reading of their chronological sequence, though he thought he had encountered a southern end to the C embankment in the form of an acute angle return of about 75 degrees (1932:294–95, correcting his earlier 90 degrees in 1928) eastward to join Wall D, producing a roughly square base for what he called a truncated pyramid confined to the acropolis. It is to be noted that his own sketch plan (1932:293–94, Abb. 3) does not show Wall C itself making the return, so the suspicion arises that his discernment of the south limit of the rampart is instead an interpretation of a section cut into the heart of the rampart.

Nor is his evidence for concluding a northern limit to his pyramid indicated.

The Joint Expedition confirmed Welter's reading of the sequence of fortification: D, then C, then A. It refuted his notion of a roughly square section of a pyramid as the base for the acropolis by finding evidence of the C Rampart at points throughout the entire northern perimeter of the site, as far as the East Gate.

Three narrow probe trenches designed to test Wall C, together designated Field V, Area 7, were dug in 1960. The southernmost of these, off the southwest corner of the Fortress Temple, was not sited far enough south to disprove Welter's sense of a turn of the rampart eastward. It did succeed, however, in displaying more clearly the tip-lines associated with Wall C, as well as another prepared slope running over Wall C down to the footing of later Wall A, thus suggesting another phase in the MB IIB fortification system (see below). The layers approaching the outer face of Wall D, of *ḥuwwar*, clay, brown earth, clay, and packed brown, all probably belonged to the rampart. The latest pottery from all of them, of which 20 indicator sherds were saved, dated to MB IIB.

On Ill. 10 and more clearly in Ill. 68 ("revetment wall"), Wall C is pictured rising about 4.00 m above the slight rise in elevation of bedrock that constitutes the hillock under the Fortress Temple upon which it was founded; Welter speaks of a 5.00 m height to Wall C plus fist-sized stones on the slope above it. The angle of its batter was pronounced, more distinct than that of Wall A. Inside Wall C on Ill. 68 can be seen, approaching its top but cut into by Welter's superficial trenching, the indication of tongues of chalk interlaced with darker soil, overlying the *ḥuwwar* (=Welter's marl). This sort of tonguing is typical of the prepared surfacing of a glacis. It is regrettable that what little pottery there was in the layering inside Wall C was not effectively separated by loci during excavation; only ten forms were registered, representing Chalcolithic, EB I, and MB IIB to possible C (3 sherds). It is not clear which side of Wall C these came from, but the field diary claims that nothing later than MB IIB came from the layering outside the wall (see further below).

Judging from the nature of the horizontally laid layers beneath the Fortress Temple all the way to the top of Chalcolithic remnants, from the interrupted layering against Wall D shown in fig. 18 (above), and from Welter's discernment of what he thought was fill in back of Wall C all the way over to Wall D in his southern return of his "truncated pyramid," it seems clear that the 37.00 m distance from the outside of Wall C to the interior of Wall D was a prepared, domed rampart similar to others known from MB II—at Hazor, Yavneh-Yam, Tel Kabri, Acco and Dan in Palestine, and at Qatna, Carchemish, and Tell el-Yehudiyeh in Syria and Egypt. How high it stood cannot be ascertained, though Seger, in an article comparing the Shechem and Gezer fortifications, extrapolated it to a height of as much as 15.00 m. At its top, Seger posited a vertical wall like the one in the comparable system at Jericho (1975:36*–38*).

Recent excavation is gradually elucidating the varying ways in which such ramparts were constructed (Kempinski 1992:129–32). Judging from cuts made through the ones at Hazor (Yadin 1972:51–57) and Dan (Biran 1994:59–73), they were sophisticatedly engineered and designed to meet the vicissitudes of the location, both as to the way the core was built and as to materials and methods chosen to layer up the fill (Pennells 1983). Drainage and the stemming of erosion were pertinent considerations in the degree of slope and nature of the consolidation, but Yadin's idea that the rampart system served to frustrate the use of the battering ram remains compelling (Yadin 1955:23–32; cf. Parr 1968; G. R. H. Wright 1968; Seger 1975:42*–45*).

Field IV Beneath the 7300 Building (Ill. 58, 59). At Shechem, the evidence suggests that there was another development after the building of the C Rampart but still within MB IIB. Welter's 1932 section, the evidence from Field V.7, Dever's A-B trench through the 7300 building in Field IV dug in 1973, and hints from Field III point to another consolidated slope overlying the one coming to the top of Wall C. It too showed tongues of chalk interlaced with darker fill layers, and its tiplines extrapolated ran to the tip-line which Welter apparently picked up in a narrow trench inside Wall A, reaching Wall A at its lowermost course. When Dever made his cut in 1973, he found the same conditions (Ill. 59 = IV FF:##14–15; cf. the schematized section in Dever 1974:39, fig. 9). And indeed, his 1972 cut through the defenses north of the Northwest Gate, in the complex designated 7200 (Ill. 58 = IV EE:#37; cf. Dever 1974:34, fig. 4), probably shows corresponding conditions there, involving the segments of stony soil beneath "Glacis B" of his Phase 5.

This set of evidence does not make sense if it is taken to relate to the construction of Wall A as a defense system, itself battered so as to retain a filling behind it. Builders would not have first built Wall A as free-standing and then laid a glacis to its interior base, later to level to its top with horizontal fill layers. The consolidated slope must represent an extension of the C Rampart outward by means of a second earth-moving operation, surfaced as a glacis. As noted above, the probe in Field V, Area 7 found nothing later than MB IIB pottery in this slope.

The Wall A system was later designed on a different concept, at the beginning of MB IIC. Whether the foot of the augmented rampart was revetted, as the earlier one was with Wall C, is uncertain. It may have simply merged with the horizontal plane of the natural valley floor. Or it may have been retained by a stone revetment where Wall A now is, perhaps one represented by the current lowest course of Wall A—this suggested by Welter's section.

The construction of the original C Rampart is associated with Stratum XIX; whether it served also for Stratum XVIII cannot be shown. Either with XVIII or with XVII, the augmented rampart was developed. As the description of the interior of the acropolis will show, building spread out to cover Wall D at a point in time still within MB IIB, before Wall A and the Fortress Temple were built; perhaps the addition to the rampart took place co-terminus with that expansion.

Other Segments of the C System. The Joint Expedition probed beneath MB IIC layers where the C Rampart lines ought to run (known or extrapolated) at nine locations, two of which, Field V, Area 7, and Field IV under the 7300 building, have already been described. In clockwise order from the region of the Fortress Temple, the remain-

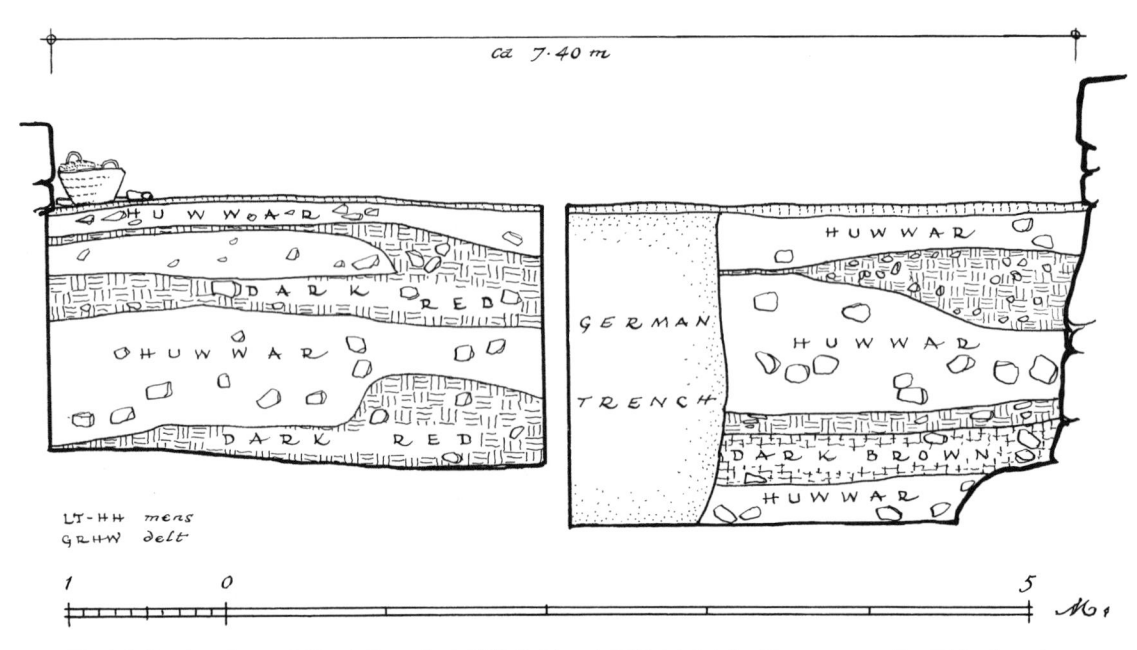

Fig. 33. Sections beneath North Gate, loci 4003 (left) and 4002 (right), looking east; see fig. 34 for locations.

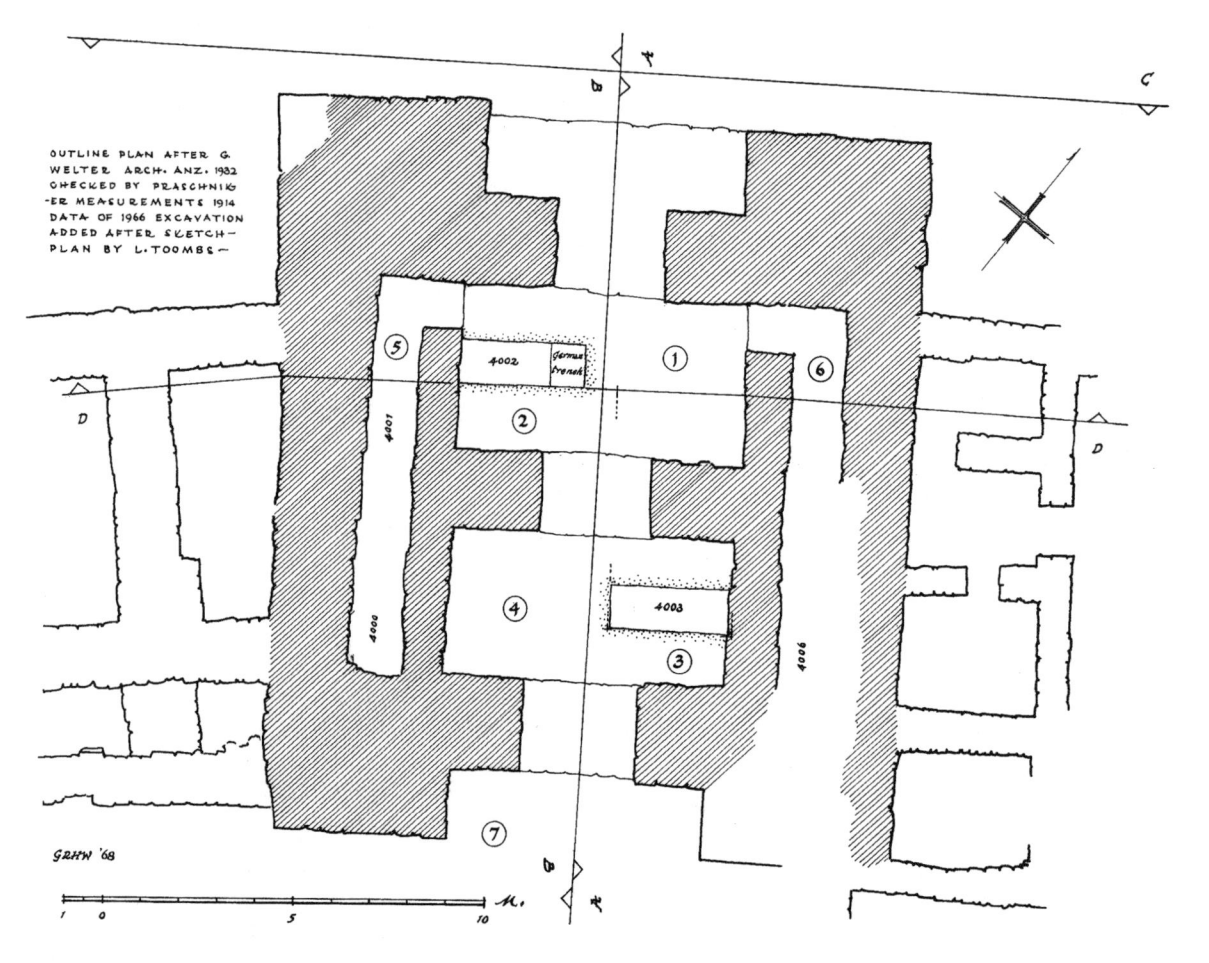

Fig. 34. Key plan of the Northwest Gate, after Welter.

ing seven are beneath the Fortress Temple itself; in Field IV beneath the Northwest Gate; in Field VI.2 at the north edge of the acropolis region; in a deep probe in Field XIII; in the lowest cut in Field VIII.1; in Field III; and in Field I beneath the East Gate. At all seven locations, excavation almost certainly encountered the rampart, in every case to some degree truncated and its soil used to cover over and level up previous ruins. The quantity of soil involved, first moved in for the rampart and then redistributed after its nullification, was immense, and the fact that Chalcolithic, MB IIA and MB IIB sherds are found in soil virtually throughout the mound is as much due to this activity as to all the other later forces that resulted in redistributing sherds upward in the stratigraphy.

Beneath the Fortress Temple, the nature of the build up is difficult to deal with. A massive platform was constructed here upon which to site the Temple, and the separation of the fills that belong to that enterprise from the soil that represents the truncated rampart is impossible without dismantling the Temple building, and likely to be impossible even if that were done. Grey soil which was traced deep below the earliest flooring of the Temple, frequently interrupted by the ubiquitous Iron I pits cut deep into the Temple underpinnings, is a probable candidate for the fill in preparation for the Temple. At a point about 3.50 m below the lowest flooring of the Fortress Temple, at site elevation 16.18, excavation in the narrow cuts deep below the Temple began to discern tamped horizontal layers that now are seen likely to be stopping or working surfaces in the building up of the rampart. Two MB IIA, four MB IIA/B, three MB II/C and six Chalcolithic sherds were registered from the sparse ceramics in this layering; field diaries speak of other MB II pieces which were not registered.

In 1966, probes were made into the underpinnings of the Northwest Gate, which had been cleared to its entrance surface by the Austro-German expedition in 1927. To a depth of 1.60 m to 1.75 m below the street surface, layers of *ḥuwwar* and dark red earth containing frequent fist-sized stones (fig. 33), appeared in probes 4002 and 4003, placed in the exterior and interior gate chambers respectively (fig. 34). Similar layering appeared in another 0.40 m-deep probe against the interior (southeast) of the innermost pier of the gate. If the hypothesis of an augmented rampart holds, the layers in the innermost probe could have belonged to it; the layers within the gate chambers would fit better with the fill thrown in against Wall A as it was built up at the beginning of MB IIC.

In describing Wall D above, it was noted that loci 47 and 48 of fig. 11 = VI PP against the west face of the Wall probably belonged to the C Rampart, even though they do not lie horizontal but sloped slightly westward. While it is not impossible that locus 44 and even locus 37 belonged to the rampart also (see below), they probably fit better with Strata XVIII or XVII rather than with XIX. There is no pottery later than MB IIB in these layers, and the pottery is sparse.

In Field XIII, immediately northeast of VI.2 across a one-meter balk, deep probes were dug in Areas 1 and 3 parallel to the main north–south cross-balk of the field and 1.50 m west of it. Extrapolation of the lines of Wall A and of Wall D had suggested that the rampart, if of uniform width, would have its eastern edge approximately under the cross-balk. The probes reached superimposed sloping layers of pulverized limestone and red field earth, virtually devoid of pottery (fig. 35). Locus 3564 displayed ca. 0.40 m of this material; elsewhere in the probe in area 3 excavation penetrated a full meter of this layered fill, while in Area 1 at least 0.40 m was dug. The top of the layering was at site elevation 16.75, two full meters higher than the top of fig. 11: locus 47 at ca. 14.70 m. What few sherds there were, with no indicators, came from the Area 1 loci and were of MB II ware.

Without much doubt, this layering is again the C Rampart, here preserved to a higher elevation than is the case only 10.00 to 12.00 m to the southwest—an indication of the topography with which MB IIC builders would have had to cope. It is conceivable that some sort of retaining structure lies hidden in the barely one-meter wide balk between VI.2 and XIII.1 that would account for the drop of two meters to its south. A probe in Field XIII, Area 4, ca. 3.00 m east of the Area 3 probe, failed to encounter Wall D where extrapolation would have placed it, suggesting a curve eastward here and suggesting that the levels of rampart fill in Field

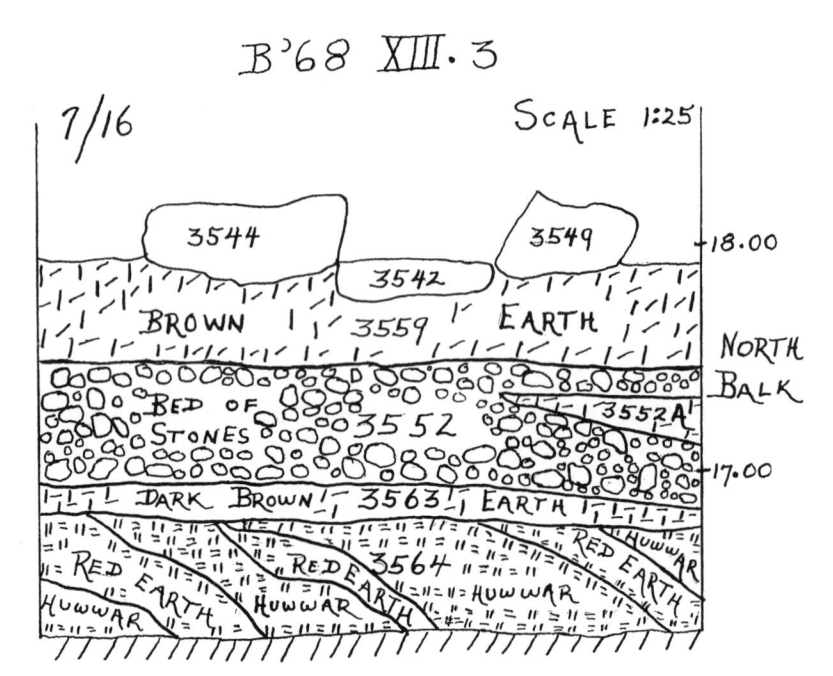

Fig. 35. Lawrence Toombs' field sketch of subsidiary section in Field XIII, Area 3, showing at its base the tiplines of the C Rampart, locus 3564.

XIII were from a location more to the interior of the rampart than the extrapolations of the fortification walls had hinted.

In Field VIII, Area 1, beginning from a cobbled or metalled surface at elevation 14.00–13.90 on fig. 7 (above, Chapter 1), the layers down to virgin soil just above bedrock probably belong to the C Rampart. They show red field earth and *ḥuwwar* layering similar to that in the Field XIII probes. As the section indicates, layers of small stones, probably constituting solidified working surfaces for the builders to stand on as they built up the fill, occurred at several points, recalling the conditions beneath the Fortress Temple and beneath the East Gate. The top of this layering, which may have been lowered by Austro-German excavation before their back-filling of the sterile, *ḥuwwar*-filled top 2.00 m of the section, was at site elevation ca. 13.85, some 37 m away from the higher dome of it in Field XIII but positioned along the appropriate curve of the rampart. The pottery from the red earth, of which 22 indicators were saved, is MB IIB except for one or two Chalcolithic/EB I.

In 1964, James Ross deepened the Field III cut (Ill. 41), shown in Ill. 44. Wall A in Field III is most likely Wall 655 on this section. To its west, light brown earth with greenish striations of *ḥuwwar* in #39 rode over damp brown layer #40 and packed green clay layer #41, all three sloping so that if extrapolated they would have reached Wall 655 deep on its interior face. Farther west, on the other side of Wall B, sloping *ḥuwwar* layer (Ill. 43:#16) over a rubbly layer of mixed *ḥuwwar* and clay (##17 and 18) would, if extrapolated, have run below Ill 44:#41. Still farther west the dome of packed green clay of Ill. 43:##20 and 31, suggested a slope that will have run deeper still. These layers had been cut into by the building of Wall B and then topped by layers of MB IIC phasing. Ill. 43:##20 and 31, ##17 and 18, and #16, and Ill. 44:#41 are tentatively identified as the C Rampart and its augmentation, although the field analysis of Ill. 43:#20 found one or two sherds to be MB IIC in date. Ill. 44:##39 and 40 appear to belong to the earliest development of the Wall A system, to be described in the next chapter; a few sherds found in these two layers are MB IIC.

Similar conditions probably existed beneath the East Gate in Field I. In probes made within the gate (Ill. 26), layered soil with lenses of *ḥuwwar* were once again encountered, and, at the base of excavation, greenish clay reminiscent of that found in Field III. These layers were virtually sterile of pottery. Field I is at a point about as low on the

Fig. 36. Overview of the acropolis, bounded by Wall 900 at the left margin. The streets ran between Wall 900 and the succession of walls to its right. The tongue of the Temple forecourt is in the center. The Hellenistic structure in Field II is at the upper left.

mound as it has been possible to conduct excavations; the top of the material that may represent the C Rampart is at site elevation ca. 7.00 m, while the greenish clay layer is at roughly 4.50 m. A proposal made in the report of the 1964 season (Bull, *et al.* 1965:35–36, and fig. 16) that the top of a wall of large ("cyclopean") boulders below the threshold of the front piers in the East Gate, at site elevation 4.90 m, might be Wall C would probably require assigning at least the upper layers just described to the augmentation of the rampart running to the line of the footing of later Wall A. It would locate Wall C at least 13.00 m from Wall A in the east where it is 8.00 m away from it in the west. The proposal remains possible, but is based on insufficient evidence and demands further excavation.

In sum, there is solid evidence for a rampart-style of fortification belonging to MB IIB all around the northern arc of the mound. It is built from varying kinds of material, although there was a tendency to include in it segments of water-impervious natural chalk (*ḥuwwar*) and to face its slopes with tongues of this chalk. Red field earth was a standard ingredient; greenish clay was characteristic of the easternmost arc. The soil was gathered from locations where there was sparse pottery, and rarely if at all did the material contain occupation rubbish such as charcoal or artifacts other than stray sherds. The rampart was at first confined to the distance between two walls, D and C, and then was augmented to extend to the point where the base of Wall A sits.

An intriguing question for the historian is the value and utility of such a rampart in a narrow valley between two flanking mountains, as opposed to the usual circumstance where such fortifications are found, namely surrounding cities on flat plains.

The Acropolis in Stratum XIX (Ills. 82–84, 86–87, 91, figs. 4, 20)

With the development of the C Rampart in Stratum XIX and its augmentation out to the line of the foot of Wall A (Strata XVIII-XVII) went a succession of changes in the structures on the adjacent acropolis, Field VI, defined as separate from the rest of the city by the use, rebuild and maintenance of Wall 900 (fig. 36). This succession defines MB IIB stratigraphy at Shechem and provides the close separation for the pottery typologies.

The Street. The foundation for Street 6, overlying Street 7 of Stratum XX, was locus 62, a layer of medium grey earth with considerable ash, bone, sherds and occasional cobblestones (Ill. 82 = VI AA I:#16; figs. 4 and 20:#13; Ill. 83 = VI BB I:#13; Ill. 87 = VI FF II:#4). It filled the foundation trench

Fig. 37. The balk between Areas 3D and 3E with Wall 900 at left. Street 6 is marked by numbers on the wall at left margin.

for 902 of Stratum XIX (AA I:#17; fig. 20:#14), and the same type of earth was found between the stones of Wall 902 itself. The eastern curb of the drain contemporary with Street 6 (locus 120; AA I:#15; BB I:#12) was constructed of large unhewn stones while the cobblestones of the street foundation were somewhat smaller. A few fragments of the paving lining the bottom of the drain were noted, but there was no evidence the drain was covered; it was an open channel (locus 126) about 0.60 m wide, slightly lower than the elevation of the street. An east–west drain, locus 17:6, led through the mudbrick superstructure of Wall 902 from Room 16 into the street drain, eventually washing away the western curb at this point.

Street 6 is unique in that its cobblestone and earth foundation, locus 62, was paved with chunks of soft marl averaging 0.10 m in thickness (locus 61; VI AA I:#14; VI AA I/1:#12; VI BB I:#11; VI FF II:#3; fig. 37). This construction, in addition to its well-preserved drain, made it the most impressive of the nine streets of MB IIB. It led north directly to the Entrance Hall, as had Streets 9–7 of Stratum XX. The northern end of Street 6 was at site elevation 13.60, nearly the same as Floor 602 of the hall, at 13.55.

Preparation and Construction. In several respects, Stratum XIX construction represents reuse and reconstruction of the Stratum XX plan, while in other respects it involves a new configuration of space (Ill. 73). Reconstruction was more common in the south. Walls 934 (partly) and 933 of XX were simply reused in XIX. Walls 922A, 904A, 938A, 984A and 902 were built on the stumps of their predecessors 922B, 904B, 983, 986 and 939, at least for parts of their lengths. Foundation trenches for this process of rebuild were discerned in a few cases, notably locus 320 for Wall 922A (BB III:#8) and locus 231 for Wall 902 (BB II:#10; AA II:#7). The walls defining Rooms 29–32 and 25–28 of Stratum XX were nullified, and the Northern Complex greatly altered. Wall 924A was rebuilt on the line of Stratum XX Walls 976 and 924B, and Wall 958A was reused as the north boundary of the Entrance Hall, but Storerooms 21–24 of Stratum XX were abandoned and Wall 951A displaced Stratum XX Wall 989 slightly east of its line (Ill. 86 = VI EE:#1 is the foundation trench for 951A cutting into the brick east face of 989). Wall 951A served as the eastern limit of a large courtyard whose earliest floor (locus 426) ran over the storeroom partition walls (Ill. 84 = CC II:#16). Wall 900, it is to be recalled, was rebuilt in Stratum XIX beginning at a point about 4.00 m south of the Entrance Hall. While there was architectural continuity from Stratum XX to Stratum XIX, far more than from XXI to XX, it was confined to the Southern Complex and to the Entrance Hall.

Fill over Stratum XX and beneath makeup for Stratum XIX floors also suggested continuity more than discontinuity. It appears to be purposeful leveling for Stratum XIX rather than erosion accumulation after abandonment of Stratum XX. Its nature varied. It was a layer of compact brown earth as much as 0.75 m thick under Room 9 along the eastern side of the Southern Complex up to the Entrance Hall (loci 6:15, 600A, 607A; Ill. 91 = VI KK:##9 and 16), but was grey earth with rubble (locus 17:11) under Room 16 a few meters south. It was as much as a meter thick to the west under Rooms 12, 13 and 15 (locus 334; BB IV:#7 and the red-brown earth of FF IV:#20 cut by the foundation trench for Wall 938A). It was thinnest or entirely absent in the center of the south and throughout the Northern Complex. The floors of the Stratum XX Northern Complex and the Entrance Hall were immediately overlaid by the makeup for Stratum XIX floors, respectively locus 464 under Floor 426 (CC II:#17) and 604 and 610 under Floor 602 (EE:#6). In Room 10, hard brown fill 301 was under pebbly makeup #17 south of Wall 915 (CC III:#25), but pebbly makeup #17 was directly on the Stratum XX floor north of Wall 915 in Room 11; a thin deposit, locus 303-307 (the lower part of CC III:#7; BB III:7), under part of Room 11 was probably fill rather than makeup. Nowhere was this fill as thick as that laid in beneath Stratum XX, nor as that between XIX and XVIII, another indication that XX and XIX were closely related in time and concept.

Structures. Almost every room and court of Stratum XIX excavated to sufficient depth showed evidence of two floorings, usually separated by 0.05–0.10 m of new makeup. The Northern Complex showed additional resurfacings. Only the room segment to the east of Wall 900 running to Wall 987 showed one flooring (at elevation 14.10), and here disturbance by or subsequent to the Austro-German excavation work at the exposed surface may have removed evidence of later phases. Two walls, 915 between Rooms 10 and 11 and 921 in Room 13, related only to the upper phase. The lower phase is XIXB, the upper XIXA.

The Northern Complex. The eastern and southern boundaries of this court are clear. The northern limit was beyond Wall 943 of MB IIC, since Stratum XIX floorings ran well beneath its foundation (CC II:#13); Wall 3906 exposed in Field XIII:6 and shown on Ills. 147 and 167 is a candidate. Wall D may have formed the western limit, since the lowest Stratum XIX floor, 426 (Ill. 89 = VI HH:#13), was traced to a point about 2.00 m from its east face at an elevation more than a meter below its preserved top. Wall 951A was the eastern limit, and served as western limit of the Entrance Hall. As preserved, 951A was 0.60 m wide and stood three courses, to a height of 0.50 m. (The later rebuild of 951A, Wall 951 of Stratum XVIII, was only 0.40 m wide.) Wall 924A, which served as south boundary of both the Northern Court and the Entrance Hall, was built upon and thus replaced Stratum XX Walls 976 and 924B. Over the 1.00 m wide 924B, 924A was two stones wide spanning 0.75 m; over the mudbrick top of Stratum XX Wall 976, 924A narrowed to 0.50 m. Here it was made of well-hewn stones, one of which had earlier been used as a door socket (fig. 38). The founding level of 951A and 924A were both at site elevation 13.40 near the Entrance Hall.

The earliest XIXB floor in the Northern Court was 426, a packed earth surface with intermittent patches of packed limestone, overlaid by a thin layer of grey ash (VI CC II:#16 and HH:#13, with occupation debris CC:II:#15 and HH:#12). Makeup for 426, narrowly separating it from Stratum XX floors below, was composed of damp brown earth (locus 464; CC II:#17; HH:#14). The CC section displays Floor 426 running over Wall 974 and beginning a slight upward slope as it approached Wall 924; Stratum XVII Pit 431 and the even later Trough 410 (CC II:##4 and 2) severed its connection to Wall 924, but the rise in slope suggests it would have run *over* the stump of Stratum XX Wall 965 and met 924A at its founding level.

About 0.35 m above Floor 426 was Floor 469 (CC II:#13; HH:#9 with occupation debris #8), traced among the interruptions of Austro-German trenching along Wall 943, Pit 431 and Trough 410 (CC II:##1, 4 and 2). It rested on a makeup of

Fig. 38. Looking south at Stratum XIX Wall 924A, resting on the mudbrick topping of Stratum XX Wall 976, in Field VI, Area 24. Wall 924A was preserved for only two to three courses of stone; riding immediately upon it is Wall 924 of Stratum XVIII. Note the door socket stone reused in 924A. In the foreground is a segment of Stratum XX Floor 451 with the stones of Wall 965 nearest the camera. Floor 406 of Stratum XVIIIB is the white surface approaching Wall 924 at the sixth decimeter from the bottom of the meter stick propped against Wall 924A-924. Surfaces of Stratum XIX were not preserved, due to the intrusions of Pit 431 and Trough 410.

pebbly grey earth with tiplines of bricky material (locus 416), mixed with large quantities of body sherds (CC II:#14, HH:##10–11). The floor was of hard packed earth with ashy debris upon it, and most probably represents XIXA surfacing.

Associated with Floor 469 is Step 429, which rose from west to east probably to a threshold in Wall 951A destroyed when LB Tower 944 was set in. If there was such a doorway, the step up suggests that the floor in the northeastern room east of Wall 951A will have been higher in elevation than Floor 469; all traces have been removed.

The step (CC II:#12; HH) was at least 1.40 m wide, its northern side having been considerably eroded. The riser, 0.25 m high, was defined by mudbricks set on their edges; one set marked the front edge and the other the back edge of the wide tread, formed of flat bricks set between them. Step 429 rested directly on Floor 469, and was built after the floor was laid; there is evidence of secondary resurfacing and local repair. Floor 457 (HH:#7), of packed limestone, proceeded from the midpoint of the riser westward, merging with Floor 469 (HH:#9) after a short distance.

The Entrance Hall. There was a slight shift eastward in the placement of this hall from where it had been in Stratum XX. The northern and southern boundaries were Walls 958A with its pillars and 924A respectively, positioned over their predecessors, but the east limit was now Wall 900 and the west limit was 951A which shifted the line of Stratum XX Wall 989 slightly eastward (VI EE). The floors in the two strata were very similar: Stratum XIX Flagstone Paving 602 was constructed of large flat pavers nearly identical with those used in Stratum XX Paving 605, quite likely borrowed from the latter (compare fig. 39 with fig. 28 above; EE:#3). Floor 602 ran over Stratum XX Wall 981 (the former east limit of the Entrance Hall) and over Buttress 601 to the base of the rebuilt Wall 900; it also ran to the lowest courses of Walls 924A and 951A. No flagstones were found in direct contact with the pillars along the north side of the hall, but the preserved height of the pillars is such as to make clear that they were reused in Stratum XIX. A few stones apparently continuous with Floor 602 ran to the south face of Wall 958A around the west end of the row of pillars.

Makeup for 602 was brown earth with a layer of decomposed brick to the east (locus 604; EE:##4–5), but a thick layer of grey earth with flecks of *ḥuwwar* further west.

Into this makeup a trench (locus 611) was cut in the southwest corner of the Entrance Hall for a child burial (608) in a storage jar (fig. 40). The jar itself (locus 614, B62 reg. #1254 = Cole 1984: pl. 35a; fig. 41) lay on its side, rim to the east; the long axis ran approximately ESE-WNW. Four large stones overlay its southern edge, perhaps

Fig. 39. Flagstone Paving 602 of Stratum XIX, in the Entrance Hall.

intended to protect the jar from being crushed, like the stone slabs surrounding Burial 16:21 (below). Inside the jar was the skeleton of a six- to seven-year-old child, lying on its right side with knees flexed and arms raised under the chin (fig. 42). Not all bones were articulated, and many were displaced—e.g., the mandible near the pelvis—probably as a result of the crushing of the jar by the weight of Stratum XVIII fill on the Stratum XIX floor above. The body had been provided with a necklace of crystal and agate beads on either side of a central scaraboid (fig. 43). Four vessels were arranged on top of and next to the body (fig. 44 with 41). Two red-burnished piriform juglets were by the skull (#1081 = Cole 1984: pl. 27:1 and #1082 = pl. 28a), a narrow-necked pitcher on the chest (#1083 = pl. 30d), and a double-loop, shoulder-handled jug on the legs (#1080 = pl. 29a). All four

Fig. 40. Jar Burial 608 in Stratum XIX Entrance Hall, looking southeast.

Fig. 41. Jar 614, in which was Burial 608, with four MB IIB pots found within.

were crushed. The outside diameter of the jug was greater than the inside diameter of the rim of the storage jar, so the jar must have been split or broken for its insertion and presumably the insertion of all the contents (compare Burial 16:21 below).

Outside the burial jar, at its mouth, was a large rim-to-shoulder handled jug (#1076 = Cole 1984: pl. 30b) with red-burnished piriform juglet #1077 inside it; judging from the diameters, #1076 had been broken to place #1077 inside. A few fragments of unidentifiable bone were inside #1076. South of the base of the main jar (fig. 40) were a medium-sized handleless jug #1078 overlying a dipper juglet (#1079 = Cole 1984: pl. 27h); again there were scattered bone fragments. Just at the base of the main jar were several disconnected

Fig. 42. Remains of the skeleton in Burial 608, oriented as in fig. 40, head to southeast.

Fig. 43. Crystal and agate beads with scaraboid, strung as they lay in Burial 608.

bones and bone fragments, spilled either from the main burial or from the ##1078-79 deposit.

A related deposit, locus 612, was found just to the southwest, under the lowest course of foundation stones for Wall 951A near its juncture with 924A (fig. 45). A group of store jar fragments surrounded a pinched-mouth jar (#1075 = Cole 1984: pl. 39a), which had been purposefully broken to insert a black-slipped piriform juglet (#1073 = Cole 1984: pl. 27k). No bones or organic matter were discovered in connection with this deposit. Though Burial 608 and Deposit 612 were clearly separate from one another, they are probably closely related chronologically. Wall 951A was to be built over Stratum XX Floor 605, and the 612 deposit was made after construction had begun. Trench 611 for Burial 608 was cut through the makeup for Floor 602; the burial was placed in, the trench filled and the floor laid, probably in rapid sequence. All of this activity came as the room was being built.

The Entrance Hall apparently had the same function in Stratum XIX as in XX. One proceeded from Street 6 through a door in Wall 924A into the flagstone area. Between Walls 924A and 903A, there apparently continued westward from this entrance an alley—no partition walls across it have

Fig. 44. Four MB IIB vessels in Burial 608.

Fig. 45. Burial 612, at junction of Walls 951A and 924A in the Entrance Hall.

been found, comparable to those in the sub-complex Rooms 25–28 of Stratum XX, and it is highly unlikely that the Austro-German excavations would have removed them without a trace. There was no clear evidence of entries from this alley to the Southern Complex; one is conjectured near Wall D giving access to Room 15. There may also have been a doorway from the Entrance Hall northward at the east end of Wall 958A, against Wall 900, but, given the ruined conditions here, that is speculative.

The Southern Complex. The eastern and western limits of the Stratum XIX Southern Complex (Ill. 73) were on the same lines as those in Stratum XX. On the east, Wall 902 was a reconstruction of Wall 939; on the west, Wall 933 was re-used from Stratum XX, and for part of its length refaced with Wall 921 in Stratum XIXA.

Fig. 46. South face of Wall 903A topped by Wall 903; note the two phases of building.

For somewhat less than the northern one-half of its length, Wall 902 was built directly on the stump of Wall 939; 939 was only 0.60 m wide, however, while 902 averaged 0.90 m. Its faces were of semi-hewn stones; its core was loose rubble. The maximum preserved height of Wall 902 was 0.90 m through six courses. Just north of its junction with Wall 926 (the north limit of Room 16 on the plan), Wall 902 jogged very slightly to the west, and from this point south completely replaced 939. Its foundation trench (Ill. 82 = VI AA II:#7; Ill. 83 = BB II:#10) cut Stratum XX flooring 17:12 of Courtyard 35 which would have run to the Wall 939, and rested virtually upon Floor 214.

This southern segment of Wall 902 was wider, at 1.10 m, than the northern one, but the style of construction was the same. The southern segment showed traces of mudbrick superstructure, and this is likely to have been the case to the north also.

The northern boundary of the Southern Complex in Stratum XIX was Wall 903A, replacing Stratum XX Wall 934 and expanding the complex about 2.00 m northwards. Part of Wall 934 was reused as an interior partition wall separating Rooms 13 and 15. Wall 903A varied somewhat in its width, but averaged 0.90 m. Part of its lowest course was constructed of well-hewn square blocks

Fig. 47. Wall 915 of Stratum XIX, showing mudbrick topping. Above it, a column base of Stratum XVIII.

Fig. 48. Brick topping of Wall 916 at right, south boundary of Room 10, Stratum XIX.

Fig. 49. Brick topping on Wall 921 at its junction with Wall 919 at left margin, Room 13. Note the plaster covering the overlapping bricks.

(fig. 46) like those of Wall 924A. Its maximum preserved height is 0.65 m through four courses.

The southern boundary of the Southern Complex was not excavated by the Joint Expedition, but it may be assumed from the Austro-German plans that it was a wall now designated 995A—distinct from the slightly narrower Wall 995 of Stratum XVIII riding upon it.

Almost all walls interior to the Southern Complex consisted of a stone foundation with mudbrick superstructure; occasionally traces of mortar could be discerned between the bricks (e.g., Wall 915 shown in fig. 47 beneath the column base; Wall 916 shown in fig. 48, at right; Wall 921 in fig. 49). As noted, Wall 902 was at least partially executed in this fashion, as was Wall 933, built in Stratum XX and reused in XIX.

<u>Room 9.</u> Rooms 8 and 9 were bordered on the west by Wall 904A and separated by Wall 905A (fig. 50). On the west side of Room 9, Wall 904A was 0.60 m wide. For part of its length it was founded on the stump of Stratum XX Wall 904B. Its preserved height reached 0.75 m to the foundation course of Wall 904 of Stratum XVIII (Ill. 83 = VI BB at junctions of Zones II and III). A doorway led from Room 9 to 11 at the southwest corner of Room 9; in Stratum XIXA it was blocked with earth (KK:#1 = Ill. 91 and BB = Ill. 83) prior to the laying of XIXA Floor 16:6 (KK:#2; BB II:#2).

Wall 905A, of approximately the same dimensions as 904A, was not bonded into 902 or 904A; judging from what little was preserved, there must have been a door at its western end giving access to Room 8.

Floor 16:8 was the earliest occupation layer of Room 9. It was laid upon a makeup (locus 504; VI BB II:#8, fig. 51:#2) of grey earth with *ḥuwwar* flecks and occasional stone slabs (BB II:#9). The floor itself was of packed limestone (fig. 52; BB II:#7; fig. 51:#1; KK #6). Two ovens (locus 16:17; KK:#8; fig. 53) were found in the northwest corner of the room, along Wall 904A. The northern oven was slightly oval in plan, with diameter varying from 0.65 to 0.85 m; the southern was round with diameter of 0.80 m. Each was preserved 0.15 to 0.20 m high. Near the north jamb of the doorway into Room 11 was a stone-lined pit (locus 16:2) 0.50 m across, set down into Floor 16:8, probably a grain silo. A flat kneading block, seen in both figs. 52 and 53 (locus 16:1; KK:#7) was located nearly in the center of the room, resting directly on the floor. The room was apparently a bakery in XIXB.

Beneath Floor 16:8 was Store Jar Burial 16:21. The jar itself was oriented east-west with its neck,

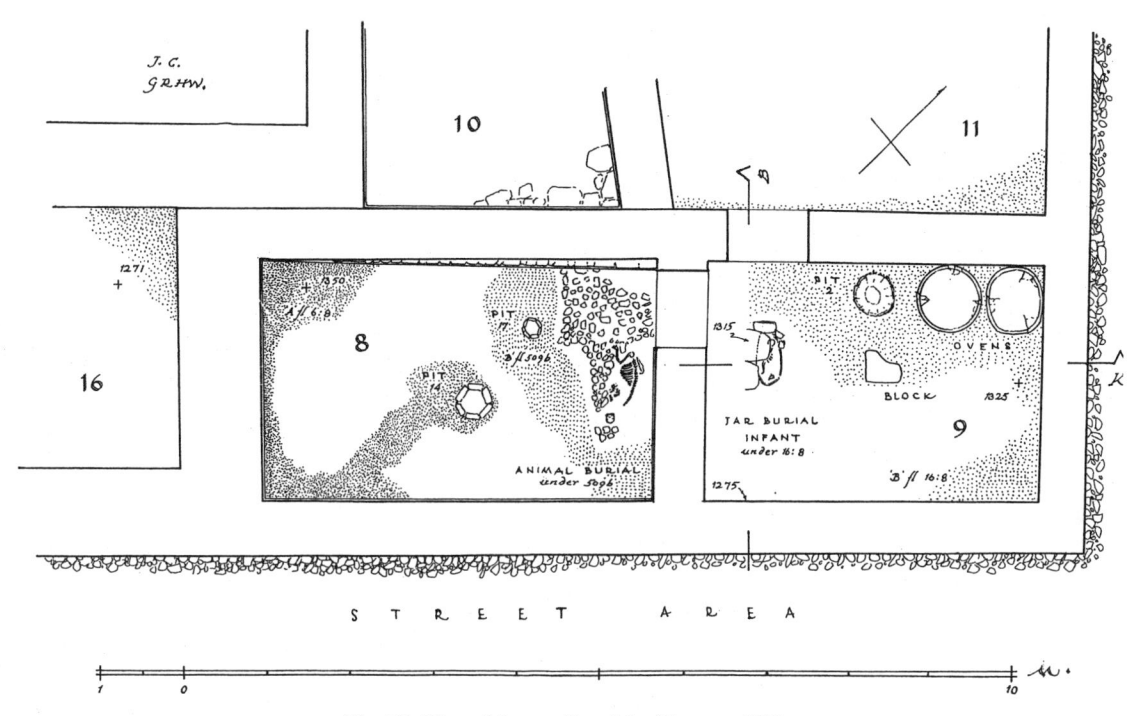

Fig. 50. Plan of Rooms 8 and 9 of Stratum XIX.

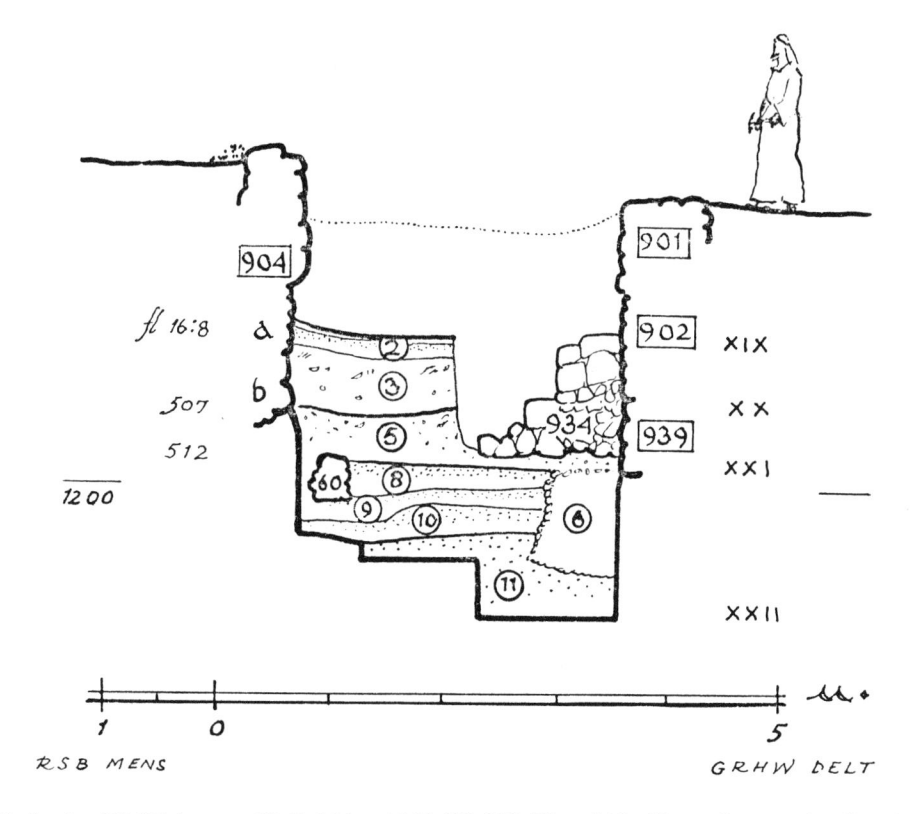

Fig. 51. Section BB II/1 between Walls 904 and 901-902-939. Floor 16.8 of Room 9 at top of undisturbed soil.

Fig. 52. A kneading rock lying on Surface 16.8 in Room 9.

broken off to permit insertion of the bones, pointing to the east (rim and handle of the main jar were inside it, at its base). A wide-necked jug (#7422 = Cole 1984: pl. 31a) and a rim-to-shoulder handled jug (#7420 = pl. 30c) were found outside the jar near the neck (fig. 54); inside the jar was a vertically burnished piriform juglet (#7421 = pl. 27j). The bones were in considerable disarray (fig. 55), and probably represent secondary burial of several individuals, one an infant. Some care was taken to protect the installation; a vault of flat stones (BB II:#5, KK:#3) was placed over the jar, and the whole was resting on a bed of small stones (BB II, below #6). This construction did not prevent settling in the deposit, and that crushed the jar.

Floor 16:6 (BB II:#3, KK:#2) represented XIXA occupation in Room 9. It was of packed limestone and rides 0.15 m above Floor 16:8 over a layer of ash from the use of the ovens (BB II:#4). Floor 16:6 covered the installations on the 16:8

Fig. 53. Ovens on Surface 16.8 in Room 9, with kneading block in foreground.

Fig. 54. Storage jar Burial 16.21 covered over by Floor 16.8 in Room 9.

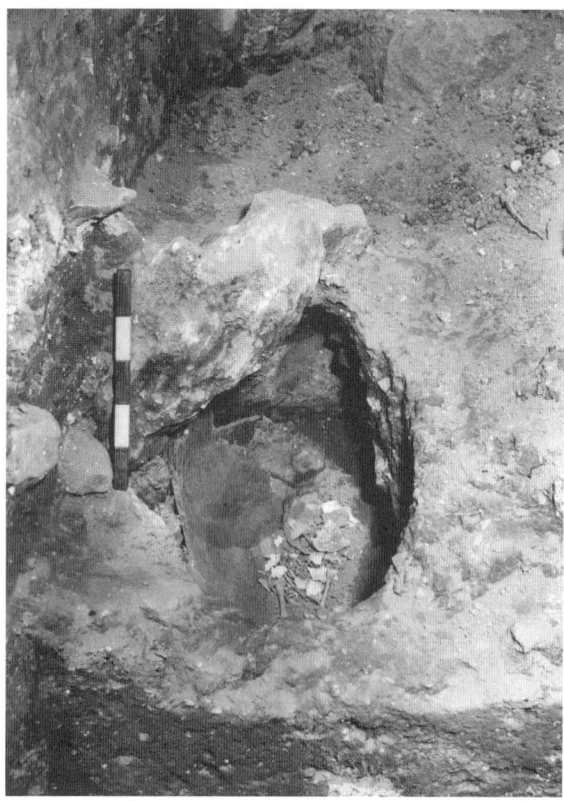

Fig. 55. Burial 16:21, with fragments of bones in its base.

floor and ran to the blockage of the door in Wall 904A (KK:#1).

Room 8. Wall 904A, 0.60 m wide in XIXB, was widened to 0.75 m in XIXA by adding a facing of flat stones along its east face—an addition not found in Room 9. Stratum XIXB Floor 509B ran beneath this widening to the original wall, while Stratum XIXA Floor 6:8, 0.05 m higher, curved up the facing of this and the other three walls of Room 8. Wall 926, the south limit of Room 8, like almost all Stratum XIX partition walls, had a stone foundation, 0.90 m wide, with a mudbrick superstructure.

Sunk into Phase B Floor 509B was a small stone-lined pit (locus 6:17), again probably a silo with a diameter of only 0.20 m, with sherds in it. Under the floor was the burial of a small animal, probably a sheep or goat (locus 6:18, fig. 56). The skeleton rested on a bed of small stones, giving the impression that the burial was special, but its significance is elusive.

Phase A floor 6:8 was again of packed limestone, laid on a thin makeup of grey pebbly earth, locus 6:19. On the floor were found a deep carinated bowl (fig. 57; #1528 = Cole 1984: pl. 11a) and several large storage jar fragments, as well as a rather large quantity of ash and burnt brick. Nearby in the center of the room was a stone-lined pit with a mortar in the bottom (locus 6:14), no doubt used for grinding grain (fig. 58).

Room 16. Wall 937 formed the western boundary for Rooms 16 through 19. Its stone foundation (locus 218) was nearly 1.00 m wide and stood 0.60 m high through four courses. At some points the mudbrick superstructure, laid on flat stones, was preserved to a height of 0.60 m (VI AA junction of zones II-III). Wall 940, separating Rooms 16 and 17, was of similar construction. Its foundation and superstructure were bonded into those of Wall 902, and the foundations of Walls 937 and 940 were bonded. The superstructure of 940 stopped at a sharp line 0.80 m. east of the east face of Wall 937, creating a doorway between the two rooms. This doorway was later blocked with stones, probably in Stratum XIXA (AA II:#2).

Fig. 56. Sheep or goat burial, locus 6:18, beneath Floor 509B in Room 8.

From the beginning of the Stratum XIX period, Room 16 was divided into two sectors by a north-south curb wall running from Wall 926 to Wall 940 at the eastern jamb of the doorway to Room 17. During Phase B, the eastern sector was floored with packed limestone (locus 501A; AA II:#6) on a makeup of grey earth and heavy stones (locus 17:9). A drain (loc 16:6) was cut through the foundation and brick superstructure of Wall 902 from the level of this floor to the street area along the east, indicated by an arrow out of Room 16 on Ill. 73. The drain sloped down very slightly as it left the room; water would have flowed out into the main street drain and then south.

West of the curb in Room 16, hard-packed earth Floor 17:3 was badly disturbed but could be traced in a few places. Where preserved, it rested on a makeup of loose grey earth (locus 17:10) without the heavy stones characteristic of the makeup in the eastern half of the room. The floor covered the threshold of the door to Room 17, continuing as Floor 209. Slag fragments were found on this floor, and more came to light in the earth associated with Street 6 outside. It is possible that Room 16 was used for casting copper and making bronze, a process requiring large amounts of water. Pertinent here is a kiln or furnace blowpipe, fragments of which came from the fill beneath the Fortress Temple. In any case, Room 16 was outfitted to deal with water.

During its Phase A occupation, Room 16 received a new packed limestone floor, Floor 17:7 (AA II:#5) about 0.05 m above the Phase B surface in both halves of the room. The curb continued in use and the drain was renewed and extended 0.50 m westward by adding a new line of stones and brick over Floor 17:7, against the superstructure of Wall 902. Like its predecessor, Floor 17:7 covered the threshold into Room 17, continuing as Floor 202.

<u>Room 17.</u> The south wall, Wall 942, had only its stone foundation preserved, 1.00 m wide and 0.45 m high through three courses; all traces of superstructure are lost, as well as any evidence of a doorway between Rooms 17 and 18. There must have been one, conjectured on the plan flush

Fig. 57. Deep carinated MB IIB bowl #1528 from Stratum XIXA, Floor 6:8 in Room 8.

Fig. 58. Stone-lined pit with stone mortar as its base in Floor 6:8, Room 8.

against Wall 937, since there would have been no other way to reach Rooms 17 and 16. The Joint Expedition excavated only part of Room 17, in two one-meter probe trenches, but they showed that the room had received two Phase B surfacings, Floors 209 and 203 (Ill. 87 = VI FF III:bottoms of ##6 and 4), both of packed limestone and both laid on makeup containing ash and charcoal (FF III:##8 and 6; Ill. 88 = GG:##11 and 9). Fragments of oven lining were in these makeups, and there were ash-filled depressions in Floor 209. There must have been ovens in the unexcavated parts of the room. Floor 203 was presumably a Phase B resurfacing necessitated by the accumulation of ashy debris from the ovens.

In Phase A, the portions of excavated Floor 202 were of packed limestone over a makeup of grey ashy earth (FF III:##3 on 4; GG:##4 on 7). This makeup also produced evidence of oven use; slabs of limestone had fallen on oven fragments in the northwest quadrant of the room and pressed them into the floor. A kneading block sat on the floor in the middle of the room—recall the similar pattern in Room 9. During Phase A, semicircular Pit 211 (GG:#6), with east-west diameter 0.50 m and a maximum depth of 0.25 m, had been dug

Fig. 59. Looking south at the junction of Walls 919 (foreground) and 908A in the southeast corner of Room 13. Wall 915 runs away from the pillar at upper left.

into the floor against the face of the north wall and lined with successive layers of small pebbles, plaster, and clay. All this may point again to baking, but the lining of unfired clay in the pit may suggest that Room 17 was a potter's workshop—though the room contained no unfinished or damaged pots and no distinctive tools.

Room 18. Only a small sector along the north wall of this room could be excavated. The remainder of the room, as well as all traces of walls and floors of Room 19 and the room adjacent to it on the west, had eroded away during the forty years since the Austro-German work. Rooms 18 and 19 on Joint Expedition plans follow the drawings the earlier excavators prepared. It should be noted that the west limit of the walls as shown here represents the way Sellin found them preserved; the continuations of Walls 994 and 995A were apparently already gone. The single fragment of flooring found in Room 18, locus 210 (GG:#5), was assigned to Phase A on the basis of its relative elevation.

Room 15 and the Western Corridor. Access to the northwestern cluster of rooms, 15, 13, and on into 11 and 10 on the plan, would have been through the alley or corridor between Walls 924A and 903A along the north of the Southern Complex, with a left (south) turn along Wall D into another corridor between D and the complex. The eastern boundary of Room 15 was Wall 922A, bonded into 903A and serving as part of the definition of Room 13 as well. The foundation trench for Wall 922A (locus 320; BB III:#8) cut through Stratum XX Floor 568 and Wall 962 running east-west under the middle of Room 13.

A layer of dark brown hard packed earth separated the founding of Wall 922A and the preserved top of Stratum XX Wall 997. South of the line of the earlier Wall 962, midway along the east limit of Room 13, Wall 922A rested directly on Stratum XX Wall 922B—which was narrower than its successor, 922B at 0.50 m 922A at 0.60 m. To recall what was noted earlier, here in the west a certain amount of filling had been thrown in to level up for the construction of the XIX rooms, but Stratum XX wall lines were being used in some ways as anchorage.

Wall 934 was reused as the partition between Rooms 13 and 15. Wall 903A formed its north limit. Stratum XVII Pit 4:4 combined with Austro-German excavation had destroyed the western end of this wall, shown as extrapolated on the plan to a conjectured doorway near Wall D, leading to the western corridor. Traces of plastered flooring, locus 9:10 (BB IV:#4) ran to the top course of the west face of Wall 933, over a makeup of dark brown earth containing large quantities of sherds (locus 8-9:15; BB IV:#6).

In Room 15, only a few traces of XIXB hard packed earth Floor 13:12 overlaid with grey ash were preserved, at elevation 13.70 on the plan. They ran to and curved up the face of Wall 934, and ran to the founding level of 922A. Still within Phase B, Floor 13:11, of packed limestone, rode on a makeup of dark crumbly soil (locus 403A) 0.10 to 0.15 m thick over Floor 13:12 (Ill. 85 = VI DD). From this makeup came a large sherd providing most of the profile of a MB IIA-B comb-decorated single-vertical-handled jug, #62.720 = Cole 1984: pl. 44a. Two flat stones in the corner of Walls 903A and 922A may have constituted a working surface used with this phase of the room; two very poorly preserved ovens (locus 405A) were in place against Wall 903A, the diameter of the western one at 0.60 m. The base of a storage jar, locus 15:4, was found imbedded in the floor just west of the western oven. The room must have been used for baking, though no grain remnant was found in the storage jar base.

Earlier disturbance had removed all but a few traces of Phase A occupation. Cobbled Floor 13:4 seems to represent this phase, laid on a makeup of dark grey earth (VI DD).

Room 13. From Room 15 one entered Room 13 at its northeast corner; its position is indicated by two courses of flat stones against the line of Wall 934 and touching Wall 922A, the lower course jutting out 0.10 m beneath the upper. Phase B Floor 332 (VI BB IV:#3) ran to the lower course, while Phase A Floor 8:6 (BB IV:#2; DD:#7) ran to the upper and was continuous with the plaster facing on Wall 934. The flat stones were probably a step up from the floor of Room 13 to that of Room 15. As preserved, their elevation was higher than the top of Wall 934, which had probably been robbed out by Stratum XVIII rebuilding.

The ill-preserved Wall 922A (the deep early Stratum XVII Pit 4:4 cut into it) continued in its lowest course to join Wall 908A, which was bonded into Wall 916 and buttressed on its west by a stump of masonry 0.35 m long at the east end of mudbrick Wall 919—that is, at the far southeast corner of Room 13. This buttress preserved a high-standing pillar of Wall 908A from being destroyed; Stratum XVIII builders used the pillar and rebuilt Wall 908A as 908 from this point southward (fig. 59). The north end of Wall 908A then was the southern jamb of a doorway from Room 13 into Room 11; the north jamb, which would have been formed by the upper courses of Wall 922A, is lost (fig. 60).

Wall 919 on the south of Room 13 was well preserved, made of mudbrick on stone foundation; the foundation was bonded into 908A as already noted, but Wall 919 abutted Wall 933, reused from Stratum XX. Wall 919's foundation was 0.65 m high and carried more than a meter of superstructure (fig. 61); it averaged 0.65 m in width. As preserved, it bowed to the north (fig. 62, center foreground, running away from the camera).

Phase XIXB Floor 332 (BB IV:#3), laid on a makeup of hard packed brown earth (locus 327; #5), ran to the base of Wall 933 and was continuous with traces of plaster running up the faces of Wall 934 and 919, traces protected from loss when XIXA Wall 921 was set in against Wall 933 and sealed them in place at each of its ends. Wall 921, then, represents Stratum XIXA. It was founded on Floor 332, and consisted of a mudbrick superstructure on a foundation of two courses of large, flat stones leveled off with rubble. Apparently 921 was a strengthening of 933 necessitated by its threatened collapse. Floor 8:6 of XIXA (BB IV:#2; DD:#7) was barely separated from XIXB Floor 332 (VI DD), but it continued as plaster on the east face of Wall 921. A fragment of a figurine was found on Floor 8:6, but no installations or artifacts indicated the purpose of Room 13.

The Courtyards: Room 14. The Joint Expedition excavated minimally in the L-shaped Southern Courtyard designated Room 14, but its outlines are quite clear from the Sellin and Welter plans. It was separated from Rooms 16–19 along Wall 902 by Wall 937, from the Northern Court's Room 10 by Wall 916, and from Central Court 12 by Walls 938A and 984A. Its western limit is undetermined; possibly it was Wall 933 extended, but more probably it was Wall D. The southern boundary, Wall 994, has eroded away since Sellin's recovery of it; he could not trace it, or Wall 995A, beyond a point about 6.00 m from their respective junctions with Wall 902.

Fig. 60. Looking slightly west of north from within the southwest corner of Room 11, into Room 13. The pillar of 908A is at left center, constituting the south jamb of the door from Room 11 to 13. Wall 919 runs away from the pillar at the upper left.

Wall 916 at the north end of the east extension of the court, like other partition walls of Stratum XIX, was of mudbrick on stone, and was bonded into both 908A and 937. The junction of 916 and 937 is noteworthy in that it doubled the thickness of walling at this point. Which wall was built first, and why is it doubled? The width of Wall 916 varied between 0.60 and 0.80 m; the wall was preserved to a height of 1.10 m.

Only Phase A occupation was discerned in the small sector excavated; excavation did not go below it. Packed limestone Floor 7:6 (CC IV:#6; AA III:#23) on a makeup of hard brown earth (locus 361; AA III:#24; CC IV:#7) ran south from Wall 916, under Stratum XVIII Wall 907. It was fragmentary, and could be traced to Wall 938A but not against Wall 937, where there was considerable intrusion (AA III:##18 and 17).

Rooms 10 and 11. The Northern Court in Phase B was one large rectangular room; Wall 915, dividing it into Rooms 10 and 11, belonged to Phase A. Wall 915 had a doorway in its western end to allow passage between the rooms. Phase B packed limestone floor 302-306 (CC III:#16; BB III:#6) at elevation 13.25 was traced from Wall 916 under Wall 915 and over the remains of Stratum XX Wall 962 to the line of Wall 934 extended; north of that it was apparently destroyed by preparations

Fig. 61. The northeast face of Wall 919 in Room 13, joining southeast face of Wall 921 at right. The surface on which the meter stick rests is Stratum XIXB Floor 332, its plaster evident in the probe trench through the floor to left of center.

Fig. 62. Looking southeast from the Fortress Temple elevation toward Wall 900, with Field II Hellenistic House in upper right corner. The bow in Wall 919 is visible in the center foreground.

for building Sleeper Wall 11:14 and by the intrusion of Burial 11:5b, both of Stratum XVIII. It is barely possible that Wall 934 was reused in Stratum XIX across Room 11 as it was to the west between Rooms 13 and 15; at some points Floor 302-306 ran to the very preserved top of 934 (see CC III) but at other points there was no connection, and parts of Wall 934 had been robbed out. Probably, the top of 934 was a hump in the floor of Room 11 and not a room divider.

Floor 302-306 rested on a makeup of hard-packed earth with occasional patches of loose stones (loci 303, 307; CC III:#17; BB III:#7). Makeup 303 under Floor 302 produced a clay figurine and 307 under 306 produced a steatite weight or toy. An overturned stone mortar (locus 549)

Fig. 63. Looking east at the junction of Wall 903/903A and Wall 904/904A in the northeast corner of Room 11. The meter stick stands on a flagstone of Stratum XIXA surface.

Fig. 64. Looking north into the northeast corner of Room 11, at junction of Walls 922/922A and 903/903A, with flagstones of Stratum XIXA surface under the meter stick.

was sunk into Floor 302 toward the southern end of the court, its base used as a work surface.

In Phase A, Wall 915 was built. It averaged 0.55 m in width; its stone foundation stood 0.80 m high through five courses, on which 0.30 m of brick superstructure was preserved. It rested directly on XIXB Floor 302-306 (CC III) and butted against Walls 904A and 908A. At the doorway, no brick was found, and traces of flat threshold stones as well as the eastern jamb of the door were preserved.

In Room 10, packed limestone Floor 7:4 (CC III:#12) rode on a makeup (#14) of grey ashy material 0.05–0.07 m thick above Floor 302 (#16). The floor merged with 302 just north of Wall 916 and continued up the wall as a plaster facing. Wall 915 was similarly faced by a continuation of the same floor. In the northeast corner of Room 10, several flagstones at elevation 13.50 (locus 550) lay on the floor, possibly remnants of a secondary surfacing once covering the whole room, similar to the flagstones in Court 12 and in the Entrance Hall in Phase A.

In Room 11, Floor 4:2 was also of packed limestone on a makeup of grey ashy earth (CC III:##11 on 13; BB III:#5 which lay on a thin layering of resurfacing and makeup over #6); it merged with Floor 306 just west of the junction with Wall 904A (BB III). It was preserved from the line of Wall 934 extended to Wall 915, where it merged with the plastering on the face of the wall. Like its predecessor, it was interrupted north of the line of Wall 934. A flagstone in the corner of Wall 903A with 904A (fig. 63, under the meter stick) and a line of similar stones along the east face of Wall 922A (fig. 64) may have been additional XIXA floor elements. The site elevation on these stones was at 13.64; if the line of Floor 4:2 is projected over the top of Wall 934, it would have reached the walls at about this elevation. There were traces of white and red plaster on the south face of Wall 903A above the single flagstone, up to the base of Stratum XVIII Wall 903 (fig. 63, the extent of the half-meter stick; note the difference in construction in the two portions of the wall). Similar traces at nearly the same elevations were on the western face of Wall 904A. The evidence indicates the flagstones were a secondary Phase A flooring as in Room 10 (cf. Court 12 and Floor 8:8, below). The secondary phase of XIXA seems to have had decorated walls in this court.

Room 12. The Central Court (Court 12) was bounded by Wall 919 on the north, 938A on the east, and 984A on the south, the two latter walls founded on the stumps of Stratum XX walls. Only the stone foundations of Walls 938A and 984A were preserved, two to three courses high; their

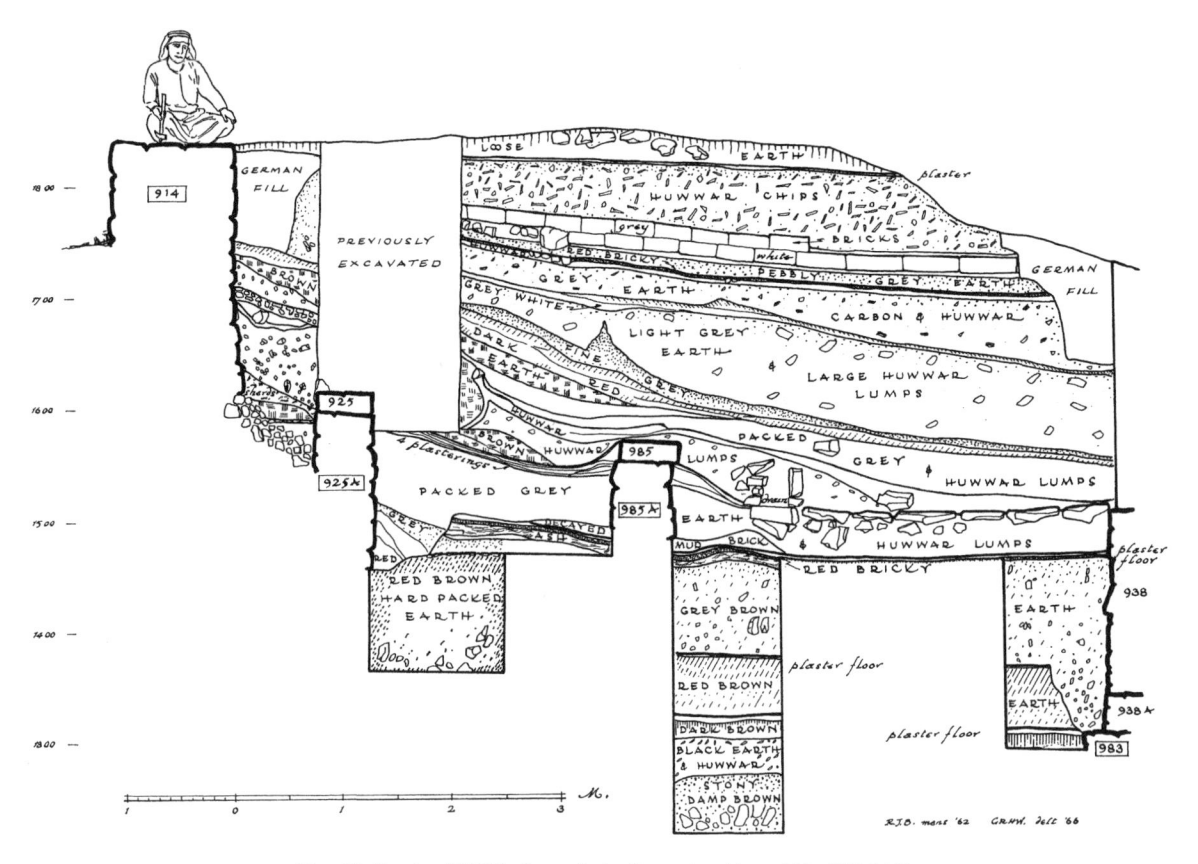

Fig. 65. Section VI FF, through the forecourt (Area 13) of Field V.

mudbrick superstructure was replaced by Stratum XVIII Walls 938 and 984. Much of this court lay beneath the preserved tongue of forecourt of the Fortress Temple, but a probe through the forecourt encountered the succession of walls. The western wall of Court 12 was most probably 933, a short segment of which was traced to the edge of the forecourt tongue. It is extrapolated on plan to meet 984A and form the southwest corner of the court. Walls 908A and 916, forming the southwest corner of the Northern Court (Room 10), created a jog in the northeast corner of the Central Court.

As virtually everywhere in the complex, the Central Court had two floors. The Phase B surface, attested only in the northeast quadrant, was hard-packed earth Floor 335A, at elevation 13.45, laid on a makeup of hard brown earth (locus 336) characteristic of XIXB makeups. The floor ran to the stone foundations of Walls 919 and 908A, but could not be traced further south, to the line of the FF section which fails to show it. The Phase A floor in the corner of Walls 938A and 916 was of fine plaster, Floor 18:12, and was most probably continuous with a segment of plaster floor on red brown earth found in the Field V, Area 13, probe through the forecourt (VI FF IV:##19 on 20; fig. 65). This floor ran probably to the mudbrick superstructure of Wall 938A before the construction of Stratum XVIII Wall 938, whose foundation trench cut through the floor and its makeup all the way to the top of Stratum XX Wall 983. The elevation of these floor fragments, at about 13.70, agrees with XIXA Floor 7:6 in Room 14 and Floor 8:6 in Room 13.

A large patch of flagstones, locus 8:8 (fig. 66), was found in the corner of Walls 919 and 908A (VI DD:#6), running up to the brick superstructure of 919. Traces of plaster could be seen beneath the stones, probably Floor 18:12; as in Rooms 10 and 11, the flagstones were probably a secondary repaving with XIXA. Beneath the flagstones (and the plaster floor traces) was a stony

Fig. 66. Flagstones of Floor 8:8 of Stratum XIXA in Room 12, looking west from the top of Wall 908 visible in the lower left corner.

grey makeup, locus 335, separating the Phase B Floor 335A from the Phase A surfaces 18:12 and 8:8. On the flagstone paving there were recovered a limestone pendant, a whetstone and a bronze pin.

Stratum XIX Occupation East of Wall 900. The Sellin excavations had destroyed virtually all evidence of Stratum XIX structures east of Wall 900, so that Iron Age pottery in refilling of earlier trenches was found almost as low as Stratum XX elevations. Discernible in the FF balk were a few foundation stones of Wall 987, as well as the line of packed limestone Floor 501B, running from 987 to Wall 900 (Ill. 87 = VI FF I). Floor 501B rested on a makeup of grey-brown bricky earth with sporadic slabs of clay (locus 501, FF I:##3–4) 0.50 m thick. It is not certain that this complex belonged to Stratum XIX; the elevation of 501B is 14.10, high for this stratum on the other side of Wall 900, where Street 6 is at 13.65 and Floor 202 of Phase A in Room 17 is at 13.70. Since Floor 501B ran just over the top of Wall 998, founded in Stratum XXI and reused in Stratum XX, without any intervening deposits, its assignment to Stratum XIX makes sense.

Structures off the acropolis during this period should presumably relate to the remains in "downtown" Shechem, notably to those in Field IX to be portrayed below. It is approximately 45 m from the east face of Wall 900 to the middle of Field IX. Floor elevations dropped roughly 7.50 m across that distance, suggesting that there is terracing between the two locations.

The Date of Stratum XIX

Stratum XIX fill over Stratum XX contains a wide range of pottery; all loci (6:15, 17:11, 17:12, 301, 312, 334, 338, 600A, 607A) have wares ranging from Chalcolithic to MB IIB. Given this mix, Cole selected only some seven sherds from this fill (Cole 1984:30–31). In the makeups laid for XIXB occupation surfaces and the foundation trenches for XIX walls, the pottery was more consistently MB IIA and MB IIB, with much less Chalcolithic. Cole selected 14 forms from these loci (307, 327, 336, 403A, 416, 464, 8-9:15); an especially significant group was drawn from the makeup for Street 6, locus 62 and from Fill 118 in the adjacent drain (32 forms). Stratum XIXB floors and Street 6 (locus 61), produced nearly pure MB IIB pottery. The whole vessels from Burials 608, 612 and 16:21 are definitive: Pls. 27:h, j and k; 28:p; 30:b and c, 31:a, and 39:a. A scarab was found on Floor 16:8 in Room 9, sealed beneath XIXA Floor 16:6; it is therefore of crucial significance for the date of XIXB. It was analyzed by S. H. Horn (1962:18) as "not later than the early

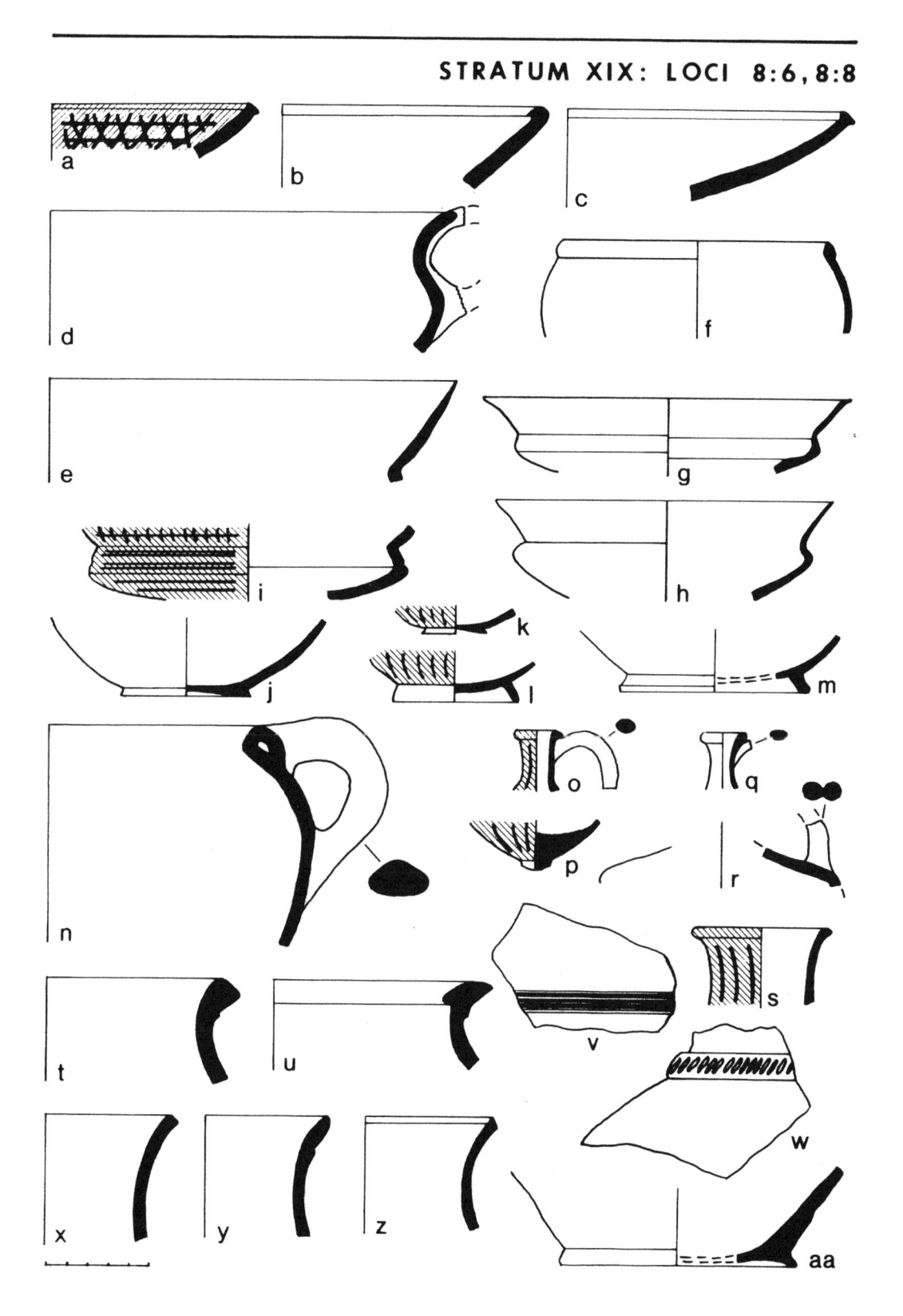

Fig. 67. Range of Stratum XIX pottery forms, from Floors 8:6 in Room 13 and 8:8 in Room 12, reproduced from Cole 1984: pl. 47.

Hyksos period, and it is quite possible that it originated in an earlier time, possibly during the Twelfth Dynasty."

Nearly the same range of pottery characterized Stratum XIXA, although in the makeups for XIXA floors there was relatively little MB IIA and less Chalcolithic. Occupation surfaces were associated with rather consistent early MB IIB sherds. Cole selected 35 of his XIX forms from Stratum XIXA surfaces and installations loci 4:2, 6:8, 7:4, 8:6, 8:8, and 17:7. Of special interest is Cole 1984: pl. 11:a, a deep carinated bowl, from Floor 6:8 (above, fig. 57). Drain 17:6 of Stratum XIX, which could not be assigned to one of the sub-phases, yielded nine of Cole's key sherds.

The evidence as a whole points to a date for Stratum XIX in the last quarter of the 18th century BCE. Fig. 67 reproduces Cole 1984: Plate 47, as a representative corpus from Floors 8:6 and 8:8, both of Stratum XIXA.

STRATUM XVIII

The problem in understanding Stratum XVIII gives classic illustration to the importance of soil in modern archaeological technique. When the Joint Expedition came to work in Field VI, it was confronted by a maze of wall tops exposed by the Sellin and Welter excavations; that work had scooped out the soil within the rooms, with its succession of fills, makeups and floors. It became a matter for the Joint Expedition to propose plausible architectural patterns, and in one key instance, that of the Central Court, there is disagreement among the Joint Expedition staff about what the pattern was. Nevertheless, some clarity emerges from toiling with the scraps of preserved evidence. Where disagreement persists, the alternatives will be presented.

Fortification and Preparation

Here and there in the final phase of Stratum XIX there was evidence of ash and possible destruction. Most of the indications, however, were local, and were probably related to the type of activity in the various rooms—ovens for baking and pottery firing produce ash and charcoal which has nothing to do with violent destruction. Stratum XIX did not end with the sort of wholesale destruction an enemy incursion might produce.

But something significant did happen at Shechem around 1700 BCE which caused a major shift in the fortifications and a set of important changes on the Acropolis. The earthen embankment which defended the city in the last quarter of the eighteenth century, originally based on Walls C and D, was augmented and spread outward. Wall D went out of use as the internal retaining wall for the embankment. A new wall (914A) was founded which served as the western limit of at least part of the compound, while perhaps serving to retain the rampart to the west of it.

The Acropolis in Stratum XVIII (Ills. 74–75, 82–85, 87, 89)

Stratum XVIII builders reused some wall lines of Stratum XIX, while nullifying many others (Ill. 75; note well, this plan is the same as Plan 3 in Cole [1984], but a printing mistake called the latter "Stratum XVII"). Wall 900 continued to form the eastern boundary, with Streets 5 and 4 running along its west face. The northern and eastern walls of the Southern Complex, and possibly also the southern one, remained on the same lines: 903 replaced 903A, 901 was built on the mudbrick superstructure of 902, and 995 was a rebuild of 995A on a slightly different line. On the west, Wall D seems no longer to have served as the boundary. Wall 912, built during Stratum XVIII, was founded higher than the preserved top of Wall D; Wall 914A ran over Wall D. In the Northern Complex, Wall 924 was built on top of 924A, 951 on 951A and 958 on 958A. New construction, Walls 948 and 949, ran onto the augmented embankment, which now reached farther into the city than the line of Wall D.

As with the transition from XX to XIX, there was a degree of continuity, but the overall picture is one of discontinuity. Stratum XVIII builders significantly changed the internal pattern of both the southern and northern complexes on the acropolis. On the one hand, they kept two crucial lines of the Central Court, rebuilding 908 and 922 on 908A and 922A as the western boundary of the Northern Court (Room 2), and they preserved closely the dimensions of Rooms 8 and 9 along the eastern boundary in the form of Rooms 1 and 3, though Wall 906 was on a slightly different line from that of 926, the south boundary of these rooms. On the other hand, they abandoned the layout of Rooms 16–19 and their defining western Wall 937, thus expanding the Southern Courtyard to the east and north as Room 5. A Western Court (Room 4) replaced Rooms 13 and 15—which later in Stratum XVIII was redivided in still another new configuration of space. On the north side of the alley or corridor, the large Northern Courtyard of Stratum XIX was replaced by a maze of small rooms and corridors, the Northern Complex.

The most striking mark of discontinuity was the fill used to cover the ruins of Stratum XIX. It was up to a meter and a half deep, forming a heightened bed for the renewed structure. Over the earlier Rooms 10 and 11 and under Room 2 of the Southern Complex, this fill of a mixture of loose grey earth and chunks of *ḥuwwar* (locus 7:2; Ill. 83 = VI BB III:#4; Ill. 84 = VI CC III:#10) averaged 1.25 m in thickness. Beneath Room 4, fill locus 8:2, of light brown-grey ashy material with pockets of loose stones and bricky detritus was nearly a meter thick (Ill. 85 = VI DD:##3–5, to the top of Wall 919 of Stratum XIX; fig. 14 = VI LL:##6, 7 and 9), while nearby in another probe, locus 13:9 was brown rocky earth about 0.80 m thick. Under the Southern Courtyard (Room 5), locus 17:2, encountered in the probe through the Fortress Temple forecourt, was brown bricky earth of similar thickness (CC IV:#4; Ill. 82 = AA III:##20, 22). In the Central Court, locus 18:6 was grey-brown earth 0.80 m thick (Ill. 87 = FF IV:##18 & 21; AA III:#21). Only in the north was the fill less massive: 0.50 m thick under XVIIIB Floor 421 (locus 408; CC II:#10; Ill. 89 = HH:#6; and locus 409 in CC II:#11, under XVIIIB Floor 406).

The sequence, then, seems to have been this: rebuild a few old walls, construct deep foundations for new walls (e.g. Wall 955 on CC II and 907 at the junction of CC III and IV) and then level the whole area with huge quantities of fill. The operation was comparable in scope to the original MB II leveling of the site prior to the construction of Stratum XXII and to the great artificial platform laid for the Fortress Temple of Stratum XVI. The different character of the Stratum XVIII fill at the few places where Sellin and Welter had left it untouched suggests that it was gathered from a variety of locations, but the pottery in it was overwhelmingly MB IIB, with a few MB IIA. Cole selected 85 of his 157 forms defining his pre-XVIII ("XVIIIs") phase from these fills.

With discontinuity exceeding continuity in the transition from Stratum XIX to Stratum XVIII, it is noteworthy that at least the southern two-thirds of the Central Court was left in the same position. This remained the case through the two sub-phases of Stratum XVIII, and through local changes within the period, including alterations in the Central Court itself.

Within Stratum XVIII these alterations call for making a distinction between XVIIIB and XVIIIA, and for speaking of hints of a Stratum XVIIIA+. Walls reused from Stratum XIX went with scraps of flooring that are the first discerned above XIXA floors and the intervening fill to define XVIIIB. For XVIIIA, new walls defined two small corner alcoves in the courtyards. In Room 4, Walls 911, 912 and 913 (defining Room 7) were founded higher than Wall 927A and its Floor 1R (fig. 14:#5); Wall 912 was founded at 14.77, while Floor 1R was at 14.75 and Wall 927A was founded at 13.89. Wall 927A itself was rebuilt as 927. There is evidence that still another set of changes was made near the end of Stratum XVIIIA, in XVIIIA+.

In the Central Court just to its south, Walls 925, 932 and 985 either were cut into or were built over the XVIIIB Floor 4R in the shift to XVIIIA.

Most of the walls breaking up the space in the Northern Complex are to be assigned to XVIIIA—though here Sellin's work had removed almost all soil layering that might prove this conclusion.

The Streets. Locus 37 designates the grey earth fill, 0.30 m thick, containing large quantities of bone, ash and sherds as well as tumbled stones and brick fragments (VI BB I:#10; cp. VI AA I:#13; fig. 20:#11). It extended to the top of Wall 902 and under the foundation of Stratum XVIII Wall 901, and was the makeup for Street 5. From it, Cole selected 49 of his forms for defining Stratum XVIIIs. The street must have been laid at the same time as the Stratum XVIII buildings were originally constructed, and the brick in the makeup may well have come from the superstructure of Wall 902. The paving for Street 5, locus 113 (AA I:#11; figs. 5 and 20; BB I:#9 at elevation 14.00 to 13.90), was poorly laid of cobblestones averaging 0.20–0.30 m in diameter, and was much rougher than that of the other street surfaces. There were a few indications of a brick curb at the western edge of Street 5 (AA I:#12). The western curb of the drain (fig. 20:to left of #8) rested against the mudbrick superstructure of Wall 902. As with all the other streets, Street 5 sloped down from north to south.

Street 4, paved with cobblestones 0.10–0.15 m in diameter, was laid on a makeup of compact grey ashy earth with only a few stones (the street is locus 85 on makeup locus 35; AA I:##9 on 10; fig. 20:Street 4 on #8; BB I:##6 on 8). Its elevation was at 14.20. There was no evidence of a curb. It makes sense that Street 4 went with Phase A, Street 5 with Phase B. The Sellin excavations tracing Wall 900 removed all connections of these two street surfaces with Stratum XVIII walls to the west. It is surmised that they extended northward only to the south end of Wall 979, since there was only a corridor about 0.80 m wide between Wall 979 and Wall 900.

The Structures: The Northern Complex. As shown on Ill. 75, north of the alleyway between Walls 903 and 924 that divided the acropolis layout in both Stratum XIX and Stratum XVIII, a maze of walls was exposed by Sellin and Welter; only the foundation courses, at most, remain, and many stones were removed in the years between 1934 and 1957. Welter's plan shows Wall 971 preserved to elevation 14.71, but by 1957 it was two courses lower at 14.30. Furthermore, at least one course of most walls of the Southern Complex had been removed in modern times. Balâṭah villagers report that many surface stones were taken from all over the site for modern building. Such fragments of surface as survived are assigned to Stratum XVIII by relative reference to XIX floorings and to the even more fragmentary remains of Stratum XVII above them.

Walls 924 continued in Stratum XVIII a line begun in Stratum XX, in the sequence 976 + 924B under 924A in turn under 924. Other indications of continuity between Strata XVIII and XIX are Wall 951 built on the stump of XIX Wall 951A, and Wall 958's stone foundation directly on the mudbrick top of 958A. Walls 950 and 979, on the other hand, were founded 0.30 m above Floor 602 of the XIXA Entrance Hall. Wall 950 ran right across the middle of what had been the Entrance Hall, while 979 relocated the eastern limit (Ill. 86 = VI EE), turning the impressive Entrance Hall of the previous two strata into a pair of small rooms. It is difficult to discern which phase within XVIII these changes belonged to, but they altered the Stratum XIX plan significantly.

A more satisfactory clue to two phases in Stratum XVIII in the Northern Complex comes from the rooms to the west. Floor 421 (Ill. 84 = CC II:#8, Ill. 89 = HH:#4) was of hard packed earth resting on a makeup of grey ashy earth (HH:#5); the floor was overlaid by ashy debris (locus 423). Floor 421 ran immediately under the foundation of Wall 955, which, according to the Welter plan, joined Walls 951, 952–954 and 956. The foundation trench for Wall 971 (HH:#3) cut through Floor 421, but the floor was probably continuous with packed limestone Floor 406 (CC II:#9) which in turn ran to Wall 924; Floor 406 was cut by Trough 410 late in the MB IIB period. The relative stratigraphy is clear: Floors 406 and 421 were contemporary with Wall 924, but earlier than Walls 955, 971 and Trough 410 (and then Pit 431 = CC II:#4, which was probably dug from Stratum XVII). The phase is uncertain; first assigned to XIXA, these two floors are now taken as XVIII for two reasons. First, the Northern Courtyard of Stratum XIX already has two floors, 426 and 469 (XIXB and XIXA respectively). Second, the elevation of 406–421 fits XVIII better than XIX, judging from Floor 7:12 of XVIIIB in the Southern Complex, just the other side of the alleyway and Wall 903 (CC II:#9 compared with CC III:#7).

The relative stratigraphy suggests placing Floor 406-421 in XVIIIB and assigning Walls 920, 955, 952-953-954, 956, 957 and 971 to XVIIIA, along with other walls continuous with them which appear on the Welter drawings but are no longer extant (948, 949 and 973). Only Walls 924, 951 and 958 were there in XVIIIB, all anchored on XIX walls below. If Wall 950 cutting across the region of the old Entrance Hall is also taken to be XVIIIA, the general plan of the Northern Complex in XVIIIB was much the same as that of Stratum XIX, a large open courtyard and a room the size of the Entrance Hall. Phase A saw the whole complex converted into small rooms (cf. the suggestion of G. R. H. Wright 1975:56–64 that the maze of walls resembles that of the fifteenth-century BCE temple found at the Amman airport in 1955 and excavated by J. Basil Hennessy in 1966 [Hennessy 1966; Herr 1983] and the MB IIC temple at Tananir on the slopes of Mt. Gerizim on the east edge of Balâṭah—on which see the MB IIC chapter below).

A small fragment of paving (locus 19:4) was found in the alley or corridor between Walls 903 and 924, over a makeup of loose grey earth (locus 453), but its attribution is unsure; possibly it was laid in Phase B and reused in Phase A. Little more can be said.

The Structures: The Southern Complex. As already noted, the outside walls of the Southern Complex continued the tradition of Stratum XIX. The Sellin plans show Wall 995 on Wall 995A, although running on a slightly different line. Wall 901 on the east (locus 6:12 designates its foundation and the pottery in its core) followed Stratum XIX Wall 902, its south portion founded on the mudbrick superstructure of 902 (Ill. 82 = VI AA I-II junction), its northern segment resting on the stone foundation of 902 (Ill. 83 = BB I-II junction). As it bordered Room 3, 901 was 0.90 m wide, constructed of heavy courses of facing stones with a rubble core; it narrowed to 0.75 m along Room 1, widened to 1.50 m along Room 5 (VI AA; VI FF). Just south of Wall 906 (the wall separating Rooms 1 and 5) it rested on the row of mudbricks used to extend Drain 17:6 in Stratum XIXA. The maximum preserved height of 901 is 0.90 m.

Wall 903 (locus 11:19) on the north bonded to 901 and ran 10.20 m to the west where it was cut off by the intrusion of Stratum XVII Pit 4:4 and the Sellin/Welter excavation. The eastern segment of Wall 903 was 0.90 m wide; to the west it narrowed to 0.75 m. There was probably a door from the alleyway/corridor running east-west along its north face into Room 4, conjectured on Ill. 75. Unlike its XIX predecessor 903A, 903 was not faced with plaster and was more roughly laid.

The western limit is a problem. Pit 4:4 took a huge bite out of the northwest corner of the complex and prevents certainty about how far Wall 903 ran and to what western wall it attached. Most plausibly, the first western limit of the plan was Wall 914A. The problem is that Wall 914A and its rebuild Wall 914 clearly had another function. Sellin and Welter had taken this wall as the retain-

Fig. 68. Looking south along Wall 914, with Wall 925 in the center. Note the phasing in Wall 914: 914A of Stratum XVIII is the battered segment at the top of which are large semi-hewn mizzi *blocks.*

Fig. 69. Looking northeast into the junction of Wall 902 (right) and Wall 906 (left). Floor 17:7 runs beneath Wall 906. Wall 906 is the south wall of Room 1, Stratum XVIII.

ing wall for the platform built for the Fortress Temple of Stratum XVI, and the Joint Expedition confirmed this judgment. As preserved (the Sellin and Welter excavations removed large parts of it), Wall 914 had a pronounced batter toward the west, comparable to Wall A but in reverse. Equally clear, though, is that it was built in two stages, 914A the lower, 914 the upper (VI AA III; VI FF IV).

Fig. 68 shows the phasing: the stone in the extreme lower right corner together with the five rather smoothly-faced (probably *mizzi* limestone) stones continuing its line away from the camera formed the top course of the MB IIB phase, while from there up is the rebuild in MB IIC. Note the layer of chalk chips running just over Wall 925 in the center of the picture, encountering 914 at what would be its lowest MB IIC course. The lowest courses of 914A are the candidate for the western wall of the Stratum XVIII courtyard complex. Furthermore, since Wall 914A sat through part of its length on top of old Wall D, it is quite possible that it also served the same purpose D had, that of retaining the fortification bank behind it. Wall 914A was not on line with the Fortress Temple as Ill. 75 shows. It was also not parallel to the major north-south wall of the Courtyard Complex, 925-912, which seems to have jogged to adjust to it. Apparently the original line of 914A was oriented as it was to retain the remains of the great C embankment beneath it and behind it. If Wall 914A was the original western boundary of the XVIII courtyard complex, the Wall 912 extension northward would represent a development within Stratum XVIII (see below on the Western and Central Courts, Rooms 4-6-7 and the room to the south of them).

Rooms 1 and 3. Wall 904 (locus 6:10 represents the soil of its dismantling) was the western boundary of Rooms 1 and 3. It was 0.65 m wide and resembled 903 in having no plaster facing and being made of rough stones, unlike 904A its predecessor in Stratum XIX. It was preserved to a height of 0.60 m through three courses. Austro-German plans show at least one more course, entrances from Room 2 into both rooms and a doorway from Room 3 into the street area (none of these were still in place when the Joint Expedition worked).

Wall 905 rebuilt Stratum XIX Wall 905A, again without plaster facing. Wall 906 (locus 6:11) was founded on the stone foundation of Wall 926, but its south face overlapped the south face of 926 by 0.20 m and the north face of 926 was not covered, retaining its superstructure of mudbrick. Stratum XIX Floor 17:7 ran under the foundation of 906 to the south face of 926 (fig. 69).

There were no preserved occupation surfaces in Rooms 1 and 3; Sellin had cleared nearly to XIX

Fig. 70. Bench 6:5 along Wall 901 in Room 1.

floors here. Bench 6:5 was in place along the east wall of Room 1 (fig. 70); it was two stones, 0.85 m wide and was preserved for 3.00 m from Wall 905 south; Welter's plans show it 3.50 m long. Only one course of stones was preserved, not bonded into the adjacent walls. Some traces of lime mortar were found between and beneath the stones. The site elevation on the preserved surface is at 14.75; were the Stratum XVIII Floor 7:12 elevation in Room 1 to have been the same as that of the Northern Court immediately to the west, the bench would have risen only 0.20 m above the floor.

Room 5. This, the Southern Court, was bounded by Walls 984, 938, 907, 906, 901 and 995, all previously described. Wall 907 (locus 7:17), which separated the court from the Northern Court (Room 2), was not bonded into 904, suggesting that 904 had rebuilt XIX 904A before 907 was constructed. Wall 907 was 0.80 m wide and preserved nearly a meter high. If there once was a mudbrick superstructure, its exposure since the Sellin excavations has resulted in its complete disappearance.

Stratum XVIIIB Floor 18:5 = 3R (Ill. 84 = VI CC IV:#2; Ill. 82 = AA III:#16) was preserved in the corner of Walls 907 and 938, but could not be traced to the east or south. Extrapolated at its known elevation, it must have run over the top of Stratum XIX Wall 937 (VI AA II-III). Of packed limestone over a makeup of bricky earth (AA III:19, CC IV:#3), its elevation was 14.55, nearly identical with Floor 7:12 in the Northern Court and about 0.20 m lower than that of Floor 4R in the Central Court. Street 5 was somewhat lower, at 13.90; the extensive filling and leveling operation which raised the elevations of Stratum XVIII floors inside did not affect the street levels as much, so one must have stepped down into the street from the Southern Complex.

Only a small fragment of a later Stratum XVIII surface, Floor 18:2, was preserved (VI AA III:#13), resting on a makeup of grey, *huwwar*-rich earth (#15) as much as 0.50 m thick. This floor's elevation was nearly the same as that of Floor 6R in the Central Court, but was again higher than that of Street 4 (see AA I:#9 with AA III:#13).

Room 2. In Stratum XIXB, the Northern Court had been bounded by Walls 903A, 904A, 916 and 908A-922A, with a doorway to the west. In XIXA, Wall 915 divided the space into Rooms 10 and 11. In Stratum XVIII, the court reverted to one large room, expanded to the south by about 0.75 m as Wall 907 replaced 916. Stratum XIX Walls 916 and 915 were covered over by XVIIIB floor 7:12 (VI CC III:#7). Wall 908 along the west made a straight join with the post of 908A described earlier (p. 65) and continued south to a bonded cor-

Fig. 71. Six column bases in the north part of Court 2 viewed looking north.

ner with 907. North of the post was a gap, before the line continued as Wall 922. The gap was apparently the entrance to Room 2 from the west. Wall 922 was very poorly preserved, and the width of the entryway can no longer be determined. Again the distinction between 922A and 922 is clear, however; the XIX wall was of well-hewn stones, the XVIII rebuild much rougher (fig. 64, above). Wall 922 was bonded into 903.

Six column bases in a row ran across the north end of the court, their centers 2 m away from Wall 903 (fig. 71). They rested on a stylobate wall erected beneath the floor to take their weight (locus 11:14; CC III: column base 5 upon stylobate 8). The stylobate butted against Wall 904 but ended 0.30 m away from Wall 922, and was 0.70 m wide, 0.60 m high (fig. 72). The column bases themselves stood an average 0.40 m high. Most probably, wooden columns positioned on the bases held a roof over the northern third of the room, extending out from the top of Wall 903.

Slightly south of the center of the unroofed southern portion of the room was a lone column base (locus 52:1) of similar dimensions, its top at site elevation 14.82, resting on a stylobate narrower and shorter than 11:14, anchored on Wall 915 of Stratum XIXA (VI CC III:#6; fig. 47, above). There is no evidence that this base was part of a row; Sellin found no others. The pillar on 52:1, like that on Base 8-9:18 in the Central Court to be described below, must have been freestanding. Again to anticipate the debate about the use of these buildings, if the analogy to the situation at the Bethshan temple and to the evidence of standing stones at the Fortress Temple is meaningful, this pillar base suggests that the Northern Court had a cultic function.

Court 2 contained the best-preserved floor of any Stratum XVIII room, Floor 7:12 (VI CC III:#7; VI III:#2). It was traced from Wall 903 past the row of column bases out to the lone pillar base. Here it was interrupted by a trench of the Sellin excavation, but it reappeared at the south edge of the room north of Wall 907. Floor 7:12 sealed the foundation trench of Wall 904 (BB III:#3). It was of packed limestone on makeup 7:15 (CC III:#9) which contained striations of lime. There was very little associated pottery. But under the floor in the extreme northwest corner of the court was Storage Jar Burial 11:5b (fig. 73), consisting of a large upright jar filled to a depth of about 0.10 m with disarticulated small bones including fragments from at least four different skulls. The top of the jar contained hard-packed brown earth with a few bone splinters. The main burial jar had been surrounded with large sherds of another jar. A carinated bowl (Cole 1984: pl. 18c) had been placed on top of the jar, and a large dipper juglet (pl. 30a)

Fig. 72. Stratum XVIII column base on stylobate. Walls 970 and 934 of Stratum XX are visible at bottom of photograph.

Fig. 73. Burial 11:5b in a storage jar in the northwest corner of Court 2 where Walls 903 (right) and 922 meet (left).

at its base, neither containing anything but soil. The whole installation leaned against the top preserved course of Stratum XIX Walls 903A and 922A and against the foundation courses of Stratum XVIII Walls 903 and 922. A small projection had been built out from the south face of Wall 903, perhaps to protect the deposit. In addition, while Wall 903 was battered east of this protection, it had a vertical face behind the burial. In short, the jar had been put in place as the corner was being built, and then covered with fill (locus 7:2) and the floor. If so, it may have been a foundation sacrifice. No offerings or grave goods other than the bowl and juglet were found.

Room 4: The Western Court. In XVIIIB the Western Court ran to Wall 914A on the west, 927A on the south, 908-922 on the east, and 903 on the north. Apparently, one entered it from the alley/corridor through a door in the now-robbed extension of 903; from Room 4 one entered Room 2.

Wall 927A-927 is difficult to interpret; between the lines of Wall 911 and 912 (both Phase A), 927A was founded quite deeply, at elevation 13.89, almost down to XIXA Floor 8:8 (fig. 14 = LL:#8 is its foundation trench). Wall 933 built in Stratum XX and reused in XIX ran beneath XVIIIB Wall 927A. The portion of Wall 927A-927 east of the line of Wall 911, Wall 927, was founded much higher, at 15.00 (Ill. 85 = VI DD), and only two courses were preserved, as was the case with 911 of Phase A. From a point 1.35 m west of 908, a wall on the line of 927A-927 was entirely missing; the gap was probably the XVIIIA doorway between Room 6 and the Central Court. As noted before, Floor 1R (fig. 14:#5) ran under Wall 912 but to Wall 927A. The conclusion is that 927A was built in XVIIIB from Wall 914A to the line of Wall 911. In Phase A, at least Walls 911 and 912 were built and Wall 927A was extended to the east as 927, narrowing the doorway between the Western and Central Courts.

Walls 911 (locus 8:10), 912 and 913 (locus 9:7) all had been exposed to a point well below

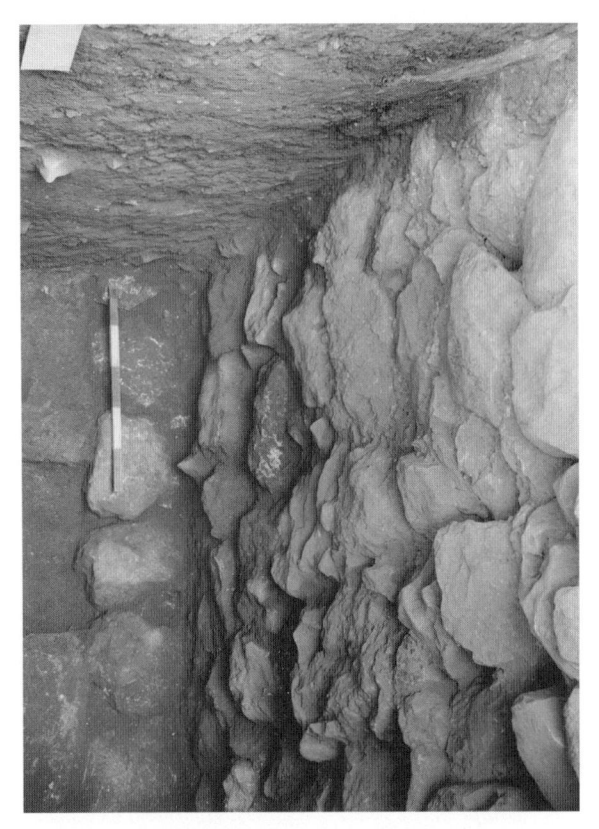

Fig. 74. Looking down at the succession of walls on the east of the Central Court. Wall 938 of Stratum XVIII on Wall 938A of Stratum XIX on Wall 983 of Stratum XX (on which the meter stick lies).

their founding elevations by the Sellin/Welter work. The Joint Expedition found 911 and 913 preserved only two courses high and their foundations were in mean elevation well above any known XVIIIB floors (VI DD). Wall 912 was relatively more deeply founded at its corner with 927, but it still ran above Floor 1R. Very little of 912 was preserved north of its juncture with 913; it was destroyed by the intrusion of Stratum XVII Pit 4:4. And the extant remains of 912 north of 913 (913 was founded at 15.44) had a much higher founding level, even above Floor 5R (fig. 14:#2), a floor of XVIIIA. Thus, Wall 912 had at least two phases: along with 911 it first formed the limit of the alcove Room 7 in the southwest corner of the Western Court; later it was extended to the north in a renovation otherwise attested in the Central Court—Stratum XVIIIA+. Judging from the elevation of its founding, Wall 913 probably also belonged to XVIIIA+.

To summarize this complicated picture: (1) In Stratum XVIIIB, Wall 914A formed the western boundary of both the Western and Central Courts, with 927A as the partition between them; there was a wide doorway connecting these two courts between the west face of Wall 908 and the east end of the original 927A. (2) Wall 912 replaced 914A as the west limit of the Western Court at the outset of Phase A. Wall 911 was built, dividing Room 7 from Room 6; 927A was extended eastward as 927, narrowing the doorway. (3) Even later in Phase A (in A+), but prior to the digging of Stratum XVII Pit 4:4, Wall 912 was extended northward to corner with Wall 903, and Wall 913 was built (more on this below).

For Phase B, virtually all remains of floors had been removed by earlier excavation. Traces of Floor 1R = fig. 14:#5 were found at the west. It was marked by an intermittent ashy layer at elevation 14.75, comparable in elevation to Floor 7:12 = 2R at 14.55 in the Northern Court, Room 4, Floor 4R at 14.90–14.50 in the Central Court, and Floor 18:5 = 3R at 14.75 in Room 5. Floor 1R rested on a makeup of hard brown earth (fig. 14:#6; Ill. 85 = VI DD:#3).

For Phase A, the only traces were preserved in the balks left by Sellin and Welter. Packed limestone Floor 5R of Room 7 at elevation 15.25 (fig. 14:#2) ran under the northern extension of Wall 912, analyzed above as a late feature of Phase A. By mean elevation, Floor 5R would have run against the south segment of Wall 912 and against Wall 927 in Phase A proper. A small portion of its makeup was locus 9:2 (#3); it was of brown earth with *ḥuwwar* flecks.

No occupation layers of the later developments in Phase A were preserved in the Western Court. It was the Central Court that provided what evidence pertains to this last development in Stratum XVIII.

The Central Court. The eastern and southern walls of the Central Court, 938 (locus 18:13) and 984, were rebuilds of 938A and 984A from Stratum XIX, and continued the tradition of Walls 983 and 986 of Stratum XX (fig. 74). Wall 938 did not bond with Wall 907, but it is difficult to say which was built earlier; probabilities are in favor of Wall 907 since it did not have a predecessor in Stratum XIX.

It seems clear that Wall 914A was the original XVIIIB west limit of the Central Court, replacing Wall 933 of Stratum XIX. In Phase A Wall 925 became the west limit. Its foundation cut XVIIIB Floor 4R (Ill. 87 = VI FF IV:#16 cut by #17). Photographs from the time of the Sellin expedition indicate that Wall 925 proceeded to a junction with 927A, and Wall 932 connected 925 to 985 defining the cubicle in the southwest corner of the court. Wall 985 ran over Floor 4R and belonged to Phase A. A doorway between its south end and the north face of Wall 984 gave access to the cubicle (fig. 75).

Stratum XVIIIB Floor 4R (VI FF IV:#16; fig. 65:plaster floor on "red bricky") was traced from Wall 938 under Wall 985 (Phase A) to a point where it was cut by the foundation trench for Phase A Wall 925 (fig. 65). Presumably it once ran to Wall 914A, but the tiny gap (note VI FF IV) between these two walls precluded investigation.

Along the north side of the Central Court as here envisioned, near the western jamb of the doorway into the Western Court, sat an isolated column base, locus 8-9:18 (fig. 76). Immediately adjacent, but at a higher elevation were flagstones of Floor 8R of Phase A, portions of which were found throughout the Central Court (see below), so Column Base 8-9:18 is to be assigned to Phase B. No clear flooring could be associated with the column base. Nevertheless, it bears such a close resemblance to Base 52:1 in the Northern Court that it may too have carried a freestanding pillar.

It is with the understanding of the phasing here that staff disagreement persists about the layout of the Central and Western Courts during Stratum XVIIIB. The area in question is a jumble of wall fragments and installations, among which the Sellin and Welter excavations probed and from which virtually all undisturbed soil had been removed. It is clear that Wall 927A-927 separated the two courts in Phase A, and this wall shows clear evidence of having been reconstructed at least once during its lifetime. The most plausible interpretation is that the wall was originally built in Phase B to a wide doorway, as noted above, then rebuilt to narrow the door in Phase A. The column base would have sat near the west jamb of the wider doorway of Phase B and logic would then posit a

Fig. 75. Looking east from the top of Wall 914, with Wall 925 in foreground. The cubicle in the southwest corner of the Central Court ran from Wall 925 to the stretch of Wall 985 and the doorway against the north face of Wall 984 at right.

partner for it on the east (Ill. 74 and fig. 77, option B). On this reconstruction, the two courts remained the same relative size throughout the period, with a shift only in the western wall line: Wall 914A in Phase B, 925-912 in Phase A.

But the column base is a puzzle. G. E. Wright remained convinced that this Phase B pillar base must have been located in the center of a court (fig. 77, option A). He thus concluded that the Phase B arrangement involved a reuse of Wall 919 of Stratum XIX, or another wall built on about that same line, some 3.50 m to the north of the line of 927A-927; it would have run beneath the line of XVIII Wall 913. This would have made the Central Court extend farther north and would have attenuated Western Court 4. Here, in the midst of the radically disturbed remnants of walls and lay-

Fig. 76. Isolated column base 8-9:18, immediately south of and below Wall 927. The context is quite disturbed.

ers, Wright invoked the requirements of architectural integrity; plausibility dictated that the base and its pillar *not* be so close to a wall as it was to Wall 927. The result was a series of proposals published in modern Hebrew (Campbell and Wright 1970:127, adopted by Jaroš 1976:28 and fig. 30). G. R. H. Wright's reconstruction shown in fig. 78 is based on this alternative.

In sum, the two courts were probably arranged as Ills. 75 and 74 suggest. But it is possible that the Central Court ran farther north in Phase B, before Wall 927A was built, and that changes in Wall 927A took place locally within the period covered by Phase A. This possibility would require that the deep founding of Wall 927A be due to the builders' having found the need to consolidate a weakness at this location or some other such explanation. Conditions here are such as to lead to presenting both alternatives and leaving the matter open.

In Phase A, the whole Central Court may have been paved with a flagstone floor. In the southeast corner, large flagstones (Floors 8R/9R, locus 5804 and 5805, Ill. 87 = VI FF IV) adjoined the upper courses of Walls 938 and 984 (fig. 79, Ill. 75). An open drain shown on Ill. 75 ran east–west in this floor, sloping down to the east and presumably running through an opening in Wall 938, now lost, into the Southern Courtyard. This drain was fed by a north-south arm, Drain 5808, which carried water from the center of the court. This system suggests the room was unroofed.

The Joint Expedition cut a vertical face on the north edge of the tongue of Fortress Temple forecourt left by Sellin. It reveals the junction of Walls 932 and 925 as shown on fig. 80 at the foot of the balk toward the right. Several stones projecting from the north face at elevation 15.70 belonged to 932, while 925 is shown coming toward the camera in the niche cut back at the right, with Wall 914A at the very right margin (see also Ill. 82, the VI AA section).

Two more flagstones remained just south of Wall 927, at elevation 15.58—the flagstones above and to the left of the lone column base (fig. 76 above).

Elsewhere in the Central Court, XVIIIA occupation surface seems to be represented by four plaster surfaces (Floor 7R) between Walls 985 and 925 (Ill. 87 = VI FF IV:#13). At their curve up to Wall 925, they are at elevation 15.70. Then, just west of the top course of Wall 938, traces of packed limestone Floor 6R (VI AA III:#12) were at the nearly identical elevation to that of Floor 18:2 (#13) of the Southern Courtyard on the other side of the wall. The whole court may have been paved in flagstones, largely robbed out, resting on the packed limestone as makeup. Note that Floor 7R of plaster and 8R of flagstones both rest on makeup described as packed grey earth with *ḥuwwar* lumps (FF IV; Ill. 75).

Still within XVIIIA, there appears to have been one more development in the Central Court. The top courses of Walls 925, 984 and 985 seem to be of different construction from that of the lower courses. The stones were larger and better hewn, and were laid on a slightly different line (fig. 81). The north segment of Wall 912 may have been

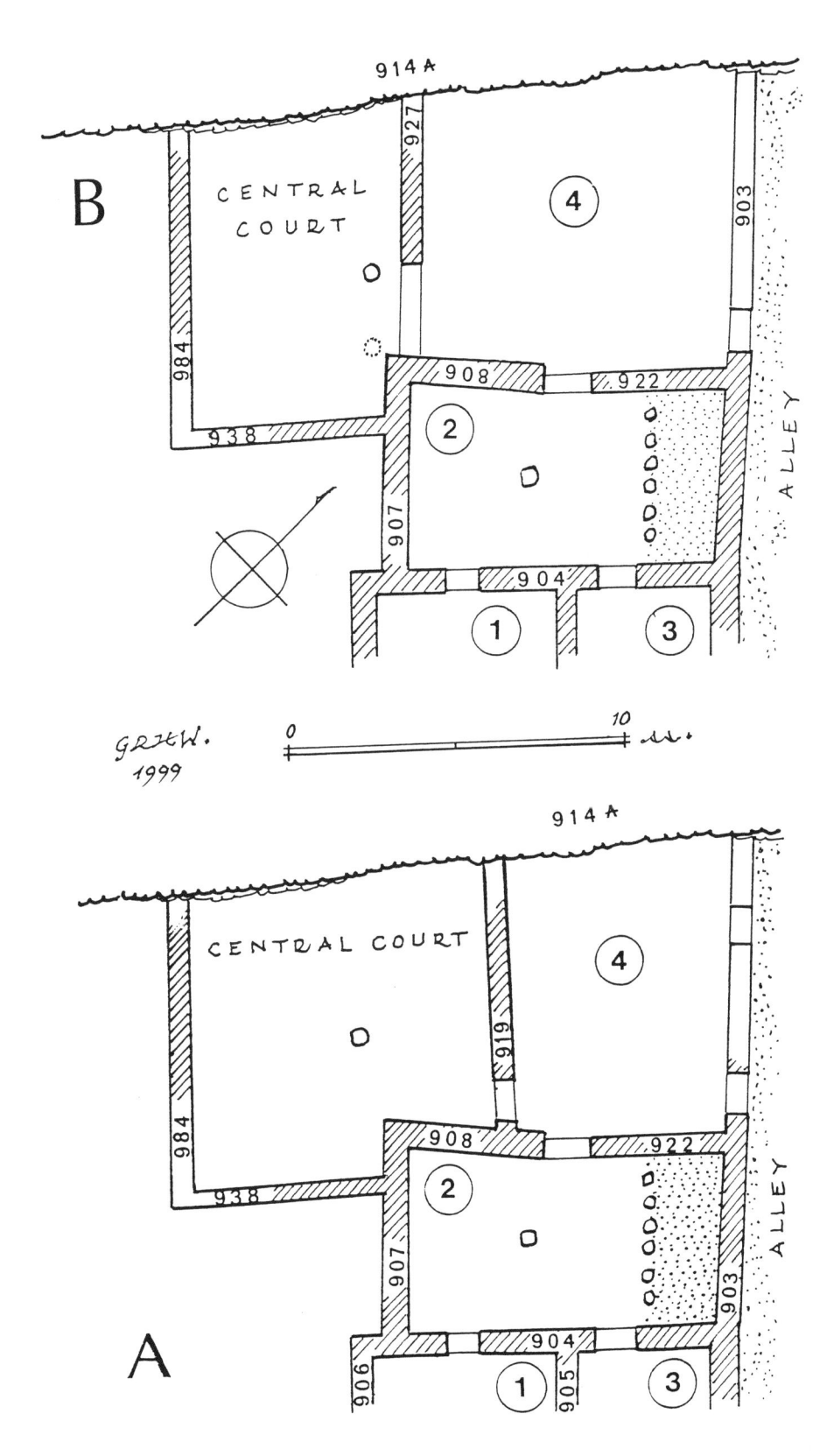

Fig. 77. Comparative block drawings of the two interpretations of the Stratum XVIII Central Court. Ernest Wright's interpretation is A; the more plausible Ross interpretation is B.

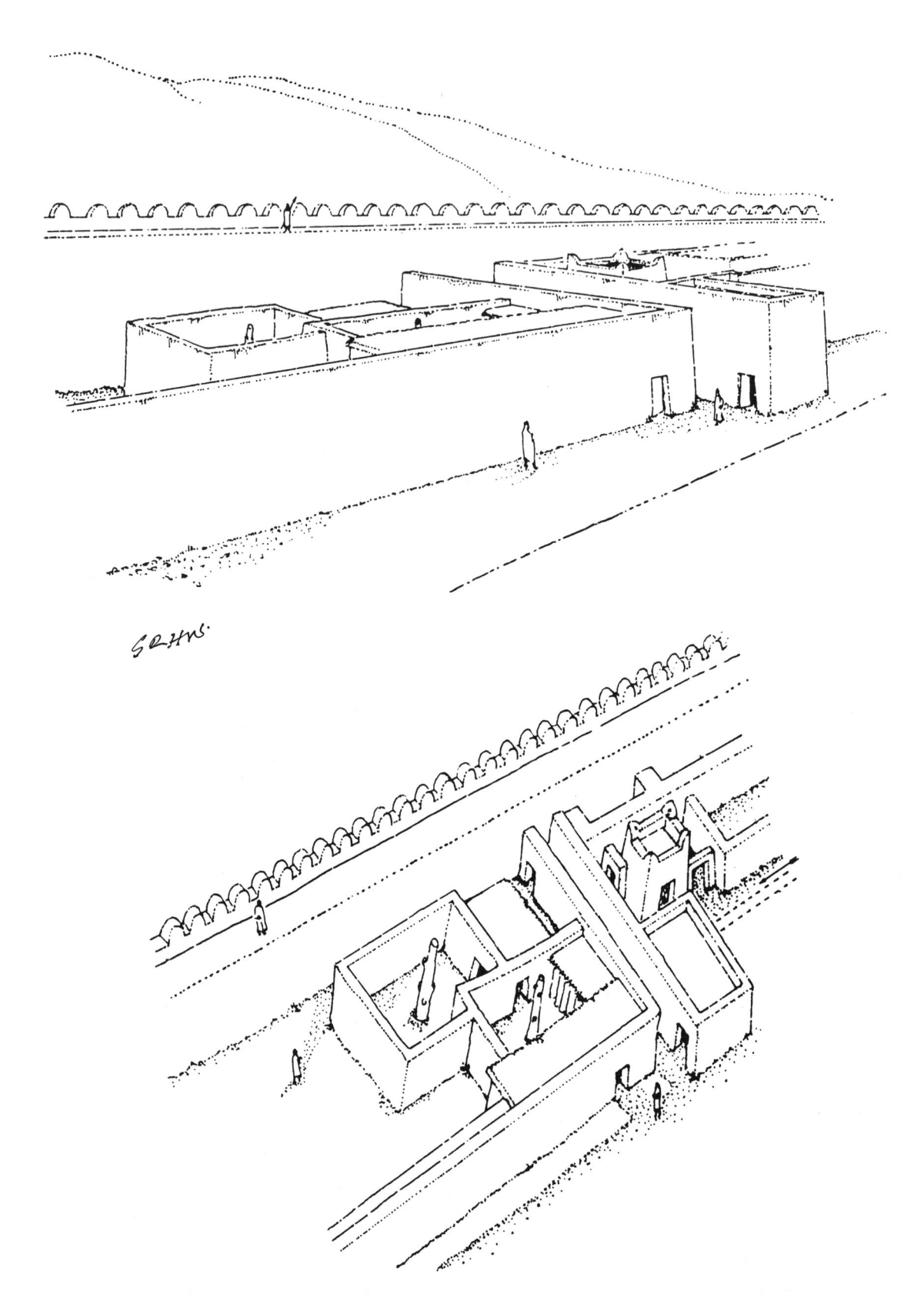

Fig. 78. G. R. H. Wright's drawings of the layout of Stratum XVIII in Field VI, based on Ernest Wright's interpretation.

Fig. 79. Flagstone Floor 8R/9R against upper courses of Walls 938 and 984.

associated with this rebuild. So may occasional flat stones, observed *in situ* in 1957 by Joint Expedition staff before excavation of Field VI, on the top of Walls 906, 907 and 938. No floorings were preserved to go with this development; probably the XVIIIA floors continued in use. Possibly Oven 5082 (fig. 82) located west of the door jamb in Wall 985 within the southwest cubicle, along with Storage Jar 5081 in the corner of Walls 984 and 925 (fig. 83), belong with the XVIIIA+ phase, though they could equally well have been installations set in with Phase A proper.

Evidence for a Phase XVIIIA+ in Room 4 has already been suggested. A further development on the division of Room 7 from Room 6 at the south of Room 4 involved extending Wall 912 northward and building Wall 913, enclosing Room 7. This is inferred from the elevation of foundations

Fig. 80. Balk face at the north edge of forecourt tongue left by Sellin. Junction of Stratum XVIII Walls 932 and 925. Stones of 932 are at the base of the balk, while stones of 925 are in the niche at right.

Fig. 81. Within the cut in the forecourt tongue, Walls 925 (foreground), 985 (center) and 984 (with meter stick resting on it) all show rebuilds belonging to Stratum XVIIIA. Compare fig. 75.

for these walls (see fig. 14 for the position of Wall 913 against the earlier portion of Wall 912), but cannot be proven.

All Stratum XVIIIA buildings and installations were finally covered over by the massive MB IIC fill upon which the Fortress Temple was built. The Sellin/Welter excavation removed any evidence of Stratum XVII remains in the area occupied by the series of Central and Southern Courts of Strata XX-XVIII. Stratum XVII remains were to be found only to the north.

The Date of Stratum XVIII

In general, this stratum's horizon is MB IIB. The overwhelming majority of pottery from the deep fill under the XVIIIB floors belongs squarely within MB IIB, with pieces of MB IIA, possible MB I, and EB occasionally appearing. Cole used 136 forms from these fills and from the makeup for Street 5 in his corpus; 32 more come from the makeup for Street 4 and the adjacent drain (Cole 1984:29, and the selection of pottery from locus 35, the makeup for Street 4, in his Plate 48 = fig. 84). Only the pottery found on the floors themselves had a somewhat later cast (notably from Floor 7:12 in Room 2), representing the end of the MB IIB tradition. It is impossible to distinguish

Fig. 82. Oven 5082 adjacent to the top of Wall 985 in Central Courtyard cubicle.

Fig. 83. Sunken storage jar base 5081 in junction of Walls 984 and 925, probably of Stratum XVIIIA+.

between the phases of Stratum XVIII on the basis of the pottery. The proposed date for Stratum XVIII is the first quarter of the seventeenth century BCE (1700–1675 BCE).

STRATUM XVII

Portions of Walls 909 (locus 50:1) and 910 (locus 51:1) were still standing when the Joint Expedition began its work (Ill. 76, incorrectly designated Stratum XVI in Cole), but had to be removed prior to stratigraphic excavation because of the danger of collapse. The Sellin/Welter excavations had removed any occupation surfaces and had reached far below their founding elevations. Welter's plan shows a site elevation of 15.26 (recalibrated) in the small room enclosed by 909-922-910-923, but Wall 909 was founded at site elevations recorded at 15.95 and 16.00, Wall 910 at 15.80 and 15.85 (Ill. 84 = VI CC III and Ill. 85 = VI DD). The stratigraphic assignment of these walls and related structures must be determined by means other than soil deposition.

Wall 909 rode immediately upon Stratum XVIII Wall 903, continuing a line going back to Stratum XIX that marked the north boundary of the Southern Complex. Wall 910 did not continue the line of any previous structure; it was constructed over the fill of the huge Pit 4:4 which had removed evidence of the entire northwest quadrant of Room 4 of Stratum XVIII. Wall 923 appears on Austro-German plans, but all traces of it were gone when the Joint Expedition began its work; presumably it too was founded on the pit's fill. Wall 922, however, continued the line of a Stratum XVIII wall, the one separating the Northern Court from the Western Court. It was widened from ca. 0.75 m to over a meter, so that its eastern face covered the westernmost column base of the XVIII Northern Court (Böhl, DuBose and German plans). Welter also considered Wall 904, the east wall of the Northern Court in Stratum XVIII, to have been reused in Stratum XVII; it is possible that the uppermost three courses (fig. 63, above) are to be assigned to XVII.

Next comes the question of Wall 901 and the uppermost three street levels between it and Wall 900. Street 3 was preserved for most of its original length, and had a paving of small cobblestones on a makeup of grey earth filled with sherds and bone fragments, with frequent ashy streaks. The street itself is shown on Ill. 82 = VI AA:I:#6, figs. 5 and 20, Ill. 83 = VI BB I:#4 and in fig. 85). Makeup 107, from which Cole drew all seven of his "XVIIs" forms (1984:29), is shown on BB I:#5 with ashy streaks as #7 as well as on AA I:#8 and fig. 20:#6. The street had a brick curb (AA II:#7; fig. 86).

Streets 1 and 2 were almost completely destroyed by Sellin trenches, except for a small fragment of the former preserved in the AA I balk (section #2, observed by the Joint Expedition but not excavated for artifacts) and a longer stretch of Street 2 further north (fig. 87; meter stick on Street 3). Street 2 (AA I:#4; BB I:#2) may have filled the whole span from Wall 900 to 901, with no drain; a few cobblestones at the appropriate elevation ran against 901 (fig. 20:on #4) but the evidence is scanty. Makeup for Street 2 (locus 110;

STRATUM XVIII: LOCUS 35

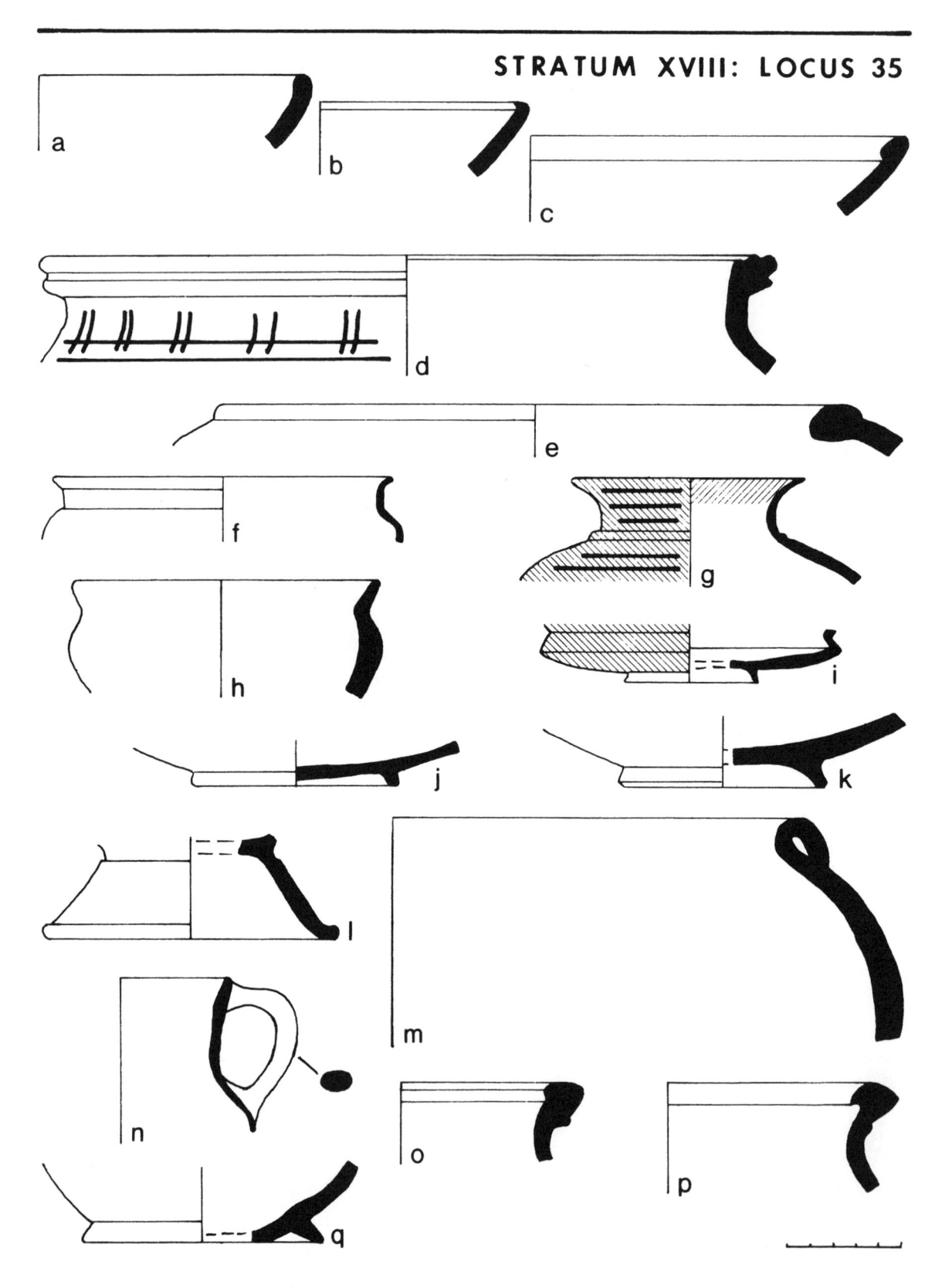

Fig. 84. Selection of pottery from Locus 35, makeup for Street 4, reprinted from Cole:pl. 48.

Fig. 85. Surface of Street 3 between Wall 900 (right) and Wall 901 (left).

AA I:#5, fig. 20:#4, BB I:#3) was of firm pinkish grey earth.

By elevation alone, Streets 3 through 1 could have belonged to Stratum XVIII, but it is questionable to assign to that stratum five street surfacings when Strata XIX and XX had only one and three respectively. It is more probable that Streets 3–1, clearly separated from Street 4 by a relatively thick makeup, belonged to Stratum XVII and therefore that Wall 901 was reused in this stratum. As ephemeral as Stratum XVII is here, then, it did involve the major eastern and northern walls of the Southern Complex. It can only be postulated that Wall 914A defined the western limits of the entire precinct.

Other walls cleared by the Sellin and Welter work and shown on their plans preserved at high elevations may belong to Stratum XVII. Wall 931, the western end of the 909-910 rectangle, paralleled 923 and 922 and may have cornered with 909; the fill beneath 931 was locus 12:3. On Ill. 76, the Stratum XVII plan, it is projected as being part of that complex.

A square structure in the northwestern quadrant of Field VI and left isolated by the Austro-German work is a candidate for Stratum XVII. It lay partially beneath Wall 930 of the 928-930-996 pair of rectangular rooms, which date to MB IIC, so relative stratigraphy of walls places it in XVII. Welter's plan records elevations on its top which recalibrated to the Joint Expedition's elevations are at 15.97. No soil was left in its interior by the previous excavators, but a Welter datum places an elevation at 15.40 in its interior, not indicated as a wall footing, but placed as though on a floor within it. The Joint Expedition did not dismantle it to seek clues to its stratification.

The square structure to the northwest of it straddling the junction of grid coordinates E and F, 4 and 5, located just inside the Northwest Gate and virtually in the way of the road through the gate is at a higher elevation and was also left isolated by Austro-German excavation. It probably belongs to MB IIC. As for the square building with walls numbered 944-945-946-947, also left high and dry by the Sellin work, an elevation on its northwest corner is at 16.25 on top of the wall and 15.25 at its foot. The assignment by the Joint Expedition to LB is speculative, and its relative height leaves doubt about stratigraphic assignment. Though its west wall, 944, was dismantled by the Joint Expedition, nothing conclusive could be learned about its date.

More information on the 909 and 910 phase can be gleaned from early photographs. Böhl 1926a: Afbb. 53, 58 and Sellin 1926b: Taf. 41

Fig. 86. Balk through the streets in Area 3A, looking south. Wall 900 to left, 901 to right. The trench at left cleared fill from the Sellin dig along Wall 900. Street 3 is marked.

show the preserved tops of 909 and 910 to be below the preserved tongue of forecourt for the Fortress Temple, and the Galling photograph (*SBBC* fig. 72) shows a pedestal of undisturbed debris with light and dark striations just off the corner of Walls 922 and 910; the striations match the striations under the forecourt, and this stratigraphy is higher than the preserved top of 910-922. In Field VI.2, the top of the fill (figs. 11 = VI PP and 12 = VI RR: locus 35) for the platform on which the XVI Fortress Temple was built was at site elevation 16.90, the same as the elevation recorded on Wall 910 and only slightly lower than the uppermost elevations on 909 (17.06 and 17.00) 17 m to the south. It is most probable that Stratum XVII walls were completely covered over prior to the construction of the Fortress Temple, with the fill to be described in the next chapter.

On the other hand, there is clear stratigraphic distinction between Strata XVIII and XVII. Although certain Stratum XVII walls (909, 922, probably 904 and 901) were built upon or continued Stratum XVIII walls, the general picture is not one of continuity. Pit 4:4 (Ill. 83 = VI BB IV:#1, Ill. 85 = DD:#2) removed the north end of Wall 912 of Stratum XVIIIA and disrupted other adjacent XVIII structures. The pit was then filled with grey, rocky earth containing *ḥuwwar* chunks, upon which Wall 910 was erected. This alone marks a sharp interruption between XVIII and XVII, during which Pit 4:4 was dug.

To summarize: the general orientation of Stratum XVII walls was similar to that of Stratum XVIII, but with a definite break. Stratum XVII was clearly earlier than the beginnings of Stratum XVI, represented by the 928-930 complex and the platform under The Fortress Temple. Stratum XVII is an intermediate phase, difficult to date. One reliable group of pottery comes from the fill of Pit 4:4, from which Cole selected 38 forms (see also his Plate 49 = fig. 88). All are clearly in the late MB IIB tradition. Cole's other group, seven sherds from the street makeup for Streets 3 and 2, is similar, with some forms moving into MB IIC.

Pit 431 (Ill. 84 = VI CC II:#4; Ill. 89 = HH:2) cut from the founding level of LB Tower 944 (at the junctions of site grid F and G, 5 and 6; seen in elevation on CC II) and intruding nearly to Stratum XIX depths, produced a mixture of pottery and has a high probability of intrusive material, so its pottery has been discounted for dating Stratum XVII. Judging from the way in which it was laid into Pit 431, Bin 410 (CC II) was stratigraphically subsequent to Pit 431, but it is on the Stratum XVII plan for location purposes. It was lined with large, smooth stones, some of which were laid flat (the

Fig. 87. Streets 2, 3, 4 and 5 against Wall 900 in Area 3E. The meter stick lies on Street 3.

bottom and the upper courses of the sides), some vertically (the lower two courses on the sides). The bin was cup-shaped, tapering from inside diameter 1.35 m at the top to 0.90 m at the bottom. A quantity of bones and restorable pottery were in the filling of the bin; two halves of a bowl (B62 ##718 and 335) were separated by 0.35 m of other debris, suggesting that the filling was drawn from one location and had a degree of uniformity. But the installation was open to the modern surface, and the likelihood of intrusion is great. The bulk of the pottery from it was MB IIB but several pieces belong to MB IIC. Bin 410 is certainly later than Pit 431, but it *may* have been dug before the MB IIC fill for the Temple platform was laid. It cannot serve as a safe arbiter of Stratum XVII date.

The conclusion is that Stratum XVII is from a very late stage of MB IIB, ca. 1675–1650 BCE.

Four Separations within MB IIB

To identify four strata within the span of a century constitutes an unusual circumstance in Palestinian archaeology. Further, to suggest a quarter of century as the time span for each of the four looks arbitrary. It is based on a sense of some duration to each of the strata, as indicated by the resurfacings of streets, relaying of floors, installation of facilities such as ovens and smelters, and burials beneath floors.

The Joint Expedition's interpretation of the Field VI series of construction, reconstruction and changes in layout has not gone unchallenged. Zvi Lederman (1985) and the staff of the Shiloh dig (Finkelstein, Bunimovitz and Lederman 1985; Ussishkin 1989) have re-examined the close stratigraphic separation at Shechem in light of their work at Shiloh; a key assumption of their approach is to remind interpreters that rebuilds and changes need not have represented large-scale interruptions in the lives of peoples, such as enemy attack, or earthquake, or plague, or the emergence of new life-styles. They have also questioned whether it is necessary to see developments in the fortifications as successive rather than co-terminus. The Joint Expedition retains its conviction that it is the *nature* of the changes in Field VI that call for extensions in time, and that there is significant change in concept, as well as need to cover over and level up for new stages in the construction. The substantial fills separating one stratum from another require time and engineering. While there is a need to explain these fills—for example, to sanitize after widespread pollution due to plague, or to level up after an earthquake—it is important not to telescope the lapse of time too readily. As for the for-

92 SHECHEM III. THE MIDDLE BRONZE IIB PERIOD

STRATUM XVIIS: LOCUS 4:4

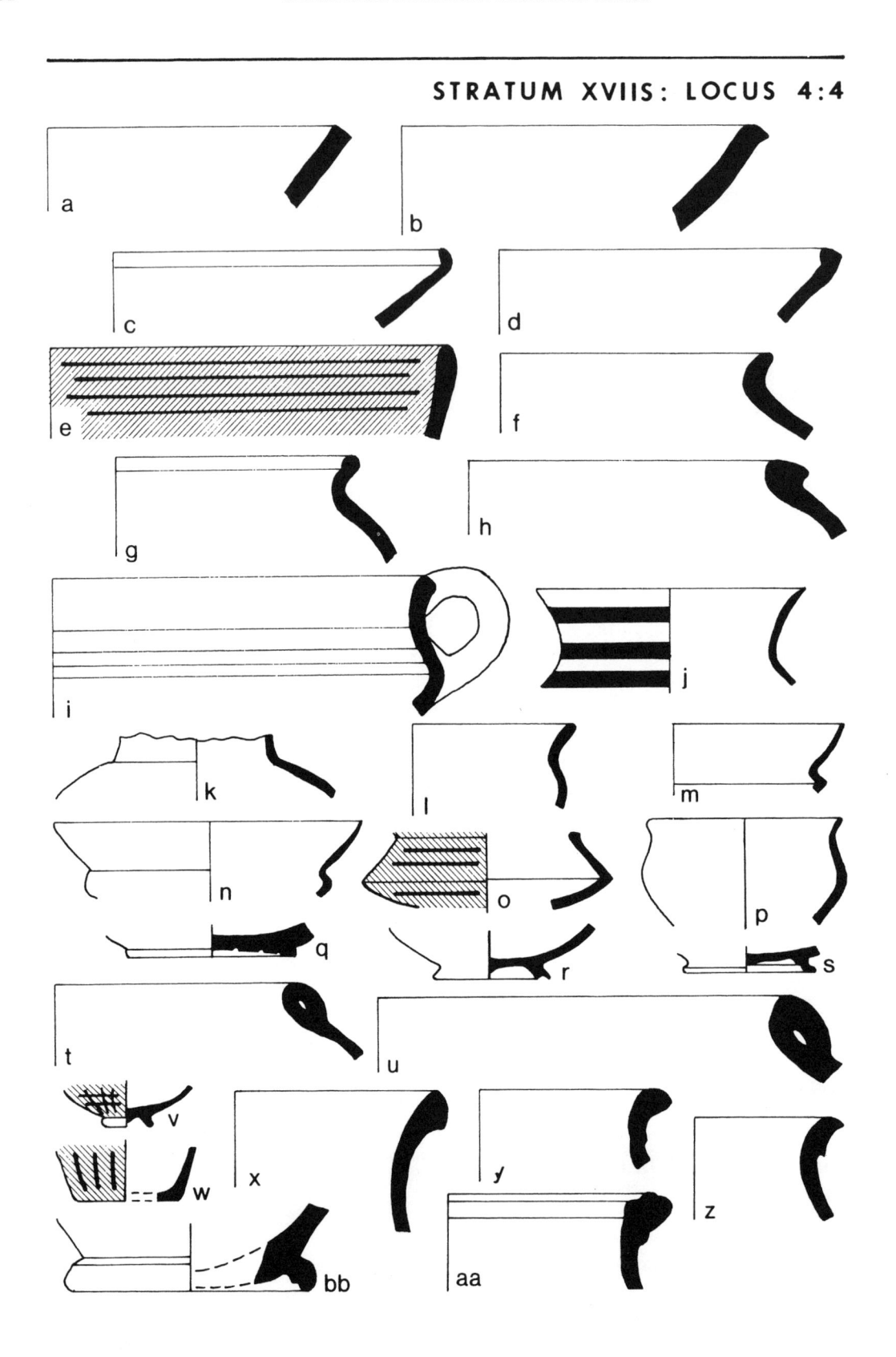

Fig. 88. Range of pottery forms from makeup for Stratum XVII, drawn from Pit 4:4 dug at the start of Stratum XVII.

tifications, it is puzzling to think of a coherent concept of protection such as that proposed for the C Rampart in its original width as only a stage in a single-phase effort that then was carried eight meters outward via another massive job of importing fill. It must be conceded, however, that the critique of the Joint Expedition reading of its MB IIB stratigraphy is valuable in its challenge to think imaginatively about the way ancient people lived and worked. And it is a caution to the Joint Expedition's archaeological tradition, which tends to see each soil layer as having chronological meaning; stratigraphic separations frequently do not provide clarity about duration, and one cannot know what a month's experience may bring in the way of change. This issue will arise again in connection with the understanding of Wall A in the following chapter.

The Purposes of the Courtyard Complexes

Three of the complexes in Field VI, representing Strata XX-XVIII and designated 939, 902 and 901, had a southern component featuring a large open court surrounded by a variety of rooms. Within the open court, an enclosure designated a Central Court, with a corner of walls that stayed in the same position throughout the three strata, lay beneath what became a focal point in the forecourt of the Fortress Temple of the succeeding MB IIC period; there is difficulty in defining the size of the Central Court in the concluding phase of the series.

All three acropolis complexes also had an adjacent complex of some sort to the north, a rather elaborate Entrance Hall or ceremonial chamber, and a system of street and alley access routes. After the 1962 Joint Expedition campaign, the project director G. Ernest Wright began to analyze the series of complexes as "Courtyard Temples."

Wright's reasoning as of 1963 is summarized in *SBBC*:108–9. His arguments, restated with observations by the present writer:

1) Wall 900 separated the complexes in Field VI from the rest of town. This *separation* suggests special function. According to Wright, to think of these as "secular public buildings" was not to think in appropriate terms.

2) One part of the complex, the central court within the larger court of the southern portion, showed continuity of wall placement throughout, and was located directly beneath where the altars and a *maṣṣebah* of the later Fortress Temple forecourt came to be placed. *Continuity* of location suggests continuity of tradition and function.

3) In the Stratum XVIII phase, two courts in the southern complex had bases for freestanding pillars—perhaps sacred pillars like the one in Beth-shan IX's cultic complex. These are indications of *cultic furnishings*.

4) True, the Courtyard Complexes lacked objects suggesting cultic activity, but then so did the Fortress Temple. If the Fortress Temple be accepted as a temple building, *absence of cultic artifacts* is not a crucial countering argument.

5) The Courtyard Complexes have too many ovens (certainly four, perhaps as many as six) to be understood as royal palaces. The ovens may point to use by families at cultic festivals. That is, *special facilities* pertain to what went on here.

6) The Courtyard Complexes were not, admittedly, comparable to typical temples. They were "open-air precincts," with some roofed portions. Perhaps this character accords with the sorts of installations the Genesis traditions refer to at Bethel (Gen. 13:3–4) or Beersheba (Gen. 26:23–25, 21:31–33). A new sense of what constituted a sanctuary needs to be imagined.

As staff deliberations continued in the excavation seasons after the 1962 campaign, attention focused on what should be in an acropolis; as with acropoleis elsewhere in the ancient world, a sanctuary could be expected. But the questions remained: were the Courtyard Complexes equivalent to sanctuaries? Did they represent *the* cultic center of MB IIB Shechem? How could one feel confidence in interpreting them?

Among the members of the Shechem staff, architect G. R. H. Wright expressed the greatest readiness to agree with the "courtyard temple" hypothesis. He placed the Shechem series in his typology of sanctuaries in Canaan (1971: 19–23; 1985: I, 43, 219; II, figs. 133–34) and adduced the Qatna high place as a better parallel than the Beth-shan and Khattusas ones Ernest Wright had cited (du Mesnil 1935: pls. 28–33; G. R. H. Wright

1985: I, 220; II, fig. 140)—but G. R. H. Wright favored identifying only a *part* of the complex as a cultic site.

Early on, Paul Lapp expressed doubts about the courtyard temple hypothesis (1963: 129–30). Then, in 1985, Lawrence E. Toombs, Associate Director of the Joint Expedition brought order and clarity into the debate and proposed abandoning the designation of the complexes as "Courtyard Temples."

Toombs proposed six "categories of argumentation," by which one can approach deciding whether a structure is a sanctuary. In doing this he sought to bring rigor of method into archaeological interpretation to go with rigor of method in field technique (cp. Coogan 1987; Dever 1983; Fowler 1981, 1985a, 1985b; Shiloh 1979; Yeivin 1973).

Toombs's six sets of criteria clearly interrelated with G. E. Wright's reasoning in 1963. Toombs presented them so as to show the interrelationship:

1) Arguments from structure. What does the layout of architecture suggest? For Wright, the complexes, set off as they were by a precinct wall, and incorporating large open spaces (courtyards), did not seem to be adequately explained by seeing them as secular public buildings for the city's rulers.

2) Arguments from architectural analogy. There are sanctuary complexes elsewhere that at least suggest analogies to the Shechem complexes; they are not, however, contemporary with Shechem's but are roughly 350 years later in date.

3) Arguments from continuity of religious function. The Fortress Temple and its forecourt furnishings override part of the courtyard complexes. Religious phenomenologists note that continuity of sacred locations over time and through cultural change is a frequent occurrence. The positioning of the Fortress Temple may mean that there is a remembered sacred location beneath it.

4) Arguments from furnishings and contents. The courtyard complexes preserved no objects that clearly point to sacred use. Wright thought that the number of ovens and kitchens suggested centers for family festivities. He was more impressed by isolated column bases in open courts, not needed to bear roof supports; perhaps they served as pedestals for sacred pillars. As for burials, pottery installations, indications of metal-casting and the like, Wright apparently felt that their force in suggesting the function of the buildings was neutral.

5) Arguments from position in the city. Toombs observes that in general it is palaces that belong on acropoleis, while temples are found throughout cities.

6) Arguments based on absence of expected installations and objects. Toombs argued that this is a more crucial consideration than Wright's reasoning would suggest (Wright's reason #4 above).

Wright did not explicitly indicate which of his reasons he found most compelling, though some ranking was implied. Toombs proposed a relative weighting of the six categories of argument, from greatest to least in force:

1. Contents and furnishing
2. Absence of expected objects and installations
3. Structure
4. Architectural analogy
5. Position in the city
6. Functional continuity

On the first of these, contents and furnishings, Toombs observed there were really not many ovens—four in the Stratum XIX complexes—and that the installations preserved were typical of domestic contexts rather than temple contexts. Pillar bases in a row point to audience chambers, while isolated pillar bases are not features of known temple plans elsewhere. Subfloor burials are more often to be found in dwellings than in temples. Industrial facilities for potters or metalworkers belong in domestic settings.

As for expected features that are absent, Toombs was struck by there being no sign of an altar; an altar is not something one removes in the face of impending disaster, and in spite of erosion and depredation in the courtyard buildings, other installations like ovens, benches, and jar sockets did survive. Why not an altar? Much broken pottery survived as well, almost all of it typically domestic. Should there not be represented some special pieces like libation stands?

On the criterion of structural layout, Toombs observed the multifunctional character of the complexes. The northern sector does not yield to a sacred interpretation (contra G. R. H. Wright 1975) but seems instead to be warehouse space or spacious rooms; this accords with Rudolf Naumann's criteria for palace complexes (1971: 389).

Toombs underscored the inconclusive character of the analogies to other courtyard sanctuary complexes; they are later in date and oblique in cultural connection. The comparable structure at Beth-shan is itself a multifunctional complex that includes a temple and a *maṣṣebah* within it. The analogies are not (G. E. Wright agreed) compelling. At best, they give an opening for conjecture.

Concerning position in the city, Toombs observes that an acropolis typically contains a palace. It is clear that an acropolis is what the precinct set off by Wall 900 and the northwestern fortifications constitutes. Temples *can* be found on an acropolis but may also be found elsewhere in town—a probable sanctuary of the Late Bronze Age was found outside the acropolis in Field IX, while more than one temple sits on the acropolis in MB IIC (the Fortress Temple and the 7300 temple), and the Tananir candidate as a sanctuary is outside town to the southeast. Typically in architecture of the Near East, the acropolis, elevated and upwind, is related to the palace, not the sacred precinct.

As for functional continuity, what seems to perdure is not simply a temple—the Fortress Temple—but a multifunctional acropolis. It is the whole public precinct that shows continuity. At the same time, it is not certain that there are perduring cultic structures. Toombs observed that the case for the lasting character of the "central court" in the courtyard complex is weaker than it might appear, especially when we recognize the changes made in two courts of Stratum XVIII that added cubicles in the southwest corners. Furthermore, evidence that the 909/910 complex carried continuity through Stratum XVII from the complexes of XX-XVIII to the Fortress Temple complex is missing and must be conjectured.

Toombs concluded that the *balance of likelihood* lies with seeing the courtyard complexes as the city's palaces. A second, *substantially less likely* possibility is that some part of the complex served a cultic purpose (G. R. H. Wright's proposal). That is often the case in known Near Eastern palaces. Which room(s) had cultic use remains for Toombs uncertain. Toombs considered it *very unlikely* that the whole structure constitutes a temple (G. E. Wright's hypothesis). *Least likely* for Toombs, is that the complex contains nothing but residences for the city's nobility.

Some countering considerations to Toombs' analysis have emerged:

1) To judge from other sanctuary locations at Shechem, it appears that isolated pillar bases, existing pillars, and *maṣṣeboth* are a Shechem hallmark. Biblical texts about Shechem sanctuaries mention standing stones (Josh. 24:26; Judg. 9:6[?]), and G. E. Wright appropriately insisted that the biblical tradition is part of the evidence in archaeological interpretation. Isolated pillar bases in the Central Court do suggest a cultic function. In his recent corpus of sanctuaries, G. R. H. Wright cites instances dating from MB and LB from Kamid el-Loz, Qatna, and Tel Mevorakh in addition to Beth-shan, where freestanding pillars are part of sanctuary architecture (1985: II, 138–40, 149, 151). This evidence calls into question the evaluation "substantially less likely" for the palace-plus-sanctuary option.

2) Functional continuity of sacred location is ranked of least weight by Toombs (cf. Fowler 1981). But at Shechem, the Fortress Temple, the Tell er-Ras sanctuaries, and probably the 7300 complex and Tananir complexes, exemplify the phenomenon that hallowed space is remembered over time and through change. This argument deserves a higher weighting. On the other hand, even a perduring holy site has to have started at some point in time. Did Shechem's tradition start with the Fortress Temple or with something in the Courtyard Complex? The argument of continuity is most compelling when it begins from a known sanctuary and tries to assess successors; it is less compelling when it reasons back in time from a known sanctuary to its predecessors.

3) What features properly go with a sanctuary? For that matter, what is "natural" to domestic complexes or to palaces? Stager and Wolff (1981) have established that an olive press next to the

sanctuary at Tel Dan is singularly appropriate to a sanctuary precinct. Based on data gathered from Nahariyah, Hazor, Taanach, and other sites, they buttress their case by mentioning other installations appropriate to sacred complexes, such as pottery-making and metal-casting facilities. Indeed, a workshop to make ceramic votive vessels may be more appropriate to a sanctuary than a domestic pottery installation would be to a palace. The same can be said of a metal-casting facility, where cultic furnishings might have been crafted. Such facilities appear to explain conditions found in Rooms 16 and 17 of the Stratum XIX complex. Questions about what is natural to a sanctuary will also apply to understanding the Tananir complex described in the next chapter.

The question of the courtyard complexes is still open; for the present writer, the balance of probability has tipped to favor Toombs's second option, that of a cultic unit within a multifunctional complex—a mediating position which would satisfy many of G. E. Wright's hunches about features in the Field VI materials, and validate G. R. H. Wright's proposal.

MB IIB Domestic Housing

The acropolis and fortification system on the west of the tell show a succession of changes all of which fall within the MB IIB period as the Joint Expedition has proposed to define it (i.e., separate from "MB IIC" and covering roughly 1750–1650 BCE). These changes cover the period of Strata XX to XVII at the west, but correlation to fortification and acropolis rebuilds can only be posited. In many cases, changes in the domestic housing may represent local rehabilitation at need.

Field IX. Approximately 45 m away from the nearest point of the acropolis, Field IX presents a succession of MB II strata, showing three distinct architectural developments, two of which have sub-phases, followed by two phases of accumulation without architecture. These five layers, local phases 17–13, cover the period from the beginning of MB IIB to the beginning of LB IB. The stratigraphy is in very thin debris layers, and there are intrusions due to robbing of walls and digging of pits from later periods. Provisionally, the lower two layerings in Field IX, constituting local phases 17 and 16 with their sub-phases, are assigned to MB IIB (equivalent to site Strata XX-XVII), while local phase 15 is assigned to MB IIC and connected to site Strata XVI and XV; local phases 14 and 13 seem to follow the destruction at the end of the Middle Bronze Age.

Local phase 17, tentatively equated with Stratum XX on the acropolis, is best discerned in relation to Wall 9623 at the eastern edge of the excavated field (Ill. 125). Wall 9623 had layer 9626 (merged with 9627) reaching to its foundation (Ill. 145 = IX EE:##78–77), the soil which lay directly upon Stratum XXI soil and in some cases could not be differentiated from the top of Stratum XXI. Pottery from 9626 (69 indicators saved) was field analyzed as MB IIA with a small admixture of MB IIB. On this layer, a surface (EE:#76) was traced from the poorly preserved collapse of Wall 9901 to Wall 9623 (Ill. 141 = IX AA:#101). Over this surface, there accumulated a series of soil layerings which were ill-defined in the field; they are loci 9618, 9618A, 9619, 9620 and 9625, here collapsed into locus 9620 (EE:#74). Pottery from this soil (100 indicators saved) showed many MB IIA characteristics, along with MB IIB (and the usual mix of Chalcolithic/EB I).

Wall 9623 was at least 1.75 m wide; its eastern face lay unexposed in the east balk of the field. Its west face was of very large field stones (shown in elevation on IX CC), forming a distinct line, while its interior was of somewhat smaller stones. Clearly there was a substantial structure lying to the east of Field IX, of which only the western edge was touched in this excavation. As Ill. 125 shows, two thin lines of stones, 9621 and 9622, define what is probably a drain to the west of Wall 9623; they appear on IX EE, interrupting layer #76. The line of flow was northward, opposite the natural slope of the mound. The drain was founded in soil layer 9626 and has 9620 soil covering it. Fig. 89 indicates cover stones over the far south end, at the confluence of 9623 and 9621. Taken together, the result was a mass of stones some 3.00 m wide at the south balk—note its depiction at the left margin of IX AA.

Soil layers 9626 and 9620 carried through into Area 4 as layers 9895A and 9895B, and reached the foundation of mudbrick-on-stone Wall 9901,

Fig. 89. Drain in Field IX, its edges made of Walls 9621 and 9622, with cover stones at its south end. Wide Wall 9623 is to its east (left).

Fig. 90. White and red bricks on top of stones of Wall 9611.

which probably extended the entire north–south width of the excavated plot. Ill. 125 displays the possible layout of spaces in Area 4, but the evidence is scant. Traces of a wall foundation beneath Wall 9880A are taken to define a Wall 9902 perpendicular to 9901, and similar traces at the south balk are taken to be an extension of 9901 to the south edge (see Ill. 142 = IX BB and Ill. 141 = IX AA). Wall 9904 was equally uncertain, but a segment of plaster Surface 9897B was preserved in the southwest corner of the area. Another small segment of flooring was discerned west of Wall 9901, on which sat the outline of an oven. If this marked an exterior courtyard, one can reconstruct a set of small rooms with entries as indicated on the plan, but there is a great deal of conjecture involved.

The failure to record elevations throughout this complex means that there may be sub-phases in local layer 17 (Stratum XX). As in Area 3, so also in the west of Area 4, locus numbers were assigned to changes in character in the soil. Loci 9895B, 9903, 9905 and 9907 correspond to 9626 and the walls previously described were all laid into this layer. Loci 9900, 9899, 9897A, 9897, 9896, and 9895A correspond to 9620, and came to the walls. On Ill. 145 = the IX EE section, it proved impossible to separate these loci (EE:#77, west of Wall 9901) A mudbrick similar to those built into Wall 9901 lay in 9900. In general, the field readings of pottery (58 indicators saved) discern more contacts with MB IIA in the lower layers, while assigning the upper layers clearly to MB IIB (91 indicators saved). Definition of Stratum XX in Field IX is less than satisfactory, while at the same time its loci may be definitive of the transition from MB IIA to MB IIB.

While the system just described may with confidence be connected with Stratum XX at the start, from this point on to the end of the Middle Bronze Age in Field IX layering is hard to correlate with the stratigraphy on the acropolis. Local changes can take place in any one building complex any time, for instance when a house changes hands or when the birth of a new generation requires reallocation of living space.

The architecture of subsequent phases of MB IIB is shown in Ills. 126 and 127. Ill. 126 shows the next phase of occupation, roughly equivalent to Strata XIX and XVIII. Wall 9623 along the east was rebuilt as Stone Wall 9611A, as wide as its predecessor and with a similar rubble core. Stone Wall 9607A bonded with 9611A, and extended into Area 4 as Wall 9880A. This wall cornered with the extremely poorly preserved Wall 9898 running into the north balk, and extending southward as the mostly robbed wall-line 9894. Wall 9898 was parallel to 9901 of the preceding phase, built flush to the west face of 9901, emerging on IX EE as the lowest course of a poorly preserved wall that was almost completely robbed out at the end of MB IIB. The region west of Wall 9898 was an open yard. The top of soil layer 9899 (IX EE:#75) blanketing Stratum XX remains under this yard probably served as the Stratum XIX surface.

Stone Walls 9898, 9880A, 9607A and a possible wall fragment poorly preserved in the balk between areas 3 and 4 at the south defined the house between the west wall of the larger building to the east and the yard on the west. Flooring is attested as chalky Surface 9893, shown on Ill. 141 = IX AA:#101 running from Wall 9611A to a hump of mudbrick and one stone making up Wall 9894, and on Ill. 142 = IX BB as the top of #85. A curious socket with lined channel set in this surface is shown on the plan; its point of entry into the south balk is indicated on IX AA as a dip in #101. The butt end of a stone and brick wall, 9619A, which seems to have belonged to this complex obtrudes from the south balk in the southwest corner of Area 3, depicted on IX AA but not on the plan.

With the addition of mudbrick Walls 9617A and 9807A, the plan of the second phase of the complex comes into view, perhaps equivalent to Stratum XVIII on the acropolis. The house then came to have four rooms. A thin beaten earth layer (IX EE:#71) over pebbly makeup #72 west of Wall 9898 belonged to this sub-phase. It ran to the edges of the robbed upper part of Wall 9898, originally of mudbrick. Apparently, when Wall 9898 was robbed only the stones and brick were removed, since the edges of the robber pit still retained slabs of plaster from the faces of the wall. Eastward from the robbery, Surface 9885 could be traced (IX EE:#70) to the remains of Wall 9617A, with slabs of plaster sloping into the subsidence of what may have been the wall's foundation trench. Plaster continued eastward from 9617A to 9611A. Floor 9886 (IX AA:#99) rode on a 0.30 m thick layer of ashy brown soil over Stratum XIX Floor 9893 (IX AA:#101).

For the final MB IIB phase in Field IX, local layer 15 taken as roughly equivalent to Stratum XVII, Wall 9611 was topped with bricks, nearly square, ca. 0.40 m by 0.15 m thick. They were white and reddish brown, laid in alternating rows (fig. 90). Walls 9607-9880 and 9878 were also of brick on stone foundation, but the bricks of the superstructure were not clearly articulated; the tops of these two walls may in fact have been of molded mud. The clear mark of the position of Wall 9889 completed a pattern of five rooms with well-defined floorings (Ill. 127). The western yard of the earlier phases had now been incorporated into the house.

The doorposts and threshold of the door connecting Rooms A and B were well-preserved. Plaster coated both doorposts and continued along the wall faces on either side of the door in both rooms; the plaster curved at the base of the walls and ran on as the floor.

Room A extended into Area 4 along the north face of Wall 9607-9880. West of the door and flush against Wall 9607 was Brick Platform 9616, shown in fig. 91; the bricks were arranged in a pattern of alternating colors, producing a parquet effect. They rested on Floor 9614, which filled the room, at elevation 6.57–6.60; at left center in the photograph are two holes in the plaster, ca. 0.20 m in diameter, filled with wood ash. Shown in section on fig. 92, they probably represent post-holes for something suspended either beside or over the platform—a covering or a spit. One of the holes ran at a slight angle, so the uprights were not quite vertical. A thin layer of ash on the platform supports the conclusion that 9616 is a hearth.

Fig. 91. Brick platform 9616, in parquet style.

On Floor 9614 in the corner of Walls 9607 and 9611 was the installation shown in fig. 93 and on the plan. It was made of bricks standing on end, and the faces at least of the west line were plastered. Its interior measured between 2.00 and 2.20 m north–south; it was ca. 0.50 m wide inside, tapering at its south end. A hole was near its south end, 0.10 m in diameter and full of wood ash, again slightly off vertical. How the hearth and this installation related is enigmatic, as is how the post holes related. There was a concentration of ash in and on the odd brick installation.

In the small triangle of Room B within the excavation field, there was another brick construction, of two layers of brick, resembling the hearth in Room A, although not enough was preserved to be sure it was a second hearth. It was located against the south face of 9607 and just east of the

Fig. 92. Post hole scars shown in section, adjacent to 9616.

Fig. 93. Installation on Floor 9614, constructed of upright bricks with their faces plastered.

doorway in Room B, reaching nearly to Wall 9611 (IX AA in the midst of #93; fig. 94). Room B showed the same use of plaster as in Room A. That there would be two hearths in adjacent rooms of a single-family dwelling seems odd. Perhaps the complex was a two-family dwelling with Wall 9607 serving as a party wall.

The walls of Room C showed plastering similar to that in Rooms A and B, continuous from wall face to Floor 9881 (fig. 95). The base of a store jar was preserved set into the thinly plastered floor (fig. 96). This photograph also shows the nature of the *ḥuwwar* surface of Floor 9882 in the west portion of Room A, running to the edge of rebuilt but robbed-out Wall 9889 (IX EE:#66), and the thick plaster of Floor 9888 in Room E in the upper left. In Room E, there was a resurfacing during Stratum XVII, an upper thicker plaster layer

Fig. 94. Vertical face at south edge of Room B, showing bricks of a second possible brick platform.

Fig. 95. Looking east in Field IX, Area 4, at Wall 9878 (meter stick is lying on it). Note the plaster line in the balk at right margin; Wall 9878 was covered with mud brick and then plastered on its face.

over a lower thinner one (IX EE:#67). Room D in the southwest corner of the complex was interrupted by Pit 9879A, but also showed a patch of poorly defined flooring.

The Field IX Stratum XVII complex was violently destroyed, though there was not a heavy mass of destruction debris. White and red-brown bricks from Wall 9611 were found on the floor at the north edge of the northeastern room. Ash overlay all of Room A, on the parquet hearth and the elongated brick installation. A whole store jar was crushed on the floor near the parquet hearth, one of its handles bearing the distinctive stamp shown in fig. 97.

There appears not to have been rebuild in Field IX during MB IIC; erosion during subsequent Strata XVI and XV probably removed further evidence of the destruction of Stratum XVII.

Field XIII. The end of MB IIB Shechem is

Fig. 96. Looking north in Area 4 of Field IX. Note the mark of robbed Wall 9889, separating plaster floorings of Rooms A and E (9882=9877A and 9888, respectively). The scraps of Wall 9880 separate these from Room C in which the base of a storage jar is set.

attested also by the domestic remains in Field XIII, Area 6. For the MB IIB period, the northern limit of the acropolis is unknown. Wall 943, built near the beginning of MB IIC in Stratum XVI, was not yet in existence to serve as the north limit of the acropolis. Stone Wall 3906 (Ills. 147 and 167) may have served that purpose; it was 0.50 m wide and preserved for at least eight courses of roughly shaped rocks selected to fit that width. The top of 3906 was at the elevation of the footing of Wall 943, and the layer of small stones (locus 3908) serving as the bedding for Wall 943 was retained by the uppermost courses of Wall 3906.

Wall 3906 did not continue eastwards along the line of Wall 943, however. Adjacent to its east preserved end was a building with mudbrick walls shown in Ill. 147. Three mudbrick walls, 3901, 3901E and 3901W contained a small portion of a room extending northwards out of the excavated field. Walls 3901 and 3901W were 1.10 m thick and preserved from one meter to almost two meters high; the thickness of 3901E was not ascertained, since it extends beyond the limit of excavation.

Within the room, Room A, the stratigraphy can be followed on Ill. 166 = XIII KK. The earliest certain flooring was 3948, of packed earth, laid over a dark brown earth makeup at the lowest point reached by excavation (KK:#30). In the southwest corner, on Floor 3948, was built the tannur shown in BASOR 205:fig. 7. It was circular, domed, lined with large store jar sherds, and ca. 0.50 m in diameter.

There built up during the subsequent years a succession of floorings displayed in XIII KK: Floor 3945 over a thin layer of ashy soil at elevation 13.57 (#29), Floor 3942 over ca. 0.10 m of reddish brown soil (#28), Floor 3939 over ca. 0.40 m of compact brown soil with broken brick and charcoal ingredients (#25), and Floor 3938 over a thin ashy layer (#23), five floorings within the room. On the uppermost floor was locus 3932 (#22), 0.07 to 0.20 m of black, ashy debris, topped by striated brown soil 0.25 m thick (#21) that looks to be erosion material. All of the floorings adjoined the sides of the tannur, accumulating over 0.75 m of soil to near its top. The oven was in use throughout, to judge from the ashy deposits on the adjacent floorings; the buildup gave the oven increasing insulation. As Seger has noted, these data speak to the question of whether such ovens were let down into floors or positioned on them; the answer seems to be "both."

West of Mudbrick Wall 3901W was Room B, defined by Mudbrick Wall 3901W and Stone Wall 3906. Here the only discerned flooring was Floor 3941 (XIII KK: top of #13) at elevation 13.78. It is only slightly higher in elevation than the lowest surface in Room A. Over Floor 3941 in Room B was a deep mass of layered destruction debris as much as 1.30 m thick, shown on KK:##7-12 and XIII LL (Ill. 167). A slab of roofing plaster 0.10 m thick, along with spills of ḥuwwar and ash, characterize the debris. Section XIII LL suggests that the north face of Wall 3906 may have collapsed northward. After the destruction, slump from Wall 3901W accumulated (KK:#6), again suggesting erosion. Pottery on the floors of both rooms and in the destruction debris was late MB IIB in date. Stratigraphically, this glimpse of a ruined house belonged to Stratum XVII, with the possibility that it reached back into Stratum XVIII.

Something calamitous ended the life of Shechem around 1650 BCE, calling for a major shift

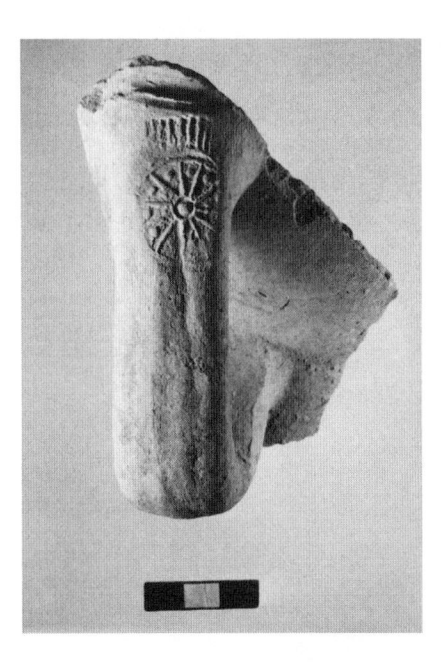

Fig. 97. Handle from a complete storage jar crushed near parquet platform of hearth 9616, with stamp impression and possible marks of quantity.

in fortifications, in the layout on the acropolis, and in domestic precincts. The massive earth movement and filling at the fortifications and in the public precinct, in preparation for Stratum XVI, apparently removed much of the evidence of destruction; it is in the two small locations where domestic housing was reached that the evidence of violent destruction is most vivid. Equally important is the evidence of at least a brief period of erosion during abandonment, before preparations for MB IIC Shechem were begun.

CHAPTER 3

THE MIDDLE BRONZE IIC PERIOD

THE SITE OF ANCIENT SHECHEM UNDERWENT a major and widespread change at a point midway through its existence as a fortified urban center in the Middle Bronze II period. A new perimeter was established which added a substantial amount of protected space within the city; accesses through the fortifications were built in locations different from where they had been in the preceding era; the acropolis was conceived in a new way, even though the sanctity of one particular location appears to have been maintained; and housing within the city spread out to cover the newly enclosed space. All of this leads the Joint Expedition staff to defend the hypothesis of a third major development within MB II, itself in two phases, for which it retains the designation MB IIC.

Strata XVI and XV mark the fifth and sixth separable units within the urban phase of MB II, and the site presents eight strata (XXII-XV) within the larger MB II, from a point well along in MB IIA to the end of the period, roughly the three and one-half centuries from 1900 to 1540 BCE. Efforts to reduce the number of strata, for example by bringing Stratum XV or some parts of it down into the Late Bronze Age (Kenyon 1971:18), have not done justice to the data from the site and have been refuted by Seger (1974).

Because Stratum XV displays continuity as it develops upon Stratum XVI, the description given here will carry through both strata in each facet of the city's life: the fortifications, the public buildings, and the domestic precincts.

THE FORTIFICATIONS: STRATUM XVI

Wall A

What Thiersch first noticed when he identified the site in 1903 was an exposed segment of wall made of huge boulders: the Cyclopean Wall, here designated Wall A. Sellin (1914a:36) measured its exposed exterior height before excavation at 2.55 m and the length at 15.20 m; he began by tracing it along its northwestern arc to the Northwest Gate, and, at least at one location, dug to its base, giving its overall height as 6.50m. In the summer campaign of 1926 he dug another vertical shaft against its exterior, and measured it as 8.50 m high to a footing on natural rock (1926b:320). Welter gives both 8.00 and 10.00 m as the height of the wall in his reports on work from 1928 to 1931. There are ten to twelve courses of Wall A proper south of the Northwest Gate, topped with three to four courses which were added when the 7300 complex was built. The total height presently visible at the site is 9.60 m.

In September, 1913, the architect Praschniker measured the run of Wall A by tape (fig. 98). He then drew a section (fig. 99) which shows a vertical rise of 7.25 m, displays the batter of the wall, and gives an early indication of the thickness. It shows the top course to be 2.30 m thick and to consist of two large rocks at the faces, two smaller rocks in the core. Sellin dug sufficiently deep inside the wall to observe that the interior face was uneven and not dressed, drawing the conclusion that the interior was not exposed. Welter's 1928 section (Ill. 10) shows that he excavated to its interior foot. On it, Wall A is 2.00 m wide at the top, widening to almost 4.00 m at the base. It suggests that the interior face is vertical and the top stone a single piece.

The American team's only exposures of the interior face are shown in a 1.80 m deep section of Field V Area 7, dug in 1962 (Ill. 68), and in two sections north and south of the Northwest Gate

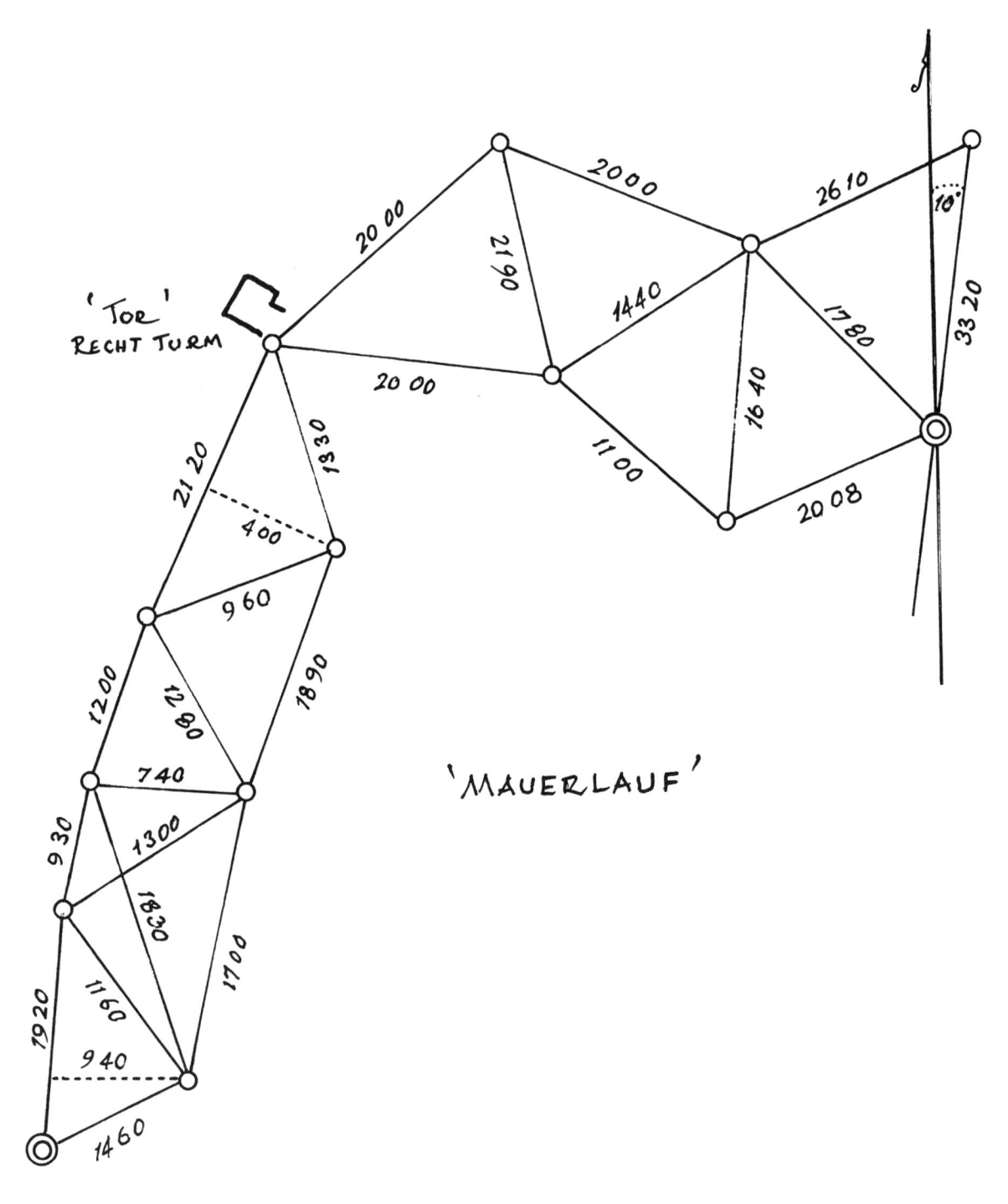

Fig. 98. Praschniker's measurements of the course of Wall A, by taped distances, from his notebook, dated Sept. 17, 1913.

dug in 1972 and 1973 (Ills. 58 and 59 = IV EE and FF). The interior face is uneven, and it slants inward. The 1962 section shows the top of Wall A 1.70 m wide, consisting of three stones. Observations made in February and March, 1994, are pertinent to the top of the wall. South of the complex Sellin called the palace, in Complex 7300 to be described later as one of the MB IIC public buildings, three boulders of what was probably the original top of the wall now lie exposed. All three are

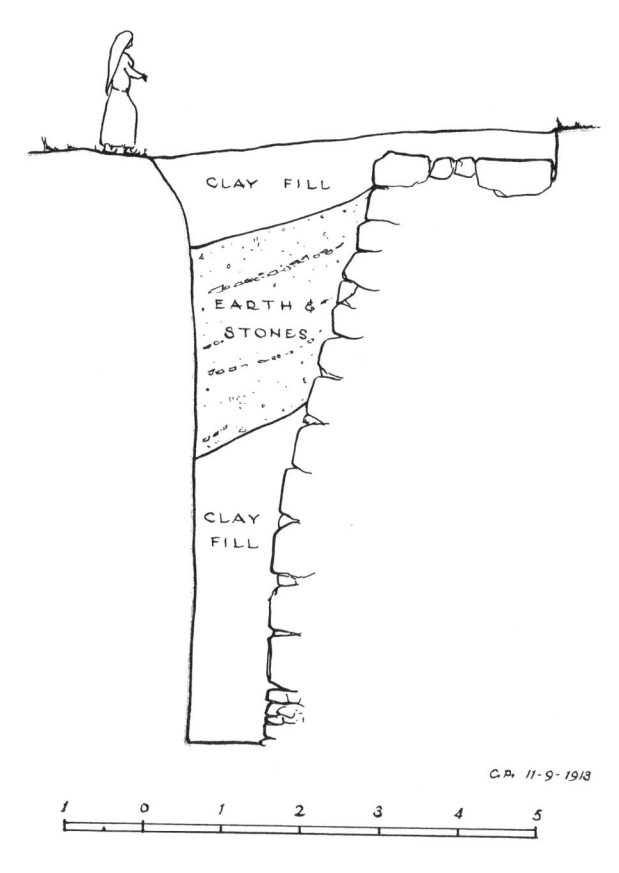

Fig. 99. Section based on the work of C. Praschniker in 1913 against the exterior face of Wall A, showing the batter of the wall and the tiplines of fill against it.

trimmed on the exterior face. One is 1.88 m long by 1.67 m wide by 0.38 m thick, the longest dimension lying through the wall. It is widest at the face of the wall and tapers almost to a point on the interior. Another is 1.55 m by 1.29 m by 0.44 m, and the third is 1.10 m by 1.66 m by 0.63 m. In sheer bulk, they approach the size of the largest boulders in the lowermost courses of Wall A. The builders levered giant stones into position all the way to the topmost course.

G. E. Wright noted that Welter had cleared the face of the wall to its foundation prior to Wright's first visit to Shechem in 1934 (*SBBC*:57). Welter exposed some of it in 1928 when he first clarified the succession of fortifications and drew the section incorporated in Ill. 10. By 1931, he had severed the connection between the deep deposit of soil that had accumulated against the wall's face all along the northwest from the gateway south, but made no drawings of what he found.

Boulders in the wall are massive, some as much as 2.20 m in length. Their faces have been rough dressed so as to present a relatively smooth and flush face, lacking projections that might have given purchase for a prying engine. The wall is not evenly coursed; the builders seem to have used natural boulders shed by the slopes of Mt. Ebal, mostly *nari* limestone which here does not lie in uniformly thick beds. Smaller stones chink the interstices; Welter speaks also of clay mortar.

The profiles show the batter, less pronounced in the lowermost courses, but reaching 15 degrees as it nears the top. The result is a lean into the mound of about a meter off vertical (correcting *SBBC*:57, where the measurement is given as 1.60 m). The "natural rock" Sellin spoke of at the foundation is a layer of *hamra* or packed clay, mixed with small stones, riding on bedrock. Sellin's plans show two drain openings in the face of the wall, the drains running from the underpinnings of the Fortress Temple. They are 1.00 m high and 0.45 m across, and emerge high on its face at the fifth to eighth courses, 5.00 or more meters above the foundation. A 1926 drawing by Heinz Johannes shows one such opening, its base at the level of excavation at the time. Whether it is one of the two Sellin found is unclear but there are three openings visible; no record from Sellin indicates the internal character of these drains, nor were explorations by James F. Ross of the Joint Expedition fruitful in discerning much about them.

Fields IV and V (Ills. 10, 52, 58–59, 68). On the northwest, Wall A was founded at the foot of the augmented earthen embankment of the C Rampart System. South of the Northwest Gate, the embankment sloped down at an angle of 40 degrees (Ills. 10, 68 and 59). Apparently the builders erected the wall a course or two at a time, filling in behind it with horizontal layers of soil as the wall grew in height. The horizontal layers probably served as construction platforms for each succeeding course, along which the stones could be rolled and levered into position. Frequently the layering in the fill shows small stones consolidating the platforms, a phenomenon to be encountered again at the East Gate. At the end of the pro-

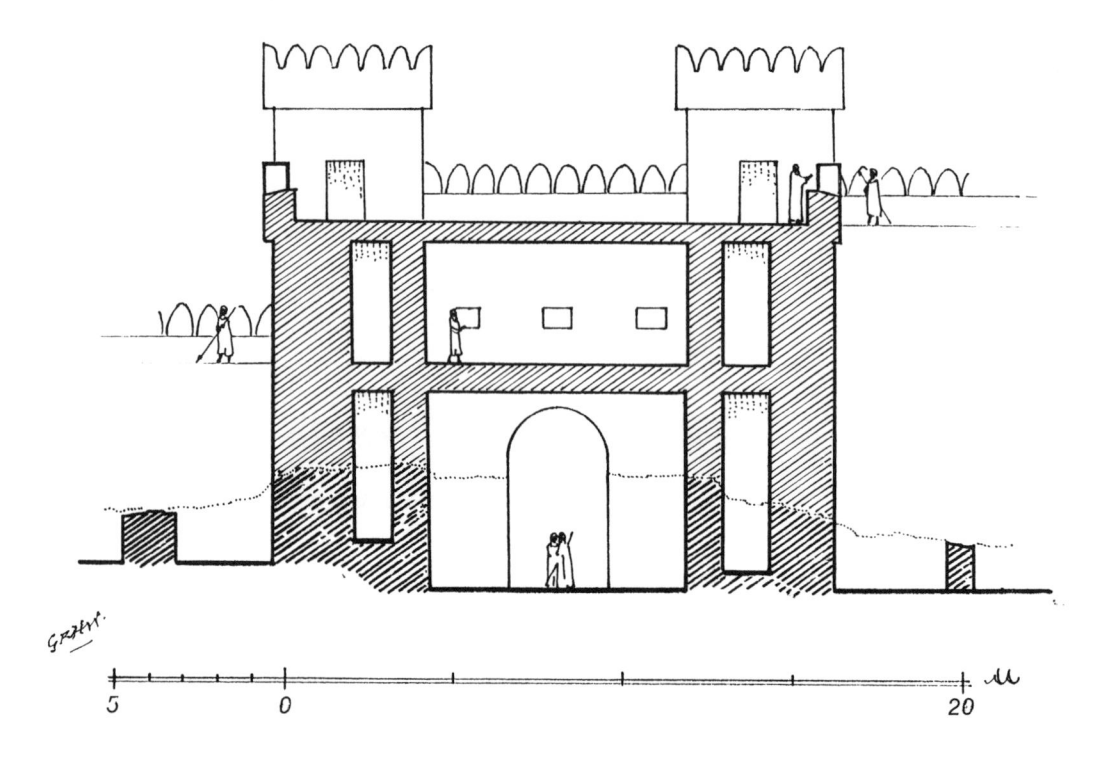

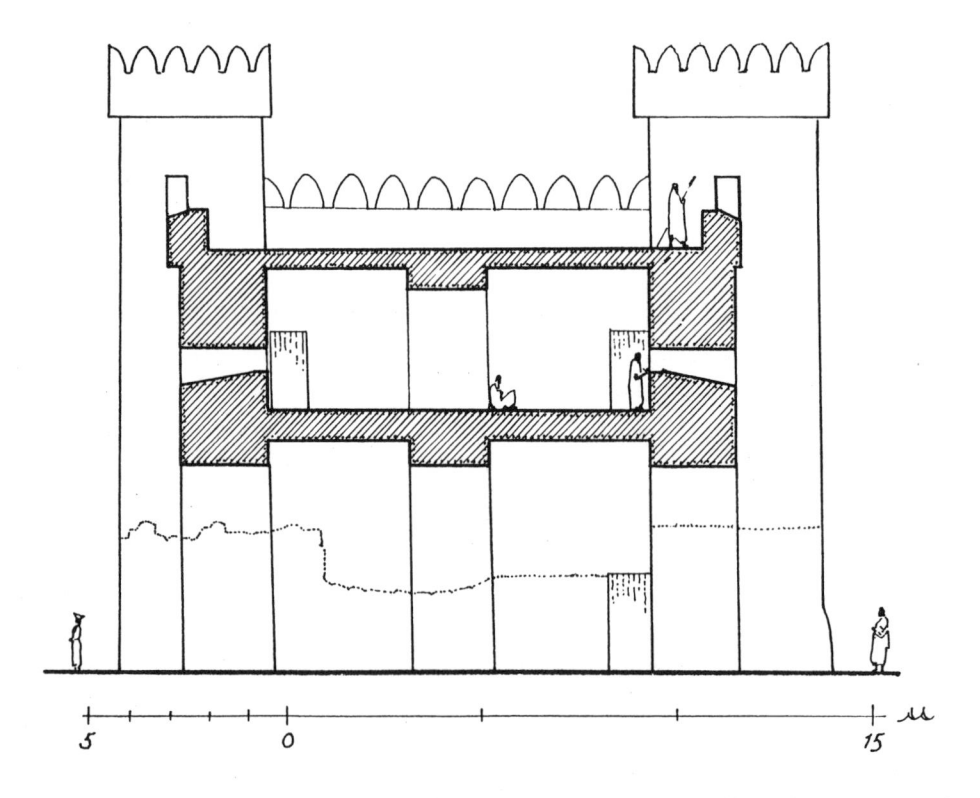

Fig. 100. *Schematic reconstructions of the Northwest Gate: longitudinally- and cross-sectioned.*

cess, the earth inside the wall was at or near the elevation of its top.

Dever's trench dug in 1973 across the fortification system south of the gate encountered two segments of the slope of the C Rampart ("Phase 4") and three or more layers of the fill thrown in to level up against the interior of Wall A (Dever 1974:39–41; Ill. 59 = IV FF:##13, 12, 11, 10). At the top of this accumulation was packed plaster floor 7318 (#9), 0.25 m thick at some places and extending inward from Wall A for more than 10.00 m to the point where it could be traced no farther, beneath the inner line (Wall 7311B) of Casemate Wall E. A similar plaster surface appears as the thin layer above the one designated "grey" at the top of the fill in Ill. 68, more than 40 m south along Wall A. This plastered surface defined what was probably an open plaza extending from the Northwest Gate southward along the wall. Near the gate Dever found a stone podium measuring 1.15 m by 2.40 m, covered with plaster; his proposal that this was the altar of an open air shrine is supported by the fact that the altar of the 7300 sanctuary was built directly upon it in Stratum XV. In Stratum XVI times, the open plaza probably filled the entire space between the top of Wall A and the Fortress Temple.

Northeast of the Northwest Gate, the picture differs. Wall A has a sawtooth style of construction, the first segment of which is shown in Ill. 52. The first segment was ca. 9.50 m long, and runs on a straight line. The plan suggests another straight segment of ca. 10.00 m, extending to a shift in the wall's direction more to the east; observations on the top of the wall in 1994 discerned a possible second sawtooth 4.00 m farther along from that point, 14.00 m from the first sawtooth. This style of wall construction is paralleled at Shiloh and other sites (Ussishkin 1989); Shechem combined in one system two different building concepts, the sawtooth style on the north and the curving battered style south of the gate.

Dever dug a salvage sounding across the system north of the gate in October, 1972 (1974:31–34). The trench crossed what Sellin had seen as the northeast wing of a "palace," its southern wing on the other side of the gate. Dever concluded Wall A here stood at first only about 3.00 m high. He encountered what he termed "Glacis B," locus 72.125 (Ill. 58 = IV EE between #36 and #37), sloping at an angle less severe than that south of the gate, reaching if extrapolated to just above the foot of the inner face of Wall A. It now seems more likely that 72.125, like the slope south of the gate, is the top of the augmented C Rampart.

Above it, tiplines of chalk and rubbish built up to a second sloping surface, Glacis A = locus 7276, which would have run if extrapolated to the top of the original Wall A. During the time of this build-up, Tower 7287 was installed, extending from Wall 7287 at the top of the slope in IV EE to Wall 72.119, 2.60 m east of it; the two were connected by a surface discerned close to Wall 7287, Floor 7291, and possibly by a resurfacing, locus 7293a, at 0.40 m above the first surface. Sloping tiplines of stony debris continued to build up from the tower down to Wall A, reaching as high as the heap of tumbled stone (locus 7285) on top of Wall 7287. Tower, slope and the lower part of Wall A constituted the first complex of Stratum XVI fortification on the northern arc of the city.

Still within Stratum XVI, defense Wall B/2 = locus 72.106B, was founded on the crest of the slope, nullifying Tower 7287, using Glacis 7276 sloping to the top of Wall A as a part of a double defense system (compare Field III, Walls 657 and 655 described below). This new arrangement, Dever's "Phase 4" constituting Stratum XVIA, was drastically destroyed.

Wall B was rebuilt on the base of the Stratum XVI Wall B/2 as what is designated B/1 = 72.106A. Wall A was heightened by the addition of ca. 4.00 m of stones smaller than those used in the lower portion. The transition from Stratum XVI to Stratum XV goes with this rebuild after the destruction. This accords with evidence from Fields I and III (below). The transition from the Wall A-plus-Tower 7287 defense to the double system of Wall A and an inner wall on the line of what would become Wall B was a development within Stratum XVI, correlating with changes in the A system in Fields I and III. The basic relationship between Wall B and Wall A was sustained throughout the entire northern half-circuit of the mound from the Northwest Gate to the East Gate: Wall A existed alone for a period of time before Wall B was added to strengthen the system of defense.

The Northwest Gate (Ills. 48–49, 56–57). Sellin's discernment of the gate in Wall A came in his first two seasons, 1913 and 1914. Its south tower projected out from the line of Wall A by 4.99 m, the north tower by 4.30 m; the edifice adapted to conditions and was not symmetrical (Ill. 48). It fit into a curve in the wall, so it necessarily narrowed from outside to inside. It was 18.30 m deep and tapered in width from 16.80 m at the outer entrance to 16.20 m at the inner. Its foundations were in a good state of preservation when Sellin found them, with mudbrick superstructure preserved upon the stone foundations, the foundations standing 1.80 to 2.00 m (Ill. 56). G. R. H. Wright has drawn proposed reconstructions of the gate in fig. 100.

Sellin removed almost all the soil from the interior. Depredations and weathering since 1914 have removed most of the brick and some of the foundation blocks, but bricks remain *in situ* on the forward towers. They are ca. 0.38 by 0.38 by 0.10–0.12 m in size, some pinkish-white and some red. Red bricks predominated in the north tower, the lighter-colored ones in the south. On the northern tower, a horizontal layer of hard plaster topped the stone foundation and the bricks rode on it. The bricks were laid with mortar, and were positioned in stacks one squarely above the other, not overlapping as might be expected.

The flanking towers ran the full depth of the gate, the south one 5.50 m wide in exterior measure tapering to 4.60 m, the north one 4.90 m wide and also tapering, but with its interior end destroyed (Ill. 49). Jutting from the flanking towers were three sets of piers, permitting three blockings of the entrance. The piers were made up of large orthostats (Ills. 56 and 57). Slabs the size of the vertically set orthostats were also laid horizontally at points in the tower foundations.

The 1966 campaign of the Joint Expedition discovered that flagstones originally paved the inner chambers of the gate. Flagstones ran under the interior lateral wall of the north tower at the inside of the outer piers, showing that this wall was constructed after the pavement was laid. The gate may originally have been asymmetrical, having a deep recess between the piers on the north side, shallow rooms between piers on the south. How long this layout lasted before the lateral wall was built and the north tower was made to correspond to the south one is impossible to tell given the complete clearance and disturbed condition of the remains. One pertinent consideration is that the walls of the 7200 complex, built late in the developments of the A system, were bonded into the northernmost wall of the gate, suggesting a major refurbishing.

Sellin discerned in the narrow passage of the southern tower evidence of a ramp running upwards from west to east, and surmised that it gave access to the trapezoidal room in the corner formed by Wall A and the gate tower, a room whose floor is at site elevation 20.25, nearly 0.75 m higher than the elevation on the gate entryway (variously 19.51, 19.53 and 19.64). Joint Expedition probes in this south gate chamber in 1966 found evidence of the ramp, but found Late Bronze pottery sealed in its makeup, pointing to an LB rebuild of the gate in Stratum XIV. The trapezoidal room probably served another purpose in Stratum XV, as the third room of tripartite Temple 7300, to be described below.

G. E. Wright (*SBBC*:59–61) presented a description of the gate piers and how they were closed based on what the Joint Expedition had discerned through its 1962 campaign. It is paraphrased in the next four paragraphs, with updated measurements and added information from the 1966 campaign.

As noted, three opposing pairs of piers jutted inward from the towers on each side. The flanks of these piers consisted of huge limestone blocks, selected from bedded limestone and smoothed, and set so there is a slot between them. The slots were plugged with debris from the collapse of the gate superstructure, or they may have been intentionally plugged when the gate was refurbished in LB. The outermost pair of piers, shown in Ill. 57, left an entryway 2.80 m wide, while the piers were ca. 2.00 m deep. Though the stone floors of the side chambers and the underpinnings of the piers were found excellently preserved by Sellin, there were no sockets for an upright doorpost to swivel in on either side of the entryway.

Fig. 101. The bank of earth against the exterior of Wall A as it looked in 1960. There is no indication of sectioning through it by Sellin or Welter.

It would seem, then, that the system involved sliding doors. To close the entrance, one slid a thick wooden door from each slot out to meet its mate at the midpoint of the entryway. For the front pair of piers this would mean that about 1.40 m of each door would have been exposed, while about 0.50 to 0.60 of each would have remained anchored in the slot. The top inside edge of the stone foundation of the southern front pier had a circular groove about 0.08 m in diameter. To strengthen the doors in the face of attack from a battering ram, the gatekeepers would have slid a long bar horizontally across the inner face of the doors and anchored it in this groove. Pushing at the door from the outside would have encountered the whole weight of the pier in which both door and bar were anchored.

The two additional sets of piers at the center and inside of the gate passage would have been closed in similar fashion. At these points, the width of the entryway was 2.85 and 2.95 m respectively, but the piers were correspondingly deeper (compare the two views in Ill. 57). Given the fact that the lower 2.00 m of each pier was built of huge rocks, as large as those in Wall A, and even better fitted, the gate entrances were able to withstand considerable force applied from outside. The exterior projections of the gate towers had foundations 6.00 m deep, doubtless designed to discourage sapping operations.

There are, of course, other ways in which the gate might have been closed. Available comparative information indicates that doors were hung from vertical posts fixed to turn in a stone socket; after the doors were swung closed, a horizontal anchor bar would be slid into place. Another possibility would have involved dropping a wide and thick wooden slab down from above on the analogy of a medieval portcullis. This system would have required the use of ropes passing over a strong horizontal beam fixed in the superstructure of the gate, probably round and suitably lubricated to reduce friction as it rotated. The slab would have been raised and lowered by the gatekeepers, stationed in the room to the northeast of the gate. This system would fit with the slotted piers and would have the advantage that there would be no weakness at the midpoint. It would put considerable strain on the brick superstructure, and there would be no need for the bolt-hole receptacle.

The sliding door theory seems the most probable. Within the gate structure itself, there were side chambers between the piers, the measurements given on Ill. 49. With the gate open, there would have been commerce of various kinds going on in the chambers. With all three sets of doors closed, if attackers breached the outer set they would have been exposed to defensive fire from upper stories of the gate while trying to bring their battering ram to bear on the next set of doors.

In many respects the Northwest Gate of Shechem resembles the MB IIC gate in Area K at Hazor, which gave access through the rampart fortifications of the great lower enclosure (Yadin 1972:60–61; Yadin, et al. 1989:276–301). Built with two flanking towers and three sets of piers like the Shechem gate, its entryway is about 3.00 m wide. The whole structure is wider than it is deep, however: 20.00 by 16.00 m compared to Shechem's 16.20 by 18.30 m. Another difference is that there appears to have been a revetment wall in front of the Hazor gate, making it more comparable to Shechem's East Gate, which is also wider than it is deep but has only two sets of piers.

The Approach to the Northwest Gate. The threshold of the gate was at site elevation 19.67, 5.00 to 6.00 m above the footing of Wall A. Welter (1932:303–4) states, "Eine senkrecht zum Tor verlaufende Rampe, zu beiden Seiten von Mauern eingefasst, führte zum Toreingang, der 5 m über dem Talniveau liegt. Ob am unteren Ende der Rampe ein Vortor liegt, konnte noch nicht fesgestellt werden." ("A ramp, running at a right angle to the gate, was enclosed on both sides by walls. It led to the gate entrance, which lay 5 m higher than the bottom of the valley. It could not yet be ascertained whether an outer gate lay at the lower end of the ramp."—S. H. Horn translation). Welter published no drawing of this ramp, but his claim that it was defined by walls would have been based upon unmistakable evidence, presumably gleaned from his cut along the wall in 1931 and then removed. His having not ascertained the presence or absence of a lower gate suggests that Welter did not cut westward into the standing bank of earth sloping up toward the wall and apparently preserved almost as high as its top (see Welter 1932:Abb.8 on 303–4, and fig. 101).

The Joint Expedition did not excavate the bank of earth outside Wall A on the northwest, nor discern anything that would support Welter's ramp. Visual assessment of the bank where it had been cut by Welter and by Sellin and Steckeweh adjacent to the Northwest Gate (1941:Fig.4; Ussishkin 1989) resulted in G. E. Wright's description of it as a purposeful fill of chalk-filled earth up to a dark streak marking where Sellin had begun excavating; above that, it was assumed to be dump from the Sellin expeditions (*SBBC*:14). When the bulldozer cleared along the wall once more in 1972, Dever noted (communication to the author in 1988, the emphasis his):

> What I can attest, with *confidence*, is simply that the material was a homogeneous fill of ḥuwwar that certainly looked to be quarried off the nearby Ebal slopes (where you can still see deep cuts today); and that, as far as I could see when it was being removed by the bulldozer was sterile, or nearly so.

Dever assumed that the fill had been previously sectioned and recorded. But Wright had inferred his conclusion that the fill was imported by John Hyrcanus to nullify the Hellenistic reuse of Shechem's old fortifications (*SBBC*:14–15). This inference was not tested archaeologically on the western edge of the city.

The matter is of importance because of Ussishkin's proposal (1989) that the fill against the outside of Wall A was put in place at the time Wall A was erected, and that it served as a constituent of the defense system, reaching well up the face of the wall. His key reason is the elevation of the threshold of the Northwest Gate, half way up the height of Wall A. He also notes the lateral thrust of the platform inside town against eight meters of exposed Wall A: even with its batter, could it hold back the pressure? And he questions whether Wall A would have been so well-preserved if exposed from the seventeenth century onward (for 1550 years to Hyrcanus, or however long until the fill was laid). Ussishkin compares the somewhat analogous circumstances at Dan and Shiloh where constructional fill is on both sides of MB II fortification walls (1989:45–46).

Several considerations weigh against Ussishkin's proposal. Welter claims to have excavated a ramp along the wall; his brief note about this cannot be ignored. Ussishkin questions a reconstruction, published in *SBBC*: fig. 21, showing a ramp approaching the Northwest Gate, not close along the wall but perpendicular to it. That reconstruction can no longer be defended. But Welter's evidence stands.

The drains Sellin found in the wall are large enough for a human being to crawl through; if they

Fig. 102. Tannur with two layers of lining from surfacing within Court I in Field I.

were at the level of the top of a slope, which Ussishkin envisions, they would have constituted a distinct vulnerability in the system—acknowledged by Ussishkin (1989:50).

It would be useful to assess the physics of the lateral thrust against the interior of Wall A, but one may be permitted to doubt that this argument is strong. Wall A has stood for more than sixty years since Welter exposed it in its entirety, and while the weight of buildings on the platform it now retains is not what it was in antiquity, there is no sign of strain on Wall A as of this time of writing. The sheer magnitude of the rocks that make up Wall A, along with the likelihood of regular reapplication of mortar to the seams, call the matter of likely deterioration of the wall into question. The care with which the rocks in the wall were rough dressed to present a flat face also suggests that they were meant to be exposed.

Field I. Welter believed that Wall A went only with the acropolis, while Wall B was the circumvallation for the whole city. He was the one, under Sellin, to excavate the gate in Wall B at the east, and to trace the offsets-insets wall from the East Gate northwards in 1927. His plans of his independent work (1932:301–2, 305–6, abb. 7 & 9) indicate that he traced Wall B for four more segments north and then west. At the East Gate, he noted how high above the valley floor this wall line ran, and probed for a retaining wall downslope, where he found a run of cyclopean masonry indicated on his plans but described very briefly: it ran parallel to the upper wall; it was of long straight sectors with at least two projections (that is, not with spaced offsets-and-insets, but with widely spaced towers jutting about 1 m outward—recalling the sawtooth style on the west); it was preserved to as much as 5 m in height. In 1931, at a point north of the axis of the East Gate in Wall B, he discerned a break in the lower wall which he deemed to be a gate; it could not be satisfactorily excavated due to the spill from an adjacent dump.

The Joint Expedition demonstrated in Fields I and III that Welter's cyclopean retaining wall is almost certainly Wall A, and that the Wall A system constituted MB IIC Shechem's outer defenses on the east as well as the west. The evidence in Field I is best seen in Ills. 15 and 20–22.

Excavation in 1956 re-encountered Welter's revetment wall in front of the East Gate designated "Revetment 1" (in G. E. Wright 1956:16, fig.4, but now seen to be Wall A), as well as another wall (Wall 112 on Ill. 21 = I BB; referred to as Revetment 2 in the 1956 plans, G. E. Wright 1956:15–17) of comparable width nearer to the gate tower and 4.90 m inside the Welter wall. From the outer face of Welter's "revetment" to the face of Wall B as it ran away from the gate's southern tower is 11.00 m, the same distance separating Wall B and Wall A on the west of the mound.

In 1957, digging against the exterior face of the outer wall showed that it was preserved through as many as sixteen courses, was battered, and showed larger and larger rocks as it went down. The exterior surfaces of its stones showed the same rough chipping away of salients as characterized Wall A on the west. At 6.30 m down from its preserved top, excavation was suspended due to the threat of collapse of Hellenistic walls at the lip of the excavation. No stones in the wall attained sizes comparable to those in Wall A on the west, south of the Northwest Gate, but some were 1.15 to 1.20 m long and .90 m thick, comparable to stones in the portion of Wall A north of the Northwest Gate. There can be little doubt that Welter's revetment is Wall A, probably continuing the sawtooth style of construction.

Wall 112—at first designated Revetment 2 and then A-2—was taken to be another revetting ingredient in a glacis running from the gate towers and Wall B down the slope. Set into a shallow foundation trench discerned along its west face (Ill. 21 = I BB:#14), it was preserved to a height of over 2.50 m and was 1.00 m thick; as I BB shows, its structure was consistent in the segment dug in 1957, but was of smaller stones in the northern segment exposed in 1966.

An opening 1.20 m wide from the street along Wall 112 gave access to Court I between it and the top of Wall A. The discovery of this doorway suggested comparison to casemate construction patterns of later periods, and raised questions about the validity of thinking of Wall 112 as a revetment. Even so, Wall 112's sturdy construction may still qualify it as part of the fortification system, somewhat analogous to Wall B/2 on the west and Wall 657 in Field III, soon to be described.

Wall 110, bonded to 112 but not to Wall A, connected them. An opening through 110 to the south near Wall A gave access to Room II. Running south from Wall 110 was Wall 114 through which was an entrance into Room III. North of Court I were other segments of walls defining Rooms IV and V; extension of the excavation northward in 1966 encountered the south face of another, ill-preserved crosswall, which like 112 showed two styles of construction.

Court I had six layers of surfacing, at least four of which showed occupation evidence. Probes 8/1 and 8/2 on Ill. 15 beneath the lowest of these surfaces encountered a dark brown fill containing many fragments of limestone; the probes reached no further evidence of occupation layers. Four beaten earth surfaces, separated by only a few centimeters, succeeded one another within the court, all at elevations lower than the threshold of the doorway through Wall 112, and thus in use with it. Two of these surfaces were clearly occupational; tannurs sat on them. One tannur (fig. 102) had two layers of interior clay lining, indicating some lapse of time. The presence of numerous animal bones with the ovens, some showing butchering marks on their surfaces, suggest that Court I was used for food preparation.

Locus 364, a cobblestone floor, lay above the four beaten earth surfaces with occupation debris in the room, but was still at an elevation below the threshold of the entrance through Wall 112, at approximate elevation 2.55; at the level of the threshold was beaten earth floor 362 on makeup 363, 0.40 m thick. Without question, there were two systems of flooring here. Field records betray confusion in numbering here which may not be resolvable and may carry over to the Expedition's registries. The problem is displayed in the discrepancy between the text of *SBBC*:68–69 and the section portrayed in *SBBC*: fig.108.

Floor 364 was marked by charcoal and ashes along with bone and sherd fragments (no whole or reconstructible pieces) and two typical MB II style loom weights, again suggesting domestic use. Whether this also constitutes evidence of violent destruction is debatable. Wright also reports charcoal on Floor 362 and takes it as possible evidence of violence.

Subsequent to the four, possibly six, phases of use of the rooms in the complex around Court I, the doorway in Wall 112 was blocked with stones, and the access to the rooms against Wall A closed off. With that, Wall 112 could have become a revetment or consolidator in the slope running from the top of Wall A to the Stratum XV system to follow, Wall B and the East Gate.

To summarize the Field I stratigraphy in Stratum XVI: Wall A was the first unit built. Dark brown, limestone rich, fill was laid in behind it, as in the west of the city, as it attained its height. Wall 112 was let down into this fill in a shallow foundation trench (Ill. 21 = I BB:#14). More of the same kind of fill was added, raising the elevation between the two walls. Then partition walls were built that divided the space between the two parallel walls, and floorings, most fully attested in Court I, marked domestic occupation of the space; the successive reflooring and the two phases of ovens mean that occupation went on here for a considerable period of time before the East Gate and Wall B were built.

Wall A was continuous across Field I where later the East Gate would be placed. Salvage work carried out in the late 1980's, under the supervision of Israeli West Bank occupation authorities and employing Balâṭah workmen who kept the Joint Expedition informed, encountered what may be a segment of the top of Wall A and the edge of a gate just off the southeast corner of the House of Salim, also called the "House of the Blind Man," the large rectangular building in the southeast quadrant of the general plans of the mound from whose foundations the weapon hoard from 1908 came (Muller 1987).

The stone top of the exposed segment of wall is 1.20 m wide, three stones across. Bricks of the superstructure ride upon a layer of fist-sized stones topped by a cushion of dark brown earth; the bricks measure 0.55 m long by 0.12 m thick. The segment of wall lay exactly on the line extrapolated on both German and American plans as the course of Wall A. The break in the visible remnants of the wall suggest that the axis of the gate would have been ca. 4.50 m south of the southeast corner of the modern house, beneath a modern paved street. It is 5.75 m from that corner to the interior face of the exposed wall segment. A rough compass bearing indicates that the wall ran 40 degrees east of north at this point. A gate here would have been positioned almost diametrically opposite the Northwest Gate on the circle of the mound.

Field III (Ills. 38, 43–44). A similar picture emerges in Field III north along the fortification line from the East Gate. It was noted in Chapter 2 on the MB IIB remains that Ill. 44:#41, at the lowest point on the far right, represented the top of the augmented C Rampart of MB IIB. Just above it, Wall 657 appeared at the foot of Wall B, serving as the foundation upon which Wall B stood. Wall 657 ran slightly oblique to the line of Wall B above it (Ill. 38). It jutted out 0.50 m from the foot of Wall B at the BB section line on the south edge of the field, 0.90 m from Wall B at the north edge of the field 6 m away. It apparently had a function of its own as a free-standing wall prior to the building of Wall B. Wall 657 was preserved for three courses of medium to large stones, which slightly overlapped a foundation course of smaller stones, the whole standing 1.30 m high. Its width was undetermined, except that it did not extend west of the foot of Wall B's west face. Illustration 43:##15, 16 and 17 ran beneath Wall B and toward Wall 657, with ##16 and 17 sloping so as to run beneath 657. There was MB IIC pottery in these layers, so they may have constituted makeup on top of the C Rampart into which 657 was set. Ill. 44:##40 and 39 (loci 535, 553, and 562) began a leveling process; they were hard to separate in excavation although their differing character is clear on the section. At least #39 accumulated after Wall 657 was built. These layers ran beneath Wall 642 and if extrapolated would have met Wall 655 (see below) well down on its east face. Pottery in ##40 and 39 was mostly MB IIB, with admixture of MB IIA and Chalcolithic suggesting the soil is imported fill, but with some MB IIC sherds, suggesting that their laying was at the transition to the new system. Wall 657 resembles Wall B/1 in Field IV.

Downslope in Ill. 44 was the top of Wall 655, 1.60 m wide (note dotted extensions on Ill. 38). The outer face of 655 was 11.50 m away from the line of Wall B, 0.50 m greater than what separated Wall B from Wall A in Fields I and IV. Discovered in 1964, Wall 655, not Wall 646 which lay above it, seems very likely to have been the top of Wall A—a conclusion which alters the interpretation emerging from the early seasons of work (*SBBC*:68). Excavation did not probe deeper than the second course of Wall 655 on the west face, nor than the top course on the east, and no surfaces were discerned against it. The conclusion is that Walls 657 and 655 constituted the Wall A system in Field III in its earliest phase.

Wall 658 butted against Wall 655 0.65 m from the south balk of Field III; it appears in elevation in the Ill. 44 section as it then attached to Wall 642. Wall 658 may have defined a room nestled against the interior face of the fortification wall, or may have been an interior divider of a quasi-casemate arrangement. In the narrow triangle along Ill. 44's section, there was a tiny segment of flooring at elevation 6.50. Wall 658 bonded into Wall 642, which in its lowest courses ran parallel to and roughly halfway between Walls 655 = Wall A and 657.

Wall 642 was the east wall of a pair of rooms defined on the west by Wall 640 and divided by Wall 641. Wall 642 was deeply founded, standing 2.10 m high through twelve courses of medium-sized, semi-hewn stones. It narrowed from 1.0 m wide at its base to 0.70 m at its top. All preserved surfaces of the rooms between Walls 640 and 642 ran to near the top of Wall 642. The reason for its deep foundation seems to have been the need to level up the slope which persisted from that of the rampart deep below.

Wall 640 was built in two stages. From the junction with Wall 641 southward it was constructed of squarish, semi-hewn stones; from the junction northward it was of larger and flatter stones. There was a slight jog at the juncture. The founding levels of the two parts were approximately the same, as are the preserved heights, so they appear to have constituted one construction phase. Two doorways lead from the corridor between Wall 657 and Wall 640 into the northern and southern rooms east of 640. The outer jamb of each doorway was hidden in the balk. The stone threshold of each was polished from use. At its greatest height, 640 was preserved 1.53 m high, through seven courses; it averaged 0.70 m in width.

In the northern room, work in 1957 was unable to discern flooring, but recovered fine MB II domestic pottery and noted patches of burn in the soil. A patch of likely flooring was discerned in 1964, shown at elevation 6.90 on Ill. 38. In the southern room, excavation in 1964 found a much clearer stratification and probed the leveling pro-

Fig. 103. Tannur 534 built into the junction of Walls 640 and 641, Field III, probably in use with MB IIC Floors 548 and 531.

cess beneath three preserved floorings. Ill. 44:##37 and 36 (locus 558), ##35 and 34 (locus 555), all showed the characteristics of fills: a mix of pottery extending from Chalcolithic/EB I through MB IIA, B and some C. Wall 640 was probably let down into them, its foundation trench filled with #32 greenish grey earth merging with #31 of crumbly *huwwar* (locus 551).

These layers were the makeup for the succession of floors collectively indicated as Ill. 44:#29. Three distinct floors were discerned, as well as several partial resurfacings. These are loci 550, 548 and 531, each of packed *huwwar* separated by dark brown compact earth. The earth separations were combined with the floor surfaces in separating the layers; 548 designates both the floor and the earth above it, 550 the floor and the earth above it. Twenty indicator sherds were saved from this layering, dating to early MB IIC.

Fig. 104. Looking south in Field III toward the DD balk. The rocks in center are fallen from the top of Wall 640 at left onto Floor 533. The crush of pottery lay to the right of the fallen rocks, close to Wall 657, hidden in the temporary balk at the right margin. See Ill. 44:##27, 30.

The uppermost floor, 531, went with a late addition butted against Wall 641 and running south from it, Wall 651, 0.80 m long and 0.70 m wide, preserved for two courses standing 0.50 m high. It divided the north end of the south room into compartments, in each of which there was an oven.

The oven built into the corner of Walls 640 and 641 (locus 534) was preserved to its original height, reaching to 1.50 m above Floor 531 (fig. 103). Nearly three-quarters of its original rim was intact, 0.15 m in diameter. The inside diameter of the oven was 1.76 m at the base. There were two separate walls, both made of the coarse, gritty clay typical of tannur walls, the outer preserved less well than the inner. Fragments of a large store jar lay against the outer wall on the south, but the oven does not seem to have been surrounded by body sherds as was typical elsewhere in the period.

The installation was set within two concentric rings of small stones; the outer of these circles rested immediately on Floor 548, indicating that the oven was in use later in the sequence of flooring. Inside it was a heavy layer of dark ash 0.10 m thick in the center. Beneath the ash was a layer of very fine-grained yellowish ashy soil with a few large stones; one of the stones was calcined and cracked from the heat.

The state of preservation together with the accumulation on Floor 531 does not suggest violent destruction, but does mean change. Stones had fallen on the west side of the oven, crushing it slightly, and there was crumbly yellow brown earth with a few stones filling it above the ashy layers. Fourteen indicator sherds came from the contents and the flooring immediately surrounding the oven.

Between Wall 640 and Wall 657 ran the corridor between the two rooms just described and the inner defense wall. Over the fill layers already described between Walls 640 and 642, Ill. 43:#33 constituted the makeup for a hard-packed surface at elevation 8.03 joining 640 and 657, topped by #30 (loci 528 and 533A), an ashy grey deposit. The surface riding on this makeup was Floor 533, a hard-packed earth floor with flecks of *ḥuwwar* embedded. Intermittent deposits of ash lay on it. A deposit of crushed pottery as much as 0.50 m thick, Ill. 44:#27, rested on the floor near Wall 657. More than 450 indicator sherds came from this crush, characteristic of the MB IIC period. Stones fallen from Wall 640 covered a segment of the floor near that wall, protecting occupation debris of loci 520 and 529 on Floor 531, sealing a deposit of 18 indicator sherds (fig. 104), further indication of violent destruction.

The details presented here about occupation against the interior of Wall A before Wall B was built speak to the issue of chronological separation between the A system and its successor, when Wall B was added. The construction of rooms used for domestic purposes, the resurfacing of floors, the building and relining of ovens, the construction of partition walls, and the acquiring of a polish on thresholds of doorways all call for the passage of time. More important, they define a system of use, a concept of protection and of the use of space. Most notably in Field IV, and less certainly at Fields I and III, there is evidence of sudden change, probably violent destruction, at the end of Stratum XVI, around the perimeter.

THE FORTIFICATIONS: STRATUM XV

Wall B

Wall B has served as a point of reference frequently in the description of Stratum XVI, and in both Fields III and IV a wall on the line of Wall B, upon which it was founded, has been seen to be part of the Wall A system. With the change to Stratum XV, Wall B itself came into being. Here is G. E. Wright's general description of it, written after the 1962 season:

> Sellin followed it [Wall B] from the East Gate to his east-west trench [in L-M 5–6]; it crossed our Field III...at a distance of over 50 m.... An entirely different type of fortification from that of Wall A, it was not built against the mound's sides, but like Wall D was meant to stand vertically on the edge of the mound's summit. Today it exists as a stone socket which varies between 3.25 m and 3.75 m. The average between these extremes suggests that the builders were building an 8-cubit-wide structure..., the variation being caused by the size of the stones and the manner in which they were laid together. In size these stones are medium to small, roughly coursed. On top of the socket the main part of the fortification was of brick interlaced with beams, and probably with brick and wooden battlements above that. When it was first destroyed, evidently by the Egyptian army between about 1550 and 1540 BC..., the Egyptians were able to set fire to the wall because there was so much wood in it and in battlements upon it, and to pull sufficient brick from its lower part as to cause it to fall inward, instead of outward down the slope. The great quantity of charcoal remains of the wooden beams indicates an exceedingly hot fire. The distance the fallen debris spread within the city from the wall base was at least 14 to 15 m....in Field III. This suggests that the height of the brick above the stone base was surely a minimum of 10 m.
>
> Wall B furthermore was an "offsets and insets" structure. That is, it was evidently built in straight sections, each *ca.* 15 m....long. The next section would either jut back or forward as the case may be, *ca.* 50 cm.... This type of building gave added strength, and it also enabled the builders to follow the curve of the mound's summit by simply altering the angle by which the straight sections were joined to one another.
>
> In a trench dug in the spring of 1928, Sellin followed ruined masses of brick work from Wall B around the northeast and northern sectors … (H-M, 3–4). How much of the actual stone socket of Wall B he discovered is today not clear from the surviving trench. A large section of it, however, was exposed in H-3 …. This means without question that it circled the whole eastern and northern portions of the tell and joined the Northwest Gate (*SBBC*:69–71).

Fig. 105. Looking west in Field IV, 7200 complex. Wall B/1 in center, with the doorway to the "postern gate" to its left. Dever's inked designations identify the elements.

Field IV (Ills. 52, 54, 58–60. Wall B/1 = Wall 72.106A (see Ill. 58 = IV EE) was found only north

Fig. 106. The opening in Wall A permitting visual coverage of approaches from the north to the Northwest Gate. Note the flat flooring slabs, covered with a layer of plaster.

of the Northwest Gate; its absence south of the gate must mean that Wall A's immense height there called for no supplementary fortification. Wall B/1 was placed in a deep foundation trench, locus 7217 = IV EE:#28, which permitted it to be anchored on the ruins of B/2 = 72.106B. It was preserved for only two courses in height at the point where IV EE crossed it (fig. 105), revealing the "postern gate" entryway through it. Wall B's interior half had fallen away completely; stones from the collapse and from the upper courses were probably reused later to build Wall E.

The outer face of Wall B was just under 11.00 m from the inner face of Wall A. The original massive base of Wall A was at this time supplemented with 4.00 m of new courses of smaller rocks (IV EE Wall 7210). Massive fill was brought in to level the slope of the Wall A system, EE:##27 and 32 east of the line of Wall 7222, and capped with the *ḥuwwar*-rich layer 72.127 (EE:#25 on #27) between Wall 7222 and Wall A. The first phase of the 7200 complex was then laid out on the level platform thus attained.

Complex 7200 is what Sellin in 1926 and 1927 designated the north wing of the "palace," built, as he recognized, later than the gate and bonded into rebuilt portions of the gate's north tower. His clearance here (1927b:Taf. 18) found the mudbrick superstructure of all the rooms, but as it turned out did not reach the floors and remove crucial evidence for the date of the complex. Much of the brick superstructure has eroded since Sellin's excavation, but the Dever-Zoghbi plan derived in 1972 (Ill. 52) indicates some preservation, shown by square blocks on the stone substructure. Rooms 10–14 on this plan were not re-excavated from the way Sellin left them, but constitute further rooms of the kind represented by Rooms 1–9.

Complex 7200 included the large central court, Room 4–5, with a central column base, positioned between the poorly preserved segments of Wall 7218 that divides the two portions of the square room. The central court was flanked by three rooms, 1–3, adjacent to the gate and three (to become four) rooms, 6–9, east of the court. Access was over a threshold in Wall 7212 forming the east boundary of the complex, from a narrow, 0.75 m wide, corridor along Wall B into Room 9. From here, one entered the other eastern rooms and the central court. A doorway from the court gave access to Room 2, from which one entered Rooms 3 and 1. In Room 1, a 0.85 by 0.55 m opening through Wall A permitted visual coverage of the corner created by the outward-jutting north tower of the gate and the stretch of Wall A running northeastward from the gate. Like the openings through

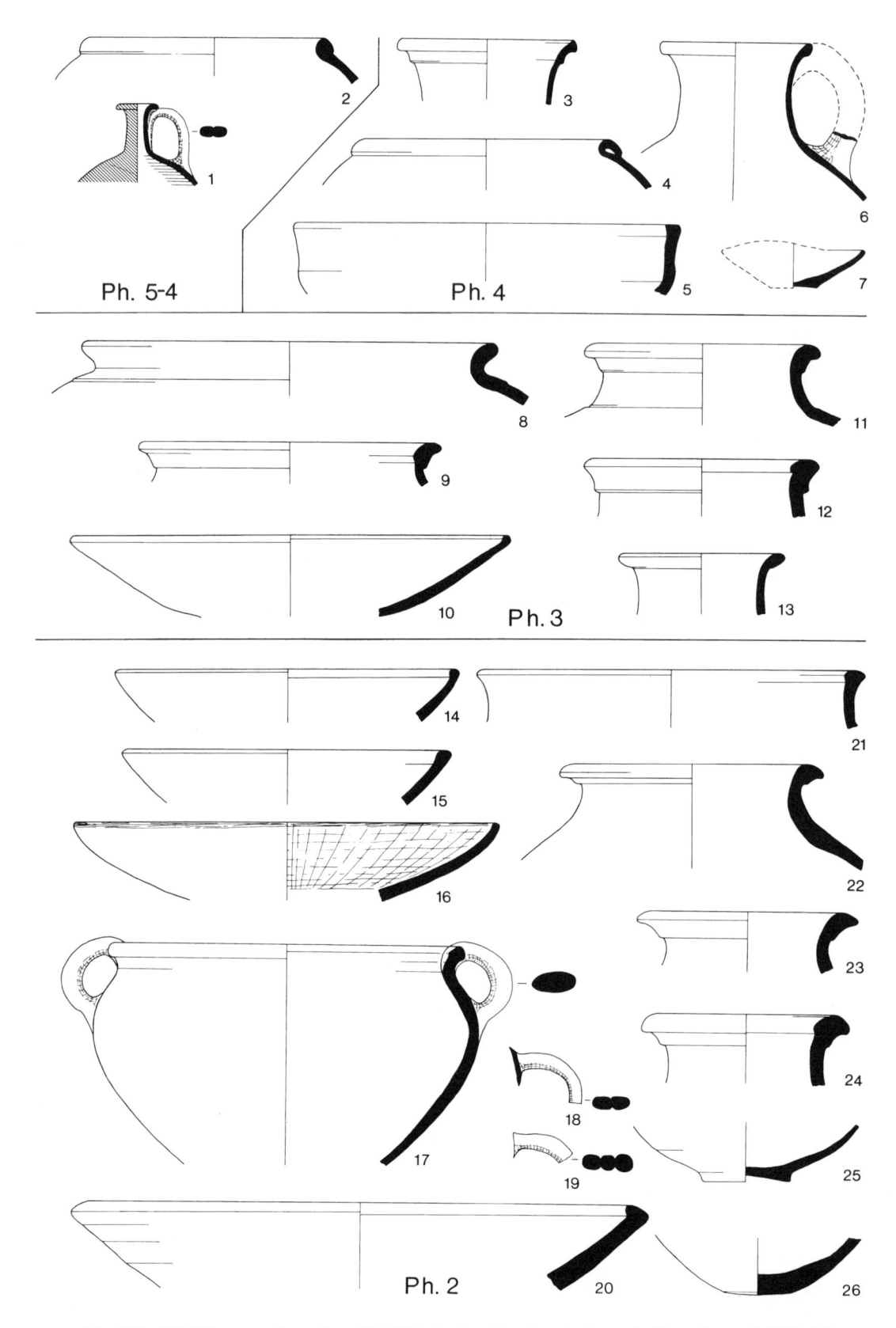

Fig. 107. MB IIC pottery forms from Field IV phasing. Note jar rim forms in Phase 3 panel, ##11–13.

Wall A south of the gate, it may have been a drain outlet, for run-off of water from the flooring in Room 1 (visible beneath Nasr Dhiab's feet in fig. 106), but it seems far too large for such a purpose. As Ill. 52 and the photograph show, two huge flat stones were part of the flooring in Room 1, with a plastered floor above them to the east but not covering them; conceivably some process was carried on in this room that required water, and the hole through the wall was related to the need to drain this room alone. However, the theory that it was a means for keeping watch on the gate approaches seems more likely.

Room 8 was cobbled, and one part of the stone work suggested a second line of walling along its east side, resulting in a curiously limited space. In view of developments in Field III to be described below, one can venture the proposal that Room 8 was housing for one or more hoofed animals.

Dever's general description of the walls and floors in the original phase of 7200:

> The building was unusually well built and well preserved. The stone foundations stood over a meter in height in places, with the lowest courses of the mudbrick superstructure often still *in situ* .... Two to four cms. of excellent white wall plaster covered the lower stone courses of most of the walls. The original Phase 3 floors were of plaster laid over a firmly-tamped make-up of chalk (*ḥuwwar*) chips (1974:36b).

MB IIC sherds dated the founding phase of the Phase 3 floors, notably four highly characteristic jar rim forms shown in fig. 107 (cf. Seger 1974:123).

Minor adjustments to this phase of the complex included raising the level of the corridor between Wall B and Wall 7212 and inserting a step at the threshold lipped with plaster, presumably to keep water from running from the corridor into the complex. There do not seem to have been resurfacings of the interior rooms, so this hardly indicates much passage of time. But this first phase of the Wall B system was subjected to massive destruction, which created the meter-thick deposit of mudbrick detritus at the left edge of IV EE :#29.

At this stage, builders dug deep into the detritus over the interior half of Wall B, robbed stones from its foundation, and built Wall 7275B, the interior wall of what would later become Casemate Wall E. Its interior face was 2.15 m from the step into the 7200 complex. As the section suggests, interior Wall E was a stack of large boulders on a foundation of small stones, either one or two rocks thick to a width of 0.85 m. Its foundation was so poor that it came to lean precariously inward. Mud plaster coated the lower courses of its inner face, an attempt perhaps to prevent water seeping in to further undermine the wall. A rough mud plaster surfacing (IV EE:#9) covered the widened corridor, combining with cobbling near the threshold into Room 9. As with Phase 3, the corridor was resurfaced once, with mud plaster surface 72.100.

Interior to the 7200 complex, structural changes included blocking the doorways from Room 8 to Room 6–7, and the introduction of mudbrick curtain walls splitting Room 6–7 in two, and dividing the central court into Rooms 4 and 5 (7220 and 7218). Repairs were made to the wall plaster. New surfaces of mud plaster were laid on a makeup of red soil 0.15 to 0.20 m above the Phase 3 fine plaster floors—in Room 6, Surface 7230 = IV EE:#7 above 72.126 (#25). A tannur was added in the northeast corner of Room 9. The overall impression is one of haste and of inferior quality. Again violent destruction struck, piling debris 7284 (EE:#8) on the corridor and onto the threshold of the entrance to Room 9.

Apparently this marked the end of the use of the 7200 complex, although Sellin's clearance had removed the destruction debris and presumably any evidence of reuse. But one more effort at fortification was yet to be made. Wall 7275A was erected at the west edge of the corridor, just at the inside of the line of the east wall of the complex, on top of about 0.25 m of the destruction debris. The space between 7275A and 7275B was provided with crosswalls, one of which, Wall 7281, appears in IV EE in elevation as #5, resulting in a casemate construction. The interior was floored with cobbling 7283, upon which, close to the interior wall, were two restorable MB IIC platter bowls (fig. 108:13 and 15). From the debris against the east face of the interior wall line 7275B came an MB IIC cooking pot (18). This pottery establishes

122   SHECHEM III. THE MIDDLE BRONZE IIC PERIOD

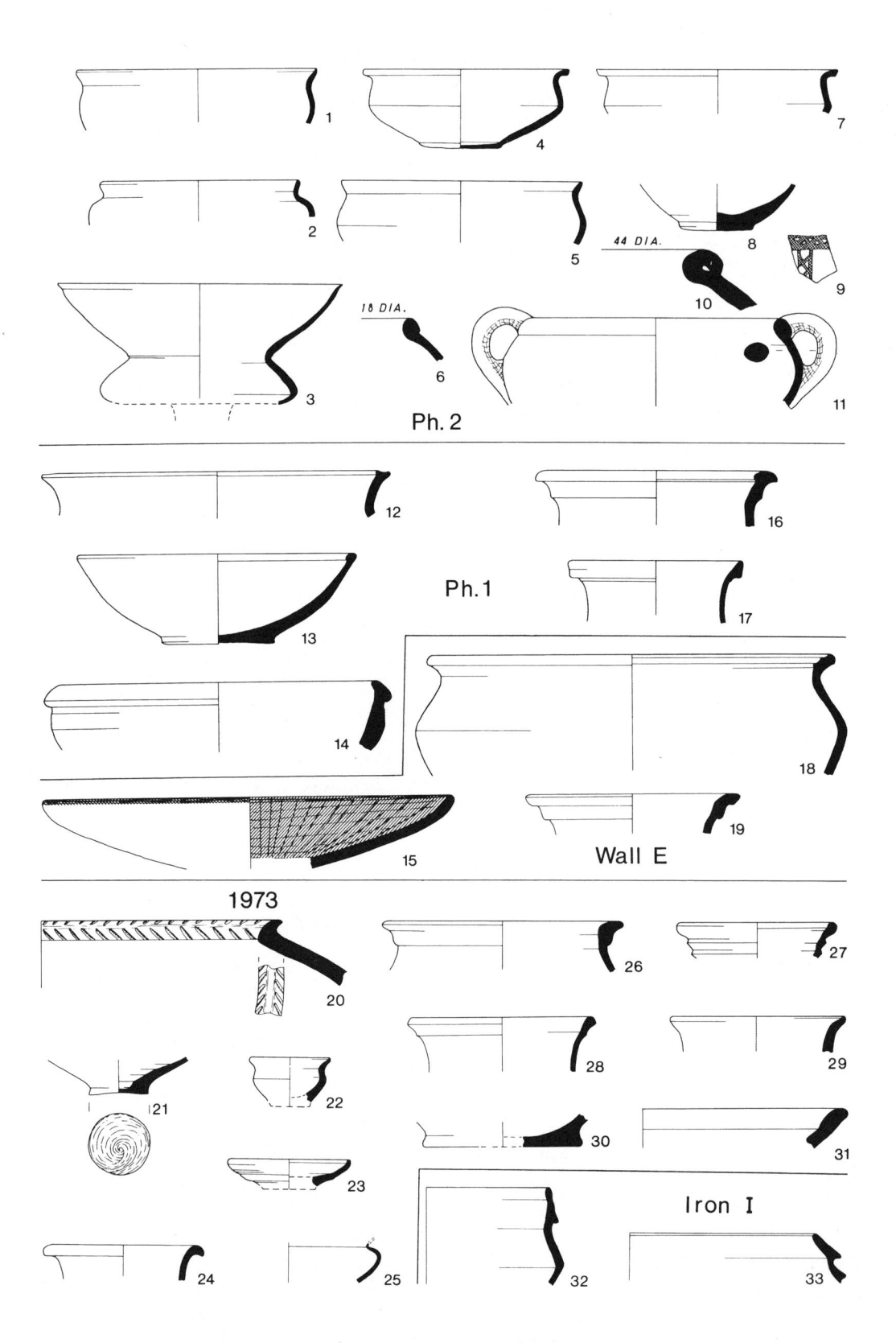

Fig. 108. More MB IIC forms, and 2 cooking pot rims from Iron I found in Field IV. The find spot of the two platter bowls (##13 nd 15) is marked in fig. 105.

that Casemate Wall E was built in MB IIC, and destroyed at the end of MB IIC—the third destruction attested on the western foundation during Stratum XV and the only place on the site where three destructions for the period are attested.

South of the Northwest Gate, Casemate Wall E continued, as Welter's 1930 plan shows, here redrawn as Ill. 50. Dever's trench dug in 1973 cut across the casemates, across the south wing of Sellin's palace, and again reached Wall A, at IV FF, depicted on Ill. 58 (see Ill. 54 for location). As noted already, no Wall B was found here, and the leveling had taken place in Stratum XVI to create a plaza between the Fortress Temple and Wall A.

Dever's team found the foundation trench (IV FF:#1; see the detailed enlargement in Ill. 60) for the exterior wall of Casemate Wall E, Wall 7310B and saw that it cut surfaces leading from the interior Wall 7311B toward a probable join to the flooring (#7) of the 7300 Complex, a three-roomed single-axis row reaching from the gate south to the colonnaded hall just outside the corner of the Fortress Temple against Wall A. It will be described below in the section on the Acropolis buildings.

Wall E as a part of the fortifications was the final development of the MB IIC fortifications, and had itself two phases of construction, first the inner wall and then the outer. Nothing corresponding to it has been identified on the north and east of the mound, so it constitutes something of an orphan in the comprehension of Shechem's fortification. But that it began its life in MB IIC is proven by the 1972–73 probes. Rebuilt much later, it was one of the few surviving indications of how Shechem was fortified in the Iron Age, as Chapter 5 will show.

Field III (Ills. 37, 43, 44). Welter and Sellin traced eight, possibly nine, offset and inset segments of Wall B from the East Gate north and west around the northern perimeter of the tell, following for the most part only the brick top of the wall. A piece of Wall B's stone foundation is exposed in grid square H3, 13.50 m in length, but no description of the superstructure or of the soil banked against its exterior face has survived. The Joint Expedition sought fuller information about this

Fig. 109. Looking west in Field III, with Wall 654 at bottom margin, Wall 646 on top of 646A in center.

system, the best complete exposure of which was made in Field III, about 50 m north of the East Gate.

In Field IV, the Wall B system made use of Wall A. The same seems to be the case in Field I. In Field III, if Wall 655 is the top of Wall A as proposed above, the Wall B system had to rebuild the line of the lower circumvallation. In Ill. 44, Wall 646/646A is shown positioned above Wall 655. It is of two phases; the lower segment is 646A, made of small, semi-hewn stones (fig. 109), which rode partly upon the packed green clay of AA:#42 to its east. The section does not depict the relation between #42 and the damp brown earth of #28 to the west of Wall 646A, and their relationship is uncertain, but they met over Wall 655 and formed a cushioning layer 0.75 m thick. Both layers then lapped against Wall 646A, suggesting that the two fill layers and the wall were built up contemporaneously. Ill. 44:#28 included at its base a spill of

Fig. 110. Looking northwest in Field III, with Wall B at the right and part of Wall 649 in lower right corner. Bench 729 is the group of flat stones against the lowest course of Wall B, left of the meter stick. Note the striated soil layer beneath Wall B.

Fig. 111. Looking west at the center part of balk on which the III BB section was drawn. Wall 649 at left, Floor 738 at 0.70 m down from the top of the meter stick.

rocks fallen probably from the top of Wall 642; the layer combines loci 532, 556, 564 and 544 assigned to various soil ingredients within it as it was dug. These loci contained a relatively large amount of MB IIA and B pottery, as well as what was field analyzed as early MB IIC. The spread of dates suggests imported fill from deep in the mound.

The second stage of filling consisted of leveling up the area where the domicile of the A system had been, between Walls 657 and 642. Pottery fill #27 was placed in first, perhaps selected as a good medium for water drainage so as not to undermine Wall B or its underpinning in Wall 657. AA:#26 = locus 519, and #25 combining loci 518, 523 and 538 and containing several whole mudbricks, brought the fill to an elevation that covered the A system walls. In these two layers, the pottery was predominantly MB IIC with some MB IIB and A. They were the first two layers to be spread after Wall B had been built.

Topping these was a thin layer of hard, smooth green clay, Ill. 44:#24, combining loci 525, 530, 536, 537 and 543, apparently the layer that sealed the filling and made ready for the construction of a glacis for the slope. Layers ##19–23, loci 511, 516, 517, 521 and 527 were ingredients in the glacis itself, merging into one another. Upon them was laid the *ḥuwwar* cap (#18), which is cut off from touching Wall B by a pit (#15) dug from a point when an upper glacis was being constructed. Downslope, the *ḥuwwar* leveled off and met the top of Wall 646A, on the east side of an intrusive Hellenistic pit, #7 in the section.

Inside Wall B, there are indications of construction that probably belong to the fortification system. Ill. 43 and Ill. 37 (top-plan) show the development. Upon the layers of fill Ill. 43:##15–

Fig. 112. Looking west inside Wall B in the domestic complex of Field III. Wall 634 in the back, 650 in the foreground. The meter stick stands on Floor 734.

17, representing either the very top of the augmented C Rampart system or cushioning layers laid down in preparation for building Wall B, Walls 649 and 650 were founded. While the founding level of Wall 649 was a few centimeters lower than that of Wall B (founded inside at elevation 9.17), it butted against and was built after Wall B. At its west end it joined Wall 650 3.20 m from Wall B. Ill. 37 shows Wall 650 running both north and south of this junction, but excavation here was limited and did not establish the north extension. Probably there were two rooms adjacent to Wall B, divided by Wall 649. Passage between them was through a 0.90 m wide doorway in 649, which, when excavated, was blocked with loose brown soil (Ill. 43:#12a). Wall 649 was 0.80 m thick, preserved through three courses to a height of 0.60 m; Wall 650 was 0.90 m thick, preserved through as many as five courses (at the section line) to a height of 1.10 m.

North of Wall 649, in the north room, a line of large, flat stones butted against Wall B's lowest course and against Wall 649 (Ills. 37 and 44, and fig. 110), at elevations varying from 9.57 to 9.73 (south to north). The line rested on smaller stones and probably served as a low bench (locus 729) along Wall B. Floor 738, of hard-packed *ḥuwwar*, ran up against the bench (Ill. 43); dark striations accumulated on Floor 738 at its north edge (Ill. 45 = III BB:#12, fig. 111), and one flat stone at the north end of the bench seems to have been embedded in the floor. Topping these dark striations and showing up intermittently elsewhere over Floor 738 was fine brown soil (BB:#11), but this soil was not separated from the fill above it in such a way as to make it a sealed locus of homogeneous pottery. It formed part of locus 729, from which 18 sherds were saved, along with a clay sealing showing a scarab impression. Loci 738 and 739 combine the pottery of the floor and the material upon it, five indicator sherds analyzed as MB IIB and A; on the floor was a piece of bone inlay. Floor 738 ran over a shallow, charcoal-lined pit filled with loose brown earth and small stones just at the west end of the southernmost stone of Bench 729, but the pit contained no pottery to help in the dating.

The room south of Wall 649 also had a hard-packed *ḥuwwar* floor, Floor 752, about 0.25 m higher in elevation than its counterpart in the north room (Ill. 45 = III BB). Pottery above and below the floor was not separated, but what little there was belonged to MB IIC.

Also founded in this first phase of the Wall B system and probably part of the fortifications was Wall 634, preserved at the line of Ill. 43 through fourteen courses to a height of 2.80 m. Thinner than 649 and 650, at about 0.70 m, it defined the western limit of a build-up of stone surfaces extending to Wall B during the founding phase and the subsequent use phase. In the founding phase, it formed the west limit of Floor 734, which joined the second courses of both Walls 650 and 634 (fig. 112), made of white, hard-packed *ḥuwwar* overlaid by 0.03 to 0.04 m of reddish clay (locus 753 = Ill. 43:#14). Nineteen sherds, from this layer mixed with the bottom of #13 just above it, range throughout MB II in date.

Fig. 113. Looking northwest in the room just inside Wall B. The balk with section III BB left of center. The succession of cobblestone surfaces, 708, 710, 711 show in the balk, while the meter stick lies on Floor 714.

On the analogy with conditions in Field I, Wall 634 may have been the inner wall of an elevated set of battlements, over seven meters wide, at the interior of Wall B. As in the Wall A system, however, the rooms at the "ground level" seem to have been used for domestic purposes. The structure interior to Wall 634 will be described as part of the interior of the city.

Subsequent to this founding phase of the Wall B system, Walls 649 and 650 were covered over with nearly a meter of fill, Ill. 43:##10 and 13 (loci 734, 738a and 752a). Upon this fill were laid a succession of stone surfaced floorings, 718, 714, 711, 710 and 708, the lower three of large enough flat stones to be termed paved while the upper two were of medium-sized cobbles (Ills. 43 and 45; fig. 113).

From bottom to top these layers are defined by confidently sealed loci with saved sherds, as follows:

1. Loci 719, 733 and 749, the upper parts of Ill. 43:##10 and 13, makeup for Floor 718, 30 sherds.
2. Loci 718, 732 and 748, brown earth with *ḥuwwar* flecks, #9 on Ills. 43 and 45, makeup for Floor 714, 13 sherds.
3. Loci 714 and 731, same material as (2), #8 on the sections, makeup for Floor 711, 14 sherds.
4. Loci 711, 717, 727 and 730, same material as (2), #7 on the sections, makeup for Floor 710, 32 sherds. Note well sherd #8819 embedded in Floor 710, sealed by hard-pack locus 728.
5. Loci 710, 716, 725, 726 and 746, same material as (2), #6 on the sections, makeup for Floor 708, 18 sherds. Locus 710 yielded a bone pendant, and locus 746 the tip of a bronze spatula.

As Ill. 43 indicates, the stratigraphy west of Wall 634 was radically different. The space between Wall B and 634 during the time of this buildup of surfaces may have been used for the stabling of equines; hoofed animals thrive on cobbled flooring, and cobbled rooms in homes at Shechem and elsewhere were probably spaces for animals (Holladay 1986).

The two phases of Stratum XV here described are deemed to have been co-terminus with the lower glacis running from Wall B down to Wall 646A, the structure which replaced Wall A and continued its line at the beginning of Stratum XV. Two more developments on the Wall B system took place in Stratum XV.

On top of Wall 646A, Wall 646, slightly wider than 646A and constructed differently, was preserved for two courses for most of its excavated

Fig. 114. The central portion of the south balk of Field III, on which Ill. 44 is drawn. Wall 657 at far right, and the layering between Walls 642 and 640 to left of center. Note the thick layer of ḥuwwar, *locus 515, running from the base of Wall 613 eastward.*

length (Ill. 44). Its stones were huge boulders, 0.75 m in diameter and largely undressed, compared to the much smaller, semi-hewn stones of 646A. At the line of Ill. 43, Wall 646 was preserved about 2.20 m high. The surface of the upper glacis sloped upward from the lowest course of the interior face of Wall 646 and was a 0.45 m thick layer of white *ḥuwwar*, Ill. 44:#13 = locus 515 (fig. 114). Hellenistic Wall 613 was cut down into the glacis, and from the line of 613 westward the glacis surface thinned to 0.05–0.06 m, thickening again as it ran to Wall B (earlier excavation cut into it without recognizing it), so its full extent cannot be ascertained (Ill. 44:#1). The white *ḥuwwar* surfacing apparently decomposed to a loose green, clay-like material constituting #12, which eroded and washed down the slope to build up against Wall 646, to a depth of 0.75 m; this is locus 505, containing rare sherds from Chalcolithic and all MB II phases, along with stray Iron Age and Hellenistic sherds.

Makeup for the glacis was packed brown earth layer Ill. 44:#14 = locus 508, from which 27 MB II B-C sherds were saved; rare Chalcolithic and MB IIA suggest the soil was imported from elsewhere on the tell. This makeup rested directly upon the lower glacis at most points. Nearer Wall B, #16 of striated green clay and #17 of brown clay = locus 510, containing pottery of similar range to that in #14, also contained intrusive Iron II sherds. At a point two meters inside Wall 646A, the upper glacis *ḥuwwar* lay directly upon that of the lower glacis for a short stretch.

The upper glacis lapped against Walls 644 and 645, an L-shaped construction forming what may be a tower foundation belonging to the fortification system (Ill. 38). Wall 644 bonded with 645, but 645 butted against Wall 646A; the lower glacis ran beneath them, the upper glacis to them. All three walls survived the destruction at the end of Stratum XV sufficiently to be reused in the Late Bronze Age.

Inside Wall B, it is uncertain what should be associated with the laying of the renewed or upper glacis. No stratigraphic connections over or through Wall B can be made. Two phases of building and flooring belonging to MB IIC are attested above the ones already described. It is unlikely that the upper glacis would have been in use only for the short period covered by the latter of these two, the years just prior to the destruction of the city at the end of Stratum XV. The relative elevations of surfaces either side of Wall B pertain: the top of the upper glacis met Wall B if extrapolated as on Ill. 44, at 11.15; the 703 flooring inside, the lower of the two phases yet to be described, was at 11.25

Fig. 115. Looking west in Field III. The meter stick leans against Wall 634. Behind and above Wall 634 is Wall 631. A fragment of Wall 635 is at the right center, and across the deep trench from it is Pit 720, set down into the point where Wall 635 would meet the uppermost course of 634.

to 11.30, the upper some 0.50 m higher, sloping to as high as 12.00. The tentative conclusion is that the upper glacis was laid in connection with the lower interior phase and continued through the upper interior phase. But it should be kept in mind that in Field IV there is evidence of a hasty rebuild in the form of Casemate Wall E as a last-ditch defensive effort, and the laying of a renewed glacis in the east might have gone with the alterations made in the west.

Floor 703 was the lower of the interior phases, a cobbled flooring similar to its predecessors 708 and 710, reaching from Wall B to the second course down from the top of Wall 634. Its makeup, III BB:#5, resembles its predecessors under the earlier cobbled floors here, hard packed brown earth flecked with ḥuwwar (loci 708, 712, 713, 715 and 745, containing 11 saved sherds of MB IIC). Its surface was at site elevation 11.26 to 11.36. With Wall 634 and cobbling 703 in place, Wall 635 was built on the cobbling (continuous under it when a small portion of the wall was removed) at an odd angle across the space near the wall. Also on 703 were two column bases, 0.60 m in diameter, the southern one with a top elevation of 11.93 and the northern one with top elevation 12.10 (Ill. 37, both dotted in). With Wall 635 running between them, these two do not seem to have been related in function, but the architectural fragments preserved here elude interpretation. Stone-lined pit 720 (fig. 115), apparently a grain silo, was set down into the junction of Walls 634 and 635; it may have belonged to the phase above, since there was a break in the upper floor above it, but the stratigraphy here is uncertain.

West of Wall 634, Cobbled Floor 803 ran at virtually the same elevation to Wall 652, a new

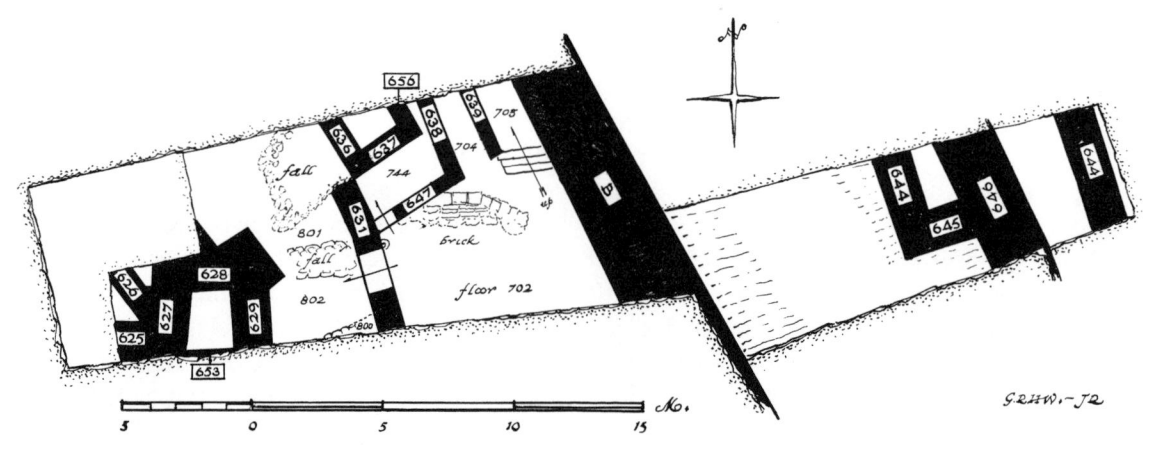

Fig. 116. Block plan of the uppermost Stratum XV phase in Field III.

Fig. 117. Looking north in Field III. Steps to platform 705, with Wall 639 in center. Parallel to 639 is Wall 638, to its left. In the lower left is the upper part of the balk on which III BB is drawn. The meter stick lies on Floor 702.

Fig. 118. Brick fall over Floor 702 in Field III, from Wall 647 southward, dating to the destruction of Stratum XV.

foundation of this period. Walls 652, 633 (stone) and 659 (mudbrick) belonged with this phase, but again their architectural interpretation is elusive and it is unclear whether they were part of the fortification system or not.

The uppermost phase of the Stratum XV development is seen on fig. 116, and displayed a number of changes. Wall 631, referred to as B/2 in early reports, was built slightly west of the line of Wall 634, now covered over; 631 was footed at the elevation of Floor 803 of the previous phase, directly upon it. It was 1.50 m thick, made of very well coursed stones chinked with small stones, and, on the east face, plastered continuously with the flooring. A doorway 1.40 m wide through Wall 631 provided access from the interior of the city into the complex near Wall B. Just inside (east) of the doorway at its north jamb was a huge stone door socket, 0.40 by 0.50 m with the socket 0.17 m in diameter, found upside down but in the right location to have swung a door for the opening.

Floor 702 ran from Wall B to Wall 631, reaching the latter at a point 0.25 m lower than the threshold in its doorway (projected on Ill. 43), and from the south balk to Wall 647. It was of mud plaster at site elevation 12.00, and topped a makeup at least 0.50 m thick of ashy grey earth.

From the open space floored with 702 plaster, a set of steps ran up to platform 705 at site elevation 12.59, curtained by Wall 639 (fig. 117). Parallel to the curtain wall 639 was Wall 638, cornering with the stone foundation of Wall 647. Between 638 and 639 was Stone Pavement 704 at site elevation 12.20. Both Walls 638 and 639 rested on this pavement. West of Wall 638, in the space defined by 638, 647 and 631 was a stone pavement, 744, sloping up from east to west, from site elevation 12.44 next to Wall 638 to 12.78 0.70 from Wall 631—and this pavement post-dated the building of Walls 638 and 647 since it ran against them, as well as against Wall 637. Wall 637 was

Fig. 119. Brick debris in south balk of Field III. Wall 635 is at right. Marks of burned beams show throughout the debris, which lies on Floor 702, Stratum XV.

the south wall of a small room bound by Walls 650 and 636, running off into the north balk of the field. In sum, there are four elevations within this relatively small space: 705 on the platform, 704 in the corridor, 744 within the northern alcove, and 702 throughout the southern space. What the various architectural ingredients define here is hard to surmise. Platform 705 may have been part of a battlement from which to shoot from the top of Wall B. Wall 631 was hardly an inner defense line, with its wide doorway, but it apparently divided the defense installations from residential areas to the west. The two rooms at the north between Wall B and Wall 631 may have been for storage, but the large area floored by 702 seems to have been open to the sky; it seems too large to have been roofed.

West of Wall 631 were a plaster floor, 802, at elevation 12.22 and a stone floor, 801 at elevation sloping from 12.59 to 12.72. Both ran west to the bastioned corner of the complex at the west edge of the field which will be described as part of the interior of town. They also ran to a small triangle of brick platform against the west face of Wall 631 at the south balk, locus 800.

What bound this whole complex together was the mass of brick fall and burn which covered all the floors, at places over two meters deep. The most striking ingredient was the collapsed brick wall in the north center of the space floored by 702 (fig. 118); it tilted at a 60 degree angle and came to rest on the floor. The bricks appear to have

Fig. 120. Smashed MB IIC cooking pot on Floor 702.

Fig. 121. Basalt tripod brazier from destruction on Floor 702, Stratum XV.

been stacked with no mortar at the seams. Each measured 0.35 by 0.35 by 0.15 m. In 1957, it was concluded that this brick wall fell from the south northward, but restudy of the deposit in 1964 after further excavation here showed that it fell from the upper part of Wall 647 southward, and probably was part of a second story or of the fortification superstructure.

Throughout the great mass of brick detritus were burn deposits representing wooden beams (fig. 119). One beam had fallen with sufficient force to make a slight depression in Floor 702. An MB IIC cooking pot lay smashed on Floor 702 under the brick fall (fig. 120). A basalt saddle quern 0.40 by 0.60 m sat on the floor, and a broken basalt brazier was in the debris just above the floor (fig. 121). The debris spilled through the doorway in Wall 631 and over the walls onto Floor 801 to the west and onto Platform 800.

Where other fields at the site suggest two destructions in close sequence at the end of MB IIC, the massive destruction on the uppermost floors in Field III seems to be all of a piece. The only hint of another destruction was the grey ashy layer of makeup beneath Floor 702.

Field I and the East Gate (Ills. 12–15, and sections and elevations in Ills. 20–22, 24, 26–27). Joint Expedition excavation of the Wall B system in Field I took place in 1956, 1957, 1962, 1964 and 1966, in all cases working with the scraps of evidence left by the Sellin and Welter work. Welter had cleared the gate in the Spring campaign of 1926 and it appears on all the German plans thereafter, shown as though completely uncovered. The 1956 Joint Expedition campaign began its work in the south part of the gate and discovered that the German work had not uncovered the entire south gate tower, nor cut deep into the foundations of the gate passageway.

The East Gate was constructed at the point farthest east on the arc of Wall B. Wall B approached the gate from the north on a straight line offset segment running slightly east of due south, and ran away from its south tower at an angle slightly west of due south. (An immense Hellenistic robber pit removed a large part of Wall B between the south tower and the south balk of Field I on its course southward, seen in Ill. 20 = I AA 47.) The gate building was, then, effectively a substitute for one of the insets in the offsets-insets system. It was structured to accommodate both the topography and this change in the line of the wall. As was the Northwest Gate, it was necessarily slightly asymmetrical (Ill. 13, which shows average dimensions and is less accurate than Ill. 14). The front facade measured ca. 18.20 m from tower

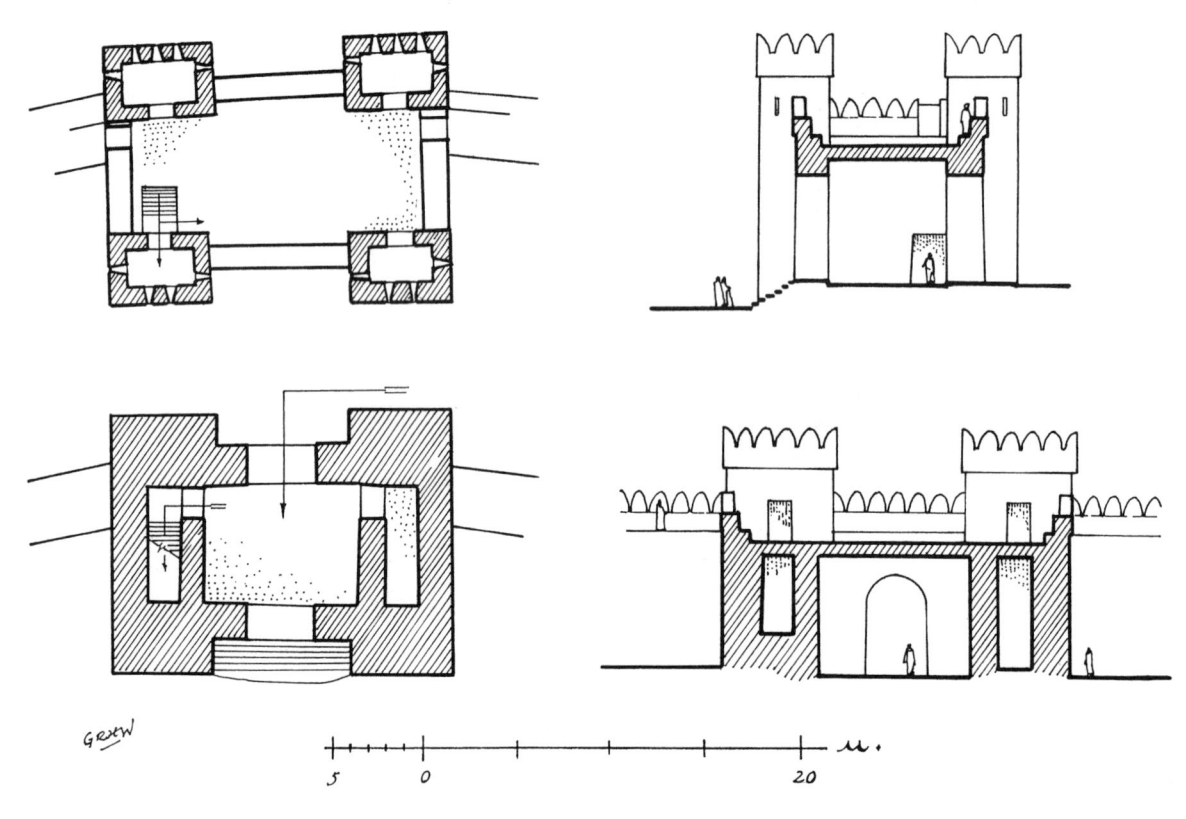

Fig. 122. Schematic reconstructions of the East Gate: roof plan, longitudinal section, ground plan, and cross section, as proposed by G. R. H. Wright.

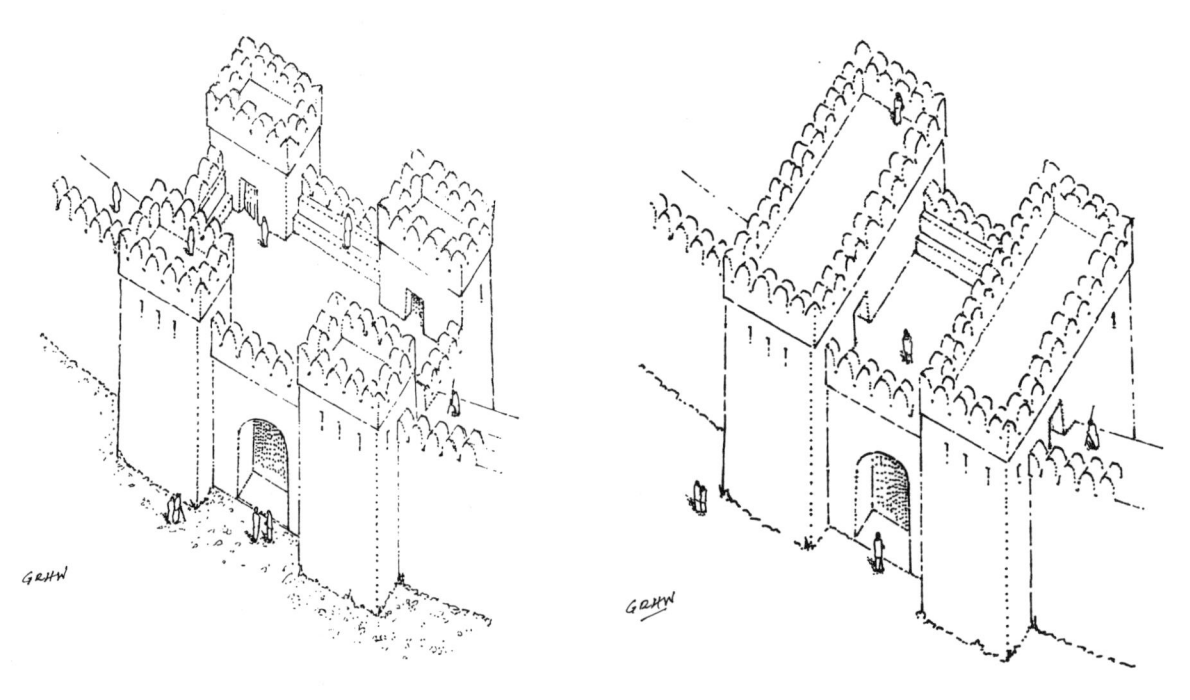

Fig. 123. Axonometric view of reconstruction of the East Gate as though it had four turrets.

Fig. 124. Axonometric view of reconstruction of the East Gate as though with two lateral massifs.

Fig. 125. Looking north between East Gate tower on left and Wall 112 (originally designated "A-2"), showing stone working surfaces 1–5, with seven more below in the section at foot of photograph.

corner to tower corner, the rear facade ca. 17.80 m. The north tower was ca. 13.30 m on its north face, while the south tower was ca. 13.80 m on its south face. The exterior face of Wall B met the north tower ca. 2.50 m in from the front facade, the south tower at ca. 2.90 m. Running away from the northern gate tower parallel to Wall B was a wall, 0.90 m thick and 1.75 m away from the inner face of Wall B. It is likely that it served as the interior bearer of the battlements on the top of Wall B, although it was much closer to the wall than the corresponding feature in Field III. Running from the south tower there are indications of a similar wall parallel to Wall B, beneath LB Wall 120, about 4.00 m away from Wall B, which may have served the same function. A crosswall ran east from this interior wall toward Wall B, defining chambers under the battlements, as in Field III.

If the three walls parallel to Wall B, in Field III, Field I north of the gate, and Field I south of the gate, are correctly understood as defining the width of the battlements, it should be noted that they are at greatly differing distances from Wall B: 7.00 m, 1.75 m and 4.00 m respectively.

While there are great similarities in concept between the East Gate and the Northwest Gate, the former had only two points of closure, a wider passageway, and a longer dimension along the wall than it does through the wall.

The gate towers were substantial masonry structures with deep foundations and brick superstructures. Elevations on the preserved remains of the southern tower were at 8.57 on the southeasternmost stone of the top and 2.93 at the base, for a preserved height of 5.64 m—the only area where excavation reached to the foundation. Dimensions of the towers are given on Ill. 13; figs. 122–124 present proposed reconstructions and axonometric views drawn by G. R. H. Wright.

Each tower contained an inner chamber which may have been guardrooms or the location of stairwells for accesses to the superstructure and its battlements—quite likely both. The interior wall defining the southern stairwell was founded at a deep enough elevation, from about 5.00 to 5.35 above datum on Ill. 24, to have gone with the founding phase of the gate, but its mate on the north may have been constructed with the second phase of use of the gate. The ponderous remnants of the final gate structure, augmented repeatedly through the history of the city, precluded further interior probing of the wall foundations, but soundings within the gate did reach the rampart layering and permitted discernment of two clear phases of use.

The Founding Phase. The East Gate builders began their work by digging a large foundation hole into the C Rampart. Its east limit was the line of Wall 112, which was made into a retaining wall for the foundation by filling up the doorway through it and perhaps by adding to its height. Archaeological excavation did not reach any other limit of the hole outside the gate structure. Within the gate, probes reached the greenish clay and chalk-filled brown earth which marked the rampart elsewhere on the site, sloping from just above to well below site elevation 5.00 (basal on Ills. 24–26).

Fig. 126. The threshold wall for the outer orthostats in the East Gate, resting on a row of stones of gate surface of Foundation Phase.

There are unanswered questions about the way the builders proceeded, but a significant degree of understanding can be gained from the 1964 and 1966 explorations, carried out after the publication of *SBBC*. Section I BB = Ill. 21 is helpful in interpreting conditions in front of the gate, notably in the segment between Wall 112 and the gate tower. The bottom of the foundation trench for the gate reached and cut into the foundation trench for Wall 112; hence, no layers originally running westward from Wall 112 were preserved. Layers of small stones were placed as footing for the tower, and are represented by the lowest meter of the wall against which the damp brown earth of I BB:#13 is placed. Loose cobbling with a layer of burn on it constituted the first of a series of building platforms as the large stones of the tower foundation were levered into place (I BB:#12). As with the construction of Wall A, so here, the builders consolidated the fill with stones as the height of the wall advanced (fig. 125). Only the uppermost layer of cobbling, at elevations rising from 4.49 to 5.01 and then to 5.59 at the threshold of the entrance was the access road to the gate. On Ill. 21 = I BB, this is the cobbling #11 slanting toward the tower from 0.70 m below the top of Wall 112.

On this reading, the top of Wall 112 constituted the road's eastern limit, although the space between it and the gate tower narrowed to 1.20 m

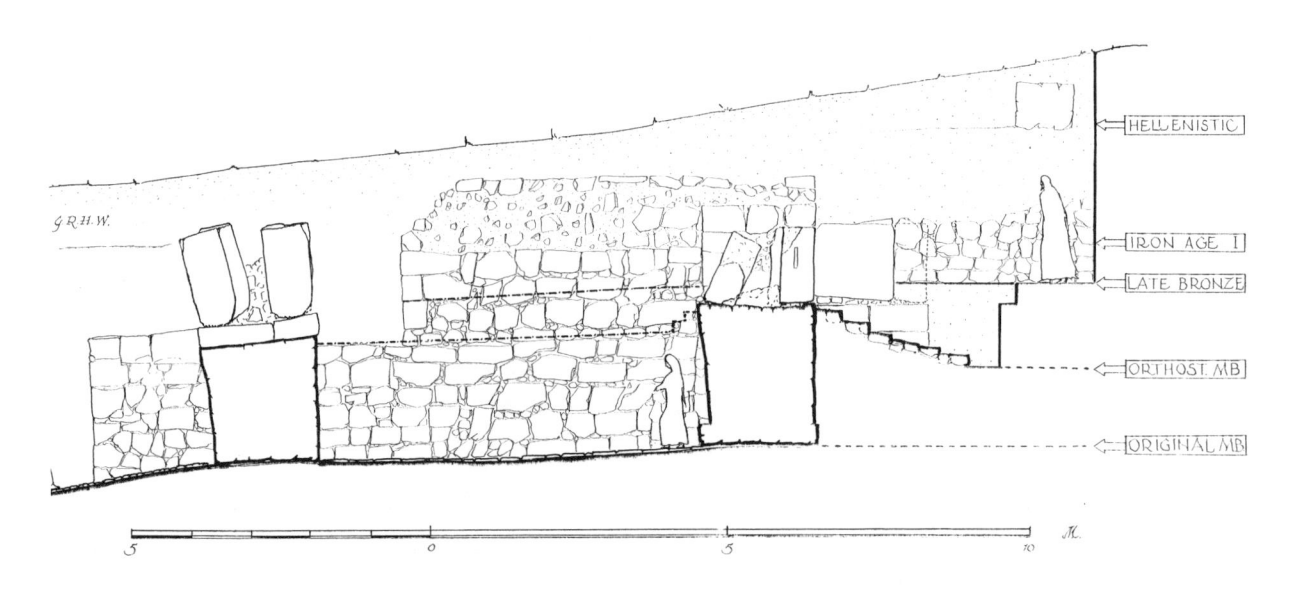

Fig. 127. Section through the East Gate showing phases of usage throughout its existence.

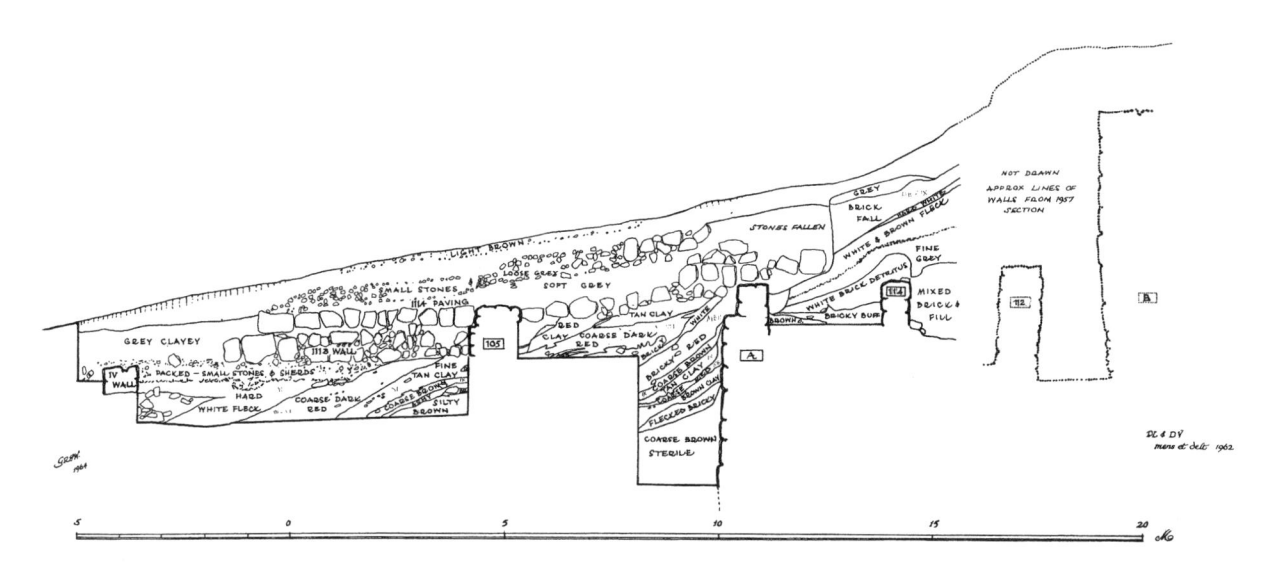

Fig. 128. Section through approach to the East Gate, set back 0.50 m from the line of I BB, as revealed by Lapp and drawn by Voelter in 1962.

at the tower's southeast corner near the edge of the excavation field. It is possible that the top of Wall 112 was actually part of the access road and not its curb, in which case there has been sag in the cobbled layer between it and the tower.

Inside the gate, work in 1957 found a segment of paving against Wall 9, the flanking wall on the south that set apart the stairwell, at elevation 5.75. The row of cobbles on Ill. 24 probably continued that surface. Inside the southern stairwell room, a segment of flooring in the southeast corner was at elevation 5.04. Inside the northern stairwell, at the west, a cobbled surface was at 5.49 (Ill. 12; Ill. 26 at right, the cobbles set in *ḥuwwar* between the layers of mud mortar and brown grey earth).

The threshold wall for the front pair of piers rested on a row of stones whose tops are at elevations 5.55 and 5.63, probably indicative of the gate's surface (Ills. 14 and 27; fig. 126). This row of stones rested on another, which was not directly in line with the walls footed upon it. It is conceivable that they are the uppermost preserved course of Wall C, the retaining wall of the original rampart (Ill. 24 = I FF). Taken together, these fragments of surface and threshold defined the first or foundation phase of the gate, which was roughly at elevation 5.50. Fig. 127 portrays a schematic elevation on the founding phase and its successors.

The fragments of surface were found covered with ash. There was charred debris at the footing of the threshold wall beneath the inner set of piers; the foundation trench for the threshold wall appears to have cut into a deep deposit of ash. Most indicative of destruction in the sections is the deep layer of compact grey on Ill. 21 = I BB:#9, which covered the street and buried Wall 112, extending down to the very top of Wall A. When the BB section was cut back 0.50 m in 1962 to check this material (fig. 128) it was found to be much less uniform than #9 of I BB, and to contain much brick detritus. Its surface was then capped with a layer of white lime close to the gate tower and one can speak of a glacis now created from the gate tower to the top of Wall A. This prepared for the second phase of the gate.

The Orthostat Phase. Definitive of the second phase of the gate was the building of threshold walls at the sites of the piers, and the placement on these threshold walls of orthostat slabs resembling those in the Northwest Gate. These orthostats may have been in place for the Foundation Phase as well, it should be noted, and then raised to their position in the concluding phase of the gate. Their arrangement and sizes are as shown on fig. 129, and their current preservation in fig. 130. The interior (western) sets are depicted in elevation in

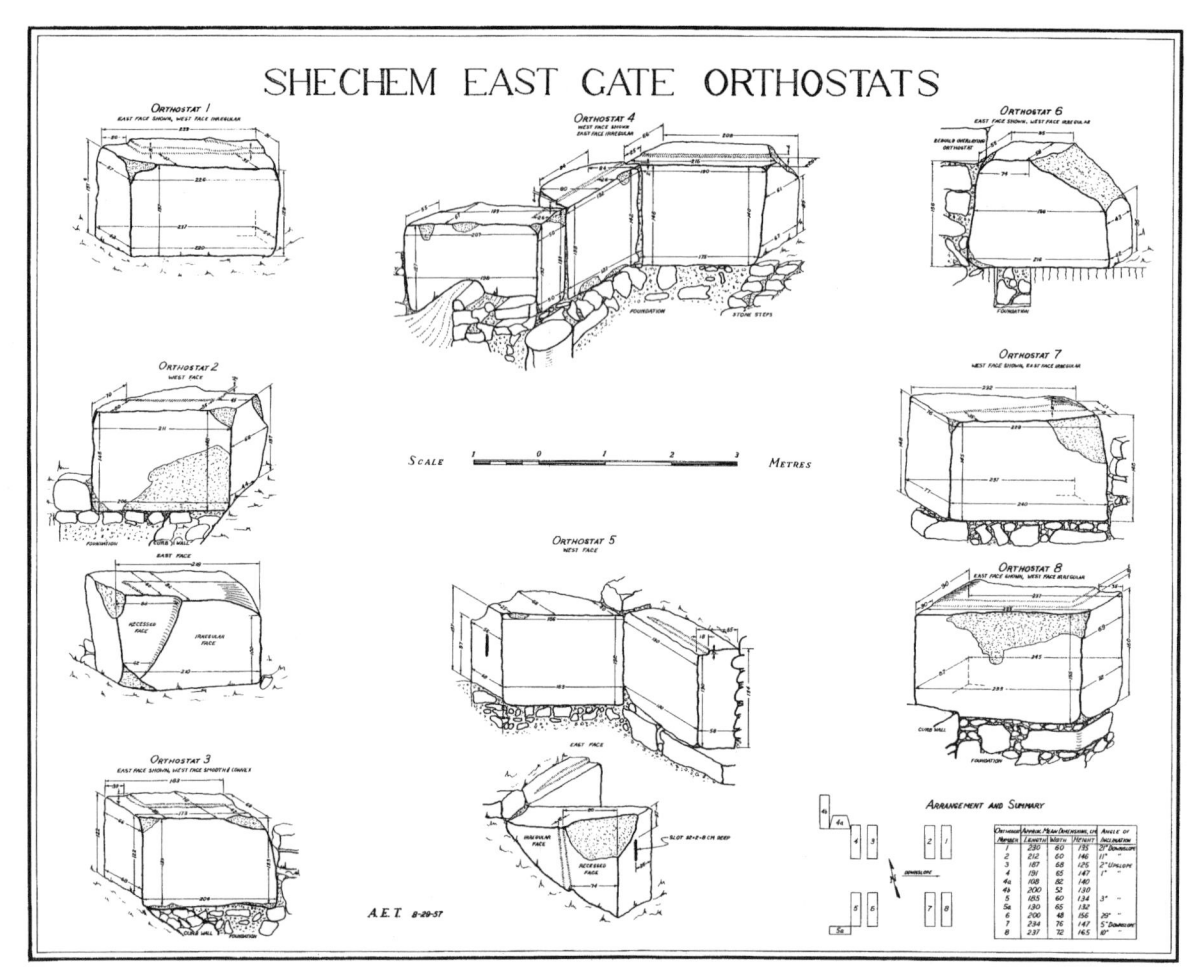

Fig. 129. The orthostats in the East Gate as measured and drawn by Talbert.

figs. 131 and 132. They were of fine-grained limestone unlike that on the two adjacent mountains; Nasr Dhiab Mansur, caretaker of the site and knowledgeable explorer of the region has identified beds of such limestone on the flanks of the plain to the east of the site, but recent difficulties have precluded studying the probable quarry. In any event, they are not of basalt (contra *SBBC*:73) and are not exotic, though they were selected and quarried for the purpose and transported some distance.

The tops of the orthostats have shallow grooves cut into them as indicated in fig. 129; the interior rectangle on the top of each was raised, while the L-shaped outer surface was trimmed lower by about 0.05 m. These cuts may have functioned as the bottoms of slots in which beams 0.30 to 0.35 m could rest and/or slide, but in the absence of information about the superstructure on the orthostats the concept is not clear. The interior orthostat in the north outer pier and the interior one of the south inner pier both showed recesses suggesting the friction that wear from doors sliding back and forth might produce. Sliding doors, as at the Northwest Gate, may have rested between the orthostats and been rolled in to close the entries, the beams serving to brace the closed doors. Affinities to orthostat construction at Hazor, and at sites in Syria, most notably in the lengthy gate at Ebla where similar grooving is to be found, demand a detailed comparative study.

The front threshold wall rested on an earlier foundation, and may have been a reconstruction of a threshold wall of the Foundation Phase. The rear threshold wall, however, was a new construction (Ill. 28). Its top at the passageway between

Fig. 130. The East Gate looking from the northwest, showing the orthostat phase and steps leading down into the city.

the piers was at elevation 8.12, and its footing at 5.69, founded upon destruction debris of the Foundation Phase. On the outer threshold, two elevations are at 7.39 and 7.62. The gate passage in the Orthostat Phase, then, had risen two meters or more. The road outside of the gate will have been at least as high as the white lime topping of the glacis, at elevation ca. 6.50, and perhaps higher; evidence here had been removed by Hellenistic rebuilding and by German trenching.

The fill to raise the gate passageway consisted first of a layer of stony brown earth as much as 0.70 m thick, overlaid by a packed grey brown layer over a meter thick. Because Sellin and Welter cleared the gate to the surface of the Orthostat Phase, it is difficult to discern whether the loose stony layer up to 0.40 m thick that followed was the makeup for the passageway or not. Over it was a layer of thick brown clay which lapped against the bottom of the orthostats at some points and may have been reflooring or may be recent accumulation (Ills. 25 and 26).

The one guide to the surface that is unimpeachable was the set of six stone stairs which started at the top of the threshold of the interior piers (Ill. 14, figs. 127 and 130) and led people entering the city down to the elevation of the cobbled street leading away from the gate. Judging from this, the threshold in the south curb wall of the passageway leading into the stairwell room required a step down from the road surface. This in turn raises the question of whether the curb walls were first built for the Orthostat Phase or were already in existence in the Foundation Phase, a question that remains open. Field diaries indicate a flooring in the south stairwell to go with the Orthostat Phase, but plans and sections do not display it.

Throughout the activity so far described, from the founding of the Foundation Phase to the preparation for the Orthostat Phase, the pottery contained in the layering tells a consistent story. It is uniformly MB IIC in date, and a selection of forms has been presented by Seger (1974, fig. 3), reproduced here as fig. 133. The Orthostat Phase then suffered a thorough destruction, comparable to that described in Field III, for which there is plenty of evidence that it was military in character and designed to put the gate out of commission. The orthostat at the front of the south inner pier was tilted 29 degrees off vertical by a blow which knocked a chunk from its surface, very likely to have been inflicted by a battering ram (see fig. 131). The outermost orthostats on both sides are off kilter as well, but lean outward, downslope, perhaps as a result of intentional dislodging which would have collapsed the superstructure.

Work in 1957 encountered the quantities of brick and burn on the steps, so deep as to have had

138　　　　　　　　　　SHECHEM III. THE MIDDLE BRONZE IIC PERIOD

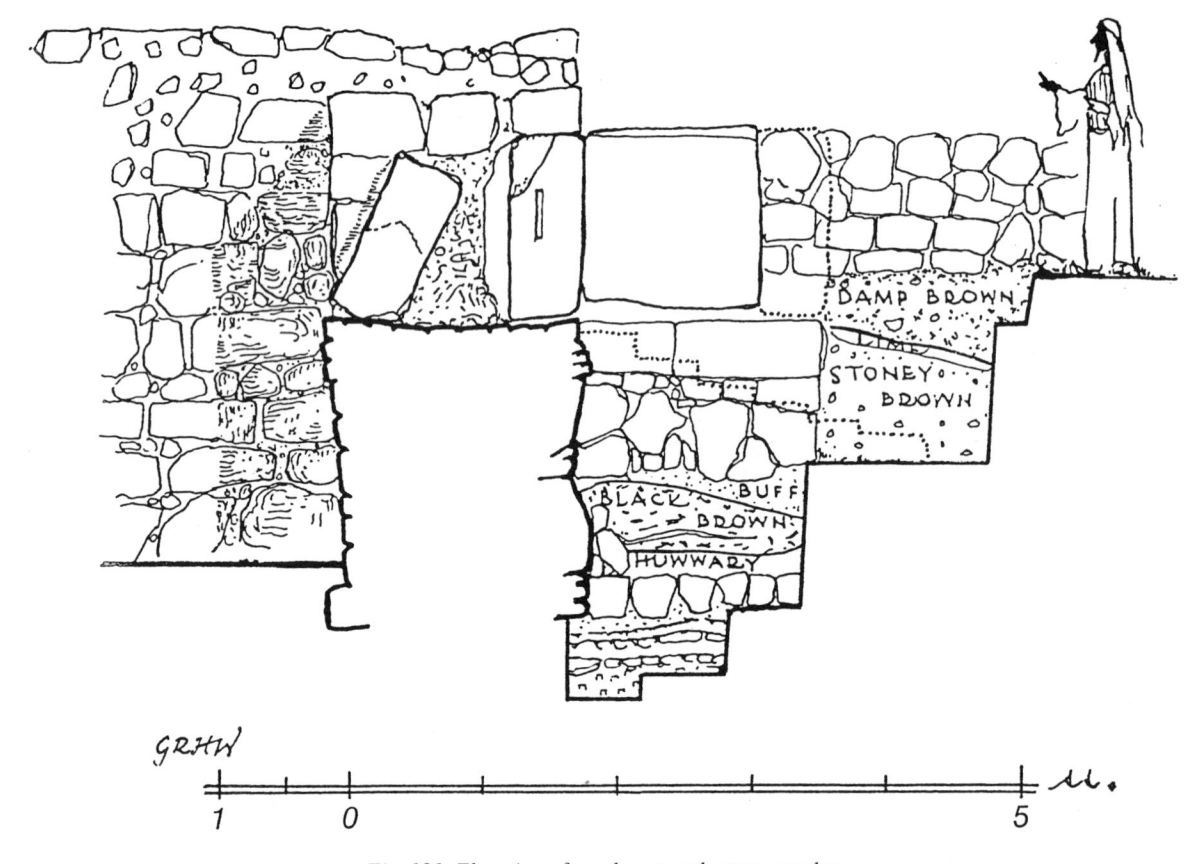

Fig. 131. Elevation of southwest orthostat complex.

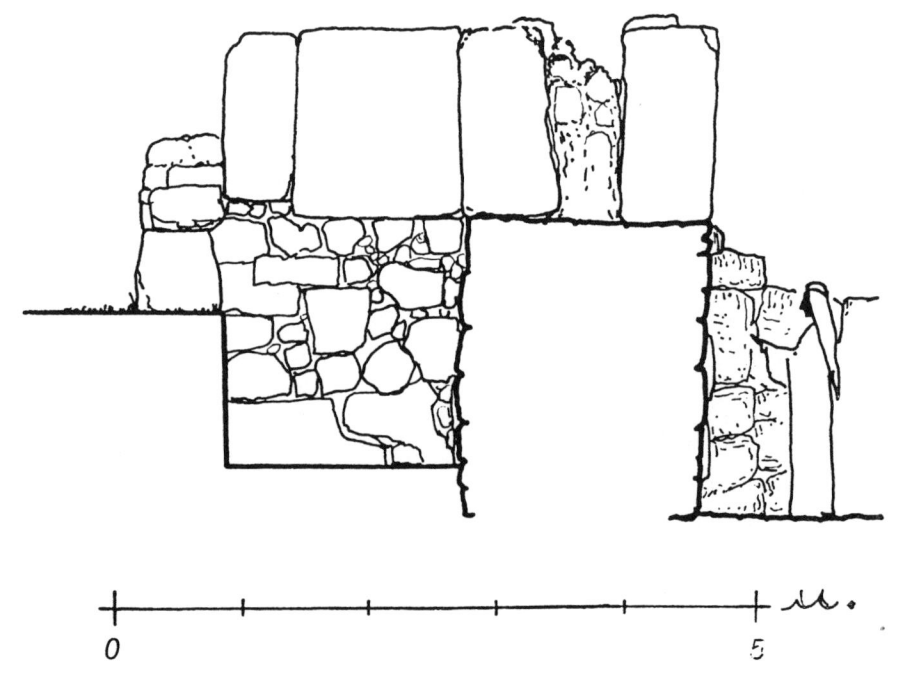

Fig. 132. Elevation of northwest orthostat complex.

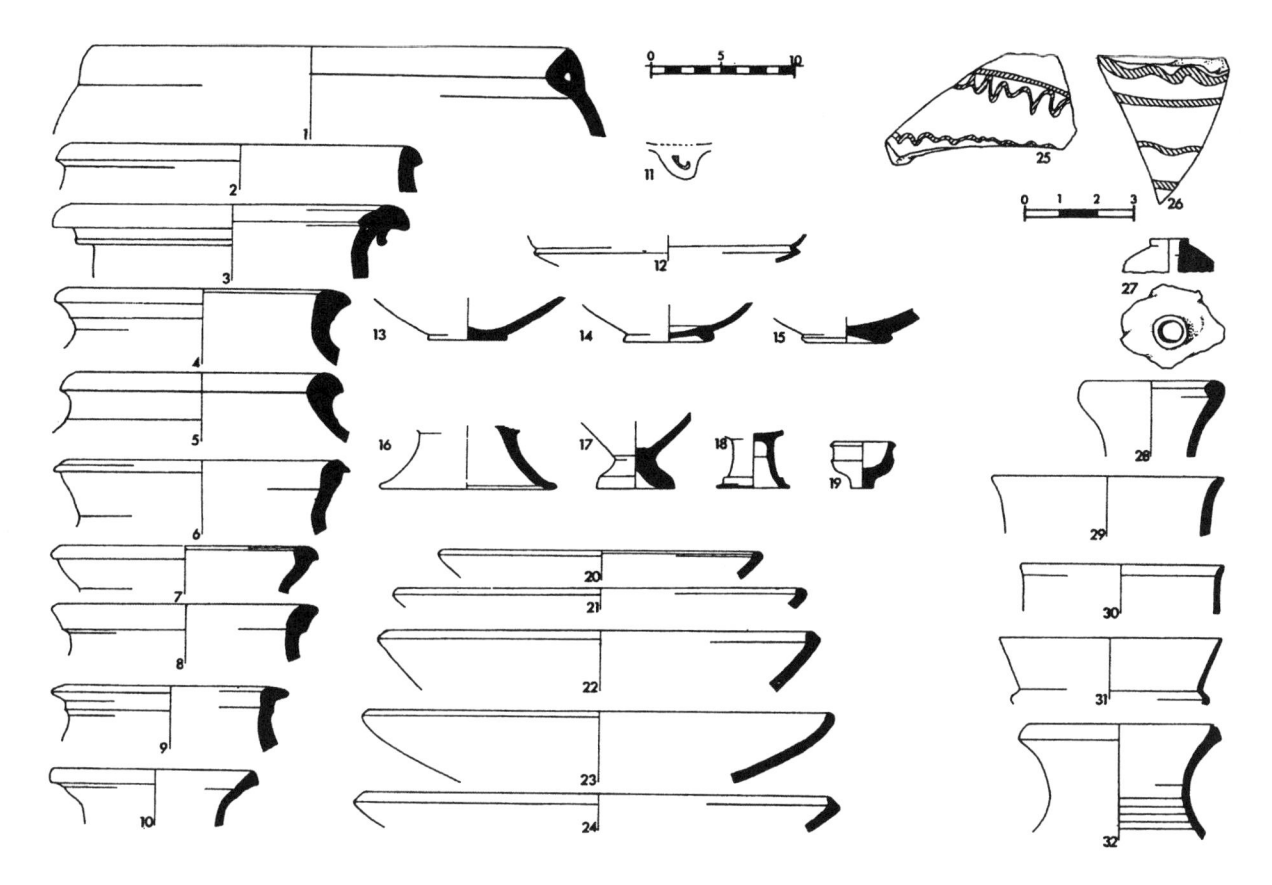

Fig. 133. Pottery forms from Foundation Phase of the East Gate (Seger 1974: fig. 3).

its top even with the threshold of the interior piers. Buried on the steps were at least two articulated skeletons and the scattered bones of another four individuals, presumably killed in the collapse of the gate superstructure, along with a great deal of broken pottery. Fig. 134 (Seger 1974: fig. 4) shows 35 forms from this location, including several "chocolate-on-white" painted pieces from shallow and deep bowls, indicative of the transition from MB IIC to the start of the Late Bronze Age tradition. A further check in 1966 provided another collection of late MB IIC pottery (fig. 135) with more bones, of a child, an adult, and of animals, lying on the cobbled surface leading away from the foot of the stairs.

G. E. Wright (*SBBC*:74) takes the layer of "brown field earth mixed with marl" overlying this debris on the steps as a resurfacing of the street, and then describes the debris of a second destruction following close upon the first one. This claim of two destructions in very close sequence, ascribed to two attacks of the Egyptians between about 1550 and 1540 BCE, continues to be the dominant interpretation of the destruction debris. Awareness of the nature of destruction debris involving two stories of buildings, especially from Field VII in the eighth century House 1727, has enhanced the possibility that all of the debris belongs to one destruction, combining attack and subsequent efforts to nullify fortifications. Whichever interpretation is correct, the south stairwell chamber was covered with 2.00 meters of ash, charcoal and brick. More of the same spilled southward into the corner made by the south gate tower and the segment of Wall B running away from the tower—to a depth of as much as 3.00 m. Pottery from this debris and from the collapse of the brick wall in Field III described above has been gath-

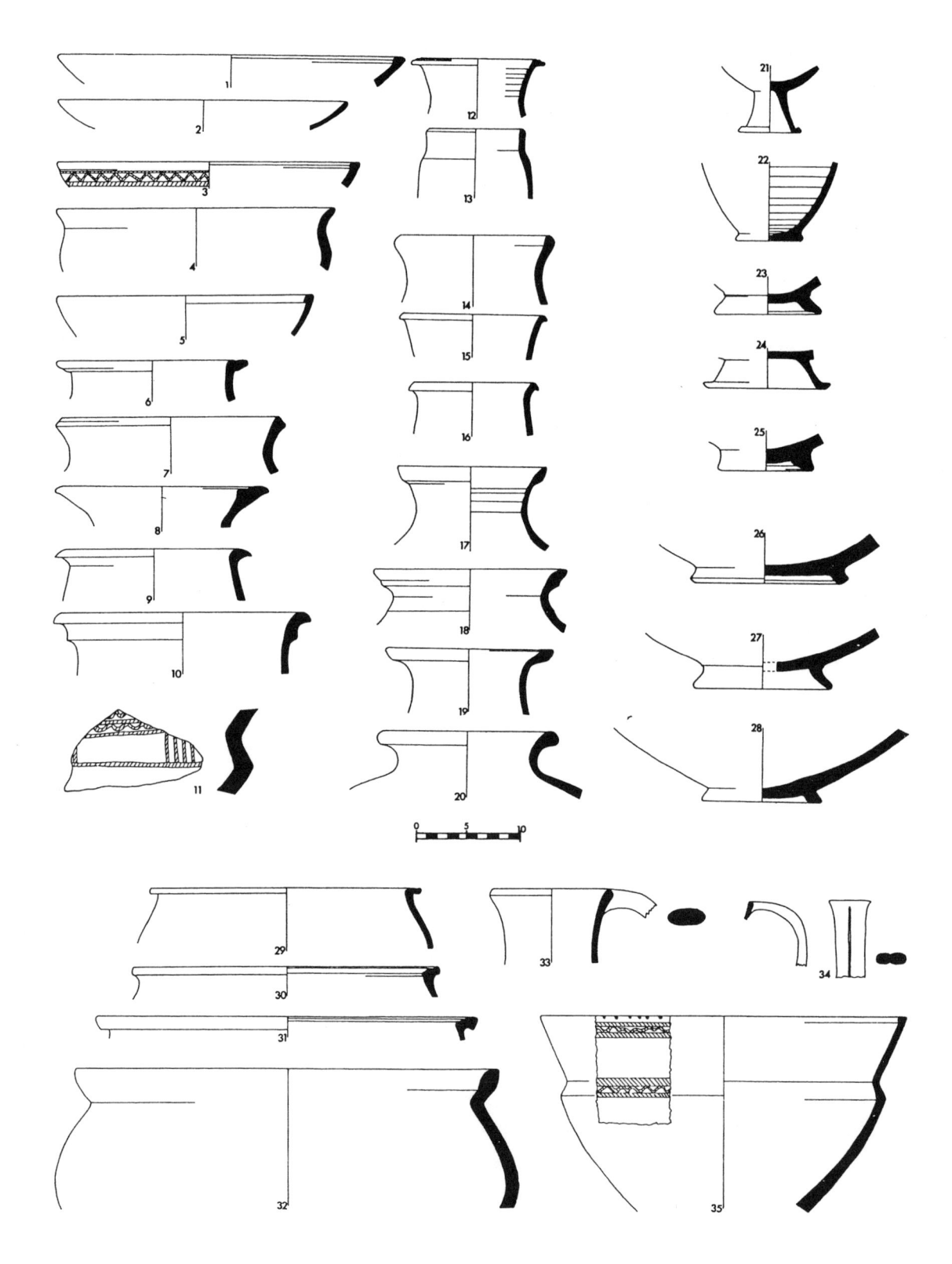

Fig. 134. Pottery forms from debris covering the steps into the city at East Gate (Seger 1974: fig. 4).

Fig. 135. Pottery and bones from the cobbled surface at the foot of steps at East Gate.

ered in figs. 136 and 137 (Seger 1974:figs. 5–6). The date is MB IIC, and represents the last decades of that period.

With this portrayal of the developments of fortification at Shechem in the MB IIC period, the issue of the sheer number of changes becomes obvious. Seger has refuted Kenyon's proposal to move the East Gate into the Late Bronze Age (Seger 1974; Kenyon 1971), and the portrayal presented here has shown why there is confidence that with the establishment of the Wall A system there began a long sequence of alterations all of which must be placed within the MB IIC (for others, MB IIB) period of about a century's duration.

To summarize:

1. Stratum XVI, earlier phase. Wall A established, filled to its top south of the Northwest Gate, the surface plastered. First phase of Northwest Gate built, approached by ramp along Wall A from the south. Wall A continued around entire northern arc of the site past the East Gate, probably with slope to it from defenses on the summit of the old rampart north of the Northwest Gate.

2. Stratum XVI, later phase. Wall B/2, Wall 657, and Wall 112 established inside Wall A. Structures built in the space between the latter two and Wall A, used for domestic purposes, their roofs perhaps as battlements. Multiple resurfacings of floors in Fields I and III. Phase ended in widespread destruction.

3. Stratum XV, earlier phase. Wall B system inaugurated. Wall A augmented north of North west Gate and Wall B/1 built; the 7200 complex constructed, showing minor modifications within the phase. Multiple phases of modifications in Field III. East Gate, Foundation Phase, in Field I. Phase ended in widespread destruction.

4. Stratum XV, later phase. Wall B continued in use. East Gate, Orthostat Phase. Possible time of building Wall E in Field IV. Two phases of modifications in Field III. Phase ended in massive widespread violent destruction, perhaps in two attacks. (Wall E construction and rapid rebuild in East Gate destroyed by second Egyptian attack might be associated, as hasty last gasp effort at defense.)

Effort has been made to indicate data pertaining to the duration of these phases, whether protracted or short. It is artificial to assign lengths of duration; any change in the series can have taken place within months or a few years of the previous change. Noteworthy are changes in conception, repeated refloorings and modifications of space, and clear evidence of destructions. Then,

142 SHECHEM III. THE MIDDLE BRONZE IIC PERIOD

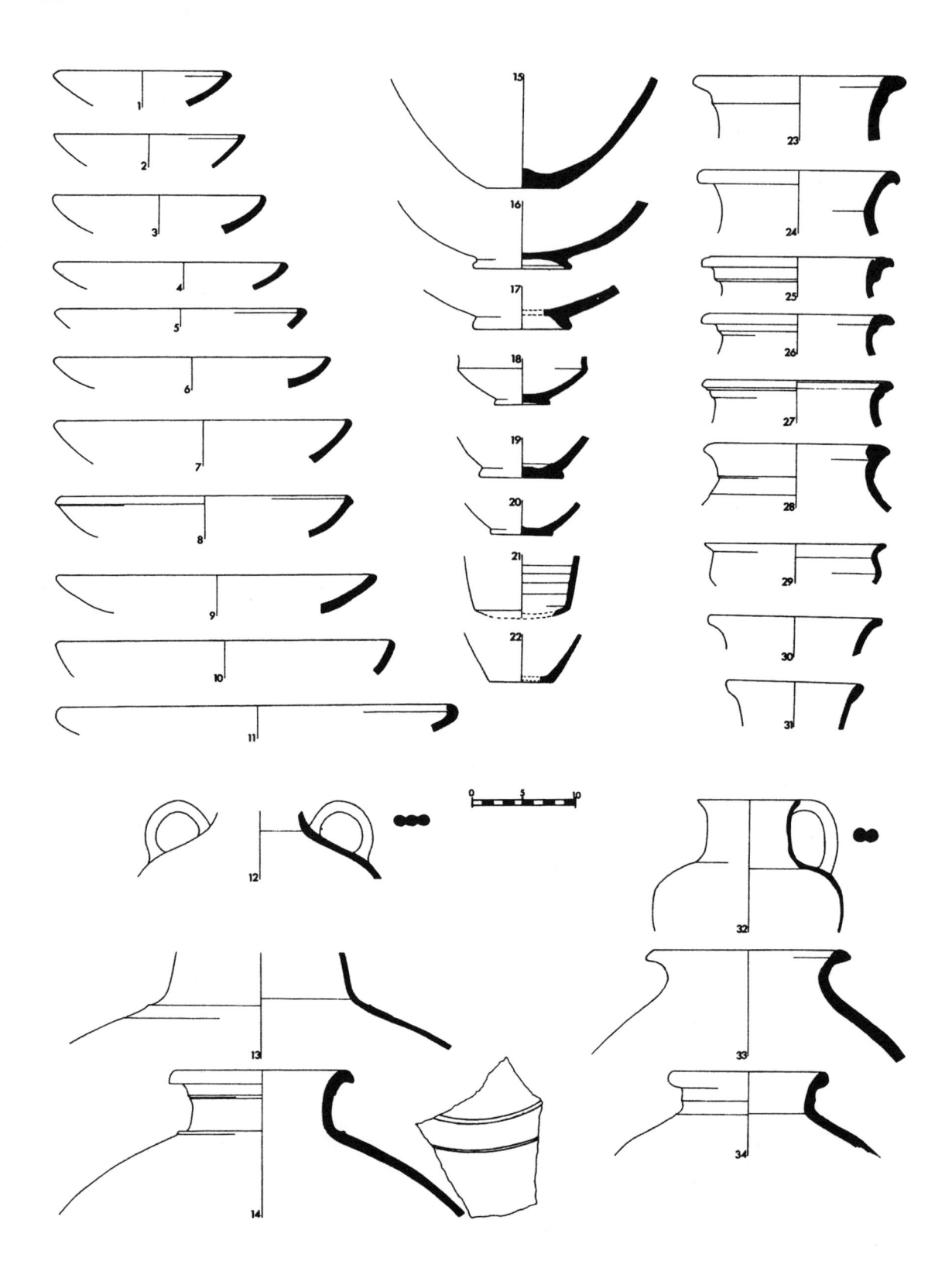

Fig. 136. Pottery forms from Stratum XV destruction in East Gate (from Seger 1974: fig. 5).

too, massive masonry construction takes time and concerted effort, requiring the overcoming of despair and lethargy following destruction as well as the assembly of labor personnel. The period from ca. 1650 to 1550 BCE at Shechem was a time of constant ferment and change.

Field XV and the Search for the South Perimeter. As the final full-scale work at Tell Balâṭah drew to a close in 1968, an attempt was made to probe the line of fortifications through the southern stretch of its course, in among the homes of the village. Ill. 173 locates the two narrow trenches in yards made available by homeowners, in grid squares D 11 and E 12. Between them ran a modern terrace wall, resulting in a 3 m difference in elevation for the modern surface. The terrace wall appears on Sellin's plans of the tell, but villagers recall that once the region was more nearly level than it is now.

Although it was not possible to carry these probes to more than three meters depth in Area 1 and roughly 1.50 m in Area 2, the evidence garnered led to the conclusion that Area 1 lay outside the fortification line, while Area 2 lay inside. The stratigraphy encountered in Area 2 showed fragments of Hellenistic walls just below the surface, and probable Iron II walls beneath them. In Area 1, however, the uppermost wall had Islamic glazed ware sealed beneath it (Ills. 174 and 175); just below them were fragments of walls and surfaces belonging to late Byzantine times, with Roman sherds in the mix.

In the deepest part of the probe in Area 1, at its north end, was a deposit of dark brown soil containing random rocks and chunks of decayed brick, with tip lines running down to the south (Ill. 175). While the small amount of pottery in this deposit represented Iron II, Iron I and Late Bronze, the strong impression was that the excavation had reached here the spill of rubbish that would lie outside the city fortifications, on which a Byzantine structure had been built after leveling of the region, to be followed by a relatively early Islamic structure. The stark difference between the stratigraphy of the two trenches strongly suggests that Trench 2 lay inside fortifications, while Trench 1 lay outside them. Especially noteworthy is that fragments of Byzantine and early Islamic buildings in Trench 1 were at elevation about 9.75, while Hellenistic was at the surface some 20 m away in Trench 2 at elevations about three meters higher.

Results of this limited excavation lead to the conclusion that the fortifications ran between the two trenches of Field XV, thus marking out an oval rather than circular configuration. Sellin's plans and the earlier site plans of the Joint Expedition presumed a circle but the final site plan shows the more probable line of fortifications.

THE PUBLIC BUILDINGS

On the acropolis, two buildings were temple structures, while two others to their north play some part in the public precinct. Another structure, not within the city bounds, belonged in the same period. In each case the purposes of these buildings has been the subject of controversy, or at least of uncertainty.

In the case of the Fortress Temple, the interpretive controversy is largely chronicled in G. E. Wright, *SBBC*, chapter 6, and is not fully reiterated here. In the cases of the Sanctuary 7300 and the structure at Tananir, the main concern here is description, with some indication of the problems of interpretation.

With regard to the two-roomed structure bounded by Walls 930, 996, 928 and 929, divided in half by Wall 927 (see Ill. 76), there is little confidence as to its interpretation or purpose. Northwest of it lay a square structure with buttresses at each corner, positioned quite close to the Northwest Gate and seemingly blocking the line of entrance through the gate.

With reference to the two enigmatic structures north of the Fortress Temple, Sellin uncovered them both, leaving the northern of the two without context and undisturbed soil to help to date it. The elevations on its preserved walls range from 19.70 to 19.76; a reading recorded by Welter on its south wall when recalibrated would be at 20.73, while a reading on its footing would recalibrate to 17.55. These are at approximately the same elevation as that of the northeast corner of the Fortress Temple, which Welter gave as 20.58. This blockhouse structure probably belonged, then, with the Temple and the Northwest Gate. Beyond this, not much can be said.

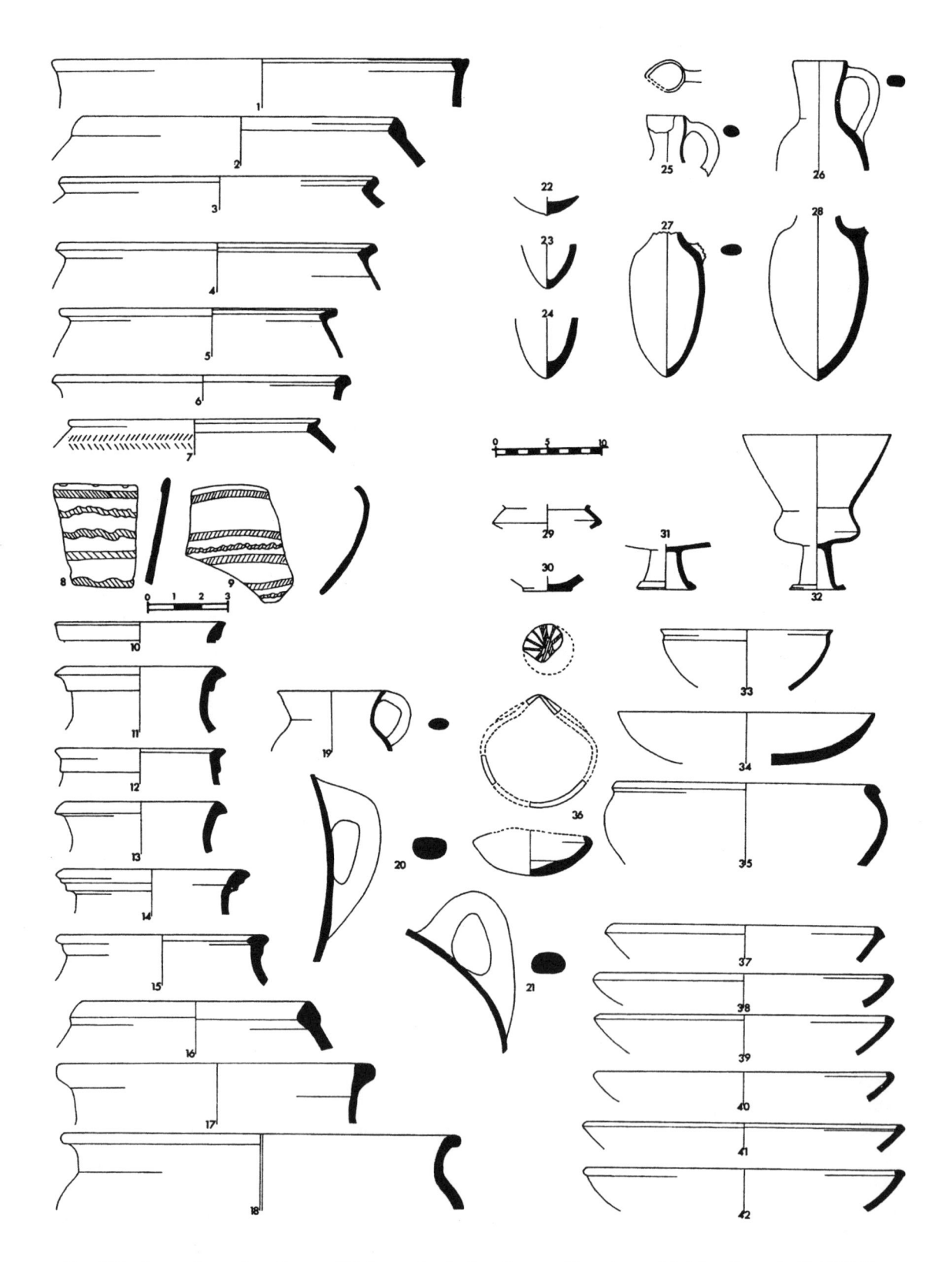

Fig. 137. *Pottery forms from Stratum XV destruction in East Gate and from beneath brick collapse in Field III (from Seger 1974: fig. 6).*

The two-roomed structure just to its east overlapped the square building below it which has been assigned to MB IIB, probably to Stratum XVII. Its north wall, Wall 996, stood approximately in line with Wall 943. The Austro-German work left part of this region undisturbed, although a trench was run along its north face that cut below its foundations. This region was the subject of a probe dug by the Joint Expedition in 1962 which sought to determine the relationships among Wall D deep beneath the building, Wall 943, and the two-roomed "930" structure. The results are seen in VI PP and RR (figs. 11 and 12). This probe established that Wall 996 and Wall 943 both belonged to the early stages of the MB IIC period, Stratum XVI, each with a deep footing of small pebbles, associated with a thick chalk or *ḥuwwar* fill (#35 on both PP and RR), and that fragments of MB IIC structures were preserved north of these walls (Walls 966, 963 and 972) which probably represent Stratum XV. The probe was so narrow that not much could be made of the architectural layout of these smaller walls. Nor is it possible to connect them effectively with MB IIC structures in Field XIII, which lay only a meter away through the balk to the north. To confirm the assignment of the "930" complex to MB IIC, however, it is noteworthy that the elevations on its preserved top and foundations comport well with the elevations on the Stratum XVI and XV buildings in Field XIII.

The Fortress Temple or Migdal (Ills. 61, 62, and 64; sections in Ills. 65–68)

Sellin found the remains of the Fortress Temple during his summer campaign of 1926. Above it, he encountered Hellenistic structures and then an Iron Age building riding over the temple. The Hellenistic remains were removed, but the walls of the Iron Age building were left in place. Sellin and Welter seem to have agreed that the Iron Age building was a sanctuary, hence the decision to preserve it—a fortunate one for the Joint Expedition in that the Iron Age walls did not in all cases lie on the underlying temple walls but instead preserved narrow banks of stratified earth *in situ* beneath them. In addition, Sellin found altars and sockets for standing stones on the platform in front of the Fortress Temple and so decided to preserve an unexcavated breadth of earth in the temple forecourt. Welter, while denying Sellin's interpretation of the MB IIC Fortress Temple as a sanctuary and ridiculing his interpretation of the altars and sockets, dug only one narrow trench through the forecourt tongue and left the rest. These undisturbed soil banks gave the Joint Expedition its most important data for both MB IIC and the LB to early Iron I periods; the forecourt tongue was not excavated in its entirety and most of it remains for future archaeologists to use in checking and augmenting conclusions here offered. A retaining wall was built in 1960 around the forecourt tongue to preserve it; a collapse of a small segment was repaired in the mid-1980s, and it stands as of the time of this writing.

Excavation of the Fortress Temple was completed in 1960 and of the forecourt stratification in 1962. Ill. 65 shows the outline of the structure in relation to the fortification systems lying beneath it at the west edge of the city.

Phase 1 = Stratum XVI. The builders of Wall A had created a plaster-topped platform against the wall's interior south of the Northwest Gate, as has been noted. It covered the fill thrown in to level up over the slope of the augmented rampart system running down to the footing of Wall A. From all indications, the top of the rampart had been shaved off and pushed both outward to Wall A and inward toward the MB IIB courtyard complexes to provide the platform on which the Fortress Temple was sited. Probes through the floors of the temple hit a layer of marl as much as 4.00 m thick which is doubtless the shaved-off rampart. It was noted during excavation at the base of the front towers of the temple, however, that the fill was somewhat different, consisting of occupation debris rather than more-or-less sterile soil.

This type of fill lay in mixed layers extending eastward from Wall 914 in fig. 65 above in Chapter 2, the forecourt section F/2-F/2 (Toombs in *SBBC*: 229–34). The tiplines suggest that it was probably thrown into place west of Wall 914 from the top of that wall. The base of Wall 914, namely 914A, was the probable western definition of the Courtyard Complexes of Strata XVIII and XVII; it had been augmented as a stout, battered wall, 2.25 m thick and preserved through some eleven

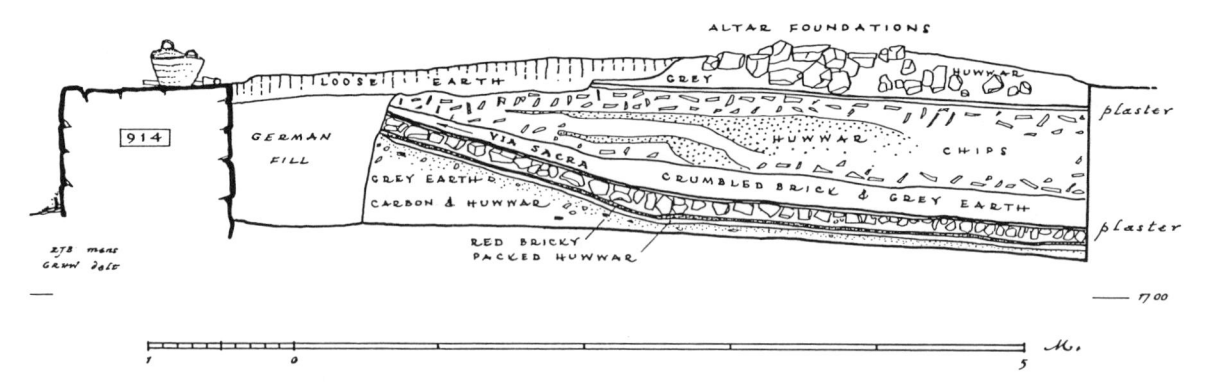

Fig. 138. Section VI F/2-F/2 through the Temple forecourt (Area 13), showing fills and the "via sacra."

courses to a height of ca. 4.00 m, angling across the front of the Fortress Temple and consolidating the underpinnings of the building, while also sustaining the fill of the forecourt.

The uppermost attested features of Stratum XVIII in the Courtyard Complexes (Chapter 2) were the floor plasterings against Wall 925 at the west and the paving stones against the very top of Wall 938 at the east (fig. 65). Above these features, the massive Pit 4:4 had been dug. All of the layers above the Stratum XVIII plasterings and paving stones belonged to the fill preparing for the Fortress Temple and its forecourt; this fill was Stratum XVII in origin and contained late MB IIB pottery, until one reached the thin *ḥuwwar* and red bricky layers below the white and grey brick courses in fig. 65, the packed *ḥuwwar* and red bricky under stones and plaster in the fig. 138. The section separates as many as thirteen interweaving tiplines of debris the uppermost of which is "grey earth with carbon and *ḥuwwar*," up to 4.00 m in depth.

The band of packed *ḥuwwar*, stones, and red bricky lining in figs. 65 and 138 constituted the sloping access way to the Fortress Temple entrance, the "via sacra." Extrapolated, it would have reached the upper courses of Wall 900, kept in use, apparently, as the defining wall of the temple precinct.

The walls of the Fortress Temple were set down into the prepared platform. A trial trench dug against the north wall in 1957 discerned its foundation trench. G. E. Wright provides a description of the temple in *SBBC*:87–91. It is summarized in what follows, with some corrections and new details resulting from more recent visits to the site, and from closer examination of Welter's original plan. Schematic reconstructions by G. R. H. Wright are shown in fig. 139.

The exterior dimensions of the stone foundation have been given at slightly differing measurements in the preliminary reports, roughly 26.30 m from west to east by 21.20 m from south to north. Variations depend upon the precise locations where the measurements were taken and upon protrusions or slight displacements on rocks at the corners. In fact the building was not quite a perfect rectangular. The south exterior line measured 27.05 m, though the top stone at the southeast corner may be ajar and protrude as much as 0.10 m. The north line measured 26.50 m long. The east or front wall measured 21.20 and the west wall 21.50. The most careful measurements were taken for dimensioned Ill. 64. Welter's plan and G. R. H. Wright's presentation based upon it (Ill. 62) vary slightly, but both show the departure from truly rectangular.

The average width of the rear and two side walls was 5.10 m, but Ill. 62 shows the variation most plainly; the widths vary from 5.05 to 5.50 m. The stones forming both inner and outer faces were of rather uniform thickness laid so that they showed horizontal courses. They were up to 0.90 by 0.50 by 0.40 m in size, chinked with small fragments which appear to be off-cuttings.

The rock in the MB IIC Temple foundation is flat-bedded *mizzi* limestone that had been pick or pointed chisel-dressed on the exterior faces, quite different from the randomly shaped *nari* rocks characteristic of Wall A and never of such large

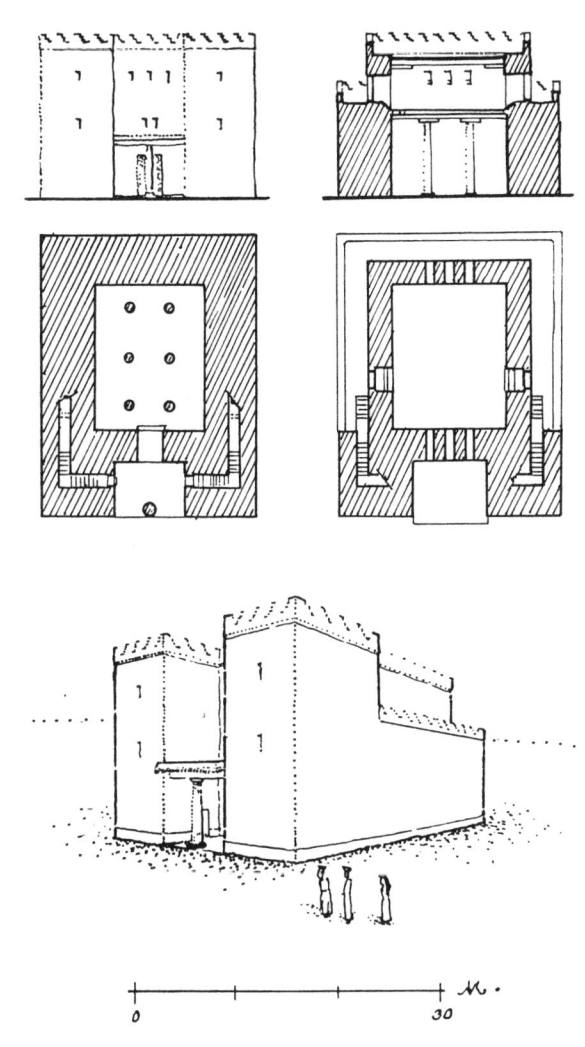

Fig. 139. Schematic reconstructions of the Fortress Temple by G. R. H. Wright: front elevation, cross section, ground plan, roof plan and perspective view. Note that these renderings presume the central pillar in the doorway.

size. They also differed from the *nari* rocks of the 5700 structure assigned to Late Bronze and Iron I to be described in the next chapter. (Fig. 140 gives an indication of these grades of stone.) *Mizzi* and *nari* are not neatly distinguishable, but the appearance and treatment in the successive phases of the Temple are distinctive. The villagers and knowledgeable masons of modern times have no trouble telling them apart. From their experience combined with his own minute observations, Robert Bull writes (personal correspondence, March 19, 1999) that *mizzi* "is harder than *nari*, is more difficult to quarry, can be shaped, does not crack or break as readily as the softer limestone." Lacking cavities ("vugs") and inclusions it is the preferred material for permanent buildings—modern and ancient. *Nari*, the softer material, "is frequently full of holes, seams, vugs and inclusions and does not stand stress as well as hard *mizzi*." Semi-hewn, it is/was used for less permanent, less expensive constructions, while unshaped *nari* stones are/were used for rough field walls and structures.

Between the faces of the Fortress Temple walls, the core was filled with smaller unhewn stones. The top was a flat and even surface of larger stones, leveled up with earth and small stones. This was plastered over and bricks set upon it. Some of the original bricks were in place under the boulders of the Iron Age building on the north wall toward the west end, at elevation 21.10 (*SBBC*:fig. 46).

The front of the temple was made up of two towers, the south one ca. 7.00 m wide and the north one ca. 6.20 m wide. Each contained a stairwell for access to the upper story or stories. Between them was the threshold of the entrance, ca. 8.00 m wide. Bull, in multiple visits to the site from 1992 to 1999, discerned that the front facade and threshold are made of *mizzi* limestone like the rest of the walls, and has proposed a different plan for the entrance. His observations conform to G. R. H. Wright's sense of the ideal interior line of the northern tower shown by the dotted line on Ill. 62, and results in slight revisions of the measurements provided in *SBBC*.

Sellin's excavation found a huge column base fallen into the region below the threshold outside the temple entrance, and he and the Joint Expedition both took it to be part of the Fortress Temple. Its angle of repose and the fact that it was carved from limestone of medium hardness, more like *mizzi* than *nari*, call into question this conclusion. Furthermore, the threshold beneath it showed no indication of an appropriate footing for such a massive column base. These data lead to the possibility that the interpretation proposed after the 1962 season (*SBBC*:89 and pictured in *SBBC*: fig. 47) is erroneous, and the current positioning of the column base with a piece of fluted column upon it at the site is inappropriate (see the discussion in

Fig. 140. Looking west along the south wall of the Temple structure. Wall 5603 is the well-hewn wide wall, its south face farthest to the left. Wall 5703 is above it, with the meter stick. There is an approximately five-degree shift clockwise of the line of 5703 off that of 5603. Wall 5603 is of mizzi *rock. Boulders on the right, north edge of 5703 represent the Iron Age Granary. Both 5703 and 5903 rocks are of* nari *limestone.*

the next chapter in connection with the 5700 LB building on top of the Fortress Temple).

Rather, one crossed a portico open to the sky, between 4.65 and 4.80 m deep, to the point where the juts from the towers separated the portico from the main room (cella), thence into the cella through a door 2.75 to 3.10 m wide and 3.25 m deep.

The cella was 10.55 m in width at the east end near the portico and 11.15 m at the west end. Its length was 13.65 m with slight variations of 0.10 either side of that figure. Sellin found four bases for columns positioned so as to lead him to think there were originally six; Welter's plan provides the locations for the four now reproduced on Ill. 62, with the elevation 20.87 on one of them. None of them were left *in situ* by the German excavators or by depredations since. Since Sellin did not recognize two floorings in the temple cella, nor discern a probable Late Bronze Age phase of the building, there is no way to be sure whether the locations on Welter's plan are correct for the first phase of the Fortress Temple. The column bases fall on lines more nearly parallel to the center line of the Late Bronze Age structure (next chapter), while the 20.87 elevation fits better with the second, later phase flooring of the MB IIC building (20.38) than with the first phase floor elevation of 19.73. Two column bases were found by the Joint Expedition preserved under the Iron Age Granary walls. Hence the proposed reconstructions in fig. 139, although these still place the column base in the entrance.

G. E. Wright was impressed by the way in which the ideal measurements of the Temple readily translated into "sacred cubits." In this he may have been on the right track, but the more exact measurements here presented suggest that the builders departed from the ideal at need. It is also important to remember that the walls would doubtless have had mud plaster facing, and perhaps fine plaster finish, with the finished construction approaching symmetry. The measurements of the portico also seem not to conform to cubit lengths.

The flooring for the foundation phase of the Fortress Temple was Floor 5010, a plaster floor from 3 to 6 millimeters thick and unmistakable where it is preserved. It, like the subsequent floorings of both the 5600 and 5700 structures, was cut through by intrusive pits belonging to Iron I which left arcs of circles through it of as much as a meter in diameter. Floor 5010 at elevation 19.73 rested directly on the marl bank without makeup, but no pottery was isolated from this brown soil locus.

Mention has been made of the Iron Age pits pocking the MB IIC flooring. One of these, Pit

Fig. 141. Cistern/silo 5099A, with the mouth of 5099B at its base.

5099, came down directly upon another excavated installation belonging to the time of Floor 5010. In the southeast quadrant of the cella was the mouth of bottle-shaped Cistern or Grain Silo 5099A, with flaring lip of grey-brown clay at the 5010 surface. The walls of the whole installation were lined with small stones and plaster, the stones set into the plaster rather than the plaster covering the stones.

The flaring mouth suggests it was capped with a cover stone. The mouth was ca. 1.00 m in diameter at the floor; the neck narrowed to 0.50 m in diameter. It then flared out to a diameter of 1.85 m at its widest, and tapered to 1.65 m at its base. The overall depth was 2.50 m, and at the base was a small plastered, flask-shaped cavity, locus 5099B, 0.55 m deep, its mouth with a diameter of 0.38 m and its base 0.73 m in diameter (fig. 141). If the excavation was a cistern, this cavity was probably a dipper hole for the last bit of water stored in it, although it was noted that the base did not incline toward the cavity; if it was a silo, perhaps the cavity served as a sump, although the plaster lining tells against this. Sellin found a similar installation in the center of the cella, 2.25 m deep and 2.50 m in diameter, which later became interpreted as a *favissa* (Thiersch 1932).

The stratigraphy argues for the date of construction of the cistern/silo to have been the same as the temple. The contents, however, show a mixture of pottery down to and including a heavy component of Iron IA. The resolution of this odd discrepancy may lie with the supposition that the cistern was empty until Pit 5099 of Iron I was dug, encountered the top of 5099A, actually was dug to a point below the lip, and intruded Iron I pottery into the early cistern as well as all around its lip.

Phase 2 = Stratum XV. Upon Floor 5010 was Layer 5009, shown on fig. 142 as grey dirt and brown earth. It was between 0.23 and 0.30 m thick and heavy with carbon, bone and pottery, along with much broken plaster in its lowest 0.10 m—all indications of occupation debris and perhaps of destruction. The pottery in it dates to MB IIC with some MB IIB. On Layer 5009 were Layers 5008 and 5007, not distinguished from one another in the section, designated "stoney marl." Layer 5007 was harder packed than 5008, but both were predominantly marl with random fist-sized rocks, and together they constituted imported fill thrown in to raise the floor level. There was little pottery in them, but the latest was MB IIC. As makeup for the floor of the second phase of the temple, a layer of red clay, Locus 5006, was put in place, topped by the 0.02 to 0.01 m thick plaster of Floor 5005 (the upper "M. B. Floor" on fig. 142). Floor

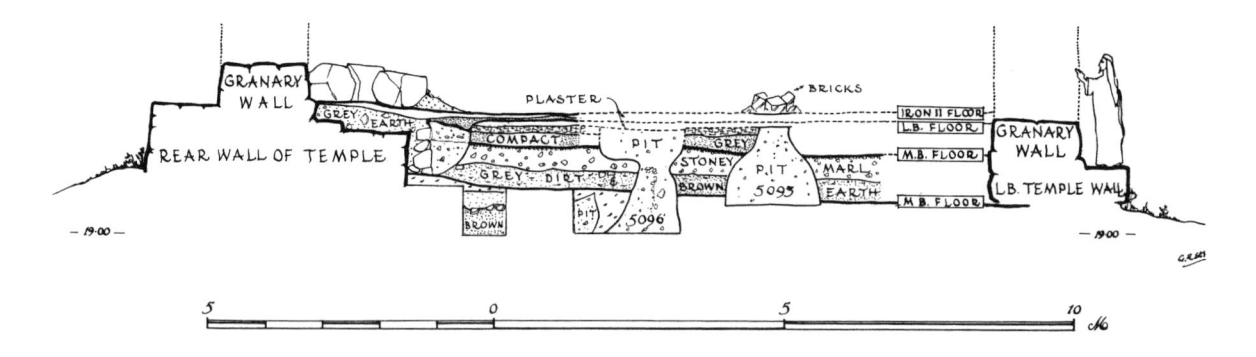

Fig. 142. Section through the granary and temple phases in Field V (portion of V BB = Ill. 67).

5005 was separated from Floor 5010 by from 0.63 to 0.75 m; one elevation taken on it was at 20.38, 0.65 m higher than the 19.73 reading on Floor 5010 nearby.

The raising of the floor level is the most salient feature of the rebuilding of the temple. This is important to recognize because the prevailing description of the Temple in all previous published reports has described a change at the front entrance of the building during the Stratum XV phase which amounted to constructing an odd bent-axis access, shown in simple plan such as that in *SBBC*:fig. 48 and described on *SBBC*:92–93. The change in arrangement at the entrance and the placement of flanking *maṣṣeboth* now are assigned to the Late Bronze Age phase of the structure described in the next chapter.

With the second phase of the MB IIC Fortress Temple belonged the layer of crumbled brick and grey earth of fig. 138 in the forecourt, and the curbing of whole white and grey bricks in figs. 65 and 143. These represented all that remained of the base of an altar Sellin had found in the forecourt, 6.55 m from the front entrance. The chunks of red brick from the "crumbled brick" layer in fig. 138 indicate a standard size from 0.35 to 0.43 m square, while the white and grey bricks in fig. 65 measure 0.35 m square. Their thickness was 0.15 to 0.16 m. This is the size of the bricks from Wall B in Field III, and appears to be typical of MB IIC at Shechem. From the stratigraphy in the forecourt already described, this brick platform, originally about 4.20 m square, belonged with the rebuilt temple; it may have displaced one for the foundation phase, but nothing now remains of an altar for that phase.

Above the brick curb in fig. 65 and the crumbled brick layer in fig. 138 was a unique layer, consisting primarily of chips of *ḥuwwar* mixed with very little earth. Toombs (*SBBC*:233–34) proposed that this material constituted the interior mass of the altar, set on the brick platform. Above the layer of chips, which was as much as 0.70 m thick, was a layer of plaster which may have topped the altar structure. As the forecourt sections show, above this were stones for the later LB altar and loose earth at the surface which Sellin and Welter left and may have disturbed.

Shechem's Fluted Columns. In the summer of 1926, while clearing the forecourt, Sellin uncovered some fragments of stone column shafts:

> Between the altar and the water trough we found two broken columns.... They had no capitals, but at the end a crown set apart by a groove. The crowns were 5 and 11 cm. high. The columns had 16 facets worked in them. The smaller one was 1.25 m high, and had a diameter of 0.36 m., while the bigger one had a diameter of 0.44 m. (1926b: 313).

By the end of the 1962 campaign, the Joint Expedition had found four such column fragments, somewhat the worse for wear, and a fifth which was unfluted but conformed to a piece in one of Sellin's photographs. Sellin had not established a connection between these column fragments and the temple, and the pieces found by the Joint Expedition were out of context. In 1968, however, a

Fig. 143. Curbing of whole white and grey-white bricks for the altar in the forecourt of the later phase of the Fortress Temple.

fragment of fluted column was found in the Stratum XIV destruction debris near Building A in Field XIII, 35 m northeast of the temple. The most reasonable conclusion is that the fluted columns belonged to the MB II C period—Fortress Temple 1. This confirmed the studies of G. R. H. Wright (1965; 1969), who analyzed the use of designed columns in Bronze Age temples, and noted that Shechem's were unique in their fluting or faceting. This design is to be connected to the category of fluted column in Egypt, known primarily from rock-cut tombs of the Middle Kingdom (1991-1784 BCE) and going out of use during the New Kingdom (after 1550 BCE). The Shechem columns may be considered provincial versions of the fluted Egyptian columns, and they are so far the only ones attested outside Egypt. Three examples were cemented by the Joint Expedition on column bases in the consolidated temple foundation at the site for display purposes, but are *not* where they may have originally stood.

The Fortress Temple is widely recognized as the best known example of a *migdal*. In *SBBC* G. E. Wright presented a comparison to its closest congener, Temple 2048 at Megiddo, and evidence for the meaning of the term *migdal* as used in the Bible, based upon ideas of B. Mazar (1968:29–30). More recent attempts to sort out the extremely complex problem of Megiddo's stratigraphy in the temple precinct (Dunayevsky and Kempinski, 1973; Kenyon, 1969; Epstein, 1965) support Wright's contention that the question of Temple 2048's date be reopened. The confidence to be placed in the date of the Shechem temple means that the Megiddo one should be dated by comparison to it, and not the other way around, as Wright insisted.

Temple 7300

Sellin excavated the structures south of the Northwest Gate in the 1926 campaigns and identified them as the south wing of the city palace; the gate was taken as the center of the complex and the 7200 structures as the north wing, added later (Sellin 1926a:233–35; 1926b:304–9). Ill. 50, a redrawing of Welter's 1930 plan with elevations recalibrated, shows what the earlier expedition saw, while fig. 144 shows an interpretive block plan with the Joint Expedition's nomenclature added. Also useful for the description to follow are Ill. 55 and IV FF = Ill. 58.

Sellin noticed that the wall riding over the eastern portion of the whole complex was a later addition—the outer part of Casemate Wall E. He tried to calculate where the interior wall of the long colonnaded hall of the south wing would lie by assuming the colonnade ran down its center, but he found no wall under Wall E that would serve. Nearer the gate, in the complex of two small rooms and one central one within the jog in Wall E (Rooms 1–3 of fig. 144), he reckoned that the eastern limit must lie under the inner line of E. He cleared these rooms to floor level and took special note of a column base near the west wall in the central room, which had a roughly rhomboid section, the points oriented on the room's axis and perpendicular to the axis (fig. 145). Sellin offered little interpretation of the complex, though he

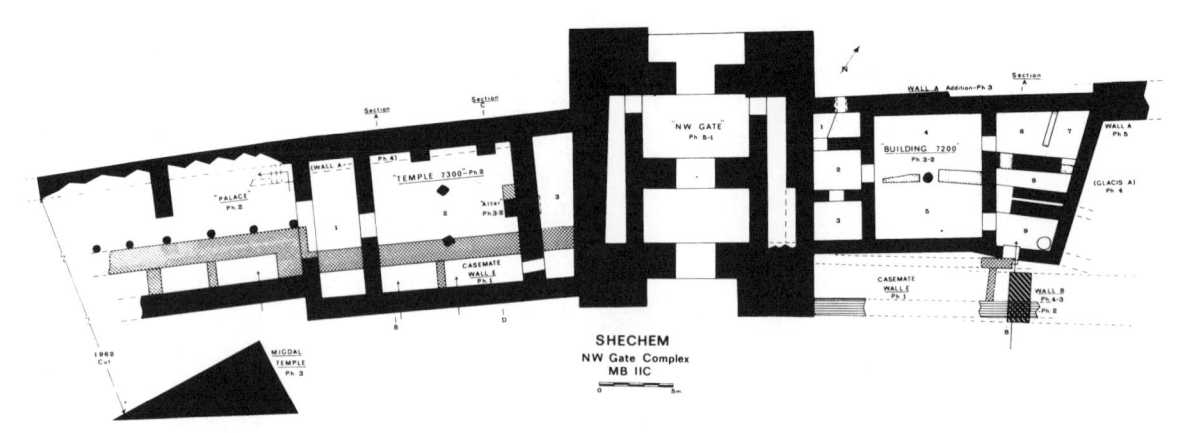

Fig. 144. Dever's block plan of Field IV, Northwest Gate and structures to either side.

called the central room the "main" room of the palace. Böhl (1927:21) thought the central room could "perhaps be called a throne hall." Welter's plan showed a complex of stone against the north wall of the central room, which goes unmentioned in Sellin's descriptions.

W. G. Dever cleaned the entire palace area in 1972–73. One focus of his attention was understanding Wall E; another was making sense of the rooms north of the colonnaded hall, the 7300 complex. He had clarified in 1972 that Wall E north of the gate had been built late in MB IIC, in two stages, first its interior line, then its exterior line and crosswalls. The same pattern made sense south of the gate. Examination of the footing of the exterior line spotted a second rhomboid-section column base (fig. 146) in line with its twin. Their spacing dictated that the central room's east wall be the core of the interior line of Wall E. The stones Welter had placed on his plan along the north wall of the central room would then be positioned centrally on that wall.

As described earlier, the Wall A building program resulted in a filled platform out to its top; this platform was extended over the C embankment eastward, to Wall 914 and on to Wall 900, and it held the Fortress Temple. The space between Wall A and the temple, stretching for forty meters north-south, was at first left open, surfaced with a thick layer of tamped plaster. A portion of this plaster is visible in the center of fig. 146, with a meter stick lying on it. The only attested architectural feature in this space was a plastered stone podium, four courses of stone high, measuring 1.15 m by 2.40 m. The tamped plaster lapped against it so that 0.50 m of the podium was above the surface, 0.60 m below. The top stones of this podium were the eastern portion of what is shown on Welter's plan at the north wall of the central room. That wall rode over the podium, so that 0.60 m of the podium protruded into the central room.

The next phase involved the construction of the 7300 complex and the long colonnaded hall (fig. 147). Three to four courses of stone were built on top of Wall A (Wall 7303) as the western limit. The 7300 building was rectangular except that its northeasternmost wall, the back wall of the gate tower, was off-line, creating a trapezoidal room as Room 3. The external measurements of the 7300 complex were ca. 12.00 m by 19.50 m. Room 1 was an antechamber, 9.00 m wide by 2.80 m deep in interior measure. There were entrances on the central axis of both its walls, leading into Room 2, the central room, which was 9.00 m wide and 10.00 deep. The central axis ran to the podium against the north wall. Room 3 was 9.00 m wide and tapered from 2.60 m at the west to 2.00 m at the east. It was entered through a narrow door near the east side wall. Even though this back room's shape was odd and its function unclear, it was an integral part of the building as constructed. All the walls were well-laid, of large trimmed rocks; their construction technique resembled that of the Fortress Temple. They were ca. 1.50 m wide. The stone foundation

Fig. 145. Column base spotted by Sellin in 7300 room, after cleaning by Dever in 1973. Wall A is to the right, Wall E outer face to left. Looking south. Photo: W. Dever.

stood ca. 1.25 m high throughout, its mudbrick superstructure preserved in many places.

The floor of Room 2 was Plaster Surface 7308 resting upon layer 7303, hard-packed light brown soil mixed with *ḥuwwar*. Makeup 7303 was from 0.30 m to 0.60 m thick, on top of Plaster 7318 of the plaza. Only ca. 0.25 m of the podium stood above this new floor level. With the construction of the 7300 building, the podium was extended westward to become 2.10 m wide; as a result, it was not centered on the wall. But it was unmistakably a feature of the room, an elevated platform at the focal point of the central space in the complex.

On the floor of the room were enough MB II C sherds to fix the general date. Sellin had found MB pottery here also, and refers to three stone pommels from dagger handles typical of MB II B/C. Of special interest are sherds of string-cut juglets which apparently were mass-produced for votive purposes (Dever, 1974: 50, n. 28), found in a disturbed location next to the podium, and sherds of miniature votive bowls found sealed on the floor in the colonnaded hall.

These data strongly suggest that the 7300 complex was a temple. As constructed, it was a three-roomed building. If it was a sanctuary, its closest analogues are temples of the Late Bronze and Iron ages: the LB II Area H temple at Hazor; Syrian examples at Alalakh, Tayinat and Hama (Dever 1974: 43, 48, notes 31, 49); and the Solomonic temple. It would be the earliest known instance of a three-room temple on a central axis, unless one invokes the D temple at Tell Mardikh of MB II A which would have to have its porch included in order to qualify (Dever 1974:8 and nn. 50–51 for implications).

Room 3 contained no functional features to suggest its purpose. It did not seem to qualify as a "holy of holies" behind the main room, which has the cultic center in the form of the podium. Dever proposed that in Shechem's 7300 building the back room may have become a *favissa*, a store room and depository for discarded furnishings—but no such material was preserved.

To summarize the succession of building: an open-air shrine with an altar occupied the space between the back corner of the Fortress Temple and the Northwest Gate, existing for the first 25 to 50 years after the Wall A system and the Fortress Temple were built—belonging to Stratum XVI, roughly 1650 to 1600. With the redesign of the Fortress Temple, a building replaced the shrine, preserving its worship center as its focus. Perhaps it served as the private "chapel" of the city's ruler, similar to the pattern in Alalakh, Stratum VII where

Fig. 146. Second rhomboid-shaped column base in line with the one in foreground, just above meter stick, built into Wall E. Note the two building phases of Wall E. Photo: W. Dever.

a "chapel" adjoins Yarim-Lim's palace of contemporary date (Woolley, 1955:59-65, fig. 35). Meanwhile, the Fortress Temple with its forecourt served as public center for the city's population. When Wall E had to be built in haste, as a last effort at defense near 1550 BCE, it was sited on the east half of 7300 and the colonnaded hall leading to it. Perhaps this nullified these buildings; perhaps, in those final desperate years, the "private chapel" and the palace structures south of it continued in use in this truncated form.

Tananir

In 1931, Welter excavated a square building with a central court surrounded on all sides by chambers, on the low slopes of Mt. Gerizim, about 300 m across the cleft of the valley from Shechem's East Gate and 500 m from the Fortress Temple. It sat on a low spur known as Tananir. Its walls were plastered. It was covered with destruction debris, including masses of burned brick. Welter concluded it was a sanctuary and proposed it as the site of the temple of El-Berith mentioned in Judges 9 (Welter 1931). Sellin (1932) provided more of a description of the structure than had Welter, agreeing that it was a sanctuary but disagreeing with the equation to the Temple of El-Berith.

Taken together, the two reports mention fetishes, incense stands, alabaster vessels, and a bronze sword or spearhead with two bronze knives. Sellin specifies a stone phallic image 0.40 m high and 0.20 m long from one of the side chambers, and a pierced clay cylinder standing 0.25 m high. Welter mentions a fetish-stand in a walled precinct outside the sanctuary, where there were also found a number of amphorae.

Many German scholars since have accepted the identification as a sanctuary (but see Fritz, 1971). Albright, on the other hand, concluded it was a patrician house, and most Americans have followed his lead.

A new factor entered the picture in 1955, when a Bronze Age ruin came to light as the old Marqa airport, now located in a northern suburb of Amman, Jordan, was undergoing expansion (Harding 1958). It was square, with chambers around a central square room. The central room had a centrally-positioned column base or perhaps altar stone in it; these and other features resemble features of the Tananir building. The Amman building was excavated in 1966 by J. B. Hennessy (1966; Hankey 1974), at which time the wealth of artifacts, many of which were imports, combined with the careful construction of the building and the mass of burnt bone, led to its interpretation as a sanctuary, possibly a locus of human sacrifice (Hennessy 1970; G. R. H. Wright 1966). Hennessy refined the building's date to LB II, roughly 1390-1200 BCE; earlier datable artifacts he saw as heirlooms. Another noteworthy feature of the building was its isolation; it seemed to have no adjacent settlement, nor were there signs of occupation any nearer than the city of Amman itself, some 4 kms away.

Expansion of the airport in 1976 called for salvage efforts at the site before it disappeared forever. L. G. Herr carried out a meticulous study of

Fig. 147. Looking north along the axis of the 7300 temple, its colonnaded wall in foreground, antechamber beyond it, and main room with pillar base. Note the altar podium against the back wall of the main chamber.

the area around the building, including a rocky installation outside it which Herr nominated a cremation pyre (1983). He proposed the whole complex then to be a mortuary, lowered its date to the 13th century alone, and connected it to Hittite practice. Herr's collection of burnt bone virtually all attested adults, not children, while Hennessy's preliminary report seemed to indicate the opposite.

The Amman building provided an architectural parallel to the Tananir one, a square structure in an isolated location, but the two are separated in chronology by 300 to 400 years. The isolation factor led to comparisons to the MB II sanctuary at Nahariyah on the coast north of modern Haifa (Ben-Dor 1950; M. Dothan 1956). It contained a number of miniature votive vessels, and their presence has become a criterion in identifying sanctuaries.

The Joint Expedition learned that the Tananir site had become partially covered by new construction. In October, 1968, R. G. Boling conducted a salvage excavation to check Welter (Boling 1975a). Two modern homes with their cisterns had been built over the east half of the ruin (fig. 148). Residents had removed soil and building stone from the west half. In spite of that, it was possible to confirm and refine the dating, and to identify four MB IIC phases, the period of Shechem Strata XVI and XV. A substantial quantity of pottery was recovered, with a strikingly high incidence of miniature votive bowls and juglets.

The complex is set into the hillside, on more or less level bedding planes of the bedrock, which had been shaped vertically and horizontally. Up-ended slabs of bedrock and outcrops had been taken advantage of. To summarize:

Earliest Phase. At the downhill edge of the site, on the lower of two bedrock planes, are parts of three rooms forming "Building B" (figs. 149–151). The row of rooms ran east-west along the terrace, forming a long, narrow structure; as the plan indicates, there may have been more to the building on down the slope. In the westernmost room was a large circular silo hewn from a bedrock outcrop and built up with stones and chalk; it reached an overall depth of 2.40 m. In the lower layers of its filling were sherds of several miniature bowls and juglets. Higher in the layered contents of the silo was a deposit of clay, along with two flat stones the excavators associated with the equipment in a potter's settling basin or sediment pit for preparing clay. For potter's installations in proximity to sanctuaries, see Yadin 1972:33–36, 85; Stager and Wolff 1981:96–97.

Fig. 148. Aerial view of the new homes covering over part of the Tananir structure, partially visible following Boling's excavation in 1968.

Pottery from Silo B is early MB IIC (Stratum XVI) and is the earliest MB at Tananir. The lower phase of Building B was the earliest structure here. Boling makes the case that what would become the central room of Welter's square structure on the next bedrock platform uphill was already in use in this earliest phase—as an open-air platform with a base for a stone pillar sunk into the bedrock in its center. He dates this first phase to the period 1650 to 1625, contemporary with the open plaza and podium inside Wall A on the city acropolis.

Second Phase. Building B was reconstructed and given a new flooring. In the western room, over Silo B, a "shelf" of this phase's surface was preserved with a large collection of smashed pottery on it, protected by a crush of destruction debris clearly indicating conflagration. Building B was destroyed, then, about 1600 BCE, probably at the same time as was Shechem Stratum XVI. Among the pottery found in the destruction debris were miniature bowls and juglets.

There is reason to think that during Building B's reconstructed phase the uphill rank of rooms in Building A, Rooms 7–10, were built, constituting a long, narrow row resembling Building B, on the uphill side of the open-air platform. This row also included a silo, Silo A, fashioned from bedrock and built out of stone and chalk. At the southwest corner of Room 7, close to Silo A, is the platformed outcrop designated the "high place" on the plan.

Third Phase. This phase is confined to the uphill plane. Boling found a first phase of Wall 502, the west limit of the square configuration, and a segment of Wall 116 which Welter had not noticed. He also found a sub-floor silo in Room 2 over which the final phase flooring was intact. Apparently the Building A platform contained an earlier structure before it came to take its final form, the one Welter rendered as his 18.00 m by 18.00 m square building with its 9.00 m by 9.00 m central court. Modern circumstances have conspired to make it impossible to recover much of the A platform, but the contents of Silo 114 provided a broad range of ceramic forms that relate most closely to the latest MB IIC pottery from Shechem (Boling, 1975a: 48, 51, 54, 61-64). Ten of its seventy indicator sherds are votive miniatures.

Most of the plan of Building A was in use, then, in the third Tananir phase. Boling dates it roughly 1600 to 1550, Stratum XV of the tell.

Final Phase. The final phase of Building A involved rebuilding and repair. Walls 502 and 116 were rebuilt, and a flooring was laid over Silo 114

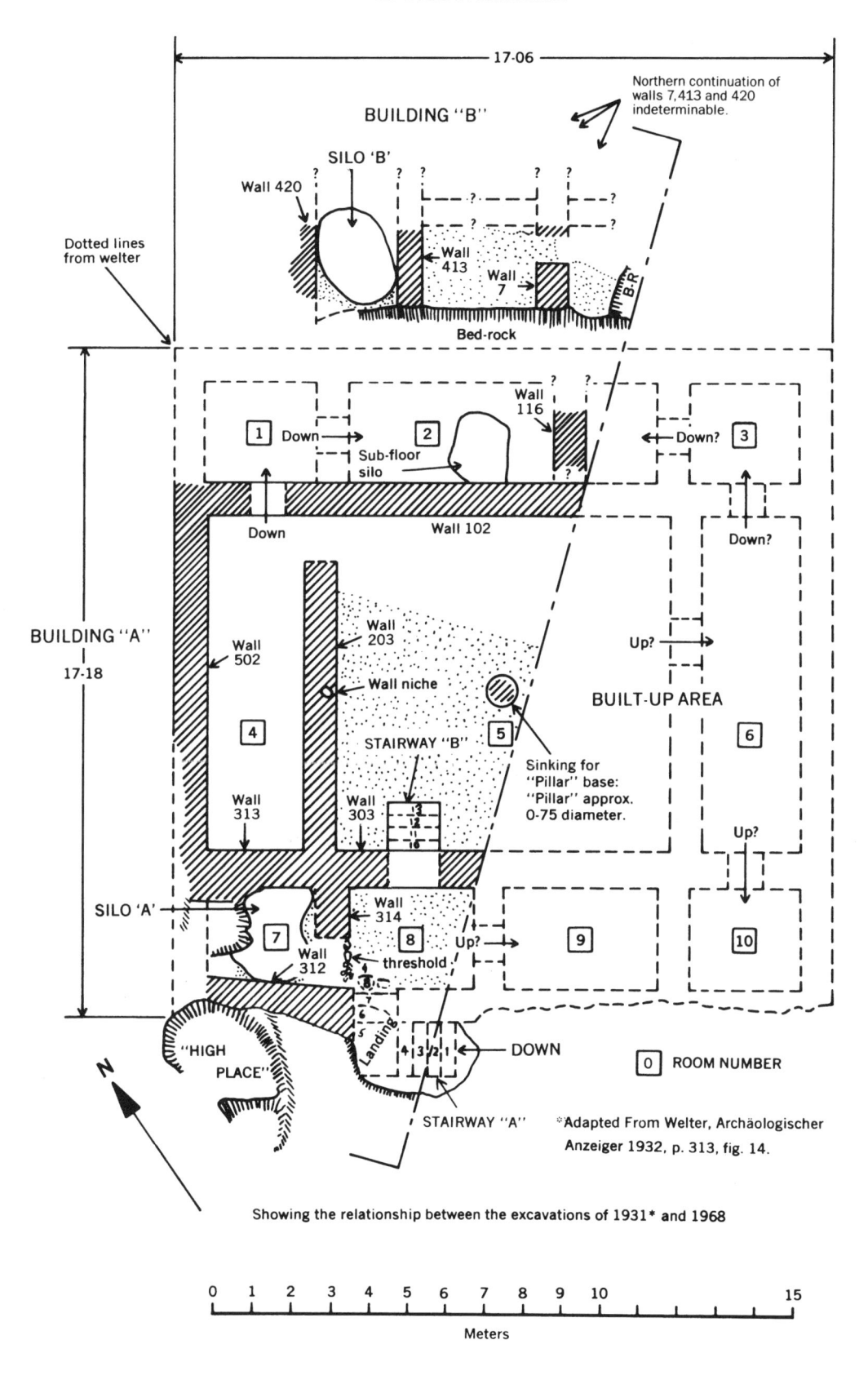

Fig. 149. Plan of the Tananir complex. (Based on Welter's drawing [1932:313, fig. 14], from Boling 1975b.)

158 SHECHEM III. THE MIDDLE BRONZE IIC PERIOD

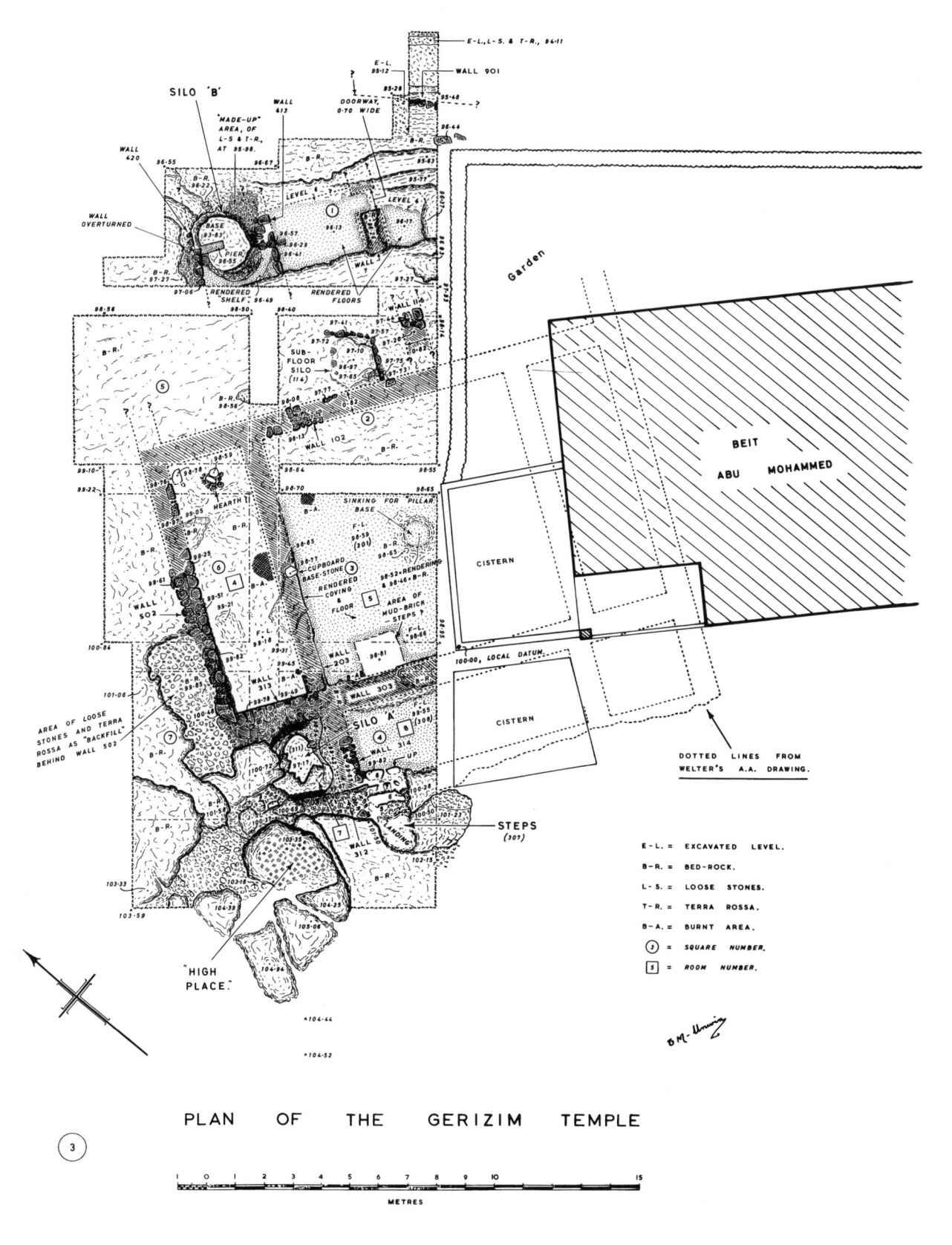

Fig. 150. Top-plan of Tananir remains found by the Boling expedition in 1968, drawn by Oliver M. Unwin.

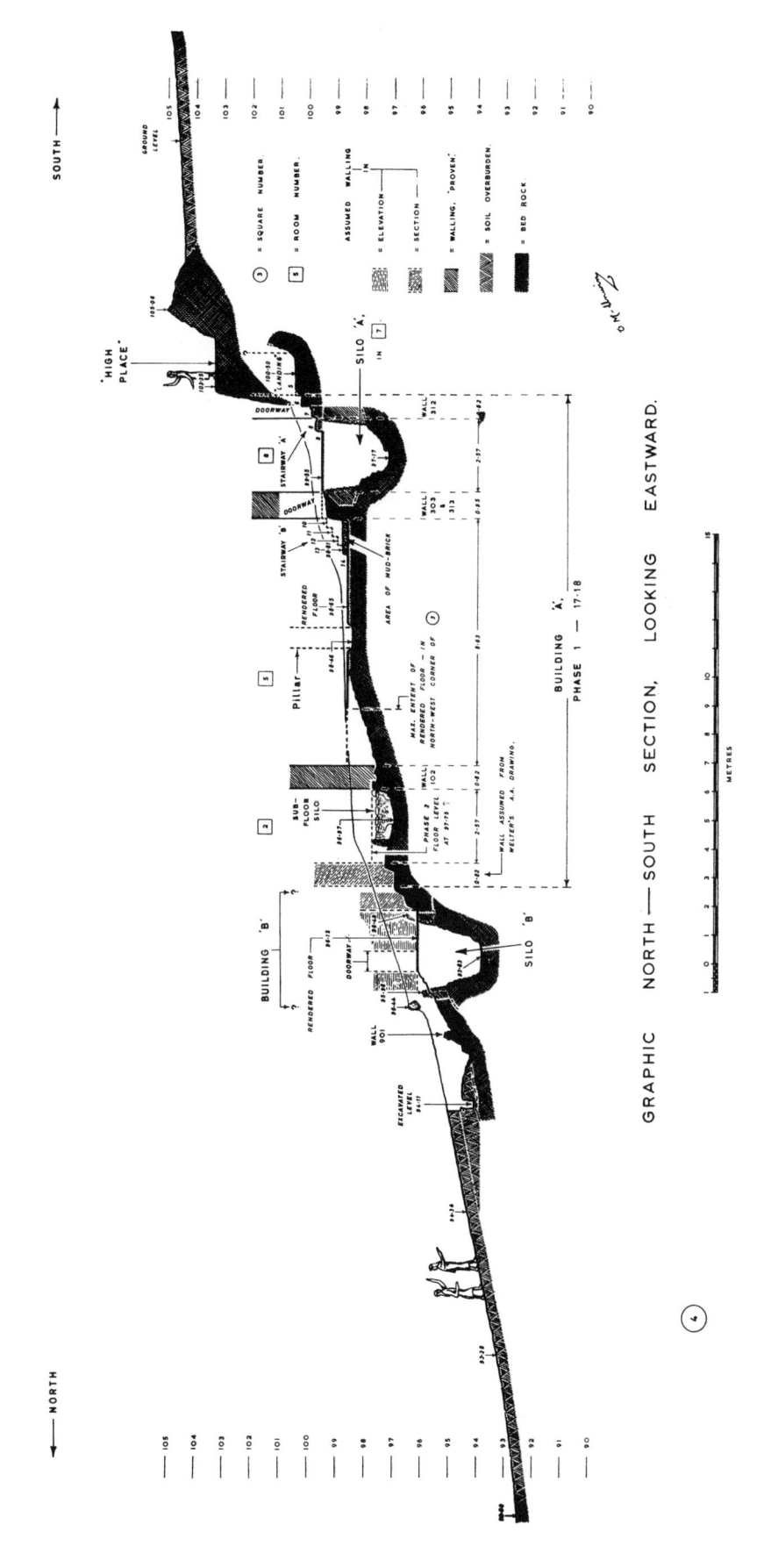

Fig. 151. North–south section through Tananir ruins, drawn by Oliver M. Unwin.

Fig. 152. Drain 3542 emerging from the corner of Building A in Field XIII (upper right).

in Room 2. If the hypothesis of a two-stage assault on Shechem by the Egyptians in 1550 and 1540 stands, it is plausible to see the final phase as repairs between the two assaults, contemporary with the construction of Wall E at Shechem.

The plan of Building A focused on a central square with rooms on all sides, these rooms showing some variety in their dimensions. To get into Building A, one came around the platformed bedrock outcrop designated "high place" (cf. Boling 1975b:172) and walked down four steps adjacent to the southern, uphill wall to a landing. One then turned right into Room 8, and entered the central court down another set of four steps. Access to the other rooms was gained from the central court directly, or indirectly from an adjacent room.

In the precise center of the central court was the pedestal for a pillar. The pillar may have been free-standing or may have held up roofing beams from the side walls of the court. Boling found two conflicting pieces of information pertinent to whether the court was roofed. The preserved chalk surfaces do not resist water effectively (cf. Hennessy 1966:159); when rain fell on them during excavation, a muddy quagmire resulted. That supports positing a roof. On the other hand, the proportion of lamps represented among the pottery fragments found was very low, suggesting that the central room was not a completely enclosed, dark room—Sellin spoke of its cave-like character (1932:305). A case can be made for partial roofing, with the pedestal under an opening to the sky. Depressions in the bedrock noted by Boling might have been post-holes for uprights to hold a partial roofing.

Two further features of the central court are noteworthy. Welter described a platform in its southeast corner which could have been an altar base, and sketched its outline on his plan. All trace of it is now gone. Boling noted one rock remaining in the line of Wall 203, the west wall of the central court. It is circular and has a flat top; architect Oliver Unwin was reminded of the base-stone of the "cupboards" built into the corresponding wall of the Amman airport building. In each case, these special stones lay on an axis that lined up with the central pillar base. On the plan of Building A it is referred to as a "wall niche;" the stone rode in a prepared depression in the bedrock.

Judgment as to the sacral character of the Tananir building is open. If the Amman building is a sanctuary, it attests the use of a singular and distinctive square architectural layout for cultic purposes. Those who accept the force of this comparison have found other structures of similar layout which may be sanctuaries; G. R. H. Wright

Fig. 153. Destruction debris of Stratum XV in Room A of Field XIII, including a tripod brazier. This crush probably represents objects from the second floor or roof.

invoked the comparison for the structure in the northern sector of the Stratum XVIII complex in Shechem's Field VI (early 17th century) and Yadin did the same for an LB I building in Area F at Hazor (1972: 95-101). The strongest evidence of cultic use is the high proportion of miniature votive vessels in all phases of the Tananir complex and the cultic equipment noted by Welter and Sellin. The central base as a possible socket for a pillar is less compelling evidence, as is the outcrop at the southwest as a "high place." Welter's fetish-stand outside the building is a mystery.

Taking everything into account, there may be three sanctuaries at Shechem in MB IIC: a major, public temple with large forecourt within the city in the form of the Fortress Temple; an open-air sanctuary behind it, developed into a "private chapel" for the city ruler(s); and a sanctuary complex outside town on the adjacent mountainside (Campbell and Wright 1969).

MB IIC DOMESTIC HOUSING

Three domestic complexes positioned against the inside of the Wall A fortification system have already been described: Building 110 outside and beneath the East Gate, the 658-642-641 complex in Field III, and the 7200 complex at the Northwest Gate. Each used the top of Wall A and a parallel wall as part of the structure. Each displayed a succession of floor resurfacings, and at one or more levels had distinctly domestic installations such as ovens or bins. The pottery found—jars, jugs and cooking pots—ran the gamut of typical domestic forms.

Two other excavation fields at Shechem reached MB IIC domestic remains. In Field XIII, it was possible to trace settlement and change from the end of Stratum XVI through Stratum XV, while in Field VII the lowest level of excavation reached two sub-phases of occupation belonging to Stratum XV. Each location provides valuable data for domestic life in MB IIC.

Field XIII (Ills. 148–150, 154 and sections Ills. 161 = XIII AA, 162 = XIII BB, 163 = XIII CC, 164 = XIII FF, and 172 = XIII RR)

Field XIII is located about 25 m inside the Northwest Gate, north of the Temple precinct. Wall 943, which marked the northern edge of the Temple precinct, was erected at the beginning of Stratum XVI as part of a preparation of the site north of the temple for houses. Between Field XIII and the Temple Precinct (Fields V-VI) ran a shallow dip in the topography. The north slope of this dip or valley was consolidated by the placement of terracing, which produced platforms for houses ascending northward and westward.

This terraced site lay on the truncated top of the great C Embankment of MB IIB. Great quantities of the top of the embankment had been removed to fill in against the interior of Wall A, as noted above. Much of it went to prepare the platform on which the Fortress Temple sat. Another platform was produced across the shallow valley from the Temple, the edge of which was encountered in the northwest corner of Field XIII. Its elevation was only about a meter lower than that of the Temple platform. On it was located Building I. About five meters eastward from it, a terrace wall let the topography drop as much as 4.00 m to the founding level of a fine housing complex, Building II.

Field XIII is best described in terms of two segments, the west and the east. The division was marked by a terrace wall slightly east of the center of the field. In Stratum XVI, this was 03626-03272 set into the C embankment, narrow segments of which appear on Ill. 148. In Stratum XV, it was the much better-preserved Terrace Wall 3792-03231-03240 on Ill. 149. East of this division is Building II, west of it a street and the corner of Building I.

In the west, the earliest development on the C embankment was a cushioning fill of dark brown earth seen on Ill. 164 = XIII FF as #57, locus 3148. At the west edge of the excavation field, occupation surfacing lay above layers ##57 and 56 in the form of Striated Floors 3137 (FF:#55) inside a circle of stones 3137A constituting a worker's hut on FF to the left of the 3137 striations.

The worker's hut served most likely for those who built Building II to the east and belonged to the period of Stratum XVI; it was soon nullified as a massive filling operation was undertaken to develop the platform for Building I. The first stage of the filling was of compact grey soil with many plaster lumps shown on XIII FF as the lower part of #52. Walls 3129-3131 and 3132 were erected as consolidators for the fill, and another fill layer was laid in as the upper part of FF:#52, comprised of a number of ingredients given separate locus numbers during digging but proving to be one continuous operation. The result was a platform at roughly elevation 18.60. Visualizing this on FF, especially the south half, to the left, is complicated by the recognition that subsequent Late Bronze Age building shaved the top of it, removing surfacing on the platform belonging to the occupation here during Stratum XV.

Before house construction could begin, streets and drainage were provided for. Although the evidence is badly disturbed, it is clear that a street, probably coming from the Northwest Gate some 25 m or 50 steps away, entered Field XIII on Flagstones 3550, the blocks above "Stone Pile not removed" in XIII FF. The steps descended from elevation 18.93 to 18.62 to 18.37 to 17.86 as shown on Ill. 154, and met a secondary street coming from the north. Building I occupied the corner northwest of this junction. As for drainage, Drain 3542 flanked by curb walls 3544 and 3549 was established; preserved for 3.70 m, it dropped 0.75 m, a drop of one in five, to a sump area against the interior of the terrace wall dividing the west of Field XIII from the east. The drain had a channel of flagstones, but was probably open to the sky, not capped, as it passed across the lateral street coming from the north (fig. 152).

The purpose of Drain 3542 was to channel flow from Building I. Building I's corner is the junction of Walls 3462B and 3496B in the far northwest corner of the field. Inside the elbow, the drain can be traced, but the accumulation above it was the filling of a deep pit cut from above the surface left by the Austro-German work in 1934, which removed all evidence of floor within Building I. To posit the elevation of its floor, one assumes that the earliest occupation was just above the drain, the sides of which were at elevations 18.69 and 18.56. What additional phases of flooring might have been present are gone. Throughout the west division of Field XIII, only the earlier phase of Stratum XV is attested.

The quality of the residence represented by this corner of Building I was high. Preparations for its construction including leveling, drainage, and street-building, together with its proximity to the Fortress Temple and the gate, lead the Joint Expedition to posit it to be a Government Residency. Excavation to the north and west of Field

Fig. 154. Fragments of decorated bone inlay from the floor of Room A, Field XIII.

XIII holds great promise for any future efforts at comprehending both MB IIC and the subsequent LB to Iron I period—Strata XIV-XI.

Across the terrace wall to the east, the phasing is more complete. With the start of Stratum XVI, prior to the building of Precinct Wall 943, a terrace wall was built attested in short preserved segments from the north balk (Wall 03626) through segment 03272 to continue in Field VI.2 as Wall 972 (Ill. 148). After Wall 943 was built, several wall lines which served throughout Strata XVI and XV were established on the terrace east of the terrace wall: the 03206-03220-03217-03223 complex, Wall 03271 at the south, and Stone Wall 03640 which came to form the foundation for Mudbrick Wall 3780. Excavation reached but did not penetrate floorings, 03642 in the north between Walls 03640 and 03641 (XIII CC = Ill. 163 and XIII AA = Ill. 161) at elevation 14.70, 03277 near Wall 03272 at elevation 14.92 sloping to 14.68 near Wall 03206, and possible floor 03294 (but this is probably an arbitrary stopping surface) along the east balk at elevation 14.15 (XIII AA; XIII:MM = Ill. 168). All these floorings appear on Ill. 148. Early MB IIC pottery characterized these floorings and the debris above them.

With the shift to Stratum XV, the new terrace line was established, Wall 3792-03231-03240 (Ill. 149), like its predecessor anchored in the C embankment (XIII CC:#61). To its east, there was erected a housing complex on two distinct levels, the portion from Wall 03217-03220-03223 northward at a *lower* elevation, as much as 1.50 m lower than the portion to the south of this wall (see XIII AA). Rooms A-D were the north portion, Rooms E-G the south. The curiosity of a "split-level" house, with the upper level downslope from the lower level, eludes explanation. Access from one level to the other would have required as many as seven stairs, not attested in the area excavated. Perhaps the two units were separate dwellings.

Changes in this housing complex were local renovations within one basic structure (compare Ills. 149 and 150). Room D and probably Room G remained unaltered throughout, but some spaces showed one alteration during Stratum XV, and two locations have two alterations. In general there were two phases of Stratum XV, Phases B and A, with the earlier Phase B showing minor changes. To connect these with alterations in the fortification system (Stratum XVA and B) would go beyond the evidence.

In the north, in Phase B, Room A was divided in two by Wall 03622, a narrow stone wall preserved to over a meter in height and marked by plaster surfacing on both faces. The floor with this

Fig. 155. Range of designs on bone inlay from Room A, Field XIII, Stratum XV destruction.

phase was 03628 to the north of the wall, at elevation 15.52, riding upon an ashy and charcoal flecked makeup (03628.1) and an ashy pit deposit 3635 apparently representing the end of Stratum XVI (XIII AA:#90, far left). On the south side of Wall 03622 was Floor 03638 (AA:#89) at elevation 15.29 (compare Ill.169 = XIII NN). At some point within Phase B, the door at the west end of Wall 03622 was blocked adjacent to the terrace wall, perhaps to buttress the terrace, but the floor was not raised.

Room B is posited in the space taken over by the intrusion of the LB sub-floor chamber. As XIII AA shows, Wall 3742 was in place for the final phase of Stratum XV, but excavation did not proceed beneath the sub-floor chamber to find what evidence of Room B may have been attested.

South of this intrusion were Rooms C and D. Room C was surfaced by Floor 03246=03211 at elevation 15.78, and given a subsequent resurfacing as 03208 (Ill. 172 = XIII RR:#16). Room D, on the other hand, attested only one floor for all of Stratum XV, Floor 03250 (with 03210 north of the wall segment 03212) at elevation 14.98 (XIII AA:##72 & 73).

Rooms E and F on either side of wall fragment 03269 had beaten earth floors 03291 at 16.64 and 03295 at 16.24. Within Room F near Wall 3840 was Cobbling 3849 at 16.60. Room G's only attested surface was a Plaster Floor 3848 at 16.76 (XIII AA:#74 and Ill. 162 = XIII BB:#70); it was not penetrated, so it is uncertain whether this surface served both Phase B and Phase A, or there is a Phase B surface deeper—though the small portion of Area 5 layering shown on AA:##74 and 77 makes the latter alternative doubtful.

A cluster of alterations belongs together to constitute Stratum XV, Phase A (Ill. 150). Mudbrick Wall 3780 was placed on top of Stone Wall 03640—the only mudbrick wall preserved

Fig. 156. Installation 16.129 against north balk of Field VII, Area 9.

in place in the complex (shown in elevation on XIII CC, and in section on XIII AA). The bricks were of varying dimensions, but were 0.13 m thick—the same as those found in Field VII Installation 16.133 to be described below. Wall 3780 was faced with purple plaster, its original color or fired to that color by the conflagration. Wall 3742, the core of the LB Sub-floor Chamber (Room B) was now clearly in place as the southern limit of Room A, while Phase B Wall 03622 was out of use and covered over. Beaten Earth Floor 3772, at elevation 16.20 to 16.09, was well-preserved from the foot of Wall 3780 to curve up the face of 3742 (XIII AA:#71).

Room B extended presumably from Wall 3742 to Wall 03260. A fragment of Surface 03210 (AA:#72) north of 03260 meant a drop to elevation below 15.00, hidden in the unexcavated region beneath the LB Sub-floor Chamber.

In Room C, Floor 03208 was laid over a filling that raised the elevation by 0.70 m from its Phase B predecessor, at 16.50. On this floor Tannur 03207 was installed in the southeast corner. Room C was now on a level with the upper portion of the Phase B split-level structure. Only Room D was still at the sunken level, over 1.50 m lower than the rest of the complex.

Across Wall 03217, in Phase B Room E, Screen Wall 03225 defined small closet-sized spaces E and F. Closet E was floored at elevation 16.81 and E/2 south of the dividing wall was floored at 16.95, about 0.30 m higher than the Phase B surfaces had been. Room G was apparently unaltered.

Destruction debris covered all of Building II (XIII AA:##68, 69–70). It reached depths of 2.50 m in Room D and 1.60 m in Room A. On the floor of Room A, along Wall 3780, 0.10 to 0.20 m of ash and charcoal lay on top of a crush of smashed store jars. Above that was a mass of bricks from Wall 3780's superstructure. Mixed with them were pieces of plaster, pockets of ash representing burnt beams, and a great deal of pottery, including restorable store jars, riding high in the debris. A three-legged basalt brazier was also in the upper layers of debris, matching one found on the floor (fig. 153). These items must have been on the floor of a second story or on the flat roof. The debris over Room D depicted in XIII AA favors seeing the house as two-storied; note the ash deposits high in the debris, separated by the designations ##69 and 70, with bricks in #69. Plaster patches suggested that upper story walls were also plastered.

The range of artifacts found on the floors of Rooms A, D and H and in the debris above them attests the quality of life of the inhabitants. Among the crushed store jars in Room A lay scorched pieces of bone inlay which had probably decorated one or more wooden boxes. Fig. 154 shows the pieces in context; fig. 155 shows the range of design: simple hatching and cross-hatching, concentric circles between incised lines, and at least two stylized birds. Over 340 decorated pieces, many of them very tiny, plus another 60 or so undecorated splinters make up the total collection.

Also lying on the floor in Room A were two scarabs. Both belong to the standard "Hyksos" corpus. The first has a geometric design, while the second (Campbell, Ross and Toombs, 1971:16) has a readable set of hieroglyphs which may, especially in its center column, contain an Egyptian name, w3h-m3 ʿt-R ʿ, "Enduring of truth (is) Re." More likely, however, the carver gathered signs into a design without reference to meaning, as often happened in this period. This scarab still showed the metal band which held it in the ring or pendant on which it was worn. A third scarab was found by a Balâṭah resident in the winter between the 1968 and 1969 excavation seasons, reportedly from the bricky debris in Area 4 and hence also part of Room A. If scarabs served to identify their owners, two and perhaps three from the same room suggest that several family members were people of status.

A typical MB IIC ring-based juglet was among the pottery on the floor of Room A; inside it were three smoothly polished goat astragali, or ankle bones. The usual interpretation is that such bones indicate cultic activity of some sort, perhaps in relation to burial ceremonies. But their presence in what clearly seems to be a typical house raises questions about this interpretation. Were they amulets, or gaming pieces? Why should they have been kept in a juglet? Study of astragali henceforth will have to take into account the context in which they were found at Shechem.

A good many bronze artifacts came from the destruction debris—a pin from the debris over Room D's floor, an earring from the floor of Room A, a finger ring and a needle from other parts of the debris. Most striking was a dagger blade found on the floor of Room D, with its rivets still holding traces of the wood handle. On the floor of Room G just south was a limestone pommel which would have capped the handle of such a dagger.

The quality of construction, finish, and artifacts from Building II led Lawrence Toombs to call it a "patrician house" after the 1968 season first encountered it. Seger's expanded evidence from 1969 fully justified this claim.

Field VII

The other location of MB IIC domestic housing is the lowest level excavated in Field VII, reached in a limited exposure next to the main terrace wall in Area 9 (Ills. 93, 113 = VII BB, and 115 = VII CC). The remains show two phases, probably both belonging to Stratum XV.

A sturdy stone wall (16.122) marked the earlier phase. With it went Tannur 16.130 north of its preserved end, and the founding phase of Tannur 16.130A north of that, partially hidden in the balk. A low bench (16.126) or platform (Plan 83, below #30) was positioned parallel to 16.122, 1.20 m to its east and continuing into the east balk. The platform was made of molded mud, the dense soil from which mudbrick is fashioned by adding straw or pebble temper and drying in the sun.

The molded mud material contrasts with the mudbricks laid flat in the space between platform and wall (locus 16.123), which apparently constituted the flooring for this phase. They were of different colors, and were roughly square, distinctly reminiscent of the parquet hearths in the Stratum XVII (MB IIB) house in Field IX. East of Wall 16.122 at the south limit of the area and continuing into the balk, there were two layers of brick beneath the surface layer. These were not square and varied in dimensions, ranging from 0.27 to 0.38 m wide, 0.51 to 0.54 m long, but all 0.13 m thick. Chocolate brown, yellow brown, and white blocks intermingled. There was shading to pink and to black at the edges of the blocks, suggesting either a thin mortar between them or the physical effect of drying in the sun. Excavation did not proceed below the bricks, so it is not certain that their top surface represents flooring of the earlier phase (Stratum XVB).

Molded mud was the material of choice for the entire later phase (Stratum XVA). Mud Wall 16.125 stood a meter high on the 16.122 foundation, and continued through the balk into Area 6 as Wall 13.174, an eroded hump shown on Ill. 113 = VII BB. Its top elevation was at 11.77. A badly eroded hummock of mud (16.128, Ill. 115 = VII CC) suggests the position of a slim wall that ran eastward from Wall 16.125 over the XVB platform.

The floor for this phase was locus 16.120 laid on makeup 16.121. Floor 16.120 was made up of thin resurfacings accumulating to 0.08–0.10 m in thickness, suggesting an extended period of use. Floor 13.173 continued 16.120 at the north limit of Area 6 at elevation 11.10, found only to the west of Wall 13.174 and curving up its west face (Ill. 113 = VII BB:#48). Several of the 16.120 floor resurfacings ran to Tannur 16.130A at the far north, indicating it was in use; the last few layers ran over it. All ran over Tannur 16.130, confined in use to Stratum XVB.

At the north balk was the curious feature 16.129 pictured in fig. 156: two blocks of *ḥuwwar* (the lower measuring 0.40 by 0.45 m) and a square pattern with rounded corners. The latter had a core of crumbly white material surrounded by rounded segments of charcoal. Beige plaster encircled this cluster of what looks like a bundle of poles.

Above the uppermost resurfacing of 16.120, riding over the walls in worn, gentle slopes, was thick destruction debris, evidence of the 1550-1540 catastrophe. In Field VII the evidence pointed to only one destruction of an occupation that lasted for some time. On top of layer 16.113, a level line of yellow plaster may have been a flooring extending westward from Wall 16.125, and thin plaster dusting lying level appeared in two places within the grey and reddish accumulations to the east of the wall which overlay the destruction debris. These may hint at ephemeral reoccupation after the destruction but before the Late Bronze Age recovery in Stratum XIV.

Field IX

The quality of domestic housing shown in Field XIII and hinted at in Field VII suggests that MB IIC was a relatively prosperous time at Shechem. Fortifications and the Fortress Temple suggest that public works demanded expenditure of time and resources. As to the extent of population, not much can be said. One hint may come from Field IX. The remains of this period, confined to Areas 3 and 4 (Areas 1 and 2 were left unexcavated), if correctly phased and understood, suggest that this part of the site was unoccupied and used perhaps as a work area. Possible remains of a brick hearth (locus 9789) on Ill. 142 = IX BB near the north balk, ashy and charcoal deposits in the accumulated erosion soil, and intrusive pits mark what Callaway's original report designated Phases 13 and 14. The layering is displayed on Ills. 141–143 and 145.

CHAPTER 4

THE LATE BRONZE AGE TO EARLY IRON I

FOUR STRATA, XIV–XI, REPRESENT the stretch of time from ca. 1450 to 1100 BCE. The period was not well discerned by Sellin's and Welter's work, although some of their finds certainly represent it. Along the fortifications, Hellenistic rebuilding dug down to the MB IIC and MB IIB systems, thus reaching a supply of good building stone to reuse and gaining anchorage for their foundations. That operation removed the intervening stratification. On the acropolis, especially in connection with the Fortress Temple, remains of this period are very thinly attested. While Sellin and Welter cannot be said to have ignored material remains of the period, their preliminary publications focused on the monumental architecture and fortifications; little was reported about their excavations inside town, where they encountered most of their evidence for the Late Bronze, Iron, Persian and Hellenistic periods. Because the Joint Expedition opened very little new ground on the fortifications or the acropolis, much of what is here reported about the Late Bronze and early Iron I periods comes from domestic housing. But something can be said about the fortifications and the acropolis.

THE FORTIFICATIONS

Evidence of the LB fortification system appears in Fields I and IV and perhaps in Field III, in every case involving at least partial reuse of the MB IIC systems. Sellin's and Welter's work removed most of the evidence on the west, and Hellenistic intrusion has badly disrupted conditions at the East Gate, but enough can be pieced together at the two gates and in Field III to show that the LB fortifications were inside the line of Wall B, reducing the extent of the city.

The East Gate: Field I

The ruins of the MB IIC East Gate were covered over by the destruction debris of its superstructure. Huge amounts of the debris filled the interior of the south gate tower and the region in front of Wall B to the south of the tower; in all likelihood the same was the case on the north side of the gate, although the German reports give little information and excavation has not probed the interior of the fortifications north of the gate edifice.

A New Gate Tower (Ill. 16, 20 = I AA, and 23 = I DD). Evidence of LB reconstruction of the fortifications occurs only to the south and west of the interior of the gate complex, centered on a new gate tower. Ill. 23 is an elevation drawn through its center. The tower showed three phases of development, but facilities against the west side of its back wall displayed four. This phasing corresponds to the domestic housing evidence of Strata XIV-XI, representing LB IB, LB IIA, LB IIB and Iron IA, roughly the period 1450–1100 BCE.

The gate tower was a rough rectangle defined by Walls 127, 126, 120 and 133 (fig. 157). Its exterior measure was 10.00 m on its west face, 9.50 m on the south, 9.00 m on the east, and 10.25 m on the north, on Wall 133. Wall 133 was a later addition, however; the original structure had no north wall, and one entered an open bay limited on the south by crosswall 128 which divided the tower in two. A wide door in

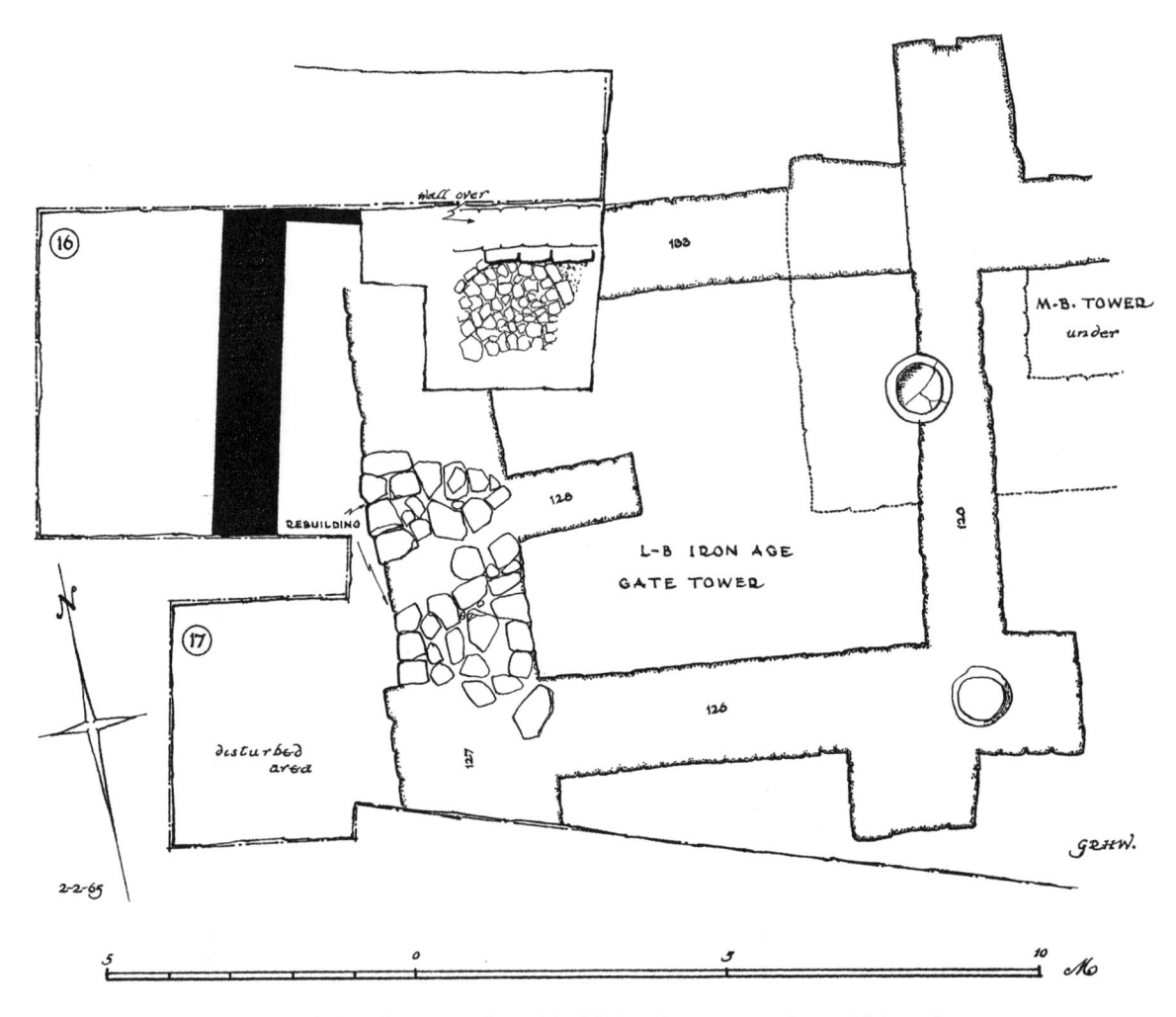

Fig. 157. Block plan showing outline of the LB/Iron I gate tower along with later features.

Wall 128 gave access to a rectangular chamber to the south.

Wall 127 was the widest and most deeply founded of these walls; it probably was the first built, and it apparently rested upon an earlier MB II wall beneath it, which remains unexcavated. Wall 126 was not bonded to it (fig. 158). The width of Wall 127 was from 2.25 to 2.50 m. It entered the south balk of the excavation field at a point ca. 0.75 m from its junction with Wall 126, and narrowed slightly to 2.15 m as it continued south. Tentatively this southern continuation is taken to be the LB city wall. The fortification line then turned east to follow Wall 126 to a buttressed corner, there to turn north again on Wall 120.

The tower then was contained within a salient of the wall and commanded the approach way, which lay downslope where it had been in MB IIC. The entryway to the city would have been at the elevation of the former MB IIC Orthostat Phase entryway, with banks of destruction debris about a meter high to each side held back by retaining walls.

The earliest phase of the open bay off the gate passageway was floored by flagstones at elevation 8.45, compared to the 8.04 elevation of the top of the stairs of the Orthostat Phase at the back of the gate that led down into the MB IIC city. Climbing two steps would have put one on the flagstone paving in the gate tower bay. West of Wall

Fig. 158. Junction of Wall 127 at right with Wall 126 within the LB/Iron I gate tower. Note that 126 abuts 127, and is founded higher.

127, the elevation on the plaza about to be described was at 8.15 m, 0.65 m higher than the MB IIC surface at the foot of the Orthostat Phase stairs (7.50). Two or three steps would have climbed to the plaza.

Phasing of the LB/Iron I remains here swings on Wall 127, notably on its interior face (Toombs 1979). The wall appears to have had a buttress against its corner inside town (fig. 157) with elevation 10.14 on one of its stones, but the "buttress" may instead be collapse off the face of the wall from early in its history, of a secondary skin as suggested on fig. 159.

The plaza mentioned above was built against Wall 127 and is preserved in two phases. The earlier cobbling, discerned only in test trenches and poorly preserved, was at elevation ca. 8.15 in the southwest corner of Area 17; excavation adjacent to Wall 127 did not reach this depth so the connection to the wall is not established. This cobbling, 127B, is taken as Stratum XIV and co-terminus with the flagstone of the tower front bay.

In the next phase, assigned to Stratum XIII, there was no change in the surfacing of the bay, but the plaza was raised by an 0.75 m fill containing bricky debris, stones and sherds. On this fill was laid Cobblestone Surface 509 (fig. 160), cut into by Pit 528. The cobbling runs flush to the face of Wall 127 to its east, at the right in the photograph, surrounding the buttress or preserved piece of the original face of the wall seen in the right foreground. If Wall 127's face did collapse, that happened between the Stratum XIV and Stratum XIII surfacings. Elevations on Cobbling 509 were 9.00 in the southwest, 9.06 in the northwest, sloping up to 9.38 in the northeast and 9.48 in the northeast of Area 17, and 9.30 on a small fragment preserved at the south edge of Area 16 (fig. 161). The cobbling was rendered smooth by a heavy coat of plaster. This may have constituted a public square or parade ground, just inside town.

Over the 509 cobbling and plaster (fig. 162) lay almost a meter of accumulated material (locus 508) before the next surfacing. Within it were

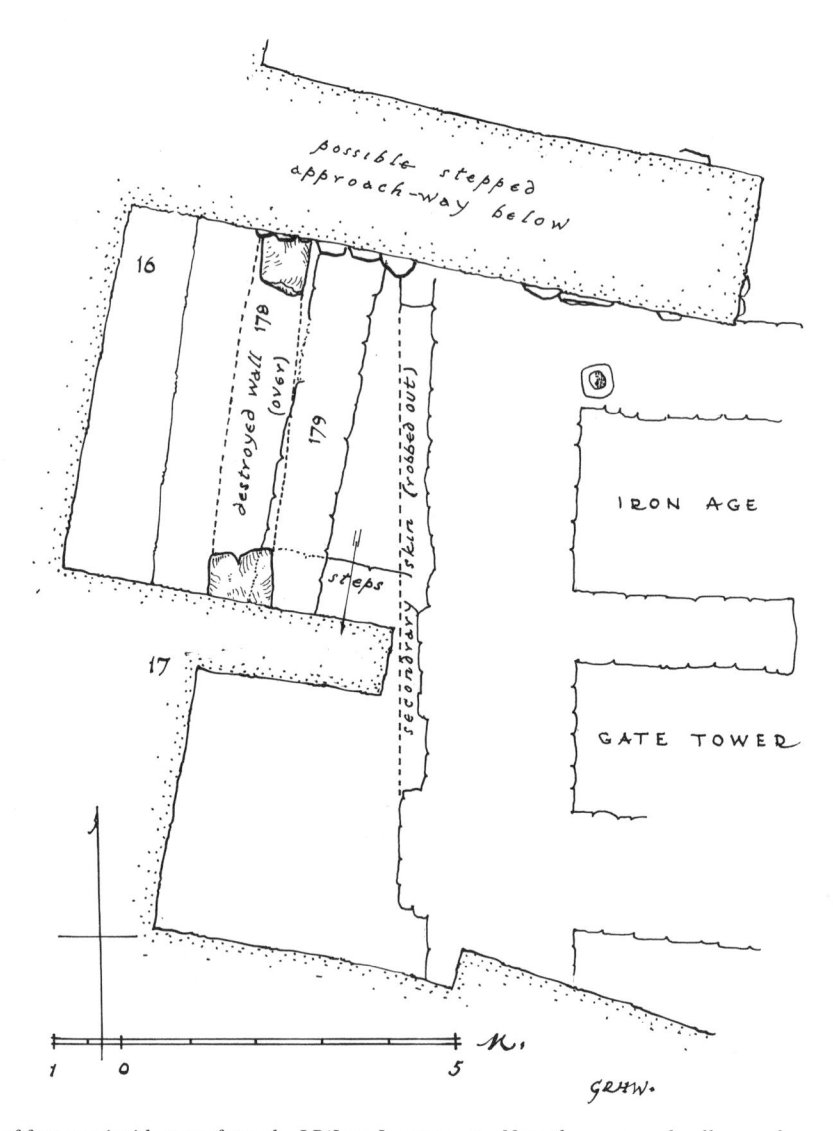

Fig. 159. Plan of features inside town from the LB/Iron I gate tower. Note the proposed collapse of a secondary skin on Wall 127, and the positions of Walls 179 and 178.

pockets of destruction debris, overlaid with a loose grey deposit containing charcoal. Elsewhere on the site, Stratum XIII ended in destruction; that destruction seems to be attested here.

In the third phase against Wall 127, equivalent to Stratum XII, the public square went out of use, and Wall 179 was built diagonally across it, as shown on Ill. 16 and fig. 157. At the very north edge of Area 16, the face of a wall perpendicular to 179, Wall 186, seems to have closed off access to the gate area. It would take removal of the bank of unexcavated earth still in place at this junction to discern what the conditions are, but apparently the public square was now occupied by a house. In Area 17, the narrow space between Walls 127 and 179 was marked by a flooring, locus 503A, interrupted from connecting to Wall 127 by a later pit (fig. 162).

In the fourth and last attested phase here, another diagonally-oriented wall, Wall 178 (fig. 159), lay partially on top but mostly to the west of Wall 179. It too joined a perpendicular wall at the north edge of the excavation, Wall 182. Indications of a surface with 178, Floor 502A, rested upon a hard bricky buildup (locus 503) over the Stratum XII floor. This surface probably repre-

Fig. 160. The tightly fitted Cobbled Surface 509, flush against Wall 127 at right margin.

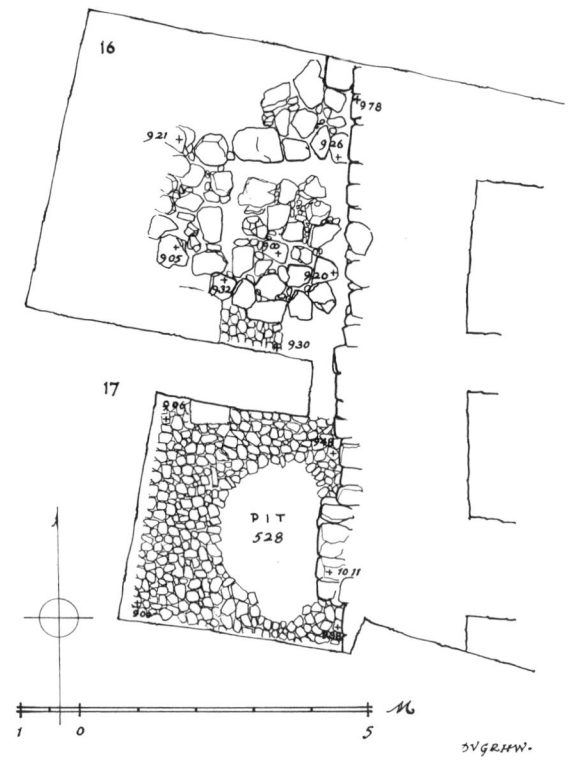

Fig. 161. Plan of Field I Areas 16 and 17, showing Cobbling 509 and jumble of fallen rock over it to the north.

sented Stratum XI. A layer of ash within the accumulation (locus 502/501) above this floor may have been the destruction debris of this phase. Above locus 502/501 was the thick striated black and grey layer 500 which resembled layering in Fields VII and XIII from Iron IA. While this layering may be destruction debris, it is more likely to be the residue of an agricultural process. It is attested only in Area 16 and the north of Area 17; in the extreme south edge of Area 17 was a fragment of a mudbrick wall corner set into the striated layering, perhaps a hut built in connection with the agricultural process.

Wall 133 was built, enclosing the north bay of the gate tower, probably in Stratum XII. Its foundation trench cut flagstone flooring of Strata XIV and XIII, but it was badly preserved, and it is not clear what the access from the gate passageway would have been. The doorway into the inner room from the former bay in Wall 128 was partially blocked (Ill. 16). Within the north room, a series of beaten earth floors was attested, probably to be distributed across Strata XII and XI. But this set of loci cannot be trusted to give definition to the phasing.

In the inner chamber, the evidence was better preserved. Five plaster floor levels, separated from one another by layers of occupational debris 0.05 to 0.10 m thick, marked the earliest usage, and conform to Strata XIV and XIII (fig. 163). The pottery is LB in date; 14 indicator sherds were saved. Against Wall 127, and extending along Wall 128 was the poorly preserved remnant of what may have been a stone bench, 0.45 m wide. Benches in guardrooms of gates are a common feature, and may mean that both rooms also served as public space for commerce or juridical activity.

On the uppermost of the five floors lay the fully articulated, but decapitated, skeleton of an equine, shown in fig. 164. It had an overall length of 0.86 m and the height at its shoulder was 0.65 m. The neck was 0.37 m long. Whether it is to be taken as a casualty of the destruction that ended Stratum XIII or represents some sort of sacrifice

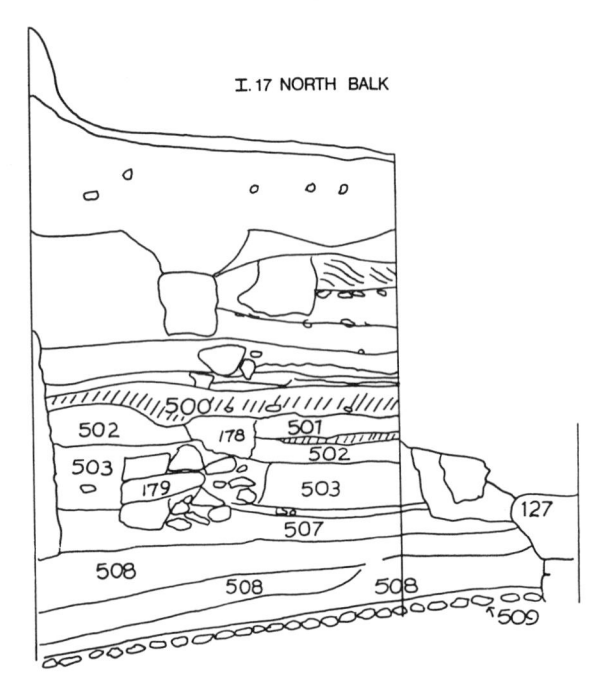

Fig. 162. Sketch drawing of section on north face of Field I, Area 17. Layer 508 represents destruction debris of Stratum XIII. Floor 503A runs east from Wall 179, its connection to Wall 127 severed by a pit.

cannot be ascertained. That there was destruction of this phase is clear, however; over the uppermost plaster floor was 0.30 m of debris, including traces of burning just above the floor, of compact grey material marked by brick and plaster fragments.

Over this accumulation, there built up fourteen separable but very thin beaten earth floorings usually dusted with plaster or lime. Here the separations were only 0.01 to 0.02 m of brown occupation debris. There was a good bit of pottery from this layering; 15 indicator sherds were kept. Preliminary analysis called them LB/Iron I, but closer analysis is called for. The hypothesis would be that the lower surfacings here are LB IIB and the upper Iron IA, spread across Strata XII and XI. Over the uppermost of these floors accumulated a thick compact grey layer with charcoal and plaster chunks in it, containing Iron I pottery including two fragmentary lamp profiles—a total of 14 indicator sherds. This layer filled up the room to the elevation which Hellenistic builders of Stratum IV leveled to place their structures.

The Northwest Gate

Nothing like as much LB evidence was found in the Northwest gate. Two hints are present. In the south gate chamber where Sellin located a ramp leading up to level of the back room of the 7300 temple, probes in 1966 discerned a sealed deposit of LB pottery on the ramp. Between the orthostats, in what was probably undisturbed soil, LB pottery was found. These two finds suggest, but hardly prove, that the Northwest Gate, like the East Gate was put back into use in LB times as access through the fortifications. Where the LB circumvallation would have run on the west and north is unknown.

Field III

Some indication of LB fortification was preserved in Field III, but the data is quite inconclusive. Ill. 39 shows a wall marked "LB Wall" riding on Wall 631 of the MB IIC complex beneath. East of this wall fragment there were no indications of LB construction, with the possible exception of Wall 654 at the far east (left) edge of the section in Ill. 44. Because of disruptions both ancient and modern (the German cutting and the intrusion #8 on the section) connections to Wall 646 were severed, and the green clay (#12) into which Wall 654 was set was virtually sterile of pottery, what little there was dating from MB and Chalcolithic. The orange brick debris in Ill. 44:#11 contained MB pottery with what may be a few LB sherds. Between Walls 646 and 644 on Ill. 39 LB phase, where the term "fill" appears on the plan, a heavy deposit of pottery with LB forms made from extremely poor clay came to light, referred to as "sewer ware" in early reports. Conceivably Wall B was reused in the region of Field III as a fortification in LB, with the LB wall rebuilt on Wall 631 as an interior reinforcement, and with Wall 654 as a retaining wall downslope, but there is little to count upon here in finding LB fortification. The pottery in all these LB deposits is in need of renewed analysis.

Fig. 163. Layering of plaster floors within the Late Bronze gate tower.

Fig. 164. Equine skeleton on the uppermost LB floor in the gate tower guard room.

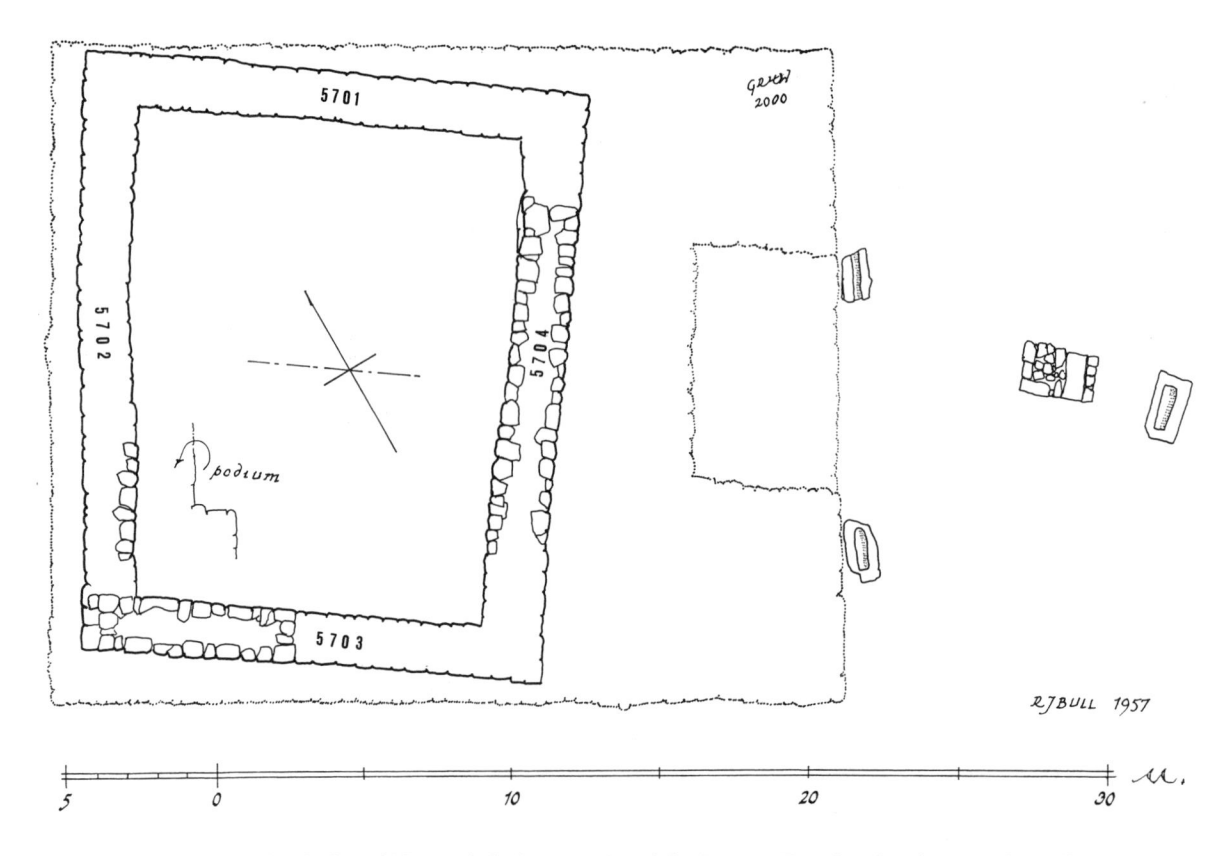

Fig. 165. Sketch plan of LB temple built over ruins of the Fortress Temple, after drawings by Bull.

THE PUBLIC BUILDINGS ON THE ACROPOLIS

Sellin and Welter left in place on top of the Fortress Temple ruins the wall fragments of the ninth century Granary, in the pattern shown on Ill. 63. The Granary walls are oriented 5 to 6 degrees south from those of the Temple foundations, at ca. 128 degrees compared to 123 degrees. Welter's plan of the ruin shows the shift plainly.

The Joint Expedition began its study of the remains in 1957, with the aim to confirm the dates of the Temple and the Granary. Part of the procedure was to lift segments of the north and west Granary walls, 5901 and 5902, to see if they had sealed any data that would point to the founding of the Granary and the last use of the Temple. What was found was a thin layer of bricky debris on top of plaster, on top of egg-sized stones. Some of the pottery within the granary walls and in the layer beneath was Iron II, of the ninth/eighth centuries, establishing the founding date of the Granary.

Regularly, though, the pottery sealed beneath the Granary walls included sherds identified as Iron I and LB. Robert Bull, supervising the work, posited an intermediate phase between the well-laid and flattened top of the MB IIC Fortress Temple foundation and the rough boulders of the Granary, to be tested in future seasons.

A Late Bronze Temple

In 1960, Bull confirmed the existence of an intermediate phase. It is on the basis of what was found within the ruins of the Temple and Granary in 1960 and what was found in the forecourt in 1962 that G. E. Wright wrote his description of "Temple 2" in *SBBC*:95–100, based on Bull's meticulous work. It is recast here to indicate more precisely what the evidence for it is and to suggest how the reasoning for its interpretation as a temple was developed (fig. 165).

Four features within the structure were definitive.

Fig. 166. Wall 5703 with meter stick on it and several boulders of the 5903 granary wall still in place.

1. Beneath Wall 5903 on the south, there appeared the fragment of Wall 5703 shown in fig. 166 sandwiched between the Temple and Granary walls. Where the granary walls consisted typically of two rows of unhewn rocks ca. 1.30 to 1.60 m wide (only one row was preserved in this particular spot, its north face flush with the north face of 5703), Wall 5703 was just under 2.00 m wide and showed two faces of semi-hewn stones with a rubble core. Both the granary walls and the walls in the 5700 series were built of *nari* limestone, typical of the rock on the slopes of Mt. Ebal above the site. Earlier, the use of the harder *mizzi* was noted as a hallmark of the MB IIC Fortress Temple. With the granary and the 5700 structure the difference is in the way the stones were cut. Those of the 5700 structure are semi-hewn and fitted to present a somewhat flat face, while those of the granary are unshaped boulders.

Wall 5703 had been seen by the Germans, and it was drawn on Welter's plan, but it was not noticed that it differed from the typical granary walls. Since Sellin's team had cleared it completely, no undisturbed soil containing sherds was left for the Joint Expedition to analyze. Its alignment was not parallel with the Fortress Temple wall beneath it. This is the only place where a wall of the intermediate phase was preserved *on* a wall of the Fortress Temple.

2. Granary Wall 5906 was left in place by the Germans, cutting diagonally across the southern half of the Temple cella. It preserved a narrow balk of earth beneath it, its south face shown in section on fig. 142. Below the granary wall and the plaster into which they were set was the typical layer of grey bricky earth (locus 5002) that served as the foundation makeup for the Granary. Beneath that was preserved a patch of yellowish plaster, 0.03 to 0.05 m thick, locus 5002A, at estimated elevation 20.90. It rested on a layer of dense, red, clay-like soil 0.15 m thick, locus 5003. Below 5003 was the 0.30 m thick layer of grey occupation soil, locus 5004, that regularly covered the upper floor of the Fortress Temple, locus 5005.

This narrow bank of preserved earth was disturbed by pits, two of which show in the section (5093 and 5096). The pits were not discerned until after excavation had proceeded below the layering just described. The pottery from locus 5003, then, may not be uncontaminated. One preserved sherd from the locus is B57 #1407, the rim of an Iron I collared-rim store jar, and other Iron I wares were present. They may have come, however, from the pit and not the layering. Nevertheless, the thin

Fig. 167. Wall 5704 of the LB Temple phase.

yellowish plaster was another feature of the intermediate phase between Temple and Granary.

3. Granary Wall 5904 ran south-north across the Fortress Temple cella. It is between 1.30 and 1.60 m wide, usually at the narrower measure. Beneath it was preserved another segment of wall, 5704, very similar in construction to Wall 5703. Preserved only one course high, it was made up of two rows of semi-hewn *nari* stones typically 0.90 by 0.65 by 0.40 m in size, with rubble core, varying from 2.00 to 2.30 m in width. It is shown in fig. 167. It was preserved for 11.80 m in length, oriented on the same lines as 5904. Its extrapolated line makes a right angle junction with Wall 5703 extrapolated, over Fortress Temple wall 5603 at the south. Since 5903 was oriented on 5703 and 5904 was oriented on 5704, the Granary layout becomes an indication of the layout of the intermediate building. Wall 5901 would suggest, then, the position of the no-longer-preserved "5701" on the north wall of the Fortress Temple. On Welter's plan, the corresponding west wall, "5702," may in fact be shown in part; the two separate segments of the west wall shown by Welter look to be of different construction technique and are not quite in line. From the way Welter has drawn them, the southern portion seems to show the external stones to be semi-hewn.

Judging from Walls 5704 and 5703 and presuming that 5701 was positioned toward the outer edge of the Fortress Wall beneath it, Building 5700 was rectangular, ca. 16.00 m wide and 12.50 m deep in interior measure, and anchored on three sides on the Fortress Temple stone foundations.

The fourth side, Wall 5704 on the east, was not anchored on the Fortress Temple foundation, and was founded substantially deeper then 5703 (fig. 142). Assuming that it in fact belonged with 5703, its position suggests that an architectural tradition is involved. Only one course of Wall 5704 was preserved, and it showed no threshold for a door in that one course. It rested, however, on a foundation Wall 5704A, 2.00 m wide and ca. 1.50 m deep. Wall 5704A stood in turn on a layer of earth 0.20 m thick which lay upon Floor 5010 of the Fortress Temple. Two baskets of pottery from this layer (no locus number) contained nine indicator sherds, including four rim and base fragments of bowls and a jug base belonging to LB, another likely LB jug rim, three MB sherds, plus an MB II scarab (B60 Obj. 659) published by Siegfried Horn (1962:8–9). Since German excavation had scooped out the adjacent soil, the limits of a foundation trench for Wall 5704 could not be defined, but the layer with these sherds doubtless belonged to it and places the first construction of Wall 5704 in the Late Bronze Age (cf. Stager 1999).

4. As mentioned above, Wall 5702 is posited to have rested on the back wall of the Fortress Temple so as to join the west end of Wall 5703. Within the bend of 5703 and putative 5702, fallen boulders of the granary walls protected a strip of undisturbed materials against Temple Wall 5602 and on top of its inner face. This strip ran from close to the preserved piece of Wall 5703 on the south, across the two banks of undisturbed debris under Granary Walls 5906 and 5905, to the interior face of 5601, and was intruded upon by at least two more of the deep pits dug in the Temple ruin

Fig. 168. Bowl of LB IIB from beneath plastered Stratum XII LB surface in the LB Temple.

from Iron I. Excavation of undisturbed soil was an intricate process.

At a point 2.20 m east of the inner face of Granary Wall 5902, between the junctions with it of 5906 and 5905, there lay Wall 5802A, one course of a single row of stones ca. 0.20 by 0.15 by 0.10 m in size, extending 1.60 m in length. The stones were set into a layer of plaster at elevation 20.89, 0.23 m lower than the preserved 5001 plaster layer of the Granary, and at the same elevation as the patch of Plaster Floor 5002A toward the east under Wall 5906. It is justifiably taken as another segment of the same floor. Wall 5802A appears to have defined a constructed platform or dais against

Fig. 169. Stone steps probably of Stratum XIV LB Temple, from disturbed flooring within the bounds of the MB IIC Fortress Temple; note MB IIC foundation at right.

Fig. 170. Socket with maṣṣebah *restored, south of entrance to Fortress Temple 1b.*

the back wall of the 5700 structure, especially erected for use with Floor 5002A.

Beneath the plaster and Wall 5802A and spreading westward was 0.70 to 0.80 m of dark earth containing LB pottery. Forty-seven LB indicator sherds were saved; among them is the profile of a large storage jar lacking its rim, the bowl shown *in situ* in fig. 168, a sherd of a Cypriote milkbowl, and a number of forms that represent LB IIB. Objects from this locus include an alabaster macehead (Obj. reg. B60 #517), a fragment of a faience vessel (#601), a faience bead (#433), a fragile faience cylinder seal with the tree of life motif (#432), a piece of ivory inlay (#648), and a tiny alabaster cosmetic mortar and pestle with red pigment preserved (#602).

Some of this collection involves Egyptian influence and some points to MB II, so the material may represent fill gathered from elsewhere, but the entire corpus requires restudy. What is important for chronology is that its latest pottery is equivalent to Stratum XII as defined elsewhere on the site, suggesting it was built after the destruction of Stratum XIII attested in the East Gate and to be confirmed in the domestic areas described below.

The date of the corpus defining Podium 5802A bears upon the interpretation of an earlier phase of the podium, found beneath the 5802A installation and directly on the lip of Wall 5602. It was defined by Wall 5802B, east of the line of 5802A by 0.15–0.20 m and 0.70 m below it, made of stones ca. 0.15 by 0.30 by 0.20 m in size. A plaster layer 0.02–0.03 m thick extended westward from 5802B over 5602 to reach the line of Granary Wall 5902. Removal of 5802B produced MB II sherds with two possible LB sherds, leading to Wright's claim in *SBBC*: 97 that it was a structure built in early LB, Stratum XIV. Stone steps attested here (fig. 169) may have led up to this earlier podium, but, if so, they ascended from a flooring no longer preserved which would have been below the top of the Fortress Temple foundation shown at the right of the photo.

North of this deposit between walls 5906 and 5905, over the northwest corner of the Fortress Temple, study of the poorly preserved layering uncovered another fragment of plaster surface, 0.03–0.04 thick, again logically related to Surface 5002A. It is at elevation 20.80. Embedded in the plaster was a bowl rim that falls in the transition from LB to Iron I; sealed beneath it were four other

Fig. 171. Socket for second flanking maṣṣebah, *north of entrance to Fortress Temple 1b.*

LB IIB bowl rims.

To the south, near Wall 5703 and in the southwest corner of the Fortress Temple, a bank of black, stony fill, contained mixed pottery including LB sherds.

This description has intentionally expressed more caution in comprehending this data than is expressed in *SBBC*. There is sound evidence for a Strata XII/XI use of the intermediate building. There is less certain indication of an earlier phase belonging to Strata XIV-XIII. There were fragments of the flooring of the upper phase, no flooring for the lower. The predominant pottery form is the LB bowl; no other kinds of artifacts are preserved from the lower phase, but the upper phase yielded interesting objects of uncertain dates, some of which were probably ceremonial but none of which were clearly cultic.

A new consideration in understanding the 5700 structure has come to light from ongoing study by Robert Bull. Frequent visits to the site between 1971 and 1999 have permitted Bull to study the kinds of rocks used, to restudy the line of the axes of the three structures (5600, 5700 and 5900), and to make new proposals about how to interpret the complex.

First, Bull determined that five large rocks running along the line of the entrance to the Fortress Temple are of *nari* limestone. Behind this row in the region of the MB IIC Fortress Temple's pronaos are more *nari* rocks which fill the region back to the line of Wall 5704. Then, Bull observed that the huge column base, originally thought to have been positioned in the entrance of the Fortress Temple and to have supported the lintel over it (cf. *SBBC*: figs. 42 and 47), is of *nari*, but of a harder kind than that used in the walls of the 5700 complex. In a forthcoming study, Bull will propose that the filling up of the region east of Wall 5704 over the Fortress Temple ruin was done as the 5700 structure was being built, resulting in a forecourt reaching back to Wall 5704. Here in the open before the 5700 building stood the column base, holding a free-standing column. This column base, by the way, stands today at the site in approximately the position it would have occupied, but erected there by the Joint Expedition in 1960 when it was thought to belong to the Fortress Temple.

Altars and Standing Stones

In front of the 5700 building, on a part of the forecourt excavated by Sellin only to the elevation of floors of the Fortress Temple, were a cluster of cultic features which must relate to the Fortress Temple and to the 5700 rectangular broadroom sanctuary proposed by the Joint Expedition.

Close to the Fortress Temple foundation were two bases for standing-stones (figs. 170 and 171). In *SBBC*, they are interpreted as relating to the second phase of the Fortress Temple ("Temple 1b"). They present the problem that they are not placed so as to flank the wide entrance of the Fortress Temple, but instead more to the south, suggesting that in the second phase of the Fortress Temple the entrance was narrower and off center. One would have entered and turned slightly to the right to walk into the cella (compare *SBBC*: figs. 41 and 48). (This shift in positioning, by the way,

Fig. 172. Kurt Galling's 1926 photograph, with the flat altar platform in place in the temple forecourt, and Maṣṣebah *1 leaning in what is probably the position as found. The squared and well-preserved corner of the Fortress Temple walls is at right center.*

Fig. 173. Re-erecting Maṣṣebah *1 on the tongue of temple forecourt. A large piece of the socket stone lies in the ruins of Field VI where it was pushed in the altercations between Sellin and Welter.*

would not have screened the view into the cella completely; morning sunlight could still enter the cella directly.)

The two *maṣṣebah* sockets were found by Sellin and appear on Welter's drawing. The southern one was 1.35 m long and 0.42 wide; it is 0.25 m deep. Sellin found a stone slab that fit the socket, the larger segment of which the Joint Expedition recovered. It is now remounted in place in the socket in front of the consolidated temple foundation, resolving the conflict of interpretation that developed between 1926 and 1928 (*SBBC*:33–34; 82–83) in favor of Sellin (fig. 170).

What remains of the northern socket was *in situ*; the ends of the socket are broken off, but what remained of its groove was 1.56 m long, 0.28 m wide, and 0.20 m deep (fig. 171). No slab for this one has ever been identified.

This reading of the evidence may stand, in which case the two phases of the MB IIC temple may have seen two treatments of the entryway. But Bull has noted that the central axis of the 5700 building runs midway between the two flanking *maṣṣebah*, and therefore has proposed that they belong with the 5700 building rather than with the Fortress Temple. For the present the matter cannot be settled, but Bull's new data are presented at this point in the portrayal of the complex because they may tip the balance of probability. This pro-

Fig. 174. Maṣṣebah 1 as the Joint Expedition remounted it.

posal would posit a column base with a pillar and two *maṣṣeboth* in front of the 5700 building.

What leads the Joint Expedition more confidently to claim that the LB building had two phases and was of cultic use is the evidence from the forecourt in connection with altars and another standing stone, *Maṣṣebah* 1. The forecourt held an altar which Sellin found, of grey brick and white marl curbing, belonging to the Fortress Temple—to both phases of it probably, but certainly to the later phase (fig. 143).

In his summer campaign of 1926, Sellin found, on a higher surface 6.55 m in front of the Temple entrance, another altar or altar foundation of stone

Fig. 175. Looking west at the reconstructed ruin of the Fortress Temple. The consolidating wall around the tongue of forecourt on which Maṣṣebah 1 stands was built by the Joint Expedition. The two flanking maṣṣeboth *are visible against the front wall of the Temple.*

Fig. 176. Storage pit 5094 filled with rubbish that includes Iron I pottery. Note the plaster floor of the 5900 Granary sealing its top.

and earth (1926a:312). He gave its dimensions at 2.20 by 1.65 by 0.35 m; it appears in Galling's 1926 photograph (fig. 172). The 1962 Joint Expedition campaign probed the extant remains of this altar, which consists of hewn stones lying on white marl and cement in turn covering a layer of black earth. The black earth contained a mix of Chalcolithic, MB IIB, several LB pieces and one probable Iron IA = Stratum XI.

Later in the same campaign, Sellin found still another altar, of mudbrick, 5.20 by 7.00 by 0.27 m (1926b:313), only 0.10 m below the one just described (the Fortress Temple altar lay 0.55–0.60 below that). The Joint Expedition was not able to find any remains of Sellin's intermediate altar. Sellin's two altars probably both belonged to the 5700 building, the later to Strata XII-XI, and the earlier probably to Strata XIV-XIII.

As the Galling photo and the Welter plan make clear, the LB altar went with the socket for *Maṣṣebah* 1, and the two together were oriented in such a way as to line up almost, but not quite, with the axis of the LB building, not with the Fortress Temple. The controverted story of the great *maṣṣebah* is told in *SBBC*:84–87—how it was disputed and thrown off the forecourt, and how the Joint Expedition re-erected it close to its original position (fig. 173).

The socket rock originally was set down into the same white marl that lay below the latest altar, 2.50 m east of it, and measured 2.40 by 1.70 m, standing 0.80 m high. The actual groove was 1.65 by 0.45 m, 0.40 m deep. The monolith was 1.48 m wide, 0.42 m thick, and preserved to a tapered top 1.45 down to 0.62 m high (fig. 174). It belonged with the Strata XII-XI phase of the LB building; perhaps it was in place with the now lost Strata XIV-XIII altar. The arrangement of the three standing stones on the consolidated piece of forecourt is shown in fig. 175.

The Late Bronze Age building then is proposed to have been a sanctuary, of broad-room style. The style is attested in various centuries throughout the third millennium, at such sites as Megiddo, Ai, Lachish, Hazor, Ugarit and Alalakh. Their orientations vary. Wright pointed out (*SBBC*:97) that between Alalakh VIII and VII there was a shift in temple orientation to the south in the seventeenth or early sixteenth centuries, reminiscent of the shift from the Fortress Temple to the LB/Iron I structure (Woolley 1955:59ff., fig. 35 & pl. XIV)—but why the axis at Shechem should have shifted 5 to 6 degrees south is not at all clear. The Joint Expedition has worked with the idea that it had something to do with a change in calendar, and the axis was shifted with the change so that the rising sun would shine directly into the cella on a particular day. The new orientation faces the rising sun approximately at the time of the winter solstice, which is probably significant. Alternatively, the orientation points to an unnamed peak on the eastern horizon, which may have been an important landmark as yet not understood.

Mention has been made throughout the description of the Fortress Temple and the LB sanctuary of numerous pits dug through the floors (fig. 176). They contain rubbish that includes Iron I = Stratum XI pottery. More about them will be said in connection with the domestic precincts, because such pits are found all over the mound. Since they are very likely to have been for grain storage, including the one or more that Sellin mistook for a cultic *favissa* (1927a:207; 1941:18), they are not treated here as part of the public buildings. On the other hand, it should be noted that they occupied what had been a sanctuary precinct, and they served as predecessors of the Granary building, a public installation.

Tower 944–947

Finally, mention must be made of Tower 944–947, the rectangle left standing by Sellin's work and drawn from his plans in place on Ill. 76, its relative elevation shown on VI HH = Ill. 89. An effort was made in 1962 to tie this structure into the stratification of the acropolis. Wall 944 was partially dismantled, and contained LB sherds within its chinking. No surface was preserved from the Sellin clearance (1941:18). The structure overrides rubbish pits probably belonging to Stratum XVII or dug from even higher. All the evidence points to this small "block-house" as belonging to the Late Bronze Age, but its precise stratum assignment is lost.

To recall, then, the data on the four isolated buildings in the north of Field VI left by the Sellin and Welter work: the farthest one west, with buttressed corners and located directly in the path of the Northwest Gate, is probably MB IIC in date. The next rectangle to its east yielded no new evidence to the Joint Expedition, but underlies the two-room 926-927-928-929-996—an MB IIC structure—so it may have belonged to MB IIB or earlier in MB IIC. The two-room structure is established as MB IIC, while the 944–947 block-house is very likely of Late Bronze date.

THE INNER CITY IN LATE BRONZE AND EARLY IRON I

The domestic areas of Field VII, IX and XIII provide the detail needed to develop a picture of Shechem during Strata XIV-XI: four distinct phases, with some local variations within the phases, and some differences from excavation field to excavation field. As the plan of MB later phase and LB scraps (Ill. 39 upper) shows, two probable refloorings in among MB IIC ruins against a fragment of an LB Wall 632 identified in Field III (see also Ill. 43) might be claimed to be a part of LB domestic use of the site, but the evidence here was too skimpy to be a factor in what the larger exposures provide. The overall picture:

1) a period of virtual abandonment in LB IA after the Egyptian conquest around 1540 BCE, lasting roughly a century;

2) a period of steady recovery, Stratum XIV, running from about 1475 to 1400 = LB IB;

3) a period of prosperity, Stratum XIII, covering much of the fourteenth century, ending in a radical destruction by unknown agency sometime in the second half of the century = LB IIA;

4) a period of recovery, Stratum XII, on a less prosperous scale but on the same lines as the preceding city = LB IIB;

5) a period of gradual and nonviolent transition, Stratum XI, to new arrangements of space and a new range of artifacts, ending in overall destruction in the late twelfth century followed by another period of virtual abandonment = LB/Iron I.

Getting Ready for Stratum XIV

Everywhere on the Shechem mound there are indications that a century or so elapsed between the end of MB IIC and recovery in the Late Bronze age. The evidence is elusive because it is largely negative. Pottery forms and decorative styles characteristic of LB IA are not found; that such forms were present in the region is indicated by their presence in the earliest LB use of Tomb C on the slope of Mt. Ebal north of the tell (Clamer 1977; 1981). When LB pottery again appears in abundance in the ruins at Shechem, it is significantly different from the MB IIC corpus preceding it. MB IIC destruction debris was left in most places to great depths, and effort was expended to smooth it out and prepare for rebuilding; MB IIC walls protruded through the subsequent fill layers and were used to anchor LB walls, but the impression is one of a gap in the use of the mound's natural surface. Remains in Fields XIII, IX, and VII give glimpses of people at work to ready the mound for a new foundation.

Field XIII

The MB IIC structures in Field XIII had been built on terracing and retained platforms. The massive destruction ending that era had left huge quantities of debris. The people who built next rearranged this debris according to a new plan. Some they dumped to the south, filling the valley between the acropolis and the Field XIII sector (VI RR section = fig. 12:#26, covered by #21, covered by makeup ##18 and 20). They scraped away the destruction debris and most of the MB IIC occupation evidence at the west. They left the destruction debris in the east and augmented it with what they scraped from the west (Ill. 161 = XIII AA:##65 on 68 south to Wall 3667 and ##69 on 70 south of Wall 3751; Ill. 163 = XIII CC:##46 and 47). Section XIII FF:#42 (Ill. 164) was a brown cushioning layer cut into the hard grey locus #52 and serving as the leveling layer for new building (loci 3538 in Area 3 and 3768 in Area 4, not seen in section, served the same purpose). Most of the pottery in these layers is MB IIC, but regularly there appeared sherds of LB IB.

Leveling. The effect was to create a relatively level area, with a gentle slope to the south and east, the wall tops of the MB IIC ruin appearing just above the surface. The idea was to secure solid foundations for new walls, which would lie in much the same pattern as those of MB IIC. The old line of the main Terrace Wall 3663-3706-3309 became the west wall of one building, while the corner of the MB IIC Stratum XV Building I, dubbed the "Government Residency," was reestablished.

The first construction in the recovery for Stratum XIV reused the tops of Walls 3751, 03231 and 03217 of Room C on the "upper terrace" part of the split-level MB IIC house, and 03271, 03220 and 03223 that had defined Rooms D-F. Ill. 151 shows the pattern of walls. A kiln was built on top of the Room C ruins. In a "yard" to the south surfaced with beaten earth at elevation 17.07, Oven

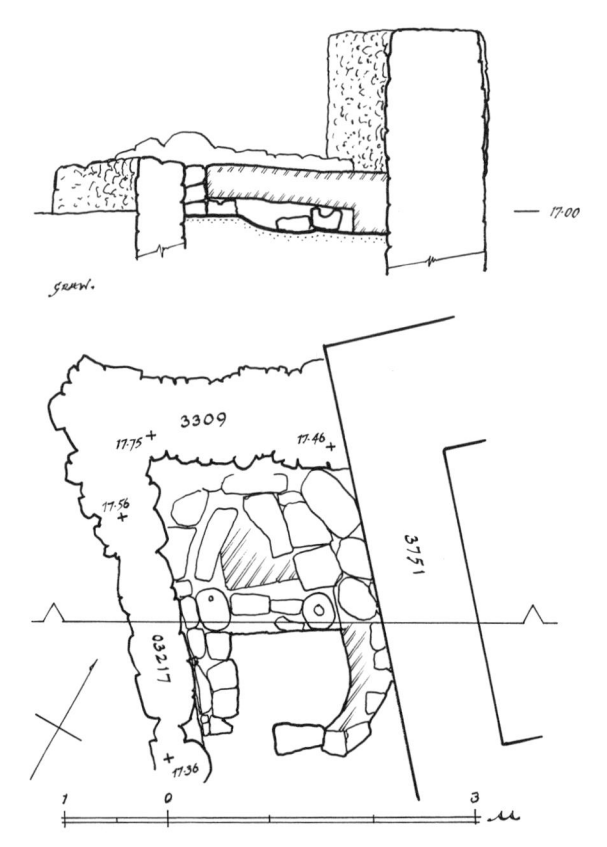

Fig. 177. Plan and section of Kiln 3396 in Field XIII, Area 2.

03274 was built against the top of Wall 03271 in the ruins of Room E. The little square, ca. 0.60 by 0.60 m, defined by walls 03224 and 03222 against the tops of 03220 and 03217 may have played some part in this combination of installations, its purpose undiscerned (see Ill. 171 = XIII QQ).

The Kiln. Kiln 3396 had two phases (fig.177). It began as a horseshoe open to the southeast, made out of rocks at least two of which were clearly reused. One had a cone-shaped depression—a door socket or jar stand or mortar depression; the other was part of a basalt rubbing stone with a hole through it. The kiln's hearth lay at 16.75 m above datum, set down below MB IIC floor levels and sunken below its surroundings. Since the opening was not toward the prevailing west wind of the mountain pass, presumably the draft was deflected into the opening or channeled from above.

The founding phase of the kiln gave way to a second phase, a larger structure with its west wall

Fig. 178. Looking west at upper layer contents of Kiln 3396. Calcined limestone rock below meter stick; another to its left, nearer camera.

placed further west. The hearth of the earlier kiln was covered with MB IIC debris and a new hearth was laid about 0.35 m higher. This phase of the hearth is better preserved, retaining its firebrick lining. The brick chunks show flat planes on the inner surface and the impression of the stones they were pressed against. Bricks also formed the cap over the kiln. Intense heat had cracked the rocks and fired the brick chunks to cement-like hardness. The ash was grey rather than black and full of charcoal, indicating open, not smothered fire.

Reuben Bullard, consulting geologist, observes that temperatures above 1000 C are required to achieve this effect; he proposes lime production, but no deposit of lime was found, nor was there evidence of pottery firing (clay puddles or broken rejects) or metalworking (slag, etc.). But bricks were everywhere here—in the structure itself but also in the surrounding area, suggesting it was a brick kiln, and that kiln-fired bricks were to be used to build here rather than sun-dried ones (figs. 178–182 document Kiln 3396).

The debris in the kiln contained noteworthy artifacts, but their date is uncertain. The pottery—including a crushed store jar and a restorable jar—belongs to MB IIC though the kiln itself was from LB IB. Apparently when the kiln was put out of use, earlier destruction debris was spread in and over it. The kiln debris contained five bullae (fig.

Fig. 179. Looking west at lower phase of Kiln 3396, with crushed MB II storage jar in situ.

Fig. 180. Looking north, with stone-lined pit set into the west end of the lower phase hearth, Kiln 3396. The meter stick lies on the hard-baked brick cap of the kiln. To the right of the meter stick is a portion of the lining of the kiln wall.

Fig. 181. Looking east at Kiln 3396, with meter stick on its collapsed cap, pit 03202 beyond.

183), probably used to seal and validate jars of some fine commodity. The mix of early debris and the debris of use means that the bullae may be LB I or MB IIC in date, but the pottery supports the earlier date as more likely.

The second phase of use for Kiln 3396 fits with another set of changes (Ill. 152; cf. Ill. 172). Wall 03218 was put in place over Oven 03274, and Wall 03219 nullified the little square structure of the earliest phase. A door was established through MB IIC Terrace Wall 3309 to give access to the two small rooms over the "yard" that held the oven. A street surfaced with pebbles and sherds as locus 03221 was at the entrance through the terrace wall at elevation 17.52, and north along the terrace at 17.67.

The Basement Room of Stratum XIII interrupted connections to the north in this preparatory phase of Stratum XIV; on current understanding, no features of the northeast complex of building in the field can be assigned to this phase.

Field VII

Not enough of Field VII was dug to gain knowledge of the overall lie of the terrain in LB IB or to learn if preparations for building involved leveling as in Field XIII. The general impression

Fig. 182. Slab of cap of Kiln 3396, removed from its position.

is one of open space with several rather randomly placed structures.

At the west edge of Area 6 was a succession of three fire pits, the lowest locus 13.175, the middle 13.169 and the upper 13.170. Fig. 184 shows 13.170 and 13.169 with the curvatures of their stone edges. Ill. 94 shows 13.170 stone-for-stone, the outline of 13.169 beneath it; no drawing of 13.175 was made, nor was a section through the firepits drawn. Firepit 13.169, the middle, best-preserved one, measured 3.48 m across at the top and 3.04 m at the base. Like the brick kiln in Field XIII, the bottoms of 13.175 and 13.169 were let down below the level of the MB IIC floors.

The walls were preserved to heights from 0.40 to 0.80 m and had bricky linings—not shaped bricks but brick-like material. The intense heat in the pits had fired the linings to hues of orange, red and red-brown. White lime found adhering to the lining and lying on the bottom of each of the pits indicate they were lime kilns. Digging did not proceed lower here, so the relationship between the lowest firepit and Wall 13.164 just to its north is not certain, but it appears that 13.175 went with the wall, its north edge touching the wall. Wall 13.164 defined an open yard for this industry. The pit was relocated slightly southward as 13.169 at the time the house walls of Stratum XIV to the

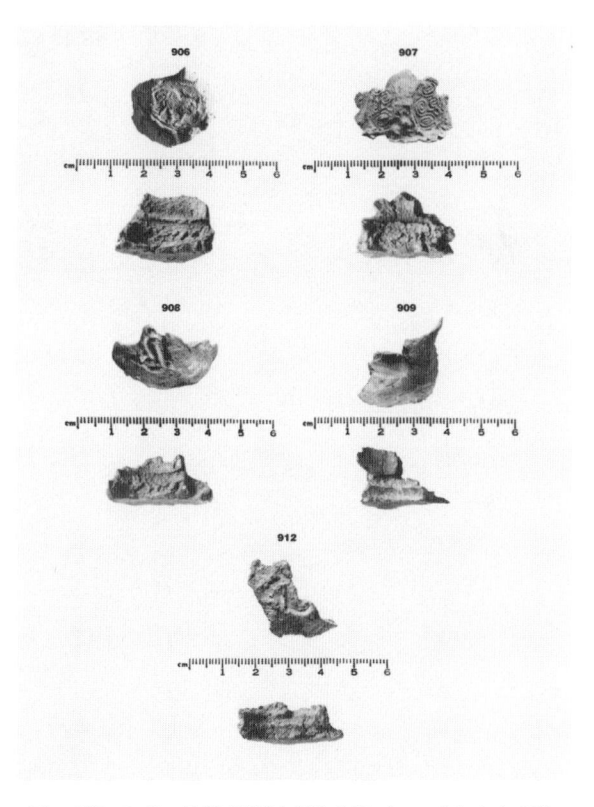

Fig. 183. Bullae B68 ##906-909, 912, from debris in Kiln 3396. It is not clear whether these belong to the kiln's use phase or are MB IIC residuals.

Fig. 184. Firepits 13.170 on top of 13.169 in Field VII, Area 6, of Strata XIV and XIII.

Fig. 185. Looking west in Room D of the eastern complex in Field XIII. Wall 3663 is at the top margin, and Wall 3667 along left margin. The meter stick lies on Floor 3763. The hole in the foreground is of unknown purpose. The earth stack at lower right is the filling of Silo 3734, left in place as the excavation proceeded to its base.

east were built. Pit 13.170 then continued the tradition into Stratum XIII. The first pit and the yard wall represent the preparatory phase.

Field IX

Field IX had evidenced no MB IIC occupation. In the layer of soil lying beneath the earliest LB architecture was one wall fragment, an arrangement of three bricks that may be a hearth, and evidence of pitting—tentatively these features are taken as more evidence of preparations for Stratum XIV housing.

THE HOUSING OF STRATUM XIV

Fields XIII and VII preserved evidence of Stratum XIV in coherent architectural units. For Field IX the evidence is compelling for Stratum XIII but less clear for XIV.

Field XIII (Ills. 153 and 169 (plans) and 161–164 (sections)

The top of the MB IIC Terrace Wall was heightened to become the west wall of a complex in the east half of Field XIII. To the west of the Terrace Wall lay open area Sector C, Yard B for Building A, and Building A continuing the "Government Residence."

Fig. 186. Crater smashed by brick lying on it, part of debris 3759 on Floor 3763. Wall 3667 (left) abuts Wall 3663 (right).

Street 3121 ran between the eastern and western complexes, its western limit clearer than its eastern along Wall 3309-3706. It was surfaced by pebbles and sherds, many of which lay horizontally. The surface built up to a thickness of 0.05 to 0.10 m (Ill. 162 = XIII BB:#54). Four Iron I pits cut through it, but it could be traced as far as Pit 3532, which cut it completely; north of Pit 3532 it apparently continued as a less certain stony layer to the line of Wall 3534, giving access to Yard B. Within the yard, a beaten earth surface 3768 continued the pathway to the north edge of the field.

The Eastern Complex: Rooms D through G. To the east of Wall 3309-3706 lay a complex of rooms the nature of which is hard to discern. Starting from the north, the row of rooms is designated D, E (ill-defined because the Stratum XIII Basement Room nullified it), F and G. At least the upper part of Wall 3663 at the north bonded into Wall 3706, but Seger has questioned on the basis of observations made in 1969 whether it was present as Stratum XIV housing was first established. Perhaps one could have walked from Yard B into an open area north of the eastern complex. Since Room D showed two surfacings with Stratum XIV, current interpretation continues with the inclusion of Wall 3663 and the definition of Room D as part of the eastern housing complex.

Only a corner of Room D was uncovered, and there are no indications of accesses through the portions of Walls 3663 and 3667 that define it; both walls were set into the MB IIC destruction debris layer 3775 and were preserved more than 1.75 m in height. In the very northeast corner of the field was Silo 3734, installed as part of Stratum XIII and reused in Stratum XII. By coincidence or design the floor of this silo was flush with the Stratum XIV floor of Room D; perhaps its diggers discerned the plaster floor and chose to stop at it, using it as a convenient lining. Intrusion of the silo limited the segments of flooring preserved in Room D. The Stratum XIVB surfacing was Plaster Floor 3774 (Ill. 161 = XIII AA:#64, Ill. 163 = XIII CC:#42) at elevation 18.09, riding on a grey makeup over debris 3775 (XIII AA:#65). The makeup shows LB IB pottery with much MB IIC.

On Floor 3774 was 0.05 m of compact grey earth (AA:#60) underlying plaster or crushed limestone Floor 3763 (AA:#56, CC:#41). In 3763 was a cylindrical hole, 0.18 m in diameter and 0.15 m deep (fig. 185), of unknown purpose. On Floor 3763 was debris 3759 (AA:#47) containing indications of destruction. Included were light-fired bricks of two sizes: 0.35 by 0.20 by 0.12 and 0.20 square by 0.14, the longer with straw binder and the shorter with less straw but inclusions of marl fragments. Three whole LB IB to LB IIA vessels were on the floor (one a crater smashed by a brick, shown in fig. 186), along with four basalt rubbing stones, a button fragment, two beads and two fragments of a bronze pin.

Room E was all but wiped out by Stratum XIII intrusion of the Basement Room, but since that intrusion involved facing the Stratum XIV walls with new construction, at least the lower parts of walls 3706, 3667, and 3381 were preserved as defining the limits of a Stratum XIV room. Thus the later walls appear *lower* than the earlier walls, a confusing state of affairs resulting from the concept of the Stratum XIII builders. At the east the situation is uncertain. The east limit was probably 3741, faced later by Wall 3752 (XIII AA, where these walls appear in elevation), but the north segment of Wall 3741, as it approached Wall 3667 in XIII AA, looks to be founded much higher, and higher than the one fragment of floor attested for Room E, Floor 3753 (AA:#57). The east balk of the field hides most of Wall 3741, so it seems likely that the wall is indeed the eastern limit of the room perhaps set back at this point and not visible.

Locus 3778 at elevation 17.60 on XIII AA:#67 lay on the 3775 debris; at first taken as the XIVB floor, it was then seen to be the weathered and tramped surface of the MB IIC debris, covered by grey makeup (#61) for beaten earth floor 3753 at elevation 18.30.

Rooms F and G were defined by Wall 3381 on the north and 3309-03239 (center of Ill. 162 = XIII BB) on the west. Access to them from Room E was through Wall 3381 to the west of its center point; a west stub of 3381 was preserved abutting Wall 3309 (not shown on Ill. 169). The south limit at its west end was probably the fragment of Wall 03205, extending 1.35 m eastward from Wall 3309, but badly disturbed by the construction of Wall 3311 belonging to Stratum XIII (XIII BB, where 3311 appears in elevation). When Seger excavated Area 5 and cut through the south limit of the field, however, he found Wall 3831 (Ill. 153) south of the line of 03205 extrapolated, and proposed it as the south limit. The east limit was probably Wall 03200-3835, preserved in elevation in XIII AA, but again badly disturbed by later construction and by two pits probably dug from Stratum XII or XI (Pits 3323 and 3324).

Wall 3390 divided this space into Rooms F and G. Its west end abutted Wall 3309, but it did not reach 03200-3835 at the east, where there may have been a door (Pit 3324 intrudes here). At the west end of Room F, Wall 3382 defined a narrow closet or annex (Ill. 169). Wall 3382, consisting of one course of six large, flat-topped stones, ended at the west edge of the presumed door through Wall 3381 in a rock with a cup-shaped depression, possibly the socket for a doorpost. The cup was not worn smooth, however, so as to suggest its use for that purpose. Wall 3382 rested directly in the debris of Kiln 3396. Within the annex was an oval stone-lined pit, locus 03202, 0.50 to 0.40 m across and 0.20 m deep, its purpose unclear.

Surrounding Pit 03202 in the closet was beaten earth Floor 3383 at elevation 17.76, laid on a thin makeup over the remains of the kiln. Floor 3383 reached Walls 3309, 3390 and 3381, tying these together. If there once had been a later floor in the closet, evidence for it was removed by Pit 3754 intruding on the junction of Walls 3309 and 3706.

The foundation trench for Stratum XIII Wall 3338 cut north-south across Room F, separating segments of preserved flooring from one another. The sequence was the same either side of this intrusion. A layer of barley-sized gravel, locus 3380, overlay the edge of Kiln 3396 and its MB IIC destruction debris adjacent to Wall 3381 at the east side of the assumed doorway, gravel taken to be bedding for a possible flagstone surface. Above 3380 was a plaster-like surface formed of compact grey ash, a good floor material, locus 3384. This patch of two floorings measured only 0.60 by 0.75 m against Wall 3381, but they merged into a layer of a mixture of ash, charcoal, patches of red field soil, limestone fragments and traces of dung—likely surfacing of a yard. To the east, adjacent to Wall 03200 on the other side of the foundation trench, was a similar sequence: locus 3391 as the tramped top of the MB IIC destruction debris (compare 3778 in Room E), 0.20 m of grey makeup, beaten earth Surface 3385 at elevation 17.74, 0.10 m of makeup and Plaster Floor 3377 at elevation 17.84 (only 3377 shows on XIII AA:#58). Although not quite as clear as in Room D, the picture is one of a B and A phase to Stratum XIV, separated by a thin layer. Overlying the two patches of upper phase floors was destruction debris, 3375 over Floor 3384 and 3371 (AA:#53) over Floor 3377, again like that in Room D. The destruction debris had MB IIC and LB IB pottery among loose soil and stones.

Foundation trenches for Stratum XIII walls also cut across Room G, leaving two segments of flooring, one from the center of the room to Wall 3309 and the other along the east edge. The sequence is familiar. In the western portion, locus 3399 at elevation 17.45 was the top of the MB IIC debris, tramped and weathered; it was topped by makeup for Plaster Floor 3392 at elevation 17.64. A second floor, preserved in small segments, was beaten earth Surface 3379, with sherds lying flat on it. Over it was locus 3370, its top at elevation 17.84, a bricky compact grey-brown layer representing Stratum XIVA destruction. Pit 3373 near Wall 3309 was dug after Floor 3379 was covered and appears to be a rubbish pit filled with destruction from Stratum XIVA; it is sealed beneath Stratum XIII floors.

Along the east, the sequence was 3391 top of destruction debris, beaten earth Floor 3378, makeup, beaten earth Floor 3376, destruction debris 3371 (the same locus number as the debris in Room F with which it is continuous).

Seger carried the excavation in the area of Rooms F and G deeper in 1969 and found remains of north-south Wall 03215 just beneath the pattern of flooring already described (Ill. 153). It divided Room G in half, with Floor 03228 to its west at elevation 17.13 and Floor 03227 to its east at elevation 17.25, sloping to 17.12 further south. In this floor was Grain Pit 3836. The fact that walls in elevation lay along the east and south balks of Area 2 where all this was located means that these features are hard to connect to other parts of the complex and results in the sections not displaying them. They may have belonged to the preparatory phase for Stratum XIV or to the first beginnings of housing here. They were higher than the MB IIC remains attested here. Clearly a great deal of rather shabby construction took place as Stratum XIV came into being and continued.

The Western Complex: Building A, Yard B, Sector C. Across the main west wall of the eastern complex and Street 3121 lay a very different arrangement of space. Except for the corner made by Walls 3462 and 3496, this area lay open, with a gentle slope eastward to the street edge. Wall fragment 3534 separated Sector C from Yard B.

Stratum XIV builders came upon the ruins of the Government Residency in the northwest corner and founded new walls on the jumbled disorder of fallen rocks. Sections through the two walls appear on Ills. 163 and 164 = XIII CC and FF; three courses up from the tops of the MB IIC foundations, both walls thickened and the Stratum XIII external surfaces reached the faces of the thickened portion. Stratum XIV portions of the wall, then, were probably the three courses between the MB IIC bases and the thickening. Within the small space inside the corner, soil layers ##10–12 on XIII CC contained Iron I pottery and the layers sloped

Fig. 187. Fragment (Object B68 #546) of fluted column from locus 3536 rubble on Surface 3537 in Room B of the Field XIII, Stratum XIV complex. The column matches those found in the temple ruins of Field V to the south.

Fig. 188. Surface 3528 in Sector C of Field XIII Stratum XIV complex. The marl ring was placed flush with the surface. The second view shows an LB zir base that would have fit it with chinking of sherds.

away from the walls; the entire space was within an Iron I pit that had removed all surfaces from MB IIC through Strata XIV-XI and created a subsidence all the way up to the mound's surface as left by the 1934 German campaign, from which the American excavation began (XIII CC and FF).

Yard B was defined by Wall 3534 and the west walls of the eastern complex. Two segments of surfacing were traced. Both lay on the preparatory cushion of earth over the MB IIC remains. This cushion was defined as 3126-3125 = 3553 along the west balk (XIII FF:#42); it is 3539 and 3538 = 3769 and 3768 on XIII CC:#43. Throughout Yard B except at the far west edge, the surface was the top of Fill 3538-3768, designated in the field reports by these same numbers and characterized by compact soil on which lay many sherds and bone fragments. Embedded in this surface (Ill. 169) was Platform 3524B, a single flat stone 0.50 by 0.40 m in size and 0.15 m thick, from which a thin wall, 3524A, curved northwestward. An oven was sited against the north edge of Platform 3524B (possibly a kneading stone?) and ash lay along 3524A's north edge, mixed with yellow-red earth—an outdoor cooking area.

Between Wall 3534 and the corner of Building A, what was almost certainly the same surface was represented by locus 3537, a crushed limestone or plaster patch near the west balk broken from connection with Surface 3538; it did not reach that balk, but it overlay Fill 3539. On it were large fragments of oven lining; the oven was probably located at the corner of Building A. Over it was locus 3536, brown to red-brown brick rubble, containing much MB IIC and LB pottery representing destruction of Stratum XIV. In this debris was a fragment of fluted column, object #546 (fig. 187), which matched those found in the temple ruins (see Chapter 3 on Shechem's Fluted Columns). Since it is fragmentary, it is likely to have been reused in a Stratum XIV wall and to have fallen into its destruction debris. Its *origin* was likely to have been Stratum XV in the temple precinct, or just possibly in the Government Residency of MB IIC. It is not impossible, however, that the fluted columns belonged to Stratum XIV, and were used in the Stratum XIV phase of the broad-roomed LB sanctuary.

Locus 3536 debris was equivalent to locus 3525A debris beneath the Stratum XIII surface 3525 on Ill. 163 = XIII CC :##34 on 38). In Yard B, there was only one flooring, and it was topped by destruction. Where there was sub-phasing to Stratum XIV in the eastern complex, in the yard there was only one surface, building up across the period of occupation.

Sector C showed the sort of irregular surfacing open areas develop; it was traced with difficulty among four pits intruding on it, and the foundation trenches for Stratum XIII walls which separated segments of the surface from one another. In the final analysis, it seems clear that surfaces 3528,

Fig. 189. Walls 16.110 and 16.110A of Stratum XIV in Field VII, Area 9. The structure was set into a saucer excavation, with Flagstone 16.118 to the right.

3117 and 3122 were all parts of the surfacing. Surfaces 3528 and 3533 (the top of the underlying fill with the same number) were an accumulation of as much as 0.15 m of build-up, containing charcoal and red to orange bricky detritus; the top, Surface 3528, was defined near Pit 3532 by crushed limestone or plaster. On it was the marl ring shown in fig. 188, apparently a jar stand, although it required chinking to hold the LB jar base upright for the photograph. Surface 3117 near the west balk can be traced on Ill. 164 = XIII FF as #41 continuous with #40, lying on makeup #42 and 47; it ran on top of the MB IIC steps 3550 to the foundation trench of Wall 3457 (#34), which apparently removed Wall 3534 defining the north edge of Sector C. At the south, Surface 3117 stepped down over the ruins of Wall 3129 into the valley to the south. Floor segment 3122 lay all along Street 3121 and was about 0.10 m thick; it was of hard bricky earth with ash and bone fragments. There was a drop in elevation from 18.83 on Floor 3117 at the west balk to 18.15 on Floor 3122 along Street 3121—a difference of 0.68 m.

Repeated reference has been made to evidence of destruction, but it does not seem to have been violent. The debris, from 0.20 to 0.40 m thick with brick ingredients, was not the sort conflagration produces. Something is needed to account for the transition from Stratum XIV to XIII, but what it was is elusive. One can speculate about disease, and the possibility that a rubbish pit was dug to bury some of the debris may point to measures against its spread. Nor was there much evidence of the duration of the gap before Stratum XIII builders changed the layout in Field XIII dramatically.

Field VII

The preparatory phase of Stratum XIV involved firepits, probably lime kilns, in an open area defined by Wall 13.164. North of the lime kiln yard, in Area 9, there was a corner of a structure, Walls 16.110 and 16.110A (fig. 189). The builders had scooped out a deep saucer (locus 16.124) in a hump of MB IIC debris, placed flat flagstones (locus 16.118) and a block of *ḥuwwar* 16.118A at its bottom to consolidate the foundations, built the walls, and then filled the saucer with less compacted earth (Ill. 112 = VII AA:#38; fig. 190, where the edge of the saucer is almost vertical, 0.80 m away from the face of the wall). The corner showed careful building technique; semi-dressed blocks 1.10 m long were laid as interleaved stretchers. The wall had been plastered, as fig. 189 shows: the dark lines representing the exterior surface turned at right angles and ran up the facing about 0.03 m away from the stone at the balk near the left margin. As with Building A in Field XIII,

Fig. 190. North balk of Field VII Area 9. The meter stick rests on Block 16.118A. Note the vertical mark of the saucer into which the 16.110 complex was set, approximately 0.35 m to the right of the meter stick. The stones at the second decimeter from the bottom of the stick lie in the crushed remains of tannur 16.114 of Stratum XIV, reused in Stratum XIII.

a pit (16.103) had been subsequently dug within the corner, disturbing any interior flooring. A patch of yellowish brick and charcoal at elevation 11.62 on VII AA near its top and to the west of the wall, but not certain on the section, locus 16.117, may be a hint of flooring.

Against the east face of Wall 16.110, just at the north balk, sat Tannur 16.114, with finger-smoothing on its outer surface. After smoothing, the builder had pressed four shallow bowls of typical Late Bronze form against the outside (VII AA and fig. 191). The surface for Stratum XIV, Floor 16.107, ran to a point halfway up the preserved side of the tannur on VII AA:#37, at elevation 11.97. Elevations elsewhere on it were read at 12.02 and 11.75, sloping to the southeast. The floor was composite in material. It appeared as patches of plaster in the center of the area, and here and

Fig. 191. Segment of Floor 16.107A under meter stick against upper stones of Wall 16.110. Tannur 16.114, first laid with 16.107 of Stratum XIV and reused in Stratum XIII, is half hidden in the balk at center right.

Fig. 192. The west face of Wall 9588 in Field IX, showing both headers and stretchers.

there a flat stone lay flush with it.

Floor 16.107 was resurfaced at least twice, as Floor 16.107A. Throughout Area 9 there was clear separation between Stratum XIV building 16.110–16.110A with its flooring 16.107 and the subsequent Stratum XIII remains with the resurfacings of 16.107A, except at the east edge of the area as shown at the junction of VII AA and VII CC = Ill. 115. Here Floor 16.107A of Stratum XIII sloped to coalesce with 16.107 of Stratum XIV (AA:#37 with CC:#23). In areas 6 and 3 to the south, and eastward at the west edge of Area 5 there is further evidence of Stratum XIV, but since excavation stopped with a mix of Stratum XIV and Stratum XIII remains showing, separation is difficult and the data untrustworthy for understanding Stratum XIV. As shown on Ill. 95, a long wall line consisting of 13.142 at the north, a gap, and Wall 13.163–10.115 to the south, ran parallel to the balk at the east of Areas 6 and 3. East-west walls bonded

Fig. 193. Looking north in Field IX Area 3, Wall 9588 to right and Wall 9585 to left. Alley surfaced by 9600 runs between them. Notice the building technique of Wall 9588 as viewed from above.

at least to the upper courses of these walls ran eastward into the balk (13.141, 13.143, and 10.125), and the northernmost of these, 13.141, continued as 14.174 in the northeast corner of Area 5.

One floor in Area 6 belonged almost certainly to Stratum XIV. Locus 13.157, at elevation 11.93, lay against the north edge of the area; the mark of a tannur 0.64–0.67 m in diameter was discernible on it near its south limit. A group of stones in the very northeast corner of the area, shown against the left (north) face of Wall 13.141 over VII CC:#28, were probably part of the MB IIC destruction debris and would have protruded through the floor; fragments of beaten earth flooring like 13.157 appeared on top of the stones (Ill. 113 = VII BB:#46), with Wall 13.147 set down into it.

There were a number of surface fragments within the yard with the firepits, including one patch against the south face of Wall 13.164 near its junction with 13.142 which may have belonged to Stratum XIV. Others may also belong to Stratum XIV, and they were so interpreted when the field report was written in 1965, but it is likely they all belonged to Stratum XIII. The foundations of Wall 13.142-13.163-10.115 were let down into the MB IIC destruction debris and were in place in Stratum XIV; Wall 13.164 was footed at elevation 10.64. The current hypothesis is that the earliest firepit 13.175 goes with the preparatory phase, the next, 13.169, with Stratum XIV, and the uppermost, 13.170 with Stratum XIII. None of the attested fragments of flooring in the firepit yard must have belonged to Stratum XIV; none may be taken as definitive of the stratum.

Field IX

Stratum XIV construction in Field IX centered on Wall 9588, and the building which it defined to the east. Excavation in Area 1 of the field had stopped at the Stratum XI level, so the building lying east of Wall 9588 was attested by what was found in a strip 2.00 m wide at the south balk of Area 3 (Ill. 141 = IX AA) narrowing to 0.60 m at the north edge of the field (Ill. 145 = IX EE); Ill. 143 = IX CC presents the stratification along the east edge of the excavated area. A *maṣṣebah* found in the Stratum XII reuse of the building, a succes-

Fig. 194. Profile of stratigraphy in east balk of Field IX Area 3. Compare IX CC section. The brick topping of Wall 9611 shows Jar 9606B buried in it with the line of Stratum XIV plaster floor running just over it.

sion of brick and stone platforms against the east face of Wall 9588, the possible base of a libation stand and a possible foundation sacrifice all lead to the hypothesis that the structure was a sanctuary.

Wall 9588 showed similar building technique to Wall 16.110/16.110A in Field VII, using rough-hewn stones in header-stretcher pattern, selected for close and compact fit. The two faces are contiguous, with virtually no rubble core (figs. 192 and 193). The interior flooring was of packed earth and chalk, with plastering at places, building up to a thickness of 0.10 m with many resurfacings, suggesting the passage of some time. It lay partially over Brick Wall 9611 of Stratum XVII (IX CC), with only the narrow band of IX CC:#48 separating the two walls. And it covered the buried jar 9606B (fig. 194) which was set down into 9611 from above (shown also on IX CC).

The late Joseph Callaway, who supervised this work, provided for the preliminary report of the 1964 campaign a description of the contents of Jar 9606B that is more complete than that found in any other record so far recovered from his relics: "a jar containing thirteen beads, a lamp, and four astragali. Two of the bones were worn smooth, apparently from use. The pot must have been a deposit for the founding of the sanctuary" (Bull, *et al.* 1965:11). Apparently the beads and astragali were not registered or photographed by the Expedition, and as of the time of writing are lost.

Strata XVI and XV layering here was all but gone; a thin black ashy layer could be traced in the balk upon which Floor 9592B rode (IX CC:#49). On the floor (#48) was a thin layer of compact grey earth on which rested a 0.40 to 0.50 m thick layer of what were discerned to be fallen stones (#47). The stone layer did not extend to touch Wall 9588; the excavators discerned a long oblique cut which may have robbed stones near the wall. At the far northeast corner of the field, 9592A lapped upon a decayed brick (locus 9606) at the junction of the north and east balks (Ills. 143 and 145 = IX CC and EE; fig. 194) against Wall 9588. In the tiny space here, the excavators also identified a line of stones parallel to 9588. The decayed brick and the hint of a defining wall may represent an altar or cultic platform; above them were platforms belonging to Strata XIII and XII. Callaway's text for the 1964 preliminary report provides one more striking detail: "Beside the small altar [i.e. locus 9606] and on the floor was the flared base of a libation stand" (Bull *et al.* 1965:11).

What part the stone layer played in Stratum XIV is not clear, but it is noteworthy that plaster against the east face of Wall 9588 belonging to Stratum XIII was discerned to run over the stone layer (fig. 194), requiring that the stone layer came from within Stratum XIV times, whether as part of the construction or of the destruction.

An alley or street with beaten earth surface lay along the west face of Wall 9588, at elevation 8.78. The surface was probably the top of layer 9600, the first layer to run over the foundation trench for Wall 9588 on IX AA and IX EE:#57. The west limit of the alley was Wall 9585, a thin but sturdy wall preserved at least 0.75 m high and reused in Stratum XIII (Ill. 128).

Walls 9864-9593, 9598, 9866 and 9870 defined part of a domestic complex to the west. Room A, with a stone-lined storage bin in its northwest corner was surfaced with beaten earth at the top of layer 9599 (IX AA:#80), resting on a makeup of ashy, bricky soil. Room B to its north was surfaced by beaten earth over IX EE:#53; Pit 9594A was probably also a storage facility in this room. In the tiny portion of Room C, north of Wall 9864, the surface was probably IX EE:#56 (see also IX BB:#74) connecting Walls 9864 and 9598. Yard D was a large open space with a hearth and a mortar set into the beaten earth surface. The most striking flooring in the complex was Flagstone Floor 9873 in Room E (IX AA:#83A), from which one passed into Yard D through the door in Wall 9870.

This description and interpretation of Stratum XIV in Field IX significantly changes and corrects that given in the preliminary report. Fig. 195, reproduced from Bull *et al.* 1965:12–13, presents a selection of pottery profiles, 26 of which come from Stratum XIV loci in Field IX (n.b., item 5 is from IX.3.93 not 43 as the legend in *BASOR* 180 has it).

THE HOUSING OF STRATUM XIII

The fortifications and broad-room sanctuary both gave indications that violent disruption marked the transition from Stratum XIII to Stratum XII. Stratum XIII was closely related to Stratum XIV, with a non-violent interruption at the shift from XIV to XIII about 1400 BCE.

Field IX

The sanctuary at the east of Field IX was slightly modified in Stratum XIII, with the building of a new floor above the stone layer 9592A. A thick plaster facing was added to the east face of Wall 9588, visible on Ill. 145. In the northeast corner of Area 3, above the location of the proposed altar of Stratum XIV, two oblong brown bricks (Ill. 143 = IX CC) may represent an altar platform for Stratum XIII. The surface for this use of the sanctuary was not entirely clear; it was probably the line of separation between IX CC:#47 and #46 and between ##77 and 72 on Ill. 141 = IX

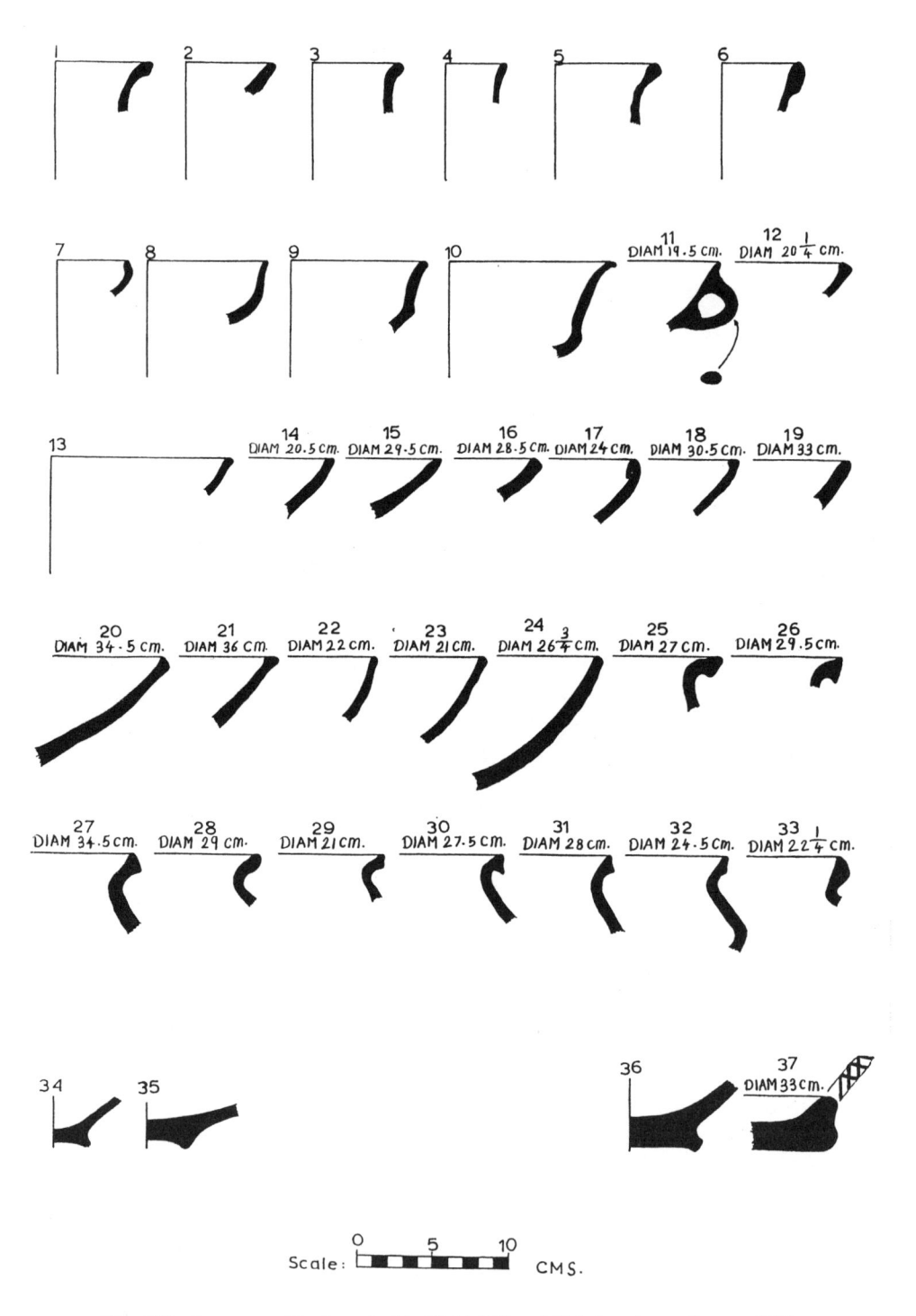

Fig. 195. Pottery profiles from loci in Fields VII and IX belonging to Stratum XIV.

Fig. 196. Looking south at south balk of Field VII Area 9. Stratum XIII Wall 16.109 in center, emerging from balk. White plaster on the surface beneath it marks Floor 16.107. Resurfacings 16.107A of Stratum XIII barely visible in the balk to west (right) of 16.109.

AA, in each case separating locus 9592A from 9592. Locus 9592, the upper layer in each case, contained brick detritus and some stones, and was topped by a layer of ash (CC:#45, AA:#69). It probably was the top of the Stratum XIII destruction in the sanctuary. A collection of 31 registered sherds from locus 9592 resembled in field analysis the Stratum XIII pottery from Field VII; they are currently being studied in relation to the control corpus from the Basement Room in Field XIII.

To the west of Wall 9588, there seems to have been little architectural change from XIV to XIII. The layering shown on IX AA:#78 and 73 and IX EE:##51–54 contained whatever new surface was in use. In Room E, the flagstone floor was covered by a *ḥuwwar* surface topping AA:#82 that rested on the flagstones. On the *ḥuwwar* surface was a layer of ash and bricky soil 9869A = IX AA:#81 and BB:#73, which represents destruction. The violent nature of the destruction of Stratum XIII indicated by Field XIII and VII was not dramatically evident in Field IX, but ash in the sanctuary and locus 9869A probably attest it.

Field VII

Stratum XIII was represented in Field VII by developments on the 16.110–16.110A complex, in the firepit yard, and in the complex to the east and south of the yard. Ill. 95 brings together the changes. What gave the entire layout definition was the evidence of massive destruction throughout (see Ill. 115 = VII CC:#19 over destruction debris #20) humping over the various wall stubs and subsiding into the rooms, and the deep debris at the south.

In Area 9, 16.110 was reused in Stratum XIII, but 16.110A was covered over. Wall 13.147 projected 0.50 m into the area from the south, on line with the top of 16.110; it continued south into Area 6 as Wall 13.147. Wall 13.147 was 0.50 m wide, much narrower than 16.110, but similar in width to all the other Stratum XIII walls in the field. Stratum XIV Floor 16.107 = 13.157 ran beneath the wall; foundation stones rested on or indented the floor (Ill. 113 = VII BB:#46 and fig. 196). Floor 16.107A, tightly banded layering of several surfacings, went with 13.147, ran north over the top of Wall 16.110A, sloped up to the top of 16.110 at the north balk (Ill. 112 = VII AA:bottom of #36), ran away from 16.110's east face over Oven 16.114 and then sloped down to become the top layering of 16.107 at the east balk (#37). In Area 6, Floor 13.154 at elevation 12.39 rode on 0.25 m of clay makeup over Stratum XIV Floor 13.157, was also of tightly banded layering as much as 0.15 m thick, and must represent the same flooring (VII

BB:#44). It ran to Wall 13.147, with the uppermost resurfacing curving up to the face of the wall.

If, as proposed earlier, Firepit 13.170 belonged to Stratum XIII, it was put out of use during the time of the stratum by a corner of walling, Walls 13.151–13.150, of the same narrow construction as others of the period. Mention has been made of the patches of surfacing preserved between the firepits and Wall 13.142-13.163. They are likely all to have belonged to Stratum XIII. East of the long wall, the one clear piece of flooring was locus 13.159, a beaten earth surface against the north face of 13.143 just inside the door through Wall 13.142. Floor 13.159 was at elevation 11.69.

At some point during the time of Stratum XIII, buttresses were built against the (presumed) exterior faces of 13.151, 13.142 and 13.163, shown on Ill. 95. The door giving access from the yard through Wall 13.142 was blocked, and the buttress covered the blocking. Surfaces at a higher level east of this wall were to be expected, but none was found.

Across the Area 6/5 balk, Walls 14.173 and 14.178 formed a right angle corner of a ruined building. Wall 14.173 stood 1.45 m high, its top showing bricks in place; as the plan suggests, the wall tilted to the south. Surfaces related to this ruined structure were probably reached in probes beside the walls, but not effectively related through the balk to the fragments of surfacing within the small chambers against the east face of the long wall in Area 6. What defined the surface was the bottom, at elevation 11.40, of a massive crush of broken store jars in firm bricky debris (locus 14.180) against the north face of Wall 14.173. At least eight pottery baskets of restorable jars came from this locus on the last day of the 1964 campaign, and await restoration. Stratigraphically definitive of the end of Stratum XIII, they are being studied with the Field XIII Basement Room corpus and other Stratum XIII destruction deposits.

To the south in Area 3, the complex shown on plan in Ill. 95 belonged to Stratum XIII, but it was not excavated below surface level. Wall 10.130 ended at its butt join with Wall 10.115. It was the north edge of a room defined on the west by 11.109 and containing a mortar near the south limit of excavation. The elevation on the lip of the mortar was 12.86, very high given the slope southward indicated in Area 6. To the east in the room were two fragments of stone surface, 10.123 and 10.124, which may have been cobbled surfaces. One gained access to this room from the north at the east edge of Area 3, through a door in Wall 10.118 which rode on top of earlier Wall 10.125. Without further excavation, the tentative hypothesis is that this complex was a late Stratum XIII addition. That it belonged with Stratum XIII was again indicated by the destruction debris lying on its surfaces (Ill. 115 = VII CC:#22).

Three superimposed surfaces were traced in a small space against the north face of Wall 10.130, with elevations from 12.28 down to 12.04. Tannur 10.127, shown on the plan, went with the lowest surface at least, and probably with all three. Ten indicator sherds with these floorings aid the study of late Stratum XIII.

The destruction debris overlying Stratum XIII occupation in Field VII is depicted on VII CC as #20. It was as much as 0.75 m thick. In Areas 6 and 9, a distinction was drawn between an upper, lighter-colored bricky layer 13.140A-16.105A and a lower, dense, damp darker layer 13.144–16.106; the distinction was particularly clear over the rooms at the east edge of Area 6. In area 3, only the lower type of soil was noted. It is not clear what caused the distinction, and what accounted for the damp and dense character of the lower debris layer—which resembles most closely the Stratum XII debris in the north of Area 9 but is otherwise unlike typical destruction debris at the site. Whole pieces of pottery were encountered high in the layering, some badly rotted and crumbling. Chunks of grey-green plaster with a pink tinge at the surface were found; whole bricks occurred. In Area 5, the debris was 14.176-14.180, again denoting a distinction between two densities of material but here less easy to discern because of the confined area of excavation. Quantities of black ash as from smothered fire characterized this part of the debris, with empty cavities at the wall junctions. From this came the crush of store jars already described.

In the southwest corner of Area 9, west of Wall 13.147 (Ill. 128), there was a thick deposit of the damper brown 16.106 material which was pulled down in one rapid operation'after all other deposits of 16.106 had been carefully dissected by the excavators. This deposit resembled 16.106, damp and dark, but from within 0.10 m of its top as defined by the ash line 16.105 there appeared the bronze figurine with its silver tunic pictured in fig. 197, its arm separated from its body. It stands 0.184 m high and has pegs in its feet for mounting. It had been exposed to fire, which had deeply oxidized the silver and fused it to the bronze. The piece awaits full publication. Reports of its context, notably that in the preliminary report (Bull, *et al.* 1965:24–5), need correction; it was from Stratum XIII destruction debris, reported as "upper layer 6" in the supervisor's field report, dated to the first half of the fourteenth century BCE. Seven baskets of pottery from 16.106 include 50 registered indicator sherds, four of which are whole vessels. Field calls on this pottery identified the presence of MB II and Iron IA, but the assemblage needs review. Objects include three bronze arrowheads, a granite bowl rim, two basalt rubbing stones, a clay bead, and a bronze spatula—domestic items plus items suggesting military action.

Field XIII

Stratum XIII in Field XIII constitutes the best-preserved Late Bronze complex anywhere at Shechem (Ill. 156). Its builders refurbished Stratum XIV remains, widening and strengthening existing walls and adding new structures in the open Sector C in the southwest. Building A was reused, and the adjacent Yard B reconstructed.

The Western Complex: Sectors A-F. The pit dug into the interior of Building A in Iron I had removed evidence of the phasing; against the exterior of the building, Stratum XIII is marked by the surface of Yard B, which is locus 3504 on Ill. 164 = XIII FF:#36, and the top of locus 3525 on Ill. 163 = XIII CC:#34. Yard B was defined on its south by a new wall line, 3457-3486 (3699), built in two separate operations. Wall 3457 was 0.65–0.70 m wide; at its east end it rested on the preserved piece of Stratum XIV Wall 3534, while the west end was built in a foundation trench cutting deep into Stratum XIV preparatory fill (XIII FF:#34). Wall 3486 was not quite in line with

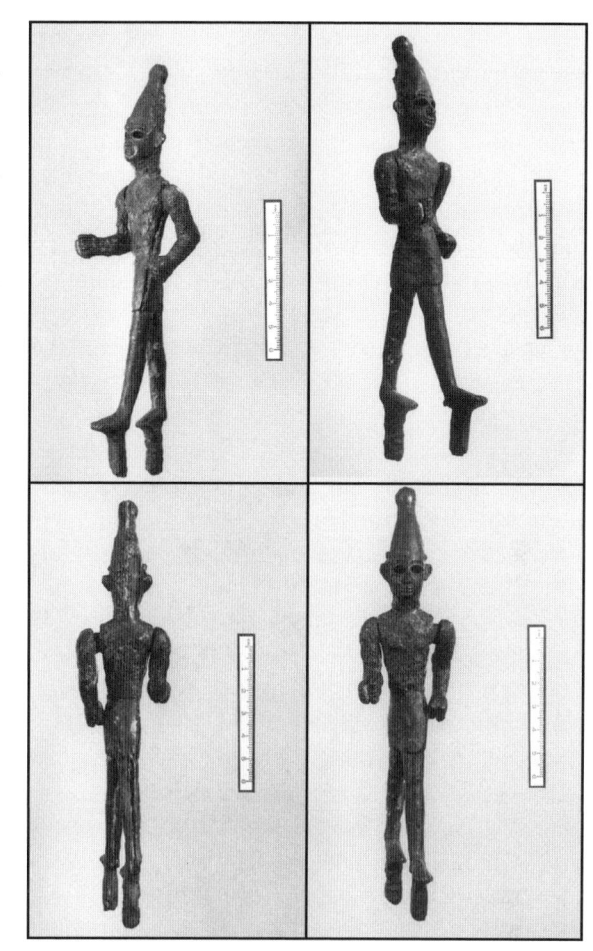

Fig. 197. Views of bronze figurine from Stratum XIII debris in Field VII.

3457, but continued it on the other side of an opening 0.80 m wide giving access south from the yard. Wall 3486 was bonded into the upper courses of Wall 3706, the west wall of the eastern complex. There was disturbance just north of this junction, but it appears that one entered Corridor H here, which in turn gave access to the house in the southeast corner of the field.

Surface 3525 in the yard was of beaten earth, the top of the layer of Stratum XIV destruction debris XIII CC:#38. The surface accumulated 0.05–0.10 m of occupation build-up, with patches of brick dust, ash, and stone-plus-sherd paving. It sloped from elevation above 19.00 at the north to 18.81 in its center to 18.62 near Wall 1663 at the east, near the opening into Corridor H. Here two resurfacings were detected but could not be connected to portions of the surfacing westward.

Yard B contained features typical of an outdoor yard: a slightly elevated brick platform (3747) possibly serving as a hearth and Jar Stand 3746 built up of marl paste on a stone basin. Over Surface 3518 (top of XIII CC:#32) of the yard was a thin layer of destruction debris, thickening toward Wall 3496 as shown on CC:##30 and 31, which are a segment of striated orange and tan debris and a deposit of orange and black brick detritus respectively—suggestions of violent destruction of Building A. Pottery was heavy on the surface and in the makeup, and included MB IIC, LB IB and LB IIA on field analysis.

In the southwest quadrant, a set of cross-walls were constructed, dividing the formerly open region of Stratum XIV Sector C into four small yards or rooms, designated C, D, E and F on the plan. The preserved height of the walls varied but none was particularly substantial. Iron I pits intruded at six places, making the tracing of surfaces very difficult. In Space D, Floor 3526 was a white, ash-covered surface on beaten earth only 0.08 m above the Stratum XIV surface. Eleven pottery pails from the makeup, the surface, and the 0.30 m of brick rubble of destruction on the surface contained sherds ranging from MB IIB to LB II.

The only patch of surface in Space C was locus 3522, the plaster layer running south from Wall 3457 as XIII FF:#35. Its makeup #38 = locus 3527 and the sherds from it were small fragments characteristic of fill, dating to MB and LB. No sherds were recovered from the surface itself.

In Yard F, Cobbled Surface 3114 was traced against Walls 3124, 3309 and 3080; together with 0.30 m of red bricky debris above it, this locus contained some MB II pottery but predominantly LB II, including White Slip II ware. In the south of the yard, an ill-defined surface, locus 3119 (Ill. 162 = XIII BB:#51) at elevation 18.49, ran to the region of Wall 3108, which appears in BB in elevation and is difficult to phase because the balk is still in place. It may have belonged to Stratum XIII, in which case 3119 went with it, or it may have been let down from Stratum XII with its foundation trench cutting 3119. Yard F contained Fire Pit 3119A and a conical depression filled with spongy earth, locus 3120—probably a jar stand.

No surface was identified in Space E. It should have been above surface 3117 = XIII FF:#40. The numerous pits and intrusions close to the west balk of the field precluded finding it.

The southwest quadrant seems to have consisted of work spaces. The walls may mean small dwellings, or the new cross walls may represent the creation of privately owned work precincts for residents of surrounding houses.

The Eastern Complex: Rooms G, H, J, K, L and M. The eastern building consisted of six units, G to the north, Corridor H, and Rooms J-M in the main structure. The main line of the western wall and several of the other wall lines continued the tradition of the previous stratum. But the builders had a different idea of how they would use the spaces, the most striking change being the construction of the subfloor storage chamber. This massive architectural intervention interfered with understanding the house plans here from the MB IIC phase on.

Room G, which may have been part of a house off to the northeast, was a storage space. It was doubtless roofed because it contained Silo 3734, an open shallow bin with a wide plaster lip that filled most of the excavated space in the room. Beaten earth Surface 3739, studded with chunks of limestone and topped by a thin grey film of chalk, extended from it to the walls (Ill. 163 = XIII CC:#35). The surface rested on a striated makeup which in turn lay on the leveled top of Stratum XIV destruction debris, layer 3759 = #39. Makeup and floor together accumulated to 0.19 m in thickness; the top was at elevation 18.35 m. The floor surface sloped down sharply to the lip of the silo, and could hardly have been a walking surface; the slope is depicted next to Wall 3667 as Ill. 161 = XIII AA:#45.

Silo 3734 was 0.60 m deep from the top of the lip; the plaster of the lip did not extend down to line it, so it was not watertight. On its bottom was a black layer of what is probably decomposed grain. Room G was probably a pantry or storeroom, or the corner of a kitchen, for a house extending north and east from it. A store jar on Floor 3739 against Wall 3663 near the lip of the silo was preserved *in situ* when Stratum XII rebuilt the lip of the silo over it.

Fig. 198. Looking east at the walls, bonded to one another, of the Sub-Floor Chamber in Field XIII, now completely cleared of its contents.

Space H most likely served as a corridor from Yard B to the complex lying to its south. Its surface seems to have been related to the series of resurfacings in Sector B, but disturbance at the line of the wall interrupted direct connection, and the wall line (3663 to 3706) was so badly damaged that it is not certain that there was a doorway through it. A doorway here makes sense and the ruins permit the conclusion; this would have provided a back entrance to the house. The surface (3745) showed a number of layers which merged into one another; the top elevation is 18.53. From Yard B to inside Corridor H there was a gradual drop of 0.15 to 0.25 m, not enough to require a step down.

Floor 3745 ran through what seems to have been a door in Wall 3742 from Room H into Room J. The top of Wall 3742 was so poorly preserved that it remains a possibility there was no division here and that Room J and Corridor H were all one space, and that Floor 3745 ran throughout. Destruction debris sat over Wall 3742, supporting this possibility. In any case, Room J's east and west walls were rebuilds of those of Stratum XIV, 3741 and 3706; the south wall was the upper part of 3751-3320.

The Sub-Floor Chamber. Beneath Room J was the sub-floor chamber. Stratum XIII builders had dug over 2.00 m down and encountered the oblong of MB IIC walls. They rebuilt on top of them, effectively facing the Stratum XIV walls in the process. The result was a rectangular cubicle of Walls 3742, 3743, 3751 and 3752, bonded to one another (fig. 198), preserved for thirteen stone courses. The chamber was roofed with wooden beams anchored on the tops of 3752 and 3743 against the faces of 3741 and 3706. Over the beams was laid Floor 3745.

Three flat stone slabs were recovered from the debris. One, 0.45 by 0.50 by 0.09 m in size, was in the destruction debris on Floor 3745; another, 0.75 by 0.90 by 0.15 m in size, was at the top of the filling of the chamber standing on end; the third, of the same size as the first, lay close to Wall 3743 well down in the fill. They were probably covers for the access, positioned at the west edge near Wall 3743. Presumably one descended from Room J by ladder.

The sub-floor chamber was probably an elaborate storage unit, used for dry storage of food stuffs at a relatively cool temperature. The walls showed no evidence of plaster lining. An LB bowl found

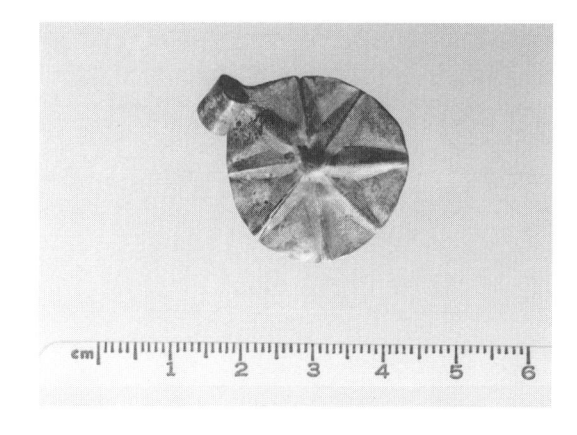

Fig. 199. Electrum pendant (B68 #821) from the silt layer at the base of the Sub-Floor Chamber.

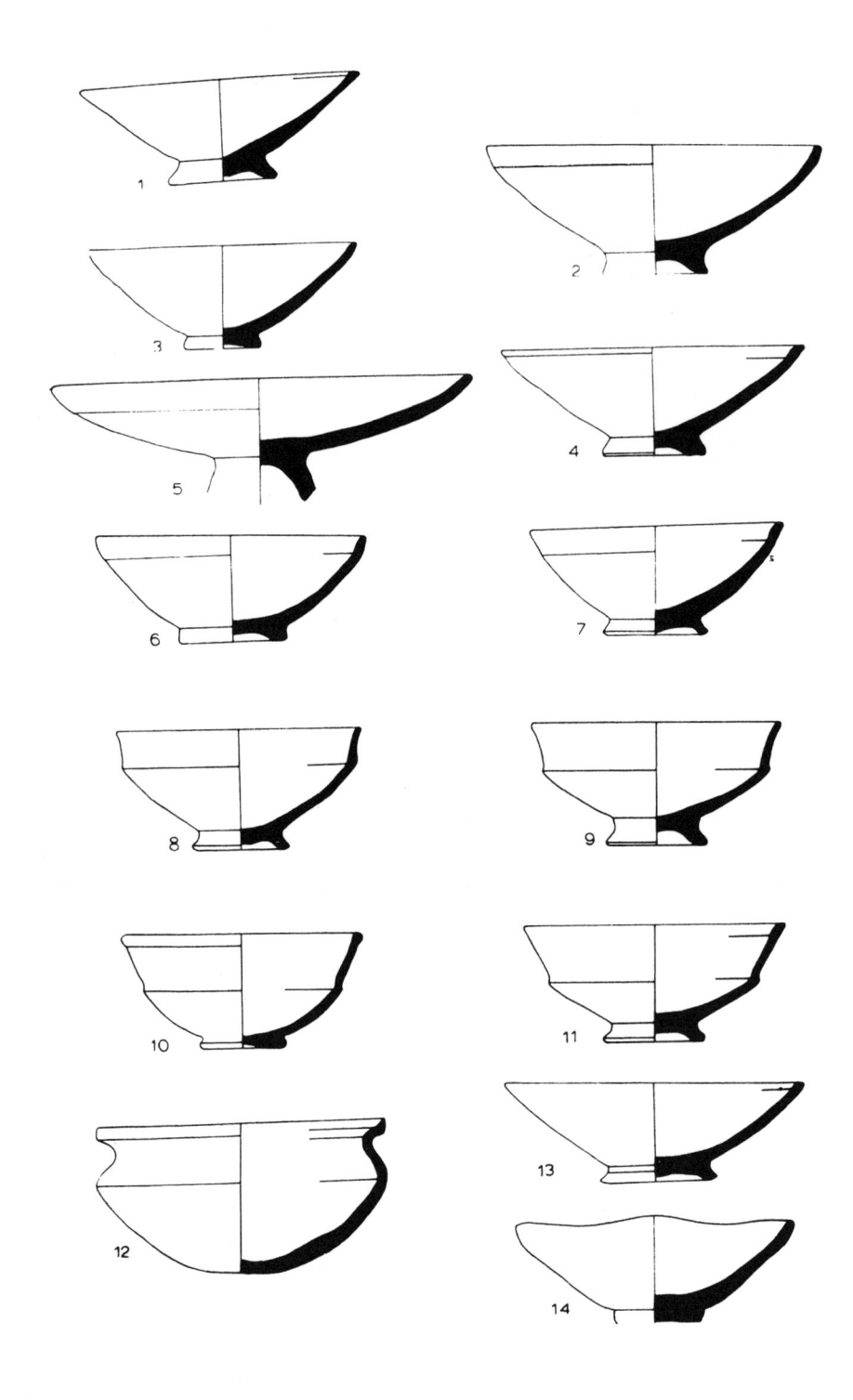

Fig. 200. Sample of the complete vessels recovered from the filling of the sub-floor chamber. Nos. 1, 2, 3, 4, 6, 7, 13, 14 are rounded or straight-sided; no. 5 is a rare trumpet-footed vessel; nos. 8–11 are typical LB carinated types; no. 12 is a small cooking pot.

Fig. 201. Looking east at the pottery beneath surface 3745, within the top layering of the Sub-Floor Chamber. The hump above the meter stick contains the skeleton, its backbone discernible.

overturned on the floor covered a mass of decomposed grain. The enclosed space, 3.00 m by 2.00 m by almost 2.50 m, is nearly 15 cubic meters.

The floor of the chamber, locus 3772, was of crushed limestone overlaid by 0.15 m of packed earth; it was at elevation 16.04, 2.49 m lower than Room J's floor above it. From the floor came five pails of pottery with a collection of 56 indicator sherds, belonging to LB IB and IIA with a very few MB sherds.

Floor 3772 showed signs of having been water-saturated; on it lay locus 3771, consisting of 0.40 m of silt, water-segregated and containing pieces of wood fiber, water-washed charcoal and decayed brick, suggesting that the basement regularly flooded, perhaps because water still collected at the low point of the drainage system built in MB IIC just to the west of Wall 9706. Locus 3771 yielded four whole LB vessels and a large number of indicator sherds, along with an electrum pendant (Obj. #821, in fig. 199), a drilled bone or ivory button (#839), a basalt grinding stone (#838) and piece of flagstone. This material was presumably dropped into the basement while it was in use, during which time it must have been becoming clear that water seepage was making storage in it untenable.

The occupants apparently gave up on the chamber because of the water problem. They filled it in with midden material, apparently brought from the town dump. The fill was tipped up toward the north and south walls as though someone stood in the middle of the room and spread it that way, in one operation to judge from the fact that pieces of various reconstructible vessels were found distributed throughout the debris. Included were bowls, kraters, cooking pots, lamps, Cypriote milk-bowls, store jars and a fine painted pitcher—a remarkable cross-cut through the domestic repertoire. Over 80 different vessels were represented, most of which have been reconstructed (fig. 200). The articulated skeleton of an unidentified large animal was found in the middle of the fill (fig. 201), either a carcass from the dump or one of the family's herd that died while the filling was going on.

The filling did not pack the chamber; when the house was destroyed, the portion of Floor 3745 over it dropped into a cavity on top of the filling. On top of the floor was 0.60 to 0.90 m of destruction debris, compact grey-brown earth filled with charred timber and brick fragments, ash, bone, shells, flints and bronze fragments. One of the bronzes is an arrow point. Among the great amount of pottery (fig. 202) was a pitcher with red monochrome painting featuring a gazelle (fig. 203). Near Wall 3741, in debris containing accretions of hard brick that probably represents the super-

Fig. 202. Pottery crush on Floor 3745, the surface over the Sub-Floor Chamber. Among the vessels was the pitcher with gazelles painted on it shown in fig. 203.

Fig. 203. Reconstructed monochrome-painted pitcher with theme of animals, including gazelle (B68 Obj. #581).

structure of the wall and perhaps the roof, was the skeleton of a small unidentified animal. The earthen surfacing of 3745 and the kinds of artifacts found indicate that Room J was a storage room, perhaps replacing the defunct sub-floor chamber.

Room K south of Room J was a corridor, entered from the east and giving access to Room L to its south. The east half of the corridor, where traffic would be heavy, was paved with Flagstones 3365. In the floor of the west alcove was a lidded, stone-lined pit, about 0.80 m deep, filled with decayed organic matter including a number of olive pits (3353). Near the west wall was an unlined and open cavity of the same depth, also containing organic matter but no seeds or pits. Layers 3349 on 3350 on 3354 accumulated on the flagstones in the heavily traveled east portion (Ill. 161 = XIII AA:#43, against the south face of 3320, below the Stratum XII floor 3333 = #42); LB pottery from these loci included sherds of a Cypriot milkbowl and of Base Ring Ware. The layers may be resurfacings, but were probably layers of destruction debris of Stratum XIII.

Room L gave evidence of two phases of use within Stratum XIII, separated by a local destruction which affected Room M as well. To construct Room L, the builders added courses to Wall 3309 on the west and laid out new walls 1.00 m wide on the east, south and north, changing the pattern from that of the preceding stratum. The east wall (Wall 3338) was built in three stages, a foundation course topped by a course 1.25 m wide, topped by the wall proper, 1.00 m in width. The top of the middle unit, 0.25 m wider than its successor, became a shelf, locus 3359, along the east edge of the room. The area enclosed is only 2.75 by 2.15 m. The wall tops were flat, their uppermost courses made of smaller rocks that would have served as good bedding for brick superstructure; two plaster-faced bricks, as well as a slab of plaster flooring over a meter square, were found in the room's debris. It was certainly roofed, and probably had a second story.

Floor 3361 of Room L, at approximate elevation 18.00, was laid on 0.15 m of makeup over the ruins of Stratum XIV rooms G and F. It was renewed over a period of time, building up 0.12 m

Fig. 204. Painted biconical vase as crushed on Floor 3355.

Fig. 205. The biconical vase as reconstructed by Ruth Amiran and Miriam Tadmor, seated in its ceramic collar stand.

of layering in thin bands to the uppermost flooring 3356. Given the strong indications that the room was roofed, it is of special note that Firepit 3360 was in the middle of the room, set 0.25 m into the floor. It was 0.80 m in diameter, and nearly filled the room; around its edge was a build-up of thinly laminated grey and black ash. Twenty-seven whole sea shells and a great number of sea shell fragments lay in the firepit or adjacent on Floor 3356, together with a crush of pottery that included a small pot painted on its outside and on its inner rim, a bowl within a whole cooking pot, part of another cooking pot, and a platter bowl. Also found in the ashes were two bone buttons, two bone needles or awls, a copper needle, and stone pestles or grinders, along with a steatite scarab (B68 Obj. #504), depicting the Horus falcon flanked by uraei, the familiar asp design of royalty—Egyptian motifs common to the New Kingdom (18th/19th dynasties). The destruction of Room L at its Floor 3356 level was local. Packed earth Floor 3355 was laid over the 0.20 m of debris and put Firepit 3360 and Shelf 3359 out of use. On 3355 fell 0.25 to 0.30 m of destruction debris, locus 3346; embedded in 3346 was Plaster Slab 3343, 1.10 by 1.10 m, lying at an angle and fallen from above, probably a piece of the second story flooring. Above it, and hence from the second story room, were three fragments of a copper or bronze vessel (Obj. B68 #245), the haft and part of the blade of a bronze sword (#246), a bone awl (#247), a bone cylinder (#248) and a partially drilled ceramic disk (#249), plus many sherds, predominantly LB II in date. On the floor itself, crushed by the fall, was the painted "biconical" jar in a jar stand shown in fig. 204 and reconstructed in fig. 205, together with a typical bowl of the period (fig. 206).

Fig. 206. Typical LB IIA (Stratum XIII) bowl from crush on Floor 3355.

Floor 3355 was traced out the door of Room L into Corridor K where Stone-lined Pit 3353 was still in service, into Room M at the east edge of the field. Here the flooring pattern was like that in Room L. Fig. 207 shows the build-up. The striations were white, grey, yellow and orange. The tags in the photograph from 3369 up to 3364 designate the thin laminations representing the protracted first period of use of the house; 3362 is local destruction debris; 3357 is the latest floor, representing the second phase of use; 3348 and 3347 represent the final, widespread destruction, 0.35 to 0.40 m thick. On XIII AA the accumulation is #50 south of Pit 7A; #48 marks Floor 3357.

There was a great deal of charcoal in the thin laminations of the first phase of use and on 3357, suggesting that a process involving fire was carried out in Room M, and the nature of the layers also suggests that Room M was open to the elements or used for an activity involving lots of water. Throughout this layering there were no noteworthy artifacts other than pottery, and relatively little of that.

The "technicolor" striations ran south into Area 5 where Seger worked in 1969 and continued to Wall 3825, the south boundary of Room M and probably the south wall of the whole house (XIII AA). From Wall 3667, the north boundary of Corridor H, to Wall 3825, the house would have measured 11.25 m along the east edge of the excavation. All indications are that it had a second story over the west row of rooms, while Room M was open to the sky. This layout, with Room M posited to be an atrium or central open courtyard, is comparable to that of the "Amarna" houses known from Egypt.

THE HOUSING OF STRATUM XII

The effect of the destruction of the fourteenth century city is plain in the succeeding layer of occupation, Stratum XII. In Fields XIII and IX, recovery took the form of rebuilding on simpler lines with inferior materials. In Field VII, the whole plan of the use of space changed, and the area began a long-lasting period of existence as an "industrial" area.

Field XIII

Ill. 157 indicates both simplification and continuity in Field XIII. In the eastern building, Stratum XIII's Room G was cleared of destruction debris and reused, as Room F on Ill. 157. Silo 3734 was cleaned, given a new plaster lip, and used for the same purpose as before. Rooms H and J over the Sub-floor Chamber became one (Room G) with the nullification of Wall 3742; its eastern limit

Fig. 207. Looking east at the east balk of Field XIII, Area 2, showing the striated surfacings in Room M of the Stratum XIII complex.

lay outside the excavation area with the nullification of Wall 3741. Its south wall was rebuilt as 3320, an inferior construction to Wall 3751 beneath. To the south, the walls that had defined Room L of the previous period were covered over, and former Rooms K, L and M became one unit (Room H). Stratum XIII Wall 3825, which defined the south limit of Room M went out of use.

Access to the eastern building probably changed: the assumed doorway from Yard B into Stratum XIII Corridor H was blocked, and the new door moved south through Wall 3309, opening into the north alcove of Room H, from which one could enter Room G to its north. Rearrangement of space in the southwest quadrant would have made this possible. This judgment is tentative, because Wall 3706 was very poorly preserved. Pit 3270-3339-3738 grossly disturbed the location of the proposed entrance, but the preserved west end of Wall 3320 at the pit's edge was made of squared stones preserved for 1.00 m in height, suggesting a doorpost for the passage between Rooms G and H.

There is nothing to indicate that the top of the Stratum XIII destruction debris eroded or lay exposed for any length of time; the occupants worked without delay to level the debris and lay floors on about 0.20 m of makeup. The stone wall foundations throughout the eastern building were usually preserved only a little higher than floor levels; they probably had mudbrick tops. In the southwest precinct, Wall 3124 was put out of use, and what had been Spaces D and F were combined into one (Space D). Wall 3108 (which may have been in place in Stratum XIII or may have been built in Stratum XII—see above) clearly defined the south limit of the complex. In the northwest corner Building A and Yard B continued in use. The rearrangement of space into larger units can be taken to mean that there were fewer people, fewer claims to accommodate.

In the eastern building, all the floors were of beaten earth and showed no plaster. In Room F, Floor 3726 at elevation 18.63 lay on 0.30 of makeup; it went with the new lip of Silo 3734, which was raised 0.15 m above the preceding lip to elevation 18.93. Floor 3726 does not reach balks and is not shown on section. Since Stratum XI surface 3716 covered the silo, the silo's contents are a sealed deposit of Stratum XII—although intrusion by Pit 3719 may have permitted later sherds to contaminate the purity of the deposit. At the silo's bottom was a deposit 0.01 m thick of water-laid reddish silt, covered by 0.01 m of black material, probably decomposed grain. A painted LB II pitcher (Obj. B68 #15) stood on the silt layer. Over these lowest layers was 0.30 m of colored striations. The rest of the filling was loose brown earth with large chunks of brick, in which were an LB

II lamp and 21 other indicator sherds.

In Room G, Stratum XII flooring sloped southward due to subsidence of the Stratum XIII debris into the cavities in the Sub-Floor Chamber below. It was best attested by 3733-3736 at elevation 19.12 in the center of the room sloping to 18.74 at the south limit, presumed to be continuous with 3729 at the east edge of the room (Ill. 161 = XIII AA:base of #36). A cache of pottery designated 3732 was embedded in 3729, and a second beaten earth surface 3731 ran beneath it, with a separation of 0.20 m. Surface 3735, the top of the Stratum XIII destruction debris, lay 0.15 m below 3731. All these scraps are to be taken together in defining Stratum XII, but the safest deposits are those with 3733 and 3736, and the cache. The cache yielded 31 indicator sherds; 3733/3736 yielded 68.

In the southeast corner of Room G, a thin wall seems to have defined a niche for a store jar to stand in. It is locus 3730, but the store jar fragment in it was not distinctive and was not registered.

In Room H, beaten earth Floor 3333 belonged with a Surface 3310 found in 1966 in a probe trench next to Wall 3309, and with a detached fragment of flooring designated 3337 north of Wall 3313 in the proposed doorway. The floor was 0.02 to 0.05 m thick and at average elevation 18.85, sloping from northwest to southeast; an elevation at the south balk was at 18.66 (XIII BB:#44 and AA:#42). Along the south, Floor 3333 topped the ruins of Stratum XIII Walls 3338 and 3311, with a line of stones as possible footing. A grey makeup, 0.20 m thick underlay Floor 3333 to the north and east.

Above Floor 3333 was a thick grey destruction debris layer, locus 3317 in XIII BB:#41 and AA:#39—about 0.20 m thick at the east but as much as 0.50 m thick at the south. In the far southeast corner of Area 2 was a small deposit of loose bricky detritus, but otherwise the debris did not point to violent destruction; the impression is one of abandonment and accumulation of erosion debris. From locus 3317, 88 indicator sherds were saved, which ought to help define Stratum XII styles, although the proposal that this is erosion debris rather than debris of violent destruction mitigates their value. Field readings regularly included MB IIB and C, rarely MB IIA and EB, along with the predominant LB II.

In the northwest of Field XIII, Building A continued in use, but no surfaces for Stratum XII were preserved inside its elbow due to the Iron Age pit (Ill. 163 = XIII CC:##10–12). Yard B continued, with the same walls as in Stratum XIII. Stratum XII surfacing was 3518, continuing into Area 4 as locus 3721; at the west balk, between Walls 3462 and 3457, it was represented by 3492. This surfacing lay on the 0.20 to 0.50 thick destruction debris of Stratum XIII. The surfacing was characterized by repeated leveling and dusting with crushed limestone. It was excavated partly in 1966 and partly in 1968; the earlier work identified evidence of burning and possible roof fall on Floor 3721 in Area 4, but the 1968 campaign recovered a ring of stones probably constituting a firepit at the west edge of Area 4 in the 3721 surface and proposed that the burn was out-throw from the firepit. Surface and makeup 3518 contained a lot of pottery, of which 148 indicator sherds from uncontaminated locations were registered (devoid, for example, of intrusion by Iron I Pit 3509A-3548). MB IIC and B sherds were present, but the great majority of sherds were LB II.

In the southwest complex, Room C is close to the west balk, and seems to have been an unroofed chamber of a building to the west. Its Stratum XII surface, Ill. 164 = XIII FF:#28, was a building up of plaster-like floorings connecting Walls 3457 and 3123; it closely resembled Floor 3518 of Yard B. Its uppermost layer (elevation 19.25) was strewn with sherds—none of which was recognizably Iron I and most of which belonged to LB II on field analysis. Room E was also a confined space next to the balk, and two pits interrupted its floors. The flooring was XIII FF:#27 at elevation 19.06, where patches of light grey ash appeared here and there. Above the surface there accumulated bricky tan-to-grey soil (FF:#25) with *ḥuwwar* chunks that contained much bone, stones, sherds, and ash deposits—suggesting an exterior yard.

The long narrow open yard D was surfaced by locus 3105/3104 and locus 3519/3758, discontinuous pieces of the same floor, extending from the south balk to Wall 3486. Elevations sloped

Fig. 208. East balk of Field IX, Area 3. The Stratum XII surface runs from the foot of the scar just right of center where the maṣṣebah *lay, north to the brick platform with plaster facing on the bricks, and beneath the bricks. Note that the upper courses of Wall 9588 had been removed prior to this photograph.*

from 19.05 to 19.01 to 18.82 to 18.76 from north to south. Section XIII BB displays the sequence of layers at the south of Yard D: 3119 (base of XIII BB:#51) is the Stratum XIII floor, covered by a thin layer of debris below Stratum XII Floor 3105, upon which lies the 0.30 m thick layer of 3105 occupation and makeup for Stratum XI. Dark organic material and light grey ash characterized the floor throughout Area 1. On it was installation 3085/3113, an undressed stone 0.70 by 0.80 m with a flat top, and a row of stones running away from it first south and then east. The installation's function is unknown.

Floor 3519 in Area 3 linked up with 3758 in Area 4 when the balks were removed; stratigraphically equivalent to 3105/3104, it was somewhat different in character, many-layered and marked by crushed limestone, resembling 3517 in Room C and 3518 in Yard B. On 3758, adjacent to Walls 3706 and 3699, a pile of loose destruction debris (locus 3757) contained 23 indicator sherds, analyzed in the field as LB II.

Stratum XII's surfaces showed renewal in layers, suggesting the passage of some time. The nature of the surfacing was poorer than that of Stratum XIII, and the walls less well-built. The picture is one of reoccupation of ruins by people with less means to expend upon building and/or less interest in working at the quality of their structures.

Field IX

The sanctuary founded in Stratum XIV and rebuilt in Stratum XIII was again refurbished for Stratum XII (Ill. 129). Wall 9588 was still its western limit; Surface 9542 of Stratum XII dished up to its top (Ill. 141 = IX AA:separation of #69 from #65), touching the bottom stone of Wall 9559 of Stratum XI, indicating that 9559 was built on the exposed top of 9588 without foundation trench.

At the north end of Wall 9588, in the far northeast corner of the field, stones of Wall 9581 appear to have run to a butt join with 9588 near its top (Ill. 145 = IX EE:right margin; Ill. 143 = IX CC:left margin). Wall 9581 may have been an east-west wall defining the north limit of the room east of Wall 9588, or a stone foundation for what was built against it, a stepped platform of bricks (IX CC); the space to excavate here was too small to decide.

A plastered floor lay on top of the destruction debris 9592 of Stratum XIII (IX CC:#44; fig. 208). It ran virtually level until it reached the brick plat-

Fig. 209. The standing-stone or maṣṣebah *on plastered floor of Stratum XII sanctuary.*

Fig. 210. Obverse face, dressed, of the Stratum XII maṣṣebah, *removed from context.*

Fig. 211. Reverse face of Stratum XII maṣṣebah.

form; the plaster curved to run up the face of the bricks, but the floor of the room is to be thought of as extending beneath the platform, either *to* Wall 9581 if it was a wall, or to the north balk if 9581 was part of the interior furnishings of the room. The platform may have been an altar, but there were no artifacts and no ashes to confirm that assumption. Throughout Strata XIV-XII there was an elevated installation here; the continuity itself suggests an altar. The strongest evidence that the room is a sanctuary, however, was the fallen *maṣṣebah*, locus 9595, found lying on the plaster floor covered by the thick layer of compacted *ḥuwwar* (IX CC:in #43; figs. 209–11).

The monolith measured 1.27 m high, 0.72 m wide and 0.24 m thick. It weighed about 250 kilograms. It had been worked with rough hammer dressing on its ends, sides and back, but had a natural face; probably it had been selected at the quarry from a flat bedding plane. The top of the stone was apparently meant to be shaped to a shallow arc, but if that was the aim, the job was not completed. No socket stone was found in the limited space available to dig. There were only seven indicator sherds from the floor and compact *ḥuwwar* layer 9578, but they were from LB II; there were no Stratum XI Iron I sherds.

It is important to note that early interpretations of the sanctuary dating it to the tenth century were wrong but were perpetuated from preliminary reports by others (Callaway in Bull *et al.* 1965:10–11; Jaroš 1976:42–43, 121–22).

In the west of Field IX, conditions were unclear. A wall, 9855A (Ill. 130), appears to have been a rebuild of Stratum XIII Wall 9864, angling across the northeast of Area 4, but the rebuild petered out and could not be connected to anything in Area 3; Stratum XIII Wall 9598 running north out of the field was probably its turn northward. Layer 9863 = IX AA:#67 and IX EE:#47 ran over XIV-XIII Wall 9866 and under Wall 9852 of Stratum XI, and offers the best prospect for Stratum XII occupation debris, while the line between #67 and #70 on IX AA may mark the flooring.

On IX EE several soil layers (#48) ran east (right) away from Wall 9864, any one of which may represent the XII surfacing. Adjacent to Wall 9588 at its north exposed end, IX EE:#50 is the best candidate for XII surfacing in the alley. None of these layers was identified as a surface at the time of digging, but the separation between IX AA:##67 and 70 is taken as the XII surface. In the southwest corner of Area 4 two soil layers, IX AA:##82 and 81 overlay the flagstones of Stratum XIII, and IX AA:#76 is probably the Stratum XII surface, but conditions in this corner were far from clear. In short, the evidence for Stratum XII west of the sanctuary in Field IX cannot effectively be defined, and it cannot be trusted to give the stratigraphic clarity to be found within the 9588 sanctuary.

Field VII

The contrast between Fields XIII and IX, where poor rebuilding of remnants from Stratum XIII characterized the transition to Stratum XII, and Field VII is noteworthy. Especially in Areas 5, 6, 8 and 9, structures and installations suggested industrial activity rather than homes. The result was as much as 1.00 m of accumulation in many layers. In Area 9, one sequence of blocky structures was built and twice remodeled. It sat among a complex of wall fragments that may have defined yards; surface indications show the yards to have been open to the sky. At the end of the period, the last of the blocky structures collapsed, leaving a pile of brick and mortar debris with no sign of burning.

To the south in Areas 2 and 3 was a building complex that may have been a home. Its western part in Area 2 rested directly on the ruins of Stratum XIII, making its assignment to Stratum XII very likely. The eastern part of the complex was at the bottom of excavation in Area 2, and since it did not quite line up with the western part across the 2/3 balk, it may be incorrectly assigned to Stratum XII. Area 2 lies exposed to this level as of the time of writing and the balk is still in place; interpretation of this structure is tentative.

The Northern Block (Ills. 96, 97, 112, 113, 115). The northern complex provided the most useful data for Stratum XII in Field VII. In Areas 8 and 9, banded layering built up over ash layer 16.105 (Ill. 115 = VII CC:#19), the top of the Stratum XIII destruction debris. First came brown clay

16.104A, then ashy layer 16.104. Above these was 16.100, 0.15 m of brown clay, topped by layer 1694 = 17.167. This layer was characterized by blue-grey, dense, finely-sedimented material 0.05 m thick that had an oily feel to the touch, on 0.03–0.05 m of soft dark brown ashy soil, on 0.02 m of reddish clay. What pottery came from this locus was battered small sherds lying flat in the soft dark brown ingredient. A band of gravelly soil lay over 1694, and that was topped by another system of banded layering, locus 1691, similar in character to 1694. Its layers were also of blue-grey clay-like material on a band of black clay. Layers chipped away like shale, and the feel was again oily. Loci 1691 and 1694 are combined on VII CC:#18, accumulating to as much as 0.70 m in depth. All of this banded layering seems to have been liquid-borne.

In the northwest corner of Area 9 was the first structure to go with this layering, two walls perpendicular to one another but not forming a corner; the west face of north–south Wall 1695 touched the north face of east–west Wall 1679 (fig. 212; Ill. 96). Layer 1694 ran to the bottommost and second courses of Wall 1679; the black-grey ingredient petered out near Wall 1695, and the soft dark brown ingredient touched the bottom of its lowest course at elevation 13.03. Along Wall 1695, the 1694 layering was topped with a thin lime wash. Apparently some process, perhaps agricultural such as olive pressing, gave this layer its definition. Whatever the process was, it was probably going on before the building was built, without foundation trench, on the layering.

In the corner formed by Walls 1679 and 1695, as many as six resurfacings of Floor 1697 built up, each with a thin lime ingredient consolidating its surface. The earliest of these floors was laid when just the two original walls existed. Then Wall 16.101 was built against the west face of Wall 1695, running west 0.70 m to the end post visible on plan; the face of a wall, Wall 1698, was visible in the west balk of the field, beneath the later Terrace Wall outlined on the plan, which would have been the other post of an entrance northward into the interior of the structure. Three more lime-dusted surfaces in the corner were associated with this new alignment of walls. Then Wall 16.102 closed off the passage past the end post, and two more resurfacings were laid.

Fig. 212. Looking north in Field VII Area 9, at the contact of Wall 1679 (east–west) and Wall 1695 (north–south). The meter stick lies on Floor 1694. Pit 1690 is in foreground. Stump of Wall 16.101 extends west from Wall 1695 for 0.70 m; Wall 16.102 continues its line westward.

Returning to the east and south of the structure, in the yard outside, two of the 1691-1694 layerings extending into Area 8 to the east proved distinctive; they are 17.158 and 17.163, at elevations 13.35 and 13.20 respectively. A cluster of flagstones, locus 17.164, formed a small dais near the west balk, also at elevation 13.35. On Floor 17.158, at least twelve rings showed in the surface around the flagstone platform (Ill. 96); a pair lay just to its south, a triangle of three just to the north. These rings, about 0.05 m in diameter, represent post-holes. Fig. 213 shows their packing, left standing as excavation proceeded lower. The holes had a pebble and mud lining around a fibrous core. In Floor 17.163, 0.15 m below 17.158, ten more post-holes were preserved. Perhaps they held up a canopy or tent over a part of the yard. No more

Fig. 213. Packing of post-holes 17.159, which appeared as rings in Floor 17.158 at the elevation of their tops. Packing is of clay and sherds.

Fig. 214. Configuration of the walls in Stratum XII later phase, in Field VII Area 9.

post-holes were found in the surfaces of other layers within the 1691-1694 system.

As a second phase of Stratum XII across the north of Field VII, a new configuration of the blocky structure (fig. 214) was built on top of the earlier complex and the area to the east was defined as a yard. In the blocky structure, Wall 1679 was rebuilt with larger, rough dressed rocks forming a flat top at elevation 14.02 to 13.92. Wall 1672 was added butting the north face of 1679, cornering with 1675 which butted Wall 1675A hidden in the east balk of the area and revealed in a rainstorm in the winter following the completion of excavation (Ill. 97). Continuing the line of Wall 1679 eastward was Wall 1670; its relationship to 1679 is not clear, since it was not bonded to it and its top was lower—perhaps it was the threshold for an entrance into the cramped chamber to its north, the east doorpost being the stub right at the east balk.

Along the north of this complex between Wall 1675 and the north edge of the field (Ill. 112 = VII AA:#27), Floor 1699 was a succession of limewashed, thinly separated surfaces at approximate elevation 13.50. Wall 1695, out of use, protruded through the floor. Floor 1699 reached Wall 1675A in the east balk and Wall 1675 (Ill. 115 = VII CC:#15). South of Wall 1675, the contemporary floor was locus 1685 at elevation 13.73, touching Wall 1670 (VII CC shows one stone of 1670 above 1685, but 1670 was founded more deeply), running through its doorway and continuing to the south balk of the area. Floor 1685 lay at the top of the 1691-1694 layering and was beaten earth with some spots of ash, quite different from the liquid-laid character of 1691-1694.

In Area 8 to the east, Walls 17.132 and 17.145, made up of segments and rather meandering in direction, defined a yard. Beaten earth surface

Fig. 215. Close-up of north balk, Field VII Area 9. Debris of locus 1688 fell to Floor 1699, which runs to the top of and over Wall 1695.

17.143, like 1699, covered the yard and consisted of a number of resurfacings dusted with lime and often showing pockets of ash. It was at the same elevation as 1699, and VII AA presumes their continuity (##28 and 29), but Wall 1675A, hidden in the balk, separated the two floorings; Floor 1699 touched Wall 1675A near its foot (VII CC:#15).

Embedded in the 17.143 layering was jar stand 17.153 near Wall 17.132 at the east edge of the area, made of a discarded mortar worn through at its bottom, lined with plaster and stone-lined above that; the uppermost resurfacing passed over it.

East of the yard, Wall 17.146 running eastward from 17.145, and a lie of flat stones at elevations 13.58 to 13.69 to its south may attest a house, but conditions here were badly disturbed by Iron Age pits and too little is known to judge. As the plan of the yard shows, the area was repeatedly dug into by pits, so much so that the excavators often were unable to discern the surfaces from which each pit was dug. In some cases the debris of destruction about to be described seemed to spill into the pits, suggesting they were open at the time of the destruction of Stratum XII, but this phenomenon is more likely due to collapse of the pit walls when they were open in Stratum XI; their contents include Iron I pottery, and the fact that Pit 17.147, at the north face of Wall 17.132, actually undercut the wall supports the supposition that the pit was not dug when the wall was in use.

The upper phase of Stratum XII, then, was floored by 1699-1685-17.143. Along the north, Debris Layer 1688, shown in fig. 215, covered 1699. In the center of the photograph lies a dark mudbrick (left of the top division of the scale) with plaster facing on its underside. Above it were two chalk slabs, the one on the upper left showing a layer of brown mud against its lower edge with a thin plaster layer covering that. The debris here was full of pieces of collapsed wall and probably roof. Nowhere in the accumulation were there signs of burning. Similar material, though not as expressive, lay above 17.143 throughout the yard.

Above 1685 was Layer 1684, 0.25–0.30 thick, continuing as 13.128 in Area 6 (VII CC:##14 and at least the upper part of 16); it was loose earth filled with pebbles, bone and many sherds. There were more than 600 registered indicator sherds gathered from 1684-13.128 and 14.170, the corresponding layer in Area 5; predominantly LB II in date, they included, on field analysis, some later pottery. Pits 1687 (VII CC: Pit C) and 1690 (discovered during the excavation of 1684 and thus not isolated) against the south face of Wall 1679, intruded upon 1684, but care was taken to discard baskets of pottery that may have been contami-

Fig. 216. Uppermost phase of Stratum XII. Wall 1679 is now rebuilt by the addition of boulders. The meter stick lies on Floor 1691. Wall 1672 runs north from its junction with Wall 1679. Wall 1675 at back and Wall 1670 at front of small room at east.

nated by their contents. This important group requires restudy.

Above 1684, and thus representing activity after the destruction, was one more phase belonging to Stratum XII—this conclusion based on the fact that it reused the blocky structure. Floor 1673, at elevation 13.97 (14.00 on VII CC:#13 between pits B and C), lay directly on 1684. It went with still another alteration of the walls in the blocky structure: Wall 1670 was covered, but a stub of wall, 1670A, was founded on 1670 butted against the east end of 1679 extending 0.70 m eastward, leaving a gap of 0.85 m between its east end and the balk. For this phase, another course of boulders, hammer dressed to provide a smooth face, was added to the top of Wall 1679; the elevation of the top of 1679 upon which the new course was laid was from 14.02 to 13.92, virtually level with Floor 1673, while the new course raised the preserved height to as high as 14.41; it is this phase of Wall 1679 that is shown on Ill. 97 and fig. 216. Floor 1673 could be traced in patches toward the south of the area and clearly ran over 1670, through the gap next to 1670A, and to Wall 1672 at elevation 13.95. A large pit, 1690, at the south face of 1679, cut off connections of the floor to that wall.

To summarize Stratum XII conditions in the north of Field VII, there were two distinct phases, the lower defined by 1691-1694-17.158-17.163, the upper by 1685-1699, covered by debris of a probably non-violent destruction. On the destruction debris a reuse of one structure in this region was attested by 1673. The nature of the surfacings suggests that this complex was a work area, involving two different agricultural or industrial activities; at least the earlier and probably both involved the use of quantities of water. No microscopic analysis of the deposits has been undertaken.

The protracted description given here is due to the expectation that this locale together with Field XIII will provide the only control for Stratum XII.

The Southern Complex. The fact that material like 1684 was not found over 17.143 in Area 8 is a signal that walls are hidden in the balks between Areas 9 and 8, 6 and 5, and 6 and 9. A portion of this walling appears as Wall 13.109 on Ill. 97 and Ill. 113 = VII BB (in elevation beneath #40). Wall 14.146, not on plan but seen in VII BB, matches 13.109 in elevation. Erosion of the balk junction where 5, 6, 8 and 9 meet revealed the east face of Wall 14.169 footed at elevation 13.75, its top at 14.29; beside and beneath 14.169 there was still another wall. Rock fall from 14.146 extended into Area 5 but yielded no architectural coherence; the region was a mass of rock and wall-lines defying portrayal in a top-plan. All of it lay embedded in Floor 14.144, an accumulation of resurfacings that accorded with the 1685-1699-17.143 system. One of the lowest of these surfacings showed the outline of a tannur at the north balk of Area 5, under the stones of Wall 14.146, meaning that the wall was built during the upper phase of Stratum XII. Floor 14.144 also touched Wall 14.169 in the 5/6 balk. This much clearly belonged with the uppermost phase of Stratum XII.

Fig. 217. Looking east in Field VII Area 2 in the Stratum XII (?) 11.156 complex. Note the post at the north end of Wall 11.139 in upper center. The meter stick lies on Floor 11.156, with pile of bones in lower right.

Another layered flooring, 14.171, appeared beneath 14.144; oily and black, it corresponds to 1691-1694, and extended to the top of the ash line 16.105-14.183-13.140, the top of the Stratum XIII destruction. Difficulty arises across the middle of Area 5, where 14.171 gave out and it proved impossible to work out the layering. A gully probably ran through the field at this point. A layer characterized by patches of yellow *ḥuwwar*, locus 14.148, at elevation 13.24 1.00 m north of the south balk of Area 5, overlay a black layer 14.149 which in turn lay on 14.171.

Locus 14.148 provided the connection to the complex in Area 2 at the south edge of the field, shown on Ill. 97. It resembled closely, notably through the unusual yellow *ḥuwwar*, locus 11.154 at elevation 13.23 in the northeast of Area 2, dotted in on the plan. It is the character of the layer that supports the connection of these two layers, not the elevation; layering sloped gently southward throughout Field VII.

Walls 11.139, 11.153 and 11.155 defined the east part of a structure in Area 2, against the north edge of which locus 11.154 ran. The walls had been built in segments. A vertical post appears in 11.139 just south of 11.153 (fig. 217), and none of the wall junctions were bonded. Surface 11.156, a beaten earth floor with brick fragments embedded, connected the interior faces of these walls, at elevations from 13.10 to 13.16. It was strewn with large bones, especially close to Wall 11.155 at the south. Resurfacings of 11.156 showed circles of white lime on them. These features are assigned to Stratum XII with a degree of uncertainty. Excavation proceeded no lower in Area 2, and surfaces of Stratum XI, which reused the walls, lay close above.

Recognition of the thick layering in loci 1691-1694 through 1685 and 1684, carefully separated in Area 9, permitted the decision to excavate rapidly the corresponding layers in Area 6. The result is loss of precise stratigraphic information about three fragments of wall, Walls 13.131, 13.136 and 13.137 (Ill. 96). Although oriented in somewhat the same directions, the three were not strictly parallel and suggested no architectural coherence. Wall 13.131 reached the east balk of Area 6, and is shown on VII CC resting directly upon the top of the Stratum XIII destruction, suggesting that it belonged to the lower phase of Stratum XII. Surface 13.132, fragmentarily preserved off its northwest end, was at elevation 13.03 and showed a deposit of white chaff in thin layering.

The complex in Area 3 is also assigned to Stratum XII, again with a degree of uncertainty as to phasing. Wall 10.105 is preserved in two portions, with a robbed out gap in the middle. Crossing the wall in the gap is the right-angled combination of Walls 10.112 and 10.114, not bonded to one another. Probably this combination was built later than 10.105, but they went with 10.105 at the point of the lowest flooring reached, 10.111 at elevations sloping from 12.95 at the east balk to 12.83 near 10.112; a tannur was preserved on this floor. Another surface, 10.104, was traced at elevation 13.18 at the east balk. Both 10.111 and 10.104 show on VII CC:#17 for 10.111 and the more ephemeral line above it. Ties from this complex to the segments of wall and flooring in Area 6 were not made. Field pottery readings found Stratum XI pottery in connection with Floors 10.111 and 10.104, calling the phasing into question. Stratigraphically, however, the complex should be Stratum XII. It is noteworthy that while Walls 10.105 and 13.131 were nearly in line with the walls of the 11.139 structure in Area 2, they were not quite perfectly aligned, and the suspicion remains that there are separating walls in the balk. In addition, it is not clear with which of the two phases of Stratum XII these complexes are to be connected (note they appear on both Ills. 96 and 97). The south half of Field VII should not be trusted for accurate data on Stratum XII.

THE HOUSING OF STRATUM XI: THE TRANSITION FROM LATE BRONZE TO IRON I

Stratum XI remains were encountered in all three domestic housing fields at Shechem. In each case, a blanket of fill 0.30 to 0.50 m thick covered Stratum XII remains. Even so, the builders of Stratum XI apparently knew where the old wall lines were. In a few cases, they dug foundation trenches and anchored their new walls on the tops of old ones; in Field XIII there are several instances where a Stratum XI wall lay directly above a Stratum XII wall, but separated from its top by the fill layer. On the other hand, there are in all the fields instances where Stratum XI walls were placed on new lines with no earlier underpinning. Pits dug during Stratum XI, but especially at its conclusion, are so numerous that the tracing of surfaces was very difficult. That the pits were dug through Stratum XI makeup from upper Stratum XI surfacing raises keenly the question of the purpose of the pits. Description here will focus on those locales where Stratum XI stratigraphy is clearest and loci are most coherent.

Field IX

The sanctuary of Late Bronze Age Strata XIV-XII was rebuilt in Stratum XI, as seen best from Ills. 130 and 131, and from the Ill. 143 = IX CC, Ill. 141 = IX AA and Ill. 145 = IX EE sections. Wall 9559 was founded on top of Wall 9588 in such a way that its east face was flush with its predecessor's east face. It was half again as wide, as much as 1.35 m, built with two clear facing lines and a wide rubble core; its west face lay on compacted *ḥuwwar* 9583A. At the lowest level reached by excavation in Area 1 to the south, Wall 9099 was discerned, poorly preserved and only a meter or less wide, which probably served as the south wall of the building. Portrayed on Ill. 130 is what was built first in Stratum XI, but the remains are so poorly preserved that it is not possible to posit two distinct phases of building. Nonetheless, there is something here to suggest a "recovery" phase leading to the main construction of Stratum XI.

From the east face of Wall 9559, two thin walls, 9566 and 9572, not bonded to 9559, ran east to the edge of the excavation, suggesting that a large room was partitioned (compare Ills. 130 and 131). Flooring for the building was 9577, a band of surfacing of beaten earth riding directly on top of the compact *ḥuwwar* layer within the building as seen on the IX CC:the separation between ##43 and 42. Floor 9577 was one exception to the usual circumstance that blanketing fill separated Stratum XI from Stratum XII, unless one takes the compact *ḥuwwar* as a special form of the fill. Section IX AA shows that 9577 (#58) came to the top of the lowest stone of 9559, its top curving to continue as plaster on the face of the wall. The IX CC section shows 9577 continuing southward but not reaching the remnants of Wall 9099; south of the poorly preserved remains of that wall, the layer that continued it (#39) merged with layers of the destruction debris over it and dipped into intrusive Pit 9098 (#38). At the north, Floor 9577 ran over the brick platform and Stone Installation 9581 (the location of 9581 is still shown on Ill. 131) and sloped up to meet Wall 9559 0.60 m up its face.

On Floor 9577 was a deposit of black and red, ashy debris, locus 9573-9095 (IX CC:#37, IX AA:#57), from 0.30 to 0.60 m thick in undulating humps. Although clearly destruction debris, it was almost devoid of pottery and artifacts—13 indicators were registered—suggesting that the building was abandoned and cleaned out in the face of threat.

While the structure defined by Wall 9588 showed clear evidence of having been a sanctuary during Strata XIV-XII, there was nothing to suggest that the 9559 structure continued that tradition. The buried *maṣṣebah* was not dug up and reused, and there was no sign of a continuation of an altar tradition at the north. The two narrow cross-walls might suggest foundation for an interior platform located south along Wall 9559, but nothing between them indicated such use. It is probable that the LB sanctuary had been nullified.

To the west of the 9559 building, a road came from the north along the 9559 building and was met by a road coming from the west which ended at Wall 9559. Neither showed cobbling or metalling; a compact fill, 9859-9583-9367 (IX AA:#60, Ill. 142 = IX BB:##65–67, IX EE:#45) lay over Stratum XII debris, its top probably serving as the road surface. Field analysis found a few Iron I sherds in this fill among predominating LB pottery (125 registered indicator sherds).

The east-west passage across Area 4 ran between the corners of two substantial structures north and south of the proposed road junction. The north building was made up of Wall 9855 and robbed Wall-line 9576A; neither was discerned at their points of entry into the north balk of the field in IX EE. The south building had Wall 9852 cornering with Wall 9867-9355 at its east end; IX BB shows both walls, without foundation trenches, 9855 founded upon earlier walls but 9852 constituting a new line. Connecting them was the Stratum XI road surface on top of 9859 (probably the separation between #60 and #64 on IX BB). A problem with the presumption of a road separating them is the thin Wall 9856 running between the two buildings, perhaps a temporary barrier or simply a step (no elevations were recorded). This thin barrier bonds to neither of the walls it connects, and again there is a suggestion of a Stratum XIA alteration on the earlier Stratum XIB ("recovery") phase. Comparison of Ills. 130 and 131 shows how uncertain this separation of phases is, especially in view of a lack of clear surfaces.

No surface could be discerned within the corner of Walls 9855-9576A; layering on IX EE is presented as running continuously, in the form of the fills over Stratum XII, but the ashy-flecked layer #42 is the likely candidate for occupation debris on a surface designated #43; IX BB:#63 may represent it. The locus is not definitive due to the lack of clear stratigraphic relationship to architecture, but its 82 registered sherds include much Iron I.

Wall 9355 was robbed out as it continued south. The thinner dividing walls within the corner, Wall 9840B, a jog of walls to its south and Walls 9369-9371-9368, partitioned the building into rooms, but disturbance from above during Stratum IX interfered with the surfaces. The partition walls appear to have belonged to the basic structure of the building, rather than being later additions, in spite of the placement on IX AA of a slim portion of the wall 9840 at its far right edge, the presumed continuation of 9840B. On Ill. 144 = IX DD stones from Wall 9355 fell on one of several layers in what the excavators designated locus 9364 (##66 and 68); it was probably one of the floorings for the structure. Pottery was not kept separate by layering within the southern building; it is predominantly Iron I, but there are intrusive Iron II sherds in it, and Area 2 is not trustworthy for defining Stratum XI.

In the south of Area 4, surfacing (IX AA:#64) was discerned directly upon 9863 debris of Stratum XII (IX AA:#68). On it lay ashy, dark grey soil (#63), upon which fell the brick wall and ashes of locus 9865 (#61). On 9865 was the collapse of Wall 9867, and over these ingredients was the ash-flecked grey soil of locus 9861 (#56). This destruction deposit went with 9573-9095 within the 9559 structure to define the end of Stratum XI in Field IX. Twenty-six indicator sherds from loci 9865 and 9861 pertain.

Field VII (Ills. 98 and 115 = VII CC)

During Stratum XI, if the phasing presented here is correct, an unusually large number of changes took place in Field VII. The field report divided the evidence into two local layers, "layers 3 and 4," both characterized by Iron IA pottery and now taken as XIA and XIB. There are indications that an effort was made after Stratum XI was destroyed to remove and bury the destruction debris, resulting in massive intrusions. Because of these intrusions, stratification from Fields I and XIII should be used to control that in Field VII, and pottery studies under way or yet to be done may require alterations in Field VII phasing. The Stratum XI pottery has been studied by Roger Boraas (1999) and is being prepared for full publication by Catherine Duff at the University of Toronto.

Four specific circumstances in Field VII complicate the interpretation. 1). By chance, some of the largest intrusions and pits straddle the control balks, affecting analysis of sections. 2). The most significant intrusion seems to have been an erosion gully running from west to east through Area 5 which interrupts connections from north to south in the field. 3). The nature of the soil, densely-packed and hard bricky detritus in outside yards, caused experienced stratigraphers to create surfaces where there had been no surfaces; on the other hand, white, circular stains where heaps of chaff or lime had rested evidenced surfacing at places where other evidence, such as soil change or flaking at an interface, was lacking. 4). Crucial loci were dug at the very end of the 1964 campaign. Plans and sections were not fully completed and are deficient, especially in showing pits and intrusions.

Stratum XIB builders began by erecting structures directly upon the Stratum XII debris (Ill. 131). Stratum XIA ended with thick deposits of destruction debris indicating a violent conclusion to the period. What the "agent" of this violence was constitutes a significant historical question.

The base of Stratum XIB in Field VII was Surface 13.103, shown on VII CC:#11, sloping from the foot of Wall 16.108 in the balk to the fragmentary remains of Wall 13.105 on top of Stratum XII Wall 13.131. Walls with this surface had no discernible foundation trenches, and seem to have been laid flush with it. Wall 16.108 was preserved only in the balk, extending 1.50 m north-south, made of two courses of small stones with a brick superstructure. Running away from the foot of 16.108 at its north preserved end was Surface 1678, which could be traced with difficulty northward into Area 9, where it reached the very top of Stratum XII Wall 1679, protruding through it from below. Surface 13.103 with 1678 marked the top of the Stratum XII debris and the beginning of Stratum XI; no cushioning blanket of makeup intervened as was the case in Fields IX and XIII.

Linked with the 13.103 surfacing was the complex in Area 6, defined by Walls 13.108, 13.113, 13.115 and 13.116 (Ill. 144). In the space east of Wall 13.113, bounded by 13.108 and 13.115, was a fragment of Flagstone Floor 13.122, at elevation 13.76, subsiding into a cavity beneath. To the east of 13.122, also at elevation 13.76, a patch of surface was identified by the appearance of a white, circular stain, locus 13.126, probably the residue of a pile of lime or chaff. The surface could not be connected to any of the walls. At elevation 14.06, 0.30 m higher, a rectangular patch of plastered flooring, 13.102, ran to within 0.02 m of Wall 13.108 and was almost certainly related to it, but it could not be traced to, or over, the subsided flagstones.

Floor 13.123A at elevation 13.94 at the south preserved end of 13.113 was resurfaced as 13.123 at elevation 14.00. Floor 13.119 at 14.47 connected the west face of 13.113 to the south face of Wall 13.116. There was a large jar base lodged in it. No resurfacing was discerned. North and east of this complex, Floor 13.103 was preserved in patches at 14.23 and 13.75 (Ill. 115 = VII CC:#11), its elevation dropping over a meter in five meters as it sloped southward on the Stratum XII debris heap.

Ill. 99 portrays the random maze of Stratum XIA walling that developed over the 13.108 complex. Wall 1381 ran parallel to 13.108 against its north face; Wall 1378 paralleled 13.113 along its west face. The tops of these two walls were preserved as high as elevation 15.36 and 15.28 at their junction; west on 1381 the elevation is 15.66. Both were found by Stratum X builders and reused. Southeast of their junction were two flat flagstones, locus 1379, at elevations 14.46 and 14.68. South still farther was plaster-lined Bin 1059, the plaster lining extending up the face of a boulder overlapping its rim. The bin may be the bottom of a silo dug from Stratum X, but its contents included only Iron I pottery and the plaster lining ran onto the boulder which has to have been in place when it was installed. An elevation was read on its preserved rim at the southwest edge at 13.79, while its base was at 13.32.

Wall 1071 to its south, reused in Stratum X, seems also to have been in place in Stratum XIA, as was the thin corner of walling at the far south of Area 2, made up of Walls 1079 and 1089, with exterior buttress 1063. A poorly attested patch of surface, locus 1085 at elevation 14.42 ran to the west face of Wall 1079. The high elevation suggests that it sat on a raised platform defined by Wall 1071. It is noteworthy that the south of Area 3 has been somewhat elevated from Stratum XIII onwards.

There has to have been Stratum XIA surfacing for the 1381-1378-1071 rectangular yard, but it was not discerned among the many intrusive pits. The two isolated flagstones and the rim of Bin 1059 suggest its elevation. The best indication of the surfacing was the patch of preserved flagstones shown on VII CC above layer #9 beneath Stratum X Wall 1069, representing the last surface for Stratum XI. On the section just to the north of these flagstones was a bricky deposit (CC:#8) which intruded through the surface and reached to Stratum XIB surface 13.103, just breaking it. The deposit was topped by a Stratum X floor (CC:#6). Extending westward from this bricky deposit but not reaching as low as the trench that cut the Stratum XIA surface at the balk was an accumulation of brick and ash, loci 1375-1376, which was traced with difficulty to Wall 1378. This deposit is tentatively taken to be Stratum XI destruction debris.

In sum, Stratum XIB in Areas 6 and 3 is defined by 13.103 and the 13.108 complex, succeeded in XIA by a rectangular yard with occasional flat flagstones perhaps used as work installations, topped by destruction debris cut into by Stratum X builders.

Getting through the main control balk on which VII CC is drawn to the complex in Areas 5 and 2 is difficult. On Ill. 131 of Stratum XIB, the significant difference in construction between Wall 13.108 and 14.147 is obvious, although the walls were roughly in line. Wall 14.158 to its east was parallel to but not aligned with Wall 14.147. Fragments of surfacing and resurfacing were identified adjacent to both faces of both walls, but connections could not be made to Floor 13.103 in Area 6 or features north of them because of the intervening erosion gully near their north faces. One surface, Flooring 14.167 at elevation 13.46, connected 14.158 to the north end of 11.139, and is the most likely candidate to go with 13.103. Wall 11.139-11.141 was probably founded in Stratum XII (note the doubt expressed in the Stratum XII description above) and rebuilt for Stratum XI. It is on a line that continued as the edge of terracing in Field VII through the Iron II period as late as Stratum VI. As in Stratum XII, it was of composite construction, rebuilt, reinforced and realigned throughout its existence. In Stratum XIB, Wall 11.153 of Stratum XII, also of composite structure, appears to have been rebuilt; with 11.139, it may have defined the northeast corner of the open yard that filled Area 3 and the west of Area 2. A curving line of stones 11.152 along the north face of 11.153 may have been continuous with Wall 13.115 of the Area 6 complex.

Surfacing of the yard near Wall 11.139 began with 11.149 at elevation 13.38, and continued through at least three resurfacings, 11.146 at approximate elevation 13.65, 11.143-11.140 at 13.73 (passing over the top of Wall 11.153, and sloping down to the west, unusual in the topography of this field) and 11.136 at 13.90. Floor 14.167 probably went with 11.149. All are assigned to Stratum XIB.

Ill. 97 shows the features on 11.140, the middle of the three surfaces. Locus 11.142 was a shallow, oval saucer 1.00 m on its east-west axis, 0.70 m on its north-south axis, lined with white residue; an elevation of 13.82 was measured on its center. It was not one of the horizontal stains of a lime or chaff heap like others noted, although the residue was the same, nor was it the bottom of a deep pit; such saucers are another of the features of Stratum XI. Adjacent on the north was stone-lined Bin 11.144; south of the saucer was a horse-

Fig. 218. Stratum XI white-lined Saucer 10.106 in Field VII Area 2.

shoe shaped ring of stones and the mud-lined emplacement for a store-jar, its base preserved, locus 11.131. On 11.140 were many chunks of yellow mudbrick, not fired, and a fall of rock at the south end of Wall 11.139 at the edge of the field.

Although there were no architectural remains from Stratum XIB in Area 3 to the west, traces of three floorings were found near the 2/3 balk and are shown on Ill. 115 = VII CC (in the featureless #7) between a stone at the south margin and a wall fragment approximately 2.00 meters north, which has not been fitted into Stratum XI phasing. The three floorings correspond in elevation with the three in area 2: 1092, another shallow saucer with white lining at elevation 13.74 in the center and 13.82 on the rim; 1093 at elevation approximately 13.70; and 1094 at 13.60. Farther west was another saucer, 10.106, shown in fig. 218 with Stra-

Fig. 219. Looking northwest in Field VII Area 2 at destruction debris, Stratum XI.

Fig. 220. Looking west in Field VII Area 2, showing 11.108 burn on 11.111 stone platform. Surface 1196 is preserved in upper right.

tum XII Wall 10.105 slightly lower in the background.

As with the complex in Areas 3 and 6, there were XIA developments on the 11.139 complex. A new wall, 11.126 was built on the west (mostly hidden in the balk), and the yard extended on the north up to Wall 14.137, which was approximately but not exactly in line with Wall 1381 of the XIA phase in Area 6. The XIA surface was a flagstone floor preserved in spots, laid upon a layer that became beaten down by the pressure of the stones, locus 11.129-11.127-11.123. Either the flagstones were continuous over this beaten earth layer or it was a beaten earth floor filling interstices between segments of flagging. Complicating the interpretation was Pit 11.103 of Stratum X, filling most of the space between Walls 11.126 and 11.139 north of the line of XIB Wall 11.153.

One preserved portion of the flagging was 11.128 along the south face of Wall 14.137, continuing through the balk to join the portion beneath Wall 1069 on VII CC. Elevations on it ranged from 14.48 to 14.26, representing unevenness but not slope. Another portion was 11.111 between Walls 11.139 and 11.126 in the south; elevations on it indicate slope from 14.30 at the north to 14.09 at the south. Between these two preserved segments was Pit 11.103.

Fig. 219 shows the jumble of destruction debris 1194 and ash 11.108 resting on top of 11.111, including one completely preserved mudbrick, 0.35 by 0.55 by 0.20 m, burned to hardness and resting at an angle in the jumble (to the left of the meter stick). Twenty-one registered sherds attest Iron I, with possible Stratum X, perhaps intrusive from adjacent Pit 11.103. Figs. 220 and 221 show the depth and intensity of the fire, which calcined stones in Wall 11.126 and accumulated to a thickness of 0.70 m.

Another extensive debris deposit was locus 14.138 3.00 m north of the north end of Wall 11.139-11.141 where no coherent architecture was preserved. It rested on Surface 14.135 of the open mound at elevation 14.02, perhaps fallen from buildings to the east outside the area of excavation. Bricks in this heap measured at least 0.53 by 0.28 by 0.115 m, the thickness being standard. A crush of pottery was among the bricks (one jar is shown in fig. 222); ten registered vessels are all from Iron I.

Two detached further deposits of destruction debris appeared among the various later disturbances in the region between the 14.138 and 1194 debris heaps, loci 14.129 and 11.134. The latter yielded five baskets of restorable pottery, which was field analyzed as belonging to Stratum X, sug-

Fig. 221. Looking west in Field VII Area 2 after cleaning of Platform 11.111. Note calcined rock and burn in balk over Wall 11.126.

gesting that some of this material may have come from later intrusions; the entire pottery collection is being restudied.

Corresponding to all this activity in the south during Stratum XIB and XIA was the remarkable accumulation in the northern part of the field. Except for wall fragment 16.108 (hidden in the balk and not drawn on Ill. 98, but see Ill. 115 = VII CC) there was no architecture throughout Areas 9 and 8 and the north half of Area 5. Over the Stratum XII debris was a series of banded layering indicating some sort of industrial activity carried out to the north and west, similar to the features of Stratum XII, but distinctive.

The banded layering was thickest at the north balk in Ill. 112 = VII AA:#24. Seven sequences were separated in Area 9 (loci 1660, 1663, 1665-1669), five in Area 8, and a similar series in the northeast corner of Area 6 (Ill. 113 = VII BB:#35 east of Pit 1392 = #30), extending as locus 14.132 in the north of Area 5. Each had a very hard buff-pink layer of clay-like sediment, 0.02 to 0.03 m thick and so dense as to yield a glossy sheen when exposed and scraped. On each buff-pink layer was a deposit of brown-black, rather oily but soft material which in some places was as much as 0.05 m thick but elsewhere thinned out completely. Interleaved were layers of sand or gravel. As with the layering in Stratum XII, the impression is one of liquid-borne material, the layers merging as they sloped south into the erosion gully cross Area 5. A round firepit 17.138 in the northeast corner of Area 8 went with the lowest layer; a horizontal lie of stones, locus 14.141A at elevations 14.33 and 14.39, at the north edge of Area 5 went with layers low in the series.

There was a substantial amount of pottery in the banded layering, in the form of worn and small sherds representing Chalcolithic, MB, LB and Iron I. The gravel and pebble layer at the bottom of the series, over Surface 1678 in Area 9, contained 2 granite spindle whorls and a granite tripod bowl, while one of the intermediate bands produced a red clay figurine.

Section VII BB = Ill. 113 provides the best evidence for relating the banded accumulation to the structures to the south. The banded layers were 14.132 (#39) covering Stratum XII Wall 14.146 and beginning from Stratum XII Floor 14.144 (#44). As noted earlier, the segment of flagstones 14.141A was a feature of one of the intermediate bands. Topping 14.132 was Stratum XIA Floor 14.124 at elevation sloping from 15.04 to 14.69 (#34). On 14.124 just to the south of the balk, and interrupting it at places suggesting that the last of the bands may have been laid just after the destruction, was the 14.138 destruction debris. The logical, but not stratigraphically proven, conclu-

Fig. 222. Looking north in Field VII Area 5 at Brickfall 14.129 on Surface 14.134, with shattered jar in foreground, all evidence of Stratum XIA destruction.

sion is that the accumulation of banded layering was coterminous with all the Stratum XI developments in the south, with the possible exception of the uppermost band.

North of this "golden spike" of connection, the mound must have been open. The topmost layer of the banded build-up in Area 8 was locus 17.108/17.113/17.114, heavily pocked with pits. The one installation in Area 8, put in place with the topmost layer, was vat 1770 on Ill. 99, to which the surface attached (##47 and 48 on Ill. 116 = VII DD). Stratum X builders found the mound at this elevation, reused and developed the vat installation, and laid their structures on and into the Stratum XI destruction debris. It is to be noted that the XI destruction debris was attested only in isolated though dramatic deposits. Makeup for Stratum X must have spread it throughout, mixed with other soil. It is also noteworthy that it filled so many of the intrusive pits, an issue to be taken up after reviewing the data from Fields XIII and I.

Field XIII

In 1934, Hans Steckeweh, working with Sellin in one final campaign of the Austro-German team, opened an extensive excavation plot from near the Northwest Gate eastward (Sellin and Steckeweh 1941). He dug by artificially horizontal levels, and stopped on a plane such that MB IIC structures were exposed at the northwest, Late Bronze remains farther southeast, Iron Age remains still more to the southeast, and Hellenistic remains at the southeastern edge. The Joint Expedition placed Field XIII where his Iron Age remains lay exposed with the intent of clarifying Shechem's Iron I and LB stratigraphy. Parts of a Stratum X building were at the surface in the south and east of the Field XIII, Stratum XI remains to the north and west. Balâṭah residents reported that they had taken stones and carbon-rich soil from the German exposure between the two expeditions.

Field XIII also proved to be riddled with ancient pits, some with their mouths at the preserved Stratum XI floor levels. In the vast majority of cases, the latest pottery in the filling of these pits belonged to Iron IA. The sections and top-plans of Field XIII locate 31 pits, discounting the modern surface robber pits; of the 31, probably six are from Iron II or later. Since the typical form of an Iron I pit is in the shape of a flask, some encroach upon the field from the side with their necks and mouth lying outside the excavated area; surface disturbance had removed the mouth and neck of others. Iron I pits tended not to remove earlier walls; if the pit diggers came down upon a wall they shifted to one side, leaving the wall and cleaning along it.

The effect of so much pitting in Field XIII was much the same as in Field VII, with walls and fragments of isolated flooring preserved as islands of undisturbed, stratified soil in a sea of disturbance.

Everywhere Stratum XI surfaces and makeup were preserved, they rode upon a cushioning fill of grey bricky soil (Ill. 162 = XIII BB:#41, 0.70 m thick; Ill. 161 = XIII AA:#39, 0.50 m thick, and #38, 0.35 m thick; Ill. 163 = XIII CC:##26 and

Fig. 223. Crush of Stratum XIA pottery on Floor 3261, Field XIII Room C.

28). Pottery from the cushioning layer was analyzed as LB IIB with a few Iron I sherds in some of its pottery pails. Over the cushion were thin layers of makeup beneath the Stratum XIB floors; XIII BB shows these layers in #40 beneath Wall 3251 and Floor 3302 and in #37 west of the wall. Wall 3251 was set in a foundation trench dug into this makeup, which again was heavy with LB IIB sherds with rare Iron I.

Illustrations 159 and 158 depict the remains of Stratum XI in Field XIII. Five pits introduced disruption and make it hard to depict coherent architecture. Toombs traced remnants of a north-south Wall 3251-3282-3679 more-or-less parallel to the Strata XIV-XII terrace wall that divided the field in half, but located well to its east. Its north end encountered a rebuild on Wall 3667 of Strata XIV-XII that ran east, stopping at a probable doorway before reaching the edge of the field. The sections display Stratum XI more effectively.

Section XIII AA = Ill. 161 on the east balk of the field gives a good depiction of Stratum XI, both in its B and A phases in the interior of Room C. On the smooth grey cushioning layer in the center of the section was Makeup 3729, ##36 on 38, topped by Stratum XIB Floor 3724 = #34; this floor was plastered on a bedding of pebbles. It ran over the mudbrick superstructure of Stratum XII Wall 3320 and continued as Floor 3327, resurfaced as 3325 from 0.02 to 0.05 above it.

South of Pit 3324 = XIII AA:#7A, the flooring continued as 3302=3318, #35, thence on Ill. 162 = XIII BB:#31 reaching Wall 3251. On it as it reached 3251 was an oven. Continuing west from Wall 3251 was Floor 3294 of Stratum XIB (BB:#32), extending to Pit 3112 (#24), a deep intrusion cut down along LB Wall 3309.

Stratum XIA in the region of Room C involved the placement of Buttress 3681 against the east face of Wall 3679, now topped with a rebuild. Wall 3633 was built parallel to and just south of the top of 3667 to form the new north limit (XIII AA shows its scar, its footing at approximate elevation 20.00 and its top poking above the surface from which Joint Expedition excavation began, where it had been robbed in modern times). Surface 3684 reached Wall 3633 from the north. Within Room C a sequence of layering developed, topped by Floor 3261=3655, shown on XIII AA:#10 interrupted by Pit 3728 = #3 south of Wall 3633, and on Ill. 158 at elevation 20.28. On it lay a crush of pottery and roof fall (fig. 223).

Surfaces 3666 at the north of XIII AA:#15 and 3271 to the south between two pits continued XIA in Area 2 (#16, probably continuing as ##17 and 19). At the junction of XIII BB and AA (##13 & 14 on AA), were segments of plastering and roof fall above Floor 3289 (#19), more evidence of destruction of Stratum XIA.

Among the pits honey-combing the rest of Field XIII, segments of surfacing and walls were preserved, from which fragmentary data for both phases of Stratum XI can be coaxed. No narrative field report for the 1966 campaign was written, but full locus lists and sketch plans were kept, and the sections have been combined with those of 1968 and 1969. Stratum XI architecture and surfacing from Field XIII was not definitive. What is clear, displayed on sections AA, BB, CC, and FF (Ills. 161–164) of Field XIII, is that Stratum XIA was topped by black deposits of varying thicknesses, interspersed with layers of soil, suggesting continual erosion and frequent burning. On XIII BB, it is plain that Pits 3228 (#7) and 3112 (#24) were dug during the process of this accumulation; their contents evidences Iron I pottery, belonging to the 12th century BCE. Almost certainly, many of the other pits in the field were dug from the same time, judging from their contents rather than on unimpeachable stratigraphic evidence such as afforded by finding their mouths sealed by surfacing or layering of Stratum XI.

Pits in Fields V and I

Pits of the sort just described occurred interrupting the stratigraphy of the temple complex and cutting through features of Stratum XIV-XI recovered just inside the East Gate complex in Field I Areas 16 and 17. The sections in figs. 3 and 142 show five such pits: 5093 and 5096 under Granary Wall 5906; and 5094, 5094A and 5087 under Granary Wall 5905. In all, seven pits and probably an eighth, all containing earth with a mix of pottery from Chalcolithic, throughout MB II and LB, ending with sherds belonging to Stratum XI, were attested in the small amount of stratified earth left by the Sellin expedition inside the temple structure. At least two more such pits, and perhaps a third encroach on the Strata XIV-XI stratigraphy in Areas 16 and 17 of Field I.

INTERPRETATION OF THE LB/IRON I STRATIGRAPHY AND THE PITS.

Understanding the LB/Iron I stratigraphy in historical terms, both political and social historical, is not easy. Toombs (1976:73–74) has proposed that the Stratum XIV recovery at Shechem, beginning with its establishment of "services" to get construction under way, took place at a time after Tuthmosis III, the Egyptian pharaoh of the heart of the fifteenth century (1490–1436), had conducted his first major Asiatic campaign in about the year 1468 BCE. This campaign consolidated an Egyptian Peace and permitted some sense of security to return to Palestine. It is not implausible to assume that he encouraged the redevelopment of city life in Palestine, and that Shechem along with other hill country towns began their new lives in these encouraging times.

With no specific occasion to point to, it is proposed to date the end of Stratum XIV around 1400 BCE, the transition between LB IB and LB IIA. This is the time when Palestine moved into the Amarna age, illuminated by the Amarna letters coming from the reigns of Amenophis III and Akhenaten, when Lab'ayu was chief of the city-state that centered on Shechem.

Toombs also reflected on the end of Stratum XIII (1979:74–76). Shechem's archaeological data attests a destruction in the fourteenth century. There is no literary evidence for such a destruction, except that the Amarna letters give many indications of conflict among fourteenth century city-state rulers in Canaan, and Lab'ayu was in the thick of the conflict (Campbell 1976). In a vertical cut at Tell Miskeh in the Wadi Far'ah, located at a key defense point for the upland, isolated city-state of Shechem, the Joint Expedition's survey team observed a layer of destruction debris containing monochrome red-painted pottery quite comparable to the Stratum XIII pottery in Field XIII destruction debris (Campbell 1991:85). Tell Miskeh, as part of the Shechem city-state, may have met a fate similar to that of Shechem.

Toombs suggested that the slim evidence of Late Bronze fortifications found in 1957 and 1964 in Field III fits this overall picture—a wall built after Stratum XIII destruction in a feeble attempt at defense in Late Bronze IIB. It is plausible to connect to this same destruction the change from the earlier to the later phase in the broad-room sanctuary in Field V. Fields I, VII, IX and XIII have presented evidence that Stratum XI began at the end of Late Bronze, developed across the transition into Iron I, and suffered widespread conflagration at its conclusion. The pottery shows development within this period, but it is *development*, not major change. The pottery from the destruction that terminated Stratum XI dates to the twelfth century BCE. These pottery forms are closely related to those from the first phase of Stratum XI and show continuity with the late LB pottery from Stratum XII. By way of contrast, the pottery from Stratum X is quite different, representing the beginning of the Iron II period. Stratum XI began in the thirteenth century and ended before 1100 BCE.

This description of Stratum XI has pointed to several features that need explaining. The *blanket of fill* over Stratum XII is one such feature. *Frequent resurfacing* is another. A third relates to the black *burn deposits*. The ones on the uppermost floors represent the destruction of the site at the end of Stratum XI. The layers of black and buff-pink in Field VII also seem to point to burning, and a possible explanation for them is the burning over of yards where chaff had accumulated. This explanation was posited on the basis of the Gezer deposits from the "acropolis," the elevated area of Field VI at Gezer which got the western wind and had a granary of the early twelfth century on it, with an open threshing-floor or food-processing area upwind from it. Reuben Bullard analyzed the Gezer black layers and found them packed with wheat and barley, along with olive pits, grape seeds, and evidence of chick-peas (see Dever, *et al.* 1986: 73–76, esp. 73, n. 120). Very similar layering of contemporary date is visible in the balks from Dothan, Shechem's central hill country neighbor 16 miles to the north, and has now been found at Aphek and Tell esh-Shariʿah (Ziklag?) in the lowlands.

The Shechem evidence is not confined, however, to one location on the site. Bands of black appear in the sides of the Austro-German cut that revealed the East Gate, inside town from the Late Bronze/Iron IA gate tower. And in Field XIII there were interrupted segments of similar black layers within the accumulation of Stratum XI soil. Sometimes these layers were thin and extensive, especially in the open area of the southwest quadrant. Sometimes, however, the black lay in thicker more confined deposits on surfaces. There seems to have been a variety of conflagrations, sometimes of the grasses in an open area, sometimes of a thicker mass of organic material. These deposits have not been chemically or microscopically analyzed, but Shechem Stratum XI seems to attest smoldering burning of various kinds of organic debris.

A fourth feature is the *circular or oval stains of white powder*, of which at least seven were found in Field VII and several more in Field XIII. Four of the Field VII examples were on surfaces, the other three set down into surfaces in very shallow depressions. While the powdery matter may be decomposed chaff or grain, one test with hydrochloric acid produced the fizzing response expected from calcium carbonate. Tentatively, they are taken to represent deposits of lime or powdered limestone. Lime is produced by burning limestone (calcium carbonate) to drive out the carbon dioxide, producing calcium oxide ("quicklime"). Adding water to quicklime produces slaked lime or calcium hydroxide. Over time, slaked lime will absorb carbon dioxide from the air and become again calcium carbonate. In archaeological deposits, quicklime will not have lasted and cannot be isolated.

There can be no question that people burned limestone to make lime in Canaan and Israel. Whether or not the Field VII and Field XIII firepits were designed as lime kilns, they produced lime by the calcining of their linings. Textual evidence from the eighth century onwards points to processes for burning that produced lime, most notably to make plaster. In Amos 2:1, Moab is to be punished for burning the bones of Edom's king to lime (Hebrew *sîd*). Isaiah 33:12, part of a late composition in the Isaiah corpus, speaks metaphorically of peoples becoming "burnings (to) lime" ("as if burned to lime," NRSV) in parallelism with a reference to burning thorny plants. Lime, *sîd*, is used for plaster according to Deuteronomy 27:2, 4. The Aramaic of Daniel 5:5 uses the term *gîr* for whitewash or plaster on the palace wall, and the same word is used in the post-exilic passage Isaiah 27:9, where altar stones are crushed the way "chalkstones" (NRSV) are—here not by fire but by pressure.

The fifth feature is the *immense number of deep pits*. There are eleven pits in one area of Field XIII that measures 5 by 6 m. Seven, perhaps eight, were cut into the interior of the Field V temple ruin. Field VII shows many more. Nor is Shechem the only site that shows a great number of pits in twelfth century BCE contexts. Paul Lapp found 17 pits in a relatively small precinct at Taanach from this period. Hazor had a great number in its contemporary stratum. On the Gezer acropolis, beneath the burned threshing floors mentioned earlier, there is a remarkable and perplexing phenomenon of wide trenching all over the acropolis area, along with a few pits. Izbet Sarta is covered with pits (usually stone-lined silos; Finkelstein 1988:264–69).

The standard and most compelling explanation for these pits is that they were used to store grain. Finkelstein has proposed that they are a feature of the new agricultural "technology" used by the Israelites, whose population was burgeoning in the hill country during this period. They had developed the new idea of terracing the hillsides to increase the area on which to grow grain, augmenting what could be grown in the small agricultural plains among the hills. To offset the effects of bad agricultural years they cut grain storage pits into the bedrock or dug pits with stone-lined sides and bottoms to store their grain supply. John Currid (1988:170–73) has shown that underground storage pits do not have to be rock-cut or stone-lined. One can produce a good underground facility by digging a small-mouthed pit in the soil, building a fire within it, covering the mouth, and thereby "seal" its walls while fumigating it.

Grain storage may explain Shechem's pits. But there are so many of them and together they would have a capacity seemingly beyond the needs of the population. Furthermore, they are packed to the brim with densely packed Iron I debris, as though deliberately filled up.

The five peculiar features of Stratum XI Shechem—the blanket of fill, many resurfacings, burn deposits and layering, lime deposits, and filled-up pits—may point in a different direction. Studies of the circumstances that allowed Israel to occupy and develop the hill country have pointed to the possibility that epidemic disease was a significant factor throughout the region during the 14th to 12th centuries (Mendenhall 1973: 105–21; Meyers 1978: 95–98 and *passim*; Stieglitz 1987). There are many hints of it in literary sources. The "Plague Prayer" of the Hittite emperor Mursilis concerns disease in the Hittite army. The Amarna letters contain a number of references to disease. The story in Numbers 25:1–18 (cf. 31:16) in which Israel yoked itself to the Baʿal of Peor speaks in verses 8 and 9 of a plague that killed many Israelites in Transjordan. The aftermath of the Korah rebellion recounted in Numbers 16, the death of the spies in Numbers 14:37, the Taberah ("burning") notice in Numbers 21:6, all specify or reflect conditions of epidemic disease. There is the curiosity that Abimelek, in Judges 9:45, not only destroys Shechem but also sows the city with salt, usually seen as rendering the area agriculturally useless.

Text and archaeology may converse on this question. Open areas throughout town seem frequently to have been burned. Burning where grass and brush grows, where refuse is thrown, where chaff or hay or straw heaps collect, would remove garbage and destroy insect and rodent habitats. That rodents at least were recognized as bearers of epidemic agents is a theme of the Ark Narrative (I Sam. 6:1–12). Burning open ground may well have been a disease-control measure. Burning in courtyards or inside houses, especially the smoldering burn that leaves black pockets rather than ash, may point to destroying contaminated clothing or food (cf. Numbers 31:21–24, Lev. 14:34–45).

The outbreak of disease may be what brought Stratum XII to an end and dictated some of the actions taken by Stratum XI inhabitants. It would explain why the thick blanket of fill was placed over the Stratum XII ruins. Repeated resurfacing of the floors would then be further measures to combat disease.

As for the remaining two features, understanding them requires even more venturesome proposals. Did Shechem's inhabitants know the properties of quicklime as agent of decay, of stench-control, of cleansing? They did burn limestone to powder, producing quicklime. They slaked it to make lime plaster, for whitewashing, and perhaps for both metallurgy and treatment of leather. Was lime used at Shechem as part of a regimen to combat disease?

As for the pits, it is conceivable that people in Iron IA would consider burying surface soil, in pits shaped like flasks, with confined mouths then plugged with stones or clay—dug on the analogy of their standard grain pits. If epidemic is a problem, it would have been easier not to transport material outside town. The soil dug up to produce the pits could become the fill and makeup for new surfaces.

These speculations attempt to explain the transition from Stratum XII to Stratum XI throughout the site. Whatever the explanation, the transition is quite marked, not only at Shechem but also at other hill country sites.

CHAPTER 5

THE IRON AGE

AFTER THE DESTRUCTION OF Stratum XIA, the Shechem site was without settlement for over a century; when renewed settlement came, soil layers contained a new range of pottery dated early within Iron II, with a distinctive red-slipped surface treatment on forms that continue in use into Stratum IX to follow.

STRATUM X

Six locations on Tell Balâṭah attest Stratum X: Field VII, with two phases of yards and structures; Field IX, a single phase with stone structures poorly attested, ending in destruction; Field II, scraps of a domicile; Field VIII, one corner of a possible domicile; Field I, inside the LB/Iron I gate tower, a probable domicile, although the stratigraphy is doubtful; Field XIII, where intrusions and modern stone-robbing between 1934 and 1966 so disturbed things that Stratum XI stratification is the highest trustworthy layer; scraps of what are probably Stratum X walls, without preserved surfaces, add nothing meaningful about Stratum X to what is attested in the other five locations.

All six sites are inside fortification lines. Contrary to the impression left by the preliminary report of the 1964 campaign (Bull, *et al.* 1965:37), the East Gate probes did not provide evidence of Stratum X fortification. The first evidence of refortification belonged to the start of Stratum IX, the date for which probably falls after any invasion of Shishak that may have hit Shechem (ca. 918 BCE). Probably, refortification by Jeroboam I should be connected to Stratum IX. G. Ernest Wright's proposal (1967a; cf. Abel 1938:81, 460) that Shechem was the administrative center for the first Solomonic district of 1 Kings 4 is called into question by the Stratum X evidence (Boling and Campbell 1986:264–70).

Stratum XB in Field VII (Ills. 100, 101, 112 = VII AA, 113 = VII BB 114 = VII CC 115 = VII DD)

The profusion of changes within Stratum X in Field VII contrasts with what is found elsewhere on the site. Stratum "XB" was a phase of walling and surfacing set into and on Stratum XI ruins, to be succeeded by a phase that alters enough features to constitute "XA."

Stratum XB architecture reused some XIA walls (1381 and 1378) and anchored new construction on others (14.117 on 14.137 and 1197 on 11.139/11.141). Vat 1770 of XI was reused by Stratum X settlers, who built on its rim to raise it to the current ground level. Walls 17.100, 1757B, 14.128 and 1197 were set down into the debris of Stratum XI destruction. Early Iron II pottery, assigned to the late tenth or early ninth centuries and defining Stratum X throughout Shechem, was in and above the earliest surfacings going with the architectural layout of XB, and in a few cases sealed between resurfacings within the phase.

The Northern Complex. Ill. 100 shows the fragmentary architectural remains. Wall 17.100 at the north edge was off-line from the somewhat rough rectangles of the two complexes to its south. The reused corner made by Wall 1381 and 1378 did not line up completely with the rectangular complexes to the east, but may have with the fragment of Wall 1071. The arrangement of walls did not suggest typical housing.

Gross disturbance interrupted the soil layering throughout Area 9 (see Ill. 115 = VII CC, pits

B and C as instances), while a cluster of huge pits from later periods severed connections from south to north in and near the balk separating Areas 5 and 8 (Ill. 114 = VII BB:##30, 37 and 32). Pit 11.103 dug later within Stratum X interrupted the east end of Wall(?) 11.116 and surface connections in the southern rectangular complex. What follows highlights the few loci that defined the first phase of recovery after the Stratum XI destruction.

Wall 14.117 was the best preserved wall of the complex, founded on the remnants of XI Wall 14.137, and later serving as the foundation for Wall 1448 of Stratum IX. Elevations on its preserved top were at 15.62 and 15.44. Its west end appears in VII CC, and its 0.95 m width shows under 1448 in Ill. 116 = VII DD. Its east end abutted Wall 14.128, a meter-wide wall poorly preserved but of good construction; this wall will have been put out of use before Stratum X ended. Wall 14.128 probably was continuous from the north segment near the north limit of Area 5 through the break shown on the plan (robbing, not a doorway) to the point at its south end where Stratum IX Wall 1152 broke into it from above. The fragment of Wall 1757B to the north may have joined 14.128, outside the limits of excavation to the northeast; alternatively, 14.128 may have run on to meet 17.100. Wall 1757B and Wall 17.100 continued in use throughout Stratum X, the latter rebuilt as 1768, and both served as foundations of Stratum IX walls. The north complex, then, was 14.117, 14.128, 1757B or 17.100; its west limit was undefined.

Because of the intrusion of Stratum IX Wall 1152 near where Wall 14.128 continued south from its junction with 14.117, it is not certain that 14.128 continued as Wall 1197, which was of different construction and off line. Both 14.128 and 1197 showed foundation trenches, discerned on the west face of 1197 and the east face of 14.128, which cut into the Stratum XI brick debris below. At the south end of 1197, just at the limit of excavation, two complexes of stone may have marked the turn of the wall to the west, 11.120 and 11.117. Neither could be effectively investigated, though the surfaces to be described below (notably 11.118) probably ran beneath them, suggesting they were XA constructions.

Thin walls 1068 and 1069, differing from one another in width and style of construction, may have completed the south rectangle (the balk between Areas 5 and 6 was not removed). Wall 1068 appears in VII CC within the featureless region designated #7; the east face of 1069 enters CC obliquely, just south of the end of Wall 14.117, resting upon Flagstone Surface 11.128 of Stratum XIA. Between the butt end of 14.117 and the west face of 1069 was a deposit of brick debris (CC:#8) that may have been a pit but appears instead to have been a bank of XI debris against which the presumed corner between the two walls was built.

Accordingly, the walls in the southern rectangle manifested four different styles of construction; only the junction of 1068 and 1069 looked bonded. The extent of the space contained within their limits was roughly 4.00 by 6.50 m and would not easily have been roofed. The short segment of Wall(?) 11.116 protruding from the 2/3 balk, rested on XI Wall 11.126, running north-south below it; the nature and function of 11.116 is obscure.

Soil stratigraphy was clearest in the north, from Wall 14.117 to 17.100, although at least five pits and the large intrusion made to install the vat and platter of the Stratum VIII house disturbed the soil layers here. Against the north face of Wall 14.117, two superimposed segments of surfacing were preserved, the upper, 1495, shown on the plan at elevation 15.00; the lower was 14.116, only 0.05 m beneath. From 1495, Pit 14.133 was cut; its filling contained mostly XI pottery, but with a few pieces analyzed as X. Sealed between 1495 and 14.116, and evidenced also beneath 14.116, was Stratum X pottery. Both almost certainly ran under Wall 14.118 of Stratum XA, but attached to Wall 14.117.

Although elevated 0.35 m higher than 14.116 and 0.30 m higher than 1495, Surface 14.123 (Ill. 113= VII BB #31), running east from late Stratum IX Pit 14.139-17.131 (#37) beneath Wall 14.118 to a flat layer of small stones on top of rock tumble 14.141, represented XB. The tumble 14.141 was apparently the filling of a pit or sump, which interrupted any attachment Surface 14.123 may have had with Wall 14.128; Wall 14.128, if it once continued northward, would have been de-

Fig. 224. Vat 1770, with its rim heightened by rows of stones for use in Stratum XB. Looking west in Field VII Area 8, Wall 17.100 at right, Floor 1794 with meter stick. A small shelf of Floor 1791 is preserved at upper center against the balk.

stroyed east of 14.141 by the gross disturbance BB:#32.

In Area 8, Stratum XB was represented by Surface 1794/1789, traceable among the intrusions of later pits to Walls 17.100 and 1757B, and to the stones (1770A) on the rim of Vat 1770. On VII DD, it is #46 south of the vat, and the interface of ##49 and 50 north of the vat. A small segment of it shows on the top plan at elevation 15.42 and VII DD shows it to have been level from north to south at this point, 0.12 m higher than the elevation on 14.123 and 0.42 m higher than Surface 1495 with Wall 14.117 to the south. The intervening intrusion of pits had destroyed the evidence that might account for the drop in elevation, although slopes to the east and south were frequent in Field VII when there was no effort to level the terrain.

Near Wall 17.100 and adjacent to 1770A, Surface 1794 was plastered (fig. 224). Whatever process was associated with the reuse of Vat 1770 seems to have called for preparation for liquid run-off into the vat. At preserved points throughout the region, Surface 1794 was marked by patches of heavy burn suggesting small fires; one such was built close to Wall 17.100 and left its mark on both the floor and the stones of the wall face, indicating that the wall was not plastered.

An array of surfacing, represented by the lower striations in VII AA:#22, down to the lowest indicated by #23 (loci 17.105 with burn 17.106 on it, 17.107, 17.109, 17.110), characterized the narrow segment of space north of Wall 17.100. Just to the west, Wall 1661A, appearing only at the northern edge of the field and shown on VII AA, was set down into the last of the Stratum XI striations and may have gone with 17.100 to hint at other constructions to the north.

The Southern Complex. All indications point to the northern complex as a work area. Within the southern rectangle, surfaces were less certain. Pit 11.103 dug late in the period of Stratum X destroyed layering and surfaces in the central north of the structure. Around it, extending to the south and discerned in places to the north, soil layers built up around a dome of XI detritus (locus 1194) close to Wall 1197 and off the southeast end of Wall 11.116. Locus 11.112 was a hard-packed soil feature suggesting a surface north of Wall 11.116; 11.118-11.115 designate similar features in the southern sector and up toward Walls 14.117 and 14.128; 11.121 was a hard-pack of earth in the elbow formed by the two walls, shown as a dotted flooring on the plan, at elevation 14.53. The character of this material suggested eroded XI debris,

Fig. 225. Looking north over Field VII Areas 3 and 6. A fragment of Floor 1077 is preserved where Wall 1071 nearest the camera and Wall 1069 at right margin meet, with a jar base and a flat stone (kneading block?) set into it.

brick, plaster and charcoal chunks, in a soil matrix. The pottery in it was of Stratum XI, with an occasional sherd analyzed as X. This mix of soil and possible surfacings was traced to the faces of Walls 14.117, 14.128 and 11.116, while Wall 1197 was cut into it. At certain points, however, 11.118-11.115 was thought to run beneath 14.117. Taken together, the evidence suggests that the combination of layers was a leveling on Stratum XI debris, accumulating prior to and with the start of Stratum X, with the various walls erected upon as well as let down into it.

East of Wall 14.128, similar material, locus 14.131, filled up around the brick of the XI destruction, without discernible surfacing; here the proportion of X pottery was higher.

Six systems of stratified soil and one pit, then, are most definitive of the start of Stratum X, from which were registered several hundred sherds:

Surfaces 1495 with 14.116, with makeups
Surface 14.123 with makeup
Surface 1794/1789 with makeup
Surfaces 11.109/11.112 with 11.118/11.115 with 11.121
Surfaces 17.105, 17.107, 17.109, 17.110
Makeup 14.131
Pit 14.133

Evidence from the western half of Field VII was much less clear. The VII CC section shows how Stratum IX Pit 1097 (Pit E) interrupted surfacing, but in fact the entire region was badly disturbed. The dotted indication of a hint of surfacing running north from Wall 1068 in #7 on the section was not isolated in digging and provides no controls for Stratum XB. At an elevation of 13.74 in the far southeast corner of Area 2, a circle of white stain, locus 1092, may mark the bottom of a silo not otherwise discerned, further interrupting XB surfacing.

Architectural fragments west and north of Wall 1069 were isolated and without identifiable surfacing in XB; it is by no means certain that 1381-1378 were in fact in use. Wall 1071, like 1381-1378 also an instance of a reuse of a Stratum XI wall, was an isolated feature unconnected to the elbow of 1068-1069; it may have continued, to join Wall 1378 extended, as the predecessors of both did in Stratum XI.

Throughout the space between Walls 1378 and 1069 was the deep deposit 1373A-10.101, the upper part of VII CC:#4. It contained much Stratum XI pottery, but with some Stratum X sherds; it underlay features assigned to Stratum XA. When Wall 1361 of Stratum XA was dismantled, a confined patch of surface (1390) was discerned with the circular stain of a pile of lime 0.65 m in diameter on it (locus 1390A) at elevation 14.95, which would be a candidate for XB surfacing.

Makeup 1373A-10.101 also overlay the small segment of Floor 1077 shown on Ill. 100 south of Wall 1071 at elevation 14.73, which *may* belong to XB. Jar base 1067 and the flat slab of stone at elevation 14.45 just north of it were probably set on and into Floor 1077, in the gap between Walls 1071 and 1069 (fig. 225). The reason for including this small complex in Stratum XB is that Surface 1077 was at the same elevation as a surface visible in the south balk of Field VII, not drawn on section, connected to a wall, locus 1078, on top of Stratum XI Wall 1079. The assignment of the 1071-1077-1067-1078 complex to Stratum XB is quite uncertain; it may have been a final feature of Stratum XI.

As difficult as it is to interpret, the data pointing to XB in Field VII is important. It represented preparations for the recovery of settlement after the destruction of the Iron I remains (recalling the preparations for Stratum XIV in Field XIII). The indications are that the recovery involved processing of agricultural products, perhaps the penning of animals, and make-shift housing. Surfaces probably built up rapidly and walls were adjusted frequently. Repeated digging into the ruins below probably sought carbon-rich soil and accessible building stone. Whether Pit 14.133 was a storage silo cannot be determined.

Stratum XA in Field VII

The layout of walls, installations and surfaces for the succeeding phase of Stratum X in Field VII is shown on Ill. 101. As with the plan of XB, this plan was not rendered to show the positions of the many intrusions from later periods; the segments of flooring indicated by dotting and dashing were all that remained among the intrusions. Two superimposed surfaces could be traced throughout the eastern half of the Field. Huge disturbance filled most of Area 9 to the west and the south of Area 3. Between, in Area 6, was a fragmentary structure with one preserved surface. Erosion disturbed the slope throughout Area 2, but two clear systems of surface were discerned, with domestic installations still in place.

Upon Wall 17.100 at the north, which was 0.95 to 1.00 m wide, a thinner wall (0.70 m), 1768, was built, its south face flush with the earlier wall's south face; stones of Wall 1768 had slipped southward off their foundation and one stone preserved at a slant in the jumble had plaster on its face, suggesting that developing Stratum X walls were being constructed with a protected face. Wall 1747B was constructed on the line of Stratum XI Wall 1747, with a cushion of soil separating them. It connected XB Wall 1757B (reused) to Wall 14.117, where 1747B continued as Wall 14.118, two stones wide to a butt junction with 14.117. The cluster of stone against the east face of 1747B-14.118 shown as 14.125 on plan may represent a wall running east. The entire system of XB Wall 14.128-1197 was covered over, and definition of the eastern limit at the south was now given by Wall 1154, a terrace wall shoring up the roughly 14.00 m wide terrace upon which structures of Strata XA through VII came to sit.

In the west half of the region, thin Walls 1369, 1361 and 1052 defined a room with Wall 1378 of Strata XI and XB strata as its western limit. Wall 1381 continued the line of Wall 1369 westward, but a pit cut the connection (Ill. 113 = VII BB:#18). Above Wall 1068 of Stratum XB and not quite in line with it, Wall 1054 extended eastward to continue as 11.110, the wall line disrupted by a collapse northward ("fall" on Ill. 101). Wall 1054 later served as the stylobate for Stratum IX pillars within Room 6 of the housing complex; it may not have existed in Stratum X, the west end of 11.110 having instead turned north on the line of a now badly robbed out wall line 1083. The entire region south of this wall was disturbed by the setting in of a Stratum VII complex that left Stratum IX walls but thoroughly disrupted surfacing.

Disturbance throughout Area 9 means that little soil stratigraphy can be assigned to XA there. Rather, it seems that Stratum XI banding continued up to the point where Stratum XA remains would be—that is, that the region of Area 9 was open ground outside the constructions of Stratum X. The one exception was Wall 1631 at its lowermost stones and the narrow segment of preserved surface shown on Ill. 112 = VII AA:#21. The foundation course of Wall 1631 was two stones wide, while the courses above that were a single stone wide, headers running through the wall, a characteristic of Stratum IX. The foundation course was preserved only very near to the north balk of the field (note the jumble beneath the Stratum IX described below). Surface #21 connecting the west terrace wall 1640 to the preserved stub of Wall 1631 was a narrow strip of probably Stratum XA surfacing at elevation 15.95 in the northwest corner of Plan 103. Disruptions by pitting in the 9/8 balk interrupted the connection of the surface to

Fig. 226. Platter Bin 1769 next to Vat 1770. Floor 1758 is in the foreground, a portion of Floor 1753 behind the bin.

Wall 1768. Were it certainly a feature of Stratum X, it would confirm what the west end of Wall 1381 suggests, that Terrace Wall 1640 was in place for Stratum X (note, as VII AA shows, excavation below this elevation did not undercut Terrace Wall 1640 and its footing was not fixed stratigraphically—terrace walls are not likely to have had foundation trenches on their downhill side).

Floors in Area 8 were well-preserved and provided good sealed loci, south of Wall 1768; north of it, tucked in against the north balk of the Field, loci 1750, 1799, and 17.101, all within VII AA:#22, were probably laid down in XA. South of Wall 1768, Surface 1791, the top line of the series shown as AA:#46, is represented by the dashing on Ill. 101, at elevation 15.65. It was plastered along the north edge of Vat 1770 and connected to its rim stones (fig. 224 above) very nearly at the same elevation as XB surface 1794. Traced eastward, it clearly connected to 1757B-1747B. Connection to the 17.100-1768 wall construction at the north is uncertain, because of slippage of 1768 and the installation of bins along 1768; it went most likely with Wall 1768. It was preserved intact beneath Platter 1769 (see below). Patches of white plaster dusted its surface at several locations near Wall 1768.

Running 0.11 to 0.16 m above 1791 was Surface 1758 sloping from elevation 16.01 next to Wall 1768 at the far north (dotted on the top plan; Ill. 116 = VII DD:top of #49) to 15.58 at the south edge of Area 8 (#45). It touched the top row of stones erected on the rim of Vat 1770. Thin lamination of red clay overlay 1758 and spilled down over the rim stones into the vat. Platter Bin 1769 was laid upon it: two large flat stones at elevation 15.82, rimmed with flat stones set vertically (fig. 226). If these were vestiges of a potter's workshop, no other evidence confirms the proposal.

Two bins, loci 1775 and 1779 were partially preserved as semicircles of stone against the south face of Wall 1768, relating to Surface 1758 and clogging the space between 1768 and the elbow of 1757B-1747B.

In the small region in the northwest corner of Area 5, north of Wall 14.117 and west of 14.118, a patch of cobbled floor 14.121 over a hard-packed surface 14.122 at 15.47 probably together corresponded to 1758 and 1791 respectively. The line connecting Pit #37 with Wall 14.118 on VII BB represented 14.122. In Area 8, within the elbow of 1757B and 1747B, Surface 1786 at 15.62 (dashed on Ill. 101) was plaster-surfaced in a manner similar to Surface 1791, while hard-pack Surface 1781, dotted on the plan, was 0.09 m higher in elevation. South of the possible Wall 14.125 and adjacent to the east face of 14.118, ephemeral segments of surfacing 14.111–14.113 (estimated elevation at 15.35) were succeeded by surfacing 14.101–14.103-14.112 at elevations ranging from 15.48 to 15.52.

Throughout the northern sector, then, were evidences of two surface systems with the only change being the setting in of Platter Bin 1769. Perhaps Wall 1747B-14.118 separated a domicile to the east from a work-yard to the west.

South of Wall 14.117 was another work-yard, extending at least from the putative line of robbed Wall 1083 to the Terrace Wall 1154. Two sloping surfaces to this yard presumably corresponded to the two systems of XA surfacing observed in the north.

The first of the two was Surface 1184-1186-1196 at elevation 14.81 adjacent to Wall 14.117, sloping to the southeast but roughly level along the arc shown on the plan, indicated by dashes. It was encountered in segments throughout the yard and combined after post-excavation analysis—note the dashing continuing to the south to the fallen stone along Wall 11.110. Wall 1185, a slim, slightly curving segment 2.00 m long and 0.40 m wide, was probably laid upon 1184, and served no clear purpose. Oven 1175 was built with its floor flush with Surface 1184; it was 0.73 m in diameter. Its construction was instructive: innermost was a layer of clay 0.06 m thick, the outer surface of which was studded with pebbles and chunks of chalk (*ḥuwwar*). At least one pottery bowl rim was set against the outside of this inner lining, on the outside of which was a clay, bricky layer 0.08 m thick. The outermost clay, bricky layer showed reddening from fire, while the inner layer showed no such effect. Apparently the oven was fired from the outside.

Eighty centimeters away to the southeast lay Oven 1179, 0.54 m in diameter, with walls only 0.06 m thick. Stains of firing were on the surface adjacent to Oven 1179. Near Wall 1154 and about 1.00 m east of Oven 1179 was Stone Mortar 1182, shown on the plan. Against the west face of Wall 1154, a small platform of stones, 0.40 m wide rested on Surface 1184; a similar installation lay southwest of Oven 1175, near Wall 11.110.

Just north of Oven 1175, the opening of massive Pit 11.103 appeared, almost certainly dug from Surface 1184. The upper part of the pit was dome-shaped and was empty. The top of the filling showed spillage of fill in a conical shape; presumably this was a refuse pit, and it must have been covered by a lid stone not discerned by the excavators. The filling was moist, dark brown, crumbly soil with small chunks of chalk, brick and charcoal; rare pieces of bone were in the uppermost layers, their number increasing the deeper the digging proceeded. Pit 11.103 material was carefully isolated as excavation continued on a horizontal plane; that is, the pit was not excavated as a separate unit, as pits should be dug. It is not certain that its bottom was reached. The domed top spread out to a diameter of 1.20 m at a point 1.20 m below its top, at which point its horizontal section was almost round. To this depth, eleven uncontaminated baskets of pottery had yielded 112 indicator sherds the great preponderance of which matched Stratum X pottery throughout the complex. Below this elevation, two baskets contained Stratum XI pottery. It is safe to take the contents of Pit 11.103 as a sealed Stratum XA locus.

The fifty baskets of pottery collected from the makeup for Surface 1184, reaching down to the Stratum XB layers 1194, 11.112 and 11.118, and sometimes into the various intrusions that cut these surfaces, also show a substantial ingredient of Stratum X pottery; this locus was not as definitive as the pit contents.

Surface 1183-1491, represented by dotting on Ill. 101, was of hard-packed earth marked by patches of distinctive orange brick detritus (Ill. 116 = VII DD:#33 next to Wall 14.117, and continuing to the south). A substantial segment of cobbling, locus 1191 at elevation 15.15, lay on 1183 and was continuous with it, beginning 1.00 m south of Wall 14.117 and continuing for 1.80 m south along and within the 2/3 balk (VII DD, north of Wall 11.105 to join #33). The hard-pack surface extended to Wall 11.110 and 1154, reached the side-walls of Ovens 1175 and 1179, lapped against both faces of Wall 1185, and touched Mortar 1182, thus reusing most if not all the features of the 1184 surfacing below it. A quern and a basalt rubbing stone were embedded in 1183 1.20 m southeast of Oven 1179, while another piece of rubbing stone was found pressed against the outer edge of Oven 1175. Elevations on 1183 were consistently 0.15

to 0.20 m higher than those on 1184. Pottery in baskets reaching down to it contained IXB pottery; sealed between it and 1184, fifteen carefully isolated baskets yielded 44 indicator sherds.

In the center of the western half of the Field, four wall fragments may have defined a hut. Foundation trenches for Stratum IX walls cut soil layers adjacent to the walls within their rough rectangle, and left isolated two patches of Floor 1373, 0.30 m lower in elevation than the Stratum IX floors above. These are located on Ill. 101 at elevations 15.34 and 15.30. The soil accumulation beneath 1373 was the thick layer of 1373A described with Stratum XB remains, which covered the Stratum XI destruction here. In this region, then, there is evidence of only one phase within XA. Both Surface 1373 and its immediate makeup, and 1373A, contained Stratum X pottery. Once again, the west half of Field VII was less useful than the east half for close definition of Stratum X.

It is noteworthy that no locus within the complex here described displayed destruction debris or extensive burning. Stratum IX construction was founded directly on top of it, in many cases reusing its walls. Field VII did not bear witness to a city-wide destruction of Stratum X.

Stratum X in Field IX (Ills. 132 [plan]; 141 = IX AA, 142 = IX BB, Ills. 143 = IX CC, 145 = IX EE)

Stratum X in Field IX was represented by poorly preserved fragments of walls that probably outlined dwelling spaces, and by open areas where soil accumulated over Stratum XI destruction debris. Wall 9559 in the northeast quadrant was in ruins and probably unused; against its east face was a collapse of rocks, locus 9565, Ill. 141 = IX AA:#53. Not on the plan, but shown on Ill. 145 = IX EE was a large pit, locus 9580, probably dug during Stratum X; another pit, 9575, was dug in the south central portion of Area 4. Soil layer 9569D-9844C accumulated throughout the northern part of the field (IX EE:#39 running west from Pit 9580; Ill. 142 = IX BB:##47 & 50). Wall 9559 protruded above the rock fall to its east and the soil build-up to its west; Stratum IX builders rebuilt on it as foundation.

In contrast to the construction style in Field VII, where Stratum X walls were often two stones wide, the walls defining the living spaces in the southern part of Field IX were all one stone wide; as was the case in Field VII, however, they were regularly founded upon thicker, ruined Stratum XI walls beneath. Wall 9852A ran from the west limit of the Field diagonally across Area 3 to the central balk, where it appears in IX BB as the single stone (designated 9848) on top of the two-stone-wide Stratum XI Wall 9852. Here it joined Wall 9867A, built on top of Stratum XI 9867, which continued into Area 2 as Wall 9352 built on Wall 9355 of Stratum XI. Wall 9840A with its east face 3.25 m away from the west face of 9867A-9352A also rode on a Stratum XI wall beneath (9840). A robbed out wall emerging from the west limit of Area 2, Wall 9347A, probably completed the rectangle of a room 3.25 by 4.00 m in size. Field notes indicate a surface within this rectangle, not given a locus number or indicated on plan; it is the interface of IX AA:##52+55 and 51. Only one sherd, which belonged to Stratum X, was saved from the soil on this surface; 39 were registered from the makeup layer #55, field-analyzed as belonging to Stratum XI.

Little sense can be made of the largely robbed out orphan walls 9361, 9356 and 9085 (the irregular jumble in the southwest corner of Area 1) along the south limit of the Field. A small segment of Wall 9350, which was later extended to the north balk of the area in Stratum IX, may have connected 9361 to 9356; it is doubtful that Wall 9352 once continued southward to link up with this early piece of 9350. Too much disturbance has taken place here to permit conclusions.

Layers of soil, loci 9346, 9347 and 9357, ran between Walls 9361 and 9347A, and appear on archived field sheets of a section HH drawn here. From these layers, 36 sherds were registered, all analyzed as belonging to Stratum X. A stone-lined pit was located in this region but not drawn on plans, and the field records are somewhat garbled, but these soil layers are probably trustworthy for Stratum X definition.

In Area 1, the outline of a partial rectangle of walls, together referred to as Wall 9088, probably defined another flimsy structure. This complex was

Fig. 227. Tower view of Field II, showing remains of Stratum X structure beneath the Hellenistic House. Wall 7051 runs at an oblique angle to the Hellenistic walls near the top of the view.

subjected to such a hot fire that the stones in the walls were largely reduced to calcined powder. The two east ends of the 9088 complex are shown on Ill. 143 = IX CC ("calcined"). Ashes and the outline of a charred beam were preserved on the surface adjacent to the southern wall at the east balk, lying on CC:#33, the interface of loci 9087 (#36) and 9087A (#34). Although the section seems to suggest that this surface runs beneath the southern wall of the 9088 complex, it in fact ran to the foundation stones, and it was the surface upon which the destruction debris fell. Twenty registered sherds from 9087 and 9087A belong to Stratum X.

The Field IX remains suggest flimsy construction on Stratum XI ruins, but the structures seem to have been living spaces, with the 9088 complex probably roofed as evidenced by the burned beam. The destruction may have been a local catastrophe. It may, on the other hand, point to widespread destruction of homes at the site.

Stratum X in Field II (Ills. 30 [plan]; 34 = II AA [section])

In the 1968 campaign, excavation proceeded beneath the Hellenistic house of Field II (fig. 227), which straddled a point in the Temenos Wall 900 of the acropolis. One aim was to see what stratification separated Hellenistic layers from the destruction debris of the Middle Bronze Age city, and gain some sense of what the Austro-German expedition may have encountered in the way of Iron Age remains in the western part of the site. Wall 900 ran beneath the northwest corner of the western room (Room 2) of the Hellenistic house, and, just to the north, had a preserved top almost at the elevation of the flooring for the house (17.95 compared to 18.03; see treatment of the Hellenistic House here in Chapter 6). Field II lies over a gap in Wall 900 which presumably was gouged when the site was ravaged in 1550–1540 BCE. Section II AA projects the position of Wall 900 to the north of the Field to display comparative elevation.

The lowest points of the 1968 probe reached layers ##19 and 20 to the south on II AA, and ashy fill deep beneath the Hellenistic house in layer #11 in the center of the section. The latest pottery in these layers was Iron I in date. Remains of Stratum X were found over the latter of these two locations; layer #10 of the center portion of II AA was the leveling makeup for a structure centered upon Wall 7051, shown running west-northwest to east-southeast under the Hellenistic house in Ill. 30. Wall 7051 was preserved 7.00 m to the point where foundation trenching for the Hellenistic house cut into it. East of it, and at an oblique angle, was Wall 7096 at the far eastern limit of excava-

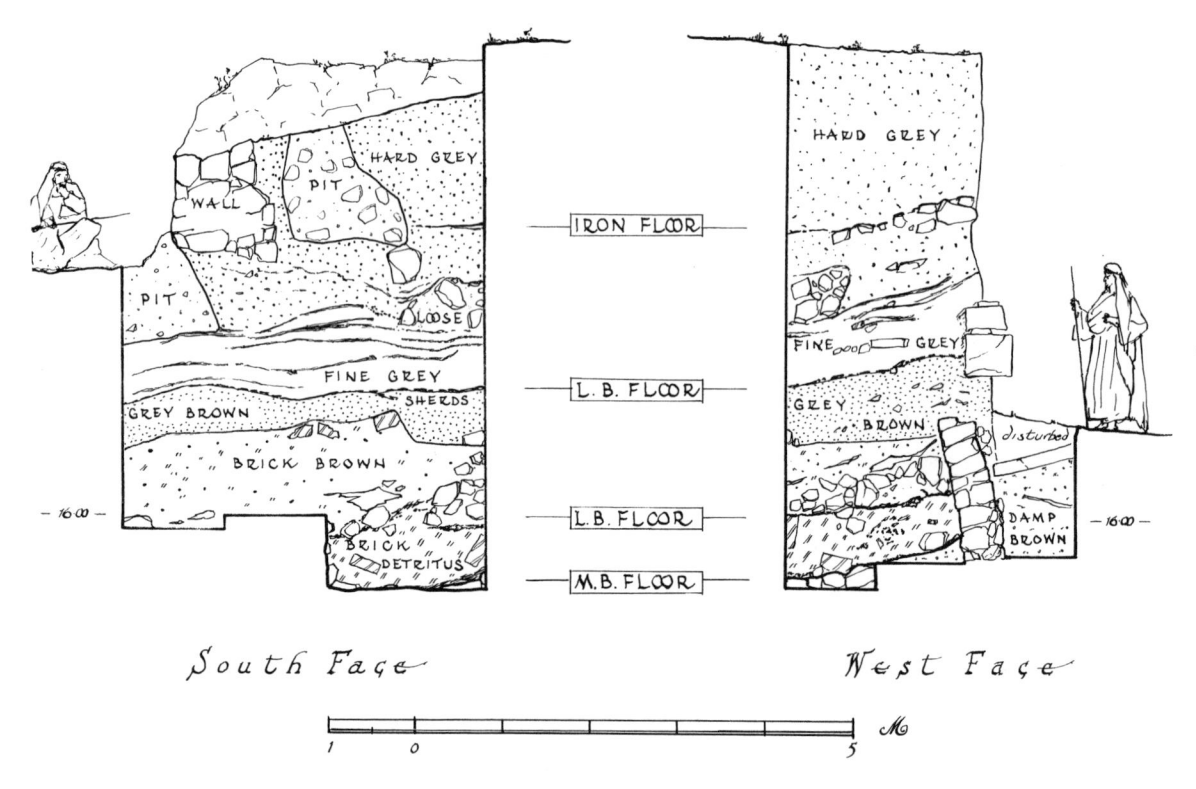

Fig. 228. Sections on south and west faces of Field VIII Area 3. Wall 8006 appears on the south face near the top, flanked by later Iron II pits. Flagstones 8013 slope down beneath the fill of "hard grey" on the west face.

tion, preserved beneath Stratum VII Wall 7026. If 7051 and 7096 intersected, their join was wiped out by subsequent intrusion.

The only surfaces to be associated with Wall 7051 during Stratum X were 7071 at elevation 15.49, represented by heavy dotting west of Stratum VII Wall 7056 and against the south face of Wall 7051, and 7076 at elevation 15.58 against the north face of Wall 7051 under the northwest corner of the east room (Room 1) of the Hellenistic house.

Surface 7077 is layer #9 in the center of II AA; it was traced beneath Walls 7056 and 7030. Pottery in its makeup, of which 56 indicator sherds were saved, include MB IIC, LB and Iron I sherds with a substantial proportion of Stratum X pieces. Sherds above Surface 7077 were in the makeup for Surface 7037 of Stratum VII and are probably not trustworthy, since the Stratum VII floor had intrusions which introduced Hellenistic pottery below its elevation. Excavation did not breach Surface 7076; 14 indicator sherds from locus 7075,

its occupation debris, showed Stratum X as the latest ingredient.

What is noteworthy in Field II is that there appears to have been no construction here following the MB IIC destruction until the time of Stratum X. Intervening was fill from LB and Iron I. The two walls and two surfaces of Stratum X hardly constitute a clear architectural complex, but a building of some sort attests the recovery at the beginning of Iron II. Judging from the adjacent ruins of the acropolis wall and the rubble and fill in layers ##19 and 20 of II AA, this building was in a saucer set down into more ancient debris.

Stratum X in Field VIII

During the 1960 campaign, an effort was made to connect 1913 Austro-German work in "Trench H" to work being started in Field VII designed to determine the full site stratigraphy from top to bottom. The earlier expedition had given very sketchy account of its long trenching efforts (Ill.

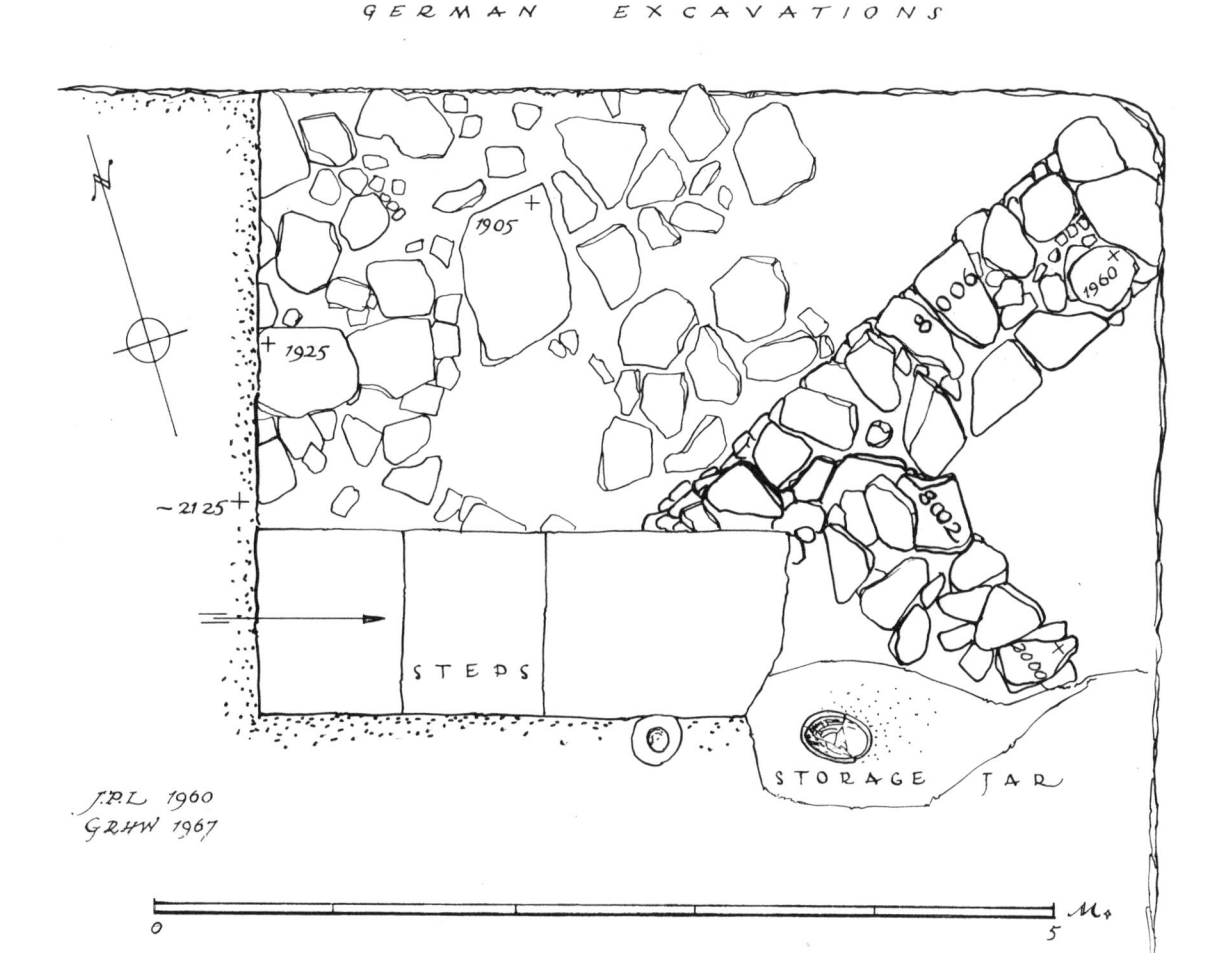

Fig. 229. Plan of upper segment of Field VIII, with Wall 8006 and Flagstones 8013 tentatively assigned to Stratum X.

119), with the result that Hellenistic and Iron Age stratigraphy was hardly described at all. Field VIII Area 3 was positioned on the edge of Trench H and began from the surface left by the earlier expedition as they made another attempt at the later stratigraphy in 1934.

The results on this upper shelf of Field VIII are shown on figs. 228 and 229. The lower phase of Iron Age remains here is tentatively assigned to Stratum X. Wall 8006 and the irregular, but originally rather fine, flagstone paving 8013 (elevations 19.05 and 19.25) were the only architecture. Twenty meters to the southeast, Stratum X elevations were roughly 4.00 m lower in elevation, which gives some sense of the slope of the tell and also indicates that the Sellin expedition peeled off roughly 4.00 m of Hellenistic and late Iron Age remains above what is now preserved.

Wall 8006 appears on the south face in fig. 228; two later Iron Age pits, their tops removed by earlier excavation, interrupted connections to any flooring either side of 8006. Flagstones 8013 are displayed on the west face, and the junction of the two sections shows the connection of wall and flooring. The structure (fig. 228) was set into a makeup fill on top of striated debris similar to that topping Stratum XI in nearby Field VII. While 97 indicator sherds were saved from on, in and under the 8006-8013 complex, field notes make it clear that the intrusion of pits was not noticed in time to forestall gross mixing, and the sherd collections were not separated by loci.

Fig. 230. Plan of Field I Areas 16 and 17 showing Iron Age features. The Stratum X surface ran from Wall 175 to a point where it was interrupted near Wall 181, under Wall 176.

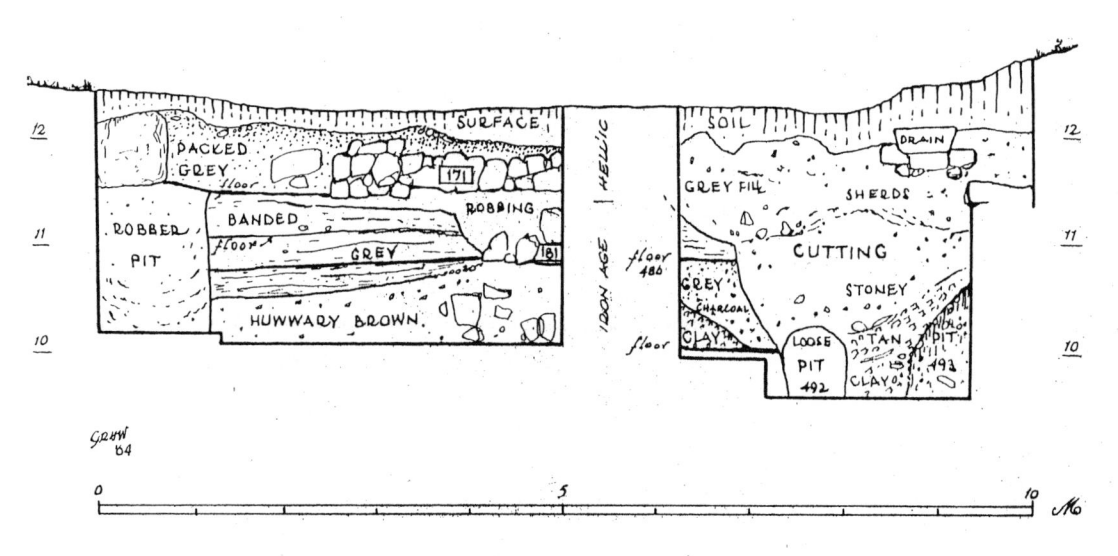

Fig. 231. Section on east face of Field I Areas 16 and 17. Surfaces in the left portion, cut by robbing from reaching Wall 181, represent Stratum X.

No confident chronological or architectural conclusions about Stratum X can be based on Field VIII results.

Stratum X in Field I

Evidence for Stratum X in the region just inside the line of the LB-Iron I gate tower was tenuous. After the destruction of the Stratum XI structures related to Wall 178/182 (shown as "lines of wall below" in outline on fig. 230 for orientation), banded accumulation comparable to that topping Stratum XI remains in Field VII collected and is visible in the north balk of Area 16. Fig. 231 also shows it. Set into two layers of leveling fill over this banding, containing pottery of earlier strata with a few Stratum X sherds included, were the foundations of Wall 175, standing to elevation 11.41 to 11.51; its line was continued at the north by a pillar of stone 177 (elevation 11.41), on the other side of a flat stone (elevation 10.97) that may have marked the threshold of an entrance through the wall-line. Perpendicular but detached was a wall fragment made of four headers, Wall 180.

A soil layer, locus 427, with a quite uncertain living surface as its interface with another layer of a very similar kind, probably represented the use of this complex, running beneath Wall 176 and interrupted from connection with Wall 181 at the far southeast corner of the area by a later intrusion (fig. 231:"floor"). Wall 181 was founded at elevation 10.85, and set into the same makeup. The oval 1.75 by 1.40 m flagstone-floored Bin 444 east of Area 16, sitting above the ruined LB-Iron I gate tower, was another possible piece of the complex. Pottery evidence is ambiguous but tends to indicate a Stratum X assignment for this complex; Wall 181 was reused with the addition of Wall 176 in later Iron II.

A correction to the charts of the overall site stratigraphy presented by Toombs (1972; 1976) is shown in the chart at the beginning of this volume. The Wall 175 complex was Stratum X, while the 176 complex belonged later, perhaps in IX. Reference to a wall "190" in the Toombs chart is to be omitted.

Adjacent to Wall 179 of Stratum XI, at the southwest corner of Area 17, a chalky surface 490 was discerned, with nothing later than Stratum X pottery sealed beneath it, but with a mix of later Iron II pottery above it. Along the south balk of Area 17, not depicted on any plan or section, note was made in the field of the corner of mudbrick structure on a shallow foundation, resting on the uppermost layer of the striated black and bricky accumulation that ends Stratum XI; it may be a Stratum X construction.

With appropriate hesitation, the claim can be made that Stratum X structures, at least some used as dwellings none of which were well-preserved, were located over the entire tell, from Field XIII at the west to the back of the gate tower of the East Gate. Resettlement and reuse of the tell for agriculture had begun, and, at least in Field IX, a structure was badly burned, but the impression is one of huts and impoverished homes among open yards. The site at this juncture does not look to be a candidate for a Solomonic district center or a prime target for a pharaonic attack. On the other hand, a passing and destructive raid on a settlement built on the ruins of a famous ancient site is entirely within the realm of possibility (Boling and Campbell 1986:269–70).

STRATUM IX

The settlement at Shechem blossomed from random reuse spread out across the tell to an organized and fortified city at the end of the tenth century, with continuity that probably covered about a century. Judging from the recorded observations of the Austro-German expedition, the entire tell, from the west perimeter to the region adjacent to the "House of the Blind Man" in the southeast, was covered with Iron Age housing. Within Stratum IX, a public building of importance came into being, identified by the Joint Expedition as a communal if not regional grain storage facility, positioned on the ruins of the sanctuary on what had been the Bronze Age acropolis.

Fortification

Because Hellenistic builders did such a thorough job of removing indications of Iron II fortifications, hints at how the city renewed its walls are sparse and difficult to interpret. The surest in-

Fig. 232. View of Field IV, looking south southeast. Wall A in foreground. Nasr Dhiab Mansoor and Jeber Muhammad Hasan Salman stand at the exterior face of Wall E, their hands on the separation between the MB IIC and Iron Age phases of the wall. Photo by W. G. Dever.

dication was the rebuilding of Wall E on the western perimeter. G. Welter's plan (Ill. 50) of the wall lines running south from the Northwest Gate depicts Wall E at the elevation of its reuse in what is almost certainly the Stratum IX period. Two casemate chambers, 8.20 m and 7.80 m in interior length, and between 1.60 and 1.70 m wide, ran south from the gate tower on top of the MB IIC foundation built as the last effort at protection before the destruction of 1550/1540 BCE. Fig. 232 shows the change in construction marking the MB IIC and Iron Age phases of the exterior wall line, as discerned during the salvage work by Dever in 1973. The two excavators have their hands on the point of separation.

Apparently to provide room for the placement of the granary on the old temple ruins, the next casemates southward were offset westward by 1.50 m; continuance of the wall southward was lost in subsequent depredations, although the first casemate in the new line, and third from the gate, had an interior chamber of at least 11.00 m in length. At the point of the IV FF section = Ill. 59, the Iron Age rebuild is depicted as Walls 7310A and 7311A on top of MB IIC walls 7310 and 7311. The Joint Expedition found the interior of the casemate devoid of defining soil, removed by the earlier expedition, and the section displays rocks probably fallen inward from Wall 7311A filling the void. Dever's visual observations (no dismantling could be done under the terms of the salvage permit) noted the bricky cushion separating 7310A from 7310.

Some stones of the interior line of Wall E at the edge of the third casemate were lifted in the concluding week of the 1962 campaign, and in the sealed makeup for their placement a small collection of sherds was found. G. E. Wright (Toombs and Wright 1963:49) described their date as "unquestionably" Stratum IX; in *SBBC*, Wright instead stated they "appeared to belong to Stratum IX," and indicated a lack of certainty about assigning Wall E to Stratum IX. As of the time of writing, it has not been possible to relocate these sherds, or to ascertain whether they were saved.

The Wall E casemate system continued to the north of the Northwest Gate, and Sellin found another segment of it in H-K 3 on the northernmost arc of the tell (Ill. 2). No similar remains were found in Field III or in the vicinity of the East Gate. Whether the northern part of the arc had two phases is also unknown. Incursions at the edge of tell between 1985 and the present have badly limited the opportunity of future work to check Wall E and the rest of the fortification system along the north.

At the East Gate, the evidence is even less certain. In the 1956 campaign, Wall "c'" was ob-

Fig. 233. Balk in Field V beneath stones of granary wall 5905, showing thick plaster layer 5001 into which the granary stones were pressed.

served, resting upon Wall 118 of the south gate tower (Ill. 12). On fig. 119 it constitutes the rocks above the upper dashed line of this otherwise unmarked depiction, above the several MB II phases of Wall 118. When digging began in 1956, it extended across the opening in Wall 118 where the figure stands just inside the orthostats in the section (see also *SBBC*:fig. 30). Against the south face of Wall "c'" a surface was traced, upon which was a burned layer with a collection of pottery, including three perfume juglets. In 1956, G. E. Wright proposed a date around 800 BCE for this collection (Wright 1956:19; 1957:23), but when excavation in Field VII in 1962 provided corpora of Shechem's Stratum VI pottery, the juglets were redated correctly to the seventh century (*SBBC*, pp. 165 and 259, n. 31). The fragment of rebuild was thus in use, and probably destroyed, in the seventh century and no ceramic evidence remained to suggest a Stratum IX phase; probably the rebuild belonged to the post-Stratum VII Assyrian destruction.

Study of the fortification slopes east of the MB II System B wall and gate in Field I in 1956 and 1957 provided evidence that Hellenistic builders had cut down to MB II levels almost everywhere at the East Gate. As a check on this stratigraphy, Paul Lapp and Nasr Dhiab trimmed back the south balk of the field approximately 0.60 m in 1962, meticulously separating each element in the tip-lines from just west of Wall 114 eastward (fig. 128). On the basis of this work, Lapp proposed that a rebuild on top of MB IIC Wall A in front of the East Gate may have been a Stratum IX structure. The fallen stones above Wall A in fig. 128 interrupt connections from a segment of brick fall directly above Wall 114 to the bricky red layer tailing away from the two-course cap on Wall A; the bricky red rested upon a layer of coarse brown soil and a layer of tan clay. The pottery from these layers recovered in 1962 showed no forms later than Stratum IX. Lapp's cut differs, then, from the conditions in the BB section from 1957 (Ill. 21), where layer #4, of striated bricky makeup contained Hellenistic pottery down to the interface with layer #9, the MB IIC debris. The inconsistency remains unresolved (G. E. Wright did not accept Lapp's conclusions, and no preliminary report mentions the finding), but it is possible that elements in the scree down the slope from the East Gate front tower wall emanated from undisturbed fragments of Iron II fortification, most but not quite all of which Hellenistic builders cleared away as they consolidated the slope.

These indications, slim as they are, suggest that Stratum IX saw a system of refortification at Shechem, positioned on the lines of the MB IIC fortifications. Presumably the street level of the East Gate, kept open by curb walls in the gate passage during Strata XIV-XI, was used again by the peoples of Stratum IX and later, to the end of the life of the city.

The Granary (Ill. 63 [plan]; sections in figs. 3 and 142)

The builders of the 5900 structure knew the layout of the LB-Iron I Temple 2, and positioned their wall lines on its wall lines, though at a slight angle. A leveling layer of makeup (5002) was topped with plaster (5001) 0.20 to 0.25 m thick (fig. 233; fig. 142 at left, against the rear granary wall). Since the Sellin Expedition cleared much of the soil within the building, layers 5001 and 5002, as also the soil layers for all but the lowest phase of the temple itself, were preserved only directly beneath the preserved 5900 wall segments; occasionally there was a tiny deposit of undisturbed soil right next to the walls. The two sections are drawn on the south faces of the balks of earth preserved beneath Walls 5905 (fig. 3) and 5906 (fig. 142).

Ill. 63 shows the walls of the 5900 building, including extrapolations in the southeast portion to fill out the likely layout (Welter's early plan also shows no walls preserved here). They were made of two rows of rough-hewn boulders laid in with a rubble core. The boulders were as much as a meter long and a half-meter or more in other dimensions. The walls were from 1.30 to 1.85 m thick. Only one course was preserved. Elevations on the preserved tops are between 0.49 and 0.76 higher than foundations.

The rocks were pressed into the wet plaster of 5001, creating a seal of sorts at the base. Mud plaster running up the walls and filling the interstices probably sustained this seal, warding off the elements and vermin.

With only the foundation course preserved, it is difficult to say how people gained access to the building and moved from chamber to chamber. There was probably a ground-level entrance indicated by the break subsequently filled with smaller stones in Wall 5902 (the western wall) where 5901 (the north wall) and 5902 would have met. Welter's plan shows Wall 5901 extending about a meter past the expected junction point, forming a screen. An earlier sketch plan by Heinz Johannes (Sellin 1927:Tafel 12) seems to indicate that 5903 also ran past the west temple wall undergirding it. The building may have been entered off a ring road along Wall E coming south from the gate—no sign of which was preserved. Alternatively, there may have been another narrow room along the west of the 5900 building.

There were no apparent ground-level accesses from one chamber to the next within the building; probably the chambers were filled from above and accessed by ladders. Ground level access would have been used primarily for cleaning.

Seventy-five sherds with recognizable form or distinctive surface treatment were collected from the strips of layers 5001 and 5002 preserved under the rocks and from within the rubble core of the walls. Ten of these are pieces of Samaria Ware, four clearly Samaria Ware B. None of the rest has to be later than ninth century in date. G. E. Wright discussed Samaria Ware B in terms of its fabric, slip, burnishing, and the forms it took (*SBBC*: 56–57). It first appeared at Shechem in Stratum IX; it was rare early in that period, grew more common as the period unfolded, and then continued through Strata VIII and VII. With Samaria Ware B in the underpinnings, these considerations point to the middle of the period covered by Stratum IX, the century from roughly 920 to 810 BCE, as the earliest date for construction.

The layout of the four rooms—accepting Welter's plan over that of Johannes—in Building 5900 recalls a broad and typical architectural concept, the "four-room" structure (Shiloh 1970; G. R. H. Wright 1970; G. E. Wright 1978a; Currid 1986: 105–27). Within this "form," there is great variation in overall size, room size and shape, division of space, and use. The concept tells little about what the structures were used for; there are instances that have been identified as citadels, storehouses, official residences, private homes, and sanctuaries.

The 5900 structure's floor with the walls pressed into it and its long narrow rooms are what points to its use as a public granary. There were three of these rooms side by side, each about 4.50 by 9.00 m with a narrower room about 16.00 by 2.00 m running perpendicular to them the width of the building. W. F. Albright commented on such buildings at Tell Beit Mirsim and other sites: "Their form is related to their function as storehouses: thick double walls and deep foundations [in the case of 5900, *sealed* foundations] were necessary to insulate as far as possible against moisture, and the long narrow design, like that of modern American farm granaries, helped to keep grain from [decaying]" (1943: 24).

As noted in the description of Stratum XI, flask-shaped and cylindrical pits with Iron I debris filling them were dug throughout the temple interior; the two sections display three with their openings at LB-Iron I elevations and two more encroaching from the side. The suggestion was made earlier that some of the great number of such pits found all over Shechem in this period related to disease control. But those in the temple area are likely to be grain silos. G. R. H. Wright proposed (1970: 275–78) that the idea of using Shechem's old acropolis for food storage may have begun around 1100, after the Abimelek destruction; that idea continued, then, in the ninth century with the construction of a very different kind of storage facility (on grain storage, see Currid 1986; cf. Currid and Navon 1986; Currid and Gregg 1988).

G. E. Wright assumed in *SBBC* that the presence of this building connected Shechem to Solomon's royal store-cities mentioned in 1 Kings 9:19 (compare 2 Chronicles 8:4, 6); see also the notices about Jehoshaphat and Hezekiah in 2 Chronicles 17:12–13 and 32:28–29, and the probable reference to store-cities as the target of Ben-Hadad in 2 Chronicles 16:4. Until a way be found to estimate the grain needs of the town and the capacity of the 5900 building, it is impossible to say whether the 5900 granary was anything more than the local "grain elevator" for Shechem. Its date does not fit well with Jeroboam I who probably used Shechem as capital of the Northern Kingdom early in his reign (prior to 900 BCE). The Omri-Ahab dynasty would be a more probable occasion. The court at Samaria, only seven miles away, would probably have called upon grain supplies from the broad Shechem plain; the Samaria Ostraca show Samaria received wine and oil from this region in the first half of the eighth century.

Domestic Complexes

Fields VII and IX provide evidence of Stratum IX settlement of some complexity; ground plans of housing and yards show local development and change indicating the passage of a period of time. The Joint Expedition preliminary reports have divided Stratum IX into A and B phases, partly because of hints of possible earthquake damage at a specific point during the period of time represented; it is equally possible, however, that the changes observed were the result of home improvements, suggesting an expanding population during a relatively quiet period in the city's life.

Field IX (Ills. 133 and 134 [plans]; 141 = IX AA, 143 = IX CC, 144 = IX DD, 145 = IX EE [sections]). A candid statement about circumstances of excavation in Field IX for Strata VIII and IX needs to be made. The top of Stratum IX features was reached at the end of the 1962 campaign, referred to as "8b and c" (Toombs and Wright 1963:47). Work was resumed at that level in 1964. The transition was poorly documented, in spite of extreme effort by experienced area supervisors. There is a paucity of elevation readings from the first week of the 1964 campaign and a lack of written field notes about the precise location of certain loci, including walls. When the balks between the areas were dismantled later in the season, wall connections through the balks were not recorded on plan; the team concentrated on the vertical. Thus the sections are continuous where the top-plans are not. The valiant efforts of the late Joseph Callaway to make sense of the architecture in Field IX during Strata IX and VIII are reflected in what is reported here; the more trustworthy data pertains to the vertical dimension of

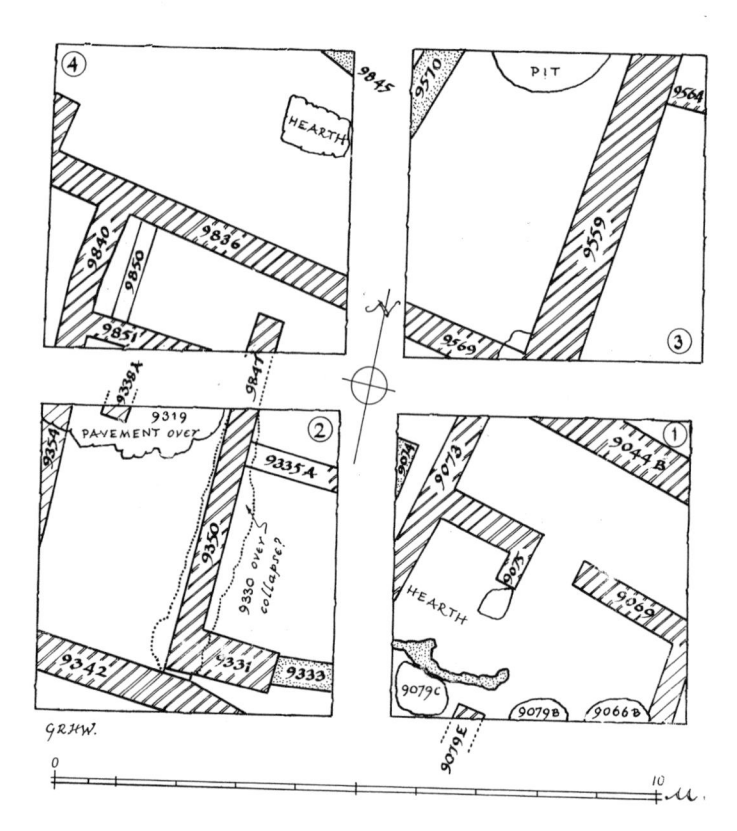

Fig. 234. Block plan of phasing in Field IX, Stratum IX. Wall lines with double hatching continued throughout the period. Walls with single hatching were original, then went out of use in Stratum IXA. Stippled walls are Stratum IXA additions.

the dig, rather than to the horizontal. That data is of importance for the study of the pottery chronology of the ninth and eighth centuries BCE, which this report is designed to enable, so it is presented here as well as it can be reconstructed.

Field IX shows in Stratum IX two extensive work yards and several probable domiciles. A series of changes suggest there were two phases in Stratum IX here (Ills. 133–134; fig. 234 combines the constructions in block plan).

In the eastern half of the field, Wall 9559 was re-established, built upon the exposed stump which had served no architectural purpose in Stratum X, but had been located on the same line since Stratum XIII. The reconstructed wall had clay and plaster included within its rubble core, a new ingredient in wall building here. Wall 9044B was constructed to meet its south end, placed along the line of calcined and ruined wall 9088 of Stratum X (Ill. 144 = IX DD). In the far northeast corner of the field, fragmentary Wall 9561 (with a possibly wider predecessor wall, Wall 9594) ran eastward. Locus 9567 = CC:#29 (Ill. 143) seems to have been the surface in use, topping makeup layer 9564 = #30, from which 43 indicator sherds were saved showing characteristics of fill (MB IIC to Stratum IX forms). Wall 9044B on IX CC looks to be placed on layer #29, but IX DD:#46 shows more clearly that this "ḥuwwary" layer reached 9044B well up on its face. CC:#26 = layer 9563 was occupation debris. No architectural changes within Stratum IX characterized this eastern portion.

West of Wall 9559 all along the north seems to have been an open yard. A shallow pit (Ill. 145 = IX EE:#35) with a partial stone lining was dug within Stratum IX along the north edge near Wall 9559, but its contents were not isolated from adjacent layering. Pit 9571, not shown on plan or section, was 1.25 m in diameter and 0.20 m deep and occupied the "disturbed" center of Area 3 west of Wall 9559. Its contents were isolated and yielded 9 indicator sherds, including IX forms. A flat segment of burned rocks marked a hearth to the west. Late within Stratum IX (Ill. 134 and fig. 234), the elbow of Walls 9570 and 9845 was constructed, its purpose obscure because of its position so close to the northern limit of excavation; 9845 served as foundation for a Stratum VIII structure, but had

Fig. 235. Looking west in Field IX Area 1, the yard. Pit 9079c cuts into Surface 9077 running to Wall 9073 in the background.

upper Stratum IX accumulation running to it, as IX EE shows (##33, 34 and 36); 9570 was built and went out of use within Stratum IX and appears in EE:#36 as two rocks in the same layer as the foot of 9845. This layer, 9569, contained a mix of earlier pottery, along with some analyzed in the field as IX.

The southern limit of this open area is Wall 9836-9569, which probably ran to intersect Wall 9559, although the point of intersection was disturbed—note the tumble of rock to the right of Wall 9559 in Ill. 141 = IX AA:#44. Running to meet the approximate point of junction of Walls 9559, 9044B and 9569 from the south was Wall 9073. Perpendicular to it was Wall 9069, which, with a doorway through it, continued to the east limit of excavation. All of these walls were built in a different construction style from those of Stratum X. Only about 0.40 m wide, they had carefully laid headers running the width of the wall. Both in Field IX and Field VII, walls of this construction were preserved to considerable height and apparently were capable of bearing considerable weight.

A chalky surface characterized the room within the partial rectangle of 9044B, 9073 and 9069, represented by the continuation of IX CC:#29 = locus 9077. This narrow room was probably a dwelling; from it one entered a yard to the south. Wall stump 9075, flanking the west of the door, defined a corner in which there was evidence of a hearth on Surface 9077 extending southward to the south limit of excavation. The yard was replete with pits; 9066B, 9079B and 9079C are shown on the plan. Pit 9079C is pictured in fig. 235 with Surface 9077 adjacent to it, running to Wall 9073. This pit was heavy with IX pottery; 78 indicator sherds make up a sound corpus for study. At least two more pits, 9066C due north of 9066B and 9078A in the same general region, neither on plan, further cut into the surfaces. If these were grain silos, it is not clear how they were covered.

Later in the period of Stratum IX (Ill. 134), a curve of small stones south of the hearth was added and Wall 9073 was extended, and a short segment of wall running south from the east point of Wall 9069 (Ill. 133), just at the east limit of excavation, was covered over. Fig. 234 shows the development schematically. A surface designated 9071 covered the later phase yard; the pottery between 9071 and 9077, of which only 8 indicator sherds were saved, may show changes in ceramic form within the period of Stratum IX.

The complex in the west of the field from wall 9836 southward underwent the most alteration during Stratum IX. Walls 9840, 9850 and 9851 in the corner of Area 4 could not be effectively dis-

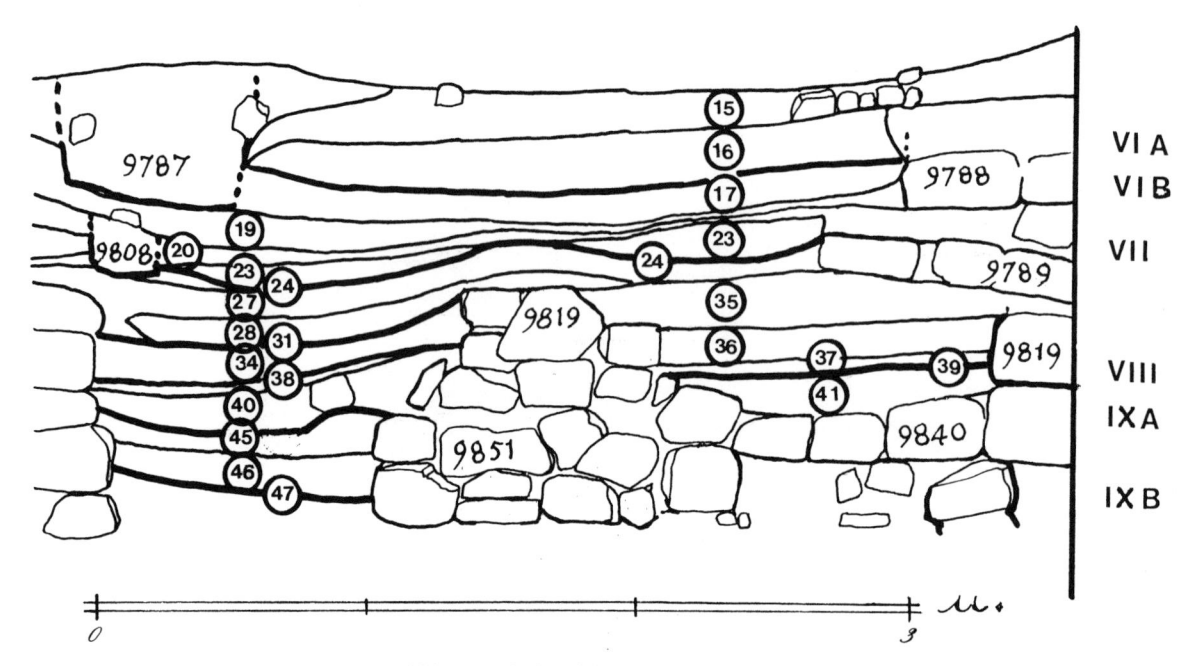

Fig. 236. Detail of Field IX AA section (cf. Ill. 141).

entangled and related to surfaces to give clarity, but two floorings were identified, shown on IX AA as thick lines between Walls 9851 and 9847 and on fig. 236 as ##45 and 47; they were chalky surface 9839A over packed earth surface 9847A.

In Area 2, Wall 9350 ran north-south through Area 2, and showed similar construction style to the other walls south of 9836-9569. During the period covered by Stratum IX, Wall 9330 was built on top of it; alternatively, 9330 may have been simply a collapse and spread of the upper courses of 9350. The plans indicate both phases. Wall 9350 butted against Wall 9342A at the south and turned right as Wall 9331, nearly flush against the north face of Wall 9342A. Access to the room defined by Walls 9350/9330, 9331, 9073 and 9569 was through a break in 9331.

West of 9350 in the earlier phase of Stratum IX was Wall 9354, the face of which appears in the west limit of excavation. Two fragments of interior partition walls, 9338A and 9335A are hard to work into a sensible plan. The entire block from 9354 and 9840 on the west to 9073 on the east, and from 9342 on the south to 9836-9569 was probably one domicile of at least three and perhaps four rooms.

Within the eastern room, straddled by the balk between Areas 1 and 2, a thick makeup over Stratum X occupation, locus 9340-9341, was topped by a surface probably representing a use phase early in Stratum IX, on which ashy soil had accumulated (Ill. 142 = IX BB:#43 on #46). These layers provided 62 indicator sherds analyzed as IX, but they include the destruction debris of Stratum X. And no later phase flooring was identified in the eastern room.

Section IX DD:#41 shows the distinctive Stone Paving 9319 in the western room which ran over Wall 9354 and divider 9338A and constituted a late Stratum IX surface. Beneath 9319 were layers of rubble and compact makeup (loci 9338 on 9339), including a hump of brick and stones (locus 9337), all within DD:#43 beneath Paving 9319; these belonged to the earlier phase of Stratum IX, and contained 46 Stratum IX indicator sherds. Close study of these corpora should help to define the period covered by Stratum IX.

The stratigraphy south of Wall 9342, which probably lay outside of the domicile just described but may have been yet another room of it, presents an important datum for the end of Stratum IX. The south face of 9342 was plastered with a

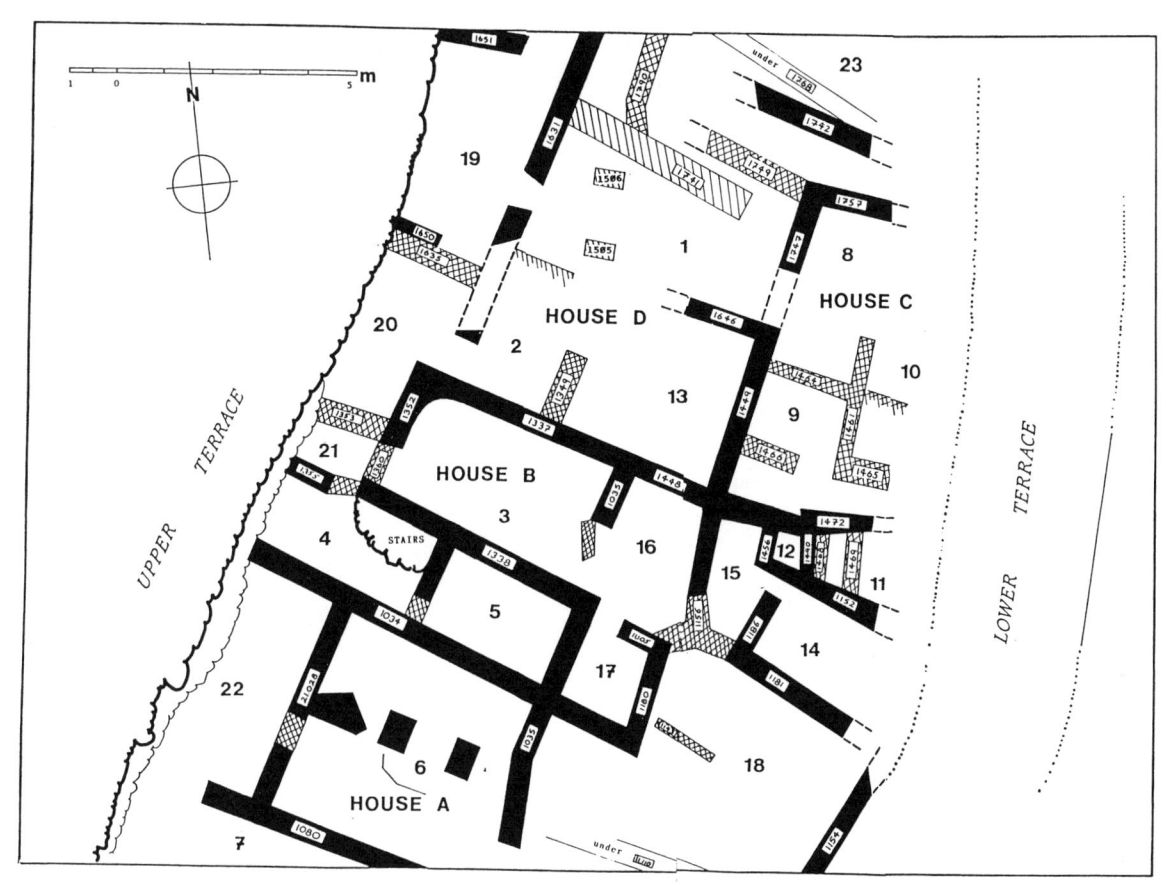

Fig. 237. Block plan of Field VII in Stratum IX. Solid walls were in use throughout Stratum IX. Single-hatched walls are later additions, and crosshatched walls are the latest additions. Drawing by K. Djerf.

continuous surface that curved down to a fragment of flooring in the far southwest corner of the excavation field. The elevation of this flooring was the same as that of the lowest layers of Stratum IX material in the room to the north of 9342 (the western room just described). Upon the chalky plastered floor was a deep accumulation of ashy black debris, locus 9359, from which a group of 15 indicator sherds were saved, all field analyzed as IX.

This ash deposit covered by soil should belong to the final deposits of the Stratum IX period but may also represent makeup for Stratum VIII. Tentatively, locus 9359 is taken to be destruction debris that terminated Stratum IX in Field IX. If that be so, the room south of 9342 was a step down from the domicile to its north.

Reasons for taking Stratum IX in Field IX as one continuous complex with local changes at various times have been distributed throughout the description given. The changes do, however, afford opportunity to study ceramic development within the period covered, notably in Areas 1 and 2, especially with the sequence beneath Paving 9319 and involving 9077 up to 9071.

Throughout Field IX, the top of Stratum IX layers showed evidence of destruction, destruction debris 9359 being one salient instance. The amount of decayed brick and ash above Stratum IX upper occupation debris merging into makeup for Stratum VIII is another (IX DD:##36 and 37; fig. 236:##40 and 41).

Field VII (Ills. 102–103 [plans]; 112 = VII AA, 113 = VIIBB, 115 = VII CC, 116 = I DD). Stratum IX followed much the same pattern in use of space that had characterized Stratum X. The terrace from Wall 1640-1357-21.039 on the west to 1154 on the east was laid out in homes. The two yards or work areas of Stratum X continued in use

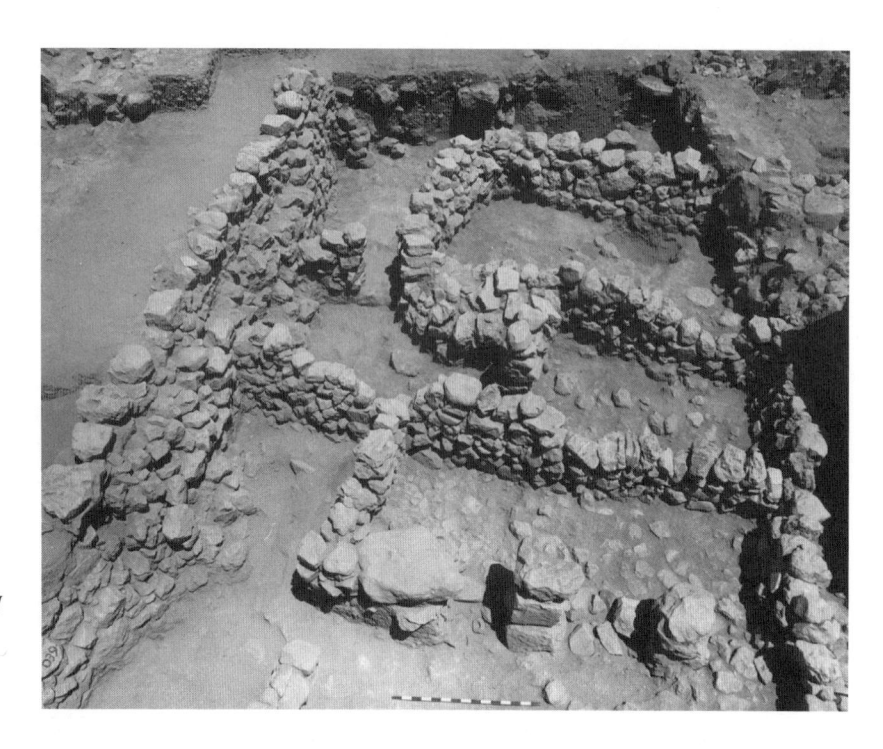

Fig. 238. Overview of Field VII Areas 3 and 6 looking north, with Terrace Wall 1640 at left. Houses A and B are depicted.

in Stratum IX (Rooms 18 and the north half of 1); the vat and platter bin installation (1769, 1770) were reused. What had been random space dividers and hut walls were now turned into houses, with features comparable to housing complexes of the Iron Age at other sites in the land.

The Terrace Walls. The western terrace wall (1640) was exposed for 18.50 m along its east face. A probe against its west face at the north limit of excavation (Ill. 112 = VII AA:#13) did not reach its footing and did not determine the elevation of Stratum IX remains to the west of the terrace wall; Stratum IX pottery was present to the bottom of the probe. On the east face at the north end the footing of Wall 1640 was at elevation 15.95 (Ills. 102 and 103, and VII AA), while the preserved top of the terrace wall, to all appearances built as one construction, reached elevations of 17.11 and 17.45 further south. There were no breaks along the stretch excavated.

Along the east face of the 1640 terrace wall, three short stretches of wall protruded, Walls 1651, 1650 and 1355, probably buttresses of some sort, because they did not extend to reach the west walls of the houses adjacent. Walls 1651 and 1650 are not recorded on the official drawing of the stratum (Ill. 102) but are reconstructed on fig. 237

from field descriptions and are shown on fig. 238. At the start of the period covered by Stratum IX, one could have passed along the terrace wall in a narrow alley from the north to Wall 1034 (through what later became Rooms 19, 20 and 21 into Room 4 and thus to House B). Later in Stratum IX, cross walls closed this alley and added a room to both Houses A and B (fig. 237).

Probes along the projected line of 1154 exposed segments of wall in the edges of balks, 1189 slightly off-line westward and 1561 (neither shown on plan), suggesting the eastern terrace wall was continuous along the dotted line on the plan. Post-excavation analysis casts doubt on this understanding.

Throughout the complex on the terrace, the masons laid headers 0.40 to 0.45 m long across the wall, faced them with mud and surfaced that with plaster, yielding finished walls 0.55 to 0.60 m thick. The construction style resembles closely that exposed in Field IX. Wall 1742 rested on the collapsed stones of Stratum X Walls 1768 and 17.100. Two party walls between homes in the complex, Walls 1449-1747 and 1448–1337, were anchored on the two-stone-wide, leveled foundations of Stratum X walls 14.118 and 14.117 respectively. Wall 1631 probably rested on one

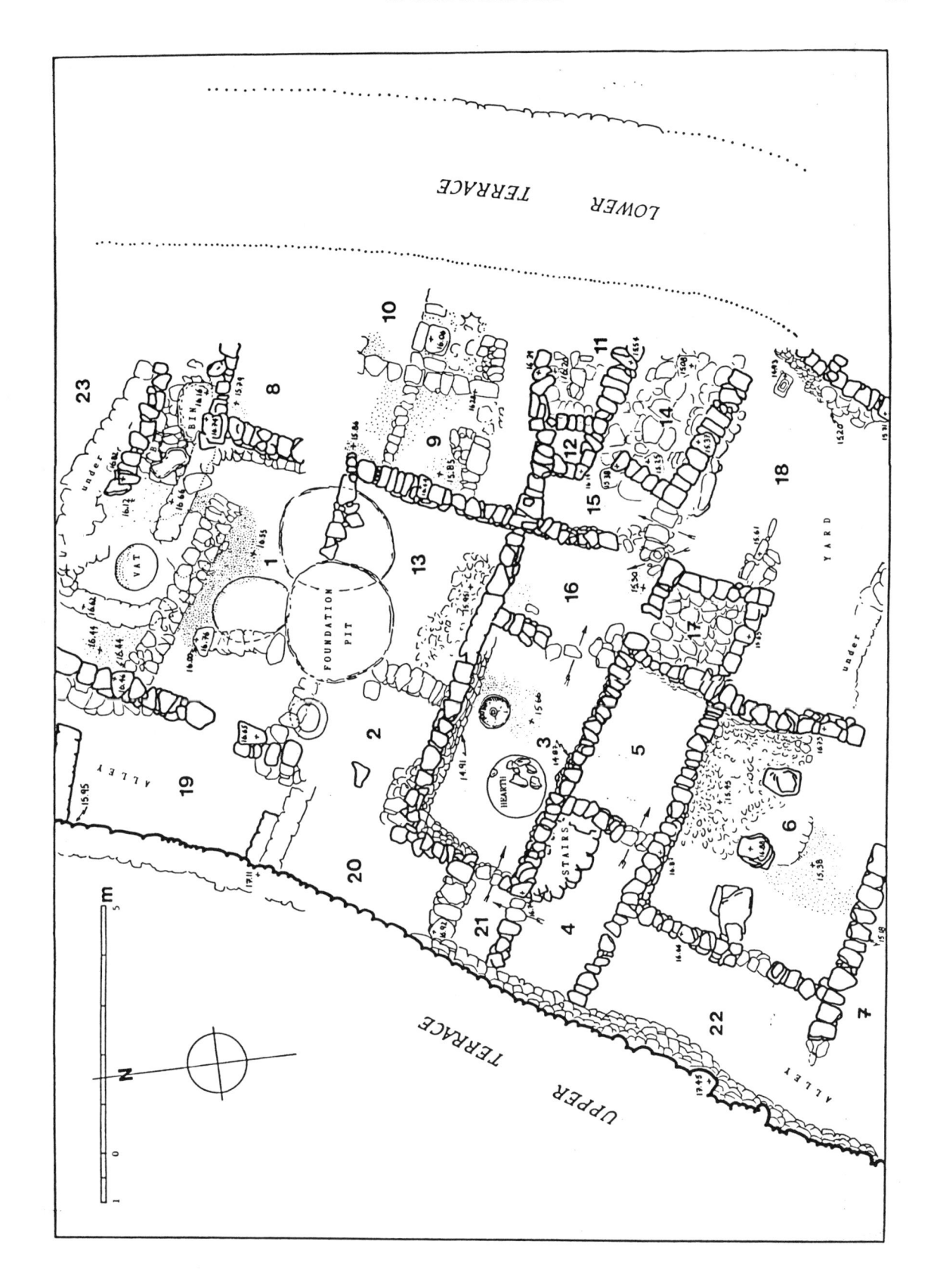

Fig. 239. Schematic stone-for-stone drawing of Field VII showing Stratum IX rooms. Drawing by K. Djerf.

Fig. 240. Looking north in Field VII Area 8 at Platter Bin 1769 and Vat 1770 (augmented) as reused in Stratum IX. The bands of red clay spilling into Vat 1770 appear in the small vertical cut at the extreme right edge.

poorly attested course of a Stratum X wall. Walls 1034 and 1080 were probably new foundations, but the pillars in House A probably reused a Stratum X wall as stylobate. All indications are that Stratum IX people represented continuity with the people of Stratum X, rebuilding promptly upon Stratum X ruins, reusing Stratum X facilities, but now developing planned use of space for houses.

House D: Rooms 1, 2 and 13. The first complex filled most of the north of the terrace. Room 1 was defined by Walls 1631, 1742, 1747 and probably 1646. Rooms 2 and 13 lay south of the line suggested by 1646, with southern definition at party wall 1337-1348.

Wall 1646 was mostly contained within the balk between Areas 5 and 8 and was very poorly preserved. Removal of the balk with care at check-ing stratification stopped when it reached 1646 and a scrap of surface attached to it. Wall 1646 did not emerge on the Area 5 side of the balk and does not show in Ill. 113 = VII BB, where it would come between Wall 1449 and the intrusion of the Stratum VIII Vat 1395 installation. Nor is the relation between it and a portion of wall west of the intrusion ("1646-west," later 1630B) at all clear; they do not constitute a straight line in the architect's measurements. Tentatively it is concluded that a wall on this line extended from Wall 1631 on the west to Wall 1449 on the east and separated Room 1 from Rooms 2 and 13.

Disturbances from above contribute to the uncertainty. Wall 1646 was undercut by Pit 17.131–14.139, a huge silo not fully defined until a site visit by some of the staff six months after the expedition had left the field in 1964. The silo was dug from late in the Stratum IX period; it was lime-lined, with three successive limed bottoms, at elevations 14.35, 14.25 and 13.90. It belled from a narrow opening probably at late Stratum IX Surface 1748, and widened to undercut Wall 1646. It reached a depth, then, of as much as 2.40 m. Its late discernment meant that no pottery collection was confined to it, and pottery in adjacent baskets may be contaminated. Noteworthy is the fact that it was so densely packed with fill that it eluded the observation of the excavators.

Pit 17.155, also dug from later Stratum IX Surface 1748, together with the trench for the installation of the Stratum VIII Vat 1395 (VII BB and DD = Ill. 116), and Pits A, B and C on Ill. 115 = VII CC, all made the tracing of surfaces exceedingly difficult. Pit 17.155, shown in section on VII DD on the west balk of Area 8, which caught only its extreme west edge, was not discerned until the last day of the 1964 campaign and had contaminated pottery collections from the tight layering adjacent to this balk. The locations of 17.155 and 17.139 (in Room 1 flanking the foundation pit for the later Strata VIII-VII installation, fig. 239) are approximate; their precise locations are irretrievable. Intrusion 1844, which cut off the east end of Wall 1757 and extended into the unexcavated region of Area 7 to the east, further complicates interpreting House D. All these intrusions mean that only a few loci were effectively isolated; Stratum IX pottery judgments focus on them.

Room 1 was approached through a break in Wall 1631 from the alley along Terrace Wall 1640. There were four changes in surfacing in Room 1, to go with three architectural arrangements: following two surface systems of the open rectangle of the original Room 1, the arrangement of space was altered first by adding Wall 1790, Wall 1749 and pillars 1655 and 1656, and then by building Wall 1741 and a probable dividing wall off-line with Wall 1646 as it might have extended westward. All this change means that Room 1 affords the best prospects in Field VII of close Stratum IX separations. The succession of changes, best followed in VII DD and the top plans, is as follows:

1. Surface 1753, VII DD:#44, is the earliest Stratum IX floor system. It almost certainly connected to Surface 1774 in the corridor between Walls 1742 and 1757, at elevation 15.93. Other elevations on 1753-1774 were at 16.25, 16.02 and 15.91, the slope running from northwest to southeast. Stratum VIII Bin 1787 (VII DD at the north limit of excavation) interrupted connections to Wall 1742 at the balk, but to the east Surface 1753 ran to the foundations of Wall 1742 at the point where they rested upon the collapsed rocks of Stratum X Wall 1768 beneath it.

A brittle band of red clay on 1753, similar to one on Stratum X Surface 1758, ran to the rim stones on Vat 1770 (1770A) and dipped into the vat (fig. 240). Flagstoned Bin 1769, founded in Stratum X, was also reused; the close proximity of layering between 1758 and 1753 is shown in fig. 226 (above). At Surface 1753, Bin 1769 would have been sunken, elevations on its sloping base being 15.82 at the west, 15.63 at the east. Several thick flagstones, locus 1755, lay flush with Surface 1753 north of Vat 1770, near Wall 1742.

Bin 1771, near the vat and between Walls 1741 and 1749 on Ill. 102, was a feature of the 1753 system. Near the west face of Wall 1747, Surface 1753 showed two laminae, through the lower of which Pit 1798-17.118 was dug before the upper covered it. The 47 indicator sherds found in this compound pit should be definitive for earliest Stratum IX. The pottery collected from beneath and within the most assured segments of Surface 1753 includes 13 indicator sherds, some field-analyzed as Stratum IX.

2. Surface 1752 also covered the entire area of Room 1. It almost certainly connected to Surface 1772 in the corridor between Walls 1742 and 1757. One portion is displayed on Ill. 102 at elevation 16.12 as widely spaced dots just to the east of Vat 1770 near Wall 1742. It is VII DD:#42. When the balk between Areas 8 and 9 was later removed, a segment of the same floor was found preserved beneath Wall 1790, shown on VII CC as #1 to the left of Pit B, and probably as the surface within #19 on VII AA.

Within the corridor between Walls 1742 and 1757, two stone-lined bins sat on 1752-1772, one against the face of Wall 1742 with rim stones as high as 16.82 and the other against Wall 1757 with rim stones at 16.16. Both connect to the 1752 system.

As with Surfaces 1753 and 1758, there was a band of brittle red clay on 1752 adjacent to the rim stones on Vat 1770, but in this case the band did not plunge into the installation but covered soil subsiding into it; with 1752-1772, the 1769-1770 installation had gone out of use.

The 1752 system was separated from the 1753 system by crumbly soil 0.05 to 0.10 m thick. Fifty-one sherds were registered from this layer, but contamination from Pit 17.155 in the southwest of Area 8 is possible. All were field-analyzed as containing no pottery later than IX; included were sherds of Samaria Ware B. A collection of 18 sherds in basket B64 VII.8.28A is trustworthy, identified as coming from within laminae of Surface 1752.

The northern portion of House D, from Wall 1646 north, was probably not a room of the house but an exterior yard through the first phases of Stratum IX. The many intrusions along the projected line separating Room 1 from Rooms 2 and 13 preclude defining whether Rooms 2 and 13 were part of the yard or were a small house opening onto the yard; the latter seems more likely.

3. The third stage of development in Room 1 involved building Walls 1790 and 1749 (fig. 237, cross-hatched). Wall 1790 was preserved only within the balk between Areas 8 and 9 and was discovered when the balk was excavated late in

Fig. 241. Looking south in Field VII Area 8. The two decayed limestone pillars 1743 are at left center, on Stratum IX Floor 1744. The meter stick lies on Stratum VIII Floor 1739.

the campaign. It bent in such a way as to suggest that it probably made some connection with Wall 1749, but the intrusion of Wall 1741, still later within Stratum IX, obscured the relation between 1790 and 1749, and the intrusion of Stratum VIII Wall 1740 further complicates interpretation. Probably with the building of Walls 1790 and 1749, one now could have entered Room 1 both from the alley along the terrace wall and from the narrow passageway between 1742 and 1757-1749 on the north.

Pit 17.155 was dug as these new walls were constructed. The surface throughout Room 1 was locus 1748-1634, which ran over the top of the pit, connecting Walls 1790, 1749 and almost certainly 1747. On VII CC this surface is at the top of what is drawn in detail. (At the beginning of the 1964 season it was recognized that VII CC section should be recorded, whereas in 1962 it had been thought that VII AA and VII DD would serve the needs of vertical portrayal.)

Surface 1748-1634 appears as VII DD:#40. It ran at elevations 16.44 in the nook between Wall 1631 and 1790 in the far north of the region (medium-spaced dots on Ill. 102) to 16.34 and 16.29 in the south. Compared to the slope in surfacings 1753 and 1752, this surface tended to be level. Lamination within the 1748 system, especially pronounced in the nook between 1631 and 1790 (loci 1793 and 1795) provided small collections of pottery, of which 8 indicator sherds were saved; another 25 indicator sherds come from the makeup for locus 1748, over surface 1752.

Section VII DD shows #40 running to join two stones just at the southwesternmost corner of Area 8, traces of a wall running westward. There may have been a dividing wall at this point, extending into Area 9 as Wall 1664 and defining the north boundary of Room 2, but the evidence is too slim to establish this.

In the former alley exterior to Wall 1631 on the west, Walls 1635 and 1353 were built, closing the passage. Room 19 became the door-yard to House D, while Room 20 became a new room attached to the house, reached from Room 2. Remnants of an irregular flooring in Room 20, locus 13.107, showed undulating elevations from 16.47 at the west to 16.37 and 16.46 at the center, to 16.42 at the east—all discerned when the balk between Areas 6 and 9 was dismantled; VII BB:#20 shows a portion of this flooring, disrupted by Pits 13.104 = #18 and 13.101 = Pit #19 to the west, and by the foundation pit for the Stratum VIII vat and platter system. These and further disruptions removed all indications of earlier Stratum IX surfacings in Room 20.

4. Wall 1741 displaced 1790 and 1749 as the northern boundary of House D late in Stratum IX, riding upon Surface 1748 at its east end but set down into 1748 toward the west. In connection with its construction, a trench (Pit A on VII CC) was dug, cutting the three previous Stratum IX surfacings, and two stone pillars erected, loci 1656 and 1655, with some hint of a stylobate between them. An elevation on the top of the northern pillar, 1656, was at 16.76, while its footing was at 16.00. Surface 1744 could be traced at elevation 16.55 along the south face of Wall 1741 (dense dotting on Ill. 102), probably appearing as surface #39 on VII DD. Other recorded elevations were at 16.51 and 16.48, again suggesting that the flooring was nearly level. On floor 1744 close to the west face of Wall 1747 stood two upright pillars of degenerate limestone, perhaps calcined by heat, which crumbled upon exposure; they are locus 1743, shown in fig. 241, their purpose unclear.

Outside the newly-defined Room 1 to the north, Surface 1638-1788 was traced from Wall 1790 westward that topped Wall 1631 at the north limit of the field (VII AA:#17), at elevation 16.54 to 16.59. At the balk, it humped over Wall 1631, indicating that the north portion of this wall was no longer in use. In the space designated Room 23 on the plan, the triangle north of Wall 1742, Surface 1762 = AA:#18, sloped from elevation 16.75 to 16.55 west to east. It met at its east end a wall face preserved in elevation in the north balk of the field, Wall 17.115 (not shown on plan), which may have defined a narrow alley at the very north edge of the complex. Surface 1750 at elevation 16.37 was defined beneath 1762 but could not be effectively traced. Both surfaces belong late in Stratum IX.

The thick jumble of walls that had by now developed along the north of House D (Walls 1790-1749-1742) may have been rebuilt into a base for stairs leading to a second story of House D. What seems clear is that what had been a yard had now been incorporated into a home, and that a pillar-style wall now defined a room at the west of Room 1, comparably to construction in Room 6 in House A to the south.

Definition of Rooms 2 and 13 is unclear because of intrusions that cut Wall 1646 and robbed any junction of the east portion of 1646 and a fragment of wall running east from Wall 1631B into the deep intrusion caused by the placement of Stratum VIII installation 1395. The combination would have been the north limit of Rooms 2 and 13, but as Ill. 102 shows they were not in line. Wall 1349, built later within Stratum IX, divided Rooms 2 and 13. When Wall 1349 was removed, a surface defined by crumbling plaster was preserved under it and either side of it, locus 1351-1486 at elevation sloping eastward from 15.64 to 15.51; it appears as layer #28 on both the VII DD and the VII BB sections. It presumably goes with the lowest Stratum IX surface in Room 1, locus 1753, in which case there would have been a drop in elevation of between 0.30 and 0.40 m from Room 1.

With the construction of Wall 1349 separating Rooms 2 and 13, a later Stratum IX surface was laid in Room 13 in the form of cobbling 1348-1450 at elevations 15.93 to 15.95 (Ill. 102; VII DD:#23). Wall 1349 was its western limit; no corresponding surface could be traced in Room 2, due to severe disruptions shown in the BB section. Apparently House D at first was a long room (Rooms 2 and 13) at a step down from the yard to its north in Room 1. At the stage when Walls 1749 and 1790 were built, the 1748 stage, the house consisted of Rooms 1, 2 and 13. When the balk between Areas 5 and 8 was excavated to just below the level of the top of Wall 1646, a tiny portion of surfacing possibly related to 1744 was discerned along the south face of 1646 at elevation 16.40.

Room 20, reached from Room 2 through the break in Wall 1354-1631 north of the corner of Walls 1352 and 1337, was filled with random stone fall, probably the collapse of the second story of House B (see below). Patches of beaten earth surfacing were noted beneath the stone fall, probably representing the surface of the early Stratum IX alleyway, but records are faulty in describing the surface and no elevations were taken, nor was pottery isolated in connection with it. In the original plan, one could enter Room 2 from the alley along the terrace wall; subsequently, Room 20 may have been incorporated into House D as a back room,

Fig. 242. Looking south at Field VII Area 5. Stone Platform 1471 left of center, with Floor 1463 of Stratum IXB in Room 9 to the right (west) of the platform. Wall 1461 separates the platform from Room 9 running toward the camera in the center.

when Walls 1353 and 1635 closed the alley. A possible late Stratum IX surface in Room 20 is locus 13.107, discerned only when the balk between Areas 6 and 9 was excavated; it sloped up to the south in this narrow strip, with elevations 16.37 at the north edge, 16.46 at the south. Stratum VIII Wall 1636 was above it. It is shown as VII BB:#20.

House C: Rooms 8 through 12. Rooms 8–12 apparently formed the western part of another home. Here there is a problem: if the projection of the eastern terrace wall, from 1154 at the south curved to include portions of Wall 1189 and 1561 (not drawn) visible in the edges of the unexcavated Areas 4 and 7 to the east, were correct, House C was not viable. The more likely limit is the line indicated on the plan farther east. There would then have been space for House C roughly equivalent to that occupied by the rest of the houses on the terrace. If that is correct, the Strata VIII and VII peoples who followed changed the terrain and brought the line of the terrace westward. In doing that they would have destroyed evidence for the east part of House C. The gross disturbance indicated on VII BB involving ##24, 25, 26 and 32 would be involved—loci 1844 and 1560 in field records. An ephemeral piece of wall designated 17.128 encountered near Wall 1757 at the north of Room 8 but not drawn on plan was in this disturbed region but its part in Stratum IX architecture could not be determined.

All of this means that little sense can be made of House C except at its west and south edges. Its south limit was probably the eastward extension of Wall 1448 combined with Wall 1472, which continued the line slightly offset northwards and off-line. Walls 1464, 1465 and 1466 were later additions to the interior architecture. As for Wall 1461, the post at the junction of 1465 and 1461 was a pillar with a deep foundation, although its relation to surfaces to be described below could not be firmly established. The post probably represented the pillar-wall style of construction attested in House A and in the later developments in House D. Another such pillar may have stood at the junction of Walls 1464 and 1461, and still another may have been at the balk face at the north of Area 5, shown in VII BB as 1461. The stones connecting these pillars and thus constituting Wall 1461 were placed later.

The complex made up of Walls 1152, 1456 and 1490 (Rooms 11 and 12) was likely to be foundation for stairs to a second story. Wall 1456, while deeply founded, butted Wall 1448 and was probably attached after 1448 was laid.

In short, then, Rooms 8–9 were probably at first one room defined by a pillar-style wall on the

Fig. 243. Looking west into Room 14 paved with Flagstones 1153. Wall 1152 at right. The other walls pictured belong to higher strata.

line of Wall 1461. A continuous surface filled the space from 1757 to 1448-1472, including Room 10. Beaten-earth surface 1497-1492-1480 was preserved in patches throughout these rooms, at elevations 15.79 in the northwest corner of Room 8 (Ill. 102), 15.60 beneath the elbow of 1461-1465, and 15.57 near Wall 1472. On VII BB, this elusive surface appears as #23, running from the very foot of Wall 1449 eastward to the pillar of 1461 preserved only in the balk. The surface clearly ran beneath the stones which were placed to fill in between the pillars and make Wall 1461 to the south; only at the balk could the surface be shown to have met what has been proposed as a pillar of the original locus 1461.

From 1492, Silo 1494 was cut deep into the ruins below. The mouth of the silo was covered by a confined locus of rough plaster, 1493, above Surface 1492. Its mouth was roughly 0.50 m in diameter and the shaft continued at this diameter to a depth of 1.25 m, at which point it was expanded to reach a diameter of 1.35 m at its bottom, 2.43 m from the mouth. The top 0.20 m of the shaft was hollow, while the remainder was filled with loosely-packed earth of uniform character. The bottom of the silo gave off a pungent odor of charred wood. Apparently the silo was filled after the earliest phase of Stratum IX, then capped when its contents settled during a subsequent phase of IX. There were 75 indicator sherds saved from the filling, none reconstructible into complete vessels. The silo was not used as a dump, then, and was probably purposely filled in one effort with fill that might have been transported from any place nearby. The collection was field-analyzed as a mixture coming down to Stratum IX in date.

The sequence of change in House C was probably as follows (fig. 237):

1. Wall 1466, only 0.35 m in width, was built abutting Wall 1449. Between its west end and the stones of Wall 1449, a portion of the mud and plaster facing of Wall 1449 was preserved, proving the succession and suggesting that the east face of Wall 1449 was indeed an interior face. Wall 1461 was made into a continuous wall. Wall 1465 ran eastward from the pillar of the earliest phase; its foundations were dug deep, to a founding elevation of 15.54, into a miasma of rock and decay from Wall 1472 northward. In this south part of Room 10, the earliest phase surface, 1492, could not be discerned, but it was found north of Wall 1465, not clearly running to meet it but instead apparently lost in the rocky collapse at its base.

Rib walls 1468 and 1469 were built in units 11 and 12, set into a loose matrix of loose, dark ashy soil that could be scooped out by hand with-

Fig. 244. Looking north at Stratum IX remains in Field VII Areas 2 and 5. The meter stick lies on Flagstones 1153 in Room 14, Surface 1142 in Yard 18 in foreground. Later Stratum IX features added (cf. Ills. 102 and 103) include Wall 1159 between Room 14 and Yard 18, Pillar 1150 to which the left end of the meter stick points, at its west end, the upright slabs of 1157 creating bins against the south face of 1159. Complex 1155 in lower right corner on Floor 1142, against Wall 1154.

out tools. If this were a stair, it had to have been rebuilt and reinforced. It also may have been a latrine.

The beaten-earth surface to go with this complex was 1474, lying on a colorful makeup of decayed brick and chalk above the earliest surface 1492-1497. It was at approximate elevation 15.69 in Room 9, and was detected beneath Wall 1464. It ran to a small stretch of cobbling (locus 1473) against the north face of Wall 1466. Thirty-nine indicator sherds were saved from the makeup of the surface, field-analyzed as Stratum IX.

The ashy soil in the stairway complex and the makeup of brick and chalk under 1474 suggests that something catastrophic, whether localized or widespread, intervened between the 1492-1497 phase and the 1474 phase in House C.

2. Wall 1464, the thinnest wall in the complex at 0.23 m in width was added after Surface 1474 was in use. Continuing its line eastward past Wall 1461 was the north limit of a stone platform, locus 1471, filling the rectangular space east of Wall 1461 between 1465 and the extended line of 1464 (fig. 242). An elevation on a stone at its north edge was at 16.06. The platform's east limit was discerned at the edge of the unexcavated area to the east, indicating it was square; it measured 1.96 m north-south. The stones in the platform were selected for their flat upper surfaces and were often rectangular, allowing for a close fit. Chalk or lime plaster appeared in places on the surface. Beneath platform 1471 was debris that was full of air pockets and contained veins of charcoal as of burnt twigs. This whole complex is pictured in fig. 244.

The system of surfacing with this third phase of Stratum IX was a thinly separated series designated 1489, topped by 1463 and then by 1467. Disturbance in the north part of Room 8, mentioned above, precluded discerning upper Stratum IX surfacing there, but the sequence was present in Room 9 and just to the north of Wall 1464. The sequence all attached to Wall 1464 and Platform 1471. Surface 1489 is shown on Ill. 102 at elevation 15.86 adjacent to Wall 1449 just at the north balk of Area 5; 1463 is shown at elevation 15.89 just to its southeast near Wall 1464. In Room 9, elevations on 1463 were at 15.83 and 15.74, while a pair of stones marking the doorsill at the east end of Wall 1466 was at 16.02. Surface 1467 was represented by the patch in the corner of Walls 1449 and 1464 in Room 9 at elevation 15.85. There were places where two of these beaten-earth surfaces were found superimposed, 0.04 to 0.10 m apart, and in one or two places all three were identified, but the separation could not be traced for large areas. A collection of 5 indicator sherds were isolated as embedded in 1463, while makeup sealed within and under this system yielded nearly 100 sherds field-analyzed as Stratum IX.

Walls 1181 and 1186 defined Rooms 14 and 15 south of the proposed stairway of House C and curving along a southern extension of Wall 1449. Walls 1181 and 1186 were built with the typical early Stratum IX construction style of headers

Fig. 245. Floor 1142 with broken Stratum IX cooking pot on it, as it comes to the west balk of Field VII Area 2. In the balk is Fill 1139.

through a 0.50 to 0.60 m width. Room 14 was paved with a fine flagstone floor, locus 1153 (fig. 243). Its elevation was at 15.25 on the west, 15.08 further east, 15.03 adjacent to Wall 1188 (probably = 1160; not on plan) in the balk between Areas 1 and 2. Wall 1188 connected Walls 1152 and 1181, but rested upon the eastward continuation of 1153 flagstones and must have been a later development within Stratum IX. The flagstones in 1153 were selected for their thickness, usually only 0.06 m, and set on a firm soil beneath except toward the east where there were air pockets. Stratum IX sherds were among the 36 indicator sherds, predominantly of Stratum X, from this makeup, 1153A.

West of Wall 1186 in Room 15 a beaten earth surface was continuous with Surface 1142 throughout Yard 18 to the south. Apparently one entered Room 15 from the yard through an opening at the east end of Wall 1181 and then went on into Room 14 through a narrow opening at the north end of Wall 1186. All in all, though, these two rooms, especially with the elegant flagstone flooring, constitute a puzzling architectural entity in relation to the layout of House C.

Yard 18 and Rooms 14 and 15. In a subsequent phase within Stratum IX, a new layout of walls was built over Walls 1181 and 1186. The new construction was not recorded on a field drawing, but it is pictured in fig. 244. A key ingredient to it was Pillar 1150 erected on the junction of 1181 and 1186, against which Wall 1159 abutted and ran eastward to the limit of excavation. Parallel to Wall 1159 and 0.35 m to its south was Wall 1157, a row of upright slabs resting on a more substantial bed of stones. Between the two were a series of bins with flat stone bottoms (locus 1165), on which rested carbonized material of an undetermined kind. At the east end of the series was a mud-packed socket for a jar base.

Another new construction was Wall 1147, positioned on the line of Wall 1186. Curved Wall 1156 ran from Pillar 1150 west and then north to reach the south end of Wall 1449, where again the junction took the form of a post. More stones then connected this walling to the corner made by Walls 1180 and 11.105 at the northwest corner of Yard 18. Apparently, then, the accesses to the region that had been Rooms 14 and 15 were all closed, and the question arises as to how one entered House B, as well as what the access from House C into Rooms 14 and 15 would have been.

Within Rooms 14 and 15, and over the surface of Yard 18, there accumulated a thick fill of chalky soil, locus 1139, with much charcoal, orange mud of what was probably decayed brick,

Fig. 246. Looking east at Field IX Areas 3 and 6, Houses A and B, Rooms 3–7.

and piles of irregularly placed rocks. Fig. 245 shows the fill in the balk at the west of Area 2. It appears as VII DD:##26 and 25; at the balk a line of ash, separating #26 from #25, was thought to suggest a later Stratum IX layer, but within the excavated area this separation was not maintained, and sherds of Strata VIII-VI appeared in the chalky build-up virtually to Surface 1142, along with Stratum IX sherds. The explanation must be that erosion balanced accumulation throughout Stratum IX. The rebuild of Walls 1147 and 1159-1157 on Walls 1181 and 1186 represented a later stage of Stratum IX, but surfacing against the south face of 1159-1157 stayed at the same elevation.

Surface 1142 in Yard 18 sloped from elevations 15.28 near the south face of Wall 1157-1181, to 15.15 in the southwest corner of Area 2 to 14.93 on the mortar rim (see below) near Wall 1154. Surface 1142 was hard-packed beaten earth with a rubbery clay feel at places and patches of bright orange mud. In a few places above the surface, chocolate brown earth, locus 1144, lay directly on 1142. In 1144 the rare pottery included sherds of Strata VIII and VII.

The west limit of Yard 18 in its northwest corner was Wall 1180, the eastern wall of Room 17. Not quite touching Wall 1180, and extending 1.90 m eastward, was Wall 1143, a row of stone slabs set upright into Surface 1142 and held in place with red mud molded against it. Wall 1143 resembles the row of slabs along Wall 1157, 1.30 to 1.40 m north of it, which defined the bins along Wall 1159. Fig. 245 shows Surface 1142 adjacent to Wall 1143, with two large sherds of a Stratum IX cooking pot lying on it. Surface 1142 was traced to Wall 1154, doubtless the limit of the terrace (its east face was not exposed in excavation).

Against the west face of Wall 1154 was a small platform of stones on 1142, including the mortar shown on plan and a small oven preserved up to its rim (fig. 244, lower right). The whole complex is locus 1155. It rested on ash and charcoal, and evidence of fire spread out on Surface 1142 adjacent to it. One of the patches of bright orange mud characterized 1142 adjacent to 1155. Two granite pestles, registered objects B62 #569 and #583, were embedded in 1142. Of great significance for the date are two complete pyxides (B62 Obj.##552 and 554) found in 1142 in the southwest corner of Area 2 as it sloped up to the top of Wall 11.110 of Stratum X protruding through the surface. An indication of the combination of erosion and accumulation of 1142 is the fact that wedges of the 1142 orange smudge ran against the faces of Wall 1157 and Wall 1181 beneath it, of Wall 1154, and of Wall 11.110. Elsewhere throughout the region among these walls 1142 was barely definable from the later 1139 chalky build-

House B: Rooms 3, 4, 5, 16, 17 and 21. At the earliest stage of Stratum IX, one entered House B from Yard 18, at the point later filled in by blockage 1156, and from the alley along the terrace wall. Wall 1034, the party wall between this complex and House A to its south, was the south termination of the alley along the terrace wall. From Yard 18, one entered Room 16, then passed through a door in Wall 1035 into Room 3. (Later, this entrance may have been partially closed by a poorly attested segment of wall shown on the top plans.) From the alley, one entered Room 3 through a door at the south end of Wall 1352, or passed on into Room 4 through a door at the east end of Wall 1355 and thence into Room 5. Room 17 is a stone platform reached from Room 16.

The walls of this complex were preserved to as many as six courses above floor levels, and the main walls had deep foundations. Wall 1337, the party wall with House D, was founded at elevation 14.91 and preserved to as high as 16.63; Wall 1338 was founded at 14.78 and preserved to as high as 16.74; no founding elevation was read on Wall 1034, but it was preserved to 16.87 (fig. 246). The corner of Walls 1337 and 1352 at the northwest of Room 3 was curved, both on the outside and the inside. A buttress at the outer face of the curve served as the south doorpost of the door into Room 2 of House D. Wall 1337 showed a lean to the north; it was more pronounced than shifts observable in other Stratum IX walls, but others in House B also suggested bowing or shifts slightly off true vertical.

Room 3 had a well-preserved beaten-earth floor, locus 1341, at elevation 15.66. Set into it (Ill. 102) was the rim and shoulder of a large store jar, rim down, which may have served as a fixed-in-place brazier (pottery registry B62, #2206, locus 1350); a smudge of burning was on the floor adjacent to it. Similar installations with marks of burning have been found in house floors at Hazor and Meṣad Hashavyahu. West of it, not drawn on the formal plan but shown in approximately the right location on fig. 239, was a cluster of stones in a shallow saucer black with ash (loci 1370-1371)—almost certainly a hearth, at elevation 15.55. The makeup for Surface 1341, above the Stratum X surfaces close below yielded 67 indicator sherds of which a few were of Stratum IX date.

Room 16 just to the east of Room 3 had two patches of preserved surface, locus 1487, at elevations 15.45 in the northwest corner and 15.30 in the southeast (VII DD:#29). Within the thickness of this surface as it built up were 37 indicator Stratum IX sherds, while from its makeup down to Stratum X another 7 sherds analyzed as Stratum X were registered. This is a good locus for Stratum IX forms.

Rooms 3 and 16 were severely disturbed by the drainage system of Stratum VII House 1727. The large intrusion shown on VII DD beneath Wall 1436 is locus 1393-1397, the stone filling of the drainage. Layer #24 in the section is featureless but seems to be further fill from later strata, reaching down to the early Stratum IX floor here; an ephemeral hard-packed surface was noted for a very short stretch in the balk between Areas 5 and 6 when it was separately excavated, a possible later Stratum IX surface. There is no firm evidence of a floor from later in Stratum IX preserved in Rooms 3 and 16. What does point to later use is the blocking of the doorways, from Yard 18 into Room 16, from Room 21 into Room 3 as well as from Room 21 to Room 4 and from Room 4 to Room 5. A wall built across the alley, Wall 1353, appears to have cut off access from the north. Elevations on the blockages suggest that such later Stratum IX surfaces as may have been present were at elevations at least 0.60 to 0.70 m above the earlier ones. Strata VIII and VII incursions destroyed them.

The northeast quadrant of Room 4 was filled with a rock-fall, some of which must have fallen from second story walls, but some of which were the foundations for stairs leading to the second floor, locus 1358 against the corner of Walls 1338 and 1343. The collapse fell onto what is presumed to be the earliest surface for Stratum IX, but the collapse rendered its nature hard to define. In the collapse was an unusually large number of registered objects: a bone tube, three spindle whorls, a flint saw, an iron chisel, an iron three-pronged digging tool and another prong of a similar tool, the foot of a faience figurine, an iron spear point, a marble scarab, and a fragment of a granite bowl.

The items in the debris, which showed no marks of burn, of brick or beam fragments, and only the spear point as an instance of weaponry, can be taken as a sample of the equipment from the living space of a typical family lost in a catastrophe.

In Room 5, a clear beaten earth Floor 1347 with scattered stones was at elevation 15.39. Seven registered sherds from above it included Stratum VIII forms, suggesting later intrusion.

Room 17 = locus 11.114 is a curiosity, a rhomboid platform of field stones laid in parallel east-west rows filling the space demarcated by Walls 1035, 1034, 1180 and 11.105. Elevations were approximately 15.59 to 15.38 on the interior stones, almost as high as the surrounding walls in many cases, although the stones in 11.105 flanking what seems to be the narrow access to this platform are at 15.90 and 15.73. There were two courses of stones within the "crib," resting upon a packed earth surface, locus 11.114A beneath them, at elevation 15.10 to 15.15.

The eastern limit of locus 11.114 is shown as the junction of Wall 1180 in elevation and Wall 11.105 on VII DD. The interior lay within the balk between Areas 2 and 3, and yielded 8 indicator sherds from among the rocks, of which some are of Stratum IX date, some earlier. It was covered by the same fill that covered Yard 18, with a mix of later period pottery, and had a pocket of the chocolate brown earth isolated as 1144 in places upon Surface 1142 on it. While Room 17 looks like an intrusion into Yard 18 and an adjunct to the adjacent houses, it was founded as deeply as the rest of the earliest Stratum IX structures and was apparently an original part of the plan. Its purpose is elusive—perhaps a bathroom?

House A: Room 6. Room 6, the main room of House A could probably have been entered from Yard 18 at its southeast corner. It ran from the deeply-founded Wall 1034 to Wall 1080, founded not so deep at elevation 15.18, a wall built in typical Stratum IX header style. Wall 21.028, the west limit of Room 6, was preserved to elevation 16.66 and at one point to 16.96, over a meter above its footing. At the start of Stratum IX, there was an access from Room 22 along the terrace wall through Wall 21.028, approached from the south since Wall 1034 terminated travel from the north along the terrace wall (fig. 246).

Room 6 was divided into two from the start of the period by the pillar-style wall represented by Pillars 1044 east and west and probably by boulder 1050, perhaps the base of a third pillar, against the east face of Wall 21.028. The two 1044 pillars, stacks of three roughly-shaped cubes 0.50 m on a side, rested upon Wall 1053 of Stratum X, now serving as stylobate. Boulder 1050 was 1.10 by 0.55 m and sat on a bed of smaller stone. Elevations on Wall 1053 were at 15.46 and 15.29, while the tops of Pillars 1044 were at 16.88 (west) and 16.15 (east).

The first Stratum IX surface north of the pillars to Wall 1034 was cobbled Surface 1047 at elevation 15.45. South of the pillars was plaster Floor 1060, which was twice resurfaced; the lowest layer was at elevation 15.38, the highest at 15.45. Between the two 1044 pillars, Floor 1060 touched an arc of small stones which may represent what was left of a bin.

A Stratum VII house was set into a deep saucer that encroached upon the south half of Room 6, removing any evidence of later developments within Stratum IX, except that the access from Room 22 was blocked up, suggesting that any surface south of the pillars would have been at a substantially higher elevation. North of the pillars, an accumulation of soil 0.60 m thick covered Cobbling 1047, topped by a later Stratum IX plastered Surface 1043. From the makeup for 1043, above 1047, six baskets of pottery yielding 22 indicator sherds were registered, including early Samaria ware frequently found elsewhere in later Stratum IX loci. No surface was discerned in Room 22, the access to Room 6; it was dug only in 1962 and left at an elevation probably above the earliest Stratum IX flooring.

Housing Units. This analysis has proposed housing units. Especially noteworthy are these features:

1. Deeply founded party walls were the strongest indication of separate housing units.

2. Three of the four houses probably had stairways leading to second stories; about House A there was no evidence for or against a second story.

3. Three houses (A, B and C) were entered from Yard 18; House D was reached from the northeast. Houses B, C and D could all have been reached from the north along the west terrace wall, while House A could have been entered from the south along the same wall.

4. All the houses showed a characteristic construction technique in their main walls, header stones across walls between 0.40 and 0.60 m wide. Their height of preservation shows this was a sturdy building technique.

5. There was a tendency to employ pillars to divide space, a style recalling similar structures in Iron II towns at Tell en-Nasbeh, Tell Beit Mirsim, Hazor, Beer Sheba and other contemporary sites. The tradition reached back to Iron I techniques, attested at Tel Masos, Giloh and Raddana, dating from the twelfth century, where the pillars were squared upright limestone blocks erected in a row on a stylobate and again dividing a room more or less in half (Fritz 1977; A. Mazar 1981: 6–11; Callaway 1983).

6. As they developed, Houses B, C and D appear to have divided larger spaces into smaller ones; some smaller spaces make one wonder how they could be used for living space, suggesting that the first floors were used more for storage and perhaps industry while the families lived upstairs. The hearth and brazier in Room 3 of House B may have been for industrial purpose just as easily as for living convenience. Cooking probably took place in the yard.

7. Houses A and B attested two phases during Stratum IX, while the north of House D suggested at least three as did House C. A frequent feature of the changes was the filling in of doorways and the erection of cross walls through the alley at the west, suggesting different traffic patterns and perhaps changes in the relationships among the occupants. Another feature is the dividing of spaces into smaller units, suggesting change of use. But some of the main walls, notably Walls 1337, 1352 and 1742, showed slippage and lean; against the outside of the corner of Walls 1337 and 1352 a reinforcement was built. Substantial rockfall suggesting upper story collapse filled Rooms 4 and 21. One set of evidence, then, suggests a major disruption during the period, while another set suggests occasional renovation.

A few hypotheses can be advanced for further testing:

a. Houses A, B and C may have constituted a cluster of dwellings belonging to one extended family, a "multiple family cluster." Yard 18 would have been for their common use, notably for baking and other food preparation. Since Houses C and D both had openings off the alley, these two homes may also have housed related families, but did not share outside yards.

b. House A was 4.00 by 4.25 m in interior space, or roughly 17 square meters, though the pillars used up some available space. House B, based on Rooms 3, 16 and 5 would have contained between 17 and 20 square meters, but with the likelihood that it had a second story it would have contained 35 to 40 square meters, and with the addition of Room 21 slightly more. House D included Rooms 13 and 2 at 5.50 by 3.00 m or 16.5 square meters, and at least in its later phases Room 1 at 5.20 by 4.00 m, another nearly 21 square meters. The extent of House C is uncertain. Both C and D probably had second stories, at least at some stage in their development.

Ethnoarchaeologists propose about ten square meters of living space required per person in typical Near Eastern village culture. The average size of a nuclear family calculated for this period is 4.1 to 4.3 (Stager 1985: 18, and bibliography there). If House A had a second story, each unit on the Field VII terrace could have housed a nuclear family. The second story may have been an addition as families grew in size.

Various of the rooms have characteristics pointing to special uses. Cobbled rooms, such as the north room of House A, may have been for housing animals (see below on the Stratum VII 1727 house). House B had no such facility and accesses to its ground floor were probably not wide enough for large cattle. Room 14 of House C, with its fine flagstone floor, ought to have had a different use; flagstones are not as good as cobbles for the care of animal feet or for the leaching of animal waste. Room 17 and the southern cubicle of Room 10 with their stone flooring, are possible candidates as bathrooms. Even smaller cubicles such as Rooms 21 and 12, and spaces beneath stairs, probably were used for storage.

c. The changes throughout the period covered by Stratum IX in this one region of the tell suggest an increase in population, with the expansion of houses outward and upward and the indications of cooperative use of space by extended families in clusters of housing as the key indications.

d. When G. E. Wright described Stratum IX in *SBBC*, his data came from the final weeks of the 1962 season, and pertained mostly to Houses A and B. That led to the confident division into two phases, IXA and IXB. The lean of Walls 1337/1448 and 1352 suggested earthquake. Alternatively, Wright suggested military destruction by the Syrian King Ben-Hadad between 860 and 855 BCE as the reason for disruption, although he acknowledged there was little evidence of military destruction. With the greater detail provided by the 1964 season, especially in Houses C and D, military attack loses cogency as the cause for the shift; earthquake remains a possibility, but much of the change seems to have come from renovation. Speaking of Stratum IXB and Stratum IXA may be of some use, but the succession of changes in specific spots may allow for even finer gradations in chronological change.

Field VIII

In Area 3 of this field, below the surface left by the Austro-German excavators just to the northwest of Field VII, a trace of Stratum IX building was set down into the previously described Stratum X complex of Wall 8006 with Floor 8013. Wall 8002 with surviving stones at elevation 20.00 ran perpendicular to Stratum X Wall 8006 and probably reused it. Two later pits flanked Wall 8002 (fig. 228, south face, uppermost left corner), but in a probe south of it, in the cut shown on plan, a surface was traced marked by three store jar bases set into sockets dug through the surface and then lined with red-brown earth and stones to prop the jar into position. The installation is of interest primarily because of this typical procedure for storage, presumably of grain, probably in a room of a home unexcavated to the south and east. The store jar bases have become lost; only their fabric could indicate their date, on comparison with the much more frequent and securely dated Stratum IX pottery from Fields IX and VII.

STRATUM VIII

Judging from the pottery forms found in what sealed deposits could be isolated, Stratum VIII was very close in date to Stratum VII, but separated in time from Stratum IXA. Poorly and thinly preserved, it provides evidence for a terminus a quo for Stratum VII. The stratigraphy in Fields VII and IX offers the best opportunities for identifying it; a phase beneath Stratum VII remains in Field I Areas 16 and 17 inside the East Gate probably belongs to it.

Field VII (Ill. 104)

The thin layer attributable to Stratum VIII in Field VII was disrupted by the builders of the 1727 house of Stratum VII. What was preserved was sealed beneath the Stratum VII house. South of that house, no layering of Stratum VIII was detected, due apparently to erosion in the Stratum VII yard there and the deep excavation dug for another Stratum VII house at the south edge of the excavation field. Scraps of ill-defined walls and surfacing to the east of the 1727 house may also belong to Stratum VIII.

The Building. The main structure occupied the terrace established by Stratum IX (Ill. 104). Stratum VIII builders added stones to the top of Terrace Wall 1628-22.011 to the west. The rebuild was set back toward the west some 0.50 m especially at the south end of the wall. The walls of the main structure did not use Stratum IX ruined walls as foundation. Preserved no more than two courses, they were set down slightly into Stratum IX destruction debris and humped over Stratum IX walls where they crossed them. As a result, elevations on the top of Stratum VIII walls are nearly the same as those on Stratum IX wall ruins, while floors of the Stratum VII building were as little as 0.10 m above them. Orientation of the main Stratum VIII structure was slightly off-line from Stratum IX below but conformed to that of Stratum VII above. With Stratum VIII a new topographic tradition began.

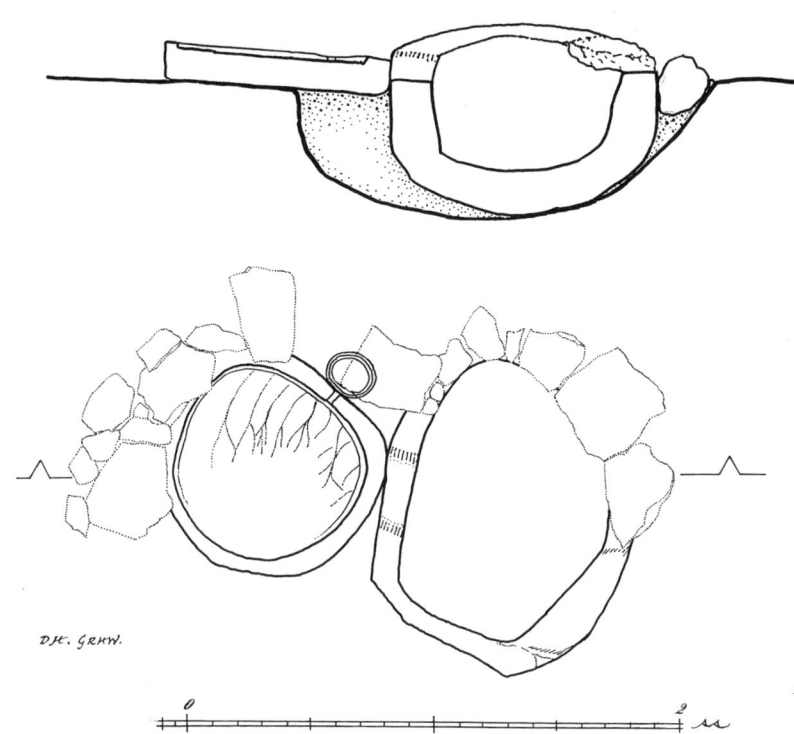

Fig. 247. Plan and section of Complex 1395–1396.

The south wall of the roughly rectangular structure, Wall 1336, ran from the Terrace Wall eastward and was preserved for two courses of rocks placed across its width of roughly 0.50 m. Elevations were at 16.76 at the west to 16.66 at the east. When the balk between Areas 5 and 6 was removed in the subsequent excavation season, the connecting portion was found, poorly preserved. It fails to show well on Ill. 116 = VII DD, but is probably represented by the rocks in #22 just to the north of Stratum VII Wall 1435, sealed by the Stratum VII flooring above.

Wall 1336 bonded to north-south wall 1746-1458, crossing VII BB. Wall 1746-1458 lay just beneath Wall 1734 of the Stratum VII house; the doorway through 1734 is positioned over 1458 on the section. Wall 1746 resembled 1336 in construction technique. It ran north to a probable junction with Wall 1740. The actual point of junction was disrupted and 1740 was of a different construction style; it was two stones wide and preserved for only one course, and came to an end after running approximately 6.50 m westward, crossing VII DD. An elevation on its preserved top was at 16.77.

These three walls formed an incomplete rectangle, with its two east-west walls running parallel to and just north of the lines which the walls of the subsequent Stratum VII house would follow, and its east wall directly beneath that of the Stratum VII house. At the west within the rectangle was an elbow of walls forming a small trapezoidal room against the terrace wall. Wall 1633 touched Wall 1636 at a disrupted junction. Elevations on the preserved tops were at 16.91 on 1633 and 16.97 on 1636.

Just east of 1633-1636, Wall 1630 ran east-west roughly 1.40 m in length, preserved to an elevation at 16.88. The westernmost stone of 1630 rested on stones of north-south Wall 1631B of Stratum IX. In line with 1630 was a poorly preserved pile of stones, suggesting an eastern termination of the wall. The builders of the Stratum VII 1727 house probably removed the portion of Wall 1630 that ran to the eastern pillar, as shown on Ill. 104.

The 1395-1396 Installation. The gap in Wall 1630 lay at the junction of the main north-south and east-west balks of the field, just north of the location of the hearth of the Stratum VII house

Fig. 248. Vat 1395 and Platter 1396. The channels in 1396 lead to groove emptying into the buried jar above the right end of the meter stick.

and Installation 1395-1396 beneath the hearth. It was further disrupted by the large pit shown on VII DD, not delineated by the excavators until after Field VII work had concluded. Current analysis proposes a change in phasing in this complex of features, assigning the Hearth 1443 to Stratum VII and the 1395-1396 complex to Stratum VIII (contra Campbell 1995).

The 1395-1396 complex (figs. 247 and 248) was probably a press or, less likely, a dyeing installation. If the complex was a press, Wall 1630 may have provided the anchorage for the carrying beam of the crushing mechanism. The installation is shown also on VII BB and DD. It first came to light in 1964 when the balks were removed to Stratum IX levels, where they remained at the conclusion of the Expedition's work; prior to that it had been noted slightly protruding from the balks and was assumed to be a platform for Hearth 1443.

Locus 1396 was a slightly saucered, grooved platter 0.90 m in diameter and 0.12 m thick. The perimeter groove was 0.05 to 0.08 m inside the outer edge and led to an outflow spout positioned over Store jar 1396A buried at its mouth. Meandering grooves on the platter lead to the perimeter groove. The platter tilted slightly to the north and east, but liquid pouring from the spout would have missed the jar opening unless some trajectory were achieved or a funneling device was used.

Touching the platter on its east edge was Vat 1395, hewn from *nari* limestone, with an irregular oval rim 0.79 m to 1.05 m in interior measure. The rim was 0.15 m thick, and the bottom was at most 0.55 m from the rim. A row of stones lay on the rim, heightening its depth; an elevation on a rim-stone at the east was at 16.83, while the vat bottom was at elevation 16.07. Some of the rim stones must have played some part in the installation's purpose, since Hearth 1443 of Stratum VII covered them. On the other hand, one of the rim stones lay over the mouth of the buried jar. Hence, the replacement of the vat and platter installation by the hearth seems to have taken place in several steps.

The foundation trench for the installation is evident on VII BB, but clarified in fig. 249. Its edge clearly cut earlier Stratum IX surfaces ##20 and 21, and the edge of Stratum VIII Surface 1398 = #17A slumped into it. Pottery from the foundation trench included one indicator form assigned in the field to Stratum VII on the basis of comparison with other forms from the house, but as has been noted, VIII and VII pottery forms are very similar.

When all the evidence is taken together, it seems clear that Stratum VII builders will have followed closely the lay-out of the Stratum VIII building, even though they did not position their

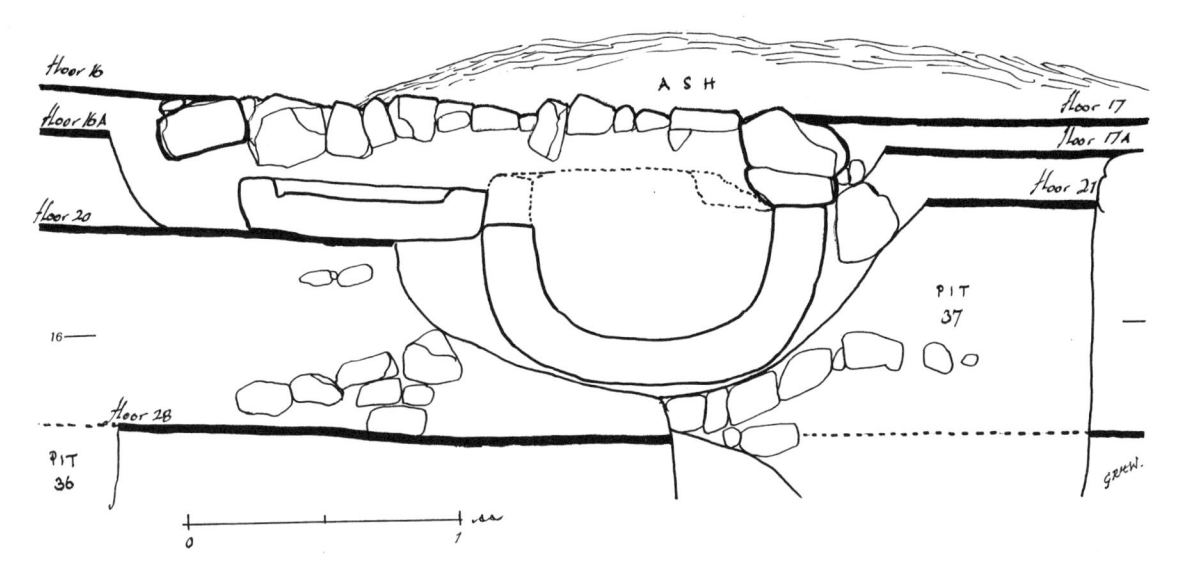

Fig. 249. Detail of section BB in Field VII, displaying Strata IX through VII layering around Complex 1395–1396.

walls on Stratum VIII foundations in every case. It is not difficult to visualize the Stratum VIII structure as an earlier design which was renovated by Stratum VII builders. Stratum VII builders preserved what parts of it they did to consolidate the foundations for the 1727 house.

Surfaces. The crucial surface for Stratum VIII was flooring 1641–1739, with elevations at 16.61, 16.64 and 16.71. It was discerned either side of the balk between Areas 8 and 9 as a limed surface with a rusty color over reddish soil passing over Wall 1741 of Stratum IX and reaching Wall 1740; the tops of the stones in 1741 were polished as if walked on as part of the surface. It appears as VII DD:#38. When the balk between Areas 8 and 9 was removed, it was clearly discerned, with a slope down to the south, but it does not show on VII CC. North of Wall 1740 a strip of cobbling beneath VII DD#36, locus 1783, connected to a stone-lined bin which was probably a Stratum VIII feature, but the region is cramped. Two segments of beaten earth floor just beneath the cobbling, loci 1784 and 1785, may also have belonged to Stratum VIII; all were observed to run above Wall 1790 of Stratum IX.

When the balk between Areas 5 and 6 was removed, either side of Wall 1336-1447 another patch of surfacing came to light at the edge of the vat and platter installation, Floor 1394 at elevation 16.44. In the 6/9 balk, at its removal, a crumbled chalk surface, locus 1398, was found; on it were fragments of crushed jar. It appears as a thick line, its western extension subsiding into Pit #19, beneath Stratum VII floor VII BB:#16, and as #16A on fig. 249. Pottery from Pit #19 = locus 13.101 is of Strata VIII and IX, and it appears to have been let down from Stratum VIII flooring. As its contents subsided over time, the plaster of Floor 1398 slumped into it, indicated by the plaster fragments between ##16 and 19 on VII BB. Finally, just west of Wall 1636 in the balk, and running 0.70 m from the wall to the edge of Pit 13.104, a fragment of Surface 13.105 was found within the balk but not reaching the south edge so as to appear on VII BB; it was at elevation 16.53. These few loci provide all the confidently stratified Stratum VIII ceramic evidence from Field VII.

To the east and north of the main structure, scraps of evidence may have been part of Stratum VIII. North of the junction of 1458 and 1740, a short stretch of Wall 1767 appeared in the north balk (VII AA). Wall 1851 probably related to it, also visible only in the section, not on plan; 1851 ran at an acute angle to the north limit of excavation and intersected a slim segment of wall, 1859, running back to the north but not reaching the north balk. Running east from the east face of Wall 1746 at its north end was Wall 1756-1850, with stone-lined pit 1844 against its south face. Surface 1852 connected Wall 1850 to Wall 1851 and was preserved to elevation 16.69. It was topped by the same sort of rust-colored limed surface as characterized 1739. Another surface, 1856, lay 0.55 m lower, also connecting these two walls. Pottery from these loci included Stratum VIII and Stratum VII forms. In this region (Area 7), there was a jumble of walls, as well as an intrusion within the elbow formed by Walls 1851 and 1859. Work stopped with the probe that reached surface 1856, so the stratigraphy is not held up from below. These features cannot be trusted to define Stratum VIII, but may augment ceramic definition.

Field IX (Ills. 135 [plan]; 141 = IX AA, 143 = IX CC, 144 = IX DD)

Conditions in Field IX were similar to those in Field VII, although in general the accumulation of Stratum VIII soil was somewhat thicker. The caveat expressed in connection with Stratum IX in this field applies here as well: excavation was divided between two seasons and the field reports do not connect well to one another. Plans were not corrected as matters clarified. The interpretation given here is worked out on the basis that the sections represent the most mature understanding of the phasing.

Stratum VIII remains (Ill. 135) in Field IX were constructed over a thick blanket of destruction debris of Stratum IXA, and as was true in Field VII few of its walls were founded on the ruined IXA walls beneath. The orientation of walls in the Stratum VIII complex was in accord with that of Stratum IX, however, and Stratum VII walls continued that orientation.

In the northeast of the field, the top course of Wall 9559 appeared at roughly the same thickness it had had since transitional Late Bronze/Iron Age times in Stratum XI. In Stratum VIII it served only to demarcate Open Yard 3 from vacant land (4) to its east. The same can be said for Wall 9044B, roughly perpendicular to 9559 at its south end.

Most of the north of the field lay within Yard 3 west of Wall 9559, bounded on the west by a poorly preserved elbow of Walls 9776A and Wall 9836 probably related to a building (1) off the northwest edge of the excavation field. The exterior face of Wall 9776A, the north-south portion of this elbow, was mud-plastered, suggesting that it was an exterior house wall. Encroaching upon the yard from the north was a corner of walls, 9528 with 9845; both wall lines continued in use in Strata VII and VI, and their location so close to the limit of excavation precluded ascertaining whether they were cut down into Stratum VIII or began in that period. If they did belong to Stratum VIII, they may have marked the corner of another house, Room 2.

A more coherent complex of small rooms lay to the south involving Walls 9819, 9313, 9310, 9314 and 9315. As Ill. 144 = IX DD shows, Wall 9313 was set down into Stratum IXA destruction debris and anchored on the flagstone floor 9319 = DD:#41, depressing it slightly. Wall 9314 was anchored upon Wall 9330 of Stratum IX at nearly the same depth, and continued northward as an ill-defined rebuild of Stratum IX Wall 9847. Decayed brick from the top of Wall 9314 (DD:#31) became part of the makeup for Stratum VII above it. Wall 9313 ran through the balk between Areas 2 and 4 to meet the elbow of Wall 9819 in the southwest corner of Area 4. Between 9313 and 9314 in the center of Area 2, Wall 9310, founded in Stratum IX, was rebuilt to cut off a small room, Room 7, here. Adjacent to it on the east was another room defined by Walls 9314 and 9315, whose eastward extent could not be ascertained, although it probably ran to the line of Wall 9068, now robbed out. This constituted Room 8. Two more small rooms, 10 and 11, lay south of the line of 9310 and 9315, separated from one another by Wall 9326, a curious wall in that its east face seems to have been a skin placed against its west face. Room 11 is obscured at its south limit by a confused jumble of stones.

Wall 9052 was founded in Stratum VIII if the surfacings here can be trusted, even though its position makes no sense in relation to the walls to its west, and even though it was reused in Stratum VII. Wall 9068 was preserved right at the balk between Areas 1 and 2, and probably joined the west end of Wall 9052, but the evidence is too slim to be sure and the outline of a room here would be no less confused were 9068 more clearly defined.

Both these walls played a part in Stratum VII to follow.

Random rocks in a rough row were in the region from Wall 9052 south to the short segment of Wall 9057 in the southwest corner of Area 1. On the plan it is designated Room 12, though it may be the extension of Room 11 eastward or may be a part of the eroded region 13 to its east. This region seems to have been outside of buildings.

Surfacings with occupation debris were traced at a number of points throughout these architectural remains, the best-defined shown on IX DD. In Room 6 within the elbow of Wall 9819, a thick plaster flooring 9820 (Ill. 141 = IX AA:#37) went with a similar flooring 9311 in Room 5 west of Wall 9313 (DD:#34). Both rode on destruction debris of Stratum IX (AA:#41 and DD:#37). Ashy soil covered this surface. Only four indicator sherds were saved from the floor and its immediate underpinning. In Room 7, Surface 9310A rested on the Stratum IXA brick and ash of Stratum IX (DD #35 on #37); it went with Surface 9827 = AA:##39 and 38 (see fig. 236 for a closer view). Again four indicator sherds were saved. East of Wall 9314 and north of 9315 and 9052 was plastered surface 9062 (DD:#35) which connected to Wall 9052 and ran just over the top of Wall 9044B both on DD and CC (Ill. 143). At the CC section, one large rock sat upon 9044B and a segment of plaster marks it (CC:#23). Three sherds were saved. Throughout its extent, this set of surfacings is topped by ashy and bricky destruction debris, but the tiny yield of pottery hardly suggests a sudden attack and destruction. In Room 12, south of Wall 9052 toward Wall 9057, two surfaces were identified, locus 9058 about 0.10 m above locus 9064. East of the random row of rocks shown on the top plan, locus 9061 designates a surface traced toward the southeast corner of the field in the eroded region 13. Together, these were probably external surfacings. Sixteen indicator sherds were saved.

Cobbling 9316 in Room 10, resting upon packed reddish soil, was poorly preserved in the region south of Wall 9307 toward the collapse of rock, locus 9319, in the far southwest corner of the field. Five sherds were registered. South of Wall 9315, in Room 11, chalky Surface 9306 rode over makeup layers 9312 and 9324 toward the pile of stone designated locus 9318 in the southeast corner of Area 2, across the balk from the wall fragment 9057. All these features yielded only nine indicator sherds.

Within the elbow formed by Wall 9776A and 9836, Room 1, layers 9821 and 9827 represent Stratum VIII, but no distinct surface was detected. Five indicator sherds came from these loci. East of 9776A, layers of compacted earth in Yard 3 yielded another six indicator sherds. The sherd counts have been given to indicate the evidence from this complex that may help to define this poorly preserved but important stratum. The total for Field IX is 52 sherds.

Field I

The difficulties in stratigraphic assignment of features in Areas 16 and 17 of Field I within the Iron II period were described earlier in treating Stratum X. In the 1964 excavation season, H. D. Lance found beneath the Wall 175 complex shown in fig. 230 a makeup containing pottery field-read as belonging to Strata VIII and VII. Floor levels of the complex shown in that plan were at that point assigned to Stratum VI. Subsequent study of this stratigraphy, which is quite disturbed by Hellenistic intrusions, has led to an alternative reading of the stratigraphy, especially the walls to the west (Walls 175, 177 and 180). The alternative is presented in Toombs (1972; 1976), and was followed in the description of Stratum X given earlier in this chapter. At the present stage of knowledge neither reading can be established, and the small selection of pottery preserved is not likely to settle the phasing. This excavation cannot be trusted to define Iron II stratigraphy.

That said, it is more probable to take Wall 176, an addition to the complex after the 175-177-180-181 structure with floor 423, as belonging to Stratum IX or possibly XA, with a mud plaster segment of surfacing just above 423 to go with it. Given the uncertainty no description of it was given in the Stratum IX stratigraphy above. Probably belonging to Stratum VIII, then, was a hard beaten earth surface, locus 419, covering most of Area 16 at elevation 11.40 near Vat 412 at the south balk, sloping to 11.30–11.25 over the back wall of

Fig. 250. Walls and surfaces of House 1727 in Field VII.

the East Gate LB/Iron I tower. In the section in fig. 231, it would have fallen within the banded layer above Floor 423.

Vat 412 was a roughly oval limestone installation with walls varying from 0.10 to 0.17 m thick and a depth of 0.45 m. To its northeast, over the gate tower and above Bin 444 assigned earlier to Stratum X, was a stretch of wall, 185, which probably belongs to this phase. Stratum VIII pottery was the latest found in the fill beneath these features, except for one store jar, crushed on Bin 444 and under Wall 185, field-assigned to Stratum VI. That one piece of pottery is now uncertain as to date, and the assignment of the first use of Vat 412, of Floor 419 and of Wall 185 to Stratum VIII prevails.

STRATUM VII

The anchor for description of Stratum VII is House 1727 in Field VII, figs. 250 and 251, one of the best preserved units among the domestic precincts at Tell Balâṭah, named from the locus assigned the floor in Room 2 (Ill. 105). Its destruction and the extensive preservation of its ruins included a wide range of artifacts, and it has been the subject of several studies in social history, including substantial contribution to museum displays in Tel Aviv and Tell Qasileh. The ferocity of its destruction, together with the recovery of an Assyrian adorant seal in its debris and the pottery characterizing the immediately subsequent building of huts on its ruins, belonging to Stratum VIB and showing Assyrian period forms, combine to place Stratum VII in absolute chronology with near certainty, in the final quarter of the eighth century BCE. For interpretation, see Campbell 1995; Holladay 1992; King 1988:62–63; Holladay 1982; *Reader's Digest Atlas* 1981:134–35; G. E. Wright 1978a; *SBBC*:158–72; Toombs and Wright 1963:38–40; 1961:49–51.

Preparations in Field VII

In Stratum VIII, as has been noted, Terrace Wall 1628-22.011-21.017 had been reinforced to retain a terrace at the west edge of Field VII. During the period of Stratum IX, a complex of dwellings on the central terrace to its east showed architectural coherence but its floors displayed the natural slope south and east of the topography of the low flanks of Mt. Ebal, stepping down almost a full meter from northwest to southeast. Because so little of the Stratum VIII floorings was preserved, it is impossible to say whether Stratum VIII builders had leveled the ground to receive the poorly preserved structures of that period.

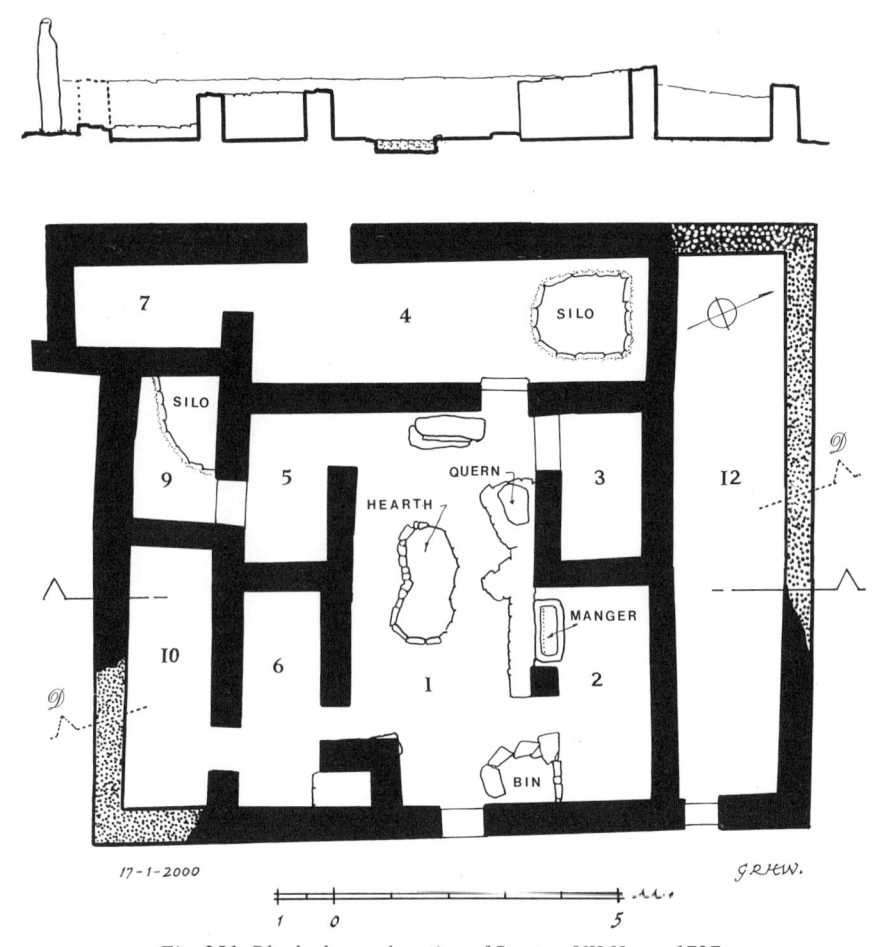

Fig. 251. Block plan and section of Stratum VII House 1727.

With Stratum VII, effort was made to create a nearly horizontal platform upon which to site the 1727 house. The platform pitched slightly to the southeast for drainage purposes, as best seen on VII BB (Ill. 112).

The circumstances of the house's destruction carried away the terrace retaining wall on the east, and resulted in collapse of the house eastward. There probably was a retaining wall at the east edge of the terrace on which House 1727 sat, with its access platform in front of the house; the platform was about 2.50 m wide, to the lip of a 30-degree slope. The collapse of the house took with it most of what defined the terrace, though a cobbled step, locus 1538, was partially preserved 0.15 m downslope from Cobbling 1429 on the pathway. The burned brick of the collapse of the 1727 house begins its plunge down the slope from the elevation of Step 1538, at elevation 16.69. Excavation in Area 7 to the north and east of these features stopped at this elevation, so the course of the terrace northward is unknown.

Just west of the edge of the terrace, under the southeast corner of Rooms 6 and 10, a deposit of large rocks mixed with soil full of chalk lumps and charcoal, locus 1141, served as underpinning. The top of this deposit was only 0.20 m below the elevation of the floor in Room 6 and 0.35 below the surface of the sump in Room 10. Apparently the builders found and used Stratum IX Wall 1147 as the core for this consolidation, but the issue of its origin and date will come up again because some Stratum VI pottery was found among its sparse yield of sherds.

A similar consolidation was installed beneath Wall 1436 separating Rooms 6 and 10, as seen on

Fig. 252. Packing of sherds and pebbles in Sump 1431.

Ill. 116 = VII DD. Drain 1345 ran adjacent to it on the south. Whether the builders placed these consolidations where they did because they intended to run a drainage system nearby, or placed the consolidations after the drainage system had undermined the house is a moot question.

On the platform between the house and the slope to the next terrace east was cobbled Surface 1429, preserved only immediately in front of the threshold of the main entrance. A segment of a beaten earth surface at the same elevation against Wall 1734 east of Room 2 continued the path or road that led from the north to the front door of the house.

Immediately to the south of the cobbling at the door, a flat flagstone at elevation 17.00 on the plan marked part of the covering over Sump 1431. The rim of the sump was flush against Wall 1734, the front wall of the house, but its stone-lining tapered away from the wall as it descended. Roughly circular, with a top diameter of 2.25 m, it bottomed at elevation 16.10, 0.90 m below the cover stone. Its interior was loosely filled with fist-sized stones and thousands of sherds, which could be scooped out by hand because there was virtually no soil. After eighteen baskets of pottery had been removed, the nineteenth was sorted *in situ* and only indicator sherds filled it to the brim. Fig. 252 shows the fill in context and suggests that the ingredients of the packing were all of roughly the same size. No large sherds of store jars and no large stones were included; most were handles, rims, bases and body sherds of cooking pots, bowls, jars and jugs. The corpus of 91 registered sherds includes pottery of all periods from Stratum XI on, with a few much earlier. Stratum VII itself is well represented, while four sherds were field-analyzed as belonging to Stratum VI.

South of Sump 1431, beaten earth Surface 1451 continued the path of access past the front door of the house, but erosion of the entire southeast corner of Room 10 cut off the continuance of this surface roughly two meters south of the sump.

As final preparation to build the house, a bed of rounded stones was spread, encountered especially beneath the cobbling of Room 6, and then a leveling blanket of chocolate brown soil beneath Rooms 1, 2, and 6. These were loci 1445A topped by 1446. Pottery within locus 1446 included MB II pieces, as well as sherds of Strata XI through VIII, so the material was probably garnered from lower levels of the site, but Strata VIII and VII sherds were present.

Fig. 253. Early view of the emerging House 1727 in Field VII. Wall 1619 has the meter stick leaning against it in the upper center. Note dressed block in the third course.

House 1727 (Ills. 105 [plan]; 112–117 [sections])

Walls. Illustrations 114 and 116 = VII BB and DD sections especially show what was regularly the case with the founding of walls in the 1727 house: they were not set deeply into foundation trenches but only 0.10–0.20 m into the makeup. Wall 1436 is something of an exception, founded on the 1141 rock underpinning stabilizing the southeast corner.

Ill. 105 provides information about the construction technique followed. The core of the house consisted of Rooms 1–6 and Room 12, which followed closely the standard plan of a typical Israelite house often called "four-room"(fig. 251). The exceptional factor is Room 12, which was integrated into the construction. The house's eastern wall, Wall 1734, made a turn at a bonded corner and ran west as Wall 1731. Room 12 cannot have belonged to another house to the north.

Walls were all between 0.40 and 0.50 m thick and built with blocks of field stone selected for their length to run across the wall's full width. The west wall of the complex was exceptional, in that it was the Terrace Wall of preceding periods; it ran between 0.55 and 0.60 m wide and did not use headers through the width. At its south end, from a passageway off Room 4, it had been faced with a skin of rocks, 22.014, which produced a straight line with its northern extent.

Wall 1724 was preserved for four to five courses to an elevation 18.67, 1.70 m above the adjacent flooring at the north end of Room 4. Although the wall leaned to the north, it stood unsupported through the two-year gap between its exposure in 1960 and its dismantling in 1962. Wall 1731 along the north limit was preserved for as many as four courses, 1.06 m in height (Ill. 112 = VII AA). Section VII DD shows the junction of Walls 1728 and 1724 in the northwest corner of Room 2, standing four courses high to 1.25 m above adjacent flooring. In general, the walls toward the southeast of the house were much less well-preserved.

While most walls were built of unshaped field stones of roughly the same size, of a weight portable by a worker, there were several places where much larger shaped blocks were placed as stretchers within walls. One such shows in the plan on Wall 1620 and another in Wall 1619, the west and south walls of Room 3 respectively. Most striking was a huge dressed block 0.80 m long and slightly wider than the rest of the wall in the third preserved course from the top of Wall 1619 shown in fig. 253.

Fig. 254. Looking south at surfaces in the balk between Areas 8 and 5 in Field VII. The balk is at the level of House 1727's central room. A small portion of Surface 1738 (Stratum VIIB) is preserved adjacent to it partially in the shadow of the boulder in the upper left. The next shelf down is Surface 1739 of Stratum VIII, and the meter stick is on Stratum IXA Floor 1744. Note the decayed pillars 1743 left of center. Cf. fig. 241.

The joins of most of the walls, with the logical exception of 1724 against the Terrace Wall at its west end, were bonded. This was apparently the case also with the joins to the eastern limiting wall 1734, but it was preserved only one course high and Wall 1724 may have met it at a butt junction. Wall 1623 separating Room 4 from Rooms 1 and 5 had been robbed for most of its length, including its junction with Wall 1436; its course could be readily traced in a robber trench. If it could be removed without disturbing Wall 1436 however, it stands to reason that it butted 1436.

Passageways from outside and from room to room are plain in the plan, except in two cases. One entered the house from the east into Room 1 and Room 12, but could not have passed from Rooms 2, 3 or 4 into Room 12. Preservation of Wall 1734 south of the main entrance into Room 1 from the east was so poor that it is not clear whether one could have entered Room 6 from the east, but on the basis of comparison to most houses of similar design throughout the Levant, it seems very unlikely. Room 1, the central room, gave access to Rooms 2 through 6, although at some time in the history of the house the passage into Room 3 was blocked. One could have entered or exited Room 4 through a passage in the Terrace Wall, probably by a set of steps mounting the 1.00 m difference in elevation up to the terrace to the west. The west end of Wall 1436 at the south end of Room 4 was ruined, but it appears that one could have exited Room 4 at the south, probably into the open yard later to be partially filled with an adjunct to the house consisting of Rooms 7, 9 and 10, yet to be described.

Rooms. Room 1 was 6.50 m by 3.15 m in interior measure, minus Bin 1444 and the alcove of Room 6 which intrude upon its eastern corners. It was filled with installations. Ill. 105 shows it as it appeared at the stage of destruction of the house. Its final surface of beaten earth was at elevation 17.02 near its northwest corner. Hearth 1443 in the center of Room 1 had its rim stones flush with this floor, so the elevation 16.83 on its east rim manifests the slight pitch southeastward.

It is in Room 1 where there was the most evidence of alterations during the life of the house. At first, excavation beneath the final surface reached Stratum VIII floors within 0.20 m and may have missed earlier Stratum VII surfaces. When the balk separating Areas 8 and 5 was excavated, a segment of an earlier Stratum VII surface 1738

Fig. 255. Looking north at Stratum VII Hearth 1443.

was found near Bin 1444 in the northeast corner of Room 1; the tight sequence of Strata IXA, VIII, VIIB and VIIA floors can best be seen in Ills. 114 and 116, along with fig. 254. Removal a season later of the balk between Areas 9 and 6 revealed two patches of earlier Stratum VII surface, 1327a and 1327b, which do not show on VII BB. They were located adjacent to Pit #19, between Stratum VIII surface #16a and #16 (fig. 249), the final floor of the room. No elevations were read on these floors, but the first floor of Room 1 was at roughly 16.90 to 16.75 from west to east.

Another feature of the early phase of Room 1 was revealed when the huge block of stone 1624, lying adjacent to the east face of Wall 1623, was removed. It sat over a shallow bin, locus 1399, filled with loose, black soil heavy with sherds field analyzed as VIII/VII.

Adjustments to the layout of Room 1 were also made along the north edge of Room 1. A break in the cobbling due east of the line of Wall 1619, at the south edge of Room 2, suggests that the original north limit of Room 1 was a straight line corresponding to the south limit; later this segment of wall was redone as load-bearing pillars. Bin 1444 built into the line of this wall at the northeast corner of Room 1, appears to have been original to the house design; a similar phenomenon occurs in the Stratum VII structure in Field IX to be described below.

Hearth 1443 (fig. 255), as was noted in the portrayal of Stratum VIII in Field VII above, rested on vat-and-platter Installation 1395-1396 of Stratum VIII. It is not at all impossible that the earlier installation was reused in the early stage of the 1727 house, perhaps with rim stones placed on the edges of the vat.

Room 2 was 3.70 m by 2.1 m in interior measure, paved with flagstones and cobbling at elevation 16.81 near its center (fig. 256). Access to it passed between two upright limestone piers in the line of wall extrapolated on the plan, separated by 0.70 m. Both were founded below the paving, and the paving came to meet them. They stood to a height 0.50 m above the paving of Room 2. As mentioned already, Room 2's south wall at the west seems to have been solid from the southwest corner to the access. Since its elevation would have been slightly higher than the earlier surface in Room 1, drainage will have been down between the stones, rather than by run-off.

Room 6 corresponded to Room 2 in the south-

Fig. 256. Looking west at Room 2 of House 1727 with stone-paved floor. Note entrance pillars at left center.

Fig. 257. Collapse of brick Wall 1319 from the top of stone Wall 1323 in Room 5, viewed from the north. Note crushed cooking pot and jug on Floor 1320.

east corner of the basic house. It was 3.70 m by 1.35 m and was also cobbled throughout, including a small alcove 1.00 m deep and 0.70 m wide. Fallen stone was in the accessway from Room 1 and the corner posts of the doorway had partially collapsed, but its position was clear.

Room 3 was 2.40 m by 1.35 m in interior measure, with a beaten earth floor at elevation 16.92. Corresponding to it on the south of Room 1 was Room 5, 2.60 m by 1.40 m, also with beaten earth surface, at elevation 16.95. In the southwest corner of Room 5 was a fireplace with a whole Stratum VII cooking pot smashed upon it (fig. 257). Adjacent lay a restorable jug.

The long Room 4 spanning the entire width of the house at the back was 2.10 m in width and 6.85 m in length. Its beaten earth surface was at elevation 17.08. At its north end was stone-lined Silo 1629, its north edge a straight line of stones parallel to the adjacent wall, while the remainder of the perimeter was curved. Its interior measures were 1.50 m north-south by 1.30 m east-west. The elevation of its bottom was at 16.74, only 0.35 below the adjacent surface of the room.

Not shown on the plan, nor discerned until the balk was removed between Areas 6 and 9 in 1964, was Pit 13.104, VII BB:#18. It was adjacent to the west wall of Room 4 (the Terrace Wall) and close to the back entrance with threshold at elevation 17.25 shown on the plan. The section shows beaten earth Floor 1630a-1327 topping this pit. A puzzling factor, though, is that the pit is filled with the same type of destruction debris as appeared over the rest of the house. It does not seem possible that Pit 13.104, at least 1.50 m deep, could have been open when the house was in use, since it is located directly in the path of the back entryway. An alternative proposal is made below in the description of the house's destruction.

Room 12 ran uninterrupted along the entire north limit of the house. It was approximately

1.90 m wide, although its north wall bent in slightly near its east end to narrow the width to 1.70 m. Assuming that the Terrace Wall continued in a straight line, Room 12 would have been 8.15 m in length. Flagstones paved the entire east half of the room but were not found to continue when the balk between Areas 8 and 9 was removed, nor was any cross wall present at that point. In the north balk of the field indications of stone paving are visible, as depicted in VII AA:#14. Probably the entire room was stone-paved originally. Elevations were measured at 17.03 on the beaten earth segment of the floor toward the west end and 16.81 on the cobbling to the east; if the cobbling was complete, the western elevation would have been at roughly 17.10 to 17.15.

Later Developments on the 1727 House Plan. Room 1 underwent a number of renovations. Hearth 1443 may have been original to the house, or may have replaced the reused Stratum VIII 1395-1396 vat and platter installation in the center of the room. Rimmed with stones of oblong shape probably selected for the purpose, the hearth's interior measure was 1.85 from east to west and from 0.80 m wide in two outer lobes to about 0.65 m at its more constricted center. An elevation on the loosely-laid stone fill was at 16.80.

All around the hearth was ash and lime deposit, and several of the rim stones had been calcined. This hearth is too large to commend itself as simply a cooking or warming fireplace; given the indications of high heat generated, it is to be taken as an industrial hearth. Just to its south, in association with the final floor of Room 1 were two rows of stone, the western one consisting of one upright slab 0.60 m long by 0.25 m wide, the eastern of smaller stones, one of which rested on a large Stratum VII bowl fragment. The purpose of this installation is elusive; possibly it was the base for a brick chimney.

West of the hearth, against Wall 1623, lay a massive block of fine-grade limestone 1.20 m long and up to 0.35 m wide propped up on stone underpinning which lay directly upon Bin 1399 of the earlier phase of Room 1 use. Its ends had been shaped to a straight face, while its upper face was rough-hewn. What this limestone block was used for is unclear, but it should be remembered that shaped blocks of large size appeared here and there in the walls of the house.

Along the north wall of Room 1 were arranged a succession of installations suggesting kitchen facilities; a smashed cooking pot lay on the floor between these installations and the north edge of Hearth 1443. Propped up on a bed of small stones at the west end was Limestone Block 1626, 0.80 m long and 0.55 m wide oriented parallel to the adjacent wall and roughly 0.20 m away from it. Its bedding held it so that its flat top surface tilted to the east. All surfaces of 1626 had been smoothed. In the destruction debris only a few centimeters above it was a granite muller, a rare material and of a size too heavy to be useful as a grain muller. Perhaps it was for shaping limestone. Also nearby was a typical basalt muller. Block 1626 was most likely a quern, not yet showing a saddle shape, but it may be that the householders were in the business of shaping better grade limestone blocks for some other use.

Connecting Block 1626 to the west pier of the access to Room 2 was a thin wall, 1735, 0.25 m to 0.35 m thick. The earlier stage surface 1738 ran beneath it, while the final surface of Room 1 ran to it. Between Wall 1735 and the corner of Walls 1619 and 1728, directly north of the center of the hearth, was a circle of stones serving as a jar holder, with the sheared-off base of a jar in it. The elevation of the rim of the jar holder was at 16.98.

Next to the east, between Wall 1735 and what would have been the south limit of Room 2, was a bin which extended through the proposed original wall line. The arrangement of Room 2, with stone-lined floor and two bins, suggested to J. S. Holladay that Room 2 was for animals, the stone flooring beneficial to their hooves and effective for drainage of urine and mucking out of dung, with the two bins as mangers (1982; 1986). If stones of an original wall here had been removed to construct this bin, a way would have had to be contrived to bear the load of the superstructure, perhaps by means of a beam, from the junction of Walls 1619 and 1728 to the western pier leading into Room 2.

A major alteration of the basic 1727 house involved the adding of Rooms 7, 9 and 10 along the south. The walls that outline Rooms 9 and 10 abut-

Fig. 258. Saddle quern and muller in the work area off the southeast corner of House 1727. Note the opening for Silo 1039 near left margin, beyond post with flagstones.

ted the south wall of the original house, and were of somewhat different construction technique. The two north-south walls employed the header construction technique, but were only about 0.35 m thick, while the south wall, Wall 1333, was built of random sized field stones, mostly smaller than typical elsewhere, and laid in two rows. Two doorways were punched through Wall 1436 at the points shown on the plan.

Room 7 between the Terrace Wall and the west wall of Room 9, Wall 1317, was in effect carved out of the former yard. The plan shows these rooms in place. Wall 1317 continued southward as Wall 1334, poorly preserved, to end in a well cut block of stone. Wall 22.013, thin and poorly preserved for only one course, connected the Terrace Wall to Wall 1334, with the possibility of a doorway at its east end against Wall 1334.

East of the post at the end of 1334, at a distance of 0.80 m, was another well-dressed post, with a threshold between them. A few flagstones north of the post suggested a work area, locus 1038, in what would be the corner of the now attenuated yard. Here sat a saddle quern enclosed in a short curve of walling with a basalt muller lying adjacent (fig. 258). South of the two posts was the circular opening of stone-lined Silo 1039. The surface of the yard among these features was strewn with sherds, many field-identified as belonging to Stratum VII, but only three indicators were registered.

Within Rooms 9 and 10 were beaten earth floors at elevations 17.04 and 17.15 respectively. Room 9 contained partially stone-lined Silo 1329 which filled nearly a third of the room, against its northwest corner. Its bottom was at elevation 16.14. In Room 10, the northwest corner contained a stone-filled sump, somewhat resembling Sump 1431 in front of the house but not packed in the same way. Excavation beneath these floors revealed Drain 1345, which ran adjacent to the south wall of the two rooms from the base of Silo 1329 in Room 9, past the sump in Room 10 and emptied into the amorphous heap of rocks shoring up the southeast corner of Room 10. Apparently the outflow of this drain undermined this corner and brought about its collapse into a region of erosion. For a drain to begin from the base of a silo seems strange; Silo 1329 may also be a sump.

Destruction: Multiple Stories. Immense quantities of brick, ash, charcoal, plaster and rocks collapsed into House 1727 at its destruction, and slid down the slope to the east. The fact that the retaining wall of the east limit of the terrace on which the house sat is missing suggests that the force of the collapse carried it with the superstruc-

Fig. 259. Looking east at the west balk of Field VII Area 5. Pottery and brick fall from the upper story of House 1727 as first encountered above the floors of Rooms 6 and 1.

West of this location, within Room 12, note was taken of two different layers of brick fall, the upper layer with a more yellow hue, with a heavy fall of stones between them. Two different kinds of mud brick seem to have been employed in building the house, although the distinction between them could not be discerned elsewhere in the ruins.

In Room 2, in the southeast corner, a rough platform of stones came to rest 0.50 m above the cobbled floor, apparently having dropped directly from above. It may have represented a cooking hearth from the second story. That there was stone in the superstructure of the house above the first floor was also suggested by the rock fall that blocked the entrance from Room 1 into Room 3. That this is collapse, rather than intentional closing of the only door into Room 3, seems likely, but it is possible that Room 3 was closed up during the course of the life of the house to become a cold storage room, with access from a hole in the ceiling.

At least half a meter above the floor of Room 6, near the top of VII DD:#18, was the accumulation down that slope. Settling and erosion of the destruction debris created pockets later used by Stratum VI occupants.

The debris provided evidence about the superstructure and roof of House 1727. Its depth is shown on the sections, VII DD:## 18 and 34, AA:##11 and 12, BB:##13 and 14. Adjacent to Wall 1724, the debris peaked at a point just over 1.00 m below the modern surface of the mound; on DD, a similar peak reached to within 0.35 of the floors of Hellenistic Stratum III flooring and was 1.35 deep over the top of the facilities along the north edge of Room 1. Over the floor of Room 12 a particularly heavy fall of rock, with much ash, collapsed onto a thin line of fine grey ash over VII DD:#5. Stones in the rock fall at first suggested a cross-wall in Room 12, but there was brick detritus beneath it, and it doubtless fell from the adjacent walls.

Fig. 260. Slab of roofing material fallen into Room 5 of House 1727.

Fig. 261. Debris in Room 1 of House 1727. The flat "terrazzo" slabs lie on brick detritus, at the foot of which are the burned half-round beams that supported the ceiling.

tion shown in fig. 259. Crushed store jars make up much of the debris. Part of a brick, about 0.30 m in length, fired by the conflagration, lies at the center left. Nearer the camera along the left margin is a piece of wall-facing, flat edge up. Similar slabs, 0.045–0.05 m thick, with one face irregular and the other smoothed were in the debris in Room 2.

Either side of Wall 1436, in Rooms 5 and 9, were piles of partially fired fallen brick. One is shown in fig. 257, standing over Silo/Sump 1329, an intact wall segment. It seems to have dropped directly downward from the second story and landed alongside the first story wall which would have borne its load. The bricks were eroded, but enough remained to show that they were approximately as wide as the stone wall, 0.40 to 0.50 m, and roughly square, of as much as 0.30 m thickness.

The brick wall crushed a collection of ring-burnished bowls, cooking pots, and plates and bowls of Samaria Ware on the floor of Room 9. Pieces of layered roofing material were also present. A huge slab of this material fell into Room 5, across the wall, pictured in fig. 260; it came to rest standing vertically. It showed at least eight mud layers 0.025 to 0.03 m thick with straw interbedding. Two patches of charcoal beneath it on the floor may represent beams; the collapse crushed another collection of domestic pottery.

This massive slab of repeatedly resurfaced roof is nearly identical to a slab found standing in Pit 13.104 in Room 4. This pit was noted earlier as located just inside the back door of the house, directly in the path of travel. How it can have been open to receive the collapsing superstructure is a mystery. Perhaps the back door was out of use when the house was destroyed, and the pit had been opened up as a silo; perhaps inhabitants of Stratum VI opened it to bury the debris; perhaps there had been an earlier collapse of a part of the roof and it was buried in the pit before the final floor was laid.

North of this, in the northwest corner of Room 1 near the two worked slabs 1624 and 1626, high in the brick debris were eight friable clay loom weights. Fallen brick from the house fell southward into the work area in the corner of the yard nearest the house. Two large store jars embedded near Wall 1334, one lying on its side on a plastered platform, were crushed by the fall.

Much of the evidence so far described points to a second story of the house and to the roof over it. More precise evidence came when the balk junction directly over the industrial hearth in Room 1 was excavated to floor levels. Throughout the high

Fig. 262. Looking north at Scree 1539, the collapse of the east wall of House 1727.

pile of brick debris here, never nearer the floor than 0.15 m above it, were chunks of flat-surfaced flooring unlike the pieces of wall plaster described over Room 5. Typically, these were 0.06 to 0.07 thick and consisted of three layers. The bottom layer, with an uneven lower face, was whitish mud with straw temper 0.025 to 0.03 m thick; it readily split along a plane from the second layer, 0.03 m thick, of red clay with pebble inclusions. The top layer was a thin, polished veneer of plaster with feldspar crystals embedded throughout. Many of the chunks of this material lay horizontal.

Below the chunks of this carefully constructed "terrazzo" floor, under a layer of bricky mud and directly on the floor of Room 1, were half-round beams, turned to charcoal by a smothered fire. At least seven were traced, six laid in pairs flush against each other. Between the pairs were separations of 0.09, 0.10, and 0.12 m width. The beams were between 0.15 and 0.22 in diameter. At several places in the floor of Room 1, round marks of charcoal probably indicated where upright wood pillars supported the beams. The beams lay flat on the floor, rounded side up, and almost certainly fell from directly above, given their symmetrical position. Two pairs of beams, the bricky material above them, and slabs of the terrazzo flooring are shown in fig. 261.

From half to a full meter of destruction debris lay above the beams and the flooring they supported. Within the debris were two burned bricks, 0.37 by 0.32 m in size and at least 0.12 m thick. With this evidence, the conclusion suggested by the rest described earlier seems inescapable: the entire core of the house, Rooms 1–6 and possibly 9 and 10, had a second story. The question of what industry was carried out on the hearth in the center of Room 1 if the room was enclosed has not been given satisfactory answer, but it appears that "cottage industries" first involving processing food or dyeing cloth and then involving a hot fire were carried on at the ground floor of the house, the "economic domain," while the "living domain" was on the second story and the roof (Holladay 1992: 312–14).

The portion to the right on the longer VII BB section (Ill. 113) shows the slope from the east edge of the platform in front of the house, starting at the point where #13 appears just to the east of the 1429 cobbling near the 1431 sump. Layer #13 is locus 1539, and includes both the rock and the brick of the scree spilling down to the point where it laps against locus 1540-1553, a strip of stones laid in a soil matrix topped by loose rocks that emanates from the eastern limit of the Field and must have gone with features of the lower terrace.

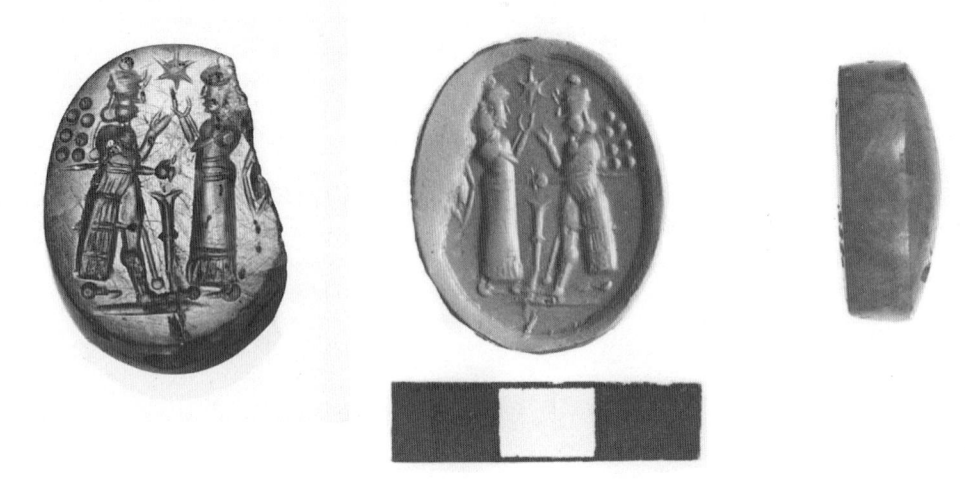

Fig. 263. Obverse, impression, and side view of Assyrian adorant seal found in Scree 1539.

Fig. 262 shows 1553 as light colored, smaller stones at the foot of the tumble, after most of 1540 had been removed; the tumble of rock from House 1727 comes down from the left. Wall 1561, shown in VII BB, is preserved just at the balk near the top of the photograph; it did not extend into the area excavated so its architectural connections are unknown, and it is not certain it was a wall.

The tumbled mass of 1539 rock was the lowest element of a spill of debris from the front of the house. Covering the rocks of 1539 and lapping over 1553-1540 was a mass of decomposed brick with inclusions of decayed plaster, calcined powdered limestone and black ash from smothered fire. At the time of excavation portions gave off an acrid smell of burning. All of this makes up layer #13 of the longer BB section; at its top is a distinct black line of ashes. The angle of repose on the bricky debris was from elevation 16.69 to 15.77, roughly 0.90 m in a distance of 2.90 m, while the stones at the base of the tumble reposed at a less severe angle.

Among the stones and beneath the decomposed brick of the tumble was found the adorant seal of Assyrian style pictured in fig. 263, presumably lost by one of the agents of the destruction of Stratum VII.

Neighboring Houses. House 1727 may have shared its yard with another house to its south at the very edge of Field VII. Wall 1048 near the south limit of the field was preserved for one course throughout much of its length and two courses near its emergence from the balk (Ill. 105; fig. 264). Running south from 1048 into the balk were three short segments of wall, 1051, 21.041 and 21.040. The location was so cramped that excavation could not make sense of this set of walls, although the complex was at first assigned to Stratum IX on the basis of its elevation. Further complicating the picture was the presence of still another fragment of wall beneath 1048, Wall 1056 with elevations on its top at 15.64 and 15.62, also visible in fig. 264 in elevation. Beneath all this was Wall 1080 which was tied by clear surfaces to the Stratum IX complex already described. No floors were discerned for either the 1048 complex or the 1056 one.

After the 1964 expedition left the field, scrutiny of the south balk of areas 2 and 3, which had not been drawn in section, noted a huge intrusion into which the 1048 house was set. It is marked in white on fig. 264. Removal of Wall 1048 had produced a basket of sherds a number of which had been field-analyzed as belonging to Stratum VII. No pottery evidence elucidated Wall 1056. While the proposal must remain hypothetical, and the inadequacy of the evidence admitted, it seems clear that another house, perhaps of the "four-room" style, was positioned here and barely touched by the excavation. If the hypothesis is valid, House 1727 was part of a housing cluster with a yard between it and the "1048 house" to its south. Fur-

Fig. 264. Field VII south balk of Areas 2 and 3. The saucer containing House 1048 is marked with white.

thermore, it seems likely that Wall 1056 belonged to Stratum VIII. Only an extension of excavation to the south could test this plausible reconstruction.

On the upper terrace at the west in Field VII were slim remains of Stratum VII structures with surfaces at elevations about one meter higher than those of the middle terrace where the 1727 house sat. Excavation of the upper terrace stopped with this level, except for a probe into Stratum IX, Area 21. Assignment of these remains to Stratum VII was decided by the discovery of Stratum VII pottery on and beneath surfaces and in the foundations of the walls. Hellenistic ruins lay directly upon or adjacent to the remains. Their builders probably removed the overburden of Stratum VII, along with any Strata VI and V remains. These Stratum VII fragments will not be useful for further elucidation of Stratum VII, but a brief description is called for. Some help is afforded by Ill. 117 = VII EE, on the west face of Areas 21 and 22.

The most coherent unit lay in Area 22 at the middle of complex. Wall lines were discerned within tumbles of fallen rock, from upper courses or from Hellenistic intrusions. Wall 22.005 ran for 2.60 m parallel to the 1628-22.011-21.107 Terrace Wall and only about 0.70 m away from it, offering an accessway somewhat similar to the one to the main entrance of the 1727 house on the middle terrace. The foundation course of 22.005 was two stones in width, but a second course on top was one stone in width, at 0.40 m, somewhat resembling walls in the 1727 house. At its north preserved end it stood to an elevation of 18.68 (Ill. 105). Traces of what was designated Wall 22.008 continued north on the other side of a threshold for a door, its north post marked by an upright stone, but this wall was so poorly preserved it was not entered on plan.

Wall 22.004, poorly preserved and tumbled, ran west from 22.005 near the probable doorway for 4.00 m to the edge of the field. Wall 22.017 ran north from the north face of 22.004; it stood four courses high to an elevation of 18.88, the best preserved wall of the complex. No northern boundary for this complex was ascertained; no connection could be established to the wall fragments in Area 23 to the north.

In the corner formed by Walls 22.004 and 22.017, in what appeared to be a yard against the Terrace Wall, was open circular Bin 22.007, stone-lined, 0.50 m deep. Adjacent to it on the southwest was installation 22.009, a pit 0.50 to 0.65 wide at its rim, belling out to 0.70 m inside, and 0.60 m deep. It was lined with 0.006 m of plaster which showed signs of fire. It may have been an oven of quite different style from the typical *tannur* found at Shechem. Alternatively it may have been a silo, its interior burned to seal it and cleanse it of vermin.

At the rim of the oven/silo was a strip of surfacing for the yard at estimated elevation 18.20; while field notes designate it 22.022, the locus number clearly was applied to the entire surrounding region and is not discreet. In one deep pocket in the corner of Walls 22.004 and 22.017 adjacent to 22.009, below the surface elevation, was a pile of store jar sherds, all typical of Stratum VII. They represent many different vessels, and efforts to restore whole pieces failed. Twenty-two indicator sherds show a range of rim forms. Great quantities of pottery characterize the half-meter thick layer of soil surrounding the oven/silo, but it was not sealed above or below by identified surfaces. Under a rock against the face of 22.005 were two juglets, one unbroken, which were field identified as belonging to Stratum X.

South of this complex, not architecturally coherent with it, was the "T" of Walls 21.015 and 21.021, both of which appear in section on Ill. 117. The south end of Wall 21.105, which was preserved for 3.30 m, formed a doorpost. Patches of plaster floor off the north end of 20.015 to its east and near the south limit of excavation sealed pottery no later than Stratum VII and may have gone with this pair of walls, but neither patch touched a wall. Access to this part of the upper terrace apparently could be gained via steps to a threshold of a break in the Terrace Wall east of Wall 21.015.

Section VII EE shows the accumulation of debris ##14–18 representing Stratum VII in this region.

In Area 23 to the north was an "L" of walls, 23.011, parallel to the Terrace Wall 1.80 m away from it with a turn west for 1.00 m. West of this was another short stretch of north-south wall and a line of stones running east-west; in their elbow at the west limit of excavation was a deep sump, 23.015, filled with loose stones reminiscent of locus 1443 in the 1727 house. A stretch of drainage channel ran to the sump from the east. All these features were exposed as excavation ended, and their stratigraphic assignment is unsure; elevations on Wall 23.015 at 18.72 and 18.70 and on features to the west at 18.08 and 18.11 would comport with the complex to the south and all lie below Hellenistic features, but none can be taken as definitive of Stratum VII. They are shown on the Stratum VII plan as probable but not certain features of it.

Stratum VII in Field IX

Separating Strata VII and VI in Field IX has proven difficult, both in the field and in analysis done since. Supervisor Joseph Callaway's field reports proposed seven phases at the end of the 1962 campaign (three of VIII, two of VII and two of VI). Work in 1964 and subsequent analysis of the records resolved these into six: IXA and VIII previously described, VIIB, VIIA, VIB and VIA. Strata VII and VI are portrayed on Ills. 136–138. Layering is displayed on all the published sections and on some subsidiary sections not published but in the archives. There is a degree of tentativity at many points.

The remains of Stratum VII include much mud brick construction, followed by erosion which decomposed the walls into ill-defined heaps. The precise courses of some wall-lines are impossible to recover, but their orientation throughout the Iron II period in Field IX remained the same.

In the northern one-third of Field IX was a corner of a house (Room 1) within a yard (2). Walls 9776 and 9528 enclosed Flagstone Floor 9833 shown on Ill. 145 = IX EE:#21. Wall 9845 appears just at the face of the north limit of the excavation field and shows in Ill. 142 = IX BB and on IX EE; it may have been the corner post of an interior wall of the house. If so, the width of Room 1 would have been about 1.00 m. between the 9845 corner post and Wall 9528 on the east, about 1.50 m between it and Wall 9776 on the south. Walls 9528 and 9845 continued Stratum VIII walls, and they with 9776 were all reused in Stratum VII. The construction technique of 9776 and 9528 resembled that of the Field VII 1727 house, oblong rocks laid across the width of the wall, measuring between 0.40 and 0.50 m in long dimension.

Over the Flagstone Surface 9833 was a thick, densely packed accumulation of chalk-rich soil, locus 9782A, virtually sterile of pottery (Ill. 137;

IX EE:#18). It appears to have been put in place during Stratum VII, and its chalk-defined top #14 appears to have been a surface within Stratum VII (VIIA). Stratum VI pottery characterized layer 9782 (IX EE:#11) immediately over it.

East of Room 1, parallel to Wall 9528 at a distance of 1.50 m, Wall 9526 ran diagonally across Area 3 to end at the south balk of the area. At its north exposed limit, it rode just over the west edge of Wall 9559, the rebuilt wall-line which had existed from Late Bronze Age times (IX EE). Wall 9526 angled away from the line of Wall 9559 as it ran southwestward; by the time it reached the IX AA section, 9526 and 9559 were 1.25 m apart. Between Walls 9528 and 9526 was the north leg of Yard 2, partly surfaced by cobbling 9543 and partly by earth surface 9544; two store jars were set deep into holes in its surface, one of them preserved in the balk (EE). The position of these two vessels suggests this space was a yard rather than a roadway giving access to the house; any doorway from yard to house must have lain outside the area excavated.

Both IX EE and AA suggest that Wall 9559 was rebuilt at the start of Stratum VII with a few stones. Wall 9559 probably was, then, the first definition of the east extent of the yard surrounding the 9776-9528 system in Stratum VII. This is what Ill. 136 portrays. Alternatively, 9559 may have served simply to consolidate the open area to the east. No surface was defined within Yard 2 along Wall 9559.

Yard 2 turned west to run along the south face of Wall 9776. Its south limit was a brick on stone wall 9830 in Stratum VIIB, dividing it from the complex to its south. Beaten earth surfaces in the yard were loci 9818 topped by 9817 and 9803 topped by 9803 (IX EE:##23, 20, 17, 13), representing VIIB and VIIA respectively; the soil layers here were nearly devoid of sherds.

East of Walls 9559 and 9526 was Region 3, extending along the eastern limit of excavation past the east end of Wall 9044A. What happened with Wall 9044A in Region 3 is not clear; some rocks suggest that it may have continued to the east balk of the field, but soil layers either side of it were similar and apparently continuous. Gravel-filled and stony soil separable into two layers (Ill. 143 = IX CC:##16 and 18) filled Space 3. Crusty plaster defined the tops of each layer. Ill. 137 of Stratum VIIA shows a hint of a brick wall running from 9526 to the east balk; its scar is just at the north edge of CC:#10 pit.

The remainder of the field contained remnants of walls whose definitions are uncertain; they are of a wide variety of construction techniques. Wall 9052, reused from Stratum VIII, is two rows of stone wide. It separated Rooms 4 and 5. Room 4, north of Wall 9052, is trapezoidal, defined by Walls 9052, 9044A, 9065 and probably a wall at the now-truncated west end of 9052. This wall, robbed out, would have been a rebuild of Stratum VIII Wall 9068 involving a right angle turn to the north. Or Room 4 may have extended to the line of Wall 9815/9803 under the junction of the balks in the center of the field.

Walls 9044A and 9052 continued in use from Stratum VIII, but 9065 was a new construction over plastered Stratum VIII floor 9062. Where these three walls met was a flat lie of stone, and the soil above it was heavy with ash, suggesting the possibility of a fireplace in this small nook. Plaster floor 9060 with bricky red occupation debris on it filled the rest of Room 4 (IX DD:#24).

Room 5 ran from Wall 9052 south to Wall 9057, also a rebuild of a Stratum VIII wall. The room's eastern limit appears to have been a poorly preserved brick wall 9051A running south on a foundation of rocks from a stone-lined bin 9051 built against the south face of Wall 9052. The north limit of the room was Wall 9052 to its junction at its west end with the stub of 9068 continuing westward as Wall 9302. Wall 9302 seems to have been rebuilt within Stratum VII as Wall 9301. At the south, Wall 9057 may have continued into the ill-defined ruins portrayed in Area 2 as Wall 9303, then turned north on a poorly preserved rough line of stones to form the western limit of Room 5. The surface for Room 5 was floor 9054 topped by rubble debris 9053 at the south limit of the field.

The plan of the later phase of Stratum VII in the southern two areas of Field IX is not clear; sections IX CC and BB fail to display surfacing for Stratum VIIA, and none could be discerned in the south balk of the field.

Wall 9830, separating the north complex from the south one at the start of Stratum VII, was difficult to trace and seems to have been a rebuild upon Stratum VIII wall 9836A. Later in Stratum VII, it was rebuilt as 9816A. Apparently, it continued to meet the south end of Wall 9526 in the form of mudbrick Wall 9558A, built on a stone foundation. This set of walling appears in the IX BB section, although the state of preservation at that point does not depict them as a stack. A series of soil layers filled Yard 2 between it and Wall 9776 (IX BB:##24, 30 and 31); one Stratum VII surface here was locus 9812 with debris 9811 over it (BB:#33).

Running south from Wall 9830 in Area 4 was Wall 9789, close to the west edge of the excavation plot, which used the stone construction typical of Room 1; it rested close to the line of underlying Wall 9819 of Stratum VIII, but not directly upon it. To the east, the stone foundation of a brick wall 9808 also ran south from 9830. Still another wall fragment, brick Wall 9803 over stone and brick Wall 9815, was just west of the central balk junction of the field.

Wall 9813 ran from a join with Wall 9789 outside the field to the west eastward to continue the line of Wall 9302-9068, although the brick that marked it is hard to define at the north edge of Area 2 (note "bricky" in IX DD:#18). Wall 9813-9302-9068 would then have met 9808 and 9815 perpendicularly to form small Rooms 6 and 7.

A succession of floor surfacings within Room 6 appears on the inset of Section IX AA in fig. 236: Floor 9810 (#31) topped with bricky red soil (#28), then 9809 (#27) with more bricky red accumulation, and finally 9805 (#24) with ashy deposit 9804 (#23) upon it. There is no certainty that this succession comports with the separation of Stratum VIIB from VIIA elsewhere in the field, though it makes sense. The VIIA plan displays the 9805 surfacing.

This succession in Room 6 provided close definition of Stratum VII pottery in Field IX, although only 13 indicator sherds were registered and some were field-identified as representing Stratum VI. The tight layering here may mean separations were not perfect. Room 7 was much narrower, but also had two (less well-defined) surfaces; only three indicator sherds were saved.

Matters are even less clear south of Wall 9813-9302-9068 in Room 8, because the lines of decomposed brick were nearly impossible to define. Field notes describe a stone wall running on top of the line of Stratum VIII Wall 9310-9315, designated Wall 9307 and drawn on Ill. 136. A short segment of Wall 9300 appears at the far western limit which probably marked the west edge of Room 8. The southern limit of Room 8 was uncertain, but the entire region was covered with layers of soil of which the lowest, locus 9308, was probably the earliest Stratum VII surface.

A collapse of stones on top of stone-heap 9318 of Stratum VIII in the southeast corner of Area 2 may mark another place where an earlier Stratum VIII wall was reused. Above Surface 9308 and covering the 9318 heap, there accumulated within Stratum VII soil deposits 9305, 9304 and 9303 with pottery forms representing Strata X down to VII; some 50 registered pieces were saved from these loci. Both plans of this region (Ill. 136 and 137) are presented as they were drawn after the 1964 season without confidence that they show discrete complexes, and indeed any attempt to make sense of Areas 1 and 2 during VIIA proved futile. Field drawing and efforts at making sense of this region are archived.

Repeated mention has been made of brick detritus and ash. Fire may have struck Stratum VII buildings in Field IX, but there were none of the usual indications of sudden and disruptive destruction. No bricks had been hardened, artifacts were few, there was no weaponry, and there were no crushed vessels on surfaces. Rather the impression is one of decay. Rooms in the south complex were small and of sun-dried brick, which may suggest relative poverty. Field IX, except for Room 1 within Yard 2, seems to have been a less affluent part of town than was Field VII.

Stratum VII in Field II

At an earlier point, brief description was given of Stratum X scraps in Field II adjacent to the acropolis, beneath a two-room Hellenistic house first revealed in 1957. Within less than a meter below Hellenistic floors, and intruded upon by the footings for Hellenistic walls, excavation by the

Fig. 265. Looking north in Field II, out the door in Wall 7007. Cobble floor 7024 at right and left, and in the balk beneath the threshold of the door.

Joint Expedition during the 1968 season first encountered part of a Stratum VII building resting on and in some cases reusing the Stratum X structure. The tight stratigraphy is shown on section in II AA = Ill. 34 and BB = Ill. 35, and the walls and floor superimposed on Stratum X and topped by the Hellenistic house in Ill. 30.

Wall 7051 running roughly east-west was founded in Stratum X and reused in Stratum VII. It was a rubble wall of small stones, differing from the Stratum VII constructions which made use of its top. Wall 7030 to its south did not parallel it, but Wall 7056 and surfaces tied Walls 7030 and 7051 together. Perpendicular to the extended line of 7030 was Wall 7026, sited on top of Stratum X Wall 7096, but less wide than its predecessor by 0.12 m. Walls 7026 and 7030, then, seem to have been two new Stratum VII constructions, and they resembled the Stratum VII walls in Field VII, being 0.45 to 0.50 m wide and built of headers across the width of the wall of style similar to those used in the 1727 house.

Wall 7056 abutted both 7051 and 7030. Makeup for the floorings that went with Wall 7030 ran beneath 7056 but not beneath 7051. Unlike 7030 and 7026, 7056 was of rubble construction and ran to a width of 0.60 m.

In the northeast of the complex, against the robbed out continuation of Wall 7051 and touching Wall 7026 was Cobbling 7024 at elevation 15.88. Wall 7026 was preserved for only one course, with an elevation of 15.95, but the cobbling ran to that one course. The foundation trench for Hellenistic Wall 7007, shown in outline on the plan, was at 16.12, which suggests how thin was the preservation of Stratum VII here. A large intrusion dug by Hellenistic builders had robbed the connection of Wall 7051 and 7026. Cobbling 7024 ran beneath Wall 7007 and could be traced in the side of the excavation on its north side, as well as into the adjacent eastern balk of the field. Fig. 265 shows these features.

In the small triangle east of Wall 7026 and within the corner of the Hellenistic walls 7012 and 7008 above was beaten earth Floor 7035, covered with a spill of broken store jars of Stratum VII date. Floor 7035 was at elevation 15.61, lapping over the Stratum X Wall 7096 beneath it to reach Wall 7026.

No surface was traced with confidence west of Wall 7026 toward where Hellenistic Wall 7006 crosses the plan, but a segment of destruction debris, locus 7032, was preserved against the west face of 7026 with orange brick as a major ingredi-

Fig. 266. Looking north in Field II with the meter stick on Wall 7026. Crush of pottery at right lies on Floor 7035, decayed brick to left of the wall.

ent, which must have come to rest on what served as surface. More store jar sherds and pieces of oven lining were heavy in this debris, which was Iron Age in date, the latest forms belonging to Stratum VII with the possibility of Stratum VI forms. Fig. 266 shows the conditions either side of Wall 7026.

Under the larger room of the Hellenistic structure (7006-7009-7013-7005), flooring from Stratum VII was traced either side of Wall 7056 and touching 7030 and 7051. Floor 7037 at elevation 15.80 is II AA:#7 between the two walls. South of Wall 7030, Surface 7038, less clearly defined than 7037, appears as AA:#17; it is basal to II BB = Ill. 35 and runs only about 0.30 m below the foundation of Wall 7009 seen in elevation. Stratum X floor here is AA:#9, as little as 0.15 to 0.30 m below 7038. On 7038 was the center part of a store jar, with its handles included but no rim or base, apparently used as a storage bin.

Destruction of these slim Stratum VII remains left brick and ash, broken storage jars and fallen stones on the small segments of flooring found. The destruction does seem to have been violent, but the collapse is poorly attested. Section II AA displays, in layers ##14, 15 and 16 near where Wall 7009 was set in by Hellenistic builders, and ##6, 5, 4 and 3 between Walls 7030 and 7051, the accumulated fill under Hellenistic floors. Pottery in these layers showed no Hellenistic, but included sherds from all periods of the site's history from MB to Iron II, including one clear Stratum VI bowl fragment. The fill was probably imported from elsewhere on the site.

The noteworthy contribution of the Field II probe below Hellenistic levels may be this: the stratigraphy of all periods subsequent to the Late Bronze Age at the west of the tell was probably badly disturbed. Study of the sequence of domestic housing at Shechem was probably best to be done in fields such as VII and IX more interior to town. Perhaps, after all, the loss of Sellin's records of what he found over the acropolis is not as severe as it might seem.

Stratum VII in Field I:16 and 17. In describing Strata X and VIII, the problems with the finds in Field I, Areas 16 and 17, have been stated. Tentatively, Wall 171 along the easternmost edge of Area 16 is assigned to Stratum VII (fig. 231). It ran for 5.10 m well above the tower of the East Gate, with a width of 0.65–0.70 m. A meter-wide doorway through it was clearly delineated by doorjambs of hewn stone, the one on the north with a notch to receive the door pivoted off the south jamb. The wall was founded on Floor 419 assigned to Stratum VIII, and Surface 420-421 sloped from it at elevation 11.35 down to the west at 11.30 until

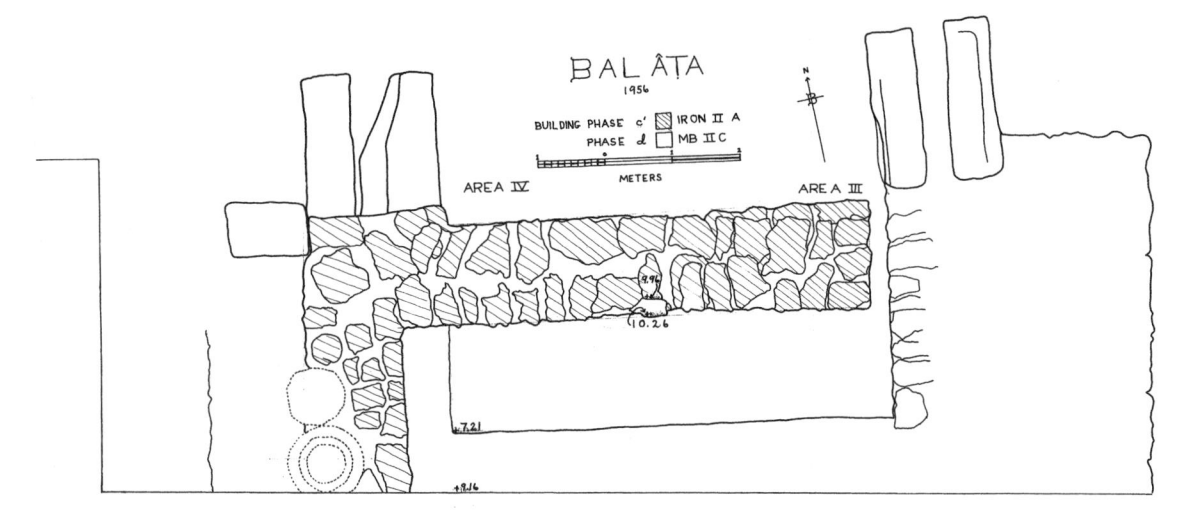

Fig. 267. 1956 plan by Robert J. Bull, showing "Wall c'" of the Iron age, over the East Gate tower.

it merged with Floor 419. Vat 412 was reused with this complex. Surface 420-421 was as much as 0.05 m thick, made of lumpy plaster. A stretch of wall, 184, perpendicular to the north preserved end of Wall 171 but not meeting it, ran above Wall 185 of Stratum VIII to the northwest, and may have been part of this system. Once again, the tentative nature of this phasing is emphasized, and its untrustworthiness for definition of Stratum VII acknowledged. Nevertheless, the amount of Stratum VIII and VII pottery in the fills and occupation levels of these ephemeral remains over the back of the gate area must not be ignored.

STRATUM VI

Three locations on the site provide the evidence of Stratum VI. At the East Gate, there is evidence of an effort at refortification and of domestic facilities just inside the fortification, ending in violent destruction. In Fields VII and IX, structures founded in Stratum VII were partially cleared and poorly rebuilt; in each of these domestic contexts, there was evidence for two destructions in close proximity of time.

If Stratum VII is correctly placed in the eighth century, terminated by the Assyrian invasion of 724–721 BCE, Stratum VI is to be dated in the seventh century. The mudbrick of the structures in Fields VII and IX belonging to Stratum VII was decayed and the destruction debris eroded before Stratum VI people rebuilt. The pottery of Stratum VI continues Stratum VII traditions but shows developments, and includes a characteristic bowl form influenced by Mesopotamian styles, a locally made version of Assyrian Palace Ware. The store jars of Stratum VI are made of a clay that fires to a rich red, unlike those of Stratum VII. An inscribed seal probably representing Stratum VI dates paleographically to the late seventh or early sixth century.

Stratum VI in Field I

Over the Middle Bronze period gate tower of the East Gate, a wall, 1.35 m wide, made of stones with a rubble and earth core (designated c' in Bull's drawing in fig. 267), is assigned to Stratum VI (shown on Ill. 12 as part of the complex of Walls 118 and 120, but not fully identifiable). It stood on the interior wall of the south gate tower, and was slightly wider than the underlying well-built stone wall of the Orthostat Phase of the gate, spreading north over the orthostats and resting upon their southern edges, and south on the fill within the MB II guardroom. It ran over the blockage of the entrance from the gateway into the guard tower. Presumably the entryway to town was through the narrow defile of the ruined gate between the orthostats, and the Stratum VI wall was one part of a guard-room above the entrance. Against the south face of Wall c' at its eastern end was a surface with a burn layer on it. Among the pottery in the burn layer were three seventh century juglets which G. E. Wright at first dated to around 800 BCE (1956:19; his revision in date is given in *SBBC*:165).

Paul Lapp, in cutting back the south balk line (fig. 128) at the East Gate in 1962, isolated two pockets of "tan clay" wash on the slope, east from Wall A and east from Wall 105, that contained Stratum VI as their latest pottery. Over the pocket east of Wall 105, a "coarse dark red" layer also contained VI pottery as its latest, as did the "hard white fleck" deposit; all ran beneath the Stratum IV Hellenistic remains in this region. Lapp placed these erosion layers with the Stratum VI rebuilding on top of the gate towers. Indeed, he noted that another "coarse dark red" layer with ash in it over a bricky white sloping surface extending up toward the top of Wall A, probably to reach it if it were originally higher, represented Stratum VII debris. G. E. Wright disagreed with this proposal, but it should be treated seriously.

Some 10.00 m west of the burned surface next to Wall c', at the back of the MB II gate tower, was the vat and platter installation drawn with dashes on fig. 267, an industrial complex first dated to the Hellenistic period, with a buried jar positioned at the outflow of the grooves on the platter, strikingly similar to the 1395-1396 installation in the Stratum VIII structure (reused in Stratum VII) of Field VII. The jar belongs to Stratum VI, though the complex was set into what may be the extension south of the proposed guard room. Another ca. 12.00 m farther west was Vat 412 in Area 16, which continued in use into Stratum VI according to the slim evidence from the location: the final use of the vat is linked by elevation with the blocking of a doorway in Wall 171 (its first phase assigned to Stratum VII), and the pottery within the blockage belongs to Stratum VI. While there are plans showing these features, no soil layers linked them and no sections could show their connections. Hellenistic construction lay above them, so they must belong to either Stratum VI or Stratum V; the pottery supports Stratum VI.

Stratum VI in Field IX (Ills. 138, 141 = IX AA, IX AA inset = figs. 236, 144 and 145 = IX DD and IX EE)

In the north half of Field IX, Stratum VI inhabitants reused Stratum VII remains. Walls 9776, 9528 rebuilt as 9528A and 9526 rebuilt as 9526A all continued. Over what had been Room 1 of Stratum VII, as the upper part of a dense chalk-filled soil layer, Stratum VI was represented by soil layer IX EE:##7 over 8 to Wall 9528A, covering over Wall 9845 of Stratum VII. The two layers suggest two phases of use (VIA over VIB), within reused Room 1. The upper surface of this Stratum VI soil was ashy, evidencing destruction. In the ash was a bronze spear head.

The line of Stratum VII Wall 9830 was re-established, offset slightly southward but perhaps simply slumped that way, as Wall 9801. Walls 9789 and 9300 were reused, and a wall on top of 9803, junctioned with 9801, served as the eastern boundary of a room crossed by IX AA. During Stratum VI, new Wall 9787 replaced Walls 9808 and 9803, defining a room in much the same position as Room 6 of Stratum VII. A barely discernible line of wall, collapsed into the northeast corner of Area 2, ran close to the line of Walls 9302/9301 of Stratum VII, probably defining the south limit of this room. Then, irregular and very poorly preserved humps of brick debris hint at wall lines to the south, although their depiction on Ill. 138 is quite uncertain.

All the walls of Stratum VI were mudbrick on a foundation of occasional, not continuous rock. The brick was quite distinctive to the period, with a markedly yellowish color, recalling brick debris of this stratum also found in Field VII. The field records do not provide definition of architecture south of the middle cross-balk, though there was clearly a thick layer of destruction debris, locus 9281, over most of Area 2 and a corresponding accumulation over Area 1.

As with Stratum VII remains, it is at IX AA, along the south edge of the room defined by Walls 9789, 9788 cornering with 9300, 9787 and 9801, where a succession of Stratum VI layering could be traced. It is depicted on the IX AA inset, fig. 236. The lowest flooring was a plaster surface at the base of locus 9793A (#19), which marked destruction on a VIB surface that connected Walls 9788, 9808 and 9801. There was probably still another VIB surface in the tight stratigraphy here, mentioned in field notes but not visible on section. In the comparable layer on the south side of the balk between Areas 2 and 4 (IX DD:#14) was heavy ash and destruction debris, and in it an iron spear head. About 40 indicator sherds from these loci define Stratum VI, although there are earlier Iron II sherds among them. Further east, either side of the balk between Areas 2 and 1 from the region of the collapse over Wall 9301 and the poorly preserved Wall complex 9040A, was another crush of Stratum VI pottery.

Stratum VIA occupancy is marked by IX AA inset:#17, a plaster floor covered by ashy layer 9793 and destruction debris in Layer #16 (locus 9781) which connects Walls 9788 and 9787, the new construction. This layer 0.12 m thick contained crushed store jars and other crushed pottery, and an overturned mortar. Two slingstones and an iron arrowhead were in the debris. Over the destruction debris there accumulated layer #15 on the AA inset, locus 9779, made up of collapsed and eroded mudbrick from the adjacent walls suggesting that considerable time passed before anyone took up occupancy here again. Locus 9779 corresponded to the thick destruction debris covering Area 2 noted above.

In summary, Field IX, presented two phases within Stratum VI, one built immediately after the destruction of the other. Both were violently destroyed. Three locations in the otherwise poorly preserved remains afford good sequences for control: Room 1, Room 6, and the area at the point where the central balks crossed. After the second destruction, the evidence indicates a hiatus in occupation.

Stratum VI in Field VII (Ill. 116)

A similar picture of two closely succeeding occupations, both destroyed, built into Stratum VII remains and followed by a hiatus, emerged in Field VII. A few refurbishings on the upper terrace to the west may stem from Stratum VI, but none are confidently to be assigned to it. The only strong evidence is displayed on Ill. 116 = VII DD. It was preserved only in a narrow gully off the southeast corner of the 1727 house, nestled into the Stratum VII debris. Little architecture was preserved; no plan could be drawn. First detected in 1962 as the 1727 house was being dismantled, the evidence was significantly augmented when the 1.00 m wide balk between Areas 2 and 3 was removed early in the 1964 campaign.

The destruction of the 1727 house included the collapse of much of its eastern facade, as has been noted. Particularly vulnerable seems to have been Room 10. Its entire east half collapsed and then eroded downslope to the south and east. In the process, the rock undergirding around Wall 1157 gave way, doubtless undercut by the flow of water through the drain system that underlay Rooms 9 and 10. This is probably what produced the gully in which Stratum VI people placed brick on stone huts.

Field reports first posited a reconstruction of the cobbled floor of Room 10 in Stratum VI, because there were a few sherds assigned to the Stratum VI corpus beneath it; a few Stratum VI sherds were also identified beneath the floor of Room 5 and in the foundations of Wall 1333. This hypothesis, while possible, is questionable. The degree of disturbance here may have introduced stray sherds from above, and the pottery needs to be reviewed. Cobbling 1332, although at a slightly higher elevation (17.15) than other surfaces in the house, was the only one attested for Room 10.

As VII DD shows, beneath Stratum IV remains (#8) was a thick leveling fill of grey soil with random stones in two layers, both included in #9. Pottery in the fill was of all periods of Iron II including Stratum V, with one or two Hellenistic Stratum IV sherds. It covered a layer of crusty lime, between layers ##9 and 10 on the section, about 0.05 m thick which yielded upon exposure a distinct smell of burning and rubbish. The lime crust and marks of burning attached to the surfaces of a quantity of brick red pottery, whose slip flaked off upon exposure. The pottery lay on and in layer #10, locus 1131, which showed a lens of ash and a high concentration of fired brick lumps along with charcoal lumps and flecks. The source of this spill was lost, due to the fact that the cross-balk between Areas 2 and 5, just at its point of origin, was

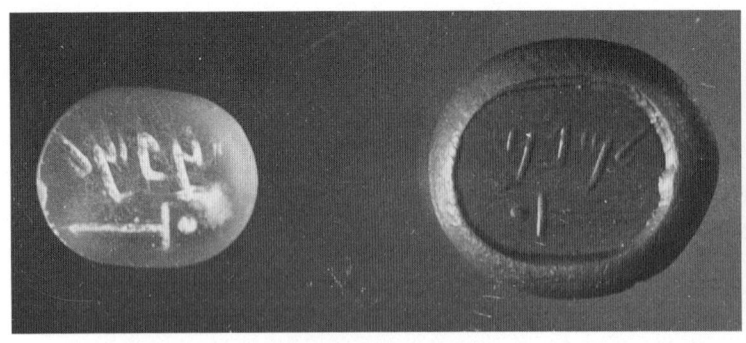

Fig. 268. Chalcedony lmbn *seal from Hellenistic fill 1202, paleographically to the time of Stratum VI.*

torn down without appropriate recording (note the dotted lines in the VII DD section drawing).

Below locus 1131 was 1132A, DD:#12, grey soil of a softer texture with the same characteristic pottery but with fewer fired brick chunks and less charcoal. It covered ash layer #13 on Surface 1132 = #14. On the ash layer was a jumble of stone which fell southward from the point where Wall 1137 is reconstructed in the section. The wall must have been brick on stone and was very poorly preserved. It apparently was the north edge of a hut positioned in the balk and extending only a little ways into Area 2 adjacent to it. Floor 1132 went with it; the ash accumulated on the floor; the wall collapsed over the ash. To all appearances, Wall 1137 was built *on* the floor after it had been established. Within the balk, but not shown on section, was a lie of stones at its south end, locus 1169, probably the southern limit of the hut. A hump of fired brick lay between the two jumbles of stone on Floor 1132 within the balk. A collection of over 50 indicator sherds attests Stratum VI forms from this complex within the balk alone. Another 65 were recovered from the debris within Area 2.

The ash layer on 1132 is clearly visible on the south balk of Area 2 where it runs almost level. Its west end reaches the region of the "1048 house," the Stratum VII building set into a depression at the south limit of the field which has been posited as the companion home sharing a yard with the 1727 house. Apparently the Stratum VI 1137-1132 hut nestled not only into the south ruins of the 1727 house but also into the ruined east edge of the 1780 complex.

Beneath the 1137-1132 complex was locus 1138, as much as 0.50 m thick of yellow-to-orange bricky soil, VII DD:#16. The color contrasted with a pink brick deposit found to the south and east throughout much of Area 2. An "eye" of this pink debris appears in the section as #15. At removal of the balk, detailed analysis of this deposit revealed a layer of white plaster, locus 11.100, 0.02–0.03 m thick, at the top of the eye, lying upon two segments of fallen brick arching up to produce the configuration of the eye. The arched brick, Loci 11.101 and 11,102, lay over horizontal bricks and a few flat stones, again suggesting fall from a hut wall, shown at the north limit of the eye in the section. More Stratum VI pottery was preserved within this collapse. The lower complex lay on a surface, DD:#17, which had makeup 1139 (#19) beneath it, of Stratum VII debris. The rubbly soil beneath the eye at its south end is apparently an intrusion from outside the field of excavation; there was Hellenistic pottery in it, as well as Stratum VI sherds.

This set of finds suggests that as with Field IX there were two stages to Stratum VI occupation, both of which suffered destruction. Weaponry was not found in the Stratum VI ruins in Field VII, as it had been in Field IX. The nature of the collapse of the buildings and the amount of broken pottery do suggest violence, and the rebuild of the 1137 hut on 1138 ruins suggests little lapse of time between the two stages.

One other artifact throws light on Stratum VI and belies perhaps the sense of poverty one gets from the ruins. It is a seal (fig. 268) found in mixed Hellenistic fill 1202 high in Field VII (Cross 1962). Carved in a rare piece of clear, blue chalcedony, it contains four Hebrew letters, *lmbn*, a

Fig. 269. Looking north at Field IX Area 1 balk, with the meter stick on plaster Floor 9037.

hypochoristicon for a name such as *mibneyahu* (note also Mebunnai of 2 Samuel 23:27; Zeron 1979). Beneath the letters is a symbol in the tradition of a mace—a mark of divinity often included in the depictions of deities in neo-Assyrian and neo-Babylonian iconography. The Assyrian seal from the 1727 house debris shows the goddess carrying a mace consisting of a handle and a globe, though it lacks the crossbar shown on the *lmbn* seal.

Cross's paleographic analysis led him to propose a broad date range: seventh or sixth century. If Stratum VI belonged to the seventh century and Stratum V to the sixth, the seal might represent either. But Stratum V falls late in the sixth century, from 525 BCE on, and that is late for the letter forms, especially of the *lamedh* (cf. Avigad 1986). The *lmbn* seal fits Stratum VI.

STRATUM V

Stratum V at Shechem is better attested by its artifacts than by its architecture or stratigraphy. In Field IX, as the sections attest, Stratum V was a thin layer often cut into by the Stratum IV Hellenistic builders who founded the succeeding city in the late fourth century BCE. Field observations in both Field IX and Field VII sometimes found difficulty in assigning features to Stratum IV or placing them in Stratum V. The artifact range, however, confirms that there was a Persian period settlement on the site in the late sixth to early fifth century whose character was distinctive and not poverty-ridden.

In Field IX a soil layer of nearly sterile decayed grey brick was thinly preserved throughout, with somewhat deeper pockets here and there. Typical brick size measured between 0.25 and 0.30 in length and 0.15 in thickness. Stratum V brick resembled no other found at Shechem, made of fine-textured mud devoid of binder; scraping produced a sheen, with a greasy appearance. Stratum VI bricks were yellow-orange with straw binder, as were those of Stratum IV. The rare patches of flooring were plastered with coarse, crusty lime. An example is Surface 9037 with stones spread around it, shown in fig. 269. The stones may have carried brick walls. The layer of 9037 floor and occupation debris shows on IX DD:##10 and 12 humping over Stratum VI collapsed Wall 9039, and could be discerned in the west balk of the area.

Ruins of a tannur were identified roughly 4.00 m away to the northwest in the southeast corner of Area 4, again with a pile of stones and the distinctive grey bricky detritus. Several other pockets of Stratum V layering were identified. Locus 9273 with a fragment of Wall 9274 on VII DD as #11.

300   SHECHEM III. THE IRON AGE

Fig. 270. Looking south in Field VII Area 7. Tannur 1828 is in the lower right corner, with Hellenistic Wall 1817 resting on its rim.

A fill, locus 9278, over Stratum VI remains and just beneath the tannur mentioned above is not shown on any section, but its pottery belonged to Stratum V. Locus 9524 in the north of Area 3 also contained this pottery. But the most striking thing about Stratum V in Field IX is that it virtually cannot be isolated, and loci assigned to it were very thin, presumably invaded by the Hellenistic strata to follow. No complex or pottery crush provided a deposit to define Stratum V.

In Field VII, Stratum V inhabitants made no attempt to build on top of the 1727 ruin, nor on the upper terrace to the west. Stratum V remains were on the south slope, at the far northeast, and

Fig. 271. Looking east in Field VII Area 4, with oval installation 1544-1545 at right. The thick plaster layer in the balk is Hellenistic Floor 1521, interrupted just above the meter stick by Pit 1522, cut down almost to the top of 1544-1545.

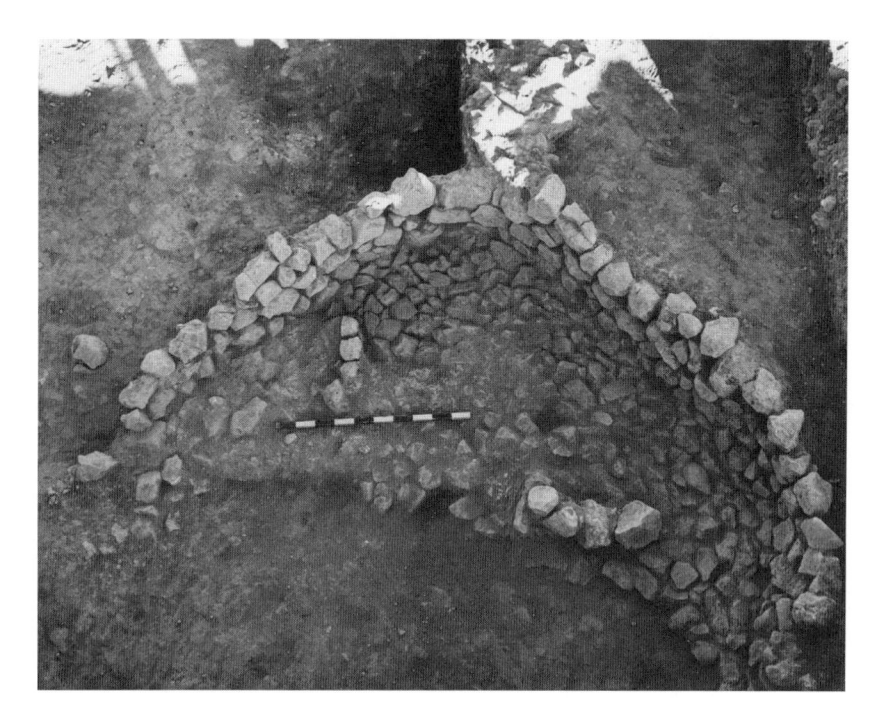

Fig. 272. Looking north in Field VII Area 2 at Installation 1127.

on the lower terrace to the east. One Stratum V installation was a tannur, 1828, placed over the Stratum VI complex in Area 7. Hellenistic Wall 1817 rested on its rim, just at its west end, as seen in the lower right of fig. 270.

Areas 4 and 2, east and south of the front door of the 1727 house, were covered with metalled Surface 1530-1229-1232-1234, beneath which another metalled surfacing, 1230, was also traced. These layers belonged to the very first stages of Hellenistic construction on the site in Stratum IV. The pottery in the soil above them had a large proportion of Stratum V forms, suggesting how much turmoil the Hellenistic builders caused. This phenomenon was typical. Most Stratum V pottery is out of stratigraphic context.

Beneath 1530 in Area 4 was fill 1556, Ill. 113 = VII BB:#11, down to the top of the Stratum VII debris 1539 = #13. Forty-six baskets of pottery were taken from this thick deposit of fill, the site's richest collection of distinctive Stratum V forms, always mixed with sherds mostly from Stratum VII with a few earlier sherds. The fill seems to have come from nearby, not imported from deep debris dug elsewhere on the site.

Placed into the 1539 destruction debris and buried within the 1556 fill was the curious installation 1544-1545, an oval pen 1.25 m wide and over 2.00 m long—its south end is hidden in the balk—which came to light by degrees in the excavation, since its surrounding wall was preserved to different heights and it had been partially dismantled by Hellenistic intrusion. It is shown in fig. 271. The western portion, Wall 1531, protruded above metalled Surface 1530, and may have functioned in Stratum IV; the rest is assigned to Stratum V. Inside the oval was a rubbery dense deposit 0.40 m thick, its top at elevation 16.15, as much as 0.40 m above the top of the Stratum VII debris, to which it reached. The deposit was devoid of distinctive pottery, though the wares suggested Iron II earlier than Stratum VI or VII. Adjacent to 1544-1545 on the east was massive Hellenistic Pit 1522, which cut its connections to the east balk of the field.

In Area 2 to the southwest of this installation was the tightly-laid cobble floor Installation 1127 shown in fig. 272. Interrupted on the south by another Hellenistic pit, it was surrounded by a curb wall 1128 which extended beneath it for 0.18 m; Wall 1128 was built before 1127 was laid. Extrapolating the curve of 1128 yielded a diameter of 3.20 m. On the 1127 cobbling were two shallow curves of stone visible in the photograph; when lifted, they

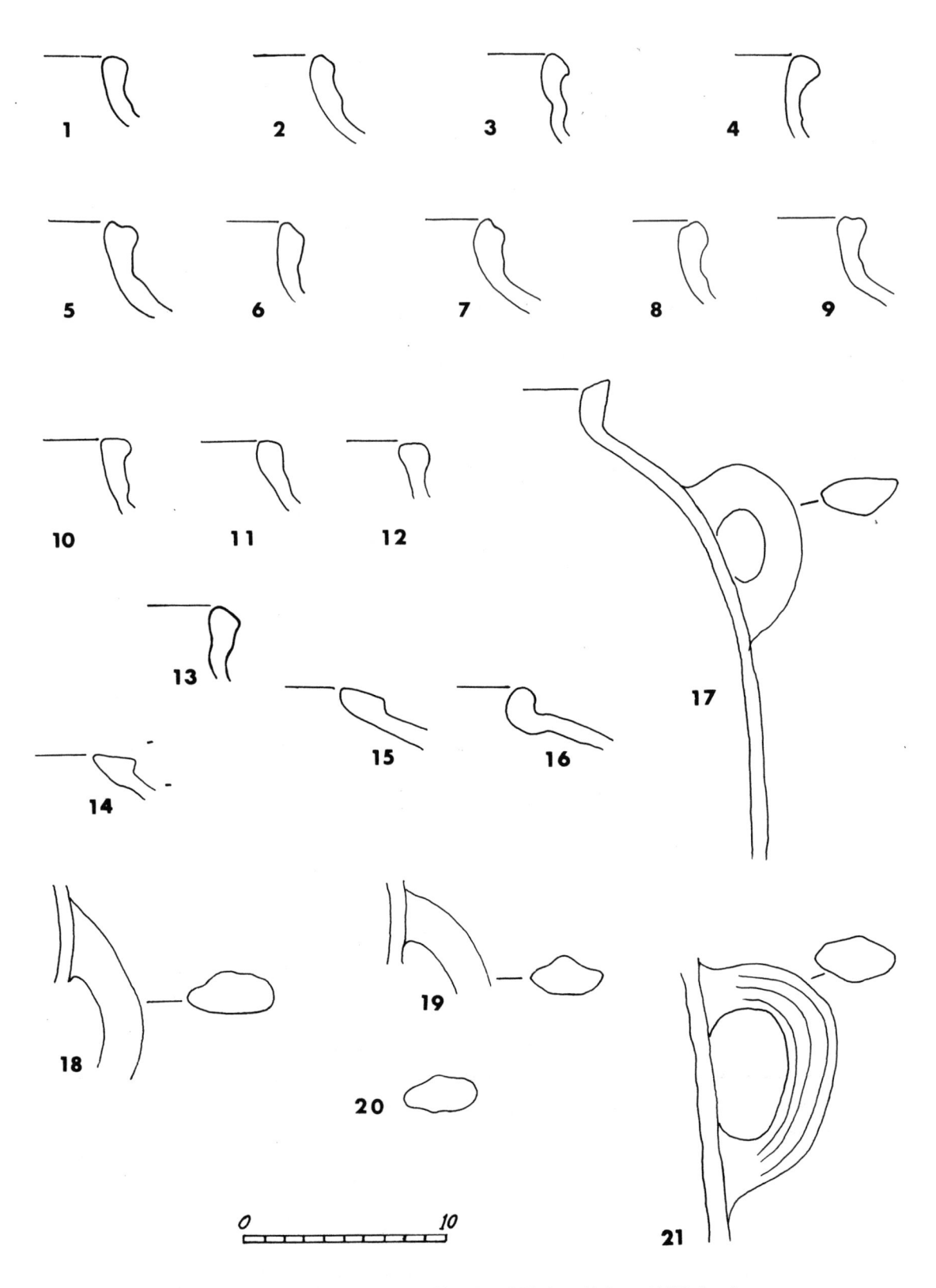

Fig. 273. Jar forms of Stratum V, Fields VII and IX, from N. Lapp (1985:fig. 4).

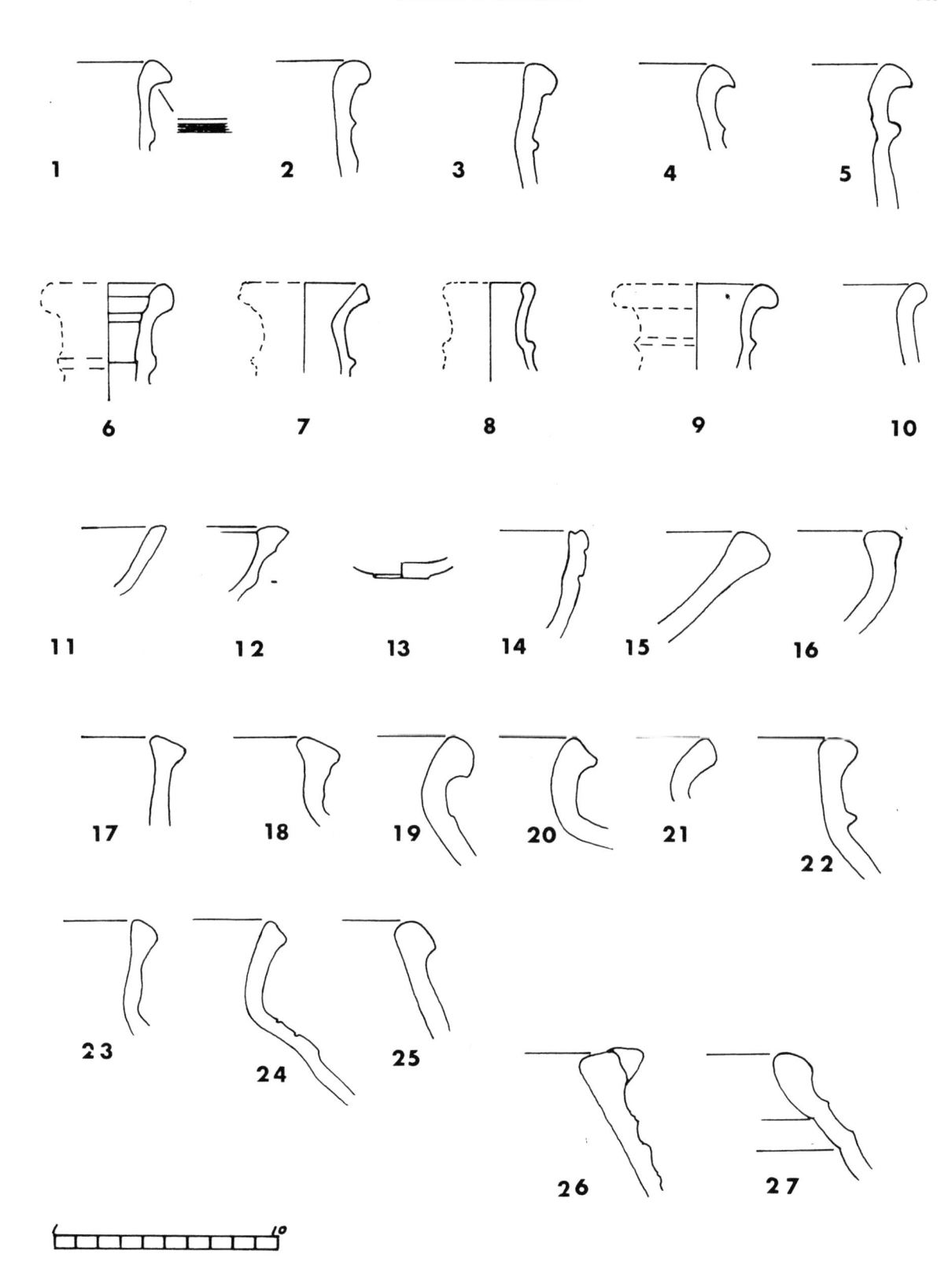

Fig. 274. Jug, bowl and crater forms of Stratum V, from Fields VII and IX, from N. Lapp (1985:fig 5).

304　　　　　　　　　　　　　　　SHECHEM III. THE IRON AGE

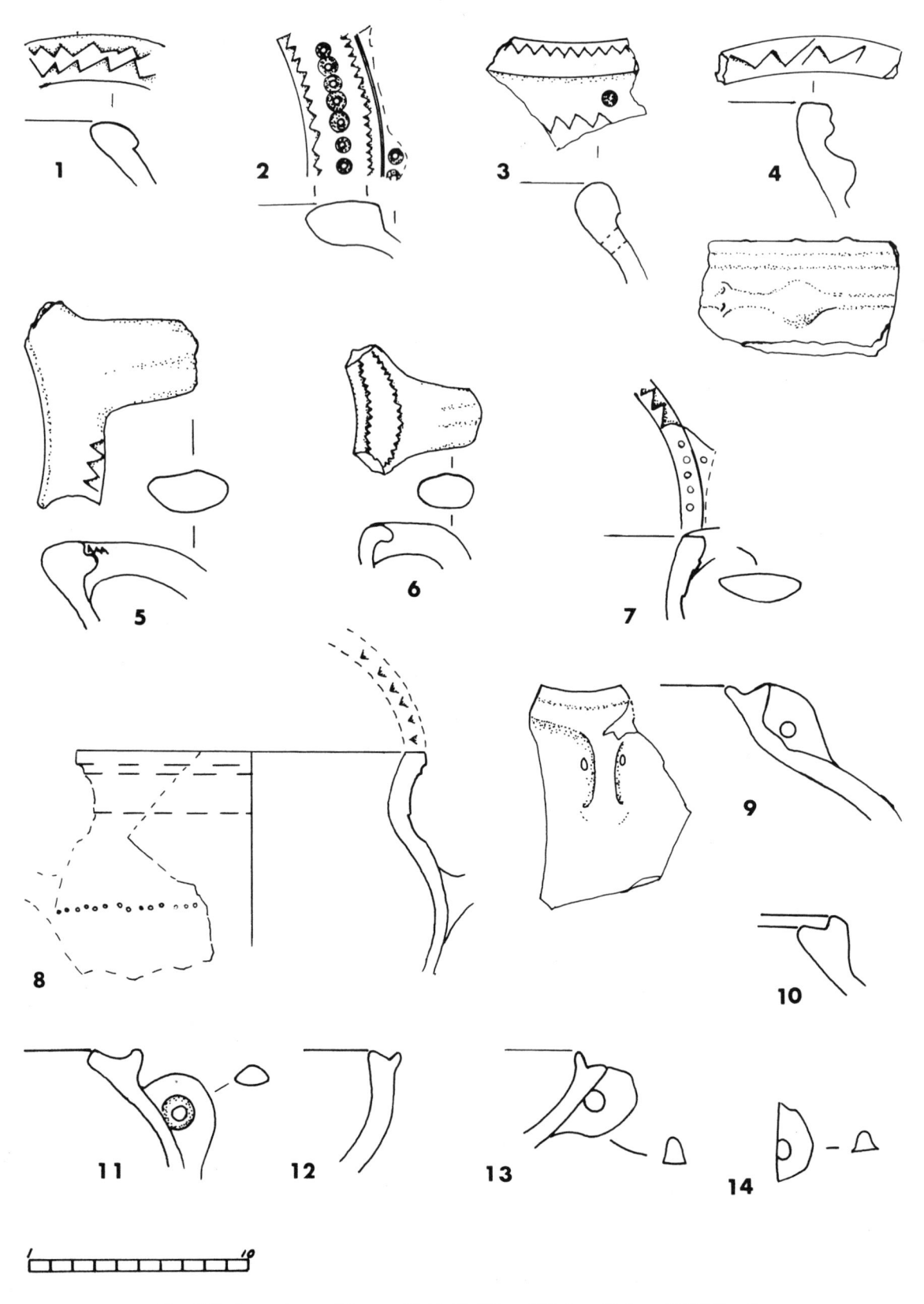

Fig. 275. Crater forms of Stratum V, Fields VII and IX, from N. Lapp (1985:fig. 6).

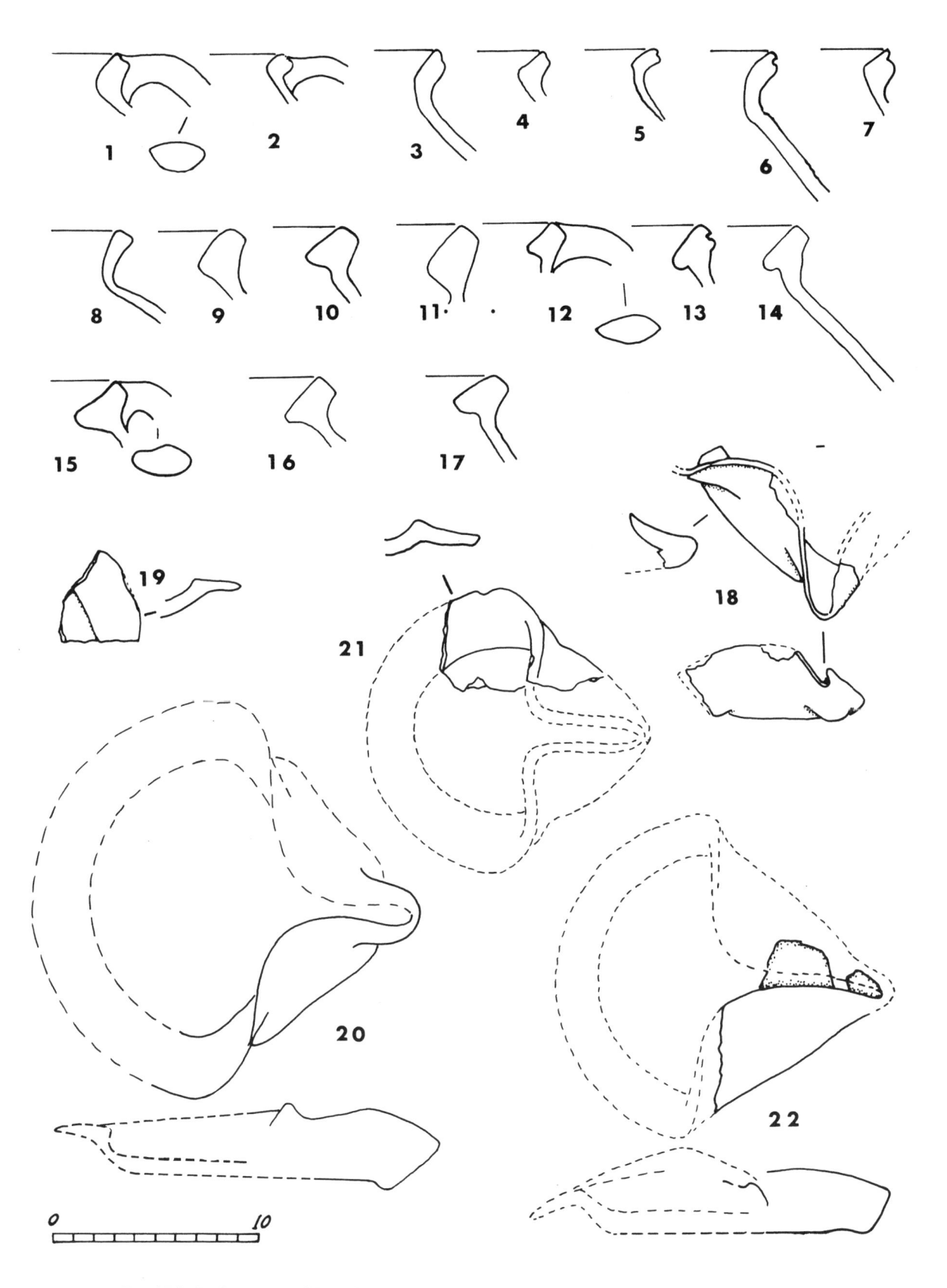

Fig. 276. Cooking pot and lamp forms of Stratum V, Fields VII and IX, from N. Lapp (1985:fig. 7).

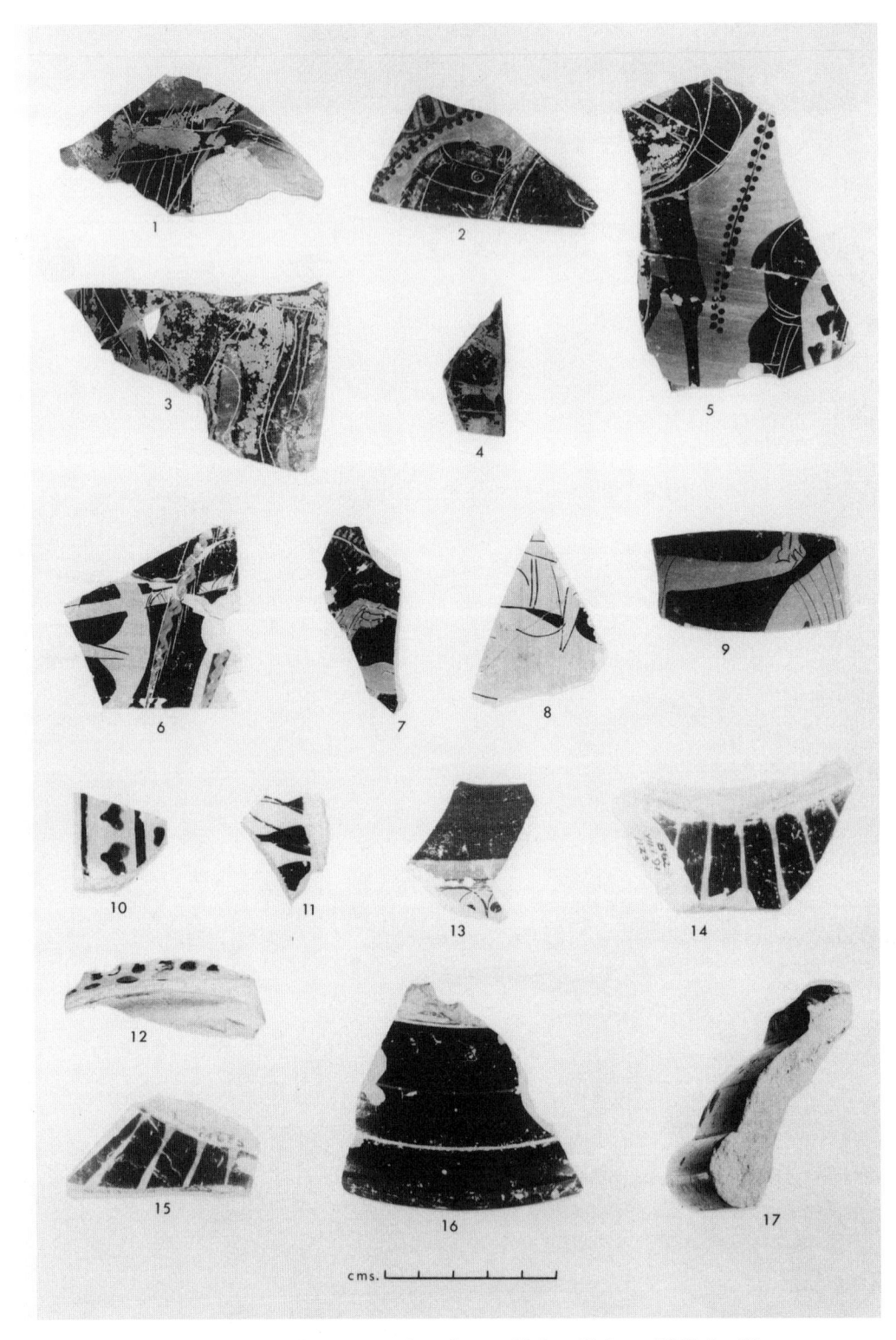

Fig. 277. Examples of Attic wares from Stratum V, from N. Lapp (1985:fig. 10).

Fig. 278. Electrum coin minted on Thasos, dated to Stratum V period.

proved to have sealed a few Stratum V sherds beneath them, but the pottery on the surface of the installation belonged to Stratum IV, and four ware sherds (not indicator forms) from beneath 1127 looked to belong to Stratum IV. The pottery yield was very slim above and below this circle. Perhaps a tent-floor or foundation for a circular hut, it probably belongs to Stratum V but cannot serve to define it.

Nancy Lapp has published the Shechem corpus of Stratum V pottery (1985), building upon work published by her late husband (P. W. Lapp 1970). Nancy Lapp culled Shechem's Stratum V forms from a selection of loci of descending order of certainty as to their trustworthiness in defining the stratum. Locus 1556 is the most confidently used, along with the layering in Field IX and the fill layers below surfaces 1530 and 1230.

The local domestic pottery is shown in figs. 273–276. It fits well with the increasing collection of pottery forms from other sites which define the "Persian Period," about 540 to 330 BCE. Of particular importance is the incised triangle or chevron design on the rims of big kraters, unique to the period and found at more than a dozen sites in the hill country north and south, as well as on the coastal plain (Stern 1982). This vessel belonged to the earlier part of the 200-year spread of the Persian period.

Of great importance is the imported Attic ware. Nancy Lapp constructed the complete catalog of 158 sherds of this highly distinctive pottery (fig. 277). It dates to the period ca. 525 to 475 BCE; the Attic decorative styles that characterize late fifth century are not represented. On this criterion, Shechem's Stratum V occupation was of short duration. The soil seems to point to the same conclusion: the top of Stratum VI debris was eroded and worn so as to indicate an interval of some years between VI and V, while Stratum V debris was eroded and blanketed over with soil before Hellenistic builders cut into it as they prepared to build upon it.

The presence of the Attic ware speaks to the issue of the material culture of Stratum V. It includes at a minimum four kraters, three cups, and several lekythoi. This rich spread of imported luxury vessels indicates a fair degree of prosperity.

Another such indicator is an electrum coin found in 1956 in mixed debris over the East Gate (fig. 278). Minted on the island of Thasos near the Thracian coast in the far north of the Aegean, it presumably came to Palestine with Greek or Phoenician traders and found its way from a port such as Dor or Tell Abu Hawam up to Shechem. G. E. Wright had Lamia Rustum Shehadeh analyze it for publication in *SBBC*:168–69. Her report is repeated here:

> [The coin] is 2 cm. in diameter and weighs 145 grains. *Obverse.* Silenus in a kneeling-running position is carrying off a nymph. An ancient incision across the coin cleaves the head of Silenus in two. There is no border. *Reverse.* A quarter incuse square; no border. The type is characteristic of the coins of Thasos in the late sixth century BCE. Thasos was rich in wine and its main deity was Dionysius, the god of wine. Its main cult was the worship of Silenus, companion of Dionysius. This type is represented on the city's earliest coins, *ca.* 560—465 BCE.
>
> The way the type is adapted to the field by making Silenus kneel is important in dating this coin. It was the custom in the early period of coinage among the Greeks to adapt the type to the field, as in reverting the head of an animal, or in a heraldic arrangement,

Fig. 279. Impression of a Persian period seal on a bulla. The reverse shows the imprint of papyrus fiber.

308   SHECHEM III. THE IRON AGE

Fig. 280. Impression of a lion figure on a Stratum V jar handle, B62, Object #349.

or the so-called kneeling (actually running) figures. This method continued to be used until the figure was represented in its natural attitude and the circular field was filled up by legends, symbols and the like.

Wright added, "The incision across the coin was common in the earliest coins of Greece. It was done to test the genuineness of the metal at a time when coinage was new and its value not trusted" (p. 169). He cited an Attic silver coin found in west Jerusalem as contemporary. A third sixth-century coin has been found at Ketef Hinnom in southwest Jerusalem minted on the island of Kos (Barkay 1986:29, 34).

Another glimpse of Stratum V material culture is afforded by the Persian seal impression

Fig. 281. Seven of the stamp impressions probably from Stratum V, showing an oval with a crossbar (resembling a "theta") with lines running away from the top of the oval. The vertical strokes have been interpreted as signifying "26."

shown in fig. 279, depicting the king as an archer, with the symbol of Ahura Mazda in the field behind his back. The seal had been pressed into a bulla affixed to a papyrus document, the impression of the fibers showing on the reverse of the bulla. Apparently, Shechem's Stratum V settlement was sufficiently important to have received a sealed official document.

A roaring lion on the jar handle seal impression shown in fig. 280 adds a different dimension. Stern (1982: 209–13) has discussed 59 examples of stamp seals depicting lions along with seven from Ramet Rahel showing a bull in a posture very similar to this lion. All of these stamps except the Shechem one come from Judean sites, and the lion is a Judean symbol. The stamp regularly marks handles of wine jars; apparently a jar of wine from a Judean site found its way to Shechem.

Finally there are the stamp impressions known so far only from Shechem (fig. 281). Counting the examples found by the Austro-German expedition (five now in Leiden and two in the Rockefeller Museum in Jerusalem), one from 1957, four from 1960 and four from 1962 (all found in Field VII), and two found in Field I Area 17 during the 1964 season, there are eighteen of these handles. None comes from a tightly stratified context; all those found by the Joint Expedition are from fills or disturbances, while the provenances of the ones the Germans found are unrecorded, so they cannot be proven to come from Stratum V. When Paul Lapp included them in a study of third century BCE stamped jar handles (1963b:26–29), he connected them to Shechem Stratum IV (around 300 BCE), the latest possible date. All are broken at the point of the upper handle join and none is a complete handle, so they are not comparable to known Stratum V rims or handle profiles. Lapp saw that the ware is not like the typical beige or tan jar handles of Shechem's Hellenistic pottery; it more closely resembles the very few handles from Stratum V. There are no examples of similar ware on other forms. Wright was probably correct to place them in Stratum V (*SBBC*:67; accepted by Stern 1982:214). This conclusion fits with the analysis of the stamp's symbols.

On the seal is an oval with a crossbar; two horizontal lines run away from the top of the oval. Beneath this symbol is a bent mark followed by six vertical strokes. There is consensus that this represents the number "26" and designates the capacity of the jar. Cross (1969: 21–22) compares a fourth century Phoenician stamp from Shiqmona on the coast at the south edge of the Mt. Carmel peninsula which reads as follows:

> Belonging to Ben-Matton, 25 [10 + 10 + 1 + 1 + 1 + 1 + 1]
> according to the royal (standard):
> Wine of Gat Karmel
> Ṭeth (symbol)

Note the indication of capacity, the notice of the royal standard, the contents and the single letter (Hebrew/Aramaic *ṭeth*) as a symbol. When these are taken with other indications from seals turning up throughout the land, they add up to this: the Shechem handles are from wine jars, of standard size assured by official seal, with an alphabetic *ṭeth* as the official marker. The Shechem *ṭeth* mark, if from Stratum V, is the earliest in a series of examples from Elephantine in Egypt, Shiqmona, and a number of Judean locations.

The architectural evidence for Stratum V might indicate that Persian period Shechem was an insubstantial settlement. But these objects suggest more: association with Judea, as well as a certain degree of prosperity. They point to a flow of Greek imports to (and through) Shechem, perhaps diverted from their travel to Samaria. They hint that Shechem had official standing in Persian administration—perhaps as district capital of the Province of Samaria (Stern 1982:244–45; Avi-Yonah 1966:24–25). They suggest that there was a prominent vineyard in the vicinity that shipped its product to Shechem in marked jars. Until the same jar stamp turns up somewhere else, it appears Shechem received the whole supply.

CHAPTER 6

THE HELLENISTIC PERIOD

LATE IN THE FOURTH CENTURY BCE, Shechem recovered, after a gap in occupation of a century and a half (G. E. Wright 1962c). Evidence of Hellenistic occupation was found over the entire mound by the Austro-German and the Joint Expeditions. At no point did all four of the phases assigned to the period lie in stratified sequence. However, four distinctive corpora of pottery were isolated in connection with Hellenistic remains, breaking into two pairs of two, based upon correlation with datable coinage. Strata IV and III go with Ptolemaic coinage and date before about 190 BCE; Strata II and I are second century in date, with Seleucid coinage; the pottery pre-dates that found at Qumran. Taken together with textual information about destruction of the site by John Hyrcanus, the data point to an end in the final decade of the second century. The resulting proposed chronology is as follows:

>Stratum IV ca. 325—250 BCE
>Stratum III ca. 250—190 BCE
>Stratum II ca. 190—150 BCE
>Stratum I ca. 150—110 BCE

Paul W. Lapp was key to developing the sense of Shechem's Hellenistic pottery typologies, working with his wife Nancy L. Lapp (P. W. Lapp 1961; N. L. Lapp 1964; Lapp and Lapp 1974). Their ongoing pottery studies, informed by participation in the Beth-zur season of 1957 and work in Mughâret Abu Shinjeh in the Wadi Daliyeh, conversed with the excavation of Hellenistic loci from 1957 to 1964. The description that follows indicates the degree of confidence felt by the Joint Expedition staff, as it developed from the time of excavation to the time of this writing. It depicts again the Joint Expedition method of discerning stratigraphy while reading pottery typology.

Hellenistic architecture lay just beneath the modern surface of the mound. Modern plowing, recent stone robbing, recent burials and the construction of relatively modern structures such as animal pens or rude huts interrupted architectural coherence and made the discernment of the stratification a particularly keen problem. The latest extensive Hellenistic architecture was built in Stratum II, with at least the Field II house persisting into Stratum I. Otherwise, Stratum I is represented by disconnected walls in several excavation fields, by a range of pottery later than that characteristic of Stratum II, and by coins of the second half of the second century BCE, the latest in context dating from 121–120 BCE and another from disturbed debris in Field III dated tentatively to 112–111 BCE.

FORTIFICATIONS

Field I (Ills. 12, 17 [plans]; 20 = IAA, 21 = IBB, 22 = ICC and fig. 128 [sections])

Evidence for Hellenistic fortification came from Fields I and III. Field I controls what can be said. The Sellin team had excavated in 1926 the central passageway of the MB IIC East Gate, revealing the south pairs of orthostats, and the entire northern gate tower. The undisturbed southern gate tower and the slope east of it were the subject of attention during the brief 1956 season of the Joint Expedition, via a three-meter wide trench running 38 meters from the interior of the gate tower and extending slightly farther east than the BB section drawn in 1957 depicts. The trench encountered the southern part of the "Hellenistic Tower," a rectangular structure some 12.50 m away from the facade of the MB IIC gate.

In 1957, broadened study of the top of the gate tower revealed later Hellenistic features, while the

Fig. 282. Fragment of Hellenistic wall on the MB IIC tower wall of the East Gate, Field I.

trench down the slope was widened to the north so as to reveal the entire Hellenistic Tower about 12.5 m downslope and outside the gate, as depicted in Ill. 12). Sections I AA = Ill. 20, I BB = Ill. 21 and I CC = Ill. 22 were all drawn during this campaign, with I CC on the north intentionally rendered as though viewed from the north to show correspondences with the other two.

In 1962, Paul Lapp and Nasr Dhiab trimmed the balk on the south edge of Field I back 0.60 m to test previous hypotheses. This work ran from a point about 3.50 m east of the front of the East Gate and permitted the extension of the south section of the field by about 5.00 m (fig. 128). With some matters still unclear, James Fennelly probed the gap Lapp had left in front of the gate tower in 1964. Even with all this checking, the interpretation of the Hellenistic fortification system in Field I remains uncertain.

The Earliest Hellenistic Phase. The top of the MB IIC fortification, with its white glacis capping, appears on I BB as the narrow layer between #8 and #9 and running beneath #7 close to the gate tower. Layer #8 was striated makeup topping the glacis and continuing down the slope to approach the top of battered Wall A, the eastern line of the Cyclopean Wall of the earlier part of MB IIC. Layer #8 was capped by a thin layer of white chalk shown between I BB:##6 and 8. Layer #8 contained a mixture of pottery, the latest of which was Hellenistic. When the trench was widened northward in 1957, this striated soil was stripped in layers over to the north balk of the same cut, depicted in I CC:#4. Hellenistic pottery mixed with pottery from all periods from MB IIA onwards characterized the fill all the way to its bottom on #7. It is indisputable that a fill imported from another location on the tell made up this layer and that it was laid down within the Hellenistic period by builders who purposely cleared to the MB IIC glacis, even cutting into it, to consolidate the slope. That process removed evidence of the intervening periods of the site's occupation.

Section I BB:#4, made up of decomposed orange-red mudbrick, spilled just over the edge of the preserved MB IIC gate tower, continuing the "decomposed mud brick" layer that covered the south guard room. Sherds taken from this brick layer in 1957 were Hellenistic in date. It is not clear from the 1956 records whether ##5 and 7 below this brick detritus contained datable pottery, but a sensible hypothesis is that these horizontal layers represent the roadways approaching the old gate passageway along the exposed face of the old MB IIC gate tower. Bricks and a few stones at their eastern lip, beneath #7 only about 2.00 m. wide and with #5 either 2.00 or nearly 3.00 m wide, represented curbs for the roads. Section I BB:#7 bottomed at elevation ca. 7.50 and reached the exposed tower wall about 2.00 m below its preserved top. Layer #5 was at elevation ca. 8.50.

The first Hellenistic approach to the city apparently ran next to the exposed top of the MB IIC gate tower and made a right angle turn between the towers, as had happened in MB IIC times. Within the old gate passage, the entrance was then at approximately the same level as that of the last MB IIC, which was at 7.90 to 8.20 within the gate before descending steps at the back from 8.09 to 7.50 (Ill. 12). The Hellenistic gateway was essentially a gully between ruins more than 1200 years old, with the ends of the orthostats protruding from accumulated debris filling around them. The two narrow curb walls continued to function to hold back ancient debris, from the inner ends of the front pair of MB IIC orthostats to the back pair, shown on the overall gate plan. Elevations on the tops of these walls were at 8.02 and 7.94 on the north side, where the wall was wider and built of facing stones with a rubble core, and 7.88 on the south side where the wall was a single stone wide and thinner. These curbs, then, were virtually at the level of the passageway between them.

On top of the gate, two fragments of walling with flat tops were preserved for only one course of stone. They are drawn on Ill. 17 labeled "Hellenistic additions," with elevations on their tops at 10.19 and 9.15. The fragment resting on the interior of the thick MB IIC gate tower was about 1.30 m wide and appears on fig. 282 with the southeast pair of orthostats in the background. The brick spill lying on the white tamped top of the Hellenistic "glacis" may have come from the brick superstructure placed on these stone foundations.

Probably the fortification then followed the line of Wall B as it ran south from the gate. Two faces of walling, separated by 3.40 m of loose earth and large stones mixed with much broken pottery, were sited on top of Wall B. Ill. 20 = I AA shows the western face, bowed westward, at the edge of the huge robber pit which took the core and the east face away. The robber pit was filled with rubble and garbage from upper Hellenistic strata; apparently the contents of the pit and the remains of the rubble and loose earth core of the wall were not distinguished at the time of digging, and the pottery from this spot is not a trustworthy guide to the dating of these features. Since the upper part of the robber pit reached into the plow zone, it is impossible to tell whether the Hellenistic rebuild of Wall B would have been stone to its top or brick on a stone foundation.

Section I AA:##9–11 shows layers of fill running away from the east face of the proposed Hellenistic rebuild of Wall B, resting on packed grey soil over striated makeup—very much like the conditions against the gate tower in I BB:##4, 5 and 7 (Ill. 21). A plausible hypothesis would be that the approach road to the gate hugged rebuilt Wall B as well as the gate tower, riding on the striated makeup below the packed grey and curbed by the rise at its east edge, before the striated fill sloped sharply down to the east. There was no accumulation of decomposed mud brick over the gate tower at the line of I AA as there was at the line of I BB, where it made up a large part of the spill (#6).

It is thus unclear whether the brick collapse down the slope resulted from destruction of the fortifications in battle, or was part of the consolidation of the slope and was reused brick detritus from earlier periods of the city's life. Within the brick debris, such pieces of brick as could be measured were rough squares about 0.15 to 0.20 m in size (Wright 1956:14); in 1957 bricks were found in the domestic housing debris inside the gate which measured 0.16 by 0.14 by 0.12 m. This brick is far smaller than bricks subsequently found to be characteristic of earlier periods of the site's history, and also smaller than a brick found in Field VII in a Stratum III context. The question of whether a destruction of fortifications is attested here remains unsettled, but inside the gate a housing complex showed violent destruction probably belonging to Stratum IV or III.

The system thus far described was the earliest Hellenistic fortification attested at the gate. It involved clearing to the MB IIC glacis, the laying in of the striated fill, consolidation with tamped chalk constituting what amounts to being another glacis, the building of a set of walls (mostly of brick?) on the foundations of the old tower and Wall B, and a collapse of brick detritus on the consolidated slope.

Later Hellenistic Phasing at the Gate. Section I BB shows this system plainly down to the top of Wall A, but difficulty arises at this point. The line of the Hellenistic consolidated slope may have dipped steeply east of Wall A and continued beneath I BB:#6 to a point below what the section shows, deep beneath Wall 105 of the rectangular Hellenistic Tower. Or it may have run on one of the two white lime layers inclining toward the foot of Wall 105.

This is what was illuminated by Lapp's 1962 work and his report prepared about it written in mid-1963. By that time, excavation in Fields II, VII and IX had provided greater precision about

Fig. 283. Stone-lined flagstone bin outside the fortifications east of the East Gate, assigned to a domestic complex belonging to Stratum IV. Robert J. Bull serves as scale.

the sequence of Hellenistic pottery collections, precision which Lapp had established both in his doctoral dissertation (P. W. Lapp 1961) and through the salvage excavation at Mugharet Abu Shinjeh where evidence of Samaritans fleeing Alexander's capture of Samaria in 331 BCE was found.

Lapp discerned a rebuild on top of Wall A shown on the section in fig. 128 with a foundation trench against its western face. His careful study of the layering against the east face of Wall A, however, found that layers labeled "tan clay," "coarse dark red" "coarse brown" and again "tan clay" contained Iron II pottery as their latest ingredient, and no Hellenistic. He proposed, then, that the Hellenistic consolidating layer was at a much higher elevation, just under Wall 105.

He also uncovered a wall farther east to which ran a cobbled floor of small stones packed with sherds, a floor G. E. Wright first noted in 1956 at its west extent (visible in the I BB section at the left margin within #2). A similar flooring ran east of the new wall, to the edge of the excavation; on it were a bread oven and the edge of a possible pottery kiln. A flagstone-floored bin discovered in 1956 but not shown on section (fig. 283) was positioned on the other side of the three-meter wide trench and somewhat to the west, its edge about 2.00 meters from the east wall of the Hellenistic Tower. Lapp concluded that the wall farthest east, the pebbled and sherd-packed floor, and the bin represented a home outside town and probably predated the laying in of the consolidation of the slope. It was clear from the growing knowledge of Hellenistic pottery at the site, and from its typological identity with the pottery Lapp had just been excavating at Mugharet Abu Shinjeh, that this home belonged to the late fourth century, the beginning date for Shechem Stratum IV. Lapp placed this extra-mural home earlier than the glacis, while Wright continued to maintain that the layers below the home were imported fill continuing the Hellenistic preparation even though they contained only MB IIC pottery. The disagreement has not been resolved.

Lapp then addressed the Hellenistic Tower, including Wall 105. The tower (Ill. 12) had walls from 1.00 m to as much as 1.40 m thick. It measured 7.50 m by 5.00 m on the outside; its interior chamber was about 5.00 m by 3.00 m. Wall 105 ran from the south wall of the rectangle into the south balk, its top at elevation 4.68, with its foot at 3.18, preserved to a height of 1.50 m. It appears to have been bonded into the south wall of the tower. The west wall of the tower extended

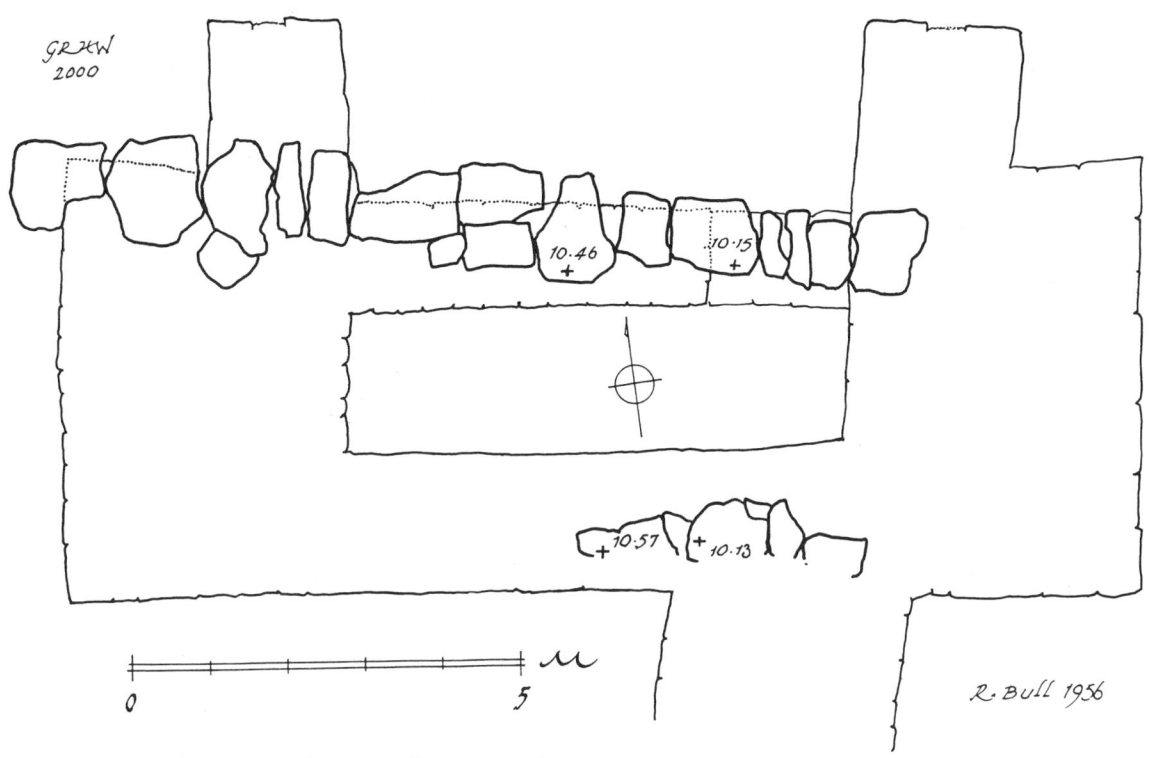

Fig. 284. Latest Hellenistic walls overlying the East Gate south tower (after 1956 drawing by Bull).

beyond the junction with the north wall, at first suggesting that a fortification wall might have run around the site with the tower integrated. But the west wall stopped 1.30 m north of the junction, without any indication of robbery of its continuation.

When Lapp cut the south balk back 0.60 m he encountered a wall perpendicular to Wall 105 and bonded with it, shown in elevation with the designation "IIIB Wall" on section in fig. 128. (Lapp's cut and this wall are not depicted on top plans.) He discerned a plastered floor in the corridor between the south wall of the tower and the new wall in elevation in the section. Wright had found the same floor in 1956 (*SBBC*:174). Pottery on it belongs to Stratum III. If this evidence is correct, the Hellenistic Tower becomes Stratum III in date.

In the fill at the foot of the Tower, but not clearly sealed beneath it nor connected to its use, a hoard of 15 Ptolemy I coins was found in 1956 (Wright 1956:13 corrected in *SBBC*:171 and 260 n. 2). The coins do not date the tower, but they loosely support the date of Stratum IV, with the caveat that coins can be kept over a long period.

Above the IIIB wall in the Lapp's section can be seen the 9.50 m extent of a heavy paving made of semi-dressed stones, assigned on pottery evidence to the latter part of Stratum III. This paving appears also on the I BB as #3 at the left. On both, it runs to and probably over Wall 105, incorporating its top. This analysis would assign the Hellenistic Tower to the earlier part of Stratum III and would propose an open court outside the city that succeeded it. In the "small stones" and "loose grey" on Lapp's section was Stratum II pottery, extending to what may have been the collapse of a Stratum II wall. Wright was dubious about the bonding of the IIIB wall and Wall 105 and continued to maintain that the Hellenistic Tower might belong later, into Stratum II (*SBBC*:183 and 260, n. 2).

In 1956, a row of rocks and a cluster of smaller stones were recorded just below the surface as the south Gate Tower was being excavated. They appear in fig. 284. Without associated surfaces, these flimsy remains are probably later than Stratum III, and may belong to Stratum II or even Stratum I.

Field III Fortification (Ills. 40 and 42)

Field III supplies two pieces of evidence that pertain to Hellenistic fortification. Wall B was traced for a substantial distance in the field, and just at the point where it enters the south balk of the field there was evidence of a rebuild on its inner face (Ills. 40 and 42). The interior face of the rebuild was plastered. Against it was pink brick detritus into which a pit had been dug; the pit contained some 15 store jars of Stratum III or possibly II date. When the locus was dug, the pit had not been noticed, so the pit contents and the surrounding bricky soil were excavated together and their ceramic contents mixed. Even so, the pottery from the locus was all Hellenistic in date. The brick detritus must have come from Hellenistic times, then, and have been earlier than the cache of jars.

The stone rebuild on Wall B and the brick debris correspond in some respects, then, to the evidence from Field I (note the zone of brick detritus inside Wall B in Field I also, as shown on Ill. 20 = I AA:#8). No brick fall was found exterior to Wall B in Field III. A trench was dug by the Sellin expedition along Wall B's exterior face which may have removed some evidence, and there are two orphaned Hellenistic walls on the shallow slope preserved outside the MB IIC fortification line, but unless erosion has removed vast quantities of evidence here, Hellenistic conditions in Field III did not confirm the proposal of Hellenistic fortification at the East Gate.

Doubtful Speculations

Three further proposals made in preliminary reports about Hellenistic fortification are inferences for which there is no direct evidence.

1. G. E. Wright speculated that the brick topping on the exterior bastions of the Northwest Gate might have stemmed from Hellenistic times, but no ceramic evidence supports this proposal; dismantling the superstructure might settle the matter.

2. Wright also speculated that the robber pit dug into Wall B at the East Gate was aimed at getting building stone for the Hellenistic Tower. But this pit was dug from too high in the preserved debris to sustain this hypothesis, and is likely to come from very late in the Hellenistic period, or even later. The heavy content of Hellenistic pottery in its filling could have come from virtually anywhere on the site.

3. Wright sought a plausible explanation for the immense bank of soil outside Wall A at the west perimeter of town, and proposed that John Hyrcanus imported quantities of earth to nullify the fortifications after 128 or 107 BCE, and even assigned to Hyrcanus responsibility for filling over Field II inside town (*SBBC*: 15, 40, 184; 1962a).

Welter cut all along the high bank to expose Wall A, and in 1964 what remained was removed by the Jordan Department of Antiquities to provide a view of the ancient wall for visitors to the site. In 1964, the bank was observed to consist of sterile layers of chalk and decomposed limestone that suggested purposeful fill. It does not make sense that this kind of deposit could result from erosion off the slopes of Mt. Ebal. But at no point did the Joint Expedition systematically trench through it to see if it could be dated. It is too late to rectify this strategic error, and the proposal that Hyrcanus was responsible must remain a conjecture.

THE DOMESTIC SECTORS

When Sellin, Welter and Steckeweh dug at various locations on the Shechem mound, they encountered remains of the "Greek" period—over the public buildings in the west, between the Northwest Gate and the location of the Joint Expedition's Field XIII, and in their long trenches in the north, east and south of the tell's interior. Their brief reports speak little about phasing within the Greek period.

The Joint Expedition encountered Hellenistic housing at every point where their work started from the mound's surface. Remnants were found above the fortifications in Fields I and III, especially at the back of the fortification complex. In Fields VII and IX there was sufficient preservation of Strata IV and III, with a few remnants of II, to permit reconstruction of five phases of building. In Field II, a well-preserved house of Late Stratum III continuing into Stratum II was set down into Iron Age layering over the Temenos Wall.

Fig. 285. Looking north in Field VII Area 4 at Stratum IV plastered Floor 1521. Metalled surface 1530 is in the upper left corner. The wall is 1531.

Stratum IV in Field VII (Ills. 106 and 107 [plans]; 112 = VIIAA, 113 = VIIBB, 116 = VIIDD and 117 = VIIEE)

In Field VII, where installations of Strata VI and V were built into the ruins of the Stratum VII complex, Hellenistic settlement first prepared the topography to receive new construction. The entire location was leveled, measuring 24 meters from east to west and 17 meters from north to south. Where there had been three terraces in Stratum VII times, and pockets of building over uneven terrain representing Strata VI and V, a gently sloping surface was created with a pitch of 7 degrees from west to east. To the west in Areas 21, 22 and 23, which expanded the field in 1962, Hellenistic remains sat on and down into Stratum VII ones. This can be seen on VII EE = Ill. 117, where Stratum IV surface 21.016 lies directly on the ruins of the Stratum VII destruction (#10 on #14). At the west of the middle terrace, the destruction debris of the 1727 house lay just below Hellenistic remains. On Ill. 112 = VII AA section, stones of Wall 1731 can be seen in contact with the foot of Hellenistic Wall 1723. On Ill. 113 = VII BB, Robber Pit #3, locus 1304A, apparently was dug to rob Wall 1623 of the Stratum VII house, which may have protruded through the surface being prepared. Since the top of the debris was undulating due to erosion, fill had to be spread in the cavities to achieve the level for new construction.

On the eastern terrace, large quantities of fill (VII BB:##10 and 11) were placed over the spill of Stratum VII debris and installations of Stratum V on the slope. As in Field I, the earliest Hellenistic builders moved a lot of earth, with its older artifacts, from elsewhere on the mound.

The top of the fill at the east was consolidated with a metalled surface, locus 1530-1232, covering all of Areas 1 and 4 (interrupted by a huge Hellenistic pit 1522 along the east balk of the field). Surface 1530-1232 is shown on VII BB as the row of pebbles beneath Floor 1521 floor (#9), at the top of the fill designated #11. The metalled surface extended 0.90 to 1.00 m into Area 2 and touched the very edge of Area 5, where it lay 0.10 m above Stratum VII cobbling 1429 at the front door of the 1727 house. Elevations at many points on it ran from 17.06 at the northwest to 16.86 at the southeast. Beneath 1530-1232 was fill 1556, but only its top-most layer, locus 1530a, 0.20 m thick and including a saucer of ash, locus 1536, contained Stratum IV pottery. In fill 1556 below 1530a, pottery was Stratum V and earlier, including several Stratum V Attic sherds, with a very few later Hellenistic intrusions probably from Pit 1522 immediately adjacent. It seems clear that 1530-1232 was the prepared surface upon which the earliest Hellenistic people founded their new settlement (fig. 285).

Throughout the rest of Field VII, it was more difficult to define Hellenistic preparations for construction. Disturbances from later Hellenistic strata, including massive pits like 1522 and 21.036, interrupted wall lines and isolated small segments of flooring at many points. All too often these intrusions were discerned too late to be sure of the elevation from which they were dug. The safest procedure is to look for sealed loci of the earliest Stratum IV material only directly beneath a preserved feature. Walls were removed during excavation with careful attention to what was sealed immediately beneath them. The same was true of patches of flooring.

Of the locations that are not sealed by preserved features, Nancy Lapp has identified certain fills as significant for isolating the earliest Stratum IV pottery, cited here by locus number:

1530-1232—already described
1530a—makeup layer beneath 1530–1232
1228—an early probe into 1530–1232
1029a—fill beneath IV levels in southeast of Area 1
1030—fill beneath IV levels in northeast of Area 1
1424—fill west of Wall 1415 in southwest of Area 5
1311—pocket of fill in brick debris over Stratum VII house Wall 1323
1836–1841—fill beneath IV levels throughout Area 7
1732 and 1727—pockets in brick debris over Room 2 of the Stratum VII house
1609–1610, 1612-1615—pockets in brick debris throughout Area 9
1622—pocket of fill in brick debris over Stratum VII house Room 3
22.020—fill surrounding Stratum VII Wall 22.005, east of Pit 22.011 and uncontaminated by the pit

To these there can now be added:

Pit 1133—sealed by 1232, cutting Stratum V installation 1127
Pit 1029B—dug from beneath IVA Wall 1025

Stratum IV showed several phases in Field VII, broadly divisible into Strata IVB and IVA. The clearest set of IVB structures and floors are shown on Ill. 106, confined to the eastern half of the field.

Walls 1517, 1426, 1415-1117 and 1123 defined one of two complexes. Of these walls only scraps were preserved, indicated by the stones within their lines on the plan, and not all connections were certain. Wall 1426 was preserved at its junction with 1415 but extended only roughly a meter toward Wall 1517, and 1517 was not quite parallel to 1415. All of these walls were preserved for only one course.

Where these walls were preserved across their width they showed similar construction: two rows of stones defining the external faces and a rubble core. They varied from 0.90 m to 1.25 m in width. In virtually every instance they were founded on makeup, without foundation trenches, but removal of the walls produced sherds sealed beneath them. Wall 1517 shows the technique most clearly. When it was removed, it was found to rest on hard-pack 1529, the top of a makeup which in turn rested upon consolidating layer 1530.

Running to the east face of 1517 and curving up its face was thick plastered surface 1521 at elevation 17.19, with a makeup beneath only 0.15–0.20 above the consolidating layer 1530. At points, 1521 was 0.07 m thick. Section VII BB = Ill. 113 shows 1521 as #9, running to Wall 1517 and beneath a press belonging later in Stratum IV. Beneath Surface 1521 in #11 is the fill over Stratum VII debris with striations of cobbling running within it. As noted above, the uppermost pebble row and striation in that portion of the fill was locus 1530, while lines of pebbles deeper in the fill are features of its accumulation.

Pit 1522 interrupted Surface 1521 so that direct connection to plaster Floor 1216 to the south could not be established (fig. 271, above). The elevation of 1216 was at 17.24. That these two represent the lowest phase of Stratum IV seems certain, and the latest pottery in the makeup beneath them (locus 1236) along with the pottery on them help to define the beginning of Hellenistic occupation. A clutter of stones near the east end of Wall 1123, probably not part of the wall, rested on Floor 1216, but another segment of 1216 ran to Wall 1123 further west.

Fig. 286. Press installation 1525 and Jar 1526, with segments of Floors 1521, 1527 and 1523 (lowest to highest), all of Stratum IV. Looking east in Field VII Area 4.

To the north of this complex was Wall 1817, built in the same style. It was founded almost directly upon Stratum VII debris; Tannur 1828 of Stratum V was in the gap between the west end of 1817 and the east end of Wall 1723, its preserved rim almost flush with the lowest Stratum IV surface going with 1817. Jar Stand 1818 made of stones in a ring was built against the south face of Wall 1817. Running south from Wall 1817 were a few stones delineating Wall 1829. If extrapolated through the major disturbance separating them, its line would not have connected with Wall 1517 to the south (note the plan).

Cobbling 1821 at elevation 17.61 extended from the line of Wall 1829 westward. East of Wall 1829 was Surface 1831 at elevation 17.68, a narrow strip of hard-packed earth topped by lime. These two surfaces were the lowest relating to the south face of Wall 1817. Against its north face, the only preserved surface was a strip of plastered floor, 1832, at elevation 17.58, shown on the plan directly against the east balk of the field at its northernmost point.

These two complexes provided the best evidence for developments during Stratum IV in Field VII. Stratum IVA is shown on Ill. 107. Wall 1817 continued in use. Near its south face at its west end, Cobbling 1826 at elevation 17.86 resurfaced 1821, 0.25 m higher. When the balk between Areas 7 and 8 was removed in 1962, more of Floor 1826 (not shown on plan) was found to have connected to the east end of Wall 1723 at its base, VII AA:#7, indicating an opening through 1723-1817 1.60 m wide. Surface 1821, however, would have run beneath Walls 1723 and 1716. These two walls represented, then, a second phase of building within Stratum IV.

Although it was not preserved above IVB Wall 1829, Floor 1826 at elevation 17.86 probably ran over it. The highest preserved stone on Wall 1829 was at elevation 17.77. East of the position of Wall 1829, Floor 1831 at elevation 17.68 was resurfaced by 1830 at elevation 17.73, again a limed beaten earth floor. Just to the south of the narrow strips of these two floorings was the substantial segment of Cobbling 1824, at elevation 17.78, which had a thin strip of limed, beaten earth floor along its south edge. Its elevation was higher than that of 1831. Conceivably 1831 was the underpinning for cobbling, but the more likely situation is that there were three successive resurfacings with Wall 1817 within Stratum IV, 1821 with 1831 in IVB, and 1826-1830 followed by 1824 in IVA.

If so, they may correlate with three phases adjacent to Wall 1517 just to the south. Over plaster IVB Floor 1521 (VII BB:#9) lay plaster Floor 1527 (#8) at elevation 17.36, and above that a third, 1523, at elevation 17.41, the latter two belonging to IVA. Pit 1522 cut all three floors at the south.

The press installation, 1525, and Jar 1526 just to its west, were set down through 1527 and reached just to the level of 1521 (VII BB, far right). Apparently both went with Stratum IVA flooring 1523, although the plaster of the floor could be traced only to within 0.07 m of the outer rim of the press and did not quite touch the jar; perhaps both were set in after 1523 was in place (fig. 286).

Fig. 287. Looking north in Field VII Area 3. Stratum IVA Wall 1025 runs through the center from north to south; Wall 1026 abuts it on the right and Wall 1027 abuts it at upper left. Crushed oven or kiln 1024A with segments of Floor 1021 lie to the west of Wall 1025 (left).

Installation 1525 has been referred to as a press, but of what commodity is unclear; alternatively it may have been used for dyeing. Its interior measure was 0.70 across (east to west) and 0.60 from the widest point of its curved back to the front (north–south). It was built of conglomerate cement with small sherds as the binder, over which had been spread a slurry of smooth plaster, both on the bottom and the sides of the interior. The cement walls were from 0.11 to 0.13 m thick around the curve; the south straight wall was approximately 0.20 m thick. The walls stood 0.12 m above the interior. Apparently the interior was originally completely enclosed by wall, but a large piece of the straight south wall had broken away. A plastered cup-hole 0.10 m from the curved back wall was 0.13 m deep and 0.22 m in diameter. There was a cover stone over the cup-hole. The bottom of the installation had been shaped to keep roughly the same thickness, from 0.08 to 0.09 under the interior and 0.07 under the cup-hole (note VII BB cuts directly through 1525). The sherds used as binder for the cement were broken to a nearly uniform size, roughly 0.03 m square. Judging from the distinctive ware, they were all from Stratum IV vessels.

The sequences of three floorings with Walls 1817 and 1517, even if they do not correlate, provide the closest Stratum IV stratigraphy anywhere on the Shechem mound. West of this narrow strip of preservation, two layers could sometimes be distinguished. IVA Walls 1723-1716 above the IVB surface in the north is one such succession.

At the south edge of the field and extending to the west was a complex involving Wall 1219-1125 probably extending to join Wall 1026 across a 4.00 m wide disturbance. Beneath 1219, in the southwest corner of Area 1, was stone-filled Pit 1239, its top sealed by the wall. Wall 1219-1125 was probably a IVA feature, while the pit was IVB. The pit contained Stratum IV pottery.

Wall 1026, the only Stratum IV wall in the field of which two courses were preserved, was bonded to a well-preserved north–south wall, 1025-1308. Drain 1028 was integrated into Wall 1026, curving northeast to southwest and cut off at both ends by disturbances. The elevation on its earthen-based channel was at 17.66; the water ran to the southwest from the northeast. When the balk between Areas 5 and 6 was removed in 1962, preserved only within the balk was the broken segment of Wall 1312, bitten into by Pit 1485 from a later period. A beaten earth surface, found only in the balk and not given a locus number, joined 1312 to the drain (Ill. 116 = VII DD:#8).

Traces of IVB Surface 1124 were found between the corner of Walls 1117 and 1123 and the drain, along the north edge of the disturbance that cut off the connection between wall segments 1125 and 1026. At elevation 17.27, the surface did not reach VII DD. It ran just to the foot of the stones lining Drain 1028 and predated it. This is another instance of Hellenistic construction on a prepared or existing surface. The entire complex from Wall 1219 at the east to 1026-1025-1308-1312 plus the drain belongs to Stratum IVA.

Still another indication of a separation between IVB and IVA was Wall 1027 under Wall 1025-1308 (both shown on Ill. 107). Wall 1027 was preserved mostly within the balk between Areas 3 and 6; the western 0.20 m of Wall 1025-1308 lay directly on it, so Wall 1027 predated the IVA complex. The short segment of 1027 preserved is built in the standard technique of the period, with two well-aligned faces and a rubble core, and was 1.10 m wide.

Along the west face of Wall 1027 were interrupted scraps of hard-packed earth Surface 1310, probably belonging to IVB. Along the west edge of Wall 1025, over the position where Wall 1027 would have run had it continued southward, scraps of Surface 1021 at elevation 17.60 and the crushed ruins of an oven or kiln, 1024A, appear to have belonged to IVA, but no earlier Hellenistic surfacing lay below them (fig. 287).

Intrusion by later Hellenistic builders again broke the connection between the features just described and patches of flooring in Area 21 to their west. Beaten earth floor 21.013 was preserved only in the southwest portion of Area 21, at elevation 17.85. Above it was another similar floor, 21.012, at elevation 18.05. Segments of a cobbled floor 21.011 filled the center of the area. Pottery between 21.012 and 21.013, on 21.012, and beneath and on Cobbling 21.011 all was analyzed as belonging to Stratum IV. These fragments of floors probably represent IVB and IVA, but it is not certain how they should be distributed between the phases. One possibility is that both 21.013 and 21.012 are IVB, while 21.011 is IVA.

A problem exists in defining 21.013 and 21.012, however, in that Pit 21.036 (Ill. 117 = VII EE:#3), at first thought to be sealed by these two floors, proved upon final analysis to have been dug from as high as Stratum III or even II. The pit contained many forms analyzed as Stratum IV and only one analyzed as late as II.

A similar but smaller pit, 22.010, was isolated in Area 22 (EE:#13); it too contained pottery analyzed as no later than Stratum IV. The featureless layer, probably still another intrusion shown as #8 on VII EE, bottomed in Stone Fall 1042, which contained pottery assigned to Stratum IV. Here it is necessary to trust the developing sense of Stratum IV forms even though the apparent stratigraphy of the pits/intrusions could mean that later sherds were introduced. Continuing analysis of Stratum IV forms suggests that Surfaces 21.012 and 21.013, Pit 22.010 and Stone Fall 1042 can all be trusted to help define Stratum IV.

In short, something of IVB is preserved in the southwest quadrant of Field VII, with better preserved remains belonging to IVA immediately above.

One further ingredient of IVA was Wall 1419 running eastward from Wall 1415, south of IVB Wall 1426. The portion of Wall 1415 preserved at the junction was bonded to 1419, involving a rebuild of 1415. North of the junction, Cobbling 1421, at elevation 17.96, was limited on the east by a stretch of stones set upright (Wall 1420), suggesting the installation was a bin. A beaten earth floor found at balk removal and not given a locus number extended north from it over Wall 1426, again demarcating the two phases of Stratum IV.

Several features are stratigraphic orphans within the period of Stratum IV, but may provide help in defining pottery forms:

1). Removal of the balks between Areas 1 and 2 and between Areas 1-2 and 4–5 revealed a metalled Surface 1233 at elevation 17.45 (Ill. 106) which may have been the surface to go with the IVB use of Wall 1517 along its west face. Direct attachment to 1517 or to Wall 1123 could not be established.

2). Removal of the balk between Areas 4–5 and 7–8 revealed beaten earth surface 1476-1548 at elevation 17.54 (Ill. 106) which may represent surfacing with Walls 1426 and 1517 north of 1426 in IVB. A segment of possible walling, 1834, also appeared in this balk, to the east of the patch of floor. Pit 1845 was discerned at the junc-

Fig. 288. Column Base 23.004 in Field VII Area 23, looking north. Flagstones 23.009 at center.

tion of this balk with the east limit of the field; it must have been what cut through Cobbling 1824 (Ill. 107).

3). A possible segment of wall, 1423, ran west from Wall 1415 for 0.75 m and ended in the disturbed area filling most of Areas 6, 8 and 9. Its phasing is unclear. Since the continuation of the line of Wall 1415 north of this point to meet Wall 1716 is conjectural, 1423 may have marked the north end of the line in IVB. Balk removal in 1962 discerned Pit 1477, probably dug in Stratum III, just north of Wall 1423 and in the conjectured line of continuation of Wall 1415.

Major disturbance characterized the northwest quadrant of the field. The VII DD section shows one Hellenistic pit (#7) which was so massive that the excavators were unable to sense its dimensions and discern any features it had not destroyed. Some that were finally discerned were hidden in balks and discovered in 1962, while their contexts had been removed in 1960. Enough survived to show that the region marked "disturbed area" on Ill. 107 was not empty of Stratum IV features, but also that later Hellenistic construction wrought havoc to what had preceded.

The disturbed area continued westward into Areas 22 and 23 above the region which had been the western terrace in the Iron II period. The most striking Hellenistic feature of Area 23 was Column Base 23.004, preserved partially within the north limit of the field and pictured in fig. 288. It is the only hint of monumental architecture to come from Field VII, carefully cut and smoothed from one block of limestone. Its rectangular plinth measured 1.02 m by 0.90 m, with the circular torus 0.60 m in diameter in its center. The torus was elevated 0.12 m above the plinth; in all, the height of the base was 0.50 m. The elevation of its top was at 19.30 m. It rested on a prepared bed of carefully laid stones; beneath this bedding was a 1.00 m thick makeup containing sherds all dated earlier than Stratum IV except for one representing the earliest Stratum IV ware. However, no surface could be detected extending away from the foundation to show what the corresponding floor was.

South of the column base and separated from it by 1.25 m of disturbed soil were five flat flagstones fitted well together (locus 23.009), their top at elevation 18.96. The preserved portion measured 0.90 by 0.96 m. It too rested on early makeup in which the latest pottery was early Stratum IV in date, mixed with Stratum V and earlier Iron II. Adjacent to the column base on its east was deep Pit 23.017 reaching to a meter below the surface of the flagstones. Preserved over the flagstones, 0.14 above them at elevation 19.10, was plastered Floor 23.008, with Stratum IV pottery sealed between the two floorings. The lower of these complexes probably belonged to Stratum IVB, the upper to IVA.

To the east and south of this stratified pair, isolated patches of beaten earth flooring, 23.005 and 23.006, belonged to Stratum IV; locus 23.016 was the fill beneath Floor 23.005 and contained Stratum IV forms. In the southeast corner of the area, a fall of random stone, locus 23.010, which cannot be certainly assigned to one of the two phases provided an additional collection of sherds of Stratum IV.

The column base and flagstone floor are hints of a monumental structure and suggest that the first

Fig. 289. Field VII Areas 4 and 7, looking west. Room A of Stratum IIIB is in the center, Room B in the foreground.

Hellenistic settlers set out to build a substantial city. The Joint Expedition's excavation sites did not recover further evidence of monumental Hellenistic architecture, while the Austro-German reports pay scant attention to the details of their Hellenistic finds.

Stratum III in Field VII (Ills. 108 and 109 [plans]; 112 = VIIAA, 113 = VIIBB, 116 = VIIDD and 117 = VIIEE)

Stratum IV remains, while divisible into two phases and local refloorings, constituted a thin stratum. Walls were not preserved above one course, were founded close to the top of the prepared fill, and were often disturbed by the intrusion of the next occupation. Stratum III builders changed virtually every feature of their predecessors, placing new walls parallel to and even partially overlapping Stratum IV ones but never directly over them. Doubtless some of the breaks in Stratum IV walls were the result of robbing by Stratum III builders. What called for the complete change in plan is unknown, and there is nothing to suggest that the change-over was due to violent destruction. Burn layers, collapsed walls, and weaponry are absent.

Two construction phases of Stratum III, designated IIIB and IIIA, were attested in the eastern half of the field. The layout of the earlier phase, IIIB, is shown on Ill. 108. Walls 1803-1807, 1805-1414 and 1506 anchor Stratum III, in use in both IIIB and IIIA. From the point opposite the west end of 1803-1807, Wall 1805-1414 had a flat-topped lower course and a rebuild directly upon it. Wall 1803-1807 showed similar phasing, the lower course with a straight north face, while the upper course was bonded to the IIIA Walls 1812-1810 with threshold 1814 (Ill. 109).

In Region D on the plan, Surface 1816 at elevation 18.05 attached to the lower course of Wall 1803 and ran beneath the portion of Wall 1805 north of the line of 1803. It appears as VII AA:#4. The extension of Wall 1805 northward was later placed on the surface as foundation. Surface 1816 was a resurfacing of 1816A at 17.97. Plastered Floor 1804, AA:#5 was cut off from 1816 and 1816A by intrusions. It ran beneath Wall 1810 and Threshold 1814. Together, 1816/1816A and 1804 constituted the IIIB surface in Region D. Wall 1803 had an opening 0.88 m wide at its west end, providing access from Region D to Room A; it was later filled with a blockage.

Room A was a small square, its east and south limits defined by Walls 1813 0.80 m wide and 1513 0.85 m wide. A break in Wall 1813, 0.70 m wide, separated its southern portion from a protrusion against the south face of 1803-1807, giving ac-

Fig. 290. Plastered Bin 1520 at the south edge of Room B, Stratum IIIB. The plaster runs up the face of Wall 1506, upon which the meter stick lies.

cess to Room B to the east (fig. 289). An elevation near the north end of Wall 1813 as preserved was at 17.90. Against the junction of 1813 and 1513 in the southeast corner of Room A was a slab of plaster coating both walls which curved to horizontal and ran a short distance out onto beaten earth Surface 1815 within the room, at elevation approximately 17.90.

The south limit of Room B was Wall 1506, founded more deeply than the IIIA Wall 1510 which continued it westward. It must have run to meet Wall 1516, the continuation of the line of Wall 1813 southward, but the junction was disrupted. Against the north face of Wall 1506 was plastered Bin 1520 (fig. 290), defined at its east edge by a flat stone 0.15 m thick and 0.60 m long standing upright. Plaster facing coated the upright stone and the face of Wall 1506 and extended horizontally on flat stones laid into the IVA Installation 1525 beneath. The rim of 1525 formed part of the layer which the plaster covered. The portion of plaster floor merged with a lightly limed earthen Surface 1808 at elevation 17.70.

Wall 1506 divided Room B from Yard C to its south. Wall 1516 was not quite in line with 1813 and was 0.10 m wider. That C was a yard is suggested by the installations in it. Tannur 1509 was positioned close to the wall junction, 0.28 m from the south face of Wall 1506 and 0.25 from the east face of Wall 1516. The tannur sat on a layer of ashy plaster, locus 1528, which sealed pre-Stratum III pottery beneath it. The interior diameter of the tannur at its widest was 0.67 m, lined with 0.02 m of clay overlaid with large body sherds from store jars, including the complete base of one jar. Between the tannur and Wall 1516 was a beaten earth surface at elevation 17.57. The tannur had been set 0.08 m down into this surface, and consisted of crumbly lime and white ash.

East of the tannur against the south face of Wall 1506 was a plastered bench, 1518, its south limit marked by a squared block of limestone 0.30 m in height and 0.13 m thick, resembling the block in Installation 1520 on the other side of the wall. The plaster ran up its face. The bench measured 0.56 m east–west and 0.80 m north–south, and slanted at an angle of 12 degrees southward. An elevation at its mid-point was at 17.68. Fig. 291 shows the tannur and the bench. As with other installations of the Hellenistic period, it is difficult to determine what process could be carried out on a plastered surface that would not chip or scar it— perhaps bread-making.

Installation 1518 was fully revealed when the east balk of the field was cut back one meter. In that extension was a 1.00 m long stretch of wall,

Fig. 291. Looking east in Field VII Area 4 at Tannur 1509 and Bench 1518, in Room C.

0.60 m wide, Wall 1547. Like other Hellenistic walls it was two stones wide, but there was no rubble core. It could not be connected to the remaining features of the yard because of interruption by Pit 1514 of later Stratum III.

Beneath these installations was Pit 1522, which cut all the Stratum IV surfaces here. The pit has to have been dug after Stratum IV ended and before Stratum IIIB construction began. There are Stratum III period sherds in its filling, presumably the earliest forms of pottery of that period; they are mixed with an abundant collection of sherds from all periods of the site's history back to MB, together with beads, a bronze ring, a spindle whorl and, notably, a fine alabastron.

West and south of this complex there was little to define more than one phase of Stratum III. Beneath IIIA flagstone floor 1203 was a stretch of Cobbling 1214 at elevation 17.75; if extended westward it would have run under Wall 1206 of Stratum IIIA founded at 17.91. To the west of Wall 1805-1414, where a IIIA cobbled street was partially preserved, a small patch of metalled surface 1719 suggested that a roadway ran here in IIIB as well. Similar rough cobbling, 1715, lay 0.15–0.20 m below IIIA Cobbling 1703 and 0.30 m beneath Paving 1602. The fill beneath these various features, carefully isolated whenever possible, contained Stratum IVA and IIIB pottery.

When the field was extended westward in 1962 to include Areas 21, 22 and 23, no architectural remains came to light. Patches of a possible surface, 22.002, were isolated, 0.55 m beneath Stratum IIIA surface 22.001, but its identification was too uncertain to be trusted as a IIIB feature.

In Stratum IIIA, the anchor walls of IIIB were rebuilt while Walls 1513 and 1813 were covered over. The coherent layout of rooms west and north of a courtyard, Room F, is shown on Ill. 109. The lettering of rooms on the plan is continuous from the four (A-D) of IIIB.

The long west wall of the complex, its central portion being a rebuild of IIIB Wall 1805-1414, ran for 14.65 m. The line of 1805 was extended northward beyond the north limit of the field (Ill. 112 = VII AA). The northern preserved point had an elevation at 18.67. Along the west edge of Room G a tapered facing was placed on the inner face of 1805 (1811) running over Wall 1513 and over the blocked doorway in Wall 1803.

A break in the long west wall was marked by clear posts, the south end of Wall 1414 (at elevation 18.37) and the north end of Wall 1408. This access is 1.20 m wide, and there were rocks partially filling it (locus 1412), which may have been an intentional blocking or may simply have fallen. A semicircle of stones within the passage, interrupted inside Room E, hint also that the passage

326   SHECHEM III. THE HELLENISTIC PERIOD

Fig. 292. Looking south in Field VII Area 4 at the two phases of Stratum III. The junction of Walls 1505 and 1510 dominates the center, the northeast limit of Room E of Stratum IIIA. Stratum IIIB Wall 1516 runs parallel to 1505 at the top center. The rim of Tannur 1509 appears under the east (left) face of 1505 at left center.

may have at one point been closed. Near its south end, Wall 1408 had an elevation at 18.33 and was footed at 18.14; all the walls of the complex except for the post of 1414 were preserved for only one course, often quite thin. Note also Wall 1206, footed at 17.91 and standing to 18.23, a height of only 0.32 m.

Wall 1408-1107 cornered with Wall 1109-1210. Where other walls in the complex ran nearly straight, and the corners were at right angles, this wall curved slightly south before curving back part of the way to a perpendicular junction with Wall 1206. Against the exterior of 1109-1210, a rock pile which at its east end looked like a wall in its own right, may have been a buttress or simply collapse from the wall to its north. This was locus 1110-1211, interrupted at its east end by Pit 1205.

Wall 1206 ran north from the east end of 1210 and ended at an access 1.00 m wide into Courtyard F, and the line continued as Wall 1505, which ran over the west half of IIIB tannur 1509. Wall 1505 extended to a rebuild on IIIB Wall 1506, but was bonded to Wall 1510 running from the doorpost of Wall 1414 eastward. The bonded junction abutted 1506 (fig. 292)

North of rebuilt Wall 1803-1807 and bonded to the rebuild was Wall 1812, the widest wall in the complex, with an elevation at 18.67. One meter north of the junction, Wall 1812 stopped, the line picked up by Wall 1810 near the north limit of the field. Between them was a neatly cobbled threshold, 1814, at elevation 18.23. The access between Rooms J and K was an impressive construction, suggesting that the main rooms of the house lay north of Wall 1803, mostly outside the excavation field.

South of Wall 1803-1807, but separated from touching it by a gap of 0.20 m, was Wall 1806, which ran 1.85 m south and stopped, leaving a 1.50 m gap between its end and Wall 1510. The narrowest of all the walls in the complex, it was 0.55 m wide, and its purpose is uncertain.

The building technique of all these walls was similar to that of previous Hellenistic ones in Field VII, with two rows of larger rocks often showing flat facets along the wall faces and smaller rough stones in the core. The varying thicknesses of the walls is noteworthy: 1806 at 0.55 m, 1206 and 1505 at 0.70–0.75 m, 1510 at 0.80 m, 1408 at 1.00 m, 1812 at 1.20 m.

Surface 1227-1511 of Room E was preserved throughout most of its northern two-thirds, to the line of stones just at the south of Mortar 1204, a stone block 0.46 by 0.43 m in size with a cup-shaped depression 0.23 m deep and 0.26 m in diameter. Flagstones and plaster marked the surface in the west center of the room, at elevation 18.04; at the base of the mortar more plaster was at 18.13.

South of the mortar was a loose lie of rocks, 1209, and no clear surface.

Through the east access from Room E was Flagstone Surface 1203 at elevation 18.07, in Courtyard F. The stones were closely fit, their interstices filled with plaster. They came through the doorway and stopped at the edge of Room E, although given the possibility that rock locus 1209 was an intrusion it is conceivable Room E also had a flagstone surface. Pit 1205, not at first discerned, seems to have been what truncated 1203 along its south edge. The semicircle of stones north of it, adjacent to Wall 1505 just north of the access, were part of the courtyard complex. North and east of it was the intrusive Pit 1514. Surface 1203 and the semicircle were the only indications of the surfacing in Courtyard F.

Rooms G and H, with screen Wall 1806 in their midst, together measured 3.70 m wide and at least 6.00 m long, into the east limit of the field. The floor was 1802-1508, with elevations at 18.30 in the northwest corner and 18.22 east of the south end of Wall 1806 (Ill. 113 = VII BB:#6), where it has sloped to an elevation of 18.00, barely topping the upright stone of Stratum IIIB Installation 1520.

In Room J, Surface 1801 was at 18.31. In the southeast corner of the room, lying on the floor was a complete brick, 0.33 by 0.32 m, its thickness unrecorded. At the north edge of the part of Room J within the excavation field, there was disruption, including the insertion of a Stratum II jar, locus 1820 (Ill. 112 = VII AA). Within the portion of AA:#2 between Walls 1805 and 1810, it proved impossible to discern Surface 1801. The surface was slightly higher than the elevation on the threshold leading into Room K. In Room K no surface was discerned.

Especially noteworthy were the range of small finds in Rooms J and G. A pair of bronze tweezers, two bronze pins, two iron points, an iron bolt, an iron knife blade or palette, a clay loom weight, a bronze spoon, and half of a fine alabaster cosmetic dish all point to G and J as rooms within a house where people carried out domestic activities. A feature of the floors throughout the entire complex is the number of iron bolts, nails and other fittings on and within the surfaces. Wood must have been prominent in the superstructure; while one whole brick was found on a floor there is otherwise little evidence of brick detritus throughout the complex. Why virtually every wall was preserved for only one course is a mystery. Probably each successive phase in Hellenistic times made use of its predecessors' building material.

If Room F was indeed a courtyard, Room E may constitute one dwelling and Rooms G-K another in a kind of insula most of which lies to the east of the field. Along its west edge ran a narrow street, between Wall 1805 and the corner of the 1707-1705-1701-1601 structure most of which lies outside the field to the north. The street was 2.15 m wide at the north limit of the field, 2.45 m wide at the south preserved end of Wall 1707. A small segment of Cobbling 1708 was preserved adjacent to Wall 1805 at elevation 18.57. In the fill below this elevation various scraps of metalled surface were noted, designated loci 1403 and 1106, as well as Cobbling 1719 assigned to Stratum IIIB. Disturbances disrupted stratigraphy throughout the whole central region to the west of the Courtyard Complex. These appear as #7 on Ill. 116 = VII DD, #4 on Ill. 113 = VII BB; contributing to the disruption would have been the robber pit 1304a (BB:#3).

North of the disturbed area was the 1601-1701-1705-1707 complex, ill-preserved wall lines which showed elevation on their preserved tops from 19.39 at the west to 18.87 at the east. Footing for 1707 was only 0.33 m below its top. Cobbling 1703-1602, patches of which were detected close to the south face of 1601-1701 at elevation 18.60, ran just beneath the wall, but attached to a one-meter long fragment of Wall 1734A discovered in 1962 when the balk between Areas 8 and 9 was removed (VII DD:#4; fig. 293). Another patch of cobbling, locus 1604 at elevation 19.16 lay at the west edge of Area 9. A hard-packed earth possible surface, 1702, was traced north of Wall 1601-1701, but could not be defined in the VII AA section.

Cobbling of two differing kinds, designated loci 1306 and 1307, formed a surface near the south edge of Area 6 (fig. 294). In Areas 22 and 23 to the west, a uniform hard-packed layer was discerned, designated 22.001 and 23.001. These features suggest that there was open ground at the far

Fig. 293. Looking south at the top of the balk in Field VII between Areas 8 and 9. Wall 1701 is in foreground, 1734A behind the meter stick, which lies on Floor 1603, all of Stratum IIIA.

west of Field VII. In this region again there were several pieces of iron bolts along with beads, a broken scaraboid, and other small finds suggesting domestic housing nearby.

In Areas 21 and 3 was a curious complex involving fragments of walls built close to one another, through the midst of which ran a capped drain (Ill. 109; the walls in Area 21 are numbered without the prefix "21"). The major wall system was 1008-21.007 cornering with 21.008 cornering with 21.003, a zig-zag line preserved two courses high through most of its length, with elevations on its preserved top from 19.37 at its west end to 19.05 at the junction of 21.003 and 21.008 and at the west end of 1008-21.007 to 18.68 further east. Running south from 21.003 were two short segments of wall (21.005 and 21.006), both butting 21.003, 0.60 m wide with a space 0.30 m between them. The north half of the intervening space was filled with random rocks, while the south half was filled with earth. North and east of this odd complex were unattached fragments of Walls 1006, 1007 cornering with 1010, and 1012 (the pile of stone with elevation 18.84 on Ill. 109).

It proved very difficult to trace surfaces within this complex. East of Wall 21.008 and south of 21.007, in the southeast corner of Area 21, a patch of beaten earth Floor 21.031 was traced, riding on makeup 21.035. North of Wall 21.003, beaten earth Floor 21.009 could be traced, riding on a thick layer of makeup and fill designated 21.034. Floor 21.009 is Ill. 117 = VII EE:#4, extending to reach Wall 21.005, but the point where Wall 21.003 would have reached that section shows no sign of the wall. Floor 21.009 may not provide a trustworthy seal for pottery analysis. Isolated from attachment to any of the walls were fragments of beaten-earth surfacing, locus 1013 and loci 1017-1019, along the north edge of Area 3, from which some help in identifying Stratum IIIB pottery forms can come.

The zig-zag course of the main wall system carried it over Drain 1016-1015-21.004. The drain meandered from the west balk of the field in Area 21, curved north and then ran for more than 7.00 m in the same southeasterly direction as other walls of IIIA in Field VII. It then turned south into the south limit of the field. Eastward from the point where it lay under Wall 21.008, it was well-built, with nicely laid-up side walls and flat capping stones. The base of the channel was earthen, and the slope was to the east. Directly under Wall 21.008, the channel was blocked with several purposefully-placed small rocks. From that point westward it was of poorer construction, was narrower, and sloped westward. Seven capping stones remained near the south end of 21.006; the rest of the channel was uncovered.

It appears that the point of drainage must have lain in the elbow of 21.003 and 21.008. At some point in time, the eastern run went out of use, was blocked, and a poorer western continuation was built, reversing the direction of flow.

The purpose of the complex is elusive. The two short walls running away from the main wall may have supported vats for some industrial activity requiring water. Conceivably the structure was a toilet or bathing installation.

Fig. 294. Field VII Area 6 within the disturbed area of Stratum IIIA. Cobbling 1306 and 1307 appear at the center near the cross balk.

All of these Stratum IIIA features lay close to the modern surface of the mound, from 0.70 to 1.00 m deep. Since Field VII provided no certain Stratum II flooring over Stratum III remains, definition of Stratum III pottery demanded careful analysis of forms that were sealed below Stratum III floors and walls and the earliest forms later than those that lay above the floors. While Field VII was being dug, data from other fields were clarifying the corpora of the four Hellenistic strata. Field VII provided a large number of floors and walls which sealed a substantial number of distinctive pottery forms and some coins beneath them, contributing to this clarification.

The evidence from coinage was especially helpful (Sellers 1962). On the plaster of Floor 1227 was a dilepton of Antiochus III. In no case was a Seleucid coin found beneath any Stratum IIIA feature. Three coins of Ptolemy II were found sealed beneath Wall 1107-1109, beneath the 1812-1814-1810 complex, and under Floor 1802—all IIIA features.

A crucial find for dating Hellenistic stratigraphy came from the disturbed area at the west edge of the street about three meters west of the 1414 post. It was a whole Hellenistic juglet with its neck broken off, buried deep in the disturbance. In it were 35 silver Ptolemaic coins, all tetradrachmas (fig. 295). One dates from Ptolemy I, 16 and probably three more from Ptolemy II, one from Ptolemy III, two from Ptolemy IV, and four certainly plus eight probably from Ptolemy V. Two of the Ptolemy V coins are datable to the year, B60 registry #566 to 198 BCE and #567 to 193 BCE. Someone hid a bank below the street containing coins minted over a period of at least 90 years, and did so after the year 193. This datum suggests that the clash that brought the change from Stratum III to Stratum II at Shechem, involving the shift from Ptolemaic to Seleucid hegemony, came between 193 and the end of Antiochus III's reign in 187.

Stratum II in Field VII (Ills. 110 [plan]; 112 = VIIAA and 116 = VIIDD)

The only wall in Field VII that belongs to Stratum II ran eastward from the vicinity of the Stratum III industrial or toilet installation in the southwest corner of the field into the south limit of the field, Wall 1005-1103-1212, traceable for 10.12 m and preserved only one course high (Ill. 110). Elevations on its preserved top were at 18.90 at the west end, 18.64 at its midpoint and 18.43 at the east end. The post at its west end rested on the slim remains of Stratum III Wall 1007. The post,

Fig. 295. Cache of silver Ptolemaic tetradrachmas from the edge of the street in Field VII Area 5.

roughly a meter square, was separated from the continuation of the wall eastward by a gap of 0.62 m, and there was another gap 1.60 m wide a meter east of the first gap. Whether either gap constituted a doorway is unclear. Indeed, the wall could easily have simply marked a boundary.

The course of 1005-1103-1212 was parallel to all the earlier east–west Hellenistic walls in Field VII, and to a line through the East Gate across the diameter of the mound. It is likely that a main street through the city ran not far south of the edge of Field VII throughout the Hellenistic period, perhaps even directly along this one preserved wall of Stratum II.

North of the wall, as excavation reached the bottom of the plow zone, there emerged hard-packed soil, VII DD:#2, where its upper surface shows the gouging of the plows. It appears as anything but a flat living surface, but within Areas 4, 5 and 6, its top was discerned as relatively flat, giving the impression of an open region. The thick layer topped by this change in soil consistency constitutes loci 1500, 1400 and 1300 as encountered in Areas 4, 5 and 6 respectively. It is the only available candidate for Stratum II occupation debris, but since there are no Stratum I remains above it and poor definition of Stratum III below it in at least Areas 5 and 6, it must be used with caution to define Stratum II. As definition of the pottery corpora for each stratum became clearer across the tell, Stratum II pottery was recognized in this hard-packed zone with great quantities of Iron II and Strata IV and III pottery. Seleucid coinage was confined to this zone, except where pits had introduced later material into lower Hellenistic contexts.

Pits intruding upon Stratum III were probably dug by Stratum II people, but since they became filled with debris from throughout the tell they likewise provide only mixtures of pottery and cannot define Stratum II. One such pit cut through Stratum III Cobbling 1203 and Floor 1214 in the southeast corner of the field and was designated locus 1205-1207; it contained what came to be seen as a larger than usual proportion of Stratum II forms. A concentration of Stratum II pottery was recovered from a loose rockfall designated locus 1208 just west of Wall 1206 of Stratum III, probably the bottom of a Stratum II intrusion. Finally, Jar 1820, inverted and set down into Stratum III remains at the north edge of the field (VII AA:"jar") is a good candidate for assignment to Stratum II.

It should be emphasized once more that the surface debris in Field VII, as elsewhere on the site, was noteworthy for the heavy proportion of Hellenistic pottery and the paucity of Roman or Byzantine evidence. Artifacts from the plow zone rarely attest anything later than the end of the second century BCE, while Seleucid coinage was regularly found. Ten coins, seven Seleucid and three Ptolemaic, came from the plow zone in Field VII. A silver coin of Demetrius II and the "Simeonides" inscribed sherd (Toombs and Wright 1961:45; *SBBC*:183) typify the situation; they came up on the first and second days of the 1960 campaign in the second and seventh pottery baskets from Field VII, Area 1. No identifiable coin of the Roman period was recovered, underscoring the actuality of the ephemeral strata II and I.

9264, 9265 and 9269 through 9271 in Area 2 (Ill. 144 = DD:##7, 8,and 10). No segment of architecture was sufficiently well-preserved to be recorded on plan, but IX AA shows what may be a fragment of a wall in the form of three stones at the right end of #9, just beneath burial 9751, topped by brick. Here the bottom of #9 can be posited as a small preserved segment of surface. As was stated in describing Stratum V in Field IX in the preceding chapter, other poorly preserved fragments of this sort now seem to have belonged in Stratum V. Apparently the only settlement in Field IX in either Stratum V or the early part of the recovery in Stratum IV consisted of mudbrick huts on skimpy stone foundations. What defined lower Stratum IV is the regular presence of Stratum IV sherds in the mixture of periods represented in the fill. If there was a IVB in Field IX corresponding to the distinct phase in Field VII, it is this preparatory layering that will have to be so designated.

The only well-preserved architectural complex of Stratum IV lay above the fill just described. It can be equated to IVA of Field VII, and is shown on Ill. 139.

Wall 9514 consisted of two segments at right angles (fig. 296). It varied in width from 0.70 to 0.85 m and was preserved for two courses. On IX DD, the deposit beneath Wall 9514 shows burnt brick. The only other hint of a foundation trench or preparation for Wall 9514 is the shallow saucer beneath the wall on IX AA = Ill. 141. It resembled Hellenistic walls in Field VII in having two rows of facing stones with rubble core. At the corner in Area 3, a large undressed stone at elevation 12.98 appears to have been selected for the bond, and larger stones flanked what was probably the doorway into the room just at the west edge of Area 3 (elevation 13.30). The top of the wall was flat and may have carried a brick superstructure; compact grey layer 9017 (DD:#3) both west and east of Wall 9514 consisted of decomposed brick.

The gaps in Wall 9514 in Area 1 were places where Islamic period burials were let down into the wall (note the one encroaching on Wall 9514 in IX DD). Field observations away from this intrusion record that decomposed brick (9016) ran to and over the stone courses. As fig. 297 shows, there were random rocks throughout the region east

Fig. 296. Looking south over Field IX Areas 1 and 3, at the 9514 complex of Stratum IVA.

Strata IV and III in Field IX (Ills. 139 [plan]; 141 = IXAA and 144 = IXDD)

Field IX was located within the orchard of the modern village of Balâṭah, where a cemetery of the Islamic period had been dug into it. Dump from the Austro-German excavation to its north and west covered the field, and the Arab graves were dug from what will have been the surface of the mound in the first millennium CE. While there had been the hope that Hellenistic remains of Strata I, II and III might be preserved here, it turned out that the highest preserved Hellenistic layer was from Stratum IV. Stratum III pottery was abundant in the mix of pottery in layers above Stratum IV but no architecture or flooring could be identified confidently.

Stratum IVB is defined by greyish rubbly soil visible on Ill. 141 = IX AA as ##9-11. These layers could be traced throughout the field, bearing locus numbers 9024, 9033 and 9035 in Area 1,

Fig. 297. Looking west in Field IX Area 1 at Wall 9514, interrupted by Islamic burial. Random rocks in foreground came to rest on probable IVA surface.

of the wall, which had probably come to rest on the surface that went with the wall. Fragments of cobbling are also visible adjacent to the wall, in soil layers ##5 and 9 = loci 9018 and 9021 of IX DD. Layer 9517B was the surface along the north side of the segment of the wall in Area 3; locus 9029 was compact occupation debris on a surface with the wall west of the wall in Area 1, the top of DD:#5.

The interior of the building suggested by the elbow of Wall 9514 could not be effectively defined. Wall 9267 is a good candidate for a wall that originally ran to meet the south end of 9514 just off the south edge of the excavation field. Just to the north of Wall 9514 as it emerges from the balk into Area 2 were three layers of silty soil 9262, 9263 and 9264 containing Stratum IV pottery, which probably accumulated on an outside surface.

Stone heap 9765 in Area 4 may also represent a wall, but is too poorly preserved to be sure. Throughout Area 4, however, was Cobbling 9760, shown in fig. 298, which apparently belonged with the complex. This was the most clearly defined surface to go with the Field IX complex. Roughly 0.12 to 0.20 m above it was a beaten earth layer 9759 which seems to have been a resurfacing of the cobbling. Set down into 9759 was Firepit 9758A, suggesting that the whole complex was a courtyard open to the sky.

At no point throughout the Field IX Stratum IV remains were there any signs of violent destruction, such as ash layers or crushed pottery and other household artifacts. One triple-spined bronze arrowhead was in layer 9759.

The latest pottery in all the layers associated with the 9514 complex, including between 9759 and 9760, belongs to the Stratum IV corpus. From these layers upwards, soil contained Stratum III and later pottery, including rare early Roman and Byzantine—but as with elsewhere in the excavations pottery any later than the end of the second century BCE was strikingly infrequent and the sherds of small size.

Hellenistic Strata in Field I (Ills. 17 and 18 [plans]; 20 = IAA and 21 = IBB)

West of the rebuild of Wall B and south of the segments of wall built over the MB IIC tower of the East Gate were remnants of Hellenistic housing representing two phases. The portions in Areas 5, 6 and 7 were excavated in 1957, and those in Areas 16 and 17 in 1964. All were badly broken up by later intrusion. The most disruptive of these was a cemetery, consisting of eleven burials in two roughly parallel rows, probably of soldiers from the Second World War. Not plotted on plan, they were in the region marked "courtyard" on Ills. 17 and 18 and were let down to varying depths.

Fig. 298. Looking east at Field IX Area 4 showing cobbling 9760 of Stratum IVA.

One effect of this disruption seems to have been to sever connections among installations in this open region. Vat and platter Installation 163, once thought to belong to Hellenistic, was reassigned to Stratum VI on the basis of the jar that caught the run-off from the platter. Stratigraphic separation of late Iron Age and Hellenistic strata here was very difficult.

The 160 complex anchors the earliest Hellenistic in the region. Wall 160, preserved for one course, resembled Hellenistic walls in Field VII and IX. It is 1.00 m wide with two rows of rocks with flat faces and a rubble core. An elevation on its top was at 11.71. Wall 160A running west from its south end had larger blocks arranged as headers across its width of 0.60 m. An elevation at its west preserved end was at 11.81. Where 160 and 160A met the elevation was at 11.50. The short stub of Wall 160B ran west from Wall 160 2.75 m north of 160A into the limit of excavation.

Within the elbow of 160 and 160A was Floor 205; outside to the south was Floor 206. Both were covered with a heavy burn layer 204 which could be traced eastward for as much as 6.00 m. Elevations on both 205 and 206 were at 11.00. On Floor 206 was a silver coin of Alexander the Great, sealed by the burn layer. There were 33 registered sherds from the burn and the floor. Above the burn were bricks and brick detritus; whole bricks measured about 0.16 by 0.14 by 0.12 m.

South of the 160 complex, two substantial walls were preserved against the south limit of excavation, Walls 159 and 159A. They apparently rested *on* Burn Layer 204 and may therefore have belonged to a later phase. They appear on Ill. 20 = I AA, 159 in elevation and 159A in section (the two unnumbered walls on #4). Alternatively, they may have gone with the 160 complex; ambiguity in the field report suggests this as possible. Fig. 299 shows the entire arrangement.

West of the Wall 160 complex by 8.25 m was the east face of Wall 170 in Area 16, a two-meter segment of wall with a squared north end and running into the limit of excavation at its south end. Of similar building technique, it was 0.75 to 0.85 m wide. Like many Hellenistic walls at Shechem, it rested upon a prepared surface 422-424 shown at elevation 11.71 on Ill. 18. Pottery in and below the surface included a very few Hellenistic pieces which need to be analyzed anew for their assignment to stratum. In Area 17, a complex of poorly preserved walls, 172, 173 and 174, apparently belonged with Wall 170, though later pits cut off connections. These features in Areas 16 and 17 were the lowest with Hellenistic pottery associated, but their elevations would demand a slope eastward not indicated by the layering in the I AA section.

Fig. 299. Looking south in Field I Area 7. The meter stick lies on Floor 205 inside the elbow of Wall 160 at left and 160A across the center. Floor 206 lies in the space beyond 160A.

Judging from the Alexander coin and the fact that fills beneath the features so far described contained no Hellenistic pottery, the lower phase inside the fortifications of Field I should belong to Stratum IV, perhaps continuing into Stratum III. Burn Layer 204 indicated it met violent destruction. This destruction may have come during the Ptolemaic era in the mid-third century, corresponding to the collapse of the fortifications described above, and thus at the end of Stratum IV. Or it may have come around 190 BCE when the Hellenistic Tower down the slope was put out of use, at the end of Stratum III. The question cannot be settled, although the interpretation given above about the fortifications favors the former.

East of the 160 complex was the lip of Stone-lined Silo 161, marked by an arched heap of stones (Ill. 21 = I BB:#3). Near its base it was 1.25 m in diameter; its interior reached 2.00 m in depth, with elevation 8.30 at its base. The arched top reached about elevation 10.70 and may have been higher. As the section shows, its top was at about the same elevation as the Stratum VI Vat 163, which would have been virtually at the Hellenistic surface. The filling of the silo was nearly sterile, but the few sherds were all Hellenistic in date.

Another vat, constructed of brick, 0.84 m in diameter and standing 0.42 m high, was adjacent to the silo. All of these features are in the region disrupted by the modern burials, and it remains an open question whether they belonged to the 160 and 159 complexes. If they did, they probably were installations in a courtyard going with a house or houses defined by 160 and 159. No early Hellenistic architecture or flooring was preserved east of them to the rebuild on Wall B.

Isolated remnants of a later Hellenistic phase in this region are shown on Ill. 17. An elbow of walls, 154 and 155, with top elevations on 154 at 11.27 and 10.97, enclosed a small segment of beaten earth flooring, 201. Not drawn on plan was a second fragment of wall (156) above the 160 complex with attached Floor 202. A third segment, Floor 203 in Area 6, near but not clearly attached to Walls 152-153, was also of beaten earth. All three segments had a thin layer of burning on them. A very few Hellenistic sherds were preserved from the burn layers on 201 and 202, combined in the registry. From one of them came a coin of Antiochus IV.

In Area 5, the complex of walls designated 151 surround a presumed surface 200 at elevations 9.01 and 9.00 but no sherds were saved to help define its date.

These features represent an upper phase of Hellenistic. If the coin is to be trusted, the date of the floors in Area 7 falls in the Seleucid era. The pottery needs new analysis. Tentatively, the upper phase here is assigned to Stratum II.

Hellenistic Strata in Field III (Ills. 40 [plan] and 42 = IIIAA)

Two phases of Hellenistic housing were preserved, very poorly, in Field III inside the line of Wall B. Trench L dug by the Sellin excavation in 1926 disturbed the entire west end of Field III (Ill. 2). None of the remains in the westernmost excavation plot, Area 1, belonged to ancient times. The architecture shown on Ill. 40 with wall numbers 601 and 602 probably represents animal pens and boundary walls built since 1926; alternatively, they may be walls encountered by the Sellin expedition, cleared of their surrounding soil, and rendered devoid of stratigraphic context.

In Areas 2, 3 and 4 scraps of Hellenistic housing were found, with a few features superimposed so as to indicate the two phases. The lower phase consisted of four wall segments (609–612) and probably a fifth, 603. Between and just to the south of Walls 611 and 612 was a stone-lined bin 0.55 m in diameter with most of four courses of the lining remaining at 0.15–0.20 m thick. It reached a maximum depth of 0.89 m down into MB II brick debris below. As the top plan shows, the walls were of a building technique comparable to that in other Hellenistic loci on the mound, although of relatively narrow width. All four were built on Bronze Age walls beneath them.

At several places on the earlier phase walls were traces of a light pink brick detritus, and another deposit of this color was banked against the interior face of the rebuild on Wall B (Ill. 42 = III AA does not distinguish between its high bulge against the rebuild and the MB IIC brick detritus beneath it). Probably the superstructure of these walls was of brick. The color differed from that of the well-preserved MB II brick below them and from that of Hellenistic brick in other fields.

No surfacings were discerned with these wall scraps; virtually no pottery was saved. What is clear, though, is that a subsequent Hellenistic phase rested on top of the complex.

The upper phase consisted of Walls 605, 606, 607 and 608, which, with a rebuild on top of the LB wall shown on Ills. 40 and 42, suggested one room of a dwelling to the south and a yard to the north. The northern part of Wall 607 lay on earlier phase Wall 609. Near Walls 606 and 608, but not clearly attached to them, was a patch of paving (elevations 14.67 and 14.73), which ran over the stone-lined bin of the earlier phase. These two data establish the separation of two phases of Hellenistic.

Close to where the stone-lined bin of the lower phase had been located was a plastered bin, its bottom at elevation 14.59. Its foundation was of sherds, of which two indicator forms were saved, embedded in clay. No sherds were isolated from beneath the patch of paving. The best collection of pottery from the later phase came from an intrusive pit between the interior face of rebuilt Wall B and the east face of Wall 606 just at the south limit of excavation (appearing on both plan and section). Field notes report parts of some 15 Hellenistic store jars, their sherds filling 17 pottery baskets, although only eight registry numbers were assigned. This cache has not yet been closely dated and is under study. Other than augmenting known groups, Field III has little to contribute to Hellenistic stratigraphy or typology, due to its poor state of preservation. The suggestion is that the lower phase represents Strata IV and III, the upper phase Stratum II.

South of Wall 605, the room running south into the balk had right angle corners, suggesting that a room of a house extended southward out of the field. No flooring could be detected, but buried in the layer marked "disturbed" on the section was a juglet containing bits of silver and gold (B57 Obj. reg. #178), including broken earrings and non-descript chunks of metal—a cache of *hacksilber* under study by Miriam Balmuth and Christine Thompson.

Fig. 300. Field II, Room 1 of the Hellenistic House, looking to the northeast. The black line in the balk at right marks the bottom of the modern overburden.

The Hellenistic House in Field II (Ills. 31 [plan]; 34 = IIAA and 35 = IIBB)

Located at the east edge of the large Austro-German excavation that revealed the acropolis, Field II was chosen by the Joint Expedition to provide information about the city remains at the foot of the acropolis, east of Wall 900. It was excavated in 1957, and again in 1968 to check the stratigraphy. In the interim, Paul Lapp published his analysis of Hellenistic pottery post-200 BCE, in which the remains in Field II played a significant role (1961:*passim*, esp. 41–49).

Dump from Sellin's work covered the site. The dump had to be excavated to ascertain the original surface of the mound; as II AA = Ill. 34 shows, the dump spilled over a slope to a depth of as much as 4.00 to 5.00 meters at the far south. Above the Hellenistic House, it thinned to as little as 0.40 m. Loci on the south (left) segment of II AA Section are lumped together in #1, and include 7000, 7058, 7065, 7070 and 7071; see also II BB = Ill. 35. Throughout the dump was the expected mix of pottery from all periods of the site's history, together with some early and late Roman and Byzantine pottery, Roman glass fragments, and trash from modern times.

The house plan appears in Ill. 31. Walls 7005 and 7104 (in section on Ill. 34) were barely covered with soil; the dump ran from approximately the position of 7005 southward. Over Room 1 of the house itself, the modern plow zone gave way to a layer of black earth not shown on either section but visible in fig. 300. It was presumed in 1957 to have marked the surface of the ancient mound. The 1968 work resulted in the conclusion that the black layer overlay all Hellenistic remains and is part of accumulation across the centuries since the end of the Stratum I period. Its utility for defining Hellenistic pottery corpora has to be secondary to what was found within the house itself (note how P. W. Lapp 1961 used it).

Room 1. At the start of Hellenistic building in Field II, the top of the Stratum VII remains below was leveled off, and a makeup was placed over them—II AA central portion:#3, which runs through Rooms 2 and 3 of the house; no section was drawn through Room 1. The makeup appears in fig. 265 (above) beneath the threshold in Wall 7007 and above Stratum VII Cobbled Floor 7024. In 1968, it was encountered under Room 1 of the house as loci 7031, 7033, 7042 and 7044, but it had been invaded by the 1957 digging and not isolated in that season.

None of these loci contained pottery later than that of Stratum VI. Removal of the walls of Room 1 in 1968 yielded foundation trenches for Walls 7006 and 7008 (locus 7036), and excavation beneath floor fragments 7048 and 7049 within Room 1 yielded sherds of Strata V, IV and III along with the familiar mix of earlier period pottery. One sherd from beneath floor 7048 and another from Foundation Trench 7036 were field analyzed as belonging to Stratum II but may be wrongly dated, or the two sherds may be intrusive. The evidence strongly supports the foundation date for the house as falling well into the time of Stratum III.

The 1968 excavation established that the first stage of the house consisted of Room 1 only. It measured 4.20 m along its west Wall 7006, 4.25 m along north Wall 7007, 4.20 m along east Wall 7012 and 3.90 m along south Wall 7008, roughly 17.60 square meters. The four walls average 0.65 m in width and show the standard Hellenistic technique of construction: two faces of stone with a rubble core. Unusual, however, was the use of well-trimmed blocks of *nari* limestone as headers through the walls. Also unusual was the laying of foundation courses 0.20 m wider than the ascending walls, extending 0.10 m to each side. Walls 7006, 7007 and 7008 had these foundations, not drawn on plan but visible in fig. 227.

These consolidating features pertain to the state of preservation of the walls in Room 1. As Ill. 31 shows, they were preserved to as much as 1.73 m (at the junction of 7007 and 7006) through as many as eight courses. Elevations are clear from the plan, which regularly shows foundation elevations.

Access to Room 1 was through Wall 7007 from the north and through Wall 7006 at its junction with 7007 (fig. 265). Both doorposts for the north door consisted of hewn oblong *nari* blocks, laid with an upright on the foundation course, a flat-lying header above it, and another upright on the header. The doorway was 0.80 m wide. The access through 7006 had a similar but less well-cut doorpost at its south end, and was 0.70 m wide. Elevation of the thresholds were 16.32 on the former (16.16 at its foundation) and 16.27 on the latter.

The junction of Walls 7006 and 7007 showed similar oblong blocks laid so as to bond the corner well and serve the north doorpost of the west access. Also at this juncture were two reused limestone fragments, a semi-engaged column drum and a section of engaged capital or base. They recall the monumental base from Stratum IV of Field VII—another hint that Room 1 in Field II was built after the destruction of Stratum IV.

The 1957 work had great difficulty in identifying surfaces in Room 1. It was noted that the room was filled to the tops of the preserved walls with soil containing Hellenistic and earlier pottery, and that *later* pottery predominated as excavation reached the elevation of the door thresholds and the base courses of the walls. But no clear beaten-earth floor was discerned. This upside-down stratigraphy has been explained (P. W. Lapp 1961:45, note 212; *SBBC*:40–41, 248, note 3) by the proposal that Room 1's floor level was kept at roughly the same elevation throughout its use and that a major importation of fill was brought from nearby and deposited in the order in which it was procured, earlier on top of later. Why Room 1 was purposefully filled up in this manner remains an intriguing question.

Though the 1957 excavation failed to discern the floor, in 1968 James Ross found Floor 7049, a hard white plastered patch in the center of the room at elevation 16.05, and a group of possible flagstones, Floor 7048, at 15.99 just to the east of 7049. Floor 7049 had a deposit of loose grey earth, locus 7050, only 0.05 m thick over it, apparently occupation debris. These elevations were, then, as much as 0.30 m down from the thresholds, a longer step down than might be expected. They were also lower than the founding elevation of Wall 7012 on the east. Either the surface saucered up toward the walls or these surfaces were relics of an earlier phase. In 1968, Ross found some indication of such saucering when clearing to the very southeast and southwest corners of Room 1—locus 7025. It is more probable that 7025, 7050, and the two floor surfaces did define the floor of Room 1 *at its last use*.

Part of this final use of Room 1 would have involved the setting in of stone-lined rectangular Bin 7011 in the northwest corner of the room, its rim at elevation at 16.74 and its founding level at 16.21, which stood directly in the way of the door through Wall 7006. Its side walls abutted the adjacent house walls. Several whole small Hellenistic bowls of second century date were found in the bin. Its foundation trench, locus 7046, contained lamp sherds probably belonging to Stratum I styles. To anticipate, the location of this bin is directly in the way of an access to Room 1 through 7006 and

Fig. 301. Structure 7015, dividing Rooms 2 and 3 in the Hellenistic House, Field II.

must belong to a stage after that access had been blocked up.

The loci defining the floor of Room 1 preserved some Stratum II sherds together with earlier Hellenistic, and of great importance two coins, one found in 1957 and the other in 1968. Object #B57:321 is a bronze of Antiochus VIII (121/120 BCE), and #B68:126 is a bronze tentatively assigned to his mother and regent Cleopatra Thea (122/121). In short, then, Room 1 was founded in late Stratum III but continued in use into the time of Stratum I, within 15 years of when the site's Hellenistic occupation ended in John Hyrcanus's attack in 107 BCE.

Out the door through Wall 7007 was a beaten earth surface mixed with ash for what was probably an open yard, at the same elevation as the foundations for Wall 7007. A wall preserved from a foundation at elevation 13.85 to a height of 15.80 may have defined the northern limit of this yard. It butted against the top of Wall 900 and ran for 3.25 m eastward, but it was not parallel to Wall 7007. Its east end was 4.25 m away from the doorway through 7007, and it angled away from the line of 7007 as it continued west to its junction with Wall 900. The surface of the yard could not be firmly connected to it.

Beneath the yard's surface only pre-Hellenistic pottery was found, but there was one coin, #B57 Obj. 348 of Ptolemy I or II. Fragments of red, orange and blue-black wall plaster were found in the debris over this surface, perhaps indicative of the wall decoration of Room 1 at some stage within its period of use.

Rooms 2 and 3. Ross's careful restudy of the complex discerned that Rooms 2 and 3 were additions to the basic house. A buttress, 7045, was built against the west end of Wall 7008 at its junction with 7008, and the walls of Rooms 2 and 3 added. The walls, built with similar technique to those of Room 1, were not so well constructed. They lack the hewn *nari* headers and the rocks in the wall faces are not so well selected as to present a flat facet. Wall 7005, butted against 7006 and 7013, is unusually wide at 1.00 m, and is slightly out of

Fig. 302. Crushed jars on Floor 7099, Field II, Room 3, probably of Stratum II.

line. All of the junctions with Room 1 exteriors were butt joins. As with Room 1, Walls 7013 and 7009 had a wider foundation course, 7014 and 7010 respectively, but the ascending wall in each case rode on the interior line of the foundation, not on its center as with Room 1.

In addition to Buttress 7045, the south end of Wall 7043 was buttressed with the rock process 7107, the elevation on its top only 0.04 m above the founding level of the wall. Another buttress, 7017 is one boulder against the interior face of Wall 7013-7014, visible on Ill. 35 = II BB where it crosses that wall. Wall 7005, at first thought to rest on a wider foundation (7109 and 7108), was found instead to have these two rows of stones as skins, a different sort of buttressing. Wall 7109 fell away after excavation, revealing Wall 7005 continuing below it (Ill. 34 = II AA). It may be that the extension northward at the west end of Wall 7005 was still another buttress. All this buttressing suggests either that the walls were known to be of less stable workmanship or that new circumstances, perhaps the threat of earthquake, had come to bear on the construction of the addition.

Dividing Room 2 from Room 3 was the Wall 7015 made of *nari* blocks 0.30 m wide ending in a block set upright (fig. 301).

Another feature of the addition of Rooms 2 and 3 was the blocking of the doorway at the north end of Wall 9006. And to be factored into the interpretation of how the expanded house was to be used is the similar blocking up of the door through Wall 7007 from the north. In the new complex, Room 1 now had no accesses at the elevation of its upper phase flooring, which was at the same elevation as its founding one.

The 1957 excavation had not discerned a floor in Rooms 2 and 3. In 1968, a 0.50 m shelf was excavated along the south edge over Room 3, and a probe was cut southward, revealing the continuation of Wall 7010 toward its junction with Wall 7014. Here was found a substantial segment of beaten earth floor, 7099, covered with ash and a crush of broken jars (II AA center series: #2 in Rooms 2 and 3; fig. 302), continuing to Wall 7009 between ## 13 and 14 in the south (left) segment of the section; on II BB it connects Wall 7009 to foundation 7014 under 7013, the west wall of the whole structure. The elevation on 7099 was at 16.80. Beneath the thin Wall 7015, more ash was found on a hard surface, at the same elevation. Apparently a living surface at this elevation filled Rooms 2 and 3 but was missed in the 1957 excavation. Wall 7015 may have been built on it; it is not certain that it was built after the destruction of Rooms 2 and 3; perhaps the ash beneath it was local and not related to that on 7099 further south.

Fig. 303. Field II looking west. Wall 7104 well above chalk surface marking uppermost use of the yard with the Hellenistic House. Wall 7104 is assigned to Stratum IA.

In any case, no higher surface was noted in Rooms 2 and 3 to suggest still another use of the house.

Although it cannot be established that they lay on the floor of Rooms 2 and 3, a collection of iron nails and an iron key were found in 1957 in the vicinity of the upright block of Wall 7015. It stands to reason that wooden doors were involved in the upper phase of the Hellenistic house. This phenomenon recalls conditions in Field VII during Stratum III.

The pottery on Surface 7099 was field analyzed as of Stratum II with possible Stratum I pieces. From locus 7100, the makeup beneath it (II BB, II AA left series:#14), came pottery of Stratum II at the latest. So far as is now known, then, the destruction of Rooms 2 and 3 fell upon Floor 7099 and is represented by the crush of jars and the burn layer. It is shown on II BB as the ashy compact layer between Wall 7009 and Wall 7013-7014, on top of which part of the latter wall collapsed as rockfall 7084.

Outside the expanded building to the north, a thick surfacing of packed chalk probably represented the upper phase use of the yard. Both phases of the house probably used the open area to the north as a yard.

An explanation for how the house functioned in the later phase is difficult to construct. How did the people who lived in Rooms 2 and 3 use the space in Room 1 or gain access to it? Conceivably it was an underground chamber during the upper phase, reached by ladder from its roof. Possibly, there was once a flooring at an elevation comparable to the one in Rooms 2 and 3, to which access would have been had over a threshold at the preserved top of Wall 7006. In that event, it remains difficult to understand why the late pottery and late coins were on the low level of floorings 7048 and 7049 in Room 1. What does seem necessary is the explanation proposed by Paul Lapp mentioned earlier, to account for the filling up of Room 1 with soil containing pottery of an earlier date

Fig. 304. Field IX Area 1 looking south. Medieval Islamic burial oriented with head to west, face turned to the south.

than what lay on its floor—probably its only floor.

One more phase within Stratum I then must have followed. Section II AA shows Walls 7104 and 7105 in the yard to the north. They rode above the thick chalk layer posited as the second surface of the yard and far above the first surface (fig. 303). A plastered storage bin 7106 within their elbow belonged with them. Running west from the line of II AA, and founded 0.65 m above the preserved top of Wall 7009 was Wall 7072, from which stones had fallen (locus 7078 = #2 and Ill. 35 = II BB) onto a skimpily preserved surface indicated as #3 in the left segment of II AA. This surface, 7098, was at elevation 17.50. Beneath it was brown-grey earth (7080) that topped the whole complex of Room 2, but contained Stratum II pottery. Locus 7074, grey rocky soil running to Wall 7072 along its north face, contained Stratum I pottery. All of this is very close to the surface upon which the German dump was deposited. Finally, Wall 7111 (not on plan) was uncovered early in the 1957 campaign parallel and to the east of Room 1's Wall 7008, with a top elevation at 17.30 and a possible surface adjacent on its north at 17.00.

All these ephemeral fragments, so near the mound's surface, may be the last evidences of Stratum I, referred to on II AA as Stratum "IA." Pottery with them supports that conclusion. But as with other places on the site (in Field III and possibly in Field I as well), these walls may be structures from much later, boundary or hut walls. If they are, however, they are not shown to be of late date by accompanying pottery of the Roman, Byzantine or Arabic periods. They are the best indications the Shechem mound affords of stratified Stratum I remains coming down to the very end of the site's Hellenistic history.

FIELD XV (ILL. 173)

In Chapter 3, mention was made of probes dug at the end of the final full (1968) season of work at the tell, designed to test the location of the southern run of fortifications. Field XV, Trench 2 (see Ill. 173), yielded at its south end a two meter stretch of wall, Wall 7523 with a beaten earth floor (7529) running to its south face. The top of the Wall 7523 was at elevation 12.68, its footing at 12.28; Floor 7529 was at elevation 12.40, and on it was a circular bin (7524) made of fired clay with a plaster interior lining, quite similar to Bin 7106 assigned to Stratum I above in the description of Field II. No signs of burning appeared, suggesting use as an oven.

Wall 7523 was 0.55 m wide and built with two contiguous rows of rock, the faces of which had been rough-hewn. Since the entire complex lay within a space roughly 2.00 by 2.50 m, little more can be said other than noting the likelihood that it represented domestic housing. North of it by about 1.75 m was a non-descript heap of rocks which may have been another wall, Wall 7527, but its nature and function could not be related to the 7523-7529-7524 complex. The remainder of the stratum in Area 2 was disrupted. But within the circular bin, the pottery belonged to Stratum II, and late Hellenistic pottery was sealed beneath Wall 7523 when it was lifted.

Just beneath this Hellenistic deposit in Field XV Area 2 were traces of a structure dated to Iron II (Strata VIII-VI) by a few sherds beneath Flagstone Floor 7535 at the south edge of the probe. Of two fragments of wall, 7527 and 7530, the former apparently cut through the latter. Again so little was preserved as to preclude contribution to the knowledge of these strata. The same is true of a pair of walls not in coherence with one another just beneath the Iron II pair just described; excavation stopped before their date was determined, but Stratum X and perhaps earlier pottery was in the soil around them.

The Iron Age layers here, if indeed they do belong to that period were not included in the description of their period earlier in this volume, but the Hellenistic phase is clearer. And once again, it is striking that virtually no Roman, Byzantine or Arabic pottery was found in XV Area 2.

THE LATEST STRATA: BYZANTINE, ROMAN AND ARABIC REMAINS

The Cemetery in Field IX

The final stratified archaeological glimpse of the life of this ancient mound is a glimpse of death. In Field IX, in the orchard of Balâṭah, the first thing encountered below the cultivation layer and the scree of excavation dump from the Austro-German excavations was a cemetery. A total of 39 skeletons were found, placed in shallow trench graves oriented east–west and capped with covering stones (fig. 304). All of the sections drawn for Field IX show them as intrusions into the surface of the mound as it was prior to the Sellin excavations and dump. It should be said that these burials are by every right a stratum of the site and should have been treated as such, but since no effort was made to study them as a part of the stratigraphy, it would belie the Expedition's method to seek to present them as a separate study (cf. the procedure, for example at Tell el-Hesi).

Of the 39 skeletons, there were ten adults, thirteen children of ages 7 to 13, one adolescent, and 15 infants and children up to age 7. What little pottery there was in the surface layering into which the graves were cut comes from early in Islamic times, probably from the Umayyad and Abbasid periods (7th-10th centuries CE). The people of modern Balâṭah, who founded the village in the mid-nineteenth century CE, did not know the cemetery was there.

Field XV, Area 1 (Ills. 174–175)

Area 2 of Field XV with its Hellenistic remains was described just above. The second trench of this probe for the line of fortifications, Area 1, lay roughly 20 m south-southeast of Area 2, and provided evidence that it lay outside the city fortification. It was here that skimpy stratification of Arabic and Byzantine occupation appeared, built apparently on a leveled portion of the talus of the tell (Ills. 174–175).

Walls 7504 and rough stone Pavement 7505 top the layering. Glazed pottery associated with the early Arabic periods appeared on and under 7505. Wall 7501, probably built earlier than 7504-7505, was set down into the same loose crumbly brown earth as underlay 7505. Sealed beneath Wall 7501 and spread throughout the fill below it was glazed Arabic pottery. Beneath this were found Walls 7509 and 7511, with associated floorings 7512 and 7515. This is the one complex on the site that dates to the Byzantine period, probably late in it (seventh century?); two Byzantine coins yet to be thoroughly studied came from the layer 7510 virtually on Floor 7512 in one case and on the top of Wall 7511. Byzantine and late Roman pottery came from the layer of *ḥuwwar* chips above Floor 7522, whose date is uncertain; in its makeup were a few sherds of Late Bronze date, but the stratigraphy is not held up from below.

REFERENCES

Abel, F. -M.
1938 *Géographie de la Palestine*. Volume 2: *Géographie politique. Les villes*. Third edition, reprinted 1967. Paris: J. Gabalda.

Albright, W. F.
1943 *The Excavations of Tell Beit Mirsim* I: *The Iron Age*. Annual of the American Schools of Oriental Research 21–22. New Haven: American Schools of Oriental Research

Alt, A.
1927 Das Institut im Jahre 1926. *Palästinajahrbuch* 23:5–51.
1938 Die Wahlfahrt von Sichem nach Bethel. In *piam memoriam Alexander von Bulmerincq*, Abhandlungen der Herder-Gesellschaft und des Herder-Instituts zu Riga, VI, 3. Riga: Ernst Plates. Reprinted in *Kleine Schriften zur Geschichte des Volkes Israel* I (1953) 79–88. Munich: Beck.

Anderson, B. W.
1962 The Drew-McCormick Archaeological Expedition. *The Drew Gateway* 32:127–34.

Avigad, N.
1986 *Hebrew Bullae from the Time of Jeremiah: Remnants of a Burnt Archive*. Jerusalem: Israel Exploration Society.

Avi-Yonah, M.
1966 *The Holy Land From the Persian to the Arab Conquests (536 B.C. to A.D. 640): A Historical Geography*. Grand Rapids, MI: Baker.

Barkay, G.
1986 *Ketef Hinnom: A Treasure Facing Jerusalem's Walls*. Jerusalem: The Israel Museum.

Ben-Dor, I.
1950 A Middle Bronze-Age Temple at Nahariya. *Quarterly of the Department of Antiquities of Palestine* 14:1–43.

Ben-Tor, A.
1992 "Notes and News: Tel Hazor, 1992." *Israel Exploration Journal* 42:154–260.

Bienkowski, P.
1989 The Division of Middle Bronze IIB-C in Palestine. *Levant* 21:169–76.

Biran, A.
1994 *Biblical Dan*. Jerusalem: Israel Exploration Society and Hebrew Union College — Jewish Institute of Religion.

Böhl, F. M. Th.
1926a De geschiedenis der stad Sichem en de opgravingen aldaar. *Medeelingen der Koninklijke Akademie van Wetenschappen, Amsterdam*, Afd. Letterkunde Deel 62, Serie B:1–24.
1926b Anhang: Die bei den Ausgrabungen von Sichem gefundenen Keilschrifttafeln. *Zeitschrift des Deutschen Palästina-Vereins* 49:321–27, pls. 44–46.
1927 *De Opgraving van Sichem: Bericht over de Voorjaars-campagne en de Zomer-campagne in 1926*. Zeist: G. J. A. Ruys' Uitgevers-Mij.

Boling, R. G.
1969 Bronze Age Buildings at the Shechem High Place: ASOR Excavations at Tananir. *Biblical Archaeologist* 32:81–103.
1975a Excavations at Tananir, 1968. Pp. 25–85 in *Report on Archaeological Work at Suwwanet eth-Thaniya, Tananir, and Khirbet Minha (Munhata)*, ed. G. M. Landes. Bulletin of the American Schools of Oriental Research Supplemental Studies 21. Missoula, MT: Scholars Press.
1975b *Judges*. AB 6A. Garden City, N. Y.: Doubleday.

Boling, R. G., and Campbell, E. F.
1986 Jeroboam and Rehoboam at Shechem. Pp. 259–72 in *Archaeology and Biblical Interpretation: Essays in Memory of D. Glenn Rose*, eds. L. G. Perdue, L. E. Toombs and G. L. Johnson. Atlanta: John Knox Press.

Boraas, R. S.
1986 Iron IA Ceramics at Tell Balâtah: A Preliminary Investigation. Pp. 249–63 in *The Archaeology of Jordan and Other Studies Presented to Siegfried H. Horn*, eds. L. T. Geraty and L. G. Herr. Berrien Springs, MI: Andrews University Press.
1999 Shechem Pottery — Locus 14.132. Pp. 18–

27 in *On the Way to Nineveh: Studies in Honor of George M. Landes*, eds. S. L. Cook and S. C. Winter. Atlanta: Scholars Press.

Borowski, O.
1987 *Agriculture in Iron Age Israel*. Winona Lake, IN: Eisenbrauns.

Bright, J.
1981 *A History of Israel*. 3rd Edition. Philadelphia: Westminster Press.

Bull, R. J.
1960 A Re-examination of the Shechem Temple. *Biblical Archaeologist* 23:110–19.
1962 The Excavation of the Temples at Shechem. *The Drew Gateway* 32:156–65.

Bull, R. J., and Campbell, E. F.
1968 The Sixth Campaign at Balâṭah (Shechem). *Bulletin of the American Schools of Oriental Research* 190:2–41.

Bull, R. J., and Wright, G. E.
1965 Newly Discovered Temples on Mount Gerizim in Jordan. *Harvard Theological Review* 58:234–37

Bull, R. J., *et al.*
1965 The Fifth Campaign at Balâṭah (Shechem). *Bulletin of the American Schools of Oriental Research* 180:7–41.

Callaway, J. A.
1983 A Visit With Ahilud: A Revealing Look at Village Life When Israel First Settled the Promised Land. *Biblical Archaeology Review* 9/5:42–53.

Campbell, E. F.
1976 Two Amarna Notes: The Shechem City-State and Amarna Administrative Terminology. Pp. 39–54 in *Magnalia Dei: The Mighty Acts of God. Essays on the Bible and Archaeology in Memory of G. Ernest Wright*, eds. F. M. Cross, W. E. Lemke, and P. D. Miller. Garden City, NY: Doubleday.
1977 Review of K. Jaroš, *Sichem: Eine archäologische und religionsgeschichtliche Studie mit besonderer Berucksichtigung von Jos 24*. *Journal of Biblical Literature* 98:420–22
1983 Judges 9 and Biblical Archeology. Pp. 263–71 in *The Word of the Lord Shall Go Forth: Essays in Honor of David Noel Freedman in Celebration of His Sixtieth Birthday*, eds. C. Meyers and M. O'Connor. Winona Lake, IN: Eisenbrauns.
1984 The Boundary Between Ephraim and Manasseh. Pp. 67–76 in *The Answers Lie Below: Essays in Honor of Lawrence Edmund Toombs*, ed. H. O. Thompson. Lanham, MD: University Press of America.
1991 *Shechem II: Portrait of a Hill Country Vale: The Shechem Regional Survey*. American Schools of Oriental Research Archaeological Reports. Atlanta: Scholars Press.
1993 Shechem/Tell Balâṭah. Pp. 1345–54 in *The New Encyclopedia of Archaeological Expeditions in the Holy Land*, ed. E. Stern. Jerusalem: Israel Exploration Society & Carta.
1995 Archaeological Reflections on Amos' Targets. Pp. 32–52 in *Scripture and Other Artifacts: Essays on the Bible and Archaeology in Honor of Philip J. King*, ed. M. D. Coogan *et al*. Louisville: Westminster-John Knox.

Campbell, E. F., and Ross, J. F.
1963 The Excavation of Shechem and the Biblical Tradition. *Biblical Archaeologist* 26:2–34.

Campbell, E. F.; Ross, J. F.; and Toombs, L. E.
1971 The Eighth Campaign at Balâṭah (Shechem). *Bulletin of the American Schools of Oriental Research* 204:2–17.

Campbell, E. F., and Wright, G. E.
1969 Tribal League Shrines in Amman and Shechem. *Biblical Archaeologist* 32:104–16.
1970 Excavations at Shechem, 1956–1969. *Qadmoniot* 3:126-33 (Hebrew).

Chambon, A.
1984 *Tell el-Far'ah I: l'age du fer*. Editions Recherche sur les Civilisations, no. 31. Paris: Association pour la Diffusion de la Pensée Francaise.

Clamer, C.
1977 Notes and News: A Burial Cave Near Nablus (Tell Balata). *Israel Exploration Journal* 27:48.
1981 A Late Bronze Age Burial Cave Near Shechem. *Qadmoniot* 14:30–34 (Hebrew).

Cole, D. P.
1984 *Shechem I: The Middle Bronze IIB Pottery*. American Schools of Oriental Research Excavation Reports. Winona Lake, IN: Eisenbrauns.

Coogan, M. D.
1987 Of Cults and Cultures: Reflections on the

Interpretation of Archaeological Evidence. *Palestine Exploration Quarterly* 119:1–8

Coote, R. B.
1981 *Amos Among the Prophets: Composition and Theology*. Philadelphia: Fortress.

Cross, F. M.
1962 An Inscribed Seal from Balâṭah (Shechem). *Bulletin of the American Schools of Oriental Research* 167:14–15.
1963 The Discovery of the Samaria Papyri. *Biblical Archaeologist* 26:110–21.
1969 Judean Stamps. *Eretz-Israel* 9 (W. F. Albright Volume):20–27.

Currid, J. D.
1985 *Archaeological Investigations Into the Grain Storage Practices of Iron Age Palestine*. Unpublished Ph.D. dissertation, University of Chicago.
1989 A Note on the Function of Building 5900 at Shechem – Again. *Zeitschrift des Deutschen Palästina-Vereins* 105:41–44.

Currid, J. D., and Gregg, J. L.
1988 Why Did the Early Israelites Dig All Those Pits? *Biblical Archaeology Review* 14/5:54–57.

Currid, J. D., and Navon, A.
1986 The Tell Halif (Lahav) Grain Storage Project. *ASOR Newsletter* 37/2:7.
in press Iron Age Pits and the Lahav (Tell Halif) Grain Storage Project.

Dever, W. G.
1974 The MB IIC Stratification in the Northwest Gate Area at Shechem. *Bulletin of the American Schools of Oriental Research* 216:31–52.
1983 Material Remains and the Cult in Ancient Israel: An Essay in Archeological Systematics. Pp. 571–87 in *The Word of the Lord Shall Go Forth: Essays in Honor of David Noel Freedman in Celebration of His Sixtieth Birthday*, eds. C. Meyers and M. O'Connor. Winona Lake, IN: Eisenbrauns.
1988 Impact of the "New Archaeology." Pp. 337–52 in *Benchmarks in Time and Culture*, eds. J. F. Drinkard, Jr., G. L. Mattingly, J. M. Miller. Atlanta: Scholars Press.
1989 Review of *Shechem I: The Middle Bronze II B Pottery*, by Dan P. Cole, in *Bulletin of the American Schools of Oriental Research*, 276, 86–88.

Donner, H.
1965 Das Deutsche Evangelische Institut für Altertumswissenschaft des Heiligen Landes: Lehrkursus 1963. *Zeitschrift des Deutschen Palästina-Vereins* 81:3–55.

Dothan, T., and Ben-Tor, A.
1983 *Excavations at Athienou, Cyprus, 1971–1972*. Qedem 16. Jerusalem: Institute of Archaeology, Hebrew University of Jerusalem.

Du Mesnil Du Buisson, R.
1930 Compte-rendu de la quatrième campagne de fouilles a Mishrife-Qatna. *Syria* 11:146–63.
1935 *Le site archéologique de Mishrife-Qatna*. Collection de Textes et Documents d'Orient 1. Paris: De Boccard.

Dunayevsky, I., and Kempinski, A.
1973 The Megiddo Temples. *Zeitschrift des Deutschen Palästina-Vereins* 89:161–87.

Finkelstein, I., and Gophna, R.
1994 Settlement, Demographic, and Economic Patterns in the Highlands of Palestine in the Chalcolithic and Early Bronze Periods and the Beginning of Urbanization. *Bulletin of the American Schools of Oriental Research* 289:1–22.

Fowler, M. D.
1981 Cultic Continuity at Tirzah? A Re-examination of the Archaeological Evidence. *Palestine Exploration Quarterly* 113:27–31.
1983 A Closer Look at the "Temple of El-Berith" at Shechem. *Palestine Exploration Quarterly* 115:49–53
1985a Excavated Figurines: A Case for Identifying a Site as Sacred? *Zeitschrift für die alttestamentliche Wissenschaft* 97:333–44.
1985b Excavated Incense Burners: A Case for Identifying a Site as Sacred? *Palestine Exploration Quarterly* 117:25–29.

Franken, H. J., and Franken-Battershill, C. A.
1963 *A Primer of Old Testament Archaeology*. Leiden: Brill

Fritz, V.
1971 Erwägungen zu dem spätbronzezeitlichen Quadratbau bei Amman. *Zeitschrift des Deutschen Palästina-Vereins* 87:140–52.
1977 Bestimmung und Herkunft des Pfeilerhauses in Israel. *Zeitschrift des Deutschen Palästina-Vereins* 93:30–45.

Galling, K.
1937 Altar. Cols. 13–22 in *Biblisches Reallexikon*. Tübingen: Mohr.

Geva, S.
1980 A Fragment of a Tridacna Shell from Shechem. *Zeitschrift des Deutschen Palästina-Vereins* 96:41–47.

Gottwald, N. K.
1985 *The Hebrew Bible: A Socio-Literary Introduction*. Philadelphia: Fortress Press.

Graesser, C.
1972 Standing Stones in Ancient Palestine. *Biblical Archaeologist* 35:34–63.

Harrison, T. P.
1993 Economics With an Entrepreneurial Spirit: Early Bronze Trade with Late Predynastic Egypt. *Biblical Archaeologist* 56:81–93

Hayes, J. H., and Miller, J. M., eds.
1977 *Israelite and Judean History*. Philadelphia: Westminster.

Hennessy, J. B.
1966a Excavation of a Bronze Age Temple at Amman. *Palestine Exploration Quarterly* 98:155–62.
1966b Supplementary Note. *Zeitschrift für die alttestamentliche Wissenschaft* 78:357–59
1970 A Temple of Human Sacrifice. *The Gazette*, Nov. 1970, pp. 307–9.

Herr, L. G.
1983 *The Amman Airport Excavations, 1976*. Annual of the American Schools of Oriental Research 48. Winona Lake, IN: Eisenbrauns.

Holladay, J. S.
1966 *The Pottery of Northern Israel in the Ninth and Eighth Centuries B.C.* Unpublished Th.D. dissertation, Harvard University.
1976 Of Sherds and Strata: Contributions Toward an Understanding of the Archaeology of the Divided Monarchy. Pp. 253–93 in *Magnalia Dei: The Mighty Acts of God. Essays on the Bible and Archaeology in Memory of G. Ernest Wright*, eds. F. M. Cross, W. E. Lemke, and P. D. Miller. Garden City, N. Y.: Doubleday.
1982 The Palestinian House: A Case Example of the Use of Ethnographic Analogy in Archaeological Reconstruction. Unpublished.
1986 The Stables of Ancient Israel: Functional Determinants of Stable Construction and the Interpretation of Pillared Buildings of the Palestinian Iron Age. Pp. 103–65 in *The Archaeology of Jordan and Other Studies Presented to Siegfried H. Horn*, eds. L. T. Geraty and L. G. Herr. Berrien Springs, MI: Andrews University.
1992 Red Slip, Burnish, and the Solomonic Gateway at Gezer. *Bulletin of the American Schools of Oriental Research* 277/278:23–70.
1993 Article, "House, Israelite." In D. N. Freedman, *et al.*, eds. *The Anchor Bible Dictionary*. New York, London, Toronto, Sydney, Auckland: Doubleday. Vol. 3, 308–18.
1994 The Use of Pottery and Other Diagnostic Criteria, from the Solomonic Era to the Divided Kingdom. Pp. 86–101 in *Biblical Archaeology Today, 1990: Proceedings of the Second International Congress on Biblical Archaeology, Jerusalem, June–July 1990*, eds. A. Biran and J. Aviram for the Israel Exploration Society. Jerusalem: Keter.

Horn, S. H.
1962 Scarabs from Shechem. *Journal of Near Eastern Studies* 21:1–14.
1966 Scarabs and Scarab Impressions from Shechem — II. *Journal of Near Eastern Studies* 25:48–56.
1968 Objects from Shechem Excavated 1913 and 1914. *Jaarbericht Ex Oriente Lux* 20:72–90 + plates and figures.
1973 Scarabs and Scarab Impressions from Shechem III. *Journal of Near Eastern Studies* 32:281–89.

Horn, S. H., and Moulds, L. G.
1969 Pottery from Shechem Excavated 1913 and 1914. *Andrews University Seminary Studies* 7:17–46 + plates.

Jaroš, K.
1976 *Sichem*. Orbis Biblicus et Orientalis 11. Göttingen: Vandenhoeck & Ruprecht.

Jaroš, K. and Deckert, B.
1977 *Studien zur Sichem-Area*. Orbis Biblicus et Orientalis 11a. Gottingen: Vandenhoeck & Ruprecht.

Josephus
1937 *Josephus* VI: *Jewish Antiquities, Books IX–XI*, with English translation by R. Marcus. Loeb Classical Library. Cambridge: Harvard University Press.
1943 *Josephus* VII: *Jewish Antiquities, Books XII–XIV*, with English translation by R. Marcus. Loeb Classical Library. Cambridge: Harvard University Press.

Kallai, Z.
1972 The Surveys: The Land of Benjamin and Mt. Ephraim. Pp. 151–93 in *Judaea, Samaria and the Golan: Archaeological Survey 1967–1968*, ed. M. Kochavi. Jerusalem: Carta (Hebrew).

Kee, H. C. and Toombs, L. E.
1957 The Second Season of Excavation at Biblical Shechem. *Biblical Archaeologist* 20:82–105.

Kempinski, A.
1986 Joshua's Altar: An Iron Age I Watchtower. *Biblical Archaeology Review* 12/1:42, 44–49.
1992 Middle and Late Bronze Age Fortifications. Pp. 127–42 in *The Architecture of Ancient Israel from the Prehistoric to the Persian Periods*, ed. A. Kempinski and R. Reich. Jerusalem: Israel Exploration Society.

Kenyon, K.
1957 *Digging Up Jericho*. New York: Praeger.
1969 The Middle and Late Bronze Age Strata at Megiddo. *Levant* 1:25–60.
1973 Palestine in the Time of the Eighteenth Dynasty. Pp. 526–66 in *The Cambridge Ancient History*, II, rev.(3rd.) ed., ed. I. E. S. Edwards, *et al.*
1979 *Archaeology in the Holy Land*. Fourth edition. New York: W. W. Norton & Co.

Kerkhof, V. I.
1966 An Inscribed Stone Weight from Shechem. *Bulletin of the American Schools of Oriental Research* 184:20–21.
1969 Catalogue of the Shechem Collection in the Rijksmuseum van Oudheden in Leiden. *Oudheidkundige Mededelingen* 50:28–109.

King, P. J.
1988 *Amos, Hosea, Micah—An Archaeological Commentary*. Philadelphia: Westminster.

Kochavi, M., Beck, P., and Gophna, R.
1979 Aphek-Antipatris, *Tel Poleg*, *Tel Zeror* and *Tel Burga*: Four Fortified Sites of the Middle Bronze Age IIA in the Sharon Plain. *Zeitschrift des Deutschen Palästina-Vereins* 95:121–65.

Kramer, K.
1979 An Archaeological View of a Contemporary Kurdish Village: Domestic Architecture, Household Size, and Wealth. Pp. 139–63 in *Ethnoarchaeology: Implications of Ethnography for Archaeology.*, ed. C. Kramer. New York: Columbia University.

1982 *Village Ethnoarchaeology: Rural Iran in Archaeological Perspective*. New York: Academic Press.

Lapp, N. L.
1964 Pottery from Some Hellenistic Loci at Balâṭah (Shechem). *Bulletin of the American Schools of Oriental Research* 175:14–26.
1985 The Stratum V Pottery from Balâṭah (Shechem). *Bulletin of the American Schools of Oriental Research* 257:19-43.

Lapp, P. W.
1961 *Palestinian Ceramic Chronology, 200 B.C.–A.D. 70*. New Haven: American Schools of Oriental Research.
1963a Palestine: Known but Mostly Unknown. *Biblical Archaeologist* 26:121–34.
1963b Ptolemaic Stamped Handles from Judah. *Bulletin of the American Schools of Oriental Research* 172:22–35.
1970 The Pottery of Palestine in the Persian Period. Pp. 179–97 in *Archäologie und Alten Testament: Festschrift für K. Galling*. Tübingen: Mohr.

Lapp, P. W., and Lapp, N. L., eds.
1974 *Discoveries in the Wadi ed-Daliyeh*. Annual of the American Schools of Oriental Research 41. Cambridge, MA: American Schools of Oriental Research.

LeBlanc, S.
1971 An Addition to Naroll's Suggested Floor Area and Settlement Population Relationship. *American Antiquity* 36:210–11.

Loud, G.
1948 *Megiddo II: Seasons of 1935–39*. In 2 volumes, *Texts* and *Plates*. Chicago: University of Chicago.

Magen, I.
1993a Shechem/Neapolis. Pp. 1354–59 in *The New Encyclopedia of Archaeological Expeditions in the Holy Land*, ed. E. Stern. Jerusalem: Israel Exploration Society & Carta.
1993b Gerizim, Mount. Pp. 484–92 in *The New Encyclopedia of Archaeological Expeditions in the Holy Land*, ed. E. Stern. Jerusalem: Israel Exploration Society & Carta.

Matthiae, P.
1979 *Ebla in the Period of the Amorite Dynasties and the Dynasty of Akkad*. Malibu, CA: Undena.

Mazar, A.
1981 Giloh: An Early Israelite Settlement near Jerusalem. *Israel Exploration Journal* 31:1–36.

Mazar, B.
1968 The Middle Bronze Age in Palestine. *Israel Exploration Journal* 18:65–97.

Milson, D.
1987 The Design of the Temples and Gates at Shechem. *Palestine Exploration Quarterly* 119:97–105.

Muller, H. W.
1987 *Der Waffenfund von Balata-Sichem*. Pp. 13–103 in *Der Waffenfund von Balata-Sichem und Die Sichelschwerter*. Munich: Bayerischen Akademie der Wissenschaften.

Naroll, R.
1962 Floor Area and Settlement Population. *American Antiquity* 27:587–89.

Naumann, R.
1971 *Architektur Kleinasiens von ihren Anfangen bis zum Ende der hethetischen Zeit*. Second edition. Deutsche Archäologisches Institut. Tübingen: Ernst Wasmuth.

Negbi, O.
1976 *Canaanite Gods in Metal: An Archaeological Study of Ancient Syro-Palestinian Figurines*. Tel Aviv: Institute of Archaeology.

Otto, E.
1979 *Jakob in Sichem (Beiträge zur Wissenschaft vom Alten und Neuen Testament: H 110 = Folge 6, H 10)*. Stuttgart: W. Kohlhammer.

Parr, P. J.
1968 The Origin of the Rampart Fortifications of Middle Bronze Age Palestine and Syria. *Zeitschrift des Deutschen Palästina-Vereins* 84:18–45.

Pennells, E.
1983 Middle Bronze Age Earthworks: A Contemporary Engineering Evaluation. *Biblical Archaeologist* 46:57–61.

Petrie, W. M. F.
1931 *Ancient Gaza I: Tell el Ajjul*. London: British School of Archaeology in Egypt.

Reader's Digest Atlas of the Bible
1981 J. L. Gardner, ed.; H. T. Frank, principal consultant. Pleasantville, NY: Reader's Digest Association.

Renfrew, C.
1984 *Approaches in Social Archaeology*. Cambridge, MA: Harvard University.

Ross, J. F.
1962 What We Do When We Dig. *The Drew Gateway* 32:149–55.

Ross, J. F., and Toombs, L. E.
1961 Three Campaigns at Biblical Shechem. *Archaeology* 14:171–79.
1967 Six Campaigns at Biblical Shechem. Pp. 119–28 in *Archaeological Discoveries in the Holy Land*, compiled by the Archaeological Institute of America. New York: Crowell.

Rowe, A.
1930 *The Topography and History of Beth-shan*. Publications of the Palestine Section of the Museum of the University of Pennsylvania 1. Philadelphia: University of Pennsylvania Museum.

Scott, R. B. Y.
1970 Weights and Measures of the Bible. Pp. 345–58 in *Biblical Archaeologist Reader 3*, eds. E. F. Campbell and D. N. Freedman. Garden City, NY: Doubleday.

Seger, J. D.
1965 *The Pottery of Palestine at the Close of the Middle Bronze Age*. Unpublished Th.D. dissertation, Harvard University.
1972 Shechem Field XIII, 1969. *Bulletin of the American Schools of Oriental Research*, 205:20–35.
1974 The Middle Bronze IIC Date of the East Gate at Shechem. *Levant* 6:117–30.
1975 The MB II Fortifications at Shechem and Gezer: A Hyksos Retrospective. *Eretz-Israel* 12 (Nelson Glueck Memorial Volume): 34*–45* (Eng.), 209 (Heb. summary).
1997 Shechem. Pp. 19–23 in *The Oxford Encyclopedia of Archaeology in the Near East*, Vol. 5, ed. E. M. Meyers. New York and Oxford: Oxford University Press.

Sellers, O. R.
1962 Coins of the 1960 Excavations at Shechem. *The Biblical Archaeologist* 25:87–96.

Sellin, E.
1914a Vorläufiger Bericht über die Ergebnisse der Ausgrabungen in Balata-Sichem. *Anzeiger der kaiserlichen Akademie der Wissenschaft in Wien*, Phil.-hist. Klasse 51.VII:35–40 and Pls. I–II.
1914b Vorläufiger Bericht und Rechnungsablage über die diesjahrige Frühjahrskampagne

der Ausgrabung in Balata-Sichem. *Anzeiger der kaiserlichen Akademie der Wissenschaft in Wien*, Phil.-hist. Klasse 51.XVIII:204–7.

1926a Die Ausgrabung von Sichem: Kurze vorläufige Mitteilung über die Arbeit im Frühjahr 1926. *Zeitschrift des Deutschen Palästina-Vereins* 49:229–36.

1926b Die Ausgrabung von Sichem: Kurze vorläufige Mitteilung über die Arbeit im Sommer 1926. *Zeitschrift des Deutschen Palästina-Vereins* 49:304–27.

1927a Die Ausgrabung von Sichem: Kurze vorläufige Mitteilung über die Arbeit im Frühjahr 1927. *Zeitschrift des Deutschen Palästina-Vereins* 50:205–11 + Tafeln 11–21.

1927b Die Ausgrabung von Sichem: Kurze vorläufige Mitteilung über die Arbeit im Sommer 1927. *Zeitschrift des Deutschen Palästina-Vereins* 50:265–74.

1928 Die Masseben des El-Berit in Sichem. *Zeitschrift des Deutschen Palästina-Vereins* 51:119–23.

1932 Der gegenwartige Stand der Ausgrabung von Sichem und ihre Zukunft. *Zeitschrift für die alttestamentliche Wissenschaft* 50:303–8.

Sellin, E., and Steckeweh, H.
1941 Kurzer vorläufiger Bericht über die Ausgrabung von *balata* (Sichem) im Herbst 1934. *Zeitschrift des Deutschen Palästina-Vereins* 64:1–20.

Shanks, H.
1987 Jeremiah's Scribe and Confidant Speaks from a Hoard of Clay Bullae. *Biblical Archaeology Review* 13/5:58–65.

Shiloh, Y.
1970 The Four-Room House: Its Situation and Function in the Israelite City. *Israel Exploration Journal* 20:180–90.

1979 Iron Age Sanctuaries and Cult Elements in Palestine. Pp. 147–57 in *Symposia Celebrating the Seventy-fifth Anniversary of the Founding of the American Schools of Oriental Research (1900–1975)*, ed. F. M. Cross. Cambridge, MA: American Schools of Oriental Research.

1980 The Population of Iron Age Palestine in the Light of a Sample Analysis of Urban Plans, Areas, and Population Density. *Bulletin of the American Schools of Oriental Research* 239:25–35.

Soggin, J. A.
1966 Bemerkungen zur alttestmentliche Topographie Sichems mit besonderem Bezug auf Jdc. 9. *Zeitschrift des Deutschen Palästina-Vereins* 83:183–98.

1986 The Migdal Temple, Migdal Sekem Judg 9 and the Artifact on Mount Ebal. Pp. 115–19 in *"Wunschet Jerusalem Frieden": Collected Communications to the XIIth Congress of the International Organization for the Study of the Old Testament, Jerusalem 1986*, eds. M. Augustin and K.-D. Schunck. Frankfurt: Peter Lang.

Stager, L. E.
1985 The Archaeology of the Family in Ancient Israel. *Bulletin of the American Schools of Oriental Research* 260:1–35.

1992 The Periodization of Palestine from Neolithic through Early Bronze Times. Pp. 22–41 in R. W. Ehrich, ed., *Chronologies in Old World Archaeology* (3rd revised ed.) Chicago: U. of Chicago Press.

1999 The Fortress-Temple at Shechem and the "House of El, Lord of the Covenant." Pp. 228–49 in P. H. Williams, Jr. and T. Hiebert, eds., *REALIA DEI: Essays in Archaeology and Biblical Interpretation in Honor of Edward F. Campbell, Jr. at His Retirement*. Atlanta: Scholars Press.

Stager, L. E., and S. R. Wolff
1981 Production and Commerce in Temple Courtyards: An Olive Press in the Sacred Precinct at Tel Dan. *Bulletin of the American Schools of Oriental Research* 243:95–102.

Stern, E.
1980 Achaemenian Tombs from Shechem. *Levant* 12:90–111.

1982 *Material Culture of the Land of the Bible in the Persian Period, 538–332 B.C.* English edition. Warminster: Aris & Phillips.

Stern, E., and Magen, Y.
1984 A Pottery Group of the Persian Period from Qadum in Samaria. *Bulletin of the American Schools of Oriental Research* 253:9–27.

Thiersch. H.
1932 Ein altmediterraner Tempeltyp. *Zeitschrift für die alttestamentliche Wissenschaft* 50:73–86.

Toombs, L. E.
1962 Daily Life in Ancient Shechem. *The Drew Gateway* 32:166–72.
1972 The Stratigraphy of Tell Balâṭah (Ancient Shechem). *Annual of the Department of Antiquities of Jordan* 17: 99-110, 173–85.
1976 The Stratification of Tell Balâṭah (Shechem). *Bulletin of the American Schools of Oriental Research* 223: 57–59.
1979 Shechem: Problems of the Early Israelite Era. Pp. 69–83 in *Symposia Celebrating the Seventy-fifth Anniversary of the Founding of the American Schools of Oriental Research (1900–1975)*, ed. F. M. Cross. Cambridge: American Schools of Oriental Research.
1985a Shechem. Pp. 935–38 in *Harper's Bible Dictionary*, ed. P. J. Achtemeier. San Francisco: Harper & Row.
1985b Temple or Palace: A Reconsideration of the Shechem "Courtyard Temple." Pp. 42–60 in *Put Your Future in Ruins: Essays in Honor of Robert Jehu Bull*, ed. H. O. Thompson. Bristol, IN: Wyndham Hall.
1992 Shechem (Place). Pp. 1174–86 in *Anchor Bible Dictionary*, vol. 5. New York: Doubleday.
1996 Shechem. Pp.1006–8 in *The HarperCollins Bible Dictionary*, ed. P. J. Achtemeier. Rev. and updated ed. San Francisco: HarperCollins.

Toombs, L. E., and Wright, G. E.
1961 The Third Campaign at Balâṭah (Shechem). *Bulletin of the American Schools of Oriental Research* 161:11–54.
1963 The Fourth Campaign at Balâṭah (Shechem). *Bulletin of the American Schools of Oriental Research* 169:1–60.

Ussishkin, D.
1989 Notes on the Fortifications of the Middle Bronze II Period at Jericho and Shechem. *Bulletin of the American Schools of Oriental Research* 276:29–53.
1992 Notes on the Middle Bronze Age Fortifications of Hazor. *Tel Aviv* 19:274–81.

Watson, P. J.
1979 *Archaeological Ethnography in Western Iran*. Tucson: University of Arizona Press.

Welter, G.
1928 Tell Balata: Report of the Summer Campaign of 1928. Eng. trans. by S. H. Horn of paper submitted to the Department of Antiquities of Palestine. [Original currently unavailable to me.]
1931 Balata-Shechem (1928, 1929, 1931). Eng. trans. by S. H. Horn of paper in Department of Antiquities of Palestine file. [Original currently unavailable to me.]
1932 Stand der Ausgrabungen in Sichem. Cols. 289–314 in *Archäologischer Anzeiger: Beiblatt zum Jahrbuch des Archäologischen Instituts*, III–IV.

Wright, G. E.
1956 The First Campaign at Tell Balâṭah (Shechem). *Bulletin of the American Schools of Oriental Research* 144:9–26.
1957 The Second Campaign at Tell Balâṭah (Shechem). *Bulletin of the American Schools of Oriental Research* 148:11–28.
1962a Archaeological Fills and Strata. *Biblical Archaeologist* 25:34–40
1962b Shechem: The City and Its Excavation. *The Drew Gateway* 32:135–48.
1962c The Samaritans at Shechem. *Harvard Theological Review* 55:357–66.
1962d Selected Seals from the Excavations at Balâṭah (Shechem). *Bulletin of the American Schools of Oriental Research* 167:5–13.
1965 *Shechem: The Biography of a Biblical City*. New York: McGraw Hill.
1967a The Provinces of Solomon. *Eretz-Israel* 8 (E. L. Sukenik Memorial Volume): 58*–68* (Eng.), 328 (Heb. summary).
1967b Shechem. Pp. 355–70 in *Archaeology and Old Testament Study*, ed. D. W. Thomas. Oxford: Clarendon.
1971 The Archaeology of Palestine from the Neolithic through the Middle Bronze Age. *Journal of the American Oriental Society* 91:276–93.
1975 The "New" Archaeology. *Biblical Archaeologist* 38:104–15.
1978a A Characteristic North Israelite House. Pp. 149–54 in *Archaeology in the Levant: Essays for Kathleen Kenyon*, eds. R. Moorey and P. Parr. Warminster, England: Aris & Phillips.
1978b Shechem. Pp. 1093–94 in *Encyclopedia of Archaeological Excavations in the Holy Land*, Vol. 4. English edition ed. M. Avi-Yonah and E. Stern. Jerusalem: Massada.

Wright, G. R. H.
1965 Fluted Columns in the Bronze Age Temple

1966   of Baal-Berith at Shechem. *Palestine Exploration Quarterly* 97:66–84.

1966   The Bronze Age Temple at Amman. *Zeitschrift für die alttestamentliche Wissenschaft* 78:351–57

1967a   Some Cypriote and Aegean Pottery Recovered from the Shechem Excavations 1964. *Skrifter Utgivna av Svenska Institutet I Athen* 4₁, XII = *Opuscula Athenesia* 7:47–75, pls. 1–5.

1967b   The Place Name Balâṭah and the Excavations at Shechem. *Zeitschrift des Deutschen Palästina-Vereins* 83:199–202

1968   Temples at Shechem. *Zeitschrift für die alttestamentliche Wissenschaft* 80:1–35.

1969   Another Fluted Column Fragment from Bronze Age Shechem. *Palestine Exploration Quarterly* 101:34–36.

1970   The "Granary" at Shechem and the Underlying Storage Pits. *Zeitschrift für die alttestamentliche Wissenschaft* 82:275–78.

1971   Pre-Israelite Temples in the Land of Canaan. *Palestine Exploration Quarterly* 103:17–32.

1973   Co-ordinating the Survey of Shechem over Sixty Years, 1913–1973. *Zeitschrift des Deutschen Palästina Vereins* 89:188–196 + plans and plates 12–15.

1975   Temples at Shechem—A Detail. *Zeitschrift für die alttestamentliche Wissenschaft* 87:56–64.

1984   The Monumental City Gate in Palestine and Its Foundations. *Zeitschrift für Assyriologie* 74:267–89.

1985a   The City Gates at Shechem: Simple Reconstruction Drawings. *Zeitschrift des Deutschen Palästina-Vereins* 101:1–8.

1985b   *Ancient Building in South Syria and Palestine* I: Text; II: Illustrations. Handbuch der Orientalistik 7.Abt.: Kunst und Archäologie. Leiden: Brill.

1986   Temple and Gate in Palestine. Pp. 173–77 in *Studies in the History and Archaeology of Palestine*, Vol. II. Aleppo: Aleppo University Palestine Archaeological Centre. [Conference papers from 1981; illustrations omitted by mistake.]

Yadin, Y.

1955   Hyksos Fortifications and the Battering-Ram. *Bulletin of the American Schools of Oriental Research* 137:23–32.

1972   *Hazor: The Head of All Those Kingdoms.* The Schweich Lectures, 1970. London: Oxford University Press.

Yadin, Y. *et al.*

1961   *Hazor III–IV: An Account of the Third and Fourth Seasons of Excavations, 1957–1958: Plates.* Jerusalem: Magnes

1989   *Hazor III–IV: An Account of the Third and Fourth Seasons of Excavations, 1957–1958: Text.* Jerusalem: Israel Exploration Society.

Yeivin, S.

1973   Temples That Were Not. *Eretz-Israel* 11 (I. Dunayevsky Memorial Volume):163–75 (Heb.), 28* (Eng. summary).

Zeron, A.

1978   The Seal of "M-B-N" and the List of David's Heroes. *Tel Aviv* 6:156–57.

Zertal, A.

1985   Has Joshua's Altar Been Found on Mt. Ebal? *Biblical Archaeology Review* 11/1:26–43.

1986   How Can Kempinski Be So Wrong! *Biblical Archaeology Review* 12/1:43, 49–53.

1987   An Early Iron Age Cultic Site on Mount Ebal: Excavation Seasons 1982–1987: Preliminary Report. *Tel Aviv* 13–14:105–65 + plates 5–19.